ATLAS OF ENERGY BUDGETS

of

PLANT LEAVES

ATLAS OF ENERGY BUDGETS
of
PLANT LEAVES

David M. Gates

Director, The Missouri Botanical Garden
Professor of Biology, Washington University

and

LaVerne E. Papian

Applied Mathematician, The Missouri Botanical Garden
Senior Programmer, Computing Facilities
Washington University, Saint Louis, Missouri

1971

ACADEMIC PRESS
LONDON · NEW YORK

ACADEMIC PRESS INC. (LONDON) LTD
Berkeley Square House
Berkeley Square, London, W1X 6BA

U.S. Edition published by
ACADEMIC PRESS INC.
111 Fifth Avenue
New York, New York 10003

Library of Congress Catalog Card Number: 79-141727
ISBN 0 12 277250 4

Printed by offset in Great Britain by
William Clowes and Sons, Limited
London, Beccles and Colchester

PREFACE

This book is written to present to the reader in a descriptive and explicit manner the concept of energy and mass flow between a leaf and its immediate environment. A leaf responds to the energy flow to and from the environment by assuming a certain temperature and a certain transpiration rate. Temperature is important to a leaf in that it affects the various biochemical events of leaf metabolism. Energy passes to and from a leaf by radiation, convection, conduction, and transpiration. These mechanisms of energy transfer are dependent upon the various radiation fluxes of the environment, including sunlight, skylight, and thermal radiation, and upon the air temperature, wind speed, and relative humidity, and in addition are dependent upon such leaf properties as absorptivity, leaf size, shape, orientation, and stomatal resistance to the diffusion of water vapor.

It is evident that many variables and parameters are involved in the evaluation of leaf temperature and transpiration rate by means of the energy transfer mechanisms. All variables and parameters act simultaneously. The result is that we are trying to understand the functional behavior of two dependent variables, e.g. leaf temperature and transpiration rate, as a function of many independent variables and parameters. In order to "navigate" so to say, in this multidimensional space we need a good "compass." Our "compass" is the energy exchange analytical method by means of which we can always locate our position in the multidimensional space.

We present in this book graphs which represent cross sections of the multidimensional space. Examples of such cross sections are: leaf temperature as a function of air temperature for specified properties of a leaf and a selected range of environmental conditions; transpiration rate of a leaf as a function of leaf diffusion resistance to water vapor for specified properties of a leaf and a selected range of environmental conditions; etc.

The book is intended for use by botanists, ecologists, foresters, agronomists, hydrologists, and others interested in the exact quantitative response of plants to environment.

November 1970   DAVID M. GATES
                                                   LAVERNE E. PAPIAN

CONTENTS

INTRODUCTION

A plant leaf is interacting with its environment through the flow of energy and the flow of gases and molecular products between the plant and the environment. If a plant leaf receives more energy than it consumes or loses it will get warmer and if it loses more than it gains it will get colder. Although the leaf may get colder or warmer for short periods of time it cannot do so for extended periods or else it will perish from freezing or burning. A plant leaf, to remain viable, must be in energy balance when averaged over long intervals of time and stay within definite broad temperature limits. However, all plant processes including photosynthesis, cell enlargement, cell division, translocation, transpiration, etc. do work and consume energy. The primary mechanism by which climate influences a plant is through the flow of energy. Photosynthesis, respiration, growth, etc. are temperature dependent events and some of these processes are light dependent as well. Transpiration, or the evaporation of water, requires 580 cal of energy for every gram of water which is vaporized. Although other processes, such as the exchange of carbon dioxide, oxygen, nitrogen, etc. are vital to the life of the plant the availability of energy is absolutely essential to carry on the processes of life.

Energy is exchanged between a plant leaf and its environment by radiation, convection, conduction, and transpiration or the vaporization of water. The climate nearby a plant is described by the parameters of radiation flux, air temperature, wind speed and relative humidity. Although these parameters are all of very different properties and each is measured in terms of its own set of dimensions, the one common denominator for the interaction of the climate parameters with a plant is the flow of energy. The radiation flux incident upon a plant leaf is coupled to the energy content or temperature of the plant by the absorptivity of the leaf and other plant parts. If the plant were to reflect all the incident radiation, and absorb none of it, the plant temperature or internal energy content would be decoupled from the incident flux of radiation. If the plant leaf was black and absorbed all of the stream of incident radiation, its internal energy content or temperature would be coupled very tightly to the incident radiation. Most plant leaves absorb about 50% of the total incident solar radiation and about 96% of infrared thermal radiation.

The air temperature and the wind speed affect the plant temperature by means of convective exchange of energy. If the leaf is small and the coefficient of convective heat exchange is large then the leaf temperature (internal energy content) and transpiration rate are strongly coupled to the air temperature and to the wind speed. If the leaf is large and the coefficient of convective heat exchange is small then the leaf temperature may depart very strongly from the air temperature, particularly with conditions of intense radiation and low wind speed.

The coupling of the leaf temperature or energy content to the water vapor pressure of the air is by means of the diffusion of water vapor from inside the leaf through the stomates to the free air beyond the boundary layer adhering to the leaf surface. Transpiration is the "evaporative cooler" which extracts energy from the leaf. Water will escape easily from the leaf if it has many large stomates which are wide open. When this is true the leaf temperature is strongly affected by the transpiration and by the external concentration of water vapor in the free air. If the stomates are nearly closed or are very small and few then the leaf temperature is affected little by the external vapor pressure through its influence on the transpiration process. Two conditions are required for the loss of water from a leaf: energy and a water vapor pressure gradient from the leaf to the air. If there is no energy available then liquid water within the leaf cannot be vaporized. If there is no vapor gradient between leaf and air then there is no force to drive the vapor from within the leaf to the free air beyond the adhering boundary layer.

Radiation, air temperature, wind and humidity all interact simultaneously with an organism and the response of the plant or animal to these factors is truly synergistic. It is this idea of synergism which is fundamental to our understanding of climate and organisms. One cannot ask the influence of the air temperature on an organism without at the same time specifying the amount of radiation, the wind speed and the humidity. Nor can one ask and receive a valid answer to the question —What is the effect of a certain amount of radiation incident on an organism?—without simultaneously specifying the air temperature, the wind speed and the humidity. The climate nearby a plant leaf is described by means of the four independent variables—radiation, air temperature, wind speed and relative humidity—each of which is time dependent. The leaf temperature and the transpiration rate of the leaf are affected by the four climate variables and hence represent two dependent variables. A conceptual space made up of two dependent variables and four independent variables is a six-dimensional regime. At any instant in time the interaction of a plant leaf with the climate is represented by a single point in this six-dimensional space. However this point traces out a volume in this space with time when all possible combinations of the values of the variables are considered. It is our task here to evaluate and describe the shape of this six-dimensional space representing the interaction of plant leaves and climate.

It is necessary to express a relation as complex as this one, between two dependent and several independent variables, in mathematical form in order that the result of any combination of values of the independent variables can be predicted in terms of values of the dependent variables. Because of the enormous complexity of the problem it is essentially impossible to experimentally explore all possible combinations of values of the variables. The power of the analytical, or mathematical method, is the fact that by carefully testing or evaluating a limited number of sets of relations between the dependent and independent variables it is then possible to predict all other possible relations. The test of such a method is to predict some specific relations and establish that indeed these predictions are confirmed by observation.

Energy Budget of a Plant Leaf

The exchange of energy between a plant leaf and the surrounding environment is described by means of the following mechanisms: chemical energy conversion through metabolism, radiative absorption and emission of energy, convective heat exchange, latent heat exchange through evaporation or condensation of moisture and conduction. For most plant leaves, in the context of the total energy exchanged, the loss or gain of energy through metabolism and conduction through the leaf petiole is small compared with the total. This does not imply that respiration and photosynthesis are not extremely important quantities, because they are from the standpoint of plant growth and productivity. The contribution of respiration and photosynthesis to the thermal or heat budget of a leaf is generally less than 3% of the total. There are a few possible exceptions such as the quick warming within the spathes of some arums caused by high respiration rates during intervals of an hour or less.

Other possible mechanisms for heat exchange between a leaf and its environment, such as interactions with fluctuating magnetic, electric, or gravitational fields are generally very small and negligible. There are special circumstances during which the energy delivered to an organism by a gradient of a gravitational, electric or magnetic field is highly significant. An organism being struck by a bolt of lightning or falling off a precipice are illustrations of special circumstances.

The exchange of energy for a plant leaf is written in the following form after many very careful laboratory measurements were done in a wind tunnel as reported by Gates *et al.* (1968) and following a long series of studies reported by Gates (1968), Parkhurst *et al.* (1968), Gates (1962), and Raschke (1956, 1960). The bibliography at the end of this book contains more references to the subject.

$$Q_{abs} = \varepsilon\sigma T_l^4 + k_1 \left(\frac{V}{D}\right)^{1/2} (T_l - T_a)$$
$$+ \frac{{}_s[d_l(T_l) - \text{r.h.}{}_sd_a(T_a)]}{Lr_l + k_2[(W^{0.20}D^{0.35})/V^{0.55}]} \quad (1)$$

where Q_{abs} is the total flux of incident radiation (sunlight, skylight, reflected light, thermal radiation from ground and atmosphere) which is absorbed by a plant leaf in units of cal cm^{-2} min^{-1}. ε is the emissivity of the leaf surface, σ is the Stefan–Boltzmann constant $(=8.132 \times 10^{-11}$ cal cm^{-2} min^{-1} $°K^{-4})$, T_l is the leaf temperature, k_1 is a proportionality constant, V is the wind speed in cm sec^{-1}, D is the leaf dimension in the wind direction measured in cm, W is the leaf width at right angles to D measured in cm, T_a is the air temperature in °C, L is the latent heat of evaporation of water in cal gm^{-1} and is temperature dependent, ${}_sd_l(T_l)$ is the saturation density of water vapor in gm cm^{-3} within the leaf mesophyll as a function of the leaf temperature T_l, ${}_sd_a(T_a)$ is the saturation density of water vapor in gm cm^{-3} of the air as a function of the air temperature T_a, r.h. is the relative humidity of the air, r_l is the internal diffusion resistance in min cm^{-1} to water vapor of the leaf, and k_2 is a coefficient which relates to the resistance of the boundary layer of air adhering to the leaf surface.

Each term of Eqn. (1) is expressed in units of cal cm^{-2} min^{-1} even though certain individual quantities, such as wind speed and resistance, contain the unit of seconds. The coefficients k_1 and k_2 are given values such that if all quantities are expressed in the dimensions indicated then each term (convection or transpiration) will automatically be in cal cm^{-2} min^{-1}. These coefficients are purely empirical and are the result of careful experimentation with real and artificial leaves mounted within a laboratory wind tunnel. The determination of the coefficients is very difficult because of the many complexities entering the exchange of heat and moisture from leaves of various dimensions and shapes. The coefficients listed below were found to be suitable for our experimental data, however a great deal of additional experimental work may lead to further refinement and modification. Different values of the coefficients were found necessary in order to fit the results of the experiments for different ranges of leaf size. A choice was made to consider two ranges of leaf size only as follows:

If $W > D$ or $W = D > 5$ cm or $D > 10$ cm
$$k_1 = 10 \times 10^{-3} \qquad k_2 = 35 \times 10^{-3}$$

If $W < D \leq 10$ cm or $W = D \leq 5$ cm
$$k_1 = 16.2 \times 10^{-3} \qquad k_2 = 26 \times 10^{-3}$$

A leaf responds to the various processes of energy exchange as expressed by Eqn. (1) by assuming a leaf temperature and a transpiration rate such that the energy flowing into the leaf is balanced by the energy flowing out from the leaf. The leaf temperature and transpiration rate are dependent variables and all other quantities are independent variables. A given leaf is described in terms of its properties which must be known. These properties are leaf dimensions W and D, internal diffusion resistance r_l, the emissivity ε to radiation from the leaf surface, and the various absorptivities and areas of the leaf surface which are presented to the incident fluxes of radiation. These absorptivities and areas are described in the next section. The climate near the leaf is described by means of the independent variables T_a, V, r.h. and the radiation fluxes contained in the quantity Q_{abs}. These radiation fluxes are described in the next section. If the amount of energy flowing into the leaf increases, the leaf temperature will increase and the transpiration rate may increase and vice versa if there is a decrease of energy flow. The leaf temperature and transpiration rate respond intimately to the flow of energy to or from a leaf and to the status of the boundary layer of air adhering to the leaf surface which comes under the domination of the air flow.

The energy content of a leaf, and hence its temperature, is coupled to the energy of the environment by means of specific coupling factors already described. The absorptivity of a leaf to radiation couples the leaf temperature to the incident flux of radiation. The convection coefficient which is $k_1(V/D)^{1/2}$ of the second term on the right-hand side of Eqn. (1) is the coupling factor between the leaf temperature and the air temperature. The convection coefficient is large in strong wind and small in low wind and is large for a small leaf and small for a large leaf. If the amount of radiation absorbed by a large leaf is very small the leaf temperature is several degrees below the air temperature. If the amount of radiation absorbed by a large leaf is of an intermediate quantity then the leaf temperature is close to the air temperature. However, for a small leaf, whether the amount of radiation absorbed by the leaf is large or small, the leaf temperature remains strongly coupled to the air temperature, i.e. remains within a few degrees of air temperature as is demonstrated by some of the graphs.

The third important coupling factor between the energy content of a leaf and the condition of the environment is the resistance of the pathway to the diffusion of water vapor from within the leaf to the air beyond the leaf.

It is clear that various leaves with different properties of absorptivity, dimensions and diffusion resistance, when in precisely the same environment, will respond in very different ways to the energy flow. Hence, one leaf may have a temperature 20°C above air temperature while another leaf may be 2°C below air temperature in exactly the same conditions of radiation, air temperature, wind and humidity.

Radiation Absorbed

The amount of radiation absorbed by a leaf is often very difficult to evaluate. This difficulty is caused by the inherent complexity of the incident radiation fluxes encountered in many natural environments; a complexity of geometry and of spectral quality. The sun is approximately a point source of strong radiation while the skylight is of relatively weak intensity but comes from a broad source—the hemisphere of the sky. Reflected sunlight and skylight may be diffuse in character off broad surfaces of soil, rock or vegetation or it may be specular off water or from certain terrain features. The direct sunlight is rich in visible radiation and near infrared radiation with a broad extension of low intensity to long infrared wavelengths and with an abrupt termination in the ultraviolet at about 2900 Å. The scattered skylight is rich in ultraviolet and blue radiation but relatively depleted of red and infrared radiation. Reflected sunlight will have the spectral quality of the product of the spectral quality of sunlight and of the reflectivity of the surface material. The thermally emitted radiation from the atmosphere and the ground originates from extended, essentially hemispherical, surfaces and has a broad spectral composition of wavelengths from about 4.0 to 30 microns and beyond, with a peak intensity at about 10 microns. The spectral qualities of the various fluxes of radiation are described by Gates (1965).

If a plant leaf of total surface area A presents an area A_i to the ith stream of incident flux R_i of radiation and if the leaf has an average absorptivity $\bar{a}_i$ to the spectral quality of this flux, then the amount of radiation absorbed $_iQ_{\text{abs}}$ per unit surface area is given by:

$$_iQ_{\text{abs}} = \frac{\bar{a}_i A_i R_i}{A} \qquad (2)$$

If there are several streams n of incident radiation fluxes then the amount of radiation absorbed per unit surface area is given by

$$Q_{abs} = \frac{\sum_{i=1}^{n} \bar{a}_i A_i R_i}{A} \qquad (3)$$

The mean absorptivity $\bar{a}_i$ of a leaf surface whose monochromatic absorptivity is $_\lambda a_i$ to an incident flux of radiation whose monochromatic intensity is $_\lambda R_i$ is given by the following product

$$\bar{a}_i = \frac{\int _\lambda a_{i\lambda} R_i d_\lambda}{\int _\lambda R_i d_\lambda} \qquad (4)$$

The spectral absorptivity $_\lambda a_i$ is determined by measuring the monochromatic reflectivity $_\lambda r_i$ and transmissivity $_\lambda t_i$ with a spectrophotometer and calculating

$$_\lambda a_i = 1 - _\lambda r_i - _\lambda t_i \qquad (5)$$

In a natural daytime situation a leaf may expose an area A_S of mean absorptivity $\bar{a}_S$ to a flux of direct sunlight of intensity S, and area A_s of mean absorptivity $\bar{a}_s$ to a flux of scattered skylight whose intensity is s, and area A_r of mean absorptivity $\bar{a}_r$ to a flux of reflected sunlight and skylight $r(S + s)$, and Area A_a of mean absorptivity $\bar{a}_a$ to a flux of atmospheric thermal radiation of intensity R_a and an area A_g of mean absorptivity $\bar{a}_g$ to a flux of ground thermal radiation of intensity R_g to result in a quantity of radiation absorbed which is calculated according to Eqn. (3) as follows:

$$Q_{abs} = \frac{\bar{a}_S A_S S + \bar{a}_s A_s s + \bar{a}_r A_r r(S + s) + \bar{a}_a A_a R_a + \bar{a}_g A_g R_g}{A} \qquad (6)$$

It is likely that the following simplifications can be made as a good approximation:

$$\bar{a}_S = \bar{a}_r; \qquad \bar{a}_a = \bar{a}_g; \qquad A_s = A_r = A_a = A_g = A/2$$

Hence, Eqn. (6) becomes

$$Q_{abs} = \frac{\bar{a}_S A_S S + \bar{a}_s(A/2)s + \bar{a}_s(A/2)r(S + s) + \bar{a}_a(A/2)(R_a + R_g)}{A}$$

$$= \frac{\bar{a}_S[\cos i \, S + r(S + s)] + a_s s + \bar{a}_a R_a + R_g)}{2} \qquad (7)$$

since $A_S = (A/2) \cos i$, where i = angle of incidence of the incident beam of direct sunlight with the normal to the surface of the plant leaf. If, as a further approximation, one assumes that $\bar{a}_S = \bar{a}_s$ then

$$Q_{abs} = \frac{\bar{a}_S[(\cos i + r)S + (1 + r)s] + \bar{a}_a(R_a + R_g)}{2} \qquad (8)$$

It is not the purpose here to give a detailed discussion of the various sources of radiation, however a few examples are given in Fig. 1. in order to indicate the range of values likely to be encountered in natural terrestrial environments. Here, for the purpose of calculating Fig. 1, a mean absorptivity $\bar{a}_s = 0.5$ for the leaf surface to sunlight is assumed. The mean absorptivity to long wave, infrared thermal radiation is assumed as $\bar{a}_a = 1.0$, which is close enough for practical purposes to the actual value of about 0.96. All calculation are accurate to ± 0.05 cal cm^{-2} min^{-1}.

The diagram presented in Fig. 1 is somewhat complicated and for that reason it may require careful study by the reader before he gets a complete comprehension of it. It is hoped that the following discussion will be useful to the reader.

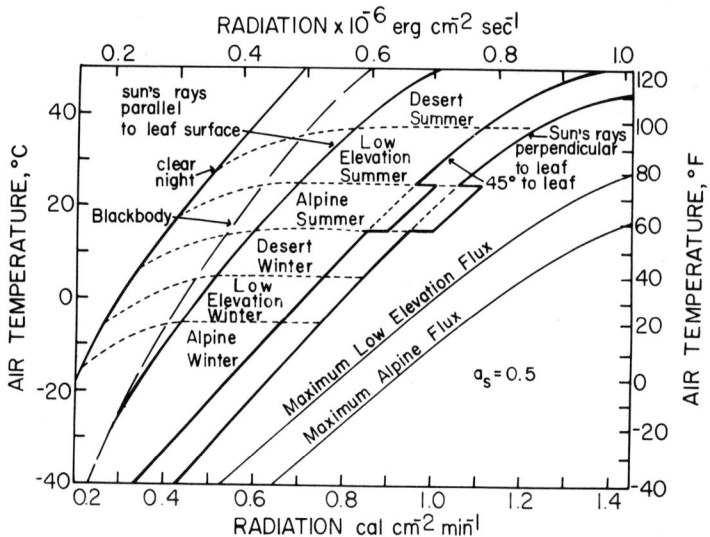

FIG. 1. Relationship between the air temperature of the environment and the total estimated radiation flux absorbed by a leaf for various leaf orientations to the direct sunshine. Leaf absorptivity to sunlight is taken as 0.5.

Figure 1 is valid only for mid latitudes, say between about 30° and 50°. There is a fairly definite relation between the intensities of the radiation fluxes within any specified environment and the air temperature. If a leaf has its surface perpendicular to the incident rays from the sun the amount of radiation absorbed by it in the daylight is given by the right-hand heavy solid line. The heavy solid line represents the amount of radiation absorbed by the leaf receiving sunlight, skylight, reflected light and thermal radiation from ground and atmosphere. If the leaf surface makes an angle of 45° with the incident rays of the sun then the amount of radiation absorbed by the leaf is shown by the intermediate heavy solid line, which is marked accordingly. If the leaf surface is parallel to the incident direct rays of the sun, the leaf still absorbs light from scattered skylight, reflected light, and thermal radiation giving the relation shown by the heavy solid line which approaches the blackbody line. The blackbody line (long dashes) is known with great precision and is shown for the sake of comparison. Leaves within a dense canopy are in a situation which approximates the blackbody radiation condition.

At night leaves in the open are exposed to the blackbody, thermal radiation from the ground and to the much weaker thermal radiation of the cold clear sky; hence they have an average amount of absorbed radiation which is less than the blackbody amount. The heavy solid line at the left-hand side of the diagram represents the amount of radiation absorbed by a leaf at night.

If a leaf absorbed all incident sunlight, skylight, reflected light and thermal radiation and had its surface perpendicular to the direct rays of the sun it would absorb the amount of radiation given by the two thin solid lines at the right-hand side of the diagram. Fluxes of sunlight are greater at high elevations in the mountains, e.g. in the alpine tundra, than at low elevation sites. If the absorptivity of the leaf is 0.6 rather than 0.5, the lines shift to the right by approximately 0.04 cal cm^{-2} min^{-1} at 0°C.

The air temperature–radiation climate of plant leaves are indicated in Fig. 1 for the following situations: a desert summer and winter, a low elevation site summer and winter, and an alpine summer and winter. Other situations could be indicated also. The boundaries for each situation are not to be considered absolute. In fact, the climate of one situation can overlap considerably with the climate of another. However, from Fig. 1 it is possible to read any other situation one wishes. A cloudy day would produce fluxes of absorbed radiation which may approximate the blackbody line or thinner clouds, and more sunlight would fall between the solid lines to the right of the blackbody line. With just a little experience one can learn to select the proper amount of radiation absorbed for a specific air temperature in a given environmental situation. With an overcast sky the amount of radiation absorbed by a leaf is nearly independent of the angle of the leaf.

A leaf in a summer desert environment, with high air temperature, may have values of Q_{abs} between 1.2 and 1.4 cal cm^{-2} min^{-1}. A leaf in a summer sea level or low elevation environment may have Q_{abs}

between 1.0 and 1.2 cal cm^{-2} min^{-1}. In the summer alpine condition the amount of radiation absorbed by a plant leaf may ordinarily be about 0.95 to 1.05 cal cm^{-2} min^{-1}, but on occasion may be as much as 1.1 cal cm^{-2} min^{-1}. The heavy solid lines showing the amount of radiation absorbed by a leaf in the alpine environment jog to the right about 0.05 cal cm^{-2} min^{-1}. Although the flux of direct sunlight is very intense in the alpine environment, the amount of scattered skylight is low because of the low-density dry atmosphere overhead and the low flux of thermal radiation from the cold sky and cold ground surface. The amount of radiation incident on a leaf in the desert environment is disproportionately greater than the flux incident in the alpine environment, not only because of the much higher ground surface temperature and air temperature affecting the thermal radiation, but also because of the generally greater albedo of the desert soils affecting the amount of reflected sunlight. Another factor taken into account when calculating the values of absorbed radiation is the relative transparency of the atmosphere to the flux of direct sunlight. The low elevation sites have the greatest amount of water vapor in the atmosphere and less direct sunlight as a result.

The nighttime air temperatures are almost always lower than the daytime air temperatures. Hence the boundaries shown for the various climates bend downward to the left until they terminate at the heavy left-hand line representing the clear night situation with a leaf fully exposed to a clear sky. If it is overcast at night the appropriate situation will fall just to the left of the blackbody line.

It is difficult to make a generalized diagram, such as Fig. 1, which applies to all situations with great accuracy. Specific cases should be evaluated carefully in order to calculate Q_{abs}. Figure 1 is intended as a general guide only.

CONVECTION

Heat and mass transfer by the flow of air across a leaf surface is a very complex phenomenon known as convection. It is not the purpose here to give a thorough discussion of the subject of convective heat transfer but to summarize the basic concept. Generally, the rate of heat transfer Q_c between a surface and the surrounding air is proportional to the temperature difference between surface temperature T_s and air temperature T_a:

$$Q_c = h_c(T_s - T_a) \tag{9}$$

where h_c = coefficient of convective heat transfer, which in itself depends upon the roughness of the surface, its size and shape, the orientation of the surface to the wind direction, the wind speed and the density of the air. Next to every surface is a boundary layer of adhering air across which there may be a temperature difference which results in the transfer of heat from the surface by conduction and into the air by convection. Actually the process of convection includes the conduction of heat across the boundary layer and the mass movement of air beyond the boundary layer transferring the energy in the fluid.

Engineers have made many detailed observations of the transfer of energy and mass between flat plates, circular plates, cylinders and spheres to and from the surrounding air. Very few of the surfaces which engineers have studied represent the surfaces of plant leaves with any precision. Nevertheless, their results for flat plates represent a reasonable approximation to plant leaves and at least give us an idea of the size of the numbers and the functional dependence of the convective heat transfer coefficient on wind speed and leaf dimension. The thickness of the boundary layer of adhering air increases with the size of the surface. The thicker the boundary layer, the smaller the amount of heat transferred by convection. Hence, the coefficient of convective heat transfer decreases with increasing leaf dimension D. The greater the wind speed the smaller is the depth of the boundary layer and the greater is the value of the coefficient of convective heat transfer. For flat plates which are warmer or colder than the surrounding air, the coefficient of convective heat transfer is inversely proportional to the square root of the dimension of the leaf in the direction of the air flow. For flat plates engineers have established the following convective heat transfer coefficients for the situations specified:

Forced laminar flow with plate at uniform temperature in air:

$$h_c = 5.73 \times 10^{-3} V^{0.5} D^{-0.5} \tag{10}$$

Forced laminar flow with plate in uniform heat flux in air:

$$h_c = 7.77 \times 10^{-3} V^{0.5} D^{-0.5} \tag{11}$$

Forced turbulent flow across a flat plate in air:

$$h_c = 5.46 \times 10^{-4} V^{0.8} D^{-0.2} \tag{12}$$

One should note that the convective heat transfer coefficient for turbulent flow is smaller than that for laminar flow at low wind speeds but at higher wind speeds it is larger. For a leaf of characteristic dimensions (10 cm) the wind speed at which the turbulent convective heat transfer rate exceeds the laminar convective heat transfer rate is 690 cm sec^{-1}, and for a 1 cm leaf it is 6900 cm sec^{-1}. Furthermore, it is known that laminar flow dominates the pattern of convective heat loss over leaves of ordinary dimensions for the wind speeds normally encountered. In fact, at a wind speed of 100 cm sec^{-1} laminar flow exists for a distance of 7.1 cm along the leaf, but at a wind speed of 500 cm sec^{-1} laminar flow changes to turbulent flow after 1.4 cm along a leaf. A leaf is generally neither at uniform temperature across its surface, nor at uniform heat flux, nor all laminar flow, nor all turbulent flow, nor with a very simple geometry. This is the primary reason for having derived the coefficients of Eqn. (1) directly from measurements with real leaves mounted in a laboratory wind tunnel. It is seen that the convective heat transfer coefficient in Eqn. (1) is as follows:

$$h_c = k_1(V/D)^{0.5} \qquad (13)$$

where $k_1 = 10 \times 10^{-3}$ when $W > D$ or $W = D > 5$ cm or $D > 10$ cm and $k_1 = 16.2 \times 10^{-3}$ when $W < D \leq 10$ cm or $W = D \leq 5$ cm.

Comparison with Eqns. (10), (11) and (12) shows that k_1 is larger than the coefficients normally used for flat plates. This is as one would expect since leaf shape and roughness will tend to produce an increase in the rate of convective heat exchange. Also, by assuming a square root function of wind speed and characteristic dimension for the convective term, the coefficient k_1 tends to take account of the increased convective heat exchange which occurs with the 0.8 power of the wind speed for turbulent flow at the greater wind speeds. At very low wind speeds one would expect, from the strictly practical standpoint, that a larger coefficient is required than the normal forced convection coefficient since free convection adds significantly to the rate of convective heat exchange when forced convection is small. All of this would indicate to us that the values of k_1 used here are very nearly correct within the context of the formulation of the problem. Rather than using a different expression for free or natural convection which does not contain the wind speed but is expressed solely as a buoyancy force as a result of the temperature difference betweeen leaf and air, we consider that free convection occurs when $V = 10$ cm sec^{-1}. Purely free convection occurs relatively rarely in nature, particularly during the daytime.

Ideally it is desired that the rate of convective heat exchange is expressed as a function of W and D instead of a function of D alone. We were able to evaluate the apparent influence of W and D on the evaporative exchange of moisture from a leaf in the way they influence the boundary layer resistance. To carry the analysis one step further, e.g. to include W in addition to D in the convection term, required an accuracy and sophistication of measurement much beyond the scope of the present observations. We had to make a judgment as to the most reasonable procedure and elected to evaluate the convective term as a function of D only and the evaporative terms as a function of W and D.

LEAVES OF VARIOUS SHAPES

There is often some question concerning the exact value of D to use for a particular leaf. Parkhurst *et al.* (1968) reported an evaluation of the characteristic dimension of leaves of various shapes and sizes. As a general rule the "effective" characteristic dimension D of a leaf in the direction of wind flow is between 0.5 and 0.8 of its maximum dimension in that direction. The laboratory experiments which led to the establishment of k_1 in Eqn. (1) involved rectangular areas of moistened and dry blotting paper which had a constant dimension in the direction of wind flow. A real leaf is tapered towards the ends and often the edge is serrated or involuted in various ways. The use of a smaller "effective" characteristic dimension than the maximum dimension in the direction of wind flow will increase the rate of convective heat exchange; a change which is probably in the right direction according to our observations and experience.

The following definitions of mean characteristic dimensions are more correct than those used in the paper by Parkhurst *et al.* (1968) and should supplant the values given there.

Assume that a leaf has an irregular shape as shown in Fig. 2 and that the dimension of the leaf in the direction of air flow at any position x is given by $w(x)$. The total length of the leaf is L. The area of the leaf is given by

$$A = \int_0^L w(x)\ dx \qquad (14)$$

For laminar flow in forced convection we know from Eqn. (10) that at constant air speed the convection coefficient is inversely proportional to the square root of the dimension in the direction of air flow. For a given temperature difference $\Delta T = T_l - T_a$, between leaf and air, the total amount of heat $\dot{q}$ convected to or from the leaf per unit time is given by:

$$\dot{q} = K \int_0^L w(x)^{-0.5} w(x)\ dx = K \int_0^L w(x)^{0.5}\ dx \qquad (15)$$

It is desired that this rate of convective heat exchange be expressed in terms of a mean characteristic dimension $\bar{D}$ as follows:

$$\dot{q} = K\bar{D}^{-0.5} \int_0^L w(x)\ dx \qquad (16)$$

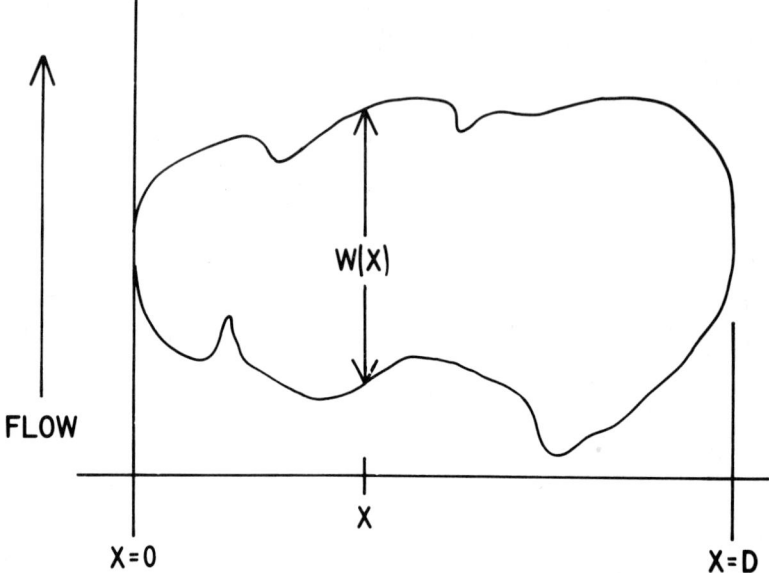

FIG. 2. An arbitrary leaf shape used for the mathematical determination of its weighted-mean width for convective heat transfer.

Hence, equating Eqns. (15) and (16) and solving for D one obtains:

$$D = \left[\frac{\int_0^L w(x) \, dx}{\int_0^L w(x)^{0.5} \, dx} \right]^2 \tag{17}$$

for the mean value the characteristic dimension for the convective heat exchange of an irregular shaped leaf in laminar forced flow.

If an identical procedure is used for the case of turbulent forced flow one finds that the mean value of the characteristic dimension is given by:

$$D = \left[\frac{\int_0^L w(x) \, dx}{\int_0^L w(x)^{0.8} \, dx} \right]^5 \tag{18}$$

For leaves of many shapes the ratio of the mean value of the characteristic dimension to the maximum dimension in the direction of wind flow is about 0.6 for laminar flow and 0.7 for turbulent flow tranversally across the leaf, and somewhat larger ratios for flow in the longitudinal direction. As a general rule, however, one can take the characteristic dimension of a leaf to be approximately 0.7 of its maximum dimension in the direction of air flow.

Evaporative Heat Exchange

In addition to radiation and convection, evaporative heat exchange at a leaf surface is often a very significant part of the total energy budget of a leaf, and therefore has a notable influence on the leaf temperature. The fact that this is true is demonstrated clearly by the graphs and tabulations to follow. The relation between the transpiration rate of a leaf and the leaf temperature was discussed in detail by Gates (1968).

The loss of moisture from a plant leaf is essentially a diffusion process by which water vapor is evaporated inside the leaf from liquid water at the mesophyll to flow along a vapor pressure gradient from the sub-stomatal cavity, through the stomates and boundary layer adhering to the leaf surface to the free air beyond the boundary layer. The pathway through the substomatal cavity and stomate offers a resistance to the flow because of the viscosity of the air. This internal resistance depends on the dimensions of the cross section at each part of the pathway and on the length of the pathway. Clearly the internal or leaf resistance r_l is a direct result of the particular leaf anatomy. In addition there is an external resistance in the diffusion pathway as a result of the adhering boundary layer of air. This external resistance r_a is affected by the wind flow along the leaf surface.

There are two requirements for the loss of moisture from a leaf by transpiration. First, there must be energy available to change the moisture from liquid water to water vapor, a process which requires 580 calories per gram at 30°C. Second, there must be a water vapor pressure or density gradient along which the water vapor will flow. The water vapor density $_sd_l(T_l)$ at the mesophyll cell walls lining the substomatal cavity is assumed saturated at the leaf temperature T_l. During conditions of great water stress there are times when saturation does not exist in the intercellular air spaces of the leaf mesophyll. If such is the case it is easily taken into account by multiplying $_sd_l(T_l)$ by a value for the relative humidity inside the leaf, a value rarely less than 0.95. The actual water vapor density $d_a(T_a)$ of the air temperature T_a beyond the adhering boundary layer is the product of the relative humidity r.h. of the air and the saturation vapor density $_sd_a(T_a)$ of the air at the temperature T_a. Hence $d_a(T_a) = $ r.h. $_sd_a(T_a)$ and the driving force for the diffusion of water vapor from the leaf is $_sd_l(T_l) - $ r.h. $_sd_a(T_a)$. The transpiration rate E is given by the following diffusion equation:

$$E = \frac{_sd_l(T_l) - \text{r.h.} \, _sd_a(T_a)}{r_l + r_a} \tag{19}$$

The boundary layer resistance r_a of the adhering layer of air on the leaf surface varies with the wind speed across the surface and with the dimensions of the leaf. Hence the following relation fitted the observations best:

$$r_a = k_2 \frac{W^{0.20}D^{0.35}}{V^{0.55}} \tag{20}$$

where k_2 is a constant of proportionality in units such that if V is in cm sec^{-1} and W and D in cm, then r_a is expressed in min cm^{-1}. At low wind speed the boundary layer resistance may be of the same magnitude as the internal leaf resistance, particularly for those leaves which have many large stomates and give off water with relative ease. Often the minimum leaf resistance for agronomic plants are about 0.01 to 0.02 min cm^{-1}. The boundary layer resistance of a leaf 10×10 cm becomes equal to these values for wind speeds of 70 and 21 cm sec^{-1} respectively. The leaves of many plants have greater internal resistances than this and for them the boundary layer resistance is often only a small fraction of the total resistance.

It is important to know the minimum internal resistance for a leaf of a particular species since the values of r_l which can occur in practice are always of this value or greater. If one can measure E by weighing a leaf or a plant during an interval of time when the leaf is strongly ventilated, so that r_a is small, and at the same time measure T_l, r.h. and T_a, one can solve Eqn. (14) for r_l. If this is done while the leaf is well watered and in full light, one may obtain a good estimate of $_{min}r_l$. The value of $_{min}r_l$ for a plant species will vary between sun and shade leaf, old and new leaf, as well as for leaves grown with different nutrients available or with various histories of photoperiod and thermoperiod. Again good judgment must be used in knowing what is the most reasonable value for $_{min}r_l$ and for values of r_l for any set of environmental conditions.

ACKNOWLEDGMENTS

This research was supported by the Center for the Biology of Natural Systems, Washington University, under PHS Grant No. ES 00139-04 and the computer facilities of Washington University under NSF Grant No. G 22296.

THE TABLES

A plant leaf responds to the energy flow as expressed by Eqn. (1) to achieve a specific temperature and transpiration rate for a given set of environmental conditions. Two leaves with different properties (e.g. different size or color or internal diffusion resistance) will respond in very different ways (e.g. different temperatures and transpiration rates) to the same identical set of environmental conditions. The numbers of combinations are many and the relations expressed by Eqn. (1) are intricate. With the aid of a digital computer, solutions of Eqn. (1) are obtained for any and all combinations of values of the variables. The Tables to follow are the result of these calculations.

The tables list leaf temperatures and rates of transpiration at specific values of leaf resistance, relative humidities and leaf temperatures for certain values of wind speed, radiation absorbed, and leaf dimensions. Leaf temperatures are given in °C and the rates of transpiration in gm cm^{-2} sec^{-1}. Results are given for relative humidities of 0 and 100% only because of the relative insensitivity of the dependent variables on relative humidity and the fact that linear interpolation for relative humidities between 0 and 100% is easy and accurate. Results are listed for air temperatures of 0, 10, 20, 30, and 40°C, which adequately cover the ranges of air temperatures normally encountered in the natural environment when broad leaves are physiologically active. The diffusion resistances listed are given in sec cm^{-1} even though the calculations of Eqn. (1) were made in min cm^{-1} (simply sec cm^{-1}/60 sec min^{-1}). The values of leaf temperature and transpiration rate are given for internal leaf resistances of 0, 1, 2, 5, 10, 20, and ∞ sec cm^{-1} with no listing of transpiration rate for an infinite resistance since the rate is always zero. When the transpiration rate is less than zero, the transpiration rate and its corresponding temperature are left blank. The tabulations are organized first under wind speeds of 10, 20, 50, 100, 200, 400, and 800 cm sec^{-1}. At each wind speed the tabulations are then organized for a constant amount of absorbed radiation of 0.4 × 10^6, 0.6 × 10^6, 0.8 × 10^6, and 1.0 × 10^6 ergs. cm^{-2} sec^{-1}. The conversion factor from one set of energy units to the other is given in the tabulation at the head of the table as 1.0 × 10^6 ergs cm^{-2} sec^{-1} = 1.433 cal cm^{-2} min^{-1}. Within a given wind speed and amount of radiation absorbed the tables are given for the following leaf dimensions of D and W: 1 and 1, 5 and 1, 1 and 5, 5 and 5, 10 and 5, 20 and 5, 1 and 10, 5 and 10, 10 and 10, and 20 and 10 cm. There are 280 tables of leaf temperatures and 280 tables of transpiration rates. It would be easy to have many others but the tables given here are considered minimal. In order to make up for the lack of more tables graphical relations are given so that inter-polation and extrapolation is done easily.

A great deal of thought was given to the choice of presenting humidity on a relative humidity basis, where air temperature is specified simult-aneously, as against the choice of using vapor pressure or absolute humidity. After considerable trial and testing we elected to present relative humidity, partly dictated by the fact that most workers will still think in terms of relative humidity and use instruments which measure relative humidity.

INFORMATION ABOUT TABLES --

VARIABLE	NAME	UNITS
AIRSPEED	V	CENTIMETERS/SECOND
AIR TEMPERATURE	TA	DEGREES CENTIGRADE
LEAF TEMPERATURE	TL	DEGREES CENTIGRADE
TRANSPIRATION EXP 6	E	GRAMS/SQUARE CENTIMETER/SECOND
RELATIVE HUMIDITY	RH	DIMENSIONLESS
INTERNAL DIFFUSION RESISTANCE	RES	SECONDS/CENTIMETER
DIMENSION ALONG AIRFLOW	D	CENTIMETERS
DIMENSION ACROSS AIRFLOW	W	CENTIMETERS
RADIATION ABSORBED	Q	ERGS/SQUARE CENTIMETER/SECOND

1.0 EXP 6 ERGS/CM2/SEC   #   1.433 CAL/CM2/MIN

LINEAR INTERPOLATION WILL YIELD LEAF TEMPERATURES AND TRANSPIRATION
RATES AT ANY DESIRED RELATIVE HUMIDITY.

AIRSPEED = 10. CM/SEC   RADIATION ABSORBED = 0.4 EXP 6 ERGS/CM2/SEC

DIMENSION ALONG AIRFLOW = 1 CM   DIMENSION ACROSS AIRFLOW = 1 CM

TA	RH	LEAF TEMPERATURES FOR RESISTANCES=							TRANSPIRATION EXP 6 FOR RES =					
		**0*	**1*	**2*	**5*	*10*	*20*	INF*	**0*	**1*	**2*	**5*	*10*	*20*
0	0	-3.1	0.4	1.2	1.9	2.2	2.3	2.5	9.0	3.5	2.2	1.0	0.5	0.3
0	100	1.7	2.2	2.3	2.4	2.5	2.5	2.5	1.4	0.5	0.3	0.2	0.1	0.0
10	0	2.9	7.8	9.1	10.3	10.8	11.0	11.3	13.7	5.7	3.7	1.8	0.9	0.5
10	100	10.7	11.1	11.2	11.2	11.3	11.3	11.3	1.0	0.5	0.3	0.1	0.1	0.0
20	0	8.3	14.8	16.6	18.3	19.1	19.6	20.1	19.5	8.8	5.8	2.9	1.6	0.8
20	100	20.0	20.0	20.0	20.1	20.1	20.1	20.1	0.1	0.0	0.0	0.0	0.0	0.0
30	0	13.0	21.1	23.6	26.1	27.2	27.9	28.7	26.3	12.9	8.7	4.5	2.5	1.3
30	100													
40	0	17.2	26.9	30.0	33.4	35.1	36.1	37.2	33.9	17.9	12.5	6.7	3.8	2.0
40	100													

DIMENSION ALONG AIRFLOW = 5 CM   DIMENSION ACROSS AIRFLOW = 1 CM

TA	RH	LEAF TEMPERATURES FOR RESISTANCES=							TRANSPIRATION EXP 6 FOR RES =					
		**0*	**1*	**2*	**5*	*10*	*20*	INF*	**0*	**1*	**2*	**5*	*10*	*20*
0	0	-1.9	1.3	2.4	3.6	4.2	4.5	4.9	5.6	3.0	2.1	1.1	0.6	0.3
0	100	3.0	3.9	4.2	4.5	4.7	4.8	4.9	1.5	0.8	0.6	0.3	0.2	0.1
10	0	3.1	7.3	8.9	10.6	11.5	12.0	12.6	7.9	4.5	3.2	1.7	1.0	0.5
10	100	11.3	11.8	12.0	12.3	12.4	12.5	12.6	1.1	0.7	0.5	0.3	0.1	0.1
20	0	7.6	12.7	14.8	17.2	18.5	19.2	20.1	10.6	6.3	4.6	2.5	1.5	0.8
20	100	20.0	20.1	20.1	20.1	20.1	20.1	20.1	0.1	0.0	0.0	0.0	0.0	0.0
30	0	11.7	17.7	20.3	23.4	25.1	26.2	27.5	13.7	8.6	6.4	3.7	2.2	1.2
30	100													
40	0	15.3	22.3	25.3	29.2	31.4	32.9	34.8	17.2	11.2	8.5	5.1	3.1	1.7
40	100													

AIRSPEED = 10. CM/SEC   RADIATION ABSORBED = 0.4 EXP 6 ERGS/CM2/SEC

DIMENSION ALONG AIRFLOW = 1 CM   DIMENSION ACROSS AIRFLOW = 5 CM

LEAF TEMPERATURES FOR RESISTANCES=   TRANSPIRATION EXP 6 FOR RES =

TA	RH	**0*	**1*	**2*	**5*	*10*	*20*	INF*	**0*	**1*	**2*	**5*	*10*	*20*
0	0	-1.9	0.6	1.2	1.9	2.2	2.3	2.5	7.1	3.2	2.0	1.0	0.5	0.3
0	100	1.8	2.2	2.3	2.4	2.5	2.5	2.5	1.1	0.5	0.3	0.2	0.1	0.0
10	0	4.6	8.1	9.2	10.3	10.8	11.0	11.3	11.1	5.2	3.4	1.7	0.9	0.5
10	100	10.8	11.1	11.2	11.3	11.3	11.3	11.3	0.8	0.4	0.3	0.1	0.1	0.0
20	0	10.3	15.2	16.8	18.4	19.1	19.6	20.1	16.1	8.1	5.5	2.8	1.6	0.8
20	100	20.0	20.0	20.0	20.1	20.1	20.1	20.1	0.1	0.0	0.0	0.0	0.0	0.0
30	0	15.5	21.7	23.8	26.1	27.2	27.9	28.7	22.2	11.9	8.3	4.4	2.5	1.3
30	100													
40	0	20.1	27.6	30.3	33.5	35.1	36.1	37.2	29.2	16.7	11.9	6.5	3.8	2.0
40	100													

DIMENSION ALONG AIRFLOW = 5 CM   DIMENSION ACROSS AIRFLOW = 5 CM

LEAF TEMPERATURES FOR RESISTANCES=   TRANSPIRATION EXP 6 FOR RES =

TA	RH	**0*	**1*	**2*	**5*	*10*	*20*	INF*	**0*	**1*	**2*	**5*	*10*	*20*
0	0	-0.5	1.7	2.6	3.7	4.2	4.5	4.9	4.5	2.7	1.9	1.0	0.6	0.3
0	100	3.4	4.0	4.3	4.6	4.7	4.8	4.9	1.2	0.7	0.5	0.3	0.2	0.1
10	0	4.9	7.8	9.2	10.7	11.5	12.0	12.6	6.5	4.0	2.9	1.6	0.9	0.5
10	100	11.5	11.9	12.1	12.3	12.4	12.5	12.6	0.9	0.6	0.4	0.2	0.1	0.1
20	0	9.8	13.5	15.2	17.3	18.5	19.2	20.1	8.8	5.7	4.3	2.4	1.4	0.8
20	100	20.1	20.1	20.1	20.1	20.1	20.1	20.1	0.1	0.0	0.0	0.0	0.0	0.0
30	0	14.2	18.6	20.8	23.6	25.2	26.2	27.5	11.6	7.8	5.9	3.5	2.1	1.2
30	100													
40	0	18.1	23.3	25.9	29.4	31.5	32.9	34.8	14.8	10.2	8.0	4.9	3.0	1.7
40	100													

AIRSPEED = 10. CM/SEC   RADIATION ABSORBED = 0.4 EXP 6 ERGS/CM2/SEC

DIMENSION ALONG AIRFLOW = 10 CM   DIMENSION ACROSS AIRFLOW = 5 CM

TA	RH	LEAF TEMPERATURES FOR RESISTANCES=							TRANSPIRATION EXP 6 FOR RES =					
		**0*	**1*	**2*	**5*	*10*	*20*	INF*	**0*	**1*	**2*	**5*	*10*	*20*
0	0	0.5	2.5	3.5	4.7	5.4	5.8	6.4	3.8	2.5	1.8	1.1	0.6	0.3
0	100	4.4	5.0	5.4	5.8	6.0	6.2	6.4	1.3	0.8	0.6	0.4	0.2	0.1
10	0	5.3	7.9	9.2	11.0	11.9	12.6	13.3	5.2	3.5	2.7	1.6	0.9	0.5
10	100	12.0	12.4	12.6	12.9	13.1	13.2	13.3	0.9	0.6	0.5	0.3	0.2	0.1
20	0	9.8	12.9	14.6	16.9	18.2	19.0	20.2	6.9	4.8	3.8	2.3	1.4	0.8
20	100	20.1	20.1	20.1	20.1	20.2	20.2	20.2	0.1	0.0	0.0	0.0	0.0	0.0
30	0	13.8	17.5	19.5	22.3	24.1	25.3	26.8	8.9	6.4	5.0	3.1	1.9	1.1
30	100													
40	0	17.4	21.7	24.1	27.5	29.7	31.3	33.4	11.1	8.2	6.6	4.2	2.6	1.5
40	100													

DIMENSION ALONG AIRFLOW = 20 CM   DIMENSION ACROSS AIRFLOW = 5 CM

TA	RH	LEAF TEMPERATURES FOR RESISTANCES=							TRANSPIRATION EXP 6 FOR RES =					
		**0*	**1*	**2*	**5*	*10*	*20*	INF*	**0*	**1*	**2*	**5*	*10*	*20*
0	0	3.7	5.2	6.2	7.7	8.7	9.5	10.5	2.7	2.1	1.7	1.1	0.7	0.4
0	100	7.2	7.9	8.4	9.1	9.6	10.0	10.5	1.3	1.0	0.8	0.6	0.4	0.2
10	0	7.1	8.9	10.1	11.9	13.2	14.1	15.5	3.3	2.6	2.2	1.4	0.9	0.5
10	100	13.2	13.7	14.0	14.5	14.8	15.1	15.5	0.9	0.7	0.6	0.4	0.3	0.2
20	0	10.2	12.3	13.7	15.9	17.4	18.6	20.3	4.1	3.3	2.7	1.8	1.2	0.7
20	100	20.1	20.1	20.1	20.2	20.2	20.2	20.2	0.1	0.0	0.0	0.0	0.0	0.0
30	0	13.2	15.5	17.1	19.6	21.5	22.9	25.0	4.9	4.0	3.4	2.3	1.5	0.9
30	100													
40	0	15.9	18.5	20.2	23.1	25.3	27.0	29.6	5.8	4.8	4.1	2.8	1.9	1.2
40	100													

AIRSPEED = 10. CM/SEC   RADIATION ABSORBED = 0.4 EXP 6 ERGS/CM2/SEC

		DIMENSION ALONG AIRFLOW = 1 CM							DIMENSION ACROSS AIRFLOW = 10 CM					
		LEAF TEMPERATURES FOR RESISTANCES=							TRANSPIRATION EXP 6 FOR RES =					
TA	RH	**0*	**1*	**2*	**5*	*10*	*20*	INF*	**0*	**1*	**2*	***5*	*10*	*20*
0	0	-0.8	1.3	2.0	2.9	3.3	3.5	3.8	4.9	2.7	1.9	1.0	0.6	0.3
0	100	2.8	3.2	3.4	3.6	3.7	3.7	3.8	1.1	0.6	0.4	0.2	0.1	0.1
10	0	5.2	8.1	9.2	10.5	11.2	11.6	12.0	7.4	4.3	3.0	1.6	0.9	0.5
10	100	11.3	11.6	11.7	11.8	11.9	12.0	12.0	0.8	0.5	0.4	0.2	0.1	0.1
20	0	10.6	14.4	15.9	17.8	18.8	19.4	20.1	10.4	6.4	4.6	2.6	1.5	0.8
20	100	20.1	20.1	20.1	20.1	20.1	20.1	20.1	0.1	0.0	0.0	0.0	0.0	0.0
30	0	15.5	20.1	22.2	24.7	26.1	27.0	28.1	14.1	9.0	6.7	3.8	2.2	1.2
30	100													
40	0	19.8	25.4	27.9	31.2	33.1	34.3	35.9	18.3	12.1	9.2	5.5	3.3	1.8
40	100													

		DIMENSION ALONG AIRFLOW = 5 CM							DIMENSION ACROSS AIRFLOW = 10 CM					
		LEAF TEMPERATURES FOR RESISTANCES=							TRANSPIRATION EXP 6 FOR RES =					
TA	RH	**0*	**1*	**2*	**5*	*10*	*20*	INF*	**0*	**1*	**2*	***5*	*10*	*20*
0	0	1.4	3.1	4.0	5.2	5.9	6.4	7.0	3.2	2.3	1.7	1.0	0.6	0.3
0	100	5.0	5.6	5.9	6.3	6.6	6.8	7.0	1.2	0.8	0.6	0.4	0.2	0.1
10	0	6.2	8.3	9.5	11.1	12.1	12.8	13.7	4.5	3.2	2.5	1.5	0.9	0.5
10	100	12.2	12.6	12.8	13.1	13.3	13.5	13.7	0.9	0.6	0.5	0.3	0.2	0.1
20	0	10.5	13.1	14.6	16.7	18.1	19.0	20.2	5.9	4.3	3.4	2.1	1.3	0.8
20	100	20.1	20.1	20.1	20.1	20.1	20.1	20.2	0.1	0.0	0.0	0.0	0.0	0.0
30	0	14.4	17.5	19.4	22.0	23.7	24.9	26.6	7.5	5.7	4.6	2.9	1.8	1.1
30	100													
40	0	18.0	21.6	23.7	26.9	29.0	30.6	32.8	9.4	7.2	5.9	3.9	2.5	1.4
40	100													

AIRSPEED = 10. CM/SEC   RADIATION ABSORBED = 0.4 EXP 6 ERGS/CM2/SEC

DIMENSION ALONG AIRFLOW = 10 CM   DIMENSION ACROSS AIRFLOW = 10 CM

TA	RH	LEAF TEMPERATURES FOR RESISTANCES=							TRANSPIRATION EXP 6 FOR RES =					
		**0*	**1*	**2*	**5*	*10*	*20*	INF*	**0*	**1*	**2*	**5*	*10*	*20*
0	0	2.7	4.3	5.1	6.5	7.3	7.9	8.7	2.8	2.1	1.7	1.1	0.7	0.4
0	100	6.2	6.8	7.2	7.7	8.1	8.4	8.7	1.2	0.9	0.7	0.5	0.3	0.2
10	0	6.9	8.8	9.9	11.6	12.7	13.5	14.5	3.7	2.8	2.3	1.5	0.9	0.5
10	100	12.8	13.2	13.4	13.8	14.1	14.3	14.5	0.9	0.7	0.5	0.4	0.2	0.1
20	0	10.7	12.9	14.2	16.3	17.8	18.8	20.2	4.7	3.6	3.0	2.0	1.3	0.7
20	100	20.1	20.1	20.1	20.2	20.2	20.2	20.2	0.1	0.0	0.0	0.0	0.0	0.0
30	0	14.2	16.7	18.3	20.8	22.6	23.9	25.8	5.8	4.6	3.8	2.6	1.7	1.0
30	100													
40	0	17.4	20.3	22.1	25.0	27.2	28.8	31.2	7.1	5.7	4.8	3.3	2.2	1.3
40	100													

DIMENSION ALONG AIRFLOW = 20 CM   DIMENSION ACROSS AIRFLOW = 10 CM

TA	RH	LEAF TEMPERATURES FOR RESISTANCES=							TRANSPIRATION EXP 6 FOR RES =					
		**0*	**1*	**2*	**5*	*10*	*20*	INF*	**0*	**1*	**2*	**5*	*10*	*20*
0	0	4.3	5.6	6.4	7.8	8.8	9.5	10.5	2.4	1.9	1.6	1.1	0.7	0.4
0	100	7.5	8.1	8.5	9.2	9.6	10.0	10.5	1.2	0.9	0.8	0.5	0.3	0.2
10	0	7.8	9.4	10.4	12.0	13.2	14.1	15.5	3.1	2.5	2.1	1.4	0.9	0.5
10	100	13.4	13.8	14.0	14.5	14.9	15.1	15.5	0.8	0.7	0.6	0.4	0.3	0.2
20	0	11.1	12.9	14.0	16.0	17.5	18.6	20.3	3.8	3.1	2.6	1.8	1.2	0.7
20	100	20.1	20.1	20.1	20.2	20.2	20.2	20.2	0.1	0.0	0.0	0.0	0.0	0.0
30	0	14.1	16.1	17.5	19.8	21.5	22.9	25.0	4.6	3.7	3.2	2.2	1.5	0.9
30	100													
40	0	17.0	19.2	20.7	23.3	25.3	27.0	29.6	5.4	4.5	3.9	2.7	1.9	1.1
40	100													

AIRSPEED = 10. CM/SEC   RADIATION ABSORBED = 0.6 EXP 6 ERGS/CM2/SEC
DIMENSION ALONG AIRFLOW = 1 CM   DIMENSION ACROSS AIRFLOW = 1 CM

TA	RH	**0*	**1*	**2*	**5*	*10*	*20*	INF*	***0*	***1*	***2*	***5*	*10*	*20*
0	0	0.4	4.6	5.7	6.6	7.0	7.2	7.5	11.5	4.6	2.9	1.4	0.7	0.4
0	100	4.8	6.4	6.8	7.1	7.3	7.4	7.5	4.3	1.8	1.1	0.5	0.3	0.2
10	0	6.0	11.8	13.4	14.8	15.5	15.8	16.2	16.8	7.3	4.8	2.3	1.3	0.7
10	100	13.3	14.8	15.3	15.8	16.0	16.1	16.2	4.9	2.3	1.5	0.7	0.4	0.2
20	0	11.0	18.4	20.6	22.7	23.7	24.3	24.9	23.1	11.0	7.3	3.7	2.1	1.1
20	100	22.0	23.4	23.9	24.4	24.6	24.8	24.9	4.9	2.6	1.8	0.9	0.5	0.3
30	0	15.4	24.4	27.2	30.2	31.6	32.5	33.5	30.4	15.5	10.7	5.7	3.2	1.7
30	100	31.1	32.1	32.5	32.9	33.2	33.3	33.5	4.2	2.5	1.8	1.0	0.5	0.3
40	0	19.4	29.8	33.4	37.3	39.3	40.5	42.0	38.5	21.0	15.0	8.2	4.7	2.6
40	100	40.4	41.0	41.2	41.5	41.7	41.8	42.0	2.7	1.7	1.3	0.7	0.4	0.2

LEAF TEMPERATURES FOR RESISTANCES=   TRANSPIRATION EXP 6 FOR RES =

DIMENSION ALONG AIRFLOW = 5 CM   DIMENSION ACROSS AIRFLOW = 1 CM

TA	RH	**0*	**1*	**2*	**5*	*10*	*20*	INF*	***0*	***1*	***2*	***5*	*10*	*20*
0	0	4.3	8.7	10.4	12.3	13.3	13.8	14.5	8.6	4.9	3.5	1.9	1.1	0.6
0	100	8.6	11.0	12.0	13.2	13.7	14.1	14.5	5.0	2.9	2.1	1.1	0.7	0.4
10	0	8.7	14.0	16.2	18.8	20.2	21.0	22.0	11.4	6.9	5.0	2.8	1.6	0.9
10	100	15.8	18.1	19.1	20.4	21.1	21.5	22.0	5.4	3.4	2.5	1.4	0.8	0.5
20	0	12.6	18.9	21.6	24.9	26.7	27.9	29.4	14.6	9.2	6.9	4.0	2.4	1.3
20	100	23.6	25.4	26.3	27.6	28.3	28.8	29.4	5.2	3.6	2.7	1.6	1.0	0.5
30	0	16.1	23.3	26.5	30.6	33.0	34.6	36.6	18.1	11.9	9.1	5.5	3.3	1.9
30	100	31.9	33.1	33.8	34.9	35.5	36.0	36.6	4.3	3.2	2.5	1.6	1.0	0.5
40	0	19.3	27.4	31.0	35.9	38.9	40.9	43.7	21.9	14.9	11.7	7.2	4.5	2.6
40	100	40.8	41.4	41.8	42.4	42.9	43.2	43.6	2.7	2.1	1.8	1.1	0.7	0.4

LEAF TEMPERATURES FOR RESISTANCES=   TRANSPIRATION EXP 6 FOR RES =

2

25

AIRSPEED = 10. CM/SEC   RADIATION ABSORBED = 0.6 EXP 6 ERGS/CM2/SEC

DIMENSION ALONG AIRFLOW = 1 CM   DIMENSION ACROSS AIRFLOW = 5 CM

LEAF TEMPERATURES FOR RESISTANCES=   TRANSPIRATION EXP 6 FOR RES =

TA	RH	**0*	**1*	**2*	**5*	*10*	*20*	INF*	**0*	**1*	**2*	**5*	*10*	*20*
0	0	1.8	4.9	5.8	6.6	7.0	7.2	7.5	9.2	4.2	2.8	1.4	0.7	0.4
0	100	5.3	6.4	6.8	7.1	7.3	7.4	7.5	3.5	1.6	1.1	0.5	0.3	0.2
10	0	7.9	12.2	13.5	14.9	15.5	15.8	16.2	13.8	6.7	4.5	2.3	1.2	0.7
10	100	13.7	15.0	15.4	15.8	16.0	16.1	16.2	4.2	2.1	1.4	0.7	0.4	0.2
20	0	13.3	18.9	20.8	22.8	23.7	24.3	24.9	19.4	10.1	7.0	3.6	2.0	1.1
20	100	22.4	23.5	23.9	24.4	24.6	24.8	24.9	4.3	2.4	1.7	0.9	0.5	0.3
30	0	18.1	25.0	27.5	30.3	31.7	32.5	33.5	26.0	14.5	10.2	5.5	3.1	1.7
30	100	31.3	32.1	32.5	32.9	33.2	33.3	33.5	3.7	2.3	1.7	0.9	0.5	0.3
40	0	22.4	30.6	33.8	37.4	39.3	40.5	42.0	33.4	19.7	14.3	8.0	4.7	2.5
40	100	40.6	41.0	41.2	41.5	41.7	41.8	42.0	2.5	1.7	1.3	0.7	0.4	0.2

DIMENSION ALONG AIRFLOW = 5 CM   DIMENSION ACROSS AIRFLOW = 5 CM

LEAF TEMPERATURES FOR RESISTANCES=   TRANSPIRATION EXP 6 FOR RES =

TA	RH	**0*	**1*	**2*	**5*	*10*	*20*	INF*	**0*	**1*	**2*	**5*	*10*	*20*
0	0	6.2	9.3	10.7	12.4	13.3	13.8	14.5	7.0	4.4	3.2	1.8	1.0	0.6
0	100	9.6	11.4	12.2	13.2	13.8	14.1	14.5	4.1	2.6	2.0	1.1	0.6	0.3
10	0	10.9	14.8	16.7	18.9	20.2	21.0	22.0	9.5	6.2	4.7	2.7	1.6	0.9
10	100	16.7	18.4	19.3	20.4	21.1	21.5	22.0	4.6	3.1	2.4	1.4	0.8	0.4
20	0	15.2	19.9	22.1	25.1	26.8	27.9	29.4	12.4	8.4	6.4	3.8	2.3	1.3
20	100	24.2	25.7	26.5	27.6	28.3	28.8	29.4	4.6	3.3	2.6	1.6	0.9	0.5
30	0	19.1	24.5	27.2	30.8	33.1	34.6	36.6	15.6	10.9	8.5	5.3	3.2	1.8
30	100	32.3	33.4	34.0	35.0	35.6	36.0	36.6	3.9	2.9	2.4	1.5	0.9	0.5
40	0	22.6	28.7	31.8	36.2	39.0	41.0	43.7	19.2	13.8	11.0	7.0	4.4	2.6
40	100	41.0	41.5	41.9	42.5	42.9	43.2	43.6	2.5	2.0	1.7	1.1	0.7	0.4

AIRSPEED = 10. CM/SEC   RADIATION ABSORBED = 0.6 EXP 6 ERGS/CM2/SEC

DIMENSION ALONG AIRFLOW = 10 CM   DIMENSION ACROSS AIRFLOW = 5 CM

TA	RH	**0*	**1*	**2*	**5*	*10*	*20*	INF*	**0*	**1*	**2*	**5*	*10*	*20*
		LEAF TEMPERATURES FOR RESISTANCES=							TRANSPIRATION EXP 6 FOR RES =					
0	0	8.8	11.8	13.4	15.5	16.8	17.6	18.6	6.5	4.5	3.5	2.1	1.3	0.7
0	100	12.0	14.0	15.0	16.5	17.3	17.9	18.6	4.4	3.1	2.4	1.4	0.9	0.5
10	0	12.9	16.5	18.4	21.1	22.7	23.9	25.3	8.4	6.0	4.7	2.9	1.8	1.0
10	100	18.4	20.2	21.3	22.8	23.8	24.5	25.3	4.7	3.5	2.8	1.7	1.1	0.6
20	0	16.6	20.8	23.1	26.3	28.4	29.9	31.9	10.6	7.8	6.2	3.9	2.5	1.4
20	100	25.3	26.9	27.8	29.3	30.2	30.9	31.9	4.6	3.6	2.9	1.9	1.2	0.7
30	0	20.0	24.7	27.3	31.2	33.8	35.6	38.3	12.9	9.7	7.9	5.1	3.3	1.9
30	100	33.0	34.0	34.7	35.9	36.7	37.4	38.3	3.9	3.1	2.6	1.8	1.1	0.7
40	0	23.1	28.3	31.3	35.8	38.9	41.2	44.6	15.5	11.9	9.8	6.5	4.3	2.5
40	100	41.3	41.8	42.2	42.9	43.5	43.9	44.6	2.5	2.1	1.8	1.3	0.8	0.5

DIMENSION ALONG AIRFLOW = 20 CM   DIMENSION ACROSS AIRFLOW = 5 CM

TA	RH	**0*	**1*	**2*	**5*	*10*	*20*	INF*	**0*	**1*	**2*	**5*	*10*	*20*
		LEAF TEMPERATURES FOR RESISTANCES=							TRANSPIRATION EXP 6 FOR RES =					
0	0	16.1	18.7	20.4	23.3	25.5	27.2	29.8	5.9	4.8	4.1	2.9	1.9	1.2
0	100	18.7	20.7	22.1	24.4	26.2	27.6	29.8	4.8	4.0	3.4	2.4	1.6	1.0
10	0	18.6	21.4	23.3	26.6	29.1	31.1	34.3	6.9	5.7	4.9	3.4	2.4	1.4
10	100	23.2	25.1	26.3	28.6	30.4	31.9	34.3	4.9	4.1	3.6	2.6	1.8	1.1
20	0	21.0	24.1	26.1	29.7	32.5	34.9	38.7	7.9	6.6	5.7	4.1	2.8	1.8
20	100	28.5	30.1	31.1	33.2	34.8	36.2	38.6	4.6	4.0	3.5	2.5	1.8	1.1
30	0	23.2	26.5	28.7	32.7	35.8	38.5	42.9	9.0	7.5	6.6	4.8	3.4	2.1
30	100	34.8	35.9	36.7	38.2	39.6	40.8	42.9	3.8	3.3	3.0	2.2	1.6	1.0
40	0	25.3	28.8	31.2	35.5	39.0	41.9	47.0	10.1	8.6	7.5	5.6	3.9	2.5
40	100	42.1	42.7	43.1	44.0	44.8	45.6	47.0	2.4	2.2	1.9	1.5	1.1	0.7

AIRSPEED = 10. CM/SEC   RADIATION ABSORBED = 0.6 EXP 6 ERGS/CM2/SEC
DIMENSION ALONG AIRFLOW = 1 CM   DIMENSION ACROSS AIRFLOW = 10 CM
LEAF TEMPERATURES FOR RESISTANCES=   TRANSPIRATION EXP 6 FOR RES =

TA	RH	**0*	**1*	**2*	***5*	*10*	*20*	INF*	**0*	**1*	**2*	***5*	*10*	*20*
0	0	4.7	7.5	8.6	9.8	10.4	10.8	11.2	7.1	4.1	2.9	1.6	0.9	0.5
0	100	7.9	9.3	9.9	10.5	10.8	11.0	11.2	3.6	2.1	1.5	0.8	0.5	0.2
10	0	10.1	13.8	15.3	17.2	18.1	18.7	19.4	10.1	6.2	4.5	2.5	1.4	0.8
10	100	15.6	17.0	17.6	18.4	18.8	19.1	19.4	4.2	2.6	1.9	1.1	0.6	0.3
20	0	15.1	19.6	21.6	24.1	25.4	26.3	27.3	13.7	8.7	6.5	3.7	2.2	1.2
20	100	23.6	24.8	25.4	26.2	26.7	27.0	27.3	4.3	2.8	2.2	1.2	0.7	0.4
30	0	19.5	24.9	27.4	30.6	32.5	33.7	35.2	17.9	11.8	9.0	5.3	3.2	1.8
30	100	32.0	32.9	33.4	34.1	34.5	34.8	35.2	3.7	2.6	2.1	1.3	0.8	0.4
40	0	23.4	29.7	32.7	36.7	39.1	40.8	42.9	22.5	15.4	12.0	7.3	4.5	2.5
40	100	40.9	41.3	41.6	42.1	42.4	42.6	42.9	2.4	1.8	1.5	0.9	0.6	0.3

DIMENSION ALONG AIRFLOW = 5 CM   DIMENSION ACROSS AIRFLOW = 10 CM
LEAF TEMPERATURES FOR RESISTANCES=   TRANSPIRATION EXP 6 FOR RES =

TA	RH	**0*	**1*	**2*	***5*	*10*	*20*	INF*	**0*	**1*	**2*	***5*	*10*	*20*
0	0	10.6	13.2	14.7	16.9	18.2	19.1	20.4	5.9	4.4	3.5	2.2	1.3	0.8
0	100	13.5	15.3	16.3	17.8	18.8	19.5	20.4	4.2	3.1	2.5	1.6	1.0	0.6
10	0	14.5	17.7	19.4	22.1	23.8	25.1	26.7	7.6	5.7	4.6	2.9	1.8	1.1
10	100	19.6	21.2	22.3	23.9	24.9	25.7	26.7	4.5	3.5	2.8	1.8	1.2	0.7
20	0	18.1	21.7	23.8	27.0	29.2	30.7	33.0	9.4	7.2	5.9	3.9	2.5	1.5
20	100	26.1	27.6	28.5	30.0	31.0	31.8	33.0	4.4	3.5	2.9	2.0	1.3	0.7
30	0	21.4	25.4	27.8	31.6	34.2	36.1	39.0	11.4	8.9	7.4	5.0	3.3	1.9
30	100	33.5	34.4	35.1	36.4	37.2	38.0	39.0	3.7	3.1	2.6	1.8	1.2	0.7
40	0	24.5	28.9	31.6	35.9	38.9	41.3	45.0	13.6	10.8	9.1	6.2	4.2	2.5
40	100	41.5	42.0	42.4	43.1	43.7	44.2	45.0	2.4	2.1	1.8	1.3	0.9	0.5

AIRSPEED = 10. CM/SEC   RADIATION ABSORBED = 0.6 EXP 6 ERGS/CM2/SEC

DIMENSION ALONG AIRFLOW = 10 CM   DIMENSION ACROSS AIRFLOW = 10 CM

		**0*	**1*	**2*	**5*	*10*	*20*	INF*	**0*	**1*	**2*	**5*	*10*	*20*
TA	RH	LEAF TEMPERATURES FOR RESISTANCES=							TRANSPIRATION EXP 6 FOR RES =					
0	0	13.8	16.2	17.8	20.2	21.9	23.2	25.1	5.7	4.5	3.7	2.5	1.6	0.9
0	100	16.4	18.2	19.4	21.3	22.6	23.6	25.0	4.4	3.5	2.9	1.9	1.3	0.7
10	0	17.0	19.8	21.6	24.5	26.6	28.2	30.5	6.9	5.5	4.6	3.2	2.1	1.2
10	100	21.7	23.3	24.5	26.4	27.8	28.9	30.5	4.6	3.7	3.2	2.2	1.4	0.9
20	0	20.0	23.1	25.2	28.5	30.9	32.9	35.8	8.3	6.7	5.7	3.9	2.6	1.6
20	100	27.6	29.0	29.9	31.7	33.0	34.1	35.8	4.4	3.7	3.2	2.2	1.5	0.9
30	0	22.8	26.2	28.5	32.2	35.1	37.3	41.0	9.7	8.0	6.8	4.8	3.3	2.0
30	100	34.3	35.3	36.0	37.3	38.5	39.4	41.0	3.7	3.2	2.8	2.0	1.4	0.9
40	0	25.4	29.1	31.5	35.7	39.0	41.6	46.0	11.3	9.3	8.1	5.8	4.0	2.5
40	100	41.9	42.4	42.8	43.6	44.3	44.9	46.0	2.4	2.1	1.9	1.4	1.0	0.6

DIMENSION ALONG AIRFLOW = 20 CM   DIMENSION ACROSS AIRFLOW = 10 CM

		**0*	**1*	**2*	**5*	*10*	*20*	INF*	**0*	**1*	**2*	**5*	*10*	*20*
TA	RH	LEAF TEMPERATURES FOR RESISTANCES=							TRANSPIRATION EXP 6 FOR RES =					
0	0	17.1	19.3	20.9	23.5	25.6	27.2	29.8	5.5	4.5	3.9	2.8	1.9	1.2
0	100	19.5	21.2	22.5	24.6	26.3	27.6	29.8	4.4	3.7	3.2	2.3	1.6	1.0
10	0	19.7	22.2	23.9	26.9	29.2	31.2	34.3	6.4	5.3	4.6	3.3	2.3	1.4
10	100	23.9	25.5	26.7	28.8	30.5	31.9	34.3	4.6	3.9	3.4	2.5	1.7	1.1
20	0	22.2	24.9	26.7	30.0	32.7	34.9	38.7	7.4	6.2	5.4	4.0	2.8	1.7
20	100	29.1	30.5	31.5	33.3	34.9	36.3	38.6	4.4	3.8	3.3	2.5	1.7	1.1
30	0	24.5	27.4	29.4	33.0	36.0	38.5	42.9	8.4	7.2	6.3	4.7	3.3	2.1
30	100	35.2	36.2	36.9	38.4	39.6	40.8	42.9	3.6	3.2	2.9	2.2	1.6	1.0
40	0	26.7	29.7	31.9	35.8	39.1	42.0	47.0	9.5	8.2	7.2	5.4	3.9	2.5
40	100	42.3	42.8	43.2	44.1	44.9	45.6	47.0	2.4	2.1	1.9	1.5	1.1	0.7

AIRSPEED = 10. CM/SEC   RADIATION ABSORBED = 0.8 EXP 6 ERGS/CM2/SEC
DIMENSION ALONG AIRFLOW = 1 CM   DIMENSION ACROSS AIRFLOW = 1 CM

TA	RH	LEAF TEMPERATURES FOR RESISTANCES=							TRANSPIRATION EXP 6 FOR RES =					
		**0*	**1*	**2*	**5*	*10*	*20*	INF*	**0*	**1*	**2*	**5*	*10*	*20*
0	0	3.6	8.7	10.0	11.2	11.8	12.1	12.4	14.3	6.0	3.9	1.9	1.0	0.5
0	100	7.7	10.4	11.1	11.8	12.0	12.2	12.4	7.6	3.3	2.1	1.0	0.6	0.3
10	0	8.9	15.5	17.5	19.3	20.1	20.6	21.1	20.2	9.3	6.1	3.1	1.7	0.9
10	100	15.6	18.4	19.3	20.2	20.6	20.8	21.1	9.1	4.5	3.0	1.5	0.8	0.4
20	0	13.5	21.8	24.3	27.0	28.2	28.9	29.7	27.1	13.4	9.1	4.7	2.6	1.4
20	100	23.9	26.5	27.5	28.6	29.1	29.4	29.7	10.0	5.5	3.8	2.0	1.1	0.6
30	0	17.7	27.5	30.7	34.2	36.0	37.0	38.2	34.9	18.5	13.0	7.0	4.0	2.2
30	100	32.5	34.7	35.7	36.8	37.4	37.8	38.2	10.0	6.1	4.4	2.4	1.4	0.8
40	0	21.4	32.7	36.6	41.0	43.4	44.9	46.6	43.4	24.5	17.7	9.9	5.8	3.2
40	100	41.5	43.2	44.0	45.1	45.7	46.1	46.6	9.2	6.1	4.7	2.7	1.6	0.9

DIMENSION ALONG AIRFLOW = 5 CM   DIMENSION ACROSS AIRFLOW = 1 CM

TA	RH	LEAF TEMPERATURES FOR RESISTANCES=							TRANSPIRATION EXP 6 FOR RES =					
		**0*	**1*	**2*	**5*	*10*	*20*	INF*	**0*	**1*	**2*	**5*	*10*	*20*
0	0	9.7	15.3	17.6	20.4	21.8	22.8	23.9	12.2	7.4	5.4	3.1	1.8	1.0
0	100	13.5	17.4	19.1	21.2	22.3	23.0	23.9	9.0	5.7	4.2	2.4	1.4	0.8
10	0	13.5	20.1	22.9	26.4	28.4	29.6	31.2	15.4	9.9	7.4	4.3	2.6	1.4
10	100	19.8	23.6	25.4	27.8	29.2	30.1	31.2	10.1	6.8	5.2	3.0	1.8	1.0
20	0	17.0	24.4	27.7	32.0	34.5	36.2	38.4	19.0	12.7	9.7	5.9	3.6	2.0
20	100	26.7	30.1	31.9	34.4	35.9	37.0	38.4	10.6	7.6	5.9	3.7	2.3	1.3
30	0	20.1	28.3	32.1	37.2	40.3	42.5	45.4	22.9	15.8	12.3	7.7	4.8	2.8
30	100	34.3	37.1	38.7	41.1	42.7	43.8	45.4	10.4	7.8	6.3	4.1	2.6	1.5
40	0	22.9	31.9	36.2	42.0	45.8	48.5	52.3	27.0	19.1	15.3	9.8	6.3	3.7
40	100	42.6	44.6	45.9	48.0	49.5	50.6	52.3	9.3	7.4	6.2	4.2	2.8	1.7

AIRSPEED = 10. CM/SEC   RADIATION ABSORBED = 0.8 EXP 6 ERGS/CM2/SEC

DIMENSION ALONG AIRFLOW = 1 CM   DIMENSION ACROSS AIRFLOW = 5 CM

TA	RH	LEAF TEMPERATURES FOR RESISTANCES=							TRANSPIRATION EXP 6 FOR RES =					
		**0*	**1*	**2*	**5*	*10*	*20*	INF*	**0*	**1*	**2*	**5*	*10*	*20*
0	0	5.3	9.0	10.2	11.3	11.8	12.1	12.4	11.6	5.5	3.7	1.8	1.0	0.5
0	100	8.6	10.5	11.2	11.8	12.1	12.2	12.4	6.3	3.1	2.0	1.0	0.6	0.3
10	0	11.0	16.0	17.7	19.3	20.1	20.6	21.1	16.8	8.5	5.8	3.0	1.6	0.9
10	100	16.5	18.7	19.4	20.2	20.6	20.8	21.1	7.8	4.1	2.8	1.5	0.8	0.4
20	0	16.1	22.4	24.6	27.0	28.2	28.9	29.7	23.0	12.5	8.7	4.6	2.6	1.4
20	100	24.6	26.8	27.6	28.6	29.1	29.4	29.7	8.8	5.1	3.6	1.9	1.1	0.6
30	0	20.6	28.2	31.1	34.3	36.0	37.0	38.2	30.0	17.3	12.4	6.8	3.9	2.1
30	100	33.0	35.0	35.8	36.9	37.4	37.8	38.2	9.0	5.7	4.2	2.4	1.4	0.7
40	0	24.7	33.5	37.0	41.2	43.4	44.9	46.6	37.9	23.0	17.0	9.7	5.7	3.2
40	100	41.9	43.4	44.1	45.2	45.8	46.1	46.6	8.5	5.8	4.5	2.6	1.6	0.9

DIMENSION ALONG AIRFLOW = 5 CM   DIMENSION ACROSS AIRFLOW = 5 CM

TA	RH	LEAF TEMPERATURES FOR RESISTANCES=							TRANSPIRATION EXP 6 FOR RES =					
		**0*	**1*	**2*	**5*	*10*	*20*	INF*	**0*	**1*	**2*	**5*	*10*	*20*
0	0	12.0	16.1	18.1	20.5	21.9	22.8	23.9	10.2	6.7	5.1	2.9	1.7	1.0
0	100	15.1	18.0	19.4	21.3	22.3	23.0	23.9	7.7	5.1	3.9	2.3	1.4	0.7
10	0	16.2	21.1	23.4	26.6	28.4	29.6	31.2	13.2	9.0	6.9	4.2	2.5	1.4
10	100	21.3	24.3	25.8	27.9	29.2	30.1	31.2	8.8	6.2	4.8	2.9	1.8	1.0
20	0	20.0	25.6	28.4	32.2	34.6	36.2	38.4	16.5	11.6	9.1	5.7	3.5	2.0
20	100	28.0	30.7	32.3	34.5	36.0	37.0	38.4	9.5	7.0	5.6	3.5	2.2	1.3
30	0	23.4	29.7	32.9	37.5	40.4	42.5	45.4	20.1	14.6	11.7	7.5	4.7	2.8
30	100	35.3	37.6	39.0	41.2	42.7	43.8	45.4	9.5	7.3	6.0	4.0	2.6	1.5
40	0	26.5	33.4	37.1	42.4	45.9	48.5	52.3	23.9	17.8	14.5	9.5	6.2	3.7
40	100	43.3	45.0	46.2	48.1	49.5	50.6	52.3	8.7	7.0	5.9	4.1	2.7	1.6

AIRSPEED = 10. CM/SEC   RADIATION ABSORBED = 0.8 EXP 6 ERGS/CM2/SEC
DIMENSION ALONG AIRFLOW = 10 CM   DIMENSION ACROSS AIRFLOW = 5 CM

TA	RH	**0*	**1*	**2*	**5*	*10*	*20*	INF*	**0*	**1*	**2*	**5*	*10*	*20*
		LEAF TEMPERATURES FOR RESISTANCES=							TRANSPIRATION EXP 6 FOR RES =					
0	0	15.8	19.8	22.0	25.2	27.2	28.5	30.4	10.1	7.3	5.8	3.7	2.3	1.3
0	100	18.5	21.7	23.5	26.0	27.7	28.8	30.4	8.2	6.1	4.9	3.1	1.9	1.1
10	0	19.2	23.8	26.4	30.1	32.6	34.4	36.8	12.4	9.2	7.5	4.8	3.1	1.8
10	100	23.9	27.0	28.9	31.7	33.5	34.9	36.8	9.2	7.0	5.7	3.8	2.4	1.4
20	0	22.4	27.5	30.4	34.8	37.7	40.0	43.2	14.9	11.3	9.3	6.2	4.0	2.4
20	100	29.9	32.7	34.5	37.3	39.3	40.9	43.2	9.7	7.7	6.4	4.3	2.8	1.7
30	0	25.3	30.9	34.1	39.1	42.6	45.3	49.3	17.5	13.6	11.3	7.7	5.1	3.1
30	100	36.6	39.0	40.5	43.2	45.2	46.8	49.3	9.5	7.8	6.7	4.7	3.2	1.9
40	0	27.9	34.0	37.6	43.1	47.2	50.3	55.4	20.3	16.1	13.6	9.4	6.4	4.0
40	100	44.1	45.9	47.1	49.4	51.2	52.8	55.4	8.7	7.4	6.4	4.7	3.2	2.0

DIMENSION ALONG AIRFLOW = 20 CM   DIMENSION ACROSS AIRFLOW = 5 CM

TA	RH	**0*	**1*	**2*	**5*	*10*	*20*	INF*	**0*	**1*	**2*	**5*	*10*	*20*
		LEAF TEMPERATURES FOR RESISTANCES=							TRANSPIRATION EXP 6 FOR RES =					
0	0	25.4	28.9	31.3	35.6	39.1	42.1	47.2	10.1	8.6	7.6	5.6	4.0	2.5
0	100	27.4	30.5	32.6	36.3	39.7	42.5	47.2	9.3	7.9	7.0	5.2	3.7	2.4
10	0	27.4	31.1	33.7	38.3	42.1	45.4	51.3	11.3	9.7	8.5	6.4	4.6	3.0
10	100	31.0	33.9	36.0	39.9	43.1	46.1	51.3	9.7	8.4	7.5	5.7	4.1	2.7
20	0	29.3	33.1	35.9	40.8	44.9	48.6	55.3	12.5	10.8	9.6	7.3	5.3	3.5
20	100	35.3	37.9	39.8	43.5	46.8	49.7	55.3	9.9	8.6	7.7	6.0	4.4	2.9
30	0	31.0	35.1	38.0	43.2	47.6	51.6	59.2	13.8	12.0	10.7	8.2	6.0	4.0
30	100	40.5	42.7	44.3	47.7	50.7	53.5	59.2	9.5	8.5	7.6	6.0	4.5	3.0
40	0	32.7	36.9	39.9	45.5	50.2	54.5	63.0	15.1	13.2	11.8	9.1	6.8	4.6
40	100	46.7	48.3	49.7	52.4	55.0	57.6	63.0	8.5	7.7	7.1	5.7	4.3	3.0

AIRSPEED = 10. CM/SEC   RADIATION ABSORBED = 0.8 EXP 6 ERGS/CM2/SEC

DIMENSION ALONG AIRFLOW = 1 CM   DIMENSION ACROSS AIRFLOW = 10 CM

TA	RH	LEAF TEMPERATURES FOR RESISTANCES=							TRANSPIRATION EXP 6 FOR RES =					
		**0*	**1*	**2*	***5*	*10*	*20*	INF*	**0*	**1*	**2*	***5*	*10*	*20*
0	0	9.7	13.2	14.7	16.5	17.4	17.9	18.6	9.8	5.9	4.3	2.4	1.4	0.7
0	100	12.6	14.9	15.9	17.1	17.8	18.1	18.6	6.6	4.1	3.0	1.6	0.9	0.5
10	0	14.6	19.1	21.1	23.5	24.8	25.6	26.6	13.4	8.5	6.3	3.6	2.1	1.1
10	100	19.5	22.0	23.2	24.7	25.4	26.0	26.6	7.9	5.2	3.9	2.2	1.3	0.7
20	0	19.1	24.4	26.9	30.0	31.8	33.0	34.4	17.5	11.5	8.7	5.1	3.1	1.7
20	100	26.8	29.2	30.4	32.2	33.0	33.6	34.4	8.8	6.1	4.7	2.8	1.7	0.9
30	0	23.1	29.3	32.2	36.2	38.5	40.1	42.2	22.1	15.1	11.7	7.1	4.3	2.5
30	100	34.6	36.6	37.8	39.4	40.5	41.2	42.2	9.0	6.6	5.2	3.3	2.0	1.1
40	0	26.7	33.7	37.2	41.9	44.9	47.0	49.8	27.1	19.1	15.1	9.5	6.0	3.4
40	100	42.9	44.4	45.4	46.9	47.9	48.7	49.8	8.4	6.5	5.3	3.5	2.2	1.3

DIMENSION ALONG AIRFLOW = 5 CM   DIMENSION ACROSS AIRFLOW = 10 CM

TA	RH	LEAF TEMPERATURES FOR RESISTANCES=							TRANSPIRATION EXP 6 FOR RES =					
		**0*	**1*	**2*	***5*	*10*	*20*	INF*	**0*	**1*	**2*	***5*	*10*	*20*
0	0	18.2	21.8	23.9	27.1	29.3	30.9	33.1	9.5	7.3	6.0	3.9	2.5	1.5
0	100	20.7	23.5	25.3	28.0	29.9	31.2	33.1	8.0	6.2	5.1	3.4	2.2	1.3
10	0	21.5	25.5	27.9	31.7	34.3	36.3	39.2	11.5	9.0	7.4	5.0	3.3	2.0
10	100	25.7	28.5	30.3	33.2	35.3	36.9	39.2	8.9	7.1	5.9	4.0	2.7	1.6
20	0	24.6	28.9	31.7	36.0	39.1	41.5	45.2	13.7	10.9	9.1	6.3	4.2	2.5
20	100	31.3	33.9	35.6	38.6	40.7	42.5	45.1	9.3	7.6	6.5	4.6	3.1	1.9
30	0	27.3	32.1	35.1	40.0	43.5	46.4	51.0	16.0	12.9	10.9	7.7	5.2	3.2
30	100	37.7	39.9	41.4	44.1	46.2	48.0	51.0	9.2	7.7	6.7	4.9	3.4	2.1
40	0	29.9	35.1	38.3	43.7	47.8	51.1	56.6	18.4	15.0	12.9	9.2	6.4	4.0
40	100	44.9	46.5	47.7	50.0	52.0	53.7	56.6	8.4	7.3	6.4	4.8	3.4	2.2

AIRSPEED = 10. CM/SEC   RADIATION ABSORBED = 0.8 EXP 6 ERGS/CM2/SEC

DIMENSION ALONG AIRFLOW = 10 CM   DIMENSION ACROSS AIRFLOW = 10 CM

TA	RH	LEAF TEMPERATURES FOR RESISTANCES=							TRANSPIRATION EXP 6 FOR RES =					
		**0*	**1*	**2*	**5*	*10*	*20*	INF*	**0*	**1*	**2*	**5*	*10*	*20*
0	0	22.5	25.8	28.0	31.8	34.5	36.7	40.3	9.5	7.8	6.7	4.7	3.2	2.0
0	100	24.6	27.4	29.3	32.6	35.1	37.1	40.3	8.4	7.0	6.0	4.2	2.9	1.8
10	0	25.1	28.7	31.1	35.3	38.5	41.1	45.4	11.1	9.2	7.9	5.7	3.9	2.4
10	100	28.8	31.6	33.5	36.8	39.5	41.7	45.4	9.1	7.7	6.6	4.8	3.3	2.1
20	0	27.5	31.5	34.1	38.6	42.2	45.2	50.3	12.7	10.6	9.2	6.7	4.7	3.0
20	100	33.7	36.2	38.0	41.3	44.0	46.3	50.3	9.4	8.0	7.1	5.2	3.7	2.4
30	0	29.8	34.0	36.8	41.8	45.7	49.1	55.1	14.4	12.1	10.6	7.9	5.6	3.6
30	100	39.4	41.5	43.1	46.0	48.6	50.9	55.2	9.2	8.0	7.1	5.4	3.9	2.6
40	0	32.0	36.4	39.4	44.7	49.1	52.9	59.8	16.1	13.7	12.1	9.1	6.6	4.3
40	100	46.0	47.6	48.8	51.3	53.6	55.7	59.9	8.4	7.4	6.7	5.2	3.9	2.6

DIMENSION ALONG AIRFLOW = 20 CM   DIMENSION ACROSS AIRFLOW = 10 CM

TA	RH	LEAF TEMPERATURES FOR RESISTANCES=							TRANSPIRATION EXP 6 FOR RES =					
		**0*	**1*	**2*	**5*	*10*	*20*	INF*	**0*	**1*	**2*	**5*	*10*	*20*
0	0	26.8	29.8	32.0	36.0	39.3	42.2	47.2	9.5	8.2	7.2	5.4	3.9	2.5
0	100	28.6	31.3	33.2	36.8	39.8	42.6	47.2	8.8	7.6	6.7	5.0	3.6	2.4
10	0	28.9	32.1	34.4	38.7	42.3	45.5	51.3	10.7	9.3	8.2	6.2	4.5	3.0
10	100	32.1	34.7	36.6	40.2	43.3	46.2	51.3	9.2	8.1	7.2	5.5	4.0	2.6
20	0	30.8	34.2	36.6	41.2	45.1	48.6	55.3	11.9	10.3	9.2	7.1	5.2	3.4
20	100	36.3	38.6	40.4	43.8	46.9	49.8	55.3	9.4	8.3	7.5	5.8	4.3	2.9
30	0	32.6	36.2	38.8	43.6	47.8	51.7	59.2	13.1	11.5	10.3	8.0	5.9	4.0
30	100	41.3	43.3	44.8	47.9	50.8	53.6	59.2	9.1	8.1	7.4	5.9	4.4	3.0
40	0	34.4	38.1	40.8	45.9	50.4	54.6	63.0	14.4	12.7	11.4	8.9	6.7	4.5
40	100	47.3	48.8	50.1	52.6	55.1	57.6	63.0	8.2	7.5	6.9	5.6	4.2	2.9

AIRSPEED = 10. CM/SEC   RADIATION ABSORBED = 1.0 EXP 6 ERGS/CM2/SEC

		DIMENSION ALONG AIRFLOW = 1 CM							DIMENSION ACROSS AIRFLOW = 1 CM					
		LEAF TEMPERATURES FOR RESISTANCES=							TRANSPIRATION EXP 6 FOR RES =					
TA	RH	**0*	**1*	**2*	**5*	*10*	*20*	INF*	**0*	**1*	**2*	**5*	*10*	*20*
0	0	6.6	12.6	14.3	15.8	16.5	16.9	17.3	17.5	7.7	5.0	2.5	1.3	0.7
0	100	10.5	14.2	15.3	16.3	16.7	17.0	17.3	11.2	5.1	3.4	1.7	0.9	0.5
10	0	11.6	19.1	21.4	23.6	24.7	25.3	25.9	24.0	11.5	7.7	3.9	2.2	1.1
10	100	17.9	21.9	23.2	24.5	25.2	25.5	25.9	13.6	6.9	4.7	2.4	1.3	0.7
20	0	15.9	25.1	28.0	31.1	32.6	33.5	34.5	31.4	16.2	11.2	5.9	3.3	1.8
20	100	25.6	29.5	31.0	32.6	33.4	33.9	34.5	15.2	8.6	6.1	3.3	1.8	1.0
30	0	19.8	30.4	34.1	38.1	40.2	41.4	43.0	39.6	21.7	15.5	8.6	4.9	2.7
30	100	33.8	37.3	38.8	40.6	41.6	42.2	43.0	16.0	9.9	7.3	4.1	2.4	1.3
40	0	23.3	35.3	39.7	44.7	47.4	49.1	51.3	48.4	28.2	20.7	11.9	7.0	3.9
40	100	42.5	45.3	46.7	48.6	49.7	50.4	51.3	15.7	10.7	8.2	4.9	2.9	1.6

		DIMENSION ALONG AIRFLOW = 5 CM							DIMENSION ACROSS AIRFLOW = 1 CM					
		LEAF TEMPERATURES FOR RESISTANCES=							TRANSPIRATION EXP 6 FOR RES =					
TA	RH	**0*	**1*	**2*	**5*	*10*	*20*	INF*	**0*	**1*	**2*	**5*	*10*	*20*
0	0	14.4	21.2	24.2	27.8	29.9	31.3	33.0	16.3	10.5	8.0	4.7	2.8	1.6
0	100	17.7	23.0	25.4	28.5	30.3	31.5	33.0	13.5	8.9	6.8	4.0	2.4	1.4
10	0	17.8	25.4	28.8	33.3	36.0	37.8	40.2	20.0	13.4	10.3	6.3	3.9	2.2
10	100	23.3	28.5	31.1	34.6	36.8	38.2	40.1	15.2	10.6	8.3	5.1	3.2	1.8
20	0	20.8	29.2	33.2	38.4	41.7	44.0	47.2	23.9	16.6	13.1	8.2	5.2	3.0
20	100	29.6	34.4	36.9	40.6	43.0	44.8	47.2	16.3	12.0	9.6	6.2	3.9	2.3
30	0	23.6	32.8	37.1	43.1	46.7	49.9	54.0	28.1	20.0	16.1	10.4	6.7	4.0
30	100	36.6	40.7	43.1	46.7	49.3	51.2	54.0	16.6	12.8	10.6	7.1	4.6	2.8
40	0	26.2	36.0	40.8	47.7	52.2	55.6	60.7	32.4	23.7	19.3	12.9	8.5	5.2
40	100	44.3	47.6	49.6	53.0	55.6	57.6	60.7	16.1	13.0	11.0	7.7	5.2	3.2

AIRSPEED = 10. CM/SEC   RADIATION ABSORBED = 1.0 EXP 6 ERGS/CM2/SEC

DIMENSION ALONG AIRFLOW = 1 CM   DIMENSION ACROSS AIRFLOW = 5 CM
LEAF TEMPERATURES FOR RESISTANCES=   TRANSPIRATION EXP 6 FOR RES =

TA	RH	**0*	**1*	**2*	**5*	*10*	*20*	INF*	**0*	**1*	**2*	**5*	*10*	*20*
0	0	8.6	13.0	14.4	15.8	16.5	16.9	17.3	14.4	7.1	4.8	2.4	1.3	0.7
0	100	11.6	14.4	15.4	16.3	16.7	17.0	17.3	9.3	4.7	3.2	1.6	0.9	0.5
10	0	13.9	19.6	21.6	23.7	24.7	25.3	25.9	20.1	10.6	7.3	3.8	2.1	1.1
10	100	19.0	22.2	23.3	24.6	25.2	25.5	25.9	11.6	6.4	4.4	2.3	1.3	0.7
20	0	18.7	25.7	28.3	31.2	32.6	33.5	34.5	26.8	15.0	10.7	5.8	3.3	1.8
20	100	26.7	29.8	31.2	32.7	33.5	33.9	34.5	13.4	8.0	5.8	3.2	1.8	1.0
30	0	22.9	31.3	34.5	38.2	40.2	41.4	43.0	34.4	20.4	14.8	8.4	4.9	2.7
30	100	34.7	37.6	39.0	40.7	41.6	42.2	43.0	14.5	9.4	7.0	4.0	2.4	1.3
40	0	26.8	36.3	40.1	44.8	47.4	49.2	51.3	42.7	26.5	19.9	11.6	6.9	3.9
40	100	43.2	45.6	46.9	48.6	49.7	50.4	51.3	14.6	10.2	7.9	4.8	2.9	1.6

DIMENSION ALONG AIRFLOW = 5 CM   DIMENSION ACROSS AIRFLOW = 5 CM
LEAF TEMPERATURES FOR RESISTANCES=   TRANSPIRATION EXP 6 FOR RES =

TA	RH	**0*	**1*	**2*	**5*	*10*	*20*	INF*	**0*	**1*	**2*	**5*	*10*	*20*
0	0	17.2	22.2	24.7	28.0	30.0	31.3	33.0	14.0	9.6	7.4	4.5	2.7	1.5
0	100	19.8	23.9	25.9	28.7	30.4	31.5	33.0	11.7	8.2	6.4	3.9	2.4	1.3
10	0	20.9	26.6	29.6	33.6	36.1	37.8	40.1	17.4	12.3	9.7	6.1	3.8	2.2
10	100	25.3	29.5	31.7	34.8	36.8	38.2	40.1	13.5	9.8	7.8	4.9	3.1	1.8
20	0	24.2	30.6	34.0	38.7	41.8	44.1	47.2	21.0	15.4	12.3	7.9	5.1	3.0
20	100	31.4	35.3	37.5	40.9	43.1	44.8	47.2	14.7	11.2	9.1	6.0	3.9	2.3
30	0	27.2	34.3	38.1	43.6	47.2	50.0	54.0	24.9	18.7	15.2	10.1	6.6	3.9
30	100	38.0	41.5	43.6	47.0	49.4	51.2	54.0	15.3	12.1	10.1	6.9	4.6	2.7
40	0	30.0	37.7	41.8	48.0	52.3	55.7	60.7	29.1	22.2	18.4	12.5	8.4	5.1
40	100	45.4	48.2	50.1	53.2	55.7	57.6	60.7	15.0	12.3	10.6	7.5	5.1	3.2

36

AIRSPEED = 10. CM/SEC   RADIATION ABSORBED = 1.0 EXP 6 ERGS/CM2/SEC

DIMENSION ALONG AIRFLOW = 10 CM   DIMENSION ACROSS AIRFLOW = 5 CM

LEAF TEMPERATURES FOR RESISTANCES=   TRANSPIRATION EXP 6 FOR RES =

TA	RH	**0*	**1*	**2*	**5*	*10*	*20*	INF*	**0*	**1*	**2*	**5*	*10*	*20*
0	0	21.7	26.7	29.5	33.7	36.6	38.7	41.7	14.3	10.8	8.9	5.9	3.8	2.2
0	100	24.0	28.2	30.7	34.5	37.1	39.0	41.7	12.7	9.8	8.0	5.3	3.5	2.1
10	0	24.6	30.1	33.3	38.1	41.5	44.0	47.9	16.9	13.1	10.9	7.3	4.9	2.9
10	100	28.7	32.9	35.4	39.5	42.3	44.6	47.9	14.1	11.1	9.3	6.4	4.2	2.6
20	0	27.3	33.3	36.8	42.2	46.1	49.2	54.0	19.7	15.5	13.0	9.0	6.1	3.7
20	100	33.9	37.8	40.3	44.5	47.6	50.0	54.0	15.1	12.2	10.4	7.3	5.0	3.1
30	0	29.9	36.2	40.0	46.1	50.5	54.1	59.9	22.6	18.1	15.4	10.9	7.5	4.7
30	100	39.9	43.4	45.7	49.7	52.9	55.5	59.9	15.4	12.9	11.2	8.1	5.7	3.6
40	0	32.2	39.0	43.0	49.6	54.6	58.7	65.7	25.6	20.8	17.8	12.9	9.1	5.8
40	100	46.8	49.6	51.6	55.2	58.3	60.9	65.7	15.1	12.9	11.4	8.6	6.1	4.0

DIMENSION ALONG AIRFLOW = 20 CM   DIMENSION ACROSS AIRFLOW = 5 CM

LEAF TEMPERATURES FOR RESISTANCES=   TRANSPIRATION EXP 6 FOR RES =

TA	RH	**0*	**1*	**2*	**5*	*10*	*20*	INF*	**0*	**1*	**2*	**5*	*10*	*20*
0	0	32.8	37.1	40.0	45.6	50.3	54.7	63.2	15.2	13.3	11.9	9.2	6.8	4.6
0	100	34.4	38.3	41.1	46.3	50.8	55.0	63.2	14.4	12.7	11.4	8.8	6.6	4.5
10	0	34.4	38.8	41.9	47.7	52.8	57.4	66.9	16.5	14.5	13.0	10.2	7.7	5.2
10	100	37.3	41.1	43.8	49.0	53.6	58.0	66.9	15.2	13.4	12.1	9.6	7.2	4.9
20	0	35.9	40.5	43.7	49.8	55.1	60.1	70.5	17.9	15.8	14.2	11.2	8.5	5.9
20	100	40.9	44.4	47.0	52.0	56.7	61.1	70.5	15.6	13.9	12.7	10.1	7.7	5.3
30	0	37.4	42.1	45.4	51.8	57.4	62.7	74.1	19.3	17.1	15.5	12.3	9.4	6.6
30	100	45.3	48.4	50.7	55.5	59.9	64.3	74.1	15.5	14.0	12.9	10.4	8.1	5.7
40	0	38.8	43.6	47.1	53.7	59.5	65.2	77.6	20.7	18.4	16.7	13.4	10.4	7.3
40	100	50.7	53.3	55.3	59.5	63.6	67.8	77.6	15.0	13.6	12.6	10.4	8.2	5.8

AIRSPEED = 10. CM/SEC   RADIATION ABSORBED = 1.0 EXP 6 ERGS/CM2/SEC
DIMENSION ALONG AIRFLOW = 1 CM   DIMENSION ACROSS AIRFLOW = 10 CM
LEAF TEMPERATURES FOR RESISTANCES=   TRANSPIRATION EXP 6 FOR RES =

TA	RH	**0*	**1*	**2*	**5*	*10*	*20*	INF*	***0*	**1*	**2*	***5*	*10*	*20*
0	0	14.2	18.6	20.5	22.8	24.1	24.9	25.8	13.0	8.2	6.1	3.4	2.0	1.1
0	100	16.8	20.1	21.6	23.4	24.4	25.1	25.8	10.1	6.5	4.8	2.7	1.6	0.9
10	0	18.7	23.9	26.4	29.4	31.2	32.3	33.7	17.1	11.2	8.5	5.0	3.0	1.6
10	100	23.1	26.6	28.3	30.6	31.8	32.7	33.7	12.1	8.2	6.2	3.7	2.2	1.2
20	0	22.7	28.8	31.8	35.6	37.9	39.5	41.4	21.6	14.7	11.4	6.9	4.2	2.4
20	100	29.8	33.2	35.0	37.5	39.0	40.1	41.4	13.6	9.7	7.6	4.7	2.9	1.6
30	0	26.4	33.3	36.7	41.4	44.3	46.3	49.1	26.6	18.7	14.8	9.2	5.8	3.3
30	100	37.0	40.1	41.8	44.4	46.1	47.4	49.1	14.5	10.8	8.7	5.6	3.5	2.1
40	0	29.7	37.4	41.3	46.8	50.3	52.9	56.5	31.9	23.1	18.6	12.0	7.7	4.5
40	100	44.8	47.3	48.9	51.4	53.2	54.6	56.5	14.5	11.4	9.4	6.3	4.1	2.4

DIMENSION ALONG AIRFLOW = 5 CM   DIMENSION ACROSS AIRFLOW = 10 CM
LEAF TEMPERATURES FOR RESISTANCES=   TRANSPIRATION EXP 6 FOR RES =

TA	RH	**0*	**1*	**2*	**5*	*10*	*20*	INF*	***0*	**1*	**2*	***5*	*10*	*20*
0	0	24.6	29.0	31.8	36.1	39.2	41.6	45.3	13.7	10.9	9.2	6.3	4.2	2.6
0	100	26.7	30.5	32.9	36.8	39.7	41.9	45.3	12.4	10.0	8.4	5.8	3.9	2.4
10	0	27.4	32.2	35.2	40.1	43.7	46.5	51.1	16.0	12.9	11.0	7.7	5.3	3.3
10	100	31.0	34.8	37.2	41.4	44.5	47.0	51.1	13.8	11.3	9.6	6.8	4.7	2.9
20	0	30.0	35.2	38.4	43.8	47.9	51.2	56.8	18.5	15.1	13.0	9.3	6.5	4.1
20	100	35.8	39.4	41.8	46.0	49.3	52.1	56.8	14.7	12.3	10.6	7.7	5.4	3.4
30	0	32.4	37.9	41.4	47.3	51.8	55.7	62.3	21.0	17.4	15.1	11.0	7.8	5.0
30	100	41.5	44.6	46.8	50.9	54.2	57.1	62.3	15.0	12.8	11.3	8.4	6.0	3.9
40	0	34.6	40.4	44.2	50.5	55.6	59.9	67.7	23.6	19.8	17.3	12.8	9.2	6.0
40	100	47.9	50.5	52.5	56.1	59.3	62.2	67.7	14.7	12.8	11.5	8.8	6.5	4.3

AIRSPEED = 10. CM/SEC   RADIATION ABSORBED = 1.0 EXP 6 ERGS/CM2/SEC

DIMENSION ALONG AIRFLOW = 10 CM   DIMENSION ACROSS AIRFLOW = 10 CM

LEAF TEMPERATURES FOR RESISTANCES=   TRANSPIRATION EXP 6 FOR RES =

TA	RH	**0*	**1*	**2*	**5*	*10*	*20*	INF*	**0*	**1*	**2*	**5*	*10*	*20*
0	0	29.5	33.7	36.4	41.3	45.3	48.6	54.5	14.1	11.9	10.4	7.7	5.5	3.5
0	100	31.3	35.0	37.5	42.1	45.7	48.9	54.5	13.2	11.2	9.8	7.3	5.2	3.4
10	0	31.7	36.1	39.0	44.3	48.6	52.4	59.2	15.9	13.5	11.9	8.9	6.4	4.2
10	100	34.8	38.4	41.0	45.6	49.5	53.0	59.2	14.2	12.2	10.8	8.2	5.9	3.9
20	0	33.7	38.3	41.5	47.1	51.8	56.0	63.9	17.7	15.2	13.5	10.2	7.5	4.9
20	100	38.9	42.3	44.8	49.4	53.3	57.0	63.9	14.9	13.0	11.6	8.9	6.6	4.4
30	0	35.7	40.5	43.8	49.8	54.9	59.5	68.4	19.6	16.9	15.1	11.6	8.6	5.8
30	100	43.9	46.9	49.1	53.4	57.3	61.0	68.4	15.1	13.3	12.0	9.4	7.1	4.8
40	0	37.5	42.5	46.0	52.4	57.8	62.8	72.8	21.5	18.7	16.8	13.1	9.8	6.6
40	100	49.7	52.2	54.1	58.0	61.7	65.2	72.8	14.6	13.1	12.0	9.6	7.3	5.1

DIMENSION ALONG AIRFLOW = 20 CM   DIMENSION ACROSS AIRFLOW = 10 CM

LEAF TEMPERATURES FOR RESISTANCES=   TRANSPIRATION EXP 6 FOR RES =

TA	RH	**0*	**1*	**2*	**5*	*10*	*20*	INF*	**0*	**1*	**2*	**5*	*10*	*20*
0	0	34.5	38.2	40.9	46.0	50.5	54.8	63.2	14.4	12.7	11.5	9.0	6.7	4.6
0	100	35.9	39.4	41.9	46.7	51.0	55.0	63.2	13.8	12.2	11.0	8.6	6.5	4.4
10	0	36.1	40.0	42.8	48.2	53.0	57.5	66.9	15.7	13.9	12.6	10.0	7.5	5.2
10	100	38.8	42.1	44.6	49.5	53.9	58.1	66.9	14.5	12.9	11.7	9.3	7.1	4.9
20	0	37.7	41.7	44.6	50.3	55.4	60.2	70.5	17.1	15.2	13.8	11.0	8.4	5.8
20	100	42.2	45.4	47.7	52.5	56.9	61.2	70.5	14.9	13.5	12.3	9.9	7.6	5.3
30	0	39.2	43.4	46.4	52.3	57.6	62.8	74.1	18.4	16.5	15.0	12.0	9.3	6.5
30	100	46.5	49.3	51.4	55.9	60.1	64.4	74.1	15.0	13.6	12.5	10.2	8.0	5.6
40	0	40.6	44.9	48.1	54.2	59.8	65.3	77.6	19.8	17.8	16.2	13.2	10.2	7.2
40	10C	51.7	54.0	55.9	59.8	63.8	67.9	77.6	14.5	13.3	12.3	10.2	8.1	5.8

39

AIRSPEED = 20. CM/SEC   RADIATION ABSORBED = 0.4 EXP 6 ERGS/CM2/SEC

DIMENSION ALONG AIRFLOW = 1 CM   DIMENSION ACROSS AIRFLOW = 1 CM

		LEAF TEMPERATURES FOR RESISTANCES=							TRANSPIRATION EXP 6 FOR RES =					
TA	RH	**0*	**1*	**2*	**5*	*10*	*20*	INF*	**0*	**1*	**2*	**5*	*10*	*20*
0	0	-3.9	0.1	0.8	1.4	1.6	1.7	1.8	12.5	3.8	2.2	1.0	0.5	0.3
0	100	1.2	1.6	1.7	1.8	1.8	1.8	1.8	1.4	0.4	0.3	0.1	0.1	0.0
10	0	2.3	8.1	9.2	10.2	10.6	10.8	11.0	19.2	6.4	3.9	1.8	0.9	0.5
10	100	10.5	10.8	10.9	10.9	11.0	11.0	11.0	1.0	0.4	0.2	0.1	0.1	0.0
20	0	7.8	15.5	17.2	18.7	19.3	19.7	20.0	27.6	10.2	6.4	3.0	1.6	0.8
20	100	20.0	20.0	20.0	20.0	20.0	20.0	20.0	0.1	0.0	0.0	0.0	0.0	0.0
30	0	12.6	22.4	24.8	26.9	27.9	28.4	29.0	37.4	15.3	9.9	4.9	2.6	1.4
30	100													
40	0	16.8	28.6	31.8	34.8	36.2	37.0	37.9	48.5	21.8	14.5	7.4	4.1	2.2
40	100													

DIMENSION ALONG AIRFLOW = 5 CM   DIMENSION ACROSS AIRFLOW = 1 CM

		LEAF TEMPERATURES FOR RESISTANCES=							TRANSPIRATION EXP 6 FOR RES =					
TA	RH	**0*	**1*	**2*	**5*	*10*	*20*	INF*	**0*	**1*	**2*	**5*	*10*	*20*
0	0	-3.2	0.6	1.7	2.7	3.2	3.4	3.7	7.5	3.3	2.2	1.1	0.6	0.3
0	100	2.3	3.0	3.3	3.5	3.6	3.7	3.7	1.6	0.7	0.5	0.2	0.1	0.1
10	0	2.1	7.3	8.9	10.4	11.1	11.5	12.0	10.8	5.2	3.5	1.7	1.0	0.5
10	100	11.0	11.4	11.6	11.8	11.9	11.9	12.0	1.1	0.6	0.4	0.2	0.1	0.1
20	0	6.8	13.3	15.5	17.7	18.8	19.4	20.1	14.8	7.6	5.2	2.7	1.5	0.8
20	100	20.0	20.1	20.1	20.1	20.1	20.1	20.1	0.1	0.0	0.0	0.0	0.0	0.0
30	0	11.0	18.9	21.6	24.6	26.1	27.0	28.1	19.4	10.6	7.5	4.1	2.3	1.3
30	100													
40	0	14.8	23.8	27.2	31.1	33.1	34.4	36.0	24.4	14.2	10.4	5.8	3.4	1.9
40	100													

AIRSPEED = 20. CM/SEC   RADIATION ABSORBED = 0.4 EXP 6 ERGS/CM2/SEC

DIMENSION ALONG AIRFLOW = 1 CM   DIMENSION ACROSS AIRFLOW = 5 CM
LEAF TEMPERATURES FOR RESISTANCES=   TRANSPIRATION EXP 6 FOR RES =

TA	RH	**0*	**1*	**2*	**5*	*10*	*20*	INF*	***0*	**1*	**2*	**5*	*10*	*20*
0	0	-2.7	0.2	0.9	1.4	1.6	1.7	1.8	9.9	3.5	2.1	1.0	0.5	0.3
0	100	1.3	1.7	1.7	1.8	1.8	1.8	1.8	1.1	0.4	0.3	0.1	0.1	0.0
10	0	4.0	8.3	9.3	10.2	10.6	10.8	11.0	15.6	6.0	3.7	1.8	0.9	0.5
10	100	10.6	10.8	10.9	10.9	11.0	11.0	11.0	0.9	0.4	0.2	0.1	0.1	0.0
20	0	9.9	15.8	17.4	18.8	19.3	19.7	20.0	22.9	9.6	6.1	3.0	1.6	0.8
20	100	20.0	20.0	20.0	20.1	20.0	20.0	20.0	0.1	0.0	0.0	0.0	0.0	0.0
30	0	15.1	22.8	24.9	27.0	27.9	28.5	29.0	31.7	14.4	9.5	4.8	2.6	1.4
30	100													
40	0	19.8	29.1	32.0	34.9	36.2	37.0	37.9	41.9	20.6	14.0	7.3	4.1	2.2
40	100													

DIMENSION ALONG AIRFLOW = 5 CM   DIMENSION ACROSS AIRFLOW = 5 CM
LEAF TEMPERATURES FOR RESISTANCES=   TRANSPIRATION EXP 6 FOR RES =

TA	RH	**0*	**1*	**2*	**5*	*10*	*20*	INF*	***0*	**1*	**2*	**5*	*10*	*20*
0	0	-1.8	0.9	1.9	2.8	3.2	3.4	3.7	6.0	3.0	2.0	1.0	0.6	0.3
0	100	2.5	3.1	3.3	3.5	3.6	3.7	3.7	1.3	0.7	0.5	0.2	0.1	0.1
10	0	3.9	7.7	9.0	10.5	11.1	11.5	12.0	8.9	4.7	3.3	1.7	0.9	0.5
10	100	11.1	11.5	11.6	11.8	11.9	11.9	12.0	1.0	0.5	0.4	0.2	0.1	0.1
20	0	9.1	13.9	15.7	17.8	18.8	19.4	20.1	12.4	7.0	4.9	2.7	1.5	0.8
20	100	20.0	20.1	20.1	20.1	20.1	20.1	20.1	0.1	0.0	0.0	0.0	0.0	0.0
30	0	13.6	19.6	21.9	24.7	26.1	27.0	28.1	16.5	9.8	7.1	4.0	2.3	1.2
30	100													
40	0	17.7	24.7	27.6	31.2	33.1	34.4	36.0	21.1	13.2	9.8	5.7	3.4	1.9
40	100													

AIRSPEED = 20. CM/SEC   RADIATION ABSORBED = 0.4 EXP 6 ERGS/CM2/SEC

DIMENSION ALONG AIRFLOW = 10 CM   DIMENSION ACROSS AIRFLOW = 5 CM
LEAF TEMPERATURES FOR RESISTANCES=   TRANSPIRATION EXP 6 FOR RES =

TA	RH	**0*	**1*	**2*	**5*	*10*	*20*	INF*	**0*	**1*	**2*	**5*	*10*	*20*
0	0	-1.1	1.5	2.5	3.6	4.2	4.5	4.9	4.9	2.8	2.0	1.1	0.6	0.3
0	100	3.3	4.0	4.2	4.6	4.7	4.8	4.9	1.3	0.8	0.6	0.3	0.2	0.1
10	0	4.2	7.6	9.0	10.6	11.5	12.0	12.6	7.1	4.2	3.0	1.7	0.9	0.5
10	100	11.4	11.9	12.1	12.3	12.4	12.5	12.6	1.0	0.6	0.4	0.2	0.1	0.1
20	0	8.9	13.2	15.0	17.3	18.5	19.2	20.1	9.6	6.0	4.4	2.5	1.4	0.8
20	100	20.1	20.1	20.1	20.1	20.1	20.1	20.1	0.1	0.0	0.0	0.0	0.0	0.0
30	0	13.1	18.2	20.6	23.5	25.1	26.2	27.5	12.5	8.2	6.1	3.6	2.1	1.2
30	100													
40	0	16.9	22.9	25.7	29.3	31.5	32.9	34.8	15.8	10.7	8.2	5.0	3.0	1.7
40	100													

DIMENSION ALONG AIRFLOW = 20 CM   DIMENSION ACROSS AIRFLOW = 5 CM
LEAF TEMPERATURES FOR RESISTANCES=   TRANSPIRATION EXP 6 FOR RES =

TA	RH	**0*	**1*	**2*	**5*	*10*	*20*	INF*	**0*	**1*	**2*	**5*	*10*	*20*
0	0	1.5	3.6	4.7	6.3	7.3	7.9	8.7	3.4	2.4	1.9	1.1	0.7	0.4
0	100	5.7	6.5	7.0	7.7	8.1	8.3	8.7	1.4	1.0	0.8	0.5	0.3	0.2
10	0	5.4	7.9	9.4	11.4	12.6	13.4	14.5	4.4	3.2	2.5	1.6	1.0	0.5
10	100	12.5	13.0	13.3	13.8	14.1	14.3	14.5	1.0	0.8	0.6	0.4	0.2	0.1
20	0	9.0	11.9	13.6	16.1	17.7	18.8	20.2	5.5	4.1	3.3	2.1	1.3	0.7
20	100	20.1	20.1	20.1	20.1	20.1	20.2	20.2	0.1	0.0	0.0	0.0	0.0	0.0
30	0	12.2	15.6	17.6	20.5	22.5	23.9	25.8	6.8	5.1	4.2	2.7	1.7	1.0
30	100													
40	0	15.2	19.0	21.2	24.7	27.0	28.7	31.2	8.2	6.3	5.2	3.4	2.2	1.3
40	100													

AIRSPEED = 20. CM/SEC   RADIATION ABSORBED = 0.4 EXP 6 ERGS/CM2/SEC

DIMENSION ALONG AIRFLOW = 1 CM   DIMENSION ACROSS AIRFLOW = 10 CM

TA	RH	**0*	**1*	**2*	**5*	*10*	*20*	INF*	**0*	**1*	**2*	**5*	*10*	*20*
		LEAF TEMPERATURES FOR RESISTANCES=							TRANSPIRATION EXP 6 FOR RES =					
0	0	-1.8	0.7	1.4	2.1	2.4	2.6	2.8	6.7	3.1	2.0	1.0	0.5	0.3
0	100	2.0	2.4	2.6	2.7	2.8	2.8	2.8	1.1	0.5	0.4	0.2	0.1	0.0
10	0	4.4	8.0	9.2	10.3	10.9	11.2	11.5	10.2	5.1	3.4	1.7	0.9	0.5
10	100	10.9	11.2	11.3	11.4	11.4	11.5	11.5	0.9	0.4	0.3	0.2	0.1	0.0
20	0	10.1	14.8	16.5	18.2	19.0	19.5	20.1	14.7	7.8	5.3	2.8	1.5	0.8
20	100	20.0	20.1	20.1	20.1	20.1	20.1	20.1	0.1	0.0	0.0	0.0	0.0	0.0
30	0	15.1	21.1	23.3	25.7	27.0	27.7	28.5	20.1	11.2	7.9	4.3	2.4	1.3
30	100													
40	0	19.5	26.8	29.6	32.8	34.5	35.6	36.9	26.3	15.5	11.3	6.3	3.6	2.0
40	100													

DIMENSION ALONG AIRFLOW = 5 CM   DIMENSION ACROSS AIRFLOW = 10 CM

TA	RH	**0*	**1*	**2*	**5*	*10*	*20*	INF*	**0*	**1*	**2*	**5*	*10*	*20*
		LEAF TEMPERATURES FOR RESISTANCES=							TRANSPIRATION EXP 6 FOR RES =					
0	0	-0.3	1.9	2.9	4.1	4.7	5.0	5.4	4.2	2.6	1.9	1.0	0.6	0.3
0	100	3.8	4.4	4.7	5.0	5.2	5.3	5.4	1.3	0.8	0.6	0.3	0.2	0.1
10	0	4.9	7.8	9.2	10.8	11.7	12.2	12.9	6.0	3.8	2.9	1.6	0.9	0.5
10	100	11.7	12.1	12.3	12.5	12.7	12.8	12.9	0.9	0.6	0.5	0.3	0.2	0.1
20	0	9.6	13.2	14.9	17.1	18.4	19.2	20.1	8.2	5.4	4.1	2.4	1.4	0.8
20	100	20.1	20.1	20.1	20.1	20.1	20.1	20.1	0.1	0.0	0.0	0.0	0.0	0.0
30	0	13.8	18.1	20.2	23.1	24.7	25.9	27.3	10.6	7.3	5.6	3.4	2.0	1.1
30	100													
40	0	17.6	22.6	25.1	28.7	30.8	32.3	34.3	13.4	9.5	7.4	4.6	2.9	1.6
40	100													

AIRSPEED = 20. CM/SEC   RADIATION ABSORBED = 0.4 EXP 6 ERGS/CM2/SEC

DIMENSION ALONG AIRFLOW = 10 CM   DIMENSION ACROSS AIRFLOW = 10 CM

TA	RH	LEAF TEMPERATURES FOR RESISTANCES=							TRANSPIRATION EXP 6 FOR RES =					
		**0*	**1*	**2*	**5*	*10*	*20*	INF*	**0*	**1*	**2*	**5*	*10*	*20*
0	0	0.8	2.9	3.8	5.2	5.9	6.4	7.0	3.6	2.4	1.8	1.1	0.6	0.3
0	100	4.8	5.5	5.8	6.3	6.6	6.8	7.0	1.3	0.9	0.7	0.4	0.2	0.1
10	0	5.4	8.0	9.3	11.1	12.1	12.8	13.7	4.9	3.4	2.6	1.6	0.9	0.5
10	100	12.1	12.6	12.8	13.1	13.4	13.5	13.7	0.9	0.7	0.5	0.3	0.2	0.1
20	0	9.6	12.7	14.4	16.7	18.0	19.0	20.2	6.4	4.6	3.6	2.2	1.3	0.8
20	100	20.1	20.1	20.1	20.1	20.1	20.1	20.2	0.1	0.0	0.0	0.0	0.0	0.0
30	0	13.5	17.0	19.0	21.8	23.6	24.9	26.6	8.2	6.0	4.8	3.0	1.9	1.1
30	100													
40	0	16.9	21.0	23.3	26.7	29.0	30.6	32.8	10.1	7.5	6.1	3.9	2.5	1.5
40	100													

DIMENSION ALONG AIRFLOW = 20 CM   DIMENSION ACROSS AIRFLOW = 10 CM

TA	RH	LEAF TEMPERATURES FOR RESISTANCES=							TRANSPIRATION EXP 6 FOR RES =					
		**0*	**1*	**2*	**5*	*10*	*20*	INF*	**0*	**1*	**2*	**5*	*10*	*20*
0	0	2.1	4.0	4.9	6.4	7.3	7.9	8.7	3.1	2.2	1.8	1.1	0.7	0.4
0	100	5.9	6.7	7.1	7.7	8.1	8.3	8.7	1.3	1.0	0.8	0.5	0.3	0.2
10	0	6.1	8.4	9.6	11.5	12.6	13.4	14.5	4.0	3.0	2.4	1.5	0.9	0.5
10	100	12.6	13.1	13.4	13.8	14.1	14.3	14.5	0.9	0.7	0.6	0.4	0.2	0.1
20	0	9.9	12.4	13.9	16.2	17.7	18.8	20.2	5.1	3.9	3.1	2.0	1.3	0.7
20	100	20.1	20.1	20.1	20.1	20.2	20.2	20.2	0.1	0.0	0.0	0.0	0.0	0.0
30	0	13.2	16.2	18.0	20.7	22.5	23.9	25.8	6.3	4.9	4.0	2.6	1.7	1.0
30	100													
40	0	16.3	19.6	21.7	24.8	27.1	28.8	31.2	7.6	6.0	5.0	3.3	2.2	1.3
40	100													

44

AIRSPEED = 20. CM/SEC   RADIATION ABSORBED = 0.6 EXP 6 ERGS/CM2/SEC

DIMENSION ALONG AIRFLOW = 1 CM   DIMENSION ACROSS AIRFLOW = 1 CM

TA	RH	LEAF TEMPERATURES FOR RESISTANCES=							TRANSPIRATION EXP 6 FOR RES =					
		**0*	**1*	**2*	**5*	*10*	*20*	INF*	**0*	**1*	**2*	**5*	*10*	*20*
0	0	-1.3	3.3	4.2	4.9	5.2	5.3	5.5	15.0	4.7	2.8	1.3	0.7	0.3
0	100	3.5	4.8	5.1	5.3	5.4	5.4	5.5	4.4	1.4	0.9	0.4	0.2	0.1
10	0	4.5	11.1	12.5	13.6	14.1	14.3	14.6	22.3	7.8	4.8	2.2	1.2	0.6
10	100	12.3	13.7	14.1	14.3	14.4	14.5	14.6	5.1	1.9	1.2	0.6	0.3	0.2
20	0	9.7	18.3	20.3	22.0	22.8	23.2	23.6	31.3	12.1	7.7	3.7	2.0	1.0
20	100	21.4	22.6	23.0	23.3	23.5	23.5	23.6	5.0	2.2	1.4	0.7	0.4	0.2
30	0	14.3	24.9	27.6	30.1	31.2	31.9	32.6	41.7	17.7	11.6	5.8	3.2	1.7
30	100	30.7	31.6	31.9	32.3	32.4	32.5	32.6	4.3	2.2	1.5	0.7	0.4	0.2
40	0	18.4	30.9	34.4	37.8	39.4	40.4	41.4	53.2	24.7	16.7	8.6	4.8	2.6
40	100	40.3	40.8	41.0	41.2	41.3	41.4	41.4	2.7	1.6	1.1	0.6	0.3	0.2

DIMENSION ALONG AIRFLOW = 5 CM   DIMENSION ACROSS AIRFLOW = 1 CM

TA	RH	LEAF TEMPERATURES FOR RESISTANCES=							TRANSPIRATION EXP 6 FOR RES =					
		**0*	**1*	**2*	**5*	*10*	*20*	INF*	**0*	**1*	**2*	**5*	*10*	*20*
0	0	1.6	6.5	8.1	9.5	10.2	10.6	11.0	10.4	5.0	3.3	1.7	0.9	0.5
0	100	6.4	8.7	9.5	10.3	10.6	10.8	11.0	5.1	2.5	1.7	0.9	0.5	0.2
10	0	6.3	12.7	14.7	16.9	17.9	18.5	19.2	14.3	7.3	5.0	2.6	1.5	0.8
10	100	14.3	16.5	17.3	18.2	18.6	18.9	19.2	5.5	3.0	2.1	1.1	0.6	0.3
20	0	10.6	18.2	20.9	23.8	25.3	26.2	27.2	18.8	10.3	7.2	3.9	2.2	1.2
20	100	22.6	24.4	25.2	26.1	26.5	26.8	27.2	5.4	3.3	2.4	1.3	0.7	0.4
30	0	14.4	23.3	26.6	30.3	32.3	33.6	35.1	23.8	13.8	10.0	5.6	3.3	1.8
30	100	31.3	32.6	33.2	34.0	34.4	34.7	35.1	4.4	3.0	2.3	1.3	0.8	0.4
40	0	17.8	27.9	31.8	36.4	39.0	40.7	42.8	29.2	17.8	13.3	7.7	4.6	2.6
40	100	40.6	41.2	41.5	42.0	42.3	42.5	42.8	2.8	2.0	1.6	1.0	0.6	0.3

AIRSPEED = 20. CM/SEC   RADIATION ABSORBED = 0.6 EXP 6 ERGS/CM2/SEC

DIMENSION ALONG AIRFLOW = 1 CM   DIMENSION ACROSS AIRFLOW = 5 CM

LEAF TEMPERATURES FOR RESISTANCES=   TRANSPIRATION EXP 6 FOR RES =

TA	RH	**0*	**1*	**2*	**5*	*10*	*20*	INF*	**0*	**1*	**2*	**5*	*10*	*20*
0	0	0.1	3.5	4.2	4.9	5.2	5.3	5.5	11.9	4.4	2.7	1.2	0.7	0.3
0	100	3.9	4.9	5.1	5.3	5.4	5.4	5.5	3.6	1.3	0.8	0.4	0.2	0.1
10	0	6.4	11.3	12.6	13.6	14.1	14.3	14.6	18.3	7.3	4.6	2.2	1.2	0.6
10	100	12.7	13.8	14.0	14.3	14.5	14.5	14.6	4.3	1.8	1.1	0.5	0.3	0.1
20	0	12.0	18.6	20.4	22.1	22.8	23.2	23.6	26.2	11.3	7.4	3.6	2.0	1.0
20	100	21.7	22.7	23.0	23.3	23.5	23.5	23.6	4.4	2.1	1.4	0.7	0.4	0.2
30	0	17.0	25.4	27.8	30.2	31.2	31.9	32.6	35.6	16.7	11.2	5.7	3.1	1.6
30	100	30.9	31.7	32.0	32.3	32.4	32.5	32.6	3.8	2.1	1.4	0.7	0.4	0.2
40	0	21.5	31.5	34.6	37.9	39.4	40.4	41.4	46.3	23.4	16.1	8.5	4.8	2.6
40	100	40.4	40.8	41.0	41.2	41.3	41.4	41.4	2.5	1.5	1.1	0.6	0.3	0.2

DIMENSION ALONG AIRFLOW = 5 CM   DIMENSION ACROSS AIRFLOW = 5 CM

LEAF TEMPERATURES FOR RESISTANCES=   TRANSPIRATION EXP 6 FOR RES =

TA	RH	**0*	**1*	**2*	**5*	*10*	*20*	INF*	**0*	**1*	**2*	**5*	*10*	*20*
0	0	3.3	7.0	8.2	9.6	10.2	10.6	11.0	8.5	4.5	3.1	1.6	0.9	0.5
0	100	7.2	9.0	9.6	10.3	10.6	10.8	11.0	4.2	2.3	1.6	0.8	0.5	0.2
10	0	8.5	13.2	15.0	17.0	17.9	18.5	19.2	11.9	6.7	4.7	2.5	1.4	0.8
10	100	15.0	16.7	17.4	18.2	18.6	18.9	19.2	4.8	2.8	2.0	1.1	0.6	0.3
20	0	13.1	18.9	21.3	23.9	25.3	26.2	27.2	16.0	9.5	6.9	3.8	2.2	1.2
20	100	23.1	24.6	25.3	26.1	26.6	26.8	27.2	4.8	3.0	2.2	1.3	0.7	0.4
30	0	17.3	24.1	27.0	30.5	32.4	33.6	35.1	20.6	12.8	9.5	5.5	3.2	1.8
30	100	31.7	32.7	33.3	34.0	34.4	34.7	35.1	4.0	2.8	2.1	1.3	0.8	0.4
40	0	21.0	28.9	32.3	36.6	39.1	40.7	42.8	25.6	16.7	12.7	7.5	4.6	2.6
40	100	40.7	41.2	41.6	42.0	42.3	42.6	42.8	2.6	1.9	1.5	1.0	0.6	0.3

AIRSPEED = 20. CM/SEC   RADIATION ABSORBED = 0.6 EXP 6 ERGS/CM2/SEC

DIMENSION ALONG AIRFLOW = 10 CM   DIMENSION ACROSS AIRFLOW = 5 CM
LEAF TEMPERATURES FOR RESISTANCES=   TRANSPIRATION EXP 6 FOR RES =

TA	RH	**0*	**1*	**2*	**5*	*10*	*20*	INF*	**0*	**1*	**2*	***5*	*10*	*20*
0	0	5.4	9.0	10.6	12.4	13.3	13.8	14.5	7.7	4.6	3.3	1.8	1.1	0.6
0	100	9.2	11.2	12.1	13.2	13.7	14.1	14.5	4.5	2.8	2.0	1.1	0.6	0.3
10	0	10.0	14.0	16.5	18.9	20.2	21.0	22.0	10.3	6.5	4.8	2.7	1.6	0.9
10	100	16.3	18.3	19.2	20.4	21.1	21.5	22.0	4.9	3.2	2.4	1.4	0.8	0.5
20	0	14.1	19.4	21.9	25.0	26.8	27.9	29.4	13.3	8.8	6.6	3.9	2.3	1.3
20	100	23.9	25.6	26.4	27.6	28.3	28.8	29.4	4.8	3.4	2.6	1.6	1.0	0.5
30	0	17.8	24.0	26.9	30.7	33.0	34.6	36.6	16.7	11.4	8.8	5.3	3.3	1.9
30	100	32.1	33.3	33.9	34.9	35.6	36.0	36.6	4.1	3.0	2.4	1.5	1.0	0.5
40	0	21.2	28.1	31.5	36.1	38.9	40.9	43.7	20.3	14.3	11.3	7.1	4.4	2.6
40	100	40.9	41.5	41.8	42.4	42.9	43.2	43.6	2.6	2.0	1.7	1.1	0.7	0.4

DIMENSION ALONG AIRFLOW = 20 CM   DIMENSION ACROSS AIRFLOW = 5 CM
LEAF TEMPERATURES FOR RESISTANCES=   TRANSPIRATION EXP 6 FOR RES =

TA	RH	**0*	**1*	**2*	**5*	*10*	*20*	INF*	**0*	**1*	**2*	***5*	*10*	*20*
0	0	11.8	15.1	17.1	19.9	21.8	23.2	25.1	6.6	5.0	4.1	2.6	1.7	1.0
0	100	15.0	17.4	18.9	21.1	22.5	23.6	25.0	5.0	3.9	3.2	2.1	1.3	0.8
10	0	14.8	18.6	20.8	24.2	26.4	28.1	30.5	8.0	6.1	5.0	3.3	2.2	1.3
10	100	20.4	22.6	23.9	26.1	27.7	28.8	30.5	5.2	4.1	3.4	2.3	1.5	0.9
20	0	17.6	21.7	24.2	28.1	30.8	32.8	35.8	9.5	7.4	6.1	4.1	2.7	1.6
20	100	26.6	28.3	29.5	31.4	32.9	34.0	35.8	4.9	4.0	3.4	2.4	1.6	0.9
30	0	20.2	24.7	27.4	31.8	34.9	37.3	41.0	11.0	8.8	7.3	5.1	3.4	2.1
30	100	33.6	34.8	35.7	37.2	38.4	39.4	41.0	4.1	3.4	3.0	2.1	1.5	0.9
40	0	22.6	27.5	30.4	35.2	38.7	41.6	46.0	12.7	10.2	8.7	6.1	4.1	2.6
40	100	41.5	42.1	42.6	43.5	44.2	44.9	46.0	2.6	2.2	2.0	1.5	1.0	0.6

AIRSPEED = 20. CM/SEC RADIATION ABSORBED = 0.6 EXP 6 ERGS/CM2/SEC
DIMENSION ALONG AIRFLOW = 1 CM   DIMENSION ACROSS AIRFLOW = 10 CM

TA	RH	LEAF TEMPERATURES FOR RESISTANCES=							TRANSPIRATION EXP 6 FOR RES =					
		**0*	**1*	**2*	**5*	*10*	*20*	INF*	**0*	**1*	**2*	**5*	*10*	*20*
0	0	2.3	5.4	6.5	7.4	7.9	8.1	8.4	8.8	4.3	2.8	1.4	0.8	0.4
0	100	5.9	7.2	7.6	8.0	8.2	8.3	8.4	3.7	1.8	1.2	0.6	0.3	0.2
10	0	8.1	12.5	13.9	15.4	16.1	16.6	17.0	13.0	6.7	4.6	2.3	1.3	0.7
10	100	14.1	15.5	15.9	16.5	16.7	16.8	17.0	4.3	2.3	1.6	0.8	0.5	0.2
20	0	13.3	18.9	20.9	23.1	24.2	24.8	25.5	18.1	9.9	6.9	3.7	2.1	1.1
20	100	22.6	23.8	24.3	24.9	25.1	25.3	25.5	4.4	2.6	1.8	1.0	0.6	0.3
30	0	18.0	24.8	27.4	30.3	31.9	32.8	33.9	24.0	13.9	10.0	5.5	3.2	1.7
30	100	31.4	32.3	32.7	33.2	33.5	33.7	33.9	3.8	2.5	1.8	1.0	0.6	0.3
40	0	22.1	30.1	33.3	37.2	39.2	40.6	42.2	30.6	18.7	13.8	7.9	4.6	2.6
40	100	40.6	41.1	41.3	41.7	41.9	42.0	42.2	2.5	1.7	1.3	0.8	0.5	0.3

DIMENSION ALONG AIRFLOW = 5 CM   DIMENSION ACROSS AIRFLOW = 10 CM

TA	RH	LEAF TEMPERATURES FOR RESISTANCES=							TRANSPIRATION EXP 6 FOR RES =					
		**0*	**1*	**2*	**5*	*10*	*20*	INF*	**0*	**1*	**2*	**5*	*10*	*20*
0	0	7.0	10.2	11.7	13.6	14.6	15.3	16.0	6.9	4.5	3.4	1.9	1.1	0.6
0	100	10.5	12.4	13.2	14.5	15.1	15.5	16.0	4.3	2.9	2.1	1.2	0.7	0.4
10	0	11.5	15.4	17.3	19.7	21.2	22.1	23.3	9.2	6.2	4.7	2.8	1.7	0.9
10	100	17.3	19.1	20.1	21.3	22.1	22.6	23.3	4.7	3.3	2.5	1.5	0.9	0.5
20	0	15.5	20.1	22.4	25.5	27.4	28.7	30.3	11.8	8.2	6.4	3.9	2.4	1.3
20	100	24.6	26.1	27.0	28.3	29.0	29.6	30.3	4.6	3.4	2.7	1.7	1.0	0.6
30	0	19.1	24.4	27.1	31.0	33.4	35.0	37.2	14.6	10.5	8.3	5.2	3.3	1.9
30	100	32.5	33.6	34.3	35.3	36.0	36.5	37.2	3.9	3.0	2.5	1.6	1.0	0.6
40	0	22.5	28.4	31.5	36.0	38.9	41.0	44.0	17.8	13.1	10.5	6.8	4.4	2.6
40	100	41.1	41.6	42.0	42.6	43.1	43.5	44.0	2.5	2.1	1.7	1.2	0.8	0.5

AIRSPEED = 20. CM/SEC   RADIATION ABSORBED = 0.6 EXP 6 ERGS/CM2/SEC

DIMENSION ALONG AIRFLOW = 10 CM   DIMENSION ACROSS AIRFLOW = 10 CM

TA	RH	LEAF TEMPERATURES FOR RESISTANCES=							TRANSPIRATION EXP 6 FOR RES =					
		**0*	**1*	**2*	**5*	*10*	*20*	INF*	**0*	**1*	**2*	**5*	*10*	*20*
0	0	9.7	12.8	14.5	16.8	18.2	19.1	20.4	6.5	4.6	3.6	2.2	1.4	0.8
0	100	13.0	15.0	16.2	17.8	18.8	19.5	20.4	4.5	3.3	2.6	1.6	1.0	0.6
10	0	13.5	17.2	19.2	22.0	23.8	25.0	26.7	8.2	6.0	4.8	3.0	1.9	1.1
10	100	19.0	20.9	22.1	23.8	24.9	25.7	26.7	4.9	3.6	3.0	1.9	1.2	0.7
20	0	17.0	21.1	23.4	26.8	29.1	30.7	33.0	10.1	7.6	6.1	4.0	2.5	1.5
20	100	25.7	27.3	28.3	29.9	31.0	31.8	33.0	4.7	3.7	3.0	2.0	1.3	0.8
30	0	20.2	24.7	27.4	31.4	34.1	36.2	39.0	12.2	9.3	7.7	5.1	3.3	2.0
30	100	33.2	34.3	35.0	36.3	37.2	38.0	39.0	3.9	3.2	2.7	1.9	1.2	0.7
40	0	23.1	28.1	31.1	35.6	38.8	41.3	45.0	14.4	11.3	9.4	6.4	4.2	2.5
40	100	41.4	41.9	42.3	43.1	43.7	44.2	45.0	2.5	2.1	1.8	1.3	0.9	0.5

DIMENSION ALONG AIRFLOW = 20 CM   DIMENSION ACROSS AIRFLOW = 10 CM

TA	RH	LEAF TEMPERATURES FOR RESISTANCES=							TRANSPIRATION EXP 6 FOR RES =					
		**0*	**1*	**2*	**5*	*10*	*20*	INF*	**0*	**1*	**2*	**5*	*10*	*20*
0	0	12.8	15.7	17.4	20.1	21.9	23.2	25.1	6.1	4.7	3.9	2.5	1.6	1.0
0	100	15.7	17.8	19.1	21.2	22.6	23.6	25.0	4.7	3.7	3.0	2.0	1.3	0.8
10	0	15.9	19.2	21.2	24.3	26.5	28.1	30.5	7.4	5.8	4.8	3.3	2.1	1.3
10	100	21.0	23.0	24.2	26.3	27.7	28.8	30.5	4.9	3.9	3.3	2.3	1.5	0.9
20	0	18.9	22.4	24.7	28.3	30.9	32.8	35.8	8.9	7.1	5.9	4.1	2.7	1.6
20	100	27.1	28.6	29.7	31.5	33.0	34.1	35.8	4.7	3.9	3.3	2.3	1.5	0.9
30	0	21.6	25.5	27.9	32.0	35.0	37.3	41.0	10.4	8.4	7.1	5.0	3.3	2.0
30	100	33.9	35.0	35.8	37.3	38.4	39.4	41.0	3.9	3.3	2.9	2.1	1.4	0.9
40	0	24.0	28.3	31.0	35.5	38.9	41.6	46.0	12.0	9.8	8.4	5.9	4.1	2.5
40	100	41.7	42.3	42.7	43.5	44.3	44.9	46.0	2.5	2.2	1.9	1.4	1.0	0.6

AIRSPEED = 20. CM/SEC   RADIATION ABSORBED = 0.8 EXP 6 ERGS/CM2/SEC

DIMENSION ALONG AIRFLOW = 1 CM   DIMENSION ACROSS AIRFLOW = 1 CM

		LEAF TEMPERATURES FOR RESISTANCES=							TRANSPIRATION EXP 6 FOR RES =					
TA	RH	**0*	**1*	**2*	***5*	*10*	*20*	INF*	**0*	**1*	**2*	***5*	*10*	*20*
0	0	1.1	6.5	7.5	8.4	8.7	8.9	9.1	17.7	5.8	3.5	1.6	0.8	0.4
0	100	5.7	7.9	8.4	8.8	8.9	9.0	9.1	7.6	2.6	1.6	0.7	0.4	0.2
10	0	6.7	14.0	15.6	17.0	17.5	17.8	18.2	25.7	9.3	5.8	2.7	1.5	0.8
10	100	14.1	16.6	17.2	17.7	17.9	18.0	18.2	9.2	3.6	2.3	1.1	0.6	0.3
20	0	11.6	21.0	23.2	25.3	26.1	26.6	27.2	35.3	14.2	9.1	4.4	2.4	1.2
20	100	22.8	25.2	25.9	26.5	26.8	27.0	27.2	10.2	4.6	3.0	1.5	0.8	0.4
30	0	16.0	27.4	30.3	33.2	34.5	35.3	36.1	46.1	20.3	13.5	6.8	3.8	2.0
30	100	31.8	33.8	34.6	35.3	35.7	35.9	36.1	10.2	5.3	3.6	1.9	1.0	0.5
40	0	19.8	33.2	36.9	40.7	42.6	43.7	44.9	58.1	27.8	19.1	10.0	5.7	3.0
40	100	41.0	42.6	43.3	44.0	44.4	44.7	44.9	9.3	5.5	3.9	2.1	1.2	0.7

DIMENSION ALONG AIRFLOW = 5 CM   DIMENSION ACROSS AIRFLOW = 1 CM

		LEAF TEMPERATURES FOR RESISTANCES=							TRANSPIRATION EXP 6 FOR RES =					
TA	RH	**0*	**1*	**2*	***5*	*10*	*20*	INF*	**0*	**1*	**2*	***5*	*10*	*20*
0	0	5.8	12.0	14.0	16.0	17.0	17.6	18.2	13.8	7.0	4.8	2.5	1.4	0.7
0	100	10.2	14.0	15.3	16.8	17.4	17.8	18.2	9.0	4.8	3.3	1.7	0.9	0.5
10	0	10.1	17.6	20.2	23.0	24.4	25.3	26.3	18.3	9.9	7.0	3.7	2.1	1.1
10	100	17.3	21.1	22.6	24.3	25.1	25.7	26.3	10.3	6.0	4.3	2.3	1.3	0.7
20	0	13.9	22.7	25.9	29.6	31.5	32.7	34.2	23.2	13.3	9.6	5.4	3.1	1.7
20	100	24.9	28.3	29.9	31.7	32.7	33.4	34.2	10.9	6.9	5.1	2.9	1.7	0.9
30	0	17.4	27.4	31.2	35.7	38.3	39.9	41.9	28.6	17.3	12.9	7.5	4.5	2.5
30	100	33.1	35.9	37.3	39.2	40.3	41.0	41.9	10.6	7.3	5.6	3.4	2.0	1.1
40	0	20.5	31.6	36.0	41.5	44.6	46.8	49.6	34.4	21.8	16.6	10.0	6.1	3.5
40	100	41.8	43.9	45.0	46.7	47.8	48.5	49.6	9.5	7.1	5.7	3.6	2.2	1.3

AIRSPEED = 20. CM/SEC   RADIATION ABSORBED = 0.8 EXP 6 ERGS/CM2/SEC

DIMENSION ALONG AIRFLOW = 1 CM   DIMENSION ACROSS AIRFLOW = 5 CM

TA	RH	LEAF TEMPERATURES FOR RESISTANCES=							TRANSPIRATION EXP 6 FOR RES =					
		**0*	**1*	**2*	**5*	*10*	*20*	INF*	**0*	**1*	**2*	**5*	*10*	*20*
0	0	2.7	6.7	7.6	8.4	8.7	8.9	9.1	14.3	5.4	3.3	1.6	0.8	0.4
0	100	6.3	8.0	8.4	8.8	8.9	9.0	9.1	6.3	2.4	1.5	0.7	0.4	0.2
10	0	8.7	14.3	15.7	17.0	17.5	17.8	18.2	21.3	8.7	5.6	2.7	1.4	0.7
10	100	14.7	16.7	17.2	17.7	17.9	18.0	18.2	7.9	3.4	2.2	1.1	0.6	0.3
20	0	14.1	21.4	23.4	25.3	26.2	26.6	27.2	29.8	13.3	8.7	4.3	2.4	1.2
20	100	23.3	25.3	25.9	26.5	26.8	27.0	27.2	8.9	4.4	2.9	1.4	0.8	0.4
30	0	18.8	27.9	30.5	33.2	34.5	35.3	36.1	39.7	19.2	13.0	6.7	3.7	2.0
30	100	32.2	33.9	34.6	35.3	35.7	35.9	36.1	9.2	5.1	3.5	1.8	1.0	0.5
40	0	23.1	33.8	37.2	40.8	42.6	43.7	44.9	50.8	26.4	18.4	9.9	5.6	3.0
40	100	41.3	42.7	43.3	44.1	44.4	44.7	44.9	8.6	5.3	3.8	2.1	1.2	0.6

DIMENSION ALONG AIRFLOW = 5 CM   DIMENSION ACROSS AIRFLOW = 5 CM

TA	RH	LEAF TEMPERATURES FOR RESISTANCES=							TRANSPIRATION EXP 6 FOR RES =					
		**0*	**1*	**2*	**5*	*10*	*20*	INF*	**0*	**1*	**2*	**5*	*10*	*20*
0	0	7.9	12.5	14.3	16.1	17.0	17.6	18.2	11.5	6.4	4.5	2.4	1.4	0.7
0	100	11.5	14.4	15.5	16.8	17.4	17.8	18.2	7.6	4.4	3.1	1.7	0.9	0.5
10	0	12.6	18.3	20.6	23.2	24.5	25.3	26.3	15.5	9.1	6.6	3.6	2.1	1.1
10	100	18.5	21.5	22.8	24.3	25.2	25.7	26.3	9.0	5.5	4.0	2.2	1.3	0.7
20	0	16.8	23.6	26.4	29.7	31.6	32.7	34.2	20.0	12.4	9.2	5.2	3.1	1.7
20	100	25.9	28.7	30.1	31.8	32.8	33.4	34.2	9.7	6.4	4.9	2.8	1.7	0.9
30	0	20.6	28.3	31.7	35.9	38.3	39.9	41.9	25.0	16.2	12.3	7.3	4.4	2.5
30	100	33.9	36.2	37.5	39.2	40.3	41.0	41.9	9.7	6.9	5.4	3.3	2.0	1.1
40	0	24.0	32.7	36.6	41.7	44.7	46.8	49.6	30.4	20.5	15.8	9.7	6.0	3.4
40	100	42.4	44.1	45.2	46.8	47.8	48.6	49.6	8.9	6.8	5.3	3.5	2.2	1.3

AIRSPEED = 20. CM/SEC   RADIATION ABSORBED = 0.8 EXP 6 ERGS/CM2/SEC
DIMENSION ALONG AIRFLOW = 10 CM   DIMENSION ACROSS AIRFLOW = 5 CM
LEAF TEMPERATURES FOR RESISTANCES=   TRANSPIRATION EXP 6 FOR RES =

TA	RH	**0*	**1*	**2*	**5*	*10*	*20*	INF*	**0*	**1*	**2*	**5*	*10*	*20*
0	0	11.1	15.8	17.9	20.4	21.9	22.8	23.9	11.0	7.0	5.2	3.0	1.8	1.0
0	100	14.4	17.7	19.3	21.2	22.3	23.0	23.9	8.2	5.4	4.0	2.3	1.4	0.8
10	0	15.1	20.6	23.2	26.5	28.4	29.6	31.2	14.1	9.4	7.1	4.2	2.5	1.4
10	100	20.6	24.0	25.7	27.9	29.2	30.1	31.2	9.4	6.5	5.0	3.0	1.8	1.0
20	0	18.7	25.0	28.1	32.1	34.5	36.2	38.4	17.6	12.1	9.4	5.8	3.5	2.0
20	100	27.4	30.5	32.1	34.5	36.0	37.0	38.4	10.0	7.2	5.8	3.6	2.2	1.3
30	0	22.0	29.1	32.5	37.4	40.4	42.5	45.4	21.3	15.1	12.0	7.6	4.8	2.8
30	100	34.9	37.4	38.9	41.2	42.7	43.8	45.4	9.9	7.5	6.2	4.0	2.6	1.5
40	0	25.0	32.7	36.7	42.2	45.9	48.5	52.3	25.3	18.4	14.8	9.7	6.3	3.7
40	100	43.0	44.8	46.1	48.0	49.5	50.6	52.3	9.0	7.2	6.1	4.2	2.7	1.6

DIMENSION ALONG AIRFLOW = 20 CM   DIMENSION ACROSS AIRFLOW = 5 CM
LEAF TEMPERATURES FOR RESISTANCES=   TRANSPIRATION EXP 6 FOR RES =

TA	RH	**0*	**1*	**2*	**5*	*10*	*20*	INF*	**0*	**1*	**2*	**5*	*10*	*20*
0	0	19.9	24.3	27.0	31.3	34.3	36.7	40.3	10.8	8.6	7.2	4.9	3.3	2.0
0	100	22.5	26.2	28.5	32.2	34.9	37.0	40.3	9.5	7.6	6.4	4.5	3.0	1.8
10	0	22.3	27.1	30.0	34.8	38.2	41.0	45.4	12.5	10.0	8.5	5.9	4.0	2.5
10	100	26.8	30.3	32.6	36.4	39.3	41.6	45.4	10.2	8.3	7.1	5.0	3.5	2.1
20	0	24.6	29.7	32.9	38.0	41.9	45.1	50.3	14.2	11.5	9.9	7.0	4.9	3.1
20	100	32.0	35.1	37.2	40.8	43.8	46.2	50.3	10.4	8.7	7.5	5.5	3.8	2.4
30	0	26.7	32.1	35.5	41.1	45.4	49.0	55.1	16.0	13.1	11.3	8.2	5.8	3.7
30	100	38.0	40.5	42.3	45.7	48.4	50.9	55.2	10.0	8.6	7.6	5.7	4.0	2.6
40	0	28.7	34.4	38.0	44.0	48.8	52.8	59.8	17.8	14.8	12.9	9.5	6.8	4.4
40	100	45.0	46.9	48.2	51.0	53.4	55.7	59.9	9.0	7.9	7.1	5.4	4.0	2.6

DIMENSION ALONG AIRFLOW = 1 CM   DIMENSION ACROSS AIRFLOW = 10 CM
LEAF TEMPERATURES FOR RESISTANCES=   TRANSPIRATION EXP 6 FOR RES =

TA	RH	**0*	**1*	**2*	**5*	*10*	*20*	INF*	**0*	**1*	**2*	**5*	*10*	*20*
0	0	6.1	10.0	11.3	12.6	13.2	13.5	13.9	11.4	5.7	3.9	2.0	1.1	0.6
0	100	9.4	11.6	12.4	13.1	13.5	13.7	13.9	6.6	3.4	2.3	1.2	0.6	0.3
10	0	11.5	16.7	18.5	20.4	21.3	21.9	22.5	16.2	8.7	6.0	3.1	1.8	0.9
10	100	17.1	19.5	20.4	21.4	21.9	22.2	22.5	8.0	4.5	3.1	1.7	0.9	0.5
20	0	16.4	22.7	25.1	27.8	29.1	30.0	30.9	21.8	12.4	8.8	4.8	2.7	1.5
20	100	25.0	27.3	28.3	29.5	30.1	30.5	30.9	9.0	5.5	4.0	2.2	1.2	0.7
30	0	20.7	28.3	31.3	34.8	36.6	37.8	39.2	28.2	16.9	12.3	6.9	4.1	2.2
30	100	33.3	35.3	36.3	37.6	38.2	38.7	39.2	9.2	6.1	4.6	2.6	1.5	0.8
40	0	24.6	33.3	36.9	41.3	43.8	45.4	47.4	35.2	22.1	16.6	9.7	5.8	3.2
40	100	42.0	43.6	44.4	45.6	46.3	46.8	47.4	8.6	6.1	4.8	2.9	1.8	1.0

DIMENSION ALONG AIRFLOW = 5 CM   DIMENSION ACROSS AIRFLOW = 10 CM
LEAF TEMPERATURES FOR RESISTANCES=   TRANSPIRATION EXP 6 FOR RES =

TA	RH	**0*	**1*	**2*	**5*	*10*	*20*	INF*	**0*	**1*	**2*	**5*	*10*	*20*
0	0	13.3	17.5	19.6	22.3	23.9	25.0	26.3	10.3	7.0	5.4	3.2	1.9	1.1
0	100	16.2	19.4	21.0	23.1	24.4	25.2	26.3	8.0	5.6	4.3	2.6	1.6	0.9
10	0	17.1	22.0	24.5	27.9	30.0	31.5	33.3	13.0	9.2	7.2	4.4	2.7	1.6
10	100	22.1	25.3	27.0	29.4	30.9	32.0	33.3	9.1	6.6	5.2	3.3	2.0	1.2
20	0	20.6	26.2	29.1	33.2	35.8	37.7	40.2	16.0	11.6	9.3	5.9	3.7	2.2
20	100	28.6	31.4	33.1	35.6	37.3	38.5	40.2	9.7	7.3	6.0	3.9	2.5	1.4
30	0	23.8	30.0	33.3	38.1	41.2	43.6	46.9	19.2	14.3	11.6	7.6	4.9	2.9
30	100	35.7	38.1	39.6	42.0	43.7	45.0	46.9	9.6	7.6	6.3	4.3	2.8	1.7
40	0	26.7	33.5	37.2	42.6	46.4	49.3	53.5	22.6	17.2	14.2	9.5	6.3	3.8
40	100	43.5	45.3	46.5	48.6	50.2	51.5	53.5	8.8	7.2	6.2	4.3	2.9	1.8

AIRSPEED = 20. CM/SEC   RADIATION ABSORBED = 0.8 EXP 6 ERGS/CM2/SEC

DIMENSION ALONG AIRFLOW = 10 CM   DIMENSION ACROSS AIRFLOW = 10 CM

TA	RH	LEAF TEMPERATURES FOR RESISTANCES=							TRANSPIRATION EXP 6 FOR RES =					
		**0*	**1*	**2*	**5*	*10*	*20*	INF*	**0*	**1*	**2*	**5*	*10*	*20*
0	0	17.1	21.2	23.5	27.0	29.3	30.9	33.1	10.2	7.6	6.2	4.0	2.6	1.5
0	100	19.8	23.0	25.0	27.8	29.8	31.2	33.1	8.5	6.5	5.3	3.4	2.2	1.3
10	0	20.3	24.8	27.5	31.5	34.2	36.3	39.2	12.3	9.4	7.7	5.1	3.3	2.0
10	100	24.9	28.1	30.0	33.1	35.3	36.9	39.2	9.4	7.4	6.1	4.1	2.7	1.6
20	0	23.2	28.2	31.2	35.8	39.0	41.5	45.2	14.5	11.3	9.4	6.4	4.3	2.6
20	100	30.6	33.5	35.3	38.4	40.7	42.4	45.1	9.8	7.9	6.7	4.6	3.1	1.9
30	0	25.8	31.3	34.6	39.7	43.4	46.4	50.9	16.9	13.4	11.3	7.8	5.3	3.3
30	100	37.1	39.5	41.1	43.9	46.2	48.0	51.0	9.6	8.0	6.9	5.0	3.4	2.1
40	0	28.3	34.2	37.7	43.4	47.6	51.0	56.6	19.4	15.6	13.3	9.4	6.5	4.1
40	100	44.4	46.2	47.5	49.9	51.9	53.7	56.6	8.7	7.5	6.6	4.9	3.5	2.2

DIMENSION ALONG AIRFLOW = 20 CM   DIMENSION ACROSS AIRFLOW = 10 CM

TA	RH	LEAF TEMPERATURES FOR RESISTANCES=							TRANSPIRATION EXP 6 FOR RES =					
		**0*	**1*	**2*	**5*	*10*	*20*	INF*	**0*	**1*	**2*	**5*	*10*	*20*
0	0	21.2	25.1	27.5	31.5	34.4	36.7	40.3	10.2	8.2	6.9	4.8	3.3	2.0
0	100	23.5	26.8	28.9	32.4	35.0	37.1	40.3	9.0	7.3	6.2	4.3	2.9	1.8
10	0	23.7	27.9	30.6	35.0	38.3	41.1	45.4	11.7	9.6	8.2	5.8	4.0	2.5
10	100	27.8	31.0	33.0	36.6	39.4	41.7	45.4	9.6	8.0	6.9	4.9	3.4	2.1
20	0	26.1	30.5	33.4	38.3	42.1	45.2	50.3	13.4	11.1	9.5	6.9	4.8	3.0
20	100	32.8	35.6	37.6	41.1	43.9	46.3	50.3	9.9	8.4	7.3	5.4	3.8	2.4
30	0	28.3	33.0	36.1	41.4	45.6	49.1	55.1	15.2	12.7	11.0	8.1	5.7	3.6
30	100	38.7	41.0	42.7	45.8	48.5	50.9	55.2	9.6	8.3	7.4	5.5	4.0	2.6
40	0	30.3	35.3	38.7	44.4	48.9	52.8	59.8	17.0	14.3	12.5	9.3	6.7	4.3
40	100	45.5	47.2	48.5	51.2	53.5	55.7	59.9	8.7	7.7	6.9	5.3	3.9	2.6

AIRSPEED = 20. CM/SEC   RADIATION ABSORBED = 1.0 EXP 6 ERGS/CM2/SEC
DIMENSION ALONG AIRFLOW = 1 CM   DIMENSION ACROSS AIRFLOW = 1 CM

		LEAF TEMPERATURES FOR RESISTANCES=							TRANSPIRATION EXP 6 FOR RES =					
TA	RH	**0*	**1*	**2*	**5*	*10*	*20*	INF*	**0*	**1*	**2*	**5*	*10*	*20*
0	0	3.4	9.5	10.8	11.8	12.2	12.4	12.7	20.7	7.0	4.3	2.0	1.0	0.5
0	100	7.7	10.9	11.6	12.2	12.4	12.5	12.7	11.1	4.0	2.4	1.1	0.6	0.3
10	0	8.7	16.9	18.7	20.3	21.0	21.3	21.7	29.3	11.1	7.0	3.3	1.8	0.9
10	100	15.7	19.3	20.2	21.0	21.3	21.5	21.7	13.6	5.6	3.5	1.7	0.9	0.5
20	0	13.4	23.6	26.1	28.4	29.5	30.1	30.7	39.4	16.4	10.7	5.3	2.9	1.5
20	100	24.1	27.6	28.7	29.7	30.2	30.4	30.7	15.4	7.2	4.8	2.4	1.3	0.7
30	0	17.6	29.7	33.0	36.2	37.7	38.6	39.6	50.7	23.1	15.5	8.0	4.4	2.4
30	100	32.7	35.9	37.1	38.3	38.9	39.2	39.6	16.2	8.7	6.0	3.1	1.7	0.9
40	0	21.3	35.3	39.4	43.6	45.7	47.0	48.4	63.1	31.1	21.6	11.6	6.6	3.5
40	100	41.8	44.4	45.5	46.8	47.5	47.9	48.4	15.9	9.6	7.0	3.8	2.2	1.2

DIMENSION ALONG AIRFLOW = 5 CM   DIMENSION ACROSS AIRFLOW = 1 CM

		LEAF TEMPERATURES FOR RESISTANCES=							TRANSPIRATION EXP 6 FOR RES =					
TA	RH	**0*	**1*	**2*	**5*	*10*	*20*	INF*	**0*	**1*	**2*	**5*	*10*	*20*
0	0	9.6	17.0	19.5	22.3	23.6	24.4	25.3	17.7	9.5	6.7	3.6	2.0	1.1
0	100	13.6	18.9	20.8	22.9	23.9	24.6	25.3	13.4	7.5	5.3	2.8	1.6	0.9
10	0	13.5	22.2	25.3	28.9	30.7	31.9	33.3	22.6	12.9	9.3	5.2	3.0	1.6
10	100	20.0	25.3	27.5	30.0	31.4	32.2	33.3	15.3	9.3	6.8	3.8	2.2	1.2
20	0	17.0	26.8	30.6	35.1	37.5	39.1	41.1	28.0	16.8	12.5	7.2	4.3	2.4
20	100	27.1	32.0	34.2	37.1	38.7	39.7	41.0	16.6	10.9	8.2	4.9	2.9	1.6
30	0	20.2	31.1	35.4	40.8	43.9	46.0	48.7	33.7	21.2	16.1	9.7	5.9	3.4
30	100	34.8	38.9	41.1	44.0	45.8	47.1	48.7	16.9	12.0	9.4	5.8	3.6	2.0
40	0	23.0	35.0	39.9	46.2	50.0	52.6	56.2	39.7	26.0	20.2	12.6	7.9	4.6
40	100	43.1	46.4	48.2	51.1	52.9	54.3	56.2	16.4	12.4	10.1	6.5	4.2	2.4

AIRSPEED = 20. CM/SEC   RADIATION ABSORBED = 1.0 EXP 6 ERGS/CM2/SEC
DIMENSION ALONG AIRFLOW = 1 CM   DIMENSION ACROSS AIRFLOW = 5 CM

TA	RH	LEAF TEMPERATURES FOR RESISTANCES=							TRANSPIRATION EXP 6 FOR RES =					
		**0*	**1*	**2*	**5*	*10*	*20*	INF*	**0*	**1*	**2*	**5*	*10*	*20*
0	0	5.1	9.8	10.8	11.8	12.2	12.4	12.7	16.8	6.6	4.1	1.9	1.0	0.5
0	100	8.6	11.0	11.6	12.2	12.4	12.5	12.7	9.2	3.7	2.3	1.1	0.6	0.3
10	0	10.9	17.2	18.8	20.3	21.0	21.3	21.7	24.4	10.4	6.7	3.3	1.8	0.9
10	100	16.6	19.5	20.3	21.0	21.3	21.5	21.7	11.7	5.2	3.4	1.7	0.9	0.5
20	0	16.0	24.0	26.3	28.5	29.5	30.1	30.7	33.5	15.5	10.3	5.2	2.8	1.5
20	100	24.8	27.8	28.7	29.7	30.2	30.4	30.7	13.6	6.8	4.6	2.3	1.3	0.7
30	0	20.6	30.3	33.2	36.3	37.8	38.6	39.6	44.0	21.9	15.0	7.8	4.4	2.3
30	100	33.4	36.1	37.2	38.3	38.9	39.2	39.6	14.7	8.3	5.8	3.1	1.7	0.9
40	0	24.7	36.0	39.7	43.7	45.7	46.9	48.4	55.5	29.6	20.9	11.4	6.5	3.5
40	100	42.2	44.6	45.6	46.8	47.5	47.9	48.4	14.8	9.2	6.8	3.8	2.2	1.2

DIMENSION ALONG AIRFLOW = 5 CM   DIMENSION ACROSS AIRFLOW = 5 CM

TA	RH	LEAF TEMPERATURES FOR RESISTANCES=							TRANSPIRATION EXP 6 FOR RES =					
		**0*	**1*	**2*	**5*	*10*	*20*	INF*	**0*	**1*	**2*	**5*	*10*	*20*
0	0	12.1	17.7	19.9	22.3	23.6	24.4	25.3	15.0	8.8	6.3	3.5	2.0	1.1
0	100	15.3	19.4	21.0	23.0	24.0	24.6	25.3	11.5	6.9	5.0	2.7	1.6	0.9
10	0	16.4	23.0	25.7	29.0	30.8	31.9	33.3	19.5	12.0	8.8	5.0	3.0	1.6
10	100	21.7	25.9	27.8	30.1	31.4	32.3	33.3	13.5	8.6	6.5	3.7	2.2	1.2
20	0	20.2	27.8	31.1	35.2	37.6	39.1	41.1	24.4	15.7	11.9	7.0	4.2	2.4
20	100	28.5	32.5	34.5	37.1	38.7	39.7	41.0	15.0	10.2	7.9	4.7	2.9	1.6
30	0	23.6	32.2	36.0	41.4	44.0	46.0	48.7	29.8	19.9	15.4	9.4	5.8	3.3
30	100	35.9	39.5	41.4	44.1	45.9	47.1	48.7	15.6	11.3	9.0	5.7	3.5	2.0
40	0	26.8	36.2	40.6	46.4	50.1	52.7	56.2	35.5	24.6	19.4	12.3	7.8	4.5
40	100	43.9	46.8	48.5	51.2	53.0	54.3	56.2	15.4	11.8	9.7	6.4	4.1	2.4

AIRSPEED = 20. CM/SEC   RADIATION ABSORBED = 1.0 EXP 6 ERGS/CM2/SEC

DIMENSION ALONG AIRFLOW = 10 CM   DIMENSION ACROSS AIRFLOW = 5 CM

LEAF TEMPERATURES FOR RESISTANCES=   TRANSPIRATION EXP 6 FOR RES =

TA	RH	**0*	**1*	**2*	***5*	*10*	*20*	INF*	**0*	**1*	**2*	***5*	*10*	*20*
0	0	16.0	21.8	24.5	27.9	30.0	31.3	33.0	15.0	10.0	7.7	4.6	2.8	1.6
0	100	18.9	23.5	25.7	28.6	30.4	31.5	33.0	12.5	8.5	6.6	4.0	2.4	1.3
10	0	19.6	26.1	29.2	33.5	36.1	37.8	40.2	18.5	12.8	10.0	6.2	3.8	2.2
10	100	24.5	29.1	31.4	34.7	36.8	38.2	40.1	14.2	10.2	8.0	5.0	3.1	1.8
20	0	22.8	30.0	33.6	38.6	41.8	44.0	47.2	22.3	15.9	12.7	8.1	5.1	3.0
20	100	30.6	34.9	37.3	40.8	43.1	44.8	47.2	15.4	11.5	9.4	6.1	3.9	2.3
30	0	25.7	33.6	37.7	43.4	47.2	50.0	54.0	26.3	19.3	15.6	10.3	6.7	4.0
30	100	37.4	41.1	43.3	46.9	49.3	51.2	54.0	15.9	12.4	10.3	7.0	4.6	2.7
40	0	28.4	36.9	41.4	47.9	52.3	55.6	60.7	30.5	22.9	18.8	12.7	8.5	5.1
40	100	44.9	47.9	49.9	53.1	55.6	57.6	60.7	15.5	12.6	10.8	7.6	5.1	3.2

DIMENSION ALONG AIRFLOW = 20 CM   DIMENSION ACROSS AIRFLOW = 5 CM

LEAF TEMPERATURES FOR RESISTANCES=   TRANSPIRATION EXP 6 FOR RES =

TA	RH	**0*	**1*	**2*	***5*	*10*	*20*	INF*	**0*	**1*	**2*	***5*	*10*	*20*
0	0	26.4	31.8	35.2	40.7	45.0	48.5	54.5	15.7	12.9	11.1	8.1	5.6	3.6
0	100	28.6	33.3	36.3	41.5	45.5	48.8	54.5	14.6	12.1	10.5	7.6	5.4	3.4
10	0	28.4	34.1	37.7	43.6	48.3	52.3	59.2	17.6	14.6	12.7	9.3	6.6	4.3
10	100	32.2	36.8	39.8	45.0	49.2	52.8	59.2	15.6	13.2	11.5	8.5	6.1	3.9
20	0	30.3	36.2	40.0	46.4	51.5	55.9	63.9	19.5	16.3	14.3	10.7	7.7	5.0
20	100	36.6	40.8	43.6	48.8	53.0	56.8	63.9	16.2	13.9	12.3	9.3	6.8	4.4
30	0	32.1	38.3	42.2	49.1	54.5	59.3	68.4	21.4	18.1	15.9	12.1	8.8	5.9
30	100	41.8	45.5	48.0	52.9	57.1	60.9	68.4	16.2	14.1	12.7	9.8	7.3	4.9
40	0	33.8	40.2	44.4	51.5	57.4	62.6	72.8	23.4	20.0	17.7	13.5	10.0	6.8
40	100	48.1	51.0	53.2	57.5	61.4	65.1	72.8	15.6	13.8	12.5	9.9	7.5	5.1

3

AIRSPEED = 20. CM/SEC   RADIATION ABSORBED = 1.0 EXP 6 ERGS/CM2/SEC

DIMENSION ALONG AIRFLOW = 1 CM   DIMENSION ACROSS AIRFLOW = 10 CM

LEAF TEMPERATURES FOR RESISTANCES =   TRANSPIRATION EXP 6 FOR RES =

TA	RH	**0*	**1*	**2*	**5*	*10*	*20*	INF*	**0*	**1*	**2*	**5*	*10*	*20*
0	0	9.6	14.3	16.0	17.6	18.4	18.9	19.4	14.4	7.5	5.1	2.7	1.5	0.8
0	100	12.7	15.9	17.0	18.2	18.7	19.0	19.4	9.9	5.3	3.6	1.9	1.1	0.6
10	0	14.7	20.6	22.8	25.2	26.4	27.1	27.9	19.7	10.9	7.7	4.1	2.3	1.3
10	100	19.8	23.3	24.6	26.1	26.9	27.4	27.9	12.1	7.0	5.0	2.7	1.5	0.8
20	0	19.2	26.4	29.1	32.3	34.0	35.0	36.3	25.8	15.2	11.0	6.1	3.5	1.9
20	100	27.2	30.6	32.1	33.9	34.9	35.5	36.3	13.8	8.6	6.4	3.6	2.1	1.1
30	0	23.2	31.6	34.9	39.0	41.3	42.7	44.5	32.6	20.1	15.0	8.6	5.1	2.8
30	100	35.1	38.2	39.7	41.7	42.8	43.6	44.5	14.7	9.9	7.6	4.5	2.7	1.5
40	0	26.9	36.3	40.3	45.3	48.2	50.1	52.6	40.0	25.8	19.7	11.8	7.2	4.0
40	100	43.4	46.0	47.4	49.4	50.6	51.5	52.6	14.8	10.7	8.4	5.2	3.2	1.8

DIMENSION ALONG AIRFLOW = 5 CM   DIMENSION ACROSS AIRFLOW = 10 CM

LEAF TEMPERATURES FOR RESISTANCES=   TRANSPIRATION EXP 6 FOR RES =

TA	RH	**0*	**1*	**2*	**5*	*10*	*20*	INF*	**0*	**1*	**2*	**5*	*10*	*20*
0	0	18.7	23.9	26.6	30.3	32.6	34.2	36.3	14.2	10.2	8.0	5.0	3.1	1.8
0	100	21.2	25.5	27.8	31.0	33.0	34.4	36.3	12.2	8.9	7.1	4.4	2.8	1.6
10	0	22.0	27.9	30.9	35.3	38.2	40.3	43.1	17.3	12.7	10.2	6.6	4.2	2.5
10	100	26.4	30.7	33.1	36.6	39.0	40.7	43.1	13.9	10.4	8.5	5.5	3.5	2.1
20	0	25.1	31.5	35.0	40.1	43.5	46.1	49.8	20.6	15.5	12.7	8.4	5.5	3.3
20	100	32.2	36.2	38.6	42.3	44.9	46.9	49.8	15.0	11.7	9.7	6.5	4.3	2.6
30	0	27.9	34.9	38.7	44.5	48.0	50.7	56.3	24.2	18.5	15.4	10.4	7.0	4.2
30	100	38.6	42.1	44.3	48.0	50.7	52.9	56.3	15.4	12.5	10.6	7.4	5.0	3.1
40	0	30.5	38.0	42.2	48.6	53.2	56.8	62.6	27.9	21.8	18.3	12.7	8.7	5.4
40	100	45.8	48.7	50.6	54.0	56.7	58.9	62.7	15.1	12.7	11.0	7.9	5.5	3.5

AIRSPEED = 20. CM/SEC   RADIATION ABSORBED = 1.0 EXP 6 ERGS/CM2/SEC

		DIMENSION ALONG AIRFLOW = 10 CM						DIMENSION ACROSS AIRFLOW = 10 CM					
		LEAF TEMPERATURES FOR RESISTANCES=						TRANSPIRATION EXP 6 FOR RES =					
TA	RH	**0*	**1*	**2*	***5*	*10*	*20*	INF*	**0*	**1*	**2*	***5*	*10*	*20*
0	0	23.2	28.3	31.3	35.9	39.1	41.6	45.3	14.6	11.4	9.5	6.4	4.3	2.6
0	100	25.5	29.8	32.5	36.6	39.6	41.8	45.3	13.2	10.4	8.7	5.9	4.0	2.4
10	0	25.9	31.4	34.7	39.8	43.5	46.5	51.1	17.0	13.5	11.3	7.9	5.3	3.3
10	100	29.8	34.1	36.8	41.2	44.4	47.0	51.1	14.5	11.7	9.9	7.0	4.7	2.9
20	0	28.4	34.3	37.8	43.5	47.7	51.2	56.8	19.5	15.7	13.3	9.5	6.5	4.1
20	100	34.8	38.8	41.4	45.8	49.2	52.1	56.8	15.3	12.7	10.9	7.9	5.5	3.5
30	0	30.7	36.9	40.8	47.0	51.7	55.6	62.3	22.1	18.0	15.5	11.2	7.9	5.0
30	100	40.6	44.1	46.4	50.7	54.1	57.1	62.3	15.6	13.2	11.6	8.6	6.1	3.9
40	0	32.9	39.4	43.5	50.2	55.4	59.9	67.7	24.7	20.5	17.7	13.1	9.3	6.0
40	100	47.2	50.0	52.1	55.9	59.2	62.2	67.7	15.2	13.2	11.7	9.0	6.5	4.3

		DIMENSION ALONG AIRFLOW = 20 CM						DIMENSION ACROSS AIRFLOW = 10 CM					
		LEAF TEMPERATURES FOR RESISTANCES=						TRANSPIRATION EXP 6 FOR RES =					
TA	RH	**0*	**1*	**2*	***5*	*10*	*20*	INF*	**0*	**1*	**2*	***5*	*10*	*20*
0	0	28.0	32.7	35.8	41.0	45.1	48.6	54.5	14.9	12.4	10.8	7.9	5.6	3.6
0	100	29.9	34.1	36.9	41.8	45.6	48.9	54.5	13.9	11.7	10.2	7.5	5.3	3.4
10	0	30.1	35.0	38.3	44.0	48.5	52.3	59.2	16.7	14.1	12.3	9.1	6.5	4.2
10	100	33.5	37.6	40.4	45.3	49.4	52.9	59.2	14.9	12.7	11.2	8.4	6.0	3.9
20	0	32.0	37.3	40.7	46.8	51.7	55.9	63.9	18.6	15.8	13.9	10.4	7.6	5.0
20	100	37.7	41.5	44.2	49.1	53.2	56.9	63.9	15.5	13.4	11.9	9.1	6.7	4.4
30	0	33.9	39.4	43.0	49.4	54.7	59.4	68.4	20.5	17.5	15.5	11.8	8.7	5.8
30	100	42.8	46.1	48.6	53.2	57.2	60.9	68.4	15.6	13.7	12.4	9.6	7.2	4.8
40	0	35.6	41.3	45.1	51.9	57.6	62.7	72.8	22.4	19.4	17.2	13.3	9.9	6.7
40	100	48.9	51.6	53.6	57.7	61.5	65.2	72.8	15.1	13.5	12.3	9.8	7.4	5.1

AIRSPEED = 50. CM/SEC   RADIATION ABSORBED = 0.4 EXP 6 ERGS/CM2/SEC

DIMENSION ALONG AIRFLOW = 1 CM   DIMENSION ACROSS AIRFLOW = 1 CM

LEAF TEMPERATURES FOR RESISTANCES=   TRANSPIRATION EXP 6 FOR RES =

TA	RH	**0*	**1*	**2*	**5*	*10*	*20*	INF*	**0*	**1*	**2*	**5*	*10*	*20*
0	0	-4.6	-0.0	0.5	0.9	1.0	1.1	1.2	19.6	4.1	2.3	1.0	0.5	0.3
0	100		0.8	1.1	1.1	1.2	1.2	1.2	1.5	0.3	0.2	0.1	0.0	0.0
10	0	1.7	8.5	9.4	10.1	10.4	10.5	10.6	30.5	7.3	4.2	1.8	0.9	0.5
10	100	10.3	10.6	10.6	10.6	10.6	10.6	10.6	1.1	0.3	0.2	0.1	0.0	0.0
20	0	7.2	16.6	18.0	19.1	19.6	19.8	20.0	44.0	12.0	7.1	3.2	1.7	0.8
20	100	20.0	20.0	20.0	20.0	20.0	20.0	20.0	0.1	0.0	0.0	0.0	0.0	0.0
30	0	12.0	24.1	26.2	27.9	28.6	29.0	29.4	60.0	18.6	11.3	5.2	2.8	1.4
30	100													
40	0	16.3	31.0	33.8	36.4	37.4	38.0	38.6	77.9	27.2	17.1	8.2	4.4	2.3
40	100													

DIMENSION ALONG AIRFLOW = 5 CM   DIMENSION ACROSS AIRFLOW = 1 CM

LEAF TEMPERATURES FOR RESISTANCES=   TRANSPIRATION EXP 6 FOR RES =

TA	RH	**0*	**1*	**2*	**5*	*10*	*20*	INF*	**0*	**1*	**2*	**5*	*10*	*20*
0	0	-4.5	0.2	1.1	1.9	2.2	2.3	2.5	11.3	3.7	2.3	1.0	0.5	0.3
0	100	1.5	2.1	2.3	2.4	2.5	2.5	2.5	1.7	0.6	0.4	0.2	0.1	0.0
10	0	1.1	7.6	9.0	10.2	10.8	11.0	11.3	16.7	6.1	3.8	1.8	1.0	0.5
10	100	10.6	11.0	11.1	11.2	11.3	11.3	11.3	1.2	0.5	0.3	0.1	0.1	0.0
20	0	6.0	14.4	16.4	18.3	19.1	19.6	20.1	23.2	9.4	6.1	2.9	1.6	0.8
20	100	20.0	20.0	20.0	20.0	20.1	20.1	20.1	0.1	0.0	0.0	0.0	0.0	0.0
30	0	10.3	20.6	23.3	26.0	27.2	27.9	28.7	30.6	13.7	9.1	4.6	2.5	1.3
30	100													
40	0	14.2	26.3	29.7	33.3	35.0	36.0	37.2	38.9	18.8	12.9	6.8	3.8	2.1
40	100													

AIRSPEED = 50. CM/SEC   RADIATION ABSORBED = 0.4 EXP 6 ERGS/CM2/SEC

DIMENSION ALONG AIRFLOW = 1 CM   DIMENSION ACROSS AIRFLOW = 5 CM

TA	RH	**0*	***1*	***2*	***5*	*10*	*20*	INF*	**0*	***1*	**2*	***5*	*10*	*20*
		LEAF TEMPERATURES FOR RESISTANCES=							TRANSPIRATION EXP 6 FOR RES =					
0	0	-3.4	0.0	0.5	0.9	1.0	1.1	1.2	15.5	3.9	2.2	1.0	0.5	0.3
0	100	0.8	1.1	1.1	1.2	1.2	1.2	1.2	1.2	0.3	0.2	0.1	0.0	0.0
10	0	3.4	8.6	9.5	10.1	10.4	10.5	10.6	24.8	6.9	4.0	1.8	0.9	0.5
10	100	10.4	10.6	10.6	10.6	10.6	10.6	10.6	0.9	0.3	0.2	0.1	0.0	0.0
20	0	9.4	16.7	18.1	19.1	19.6	19.8	20.0	36.7	11.4	6.9	3.1	1.6	0.8
20	100	20.0	20.0	20.0	20.0	20.0	20.0	20.0	0.1	0.0	0.0	0.0	0.0	0.0
30	0	14.7	24.3	26.2	27.9	28.6	29.0	29.4	51.1	17.8	11.0	5.2	2.7	1.4
30	100													
40	0	19.3	31.3	34.0	36.4	37.4	38.0	38.6	67.6	26.1	16.7	8.1	4.4	2.3
40	100													

DIMENSION ALONG AIRFLOW = 5 CM   DIMENSION ACROSS AIRFLOW = 5 CM

TA	RH	**0*	***1*	***2*	***5*	*10*	*20*	INF*	**0*	***1*	**2*	***5*	*10*	*20*
		LEAF TEMPERATURES FOR RESISTANCES=							TRANSPIRATION EXP 6 FOR RES =					
0	0	-3.1	0.4	1.2	1.9	2.2	2.3	2.5	9.0	3.5	2.2	1.0	0.5	0.3
0	100	1.7	2.2	2.3	2.4	2.5	2.5	2.5	1.4	0.5	0.3	0.2	0.1	0.0
10	0	2.9	7.8	9.1	10.3	10.8	11.0	11.3	13.7	5.7	3.7	1.8	0.9	0.5
10	100	10.7	11.1	11.2	11.2	11.3	11.3	11.3	1.0	0.5	0.3	0.1	0.1	0.0
20	0	8.3	14.8	16.6	18.3	19.1	19.6	20.1	19.5	8.8	5.8	2.9	1.6	0.8
20	100	20.0	20.0	20.0	20.1	20.1	20.1	20.1	0.1	0.0	0.0	0.0	0.0	0.0
30	0	13.0	21.1	23.6	26.1	27.2	27.9	28.7	26.3	12.9	8.7	4.5	2.5	1.3
30	100													
40	0	17.2	26.9	30.0	33.4	35.1	36.1	37.2	33.9	17.9	12.5	6.7	3.8	2.0
40	100													

AIRSPEED = 50. CM/SEC   RADIATION ABSORBED = 0.4 EXP 6 ERGS/CM2/SEC

DIMENSION ALONG AIRFLOW = 10 CM   DIMENSION ACROSS AIRFLOW = 5 CM

LEAF TEMPERATURES FOR RESISTANCES=   TRANSPIRATION EXP 6 FOR RES =

TA	RH	**0*	**1*	**2*	***5*	*10*	*20*	INF*	**0*	**1*	**2*	***5*	*10*	*20*
0	0	-2.7	0.6	1.6	2.5	2.9	3.1	3.4	7.3	3.3	2.1	1.0	0.6	0.3
0	100	2.2	2.8	3.0	3.2	3.3	3.3	3.4	1.4	0.7	0.4	0.2	0.1	0.1
10	0	2.9	7.5	9.0	10.4	11.0	11.4	11.8	10.7	5.2	3.5	1.7	1.0	0.5
10	100	10.9	11.4	11.5	11.6	11.7	11.8	11.8	1.0	0.5	0.4	0.2	0.1	0.1
20	0	7.9	13.9	15.8	17.9	18.9	19.4	20.1	14.9	7.7	5.3	2.8	1.5	0.8
20	100	20.0	20.1	20.1	20.1	20.1	20.1	20.1	0.1	0.0	0.0	0.0	0.0	0.0
30	0	12.4	19.6	22.2	25.0	26.4	27.3	28.3	19.8	10.9	7.7	4.2	2.4	1.3
30	100													
40	0	16.3	24.8	28.0	31.7	33.6	34.9	36.3	25.3	14.7	10.7	6.0	3.5	1.9
40	100													

DIMENSION ALONG AIRFLOW = 20 CM   DIMENSION ACROSS AIRFLOW = 5 CM

LEAF TEMPERATURES FOR RESISTANCES=   TRANSPIRATION EXP 6 FOR RES =

TA	RH	**0*	**1*	**2*	***5*	*10*	*20*	INF*	**0*	**1*	**2*	***5*	*10*	*20*
0	0	-1.1	2.0	3.2	4.7	5.5	5.9	6.5	4.7	2.8	2.0	1.1	0.6	0.3
0	100	4.0	4.9	5.3	5.8	6.1	6.3	6.5	1.6	1.0	0.7	0.4	0.2	0.1
10	0	3.4	7.2	8.8	10.8	11.9	12.6	13.4	6.4	4.0	2.9	1.7	1.0	0.5
10	100	11.7	12.3	12.6	12.9	13.1	13.2	13.4	1.1	0.7	0.6	0.3	0.2	0.1
20	0	7.4	12.0	14.0	16.6	18.0	19.0	20.2	8.3	5.4	4.1	2.4	1.4	0.8
20	100	20.1	20.1	20.1	20.1	20.1	20.1	20.2	0.1	0.0	0.0	0.0	0.0	0.0
30	0	11.0	16.3	18.7	22.0	23.9	25.2	26.8	10.5	7.1	5.4	3.3	2.0	1.1
30	100													
40	0	14.3	20.3	23.2	27.0	29.5	31.1	33.3	12.8	9.0	7.0	4.3	2.7	1.5
40	100													

AIRSPEED = 50. CM/SEC   RADIATION ABSORBED = 0.4 EXP 6 ERGS/CM2/SEC

DIMENSION ALONG AIRFLOW = 1 CM / DIMENSION ACROSS AIRFLOW = 10 CM

TA	RH	**0*	**1*	**2*	**5*	*10*	*20*	INF*	**0*	**1*	**2*	**5*	*10*	*20*
		LEAF TEMPERATURES FOR RESISTANCES=							TRANSPIRATION EXP 6 FOR RES =					
0	0	-2.9	0.2	0.9	1.4	1.6	1.7	1.9	10.2	3.6	2.2	1.0	0.5	0.3
0	100	1.3	1.7	1.8	1.8	1.8	1.9	1.9	1.2	0.4	0.3	0.1	0.1	0.0
10	0	3.6	8.2	9.3	10.2	10.6	10.8	11.0	16.1	6.1	3.8	1.8	0.9	0.5
10	100	10.6	10.8	10.9	11.0	11.0	11.0	11.0	0.9	0.4	0.2	0.1	0.1	0.0
20	0	9.4	15.7	17.3	18.7	19.3	19.7	20.1	23.4	9.7	6.2	3.0	1.6	0.8
20	100	20.0	20.0	20.0	20.0	20.0	20.0	20.1	0.1	0.0	0.0	0.0	0.0	0.0
30	0	14.5	22.6	24.8	26.9	27.9	28.4	29.0	32.3	14.5	9.5	4.8	2.6	1.4
30	100													
40	0	19.1	28.9	31.8	34.7	36.2	37.0	37.9	42.4	20.6	14.0	7.3	4.1	2.2
40	100													

DIMENSION ALONG AIRFLOW = 5 CM / DIMENSION ACROSS AIRFLOW = 10 CM

TA	RH	**0*	**1*	**2*	**5*	*10*	*20*	INF*	**0*	**1*	**2*	**5*	*10*	*20*
		LEAF TEMPERATURES FOR RESISTANCES=							TRANSPIRATION EXP 6 FOR RES =					
0	0	-2.0	0.9	1.9	2.8	3.3	3.5	3.8	6.2	3.1	2.1	1.0	0.6	0.3
0	100	2.5	3.1	3.4	3.6	3.7	3.7	3.8	1.4	0.7	0.5	0.2	0.1	0.1
10	0	3.6	7.6	9.0	10.5	11.1	11.6	12.0	9.1	4.8	3.3	1.7	0.9	0.5
10	100	11.1	11.5	11.7	11.8	11.9	12.0	12.0	1.0	0.6	0.4	0.2	0.1	0.1
20	0	8.6	13.7	15.6	17.7	18.8	19.4	20.1	12.7	7.1	5.0	2.7	1.5	0.8
20	100	20.0	20.0	20.1	20.1	20.1	20.1	20.1	0.1	0.0	0.0	0.0	0.0	0.0
30	0	13.1	19.3	21.7	24.6	26.1	27.0	28.1	16.8	9.9	7.1	4.0	2.3	1.2
30	100													
40	0	17.0	24.4	27.4	31.0	33.0	34.3	35.9	21.4	13.3	9.8	5.7	3.3	1.8
40	100													

AIRSPEED = 50. CM/SEC   RADIATION ABSORBED = 0.4 EXP 6 ERGS/CM2/SEC

DIMENSION ALONG AIRFLOW = 10 CM   DIMENSION ACROSS AIRFLOW = 10 CM

TA	RH	**0*	**1*	**2*	**5*	*10*	*20*	INF*	**0*	**1*	**2*	**5*	*10*	*20*
		LEAF TEMPERATURES FOR RESISTANCES=							TRANSPIRATION EXP 6 FOR RES =					
0	0	-1.3	1.5	2.5	3.7	4.3	4.6	5.0	5.1	2.9	2.0	1.1	0.6	0.3
0	100	3.3	4.0	4.3	4.6	4.8	4.9	5.0	1.4	0.8	0.6	0.3	0.2	0.1
10	0	3.8	7.5	9.0	10.6	11.5	12.0	12.6	7.3	4.3	3.1	1.7	1.0	0.5
10	100	11.4	11.9	12.1	12.3	12.5	12.5	12.6	1.0	0.6	0.5	0.3	0.1	0.1
20	0	8.4	13.0	14.9	17.2	18.4	19.2	20.1	9.8	6.1	4.4	2.5	1.5	0.8
20	100	20.1	20.1	20.1	20.1	20.1	20.1	20.1	0.1	0.0	0.0	0.0	0.0	0.0
30	0	12.5	17.9	20.4	23.4	25.1	26.1	27.5	12.8	8.2	6.2	3.6	2.1	1.2
30	100													
40	0	16.3	22.5	25.4	29.1	31.3	32.8	34.7	16.0	10.7	8.2	4.9	3.0	1.7
40	100													

DIMENSION ALONG AIRFLOW = 20 CM   DIMENSION ACROSS AIRFLOW = 10 CM

TA	RH	**0*	**1*	**2*	**5*	*10*	*20*	INF*	**0*	**1*	**2*	**5*	*10*	*20*
		LEAF TEMPERATURES FOR RESISTANCES=							TRANSPIRATION EXP 6 FOR RES =					
0	0	-0.4	2.2	3.3	4.7	5.5	5.9	6.5	4.3	2.7	2.0	1.1	0.6	0.3
0	100	4.2	5.0	5.4	5.9	6.1	6.3	6.5	1.4	0.9	0.7	0.4	0.2	0.1
10	0	4.2	7.5	9.0	10.9	11.9	12.6	13.4	5.9	3.8	2.8	1.6	1.0	0.5
10	100	11.8	12.3	12.6	12.9	13.1	13.2	13.4	1.0	0.7	0.5	0.3	0.2	0.1
20	0	8.4	12.3	14.2	16.7	18.1	19.0	20.2	7.7	5.2	3.9	2.3	1.4	0.8
20	100	20.1	20.1	20.1	20.1	20.1	20.1	20.1	0.1	0.0	0.0	0.0	0.0	0.0
30	0	12.1	16.7	19.0	22.1	24.0	25.2	26.8	9.8	6.8	5.3	3.2	2.0	1.1
30	100													
40	0	15.6	20.8	23.5	27.2	29.5	31.1	33.3	12.0	8.6	6.8	4.3	2.7	1.5
40	100													

AIRSPEED = 50. CM/SEC   RADIATION ABSORBED = 0.6 EXP 6 ERGS/CM2/SEC

DIMENSION ALONG AIRFLOW = 1 CM   DIMENSION ACROSS AIRFLOW = 1 CM

		**0*	**1*	**2*	**5*	*10*	*20*	INF*	**0*	**1*	**2*	**5*	*10*	*20*
TA	RH	LEAF TEMPERATURES FOR RESISTANCES=							TRANSPIRATION EXP 6 FOR RES =					
0	0	-3.0	2.2	2.8	3.2	3.4	3.5	3.6	22.1	4.8	2.7	1.2	0.6	0.3
0	100	2.2	3.0	3.4	3.5	3.5	3.5	3.6	4.5	1.0	0.6	0.3	0.1	0.1
10	0	3.1	10.6	11.6	12.4	12.7	12.8	13.0	33.6	8.3	4.8	2.1	1.1	0.6
10	100	11.5	12.6	12.8	12.9	12.9	13.0	13.0	5.2	1.4	0.8	0.4	0.2	0.1
20	0	8.5	18.5	20.1	21.3	21.8	22.1	22.4	47.8	13.4	8.0	3.6	1.9	1.0
20	100	20.9	21.9	22.1	22.2	22.3	22.3	22.4	5.2	1.7	1.0	0.5	0.2	0.1
30	0	13.2	25.9	28.1	30.0	30.8	31.2	31.7	64.3	20.5	12.6	5.9	3.1	1.6
30	100	30.5	31.2	31.4	31.6	31.6	31.7	31.7	4.4	1.7	1.1	0.5	0.3	0.1
40	0	17.3	32.6	35.7	38.4	39.6	40.2	41.0	82.7	29.7	18.9	9.1	4.9	2.6
40	100	40.2	40.6	40.7	40.8	40.9	40.9	41.0	2.8	1.3	0.9	0.4	0.2	0.1

DIMENSION ALONG AIRFLOW = 5 CM   DIMENSION ACROSS AIRFLOW = 1 CM

		**0*	**1*	**2*	**5*	*10*	*20*	INF*	**0*	**1*	**2*	**5*	*10*	*20*
TA	RH	LEAF TEMPERATURES FOR RESISTANCES=							TRANSPIRATION EXP 6 FOR RES =					
0	0	-1.3	4.4	5.6	6.6	7.0	7.2	7.5	14.1	5.0	3.1	1.4	0.8	0.4
0	100	4.3	6.3	6.7	7.1	7.3	7.4	7.5	5.2	1.9	1.2	0.6	0.3	0.2
10	0	3.9	11.5	13.2	14.8	15.5	15.8	16.2	20.2	7.9	5.0	2.4	1.3	0.7
10	100	12.8	14.7	15.3	15.8	16.0	16.1	16.2	5.7	2.5	1.6	0.8	0.4	0.2
20	0	8.5	18.0	20.4	22.7	23.7	24.3	24.9	27.2	11.7	7.6	3.8	2.1	1.1
20	100	21.6	23.3	23.8	24.4	24.6	24.7	24.9	5.5	2.8	1.8	0.9	0.5	0.3
30	0	12.5	23.9	27.0	30.1	31.6	32.5	33.5	35.2	16.4	11.1	5.8	3.2	1.7
30	100	30.8	32.0	32.4	32.9	33.2	33.3	33.5	4.6	2.6	1.8	1.0	0.5	0.3
40	0	16.1	29.2	33.1	37.2	39.2	40.5	42.0	43.8	22.1	15.5	8.4	4.8	2.6
40	100	40.3	40.9	41.2	41.5	41.7	41.8	42.0	2.8	1.8	1.4	0.8	0.4	0.2

AIRSPEED = 50. CM/SEC   RADIATION ABSORBED = 0.6 EXP 6 ERGS/CM2/SEC

DIMENSION ALONG AIRFLOW = 1 CM   DIMENSION ACROSS AIRFLOW = 5 CM

		LEAF TEMPERATURES FOR RESISTANCES=							TRANSPIRATION EXP 6 FOR RES =					
TA	RH	**0*	**1*	**2*	**5*	*10*	*20*	INF*	**0*	**1*	**2*	**5*	*10*	*20*
0	0	-1.6	2.2	2.8	3.2	3.4	3.5	3.6	17.6	4.5	2.6	1.2	0.6	0.3
0	100	2.5	3.3	3.4	3.5	3.5	3.5	3.6	3.6	1.0	0.6	0.2	0.1	0.1
10	0	4.9	10.7	11.6	12.4	12.7	12.8	13.0	27.5	7.9	4.6	2.1	1.1	0.6
10	100	11.7	12.6	12.8	12.9	12.9	13.0	13.0	4.4	1.3	0.8	0.4	0.2	0.1
20	0	10.8	18.7	20.1	21.3	21.8	22.1	22.4	40.1	12.8	7.8	3.6	1.9	1.0
20	100	21.1	21.9	22.1	22.2	22.2	22.3	22.4	4.5	1.6	1.0	0.5	0.2	0.1
30	0	15.9	26.1	28.2	30.1	30.8	31.0	31.7	55.0	19.7	12.3	5.8	3.1	1.6
30	100	30.6	31.2	31.4	31.6	31.6	31.7	31.7	4.0	1.7	1.1	0.5	0.3	0.1
40	0	20.4	33.0	35.8	38.4	39.6	40.2	41.0	72.1	28.6	18.4	9.0	4.9	2.6
40	100	40.2	40.6	40.7	40.8	40.9	40.9	41.0	2.6	1.3	0.8	0.4	0.2	0.1

DIMENSION ALONG AIRFLOW = 5 CM   DIMENSION ACROSS AIRFLOW = 5 CM

		LEAF TEMPERATURES FOR RESISTANCES=							TRANSPIRATION EXP 6 FOR RES =					
TA	RH	**0*	**1*	**2*	**5*	*10*	*20*	INF*	**0*	**1*	**2*	**5*	*10*	*20*
0	0	0.4	4.6	5.7	6.6	7.0	7.2	7.5	11.5	4.6	2.9	1.4	0.7	0.4
0	100	4.8	6.4	6.8	7.1	7.3	7.4	7.5	4.3	1.8	1.1	0.5	0.3	0.2
10	0	6.0	11.8	13.4	14.8	15.5	15.8	16.2	16.8	7.3	4.8	2.3	1.3	0.7
10	100	13.3	14.8	15.3	15.8	16.0	16.1	16.2	4.9	2.3	1.5	0.7	0.4	0.2
20	0	11.0	18.4	20.6	22.7	23.7	24.3	24.9	23.1	11.0	7.3	3.7	2.1	1.1
20	100	22.0	23.4	23.9	24.4	24.6	24.8	24.9	4.9	2.6	1.8	0.9	0.5	0.3
30	0	15.4	24.4	27.2	30.2	31.7	32.5	33.5	30.4	15.5	10.7	5.7	3.2	1.7
30	100	31.1	32.0	32.5	32.9	33.2	33.3	33.5	4.2	2.5	1.8	1.0	0.5	0.3
40	0	19.4	29.8	33.4	37.3	39.3	40.5	42.0	38.5	21.0	15.0	8.2	4.7	2.6
40	100	40.4	41.0	41.2	41.5	41.7	41.8	42.0	2.7	1.8	1.3	0.7	0.4	0.2

AIRSPEED = 50. CM/SEC   RADIATION ABSORBED = 0.6 EXP 6 ERGS/CM2/SEC

DIMENSION ALONG AIRFLOW = 10 CM   DIMENSION ACROSS AIRFLOW = 5 CM

		LEAF TEMPERATURES FOR RESISTANCES=							TRANSPIRATION EXP 6 FOR RES =					
TA	RH	**0*	**1*	**2*	**5*	*10*	*20*	INF*	**0*	**1*	**2*	**5*	*10*	*20*
0	0	1.8	6.1	7.5	8.8	9.4	9.7	10.1	9.9	4.7	3.1	1.6	0.9	0.4
0	100	6.3	8.2	8.8	9.4	9.7	9.9	10.1	4.6	2.3	1.5	0.8	0.4	0.2
10	0	6.9	12.6	14.5	16.4	17.3	17.8	18.4	14.0	7.1	4.9	2.5	1.4	0.7
10	100	14.2	16.1	16.8	17.6	17.9	18.1	18.4	5.1	2.8	1.9	1.0	0.6	0.3
20	0	11.5	18.5	20.9	23.6	24.9	25.7	26.6	18.7	10.2	7.2	3.8	2.2	1.2
20	100	22.6	24.2	24.9	25.6	26.0	26.3	26.6	5.1	3.0	2.2	1.2	0.7	0.4
30	0	15.5	23.8	26.9	30.3	32.2	33.3	34.6	24.1	13.9	10.0	5.6	3.2	1.8
30	100	31.4	32.5	33.0	33.7	34.1	34.4	34.6	4.3	2.8	2.1	1.2	0.7	0.4
40	0	19.2	28.6	32.3	36.7	39.1	40.7	42.6	29.9	18.2	13.5	7.8	4.6	2.6
40	100	40.6	41.1	41.5	41.9	42.2	42.4	42.6	2.7	1.9	1.5	0.9	0.6	0.3

DIMENSION ALONG AIRFLOW = 20 CM   DIMENSION ACROSS AIRFLOW = 5 CM

		LEAF TEMPERATURES FOR RESISTANCES=							TRANSPIRATION EXP 6 FOR RES =					
TA	RH	**0*	**1*	**2*	**5*	*10*	*20*	INF*	**0*	**1*	**2*	**5*	*10*	*20*
0	0	6.7	11.1	13.1	15.6	17.0	17.8	18.9	7.9	5.1	3.9	2.2	1.3	0.7
0	100	10.9	13.6	14.9	16.6	17.5	18.2	18.9	5.3	3.5	2.7	1.6	0.9	0.5
10	0	10.4	15.5	17.9	21.0	22.8	24.1	25.6	10.0	6.7	5.2	3.1	1.9	1.0
10	100	17.3	19.8	21.1	22.9	23.9	24.7	25.6	5.6	3.9	3.1	1.9	1.1	0.6
20	0	13.7	19.5	22.4	26.2	28.4	30.0	32.1	12.4	8.6	6.7	4.1	2.5	1.5
20	100	24.5	26.4	27.6	29.2	30.3	31.0	32.1	5.3	3.9	3.1	2.0	1.2	0.7
30	0	16.8	23.2	26.5	30.9	33.8	35.7	38.4	14.9	10.6	8.4	5.4	3.4	2.0
30	100	32.4	33.7	34.5	35.8	36.8	37.5	38.4	4.3	3.4	2.8	1.9	1.2	0.7
40	0	19.6	26.6	30.2	35.4	38.7	41.2	44.7	17.6	12.9	10.4	6.8	4.4	2.6
40	100	41.0	42.1	42.9	43.5	43.9	44.3	44.7	2.7	2.2	1.9	1.3	0.9	0.5

AIRSPEED = 50. CM/SEC   RADIATION ABSORBED = 0.6 EXP 6 ERGS/CM2/SEC

DIMENSION ALONG AIRFLOW = 1 CM   DIMENSION ACROSS AIRFLOW = 10 CM

		LEAF TEMPERATURES FOR RESISTANCES=							TRANSPIRATION EXP 6 FOR RES =					
TA	RH	**0*	**1*	**2*	**5*	*10*	*20*	INF*	**0*	**1*	**2*	**5*	*10*	*20*
0	0	-0.2	3.5	4.3	5.0	5.3	5.4	5.6	12.4	4.4	2.7	1.3	0.7	0.3
0	100	3.9	4.9	5.2	5.4	5.5	5.5	5.6	3.8	1.4	0.9	0.4	0.2	0.1
10	0	6.1	11.3	12.6	13.7	14.2	14.4	14.7	18.9	7.4	4.6	2.2	1.2	0.6
10	100	12.7	13.8	14.2	14.4	14.5	14.6	14.7	4.4	1.8	1.2	0.6	0.3	0.2
20	0	11.6	18.6	20.4	22.1	22.8	23.2	23.7	26.9	11.5	7.4	3.6	2.0	1.0
20	100	21.7	22.8	23.1	23.4	23.5	23.6	23.7	4.6	2.2	1.4	0.7	0.4	0.2
30	0	16.4	25.2	27.7	30.1	31.3	31.9	32.6	36.2	16.8	11.2	5.7	3.1	1.7
30	100	30.8	31.7	32.0	32.3	32.5	32.5	32.6	3.9	2.1	1.4	0.7	0.4	0.2
40	0	20.8	31.3	34.5	37.8	39.4	40.4	41.5	46.9	23.5	16.2	8.5	4.8	2.6
40	100	40.4	40.8	41.0	41.2	41.3	41.4	41.5	2.6	1.5	1.1	0.6	0.3	0.2

DIMENSION ALONG AIRFLOW = 5 CM   DIMENSION ACROSS AIRFLOW = 10 CM

		LEAF TEMPERATURES FOR RESISTANCES=							TRANSPIRATION EXP 6 FOR RES =					
TA	RH	**0*	**1*	**2*	**5*	*10*	*20*	INF*	**0*	**1*	**2*	**5*	*10*	*20*
0	0	3.1	7.0	8.3	9.8	10.4	10.8	11.2	8.8	4.6	3.2	1.6	0.9	0.5
0	100	7.2	9.1	9.7	10.5	10.8	11.0	11.2	4.4	2.4	1.6	0.9	0.5	0.3
10	0	8.1	13.2	15.0	17.1	18.1	18.7	19.4	12.3	6.8	4.8	2.6	1.4	0.8
10	100	14.9	16.7	17.5	18.4	18.8	19.0	19.4	4.9	2.9	2.1	1.1	0.6	0.3
20	0	12.7	18.8	21.2	24.0	25.4	26.3	27.3	16.4	9.6	6.9	3.8	2.2	1.2
20	100	23.0	24.6	25.3	26.2	26.7	27.0	27.3	4.9	3.1	2.3	1.3	0.8	0.4
30	0	16.7	23.9	26.9	30.5	32.4	33.6	35.2	20.9	12.9	9.6	5.5	3.2	1.8
30	100	31.6	32.7	33.3	34.1	34.5	34.8	35.2	4.1	2.8	2.2	1.3	0.8	0.4
40	0	20.3	28.6	32.1	36.5	39.1	40.7	42.9	26.0	16.7	12.7	7.6	4.6	2.6
40	100	40.7	41.2	41.6	42.1	42.4	42.6	42.9	2.6	1.9	1.6	1.0	0.6	0.3

AIRSPEED = 50. CM/SEC   RADIATION ABSORBED = 0.6 EXP 6 ERGS/CM2/SEC

		DIMENSION ALONG AIRFLOW = 10 CM							DIMENSION ACROSS AIRFLOW = 10 CM					
		LEAF TEMPERATURES FOR RESISTANCES=							TRANSPIRATION EXP 6 FOR RES =					
TA	RH	**0*	**1*	**2*	**5*	*10*	*20*	INF*	**0*	**1*	**2*	**5*	*10*	*20*
0	0	5.2	9.1	10.7	12.5	13.5	14.1	14.8	7.9	4.7	3.4	1.9	1.1	0.6
0	100	9.1	11.3	12.3	13.4	14.0	14.4	14.8	4.7	2.9	2.1	1.2	0.7	0.4
10	0	9.6	14.4	16.5	19.0	20.3	21.2	22.2	10.6	6.6	4.9	2.8	1.6	0.9
10	100	16.2	18.3	19.3	20.6	21.2	21.7	22.2	5.1	3.4	2.5	1.4	0.8	0.5
20	0	13.6	19.3	21.8	25.0	26.9	28.0	29.5	13.6	8.9	6.7	3.9	2.4	1.3
20	100	23.9	25.6	26.5	27.7	28.4	28.9	29.5	5.0	3.5	2.7	1.6	1.0	0.5
30	0	17.2	23.7	26.7	30.7	33.1	34.6	36.7	17.0	11.5	8.9	5.4	3.3	1.9
30	100	32.1	33.3	33.9	35.0	35.6	36.1	36.7	4.2	3.1	2.5	1.6	1.0	0.6
40	0	20.5	27.7	31.2	36.0	38.9	40.9	43.7	20.6	14.4	11.3	7.1	4.5	2.6
40	100	40.9	41.5	41.9	42.5	42.9	43.2	43.7	2.7	2.1	1.7	1.1	0.7	0.4

		DIMENSION ALONG AIRFLOW = 20 CM							DIMENSION ACROSS AIRFLOW = 10 CM					
		LEAF TEMPERATURES FOR RESISTANCES=							TRANSPIRATION EXP 6 FOR RES =					
TA	RH	**0*	**1*	**2*	**5*	*10*	*20*	INF*	**0*	**1*	**2*	**5*	*10*	*20*
0	0	7.6	11.4	13.3	15.6	17.0	17.8	18.9	7.3	4.9	3.7	2.2	1.3	0.7
0	100	11.4	13.8	15.0	16.6	17.6	18.2	18.9	4.9	3.4	2.6	1.5	0.9	0.5
10	0	11.5	15.9	18.2	21.1	22.9	24.1	25.6	9.4	6.5	5.0	3.0	1.8	1.0
10	100	17.8	20.0	21.2	22.9	23.9	24.7	25.6	5.2	3.8	3.0	1.8	1.1	0.6
20	0	14.9	20.0	22.7	26.3	28.5	30.0	32.1	11.6	8.2	6.5	4.1	2.5	1.4
20	100	24.8	26.6	27.7	29.3	30.4	31.1	32.1	5.0	3.8	3.1	2.0	1.2	0.7
30	0	18.1	23.8	26.8	31.1	33.8	35.7	38.4	14.0	10.3	8.2	5.3	3.3	2.0
30	100	32.6	33.8	34.6	35.9	36.8	37.5	38.4	4.2	3.3	2.7	1.8	1.2	0.7
40	0	21.0	27.3	30.6	35.5	38.8	41.2	44.7	16.6	12.4	10.1	6.7	4.3	2.6
40	100	41.1	41.7	42.2	42.9	43.5	44.0	44.7	2.6	2.2	1.9	1.3	0.9	0.5

AIRSPEED = 50. CM/SEC   RADIATION ABSORBED = 0.8 EXP 6 ERGS/CM2/SEC
DIMENSION ALONG AIRFLOW = 1 CM   DIMENSION ACROSS AIRFLOW = 1 CM

TA	RH	**0*	**1*	**2*	**5*	*10*	*20*	INF*	**0*	**1*	**2*	**5*	*10*	*20*
		LEAF TEMPERATURES FOR RESISTANCES=							TRANSPIRATION EXP 6 FOR RES =					
0	0	-1.4	4.3	5.0	5.5	5.7	5.8	5.9	24.7	5.5	3.1	1.4	0.7	0.4
0	100	3.7	5.4	5.6	5.8	5.9	5.9	5.9	7.7	1.8	1.0	0.4	0.2	0.1
10	0	4.5	12.6	13.8	14.7	15.0	15.2	15.3	36.9	9.4	5.5	2.4	1.3	0.6
10	100	12.6	14.6	14.9	15.2	15.2	15.3	15.3	9.4	2.6	1.5	0.7	0.4	0.2
20	0	9.7	20.4	22.1	23.5	24.1	24.4	24.7	51.7	15.0	9.0	4.1	2.2	1.1
20	100	21.7	23.7	24.1	24.4	24.6	24.6	24.7	10.4	3.5	2.1	1.0	0.5	0.3
30	0	14.3	27.6	30.1	32.2	33.0	33.5	34.0	68.7	22.6	14.0	6.6	3.5	1.8
30	100	31.1	32.8	33.3	33.7	33.8	33.9	34.0	10.4	4.2	2.7	1.3	0.7	0.3
40	0	18.3	34.2	37.5	40.5	41.7	42.5	43.3	87.6	32.3	20.7	10.1	5.5	2.9
40	100	40.6	42.0	42.4	42.8	43.0	43.1	43.3	9.4	4.6	3.0	1.5	0.8	0.4

DIMENSION ALONG AIRFLOW = 5 CM   DIMENSION ACROSS AIRFLOW = 1 CM

TA	RH	**0*	**1*	**2*	**5*	*10*	*20*	INF*	**0*	**1*	**2*	**5*	*10*	*20*
		LEAF TEMPERATURES FOR RESISTANCES=							TRANSPIRATION EXP 6 FOR RES =					
0	0	1.7	8.4	9.9	11.2	11.8	12.1	12.4	17.4	6.5	4.0	1.9	1.0	0.5
0	100	6.9	10.2	11.0	11.7	12.0	12.2	12.4	9.0	3.6	2.2	1.1	0.6	0.3
10	0	6.5	15.2	17.3	19.2	20.1	20.6	21.1	24.0	9.9	6.4	3.1	1.7	0.9
10	100	14.8	18.3	19.3	20.2	20.6	20.8	21.1	10.5	4.7	3.1	1.5	0.8	0.4
20	0	10.8	21.3	24.1	26.9	28.2	28.9	29.7	31.6	14.2	9.5	4.8	2.7	1.4
20	100	23.2	26.3	27.4	28.5	29.1	29.4	29.7	11.1	5.8	3.9	2.0	1.1	0.6
30	0	14.6	26.9	30.5	34.1	35.9	37.0	38.2	39.9	19.5	13.5	7.1	4.0	2.2
30	100	32.0	34.6	35.6	36.8	37.4	37.8	38.2	10.9	6.4	4.6	2.5	1.4	0.8
40	0	18.0	31.9	36.3	40.9	43.4	44.9	46.6	49.0	25.7	18.3	10.1	5.9	3.2
40	100	41.2	43.1	44.0	45.1	45.7	46.1	46.6	9.7	6.4	4.8	2.7	1.6	0.9

AIRSPEED = 50. CM/SEC RADIATION ABSORBED = 0.8 EXP 6 ERGS/CM2/SEC

DIMENSION ALONG AIRFLOW = 1 CM
DIMENSION ACROSS AIRFLOW = 5 CM

LEAF TEMPERATURES FOR RESISTANCES=   TRANSPIRATION EXP 6 FOR RES =

TA	RH	**0*	**1*	**2*	**5*	*10*	*20*	INF*	**0*	**1*	**2*	**5*	*10*	*20*
0	0	0.1	4.4	5.0	5.5	5.7	5.8	5.9	19.8	5.2	3.0	1.3	0.7	0.4
0	100	4.1	5.4	5.6	5.8	5.9	5.9	5.9	6.3	1.7	1.0	0.4	0.2	0.1
10	0	6.5	12.7	13.8	14.7	15.0	15.2	15.3	30.4	9.0	5.3	2.4	1.3	0.6
10	100	13.0	14.6	14.9	15.2	15.3	15.3	15.3	8.0	2.5	1.5	0.7	0.4	0.2
20	0	12.1	20.6	22.2	23.6	24.1	24.6	24.7	43.6	14.4	8.8	4.0	2.1	1.1
20	100	22.1	23.8	24.1	24.4	24.6	24.6	24.7	9.1	3.4	2.1	1.0	0.5	0.3
30	0	17.1	27.9	30.2	32.2	33.0	33.5	34.0	59.1	21.7	13.7	6.5	3.5	1.8
30	100	31.4	32.9	33.3	33.7	33.8	33.9	34.0	9.4	4.1	2.6	1.3	0.7	0.3
40	0	21.5	34.6	37.6	40.5	41.8	42.5	43.3	76.7	31.1	20.2	10.0	5.5	2.9
40	100	40.8	42.0	42.4	42.9	43.0	43.1	43.3	8.8	4.4	3.0	1.5	0.8	0.4

DIMENSION ALONG AIRFLOW = 5 CM
DIMENSION ACROSS AIRFLOW = 5 CM

LEAF TEMPERATURES FOR RESISTANCES=   TRANSPIRATION EXP 6 FOR RES =

TA	RH	**0*	**1*	**2*	**5*	*10*	*20*	INF*	**0*	**1*	**2*	**5*	*10*	*20*
0	0	3.6	8.7	10.0	11.2	11.8	12.1	12.4	14.3	6.0	3.9	1.9	1.0	0.5
0	100	7.7	10.4	11.1	11.8	12.0	12.2	12.4	7.6	3.3	2.1	1.0	0.6	0.3
10	0	8.9	15.5	17.5	19.3	20.1	20.6	21.1	20.2	9.3	6.1	3.1	1.7	0.9
10	100	15.6	18.4	19.3	20.2	20.6	20.8	21.1	9.1	4.5	3.0	1.5	0.8	0.4
20	0	13.5	21.8	24.3	27.0	28.2	28.9	29.7	27.1	13.4	9.1	4.7	2.6	1.4
20	100	23.9	26.5	27.5	28.6	29.1	29.4	29.7	10.0	5.5	3.8	2.0	1.1	0.6
30	0	17.7	27.5	30.7	34.2	36.0	37.0	38.2	34.9	18.5	13.0	7.0	4.0	2.2
30	100	32.5	34.7	35.7	36.8	37.4	37.8	38.2	10.0	6.1	4.4	2.4	1.4	0.8
40	0	21.4	32.7	36.6	41.0	43.4	44.9	46.6	43.4	24.5	17.7	9.9	5.8	3.2
40	100	41.5	43.2	44.0	45.1	45.7	46.1	46.6	9.2	6.1	4.7	2.7	1.6	0.9

AIRSPEED = 50. CM/SEC   RADIATION ABSORBED = 0.8 EXP 6 ERGS/CM2/SEC

DIMENSION ALONG AIRFLOW = 10 CM   DIMENSION ACROSS AIRFLOW = 5 CM

TA	RH	LEAF TEMPERATURES FOR RESISTANCES=							TRANSPIRATION EXP 6 FOR RES =					
		**0*	**1*	**2*	***5*	*10*	*20*	INF*	**0*	**1*	**2*	***5*	*10*	*20*
0	0	5.9	11.3	13.0	14.8	15.6	16.1	16.6	13.1	6.6	4.5	2.3	1.3	0.7
0	100	10.0	13.2	14.3	15.5	16.0	16.3	16.6	8.2	4.3	2.9	1.5	0.8	0.4
10	0	10.6	17.3	19.6	22.1	23.3	24.0	24.9	17.7	9.5	6.6	3.5	2.0	1.1
10	100	17.2	20.5	21.8	23.2	23.9	24.4	24.9	9.6	5.4	3.9	2.1	1.2	0.6
20	0	14.7	22.7	25.7	28.9	30.7	31.7	33.0	22.9	13.1	9.4	5.2	3.0	1.6
20	100	24.9	28.0	29.3	30.9	31.8	32.3	33.0	10.3	6.4	4.7	2.6	1.5	0.8
30	0	18.5	27.7	31.2	35.4	37.7	39.1	40.9	28.7	17.2	12.7	7.3	4.3	2.4
30	100	33.2	35.7	37.0	38.6	39.5	40.2	40.9	10.2	6.9	5.3	3.1	1.9	1.0
40	0	21.8	32.1	36.3	41.4	44.3	46.3	48.8	34.9	22.0	16.6	9.9	6.0	3.4
40	100	41.9	43.8	44.8	46.3	47.3	47.9	48.8	9.3	6.8	5.4	3.3	2.1	1.2

DIMENSION ALONG AIRFLOW = 20 CM   DIMENSION ACROSS AIRFLOW = 5 CM

TA	RH	LEAF TEMPERATURES FOR RESISTANCES=							TRANSPIRATION EXP 6 FOR RES =					
		**0*	**1*	**2*	***5*	*10*	*20*	INF*	**0*	**1*	**2*	***5*	*10*	*20*
0	0	13.1	18.8	21.6	25.2	27.4	28.9	30.9	11.9	8.2	6.4	3.9	2.4	1.4
0	100	16.6	20.9	23.1	26.1	28.0	29.2	30.9	9.7	6.8	5.4	3.3	2.0	1.2
10	0	16.2	22.6	25.7	30.1	32.8	34.7	37.3	14.4	10.2	8.1	5.1	3.2	1.9
10	100	22.1	26.2	28.4	31.7	33.7	35.2	37.3	10.6	7.8	6.2	4.0	2.5	1.5
20	0	19.1	26.0	29.5	34.6	37.8	40.2	43.5	17.1	12.4	10.0	6.5	4.2	2.5
20	100	28.3	31.9	34.0	37.3	39.5	41.1	43.5	10.9	8.4	6.9	4.6	3.0	1.8
30	0	21.7	29.2	33.1	38.8	42.6	45.4	49.6	19.9	14.8	12.1	8.1	5.3	3.2
30	100	35.4	38.3	40.1	43.1	45.3	47.0	49.6	10.5	8.4	7.1	4.9	3.3	2.0
40	0	24.1	32.1	36.4	42.7	47.0	50.4	55.6	22.8	17.4	14.4	9.8	6.6	4.0
40	100	43.3	45.3	46.8	49.3	51.3	52.9	55.6	9.4	7.8	6.8	4.9	3.4	2.1

AIRSPEED = 50. CM/SEC   RADIATION ABSORBED = 0.8 EXP 6 ERGS/CM2/SEC

DIMENSION ALONG AIRFLOW = 1 CM   DIMENSION ACROSS AIRFLOW = 10 CM

LEAF TEMPERATURES FOR RESISTANCES= / TRANSPIRATION EXP 6 FOR RES =

TA	RH	**0*	**1*	**2*	**5*	*10*	*20*	INF*	**0*	**1*	**2*	**5*	*10*	*20*
0	0	2.4	6.8	7.7	8.6	8.9	9.1	9.3	14.8	5.5	3.4	1.6	0.8	0.4
0	100	6.3	8.1	8.6	8.9	9.1	9.2	9.3	6.6	2.5	1.6	0.7	0.4	0.2
10	0	8.4	14.3	15.8	17.1	17.7	18.0	18.3	21.9	8.9	5.6	2.7	1.5	0.8
10	100	14.7	16.8	17.3	17.9	18.1	18.2	18.3	8.2	3.5	2.3	1.1	0.6	0.3
20	0	13.6	21.3	23.4	25.4	26.3	26.8	27.3	30.5	13.5	8.8	4.4	2.4	1.2
20	100	23.2	25.3	26.0	26.7	27.0	27.1	27.3	9.2	4.5	3.0	1.5	0.8	0.4
30	0	18.3	27.7	30.5	33.3	34.6	35.4	36.2	40.4	19.4	13.1	6.7	3.7	2.0
30	100	32.1	34.0	34.7	35.4	35.8	36.0	36.2	9.5	5.2	3.6	1.9	1.0	0.6
40	0	22.4	33.6	37.1	40.8	42.6	43.8	45.0	51.5	26.5	18.5	9.9	5.6	3.0
40	100	41.3	42.7	43.4	44.1	44.5	44.8	45.0	8.8	5.4	3.9	2.1	1.2	0.7

DIMENSION ALONG AIRFLOW = 5 CM   DIMENSION ACROSS AIRFLOW = 10 CM

LEAF TEMPERATURES FOR RESISTANCES= / TRANSPIRATION EXP 6 FOR RES =

TA	RH	**0*	**1*	**2*	**5*	*10*	*20*	INF*	**0*	**1*	**2*	**5*	*10*	*20*
0	0	7.7	12.6	14.4	16.4	17.7	17.9	18.6	11.9	6.6	4.6	2.5	1.4	0.7
0	100	11.4	14.5	15.7	17.1	17.7	18.1	18.6	8.0	4.5	3.2	1.7	1.0	0.5
10	0	12.3	18.3	20.7	23.3	24.7	25.6	26.6	16.0	9.3	6.7	3.7	2.1	1.2
10	100	18.4	21.6	22.9	24.6	25.4	26.0	26.6	9.3	5.7	4.1	2.3	1.3	0.7
20	0	16.3	23.5	26.4	29.0	31.8	33.0	34.4	20.5	12.6	9.3	5.3	3.1	1.7
20	100	25.8	28.7	30.2	32.0	33.0	33.6	34.4	10.0	6.6	5.0	2.9	1.7	0.9
30	0	20.0	28.1	31.6	36.0	38.4	40.1	42.2	25.5	16.4	12.4	7.3	4.4	2.5
30	100	33.8	36.2	37.5	39.3	40.4	41.2	42.2	9.9	7.1	5.5	3.4	2.1	1.2
40	0	23.3	32.4	36.4	41.7	44.8	46.9	49.8	30.9	20.6	15.9	9.8	6.1	3.5
40	100	42.3	44.1	45.2	46.8	47.9	48.7	49.8	9.1	6.9	5.6	3.6	2.3	1.3

AIRSPEED = 50. CM/SEC   RADIATION ABSORBED = 0.8 EXP 6 ERGS/CM2/SEC

DIMENSION ALONG AIRFLOW = 10 CM   DIMENSION ACROSS AIRFLOW = 10 CM

TA	RH	LEAF TEMPERATURES FOR RESISTANCES= **0*	**1*	**2*	**5*	*10*	*20*	INF*	TRANSPIRATION EXP 6 FOR RES = **0*	**1*	**2*	**5*	*10*	*20*
0	0	10.8	15.8	18.0	20.7	22.2	23.2	24.3	11.4	7.2	5.4	3.1	1.8	1.0
0	100	14.3	17.8	19.5	21.6	22.7	23.4	24.3	8.6	5.6	4.2	2.4	1.4	0.8
10	0	14.7	20.6	23.3	26.7	28.6	29.9	31.6	14.5	9.6	7.3	4.3	2.6	1.5
10	100	20.5	24.0	25.8	28.1	29.5	30.4	31.6	9.7	6.6	5.1	3.1	1.9	1.0
20	0	18.2	24.9	28.1	32.2	34.7	36.4	38.7	18.0	12.3	9.5	5.8	3.6	2.0
20	100	27.3	30.4	32.2	34.6	36.2	37.3	38.7	10.2	7.4	5.9	3.7	2.3	1.3
30	0	21.4	28.8	32.4	37.4	40.5	42.7	45.7	21.7	15.3	12.1	7.6	4.8	2.8
30	100	34.7	37.3	38.9	41.3	42.8	44.0	45.7	10.1	7.7	6.3	4.1	2.6	1.5
40	0	24.3	32.4	36.5	42.2	45.9	48.6	52.5	25.6	18.6	14.9	9.7	6.3	3.7
40	100	42.9	44.8	46.0	48.1	49.6	50.8	52.5	9.1	7.3	6.2	4.2	2.8	1.7

DIMENSION ALONG AIRFLOW = 20 CM   DIMENSION ACROSS AIRFLOW = 10 CM

TA	RH	LEAF TEMPERATURES FOR RESISTANCES= **0*	**1*	**2*	**5*	*10*	*20*	INF*	TRANSPIRATION EXP 6 FOR RES = **0*	**1*	**2*	**5*	*10*	*20*
0	0	14.3	19.3	21.8	25.3	27.5	28.9	30.9	11.2	7.9	6.2	3.8	2.4	1.4
0	100	17.5	21.3	23.3	26.2	28.0	29.2	30.9	9.1	6.6	5.2	3.2	2.0	1.2
10	0	17.6	23.1	26.1	30.2	32.8	34.7	37.3	13.6	9.9	7.9	5.0	3.2	1.8
10	100	22.9	26.6	28.7	31.7	33.8	35.2	37.3	10.0	7.5	6.1	3.9	2.5	1.5
20	0	20.5	26.6	29.9	34.7	37.9	40.2	43.5	16.1	12.0	9.7	6.4	4.1	2.5
20	100	29.0	32.3	34.3	37.4	39.5	41.2	43.5	10.4	8.1	6.7	4.5	2.9	1.7
30	0	23.2	29.9	33.5	38.9	42.6	45.4	49.6	18.9	14.3	11.8	7.9	5.3	3.2
30	100	35.9	38.6	40.3	43.2	45.3	47.0	49.6	10.1	8.2	7.0	4.8	3.3	2.0
40	0	25.7	32.9	36.8	42.9	47.1	50.4	55.6	21.7	16.8	14.0	9.7	6.5	4.0
40	100	43.6	45.6	46.9	49.4	51.3	52.9	55.6	9.1	7.7	6.7	4.8	3.3	2.1

AIRSPEED = 50. CM/SEC   RADIATION ABSORBED = 1.0 EXP 6 ERGS/CM2/SEC
DIMENSION ALONG AIRFLOW = 1 CM   DIMENSION ACROSS AIRFLOW = 1 CM

TA	RH	LEAF TEMPERATURES FOR RESISTANCES=							TRANSPIRATION EXP 6 FOR RES =					
		**0*	**1*	**2*	**5*	*10*	*20*	INF*	**0*	**1*	**2*	**5*	*10*	*20*
0	0	0.2	6.4	7.2	7.8	8.1	8.2	8.3	27.5	6.3	3.6	1.6	0.8	0.4
0	100	5.1	7.5	7.8	8.1	8.2	8.2	8.3	11.1	2.7	1.5	0.7	0.3	0.2
10	0	5.9	14.6	15.9	16.9	17.3	17.5	17.7	40.4	10.6	6.2	2.8	1.4	0.7
10	100	13.7	16.5	17.0	17.4	17.5	17.6	17.7	13.8	4.0	2.3	1.0	0.5	0.3
20	0	10.9	22.3	24.2	25.7	26.4	26.7	27.0	55.8	16.7	10.1	4.6	2.4	1.3
20	100	22.6	25.5	26.1	26.8	26.9	26.9	27.0	15.6	5.4	3.3	1.5	0.8	0.4
30	0	15.3	29.3	32.0	34.3	35.2	35.8	36.3	73.3	24.9	15.5	7.4	3.9	2.0
30	100	31.7	34.4	35.1	35.7	36.0	36.2	36.3	16.5	6.8	4.4	2.1	1.1	0.6
40	0	19.2	35.8	39.3	42.5	43.9	44.7	45.6	92.6	35.1	22.7	11.2	6.1	3.2
40	100	41.1	43.4	44.1	44.8	45.2	45.4	45.6	16.2	7.9	5.3	2.7	1.5	0.8

DIMENSION ALONG AIRFLOW = 5 CM   DIMENSION ACROSS AIRFLOW = 1 CM

TA	RH	LEAF TEMPERATURES FOR RESISTANCES=							TRANSPIRATION EXP 6 FOR RES =					
		**0*	**1*	**2*	**5*	*10*	*20*	INF*	**0*	**1*	**2*	**5*	*10*	*20*
0	0	4.5	12.3	14.1	15.8	16.5	16.9	17.3	21.0	8.3	5.3	2.5	1.4	0.7
0	100	9.3	14.0	15.2	16.3	16.7	17.0	17.3	13.2	5.5	3.5	1.7	0.9	0.5
10	0	9.0	18.7	21.2	23.6	24.6	25.3	25.9	28.1	12.2	8.0	4.0	2.2	1.2
10	100	16.7	21.6	23.1	24.5	25.1	25.5	25.9	15.5	7.3	4.9	2.4	1.3	0.7
20	0	13.0	24.5	27.7	30.9	32.6	33.5	34.5	36.2	17.1	11.6	6.0	3.4	1.8
20	100	24.6	29.2	30.9	32.6	33.4	33.9	34.5	16.9	9.0	6.3	3.3	1.9	1.0
30	0	16.5	29.8	33.8	38.0	40.1	41.4	43.0	44.9	22.9	16.1	8.7	5.0	2.7
30	100	33.1	37.0	38.7	40.6	41.6	42.2	43.0	17.3	10.4	7.6	4.2	2.4	1.3
40	0	19.7	34.6	39.3	44.6	47.4	49.1	51.3	54.3	29.5	21.3	12.1	7.1	3.9
40	100	41.9	45.1	46.6	48.5	49.7	50.4	51.3	16.7	11.1	8.5	5.0	3.0	1.6

AIRSPEED = 50. CM/SEC   RADIATION ABSORBED = 1.0 EXP 6 ERGS/CM2/SEC

DIMENSION ALONG AIRFLOW = 1 CM
DIMENSION ACROSS AIRFLOW = 5 CM

		LEAF TEMPERATURES FOR RESISTANCES=							TRANSPIRATION EXP 6 FOR RES =					
TA	RH	**0*	**1*	**2*	**5*	*10*	*20*	INF*	**0*	**1*	**2*	**5*	*10*	*20*
0	0	1.7	6.5	7.3	7.8	8.1	8.2	8.3	22.2	6.0	3.5	1.6	0.8	0.4
0	100	5.6	7.5	7.9	8.1	8.2	8.2	8.3	9.1	2.6	1.5	0.7	0.3	0.2
10	0	7.9	14.8	16.0	16.9	17.3	17.5	17.7	33.5	10.1	6.1	2.7	1.4	0.7
10	100	14.3	16.6	17.0	17.4	17.5	17.6	17.7	11.8	3.8	2.3	1.0	0.5	0.3
20	0	13.4	22.5	24.2	25.7	26.4	26.7	27.0	47.3	16.0	9.8	4.6	2.4	1.3
20	100	23.1	25.6	26.1	26.6	26.8	26.9	27.0	13.8	5.2	3.2	1.5	0.8	0.4
30	0	18.2	29.6	32.1	34.3	35.2	35.8	36.3	63.3	23.9	15.1	7.3	3.9	2.0
30	100	32.1	34.5	35.1	36.0	36.0	36.2	36.3	15.0	6.6	4.3	2.1	1.1	0.6
40	0	22.5	36.2	39.4	42.5	43.9	44.7	45.6	81.3	33.8	22.1	11.1	6.1	3.2
40	100	41.4	43.5	44.1	44.8	45.2	45.4	45.6	15.1	7.7	5.2	2.6	1.4	0.8

DIMENSION ALONG AIRFLOW = 5 CM
DIMENSION ACROSS AIRFLOW = 5 CM

		LEAF TEMPERATURES FOR RESISTANCES=							TRANSPIRATION EXP 6 FOR RES =					
TA	RH	**0*	**1*	**2*	**5*	*10*	*20*	INF*	**0*	**1*	**2*	**5*	*10*	*20*
0	0	6.6	12.6	14.2	15.8	16.5	16.9	17.3	17.5	7.7	5.0	2.5	1.3	0.7
0	100	10.5	14.2	15.3	16.3	16.7	17.0	17.3	11.2	5.1	3.4	1.7	0.9	0.5
10	0	11.5	19.1	21.4	23.6	24.7	25.3	25.9	24.0	11.5	7.7	3.9	2.2	1.1
10	100	17.9	21.9	23.2	24.5	25.2	25.5	25.9	13.6	6.9	4.7	2.4	1.3	0.7
20	0	15.9	25.1	28.0	31.1	32.6	33.5	34.5	31.4	16.2	11.2	5.9	3.3	1.8
20	100	25.6	29.5	31.0	32.6	33.4	33.9	34.5	15.2	8.6	6.1	3.3	1.8	1.0
30	0	19.8	30.4	34.1	38.1	40.2	41.4	43.0	39.6	21.7	15.5	8.6	4.9	2.7
30	100	33.8	37.3	38.8	40.6	41.6	42.2	43.0	16.0	9.9	7.3	4.1	2.4	1.3
40	0	23.3	35.3	39.7	44.7	47.4	49.1	51.3	48.4	28.2	20.7	11.9	7.0	3.9
40	100	42.5	45.3	46.7	48.6	49.7	50.4	51.3	15.7	10.7	8.2	4.9	2.9	1.6

AIRSPEED = 50. CM/SEC   RADIATION ABSORBED = 1.0 EXP 6 ERGS/CM2/SEC

DIMENSION ALONG AIRFLOW = 10 CM   DIMENSION ACROSS AIRFLOW = 5 CM

		LEAF TEMPERATURES FOR RESISTANCES=						TRANSPIRATION EXP 6 FOR RES =					
TA	RH	**0*	**2*	**5*	*10*	*20*	INF*	**0*	**1*	**2*	**5*	*10*	*20*
0	0	9.7	16.1	18.3	20.6	21.7	22.4	23.2	16.7	8.8	6.1	3.2	1.8	1.0
0	100	13.3	17.8	19.4	21.2	22.1	22.6	23.2	12.2	6.7	4.7	2.5	1.4	0.7
10	0	13.9	21.6	24.4	27.6	29.1	30.1	31.3	21.8	12.3	8.7	4.8	2.7	1.5
10	100	20.0	24.6	26.5	28.7	29.8	30.5	31.3	14.3	8.5	6.1	3.4	2.0	1.1
20	0	17.7	26.7	30.1	34.1	36.2	37.6	39.3	27.4	16.3	12.0	6.8	4.0	2.2
20	100	27.1	31.5	33.5	36.0	37.3	38.2	39.3	15.7	10.1	7.6	4.4	2.6	1.4
30	0	21.1	31.2	35.3	40.2	43.0	44.8	47.2	33.6	20.9	15.8	9.3	5.6	3.2
30	100	34.9	38.7	40.6	43.2	44.8	45.8	47.2	16.3	11.3	8.8	5.3	3.3	1.8
40	0	24.3	35.4	40.0	45.9	49.3	51.7	54.9	40.1	26.1	20.1	12.3	7.6	4.4
40	100	43.2	46.2	48.0	50.5	52.1	53.3	54.9	15.9	11.8	9.5	6.1	3.8	2.2

DIMENSION ALONG AIRFLOW = 20 CM   DIMENSION ACROSS AIRFLOW = 5 CM

		LEAF TEMPERATURES FOR RESISTANCES=						TRANSPIRATION EXP 6 FOR RES =					
TA	RH	**0*	**2*	**5*	*10*	*20*	INF*	**0*	**1*	**2*	**5*	*10*	*20*
0	0	18.6	25.4	28.8	33.7	36.9	39.1	42.4	16.6	12.0	9.6	6.2	4.0	2.3
0	100	21.5	27.2	30.2	34.5	37.4	39.5	42.4	14.6	10.8	8.7	5.7	3.6	2.1
10	0	21.2	28.6	32.4	38.0	41.7	44.5	48.5	19.3	14.4	11.7	7.8	5.1	3.0
10	100	26.3	31.7	34.8	39.4	42.6	44.9	48.5	16.0	12.2	10.1	6.8	4.4	2.7
20	0	23.6	31.6	35.8	42.0	46.2	49.5	54.5	22.2	16.9	13.9	9.5	6.3	3.9
20	100	31.7	36.7	39.7	44.3	47.7	50.3	54.5	16.8	13.3	11.2	7.7	5.2	3.2
30	0	25.9	34.3	38.8	45.7	50.5	54.3	60.3	25.3	19.5	16.3	11.4	7.8	4.8
30	100	38.1	42.3	45.0	49.5	52.9	55.7	60.3	16.9	13.8	11.9	8.5	5.9	3.7
40	0	28.0	36.9	41.7	49.1	54.5	58.8	66.1	28.4	22.3	18.9	13.4	9.3	5.9
40	100	45.4	48.7	50.9	55.0	58.3	61.1	66.1	16.2	13.7	12.0	8.9	6.3	4.1

AIRSPEED = 50. CM/SEC   RADIATION ABSORBED = 1.0 EXP 6 ERGS/CM2/SEC

DIMENSION ALONG AIRFLOW = 1 CM
DIMENSION ACROSS AIRFLOW = 10 CM

TA	RH	**0*	**1*	**2*	**5*	*10*	*20*	INF*	**0*	**1*	**2*	**5*	*10*	*20*
		LEAF TEMPERATURES FOR RESISTANCES=							TRANSPIRATION EXP 6 FOR RES =					
0	0	4.9	9.9	11.1	12.1	12.5	12.7	13.0	17.5	6.7	4.2	2.0	1.1	0.5
0	100	8.6	11.2	11.9	12.4	12.7	12.8	13.0	9.7	3.8	2.4	1.1	0.6	0.3
10	0	10.6	17.2	18.9	20.5	21.2	21.6	22.0	25.2	10.6	6.8	3.3	1.8	0.9
10	100	16.5	19.6	20.4	21.2	21.6	21.8	22.0	12.1	5.4	3.5	1.7	0.9	0.5
20	0	15.6	24.0	26.3	28.6	29.7	30.3	30.9	34.4	15.7	10.4	5.2	2.9	1.5
20	100	24.7	27.9	28.9	29.9	30.4	30.6	30.9	14.0	7.0	4.7	2.4	1.3	0.7
30	0	20.0	30.2	33.2	36.4	37.9	38.8	39.8	44.8	22.1	15.1	7.9	4.4	2.4
30	100	33.3	36.2	37.3	38.5	39.0	39.4	39.8	15.1	8.5	5.9	3.1	1.8	0.9
40	0	24.0	35.8	39.6	43.7	45.8	47.1	48.6	56.3	29.8	21.0	11.4	6.6	3.6
40	100	42.2	44.6	45.7	47.0	47.6	48.1	48.6	15.1	9.4	6.9	3.9	2.2	1.2

DIMENSION ALONG AIRFLOW = 5 CM
DIMENSION ACROSS AIRFLOW = 10 CM

TA	RH	**0*	**1*	**2*	**5*	*10*	*20*	INF*	**0*	**1*	**2*	**5*	*10*	*20*
		LEAF TEMPERATURES FOR RESISTANCES=							TRANSPIRATION EXP 6 FOR RES =					
0	0	11.8	17.8	20.1	22.7	24.0	24.9	25.8	15.6	9.0	6.5	3.6	2.0	1.1
0	100	15.2	19.5	21.3	23.3	24.4	25.1	25.8	12.0	7.1	5.2	2.8	1.6	0.9
10	0	16.0	23.0	25.9	29.3	31.1	32.3	33.7	20.0	12.3	9.0	5.1	3.0	1.7
10	100	21.5	26.0	28.0	30.4	31.8	32.6	33.7	14.0	8.9	6.6	3.8	2.3	1.2
20	0	19.7	27.7	31.2	35.4	37.8	39.4	41.4	25.0	16.0	12.1	7.1	4.3	2.4
20	100	28.3	32.6	34.6	37.4	39.0	40.1	41.4	15.3	10.5	8.1	4.8	2.9	1.6
30	0	23.0	32.0	36.0	41.1	44.2	46.3	49.1	30.3	20.2	15.6	9.5	5.9	3.4
30	100	35.7	39.4	41.4	44.3	46.1	47.4	49.1	15.9	11.5	9.2	5.8	3.6	2.1
40	0	26.1	35.9	40.5	46.5	50.2	52.9	56.5	36.0	24.8	19.6	12.4	7.9	4.6
40	100	43.8	46.8	48.6	51.3	53.2	54.6	56.5	15.6	12.0	9.9	6.5	4.2	2.5

AIRSPEED = 50. CM/SEC   RADIATION ABSORBED = 1.0 EXP 6 ERGS/CM2/SEC

DIMENSION ALONG AIRFLOW = 10 CM   DIMENSION ACROSS AIRFLOW = 10 CM
LEAF TEMPERATURES FOR RESISTANCES=   TRANSPIRATION EXP 6 FOR RES =

TA	RH	**0*	**1*	**2*	***5*	*10*	*20*	INF*	**0*	**1*	**2*	***5*	*10*	*20*
0	0	15.7	21.8	24.7	28.3	30.4	31.8	33.6	15.5	10.3	7.9	4.7	2.9	1.6
0	100	18.7	23.6	25.9	29.0	30.8	32.0	33.6	13.0	8.8	6.8	4.1	2.5	1.4
10	0	19.1	26.0	29.3	33.7	36.4	38.2	40.7	19.0	13.1	10.2	6.3	3.9	2.2
10	100	24.2	29.1	31.6	35.0	37.2	38.7	40.7	14.7	10.4	8.3	5.2	3.2	1.8
20	0	22.2	29.9	33.6	38.8	42.0	44.4	47.6	22.8	16.2	12.9	8.2	5.2	3.0
20	100	30.3	34.8	37.3	41.0	43.4	45.1	47.6	15.8	11.8	9.5	6.2	4.0	2.3
30	0	25.1	33.4	37.6	43.5	47.4	50.2	54.4	26.8	19.5	15.8	10.4	6.8	4.0
30	100	37.2	41.1	43.4	47.0	49.6	51.5	54.4	16.2	12.6	10.5	7.1	4.7	2.8
40	0	27.7	36.6	41.2	47.9	52.4	55.8	61.1	30.9	23.1	19.0	12.8	8.5	5.2
40	100	44.8	47.9	49.9	53.2	55.8	57.8	61.1	15.7	12.8	10.9	7.7	5.2	3.2

DIMENSION ALONG AIRFLOW = 20 CM   DIMENSION ACROSS AIRFLOW = 10 CM
LEAF TEMPERATURES FOR RESISTANCES=   TRANSPIRATION EXP 6 FOR RES =

TA	RH	**0*	**1*	**2*	***5*	*10*	*20*	INF*	**0*	**1*	**2*	***5*	*10*	*20*
0	0	20.0	26.0	29.2	33.9	36.9	39.2	42.4	15.7	11.6	9.4	6.1	3.9	2.3
0	100	22.6	27.7	30.5	34.7	37.4	39.4	42.4	13.9	10.4	8.5	5.6	3.6	2.1
10	0	22.7	29.3	32.9	38.2	41.8	44.5	48.5	18.3	13.9	11.4	7.6	5.0	3.0
10	100	27.3	32.2	35.1	39.5	42.6	45.0	48.5	15.3	11.8	9.8	6.7	4.4	2.7
20	0	25.2	32.3	36.2	42.1	46.3	49.5	54.5	21.2	16.4	13.6	9.3	6.3	3.8
20	100	32.7	37.2	40.0	44.5	47.8	50.4	54.5	16.1	12.9	10.9	7.6	5.2	3.2
30	0	27.6	35.1	39.3	45.9	50.6	54.3	60.3	24.1	19.0	16.0	11.2	7.7	4.8
30	100	38.9	42.8	45.3	49.6	52.9	55.7	60.3	16.3	13.5	11.6	8.4	5.8	3.7
40	0	29.8	37.7	42.3	49.4	54.6	58.8	66.1	27.2	21.7	18.5	13.2	9.2	5.9
40	100	46.0	49.0	51.2	55.1	58.3	61.1	66.1	15.8	13.4	11.8	8.8	6.3	4.1

79

AIRSPEED = 100. CM/SEC   RADIATION ABSORBED = 0.4 EXP 6 ERGS/CM2/SEC
DIMENSION ALONG AIRFLOW = 1 CM   DIMENSION ACROSS AIRFLOW = 1 CM
LEAF TEMPERATURES FOR RESISTANCES=   TRANSPIRATION EXP 6 FOR RES =

TA	RH	**0*	**1*	**2*	**5*	*10*	*20*	INF*	**0*	**1*	**2*	**5*	*10*	*20*
0	0	-5,1	-0.1	0.4	0.6	0.8	0.8	0.9	27.8	4.3	2.3	1.0	0.5	0.3
0	100	0.5	0.8	0.8	0.8	0.8	0.9	0.9	1.5	0.2	0.1	0.1	0.0	0.0
10	0	1.3	8.8	9.6	10.1	10.3	10.4	10.5	43.4	7.8	4.3	1.8	0.9	0.5
10	100	10.2	10.4	10.4	10.4	10.4	10.5	10.5	1.1	0.2	0.1	0.1	0.0	0.0
20	0	6.8	17.3	18.5	19.4	19.7	19.8	20.0	62.9	13.1	7.5	3.3	1.7	0.9
20	100	20.0	20.0	20.0	20.0	20.0	20.0	20.0	0.1	0.0	0.0	0.0	0.0	0.0
30	0	11.7	25.3	27.1	28.4	29.0	29.2	29.5	85.8	20.9	12.2	5.4	2.8	1.4
30	100													
40	0	16.0	32.7	35.2	37.3	38.1	38.5	39.0	111.6	31.3	18.9	8.7	4.6	2.4
40	100													

DIMENSION ALONG AIRFLOW = 5 CM   DIMENSION ACROSS AIRFLOW = 1 CM
LEAF TEMPERATURES FOR RESISTANCES=   TRANSPIRATION EXP 6 FOR RES =

TA	RH	**0*	**1*	**2*	**5*	*10*	*20*	INF*	**0*	**1*	**2*	**5*	*10*	*20*
0	0	-5.3	0.0	0.8	1.4	1.6	1.7	1.8	15.6	4.0	2.3	1.0	0.5	0.3
0	100	1.1	1.6	1.7	1.8	1.8	1.8	1.8	1.7	0.5	0.3	0.1	0.1	0.0
10	0	0.4	7.9	9.2	10.2	10.6	10.8	11.0	23.3	6.8	4.0	1.8	1.0	0.5
10	100	10.4	10.8	10.9	10.9	11.0	11.0	11.0	1.2	0.4	0.2	0.1	0.1	0.0
20	0	5.4	15.3	17.2	18.7	19.3	19.7	20.0	32.7	10.8	6.6	3.1	1.6	0.8
20	100	20.0	20.0	20.0	20.0	20.0	20.0	20.0	0.1	0.0	0.0	0.0	0.0	0.0
30	0	9.8	22.1	24.6	26.9	27.9	28.4	29.0	43.5	16.1	10.2	4.9	2.7	1.4
30	100													
40	0	13.7	28.2	31.6	34.8	36.2	37.0	37.9	55.4	22.7	14.9	7.5	4.1	2.2
40	100													

AIRSPEED = 100. CM/SEC   RADIATION ABSORBED = 0.4 EXP 6 ERGS/CM2/SEC

DIMENSION ALONG AIRFLOW = 1 CM   DIMENSION ACROSS AIRFLOW = 5 CM

LEAF TEMPERATURES FOR RESISTANCES=   TRANSPIRATION EXP 6 FOR RES =

TA	RH	**0*	**1*	**2*	**5*	*10*	*20*	INF*	**0*	**1*	**2*	**5*	*10*	*20*
0	0	-3.8	-0.0	0.4	0.6	0.8	0.8	0.9	22.0	4.1	2.3	1.0	0.5	0.3
0	100	0.6	0.8	0.8	0.8	0.8	0.9	0.9	1.2	0.2	0.1	0.1	0.0	0.0
10	0	3.0	8.9	9.6	10.1	10.3	10.4	10.5	35.4	7.5	4.2	1.8	0.9	0.5
10	100	10.3	10.4	10.4	10.4	10.5	10.5	10.5	0.9	0.2	0.1	0.1	0.0	0.0
20	0	9.0	17.4	18.5	19.4	19.7	19.8	20.0	52.6	12.7	7.3	3.2	1.7	0.9
20	100	20.0	20.0	20.0	20.0	20.0	20.0	20.0	0.1	0.0	0.0	0.0	0.0	0.0
30	0	14.3	25.4	27.1	28.4	29.0	29.2	29.5	73.3	20.2	12.0	5.4	2.8	1.4
30	100													
40	0	19.0	32.9	35.3	37.3	38.1	38.5	39.0	97.1	30.3	18.5	8.6	4.6	2.4
40	100													

DIMENSION ALONG AIRFLOW = 5 CM   DIMENSION ACROSS AIRFLOW = 5 CM

LEAF TEMPERATURES FOR RESISTANCES=   TRANSPIRATION EXP 6 FOR RES =

TA	RH	**0*	**1*	**2*	**5*	*10*	*20*	INF*	**0*	**1*	**2*	**5*	*10*	*20*
0	0	-3.9	0.1	0.8	1.4	1.6	1.7	1.8	12.5	3.8	2.2	1.0	0.5	0.3
0	100	1.2	1.6	1.7	1.8	1.8	1.8	1.8	1.4	0.4	0.3	0.1	0.1	0.0
10	0	2.3	8.1	9.2	10.2	10.6	10.8	11.0	19.2	6.4	3.9	1.8	0.9	0.5
10	100	10.5	10.8	10.9	10.9	11.0	11.0	11.0	1.0	0.4	0.2	0.1	0.1	0.0
20	0	7.8	15.5	17.2	18.7	19.3	19.7	20.0	27.6	10.2	6.4	3.0	1.6	0.8
20	100	20.0	20.0	20.0	20.0	20.0	20.0	20.0	0.1	0.0	0.0	0.0	0.0	0.0
30	0	12.6	22.4	24.8	26.9	27.9	28.4	29.0	37.4	15.3	9.9	4.9	2.6	1.4
30	100													
40	0	16.8	28.6	31.8	34.8	36.2	37.0	37.9	48.5	21.8	14.5	7.4	4.1	2.2
40	100													

AIRSPEED = 100. CM/SEC   RADIATION ABSORBED = 0.4 EXP 6 ERGS/CM2/SEC

DIMENSION ALONG AIRFLOW = 10 CM   DIMENSION ACROSS AIRFLOW = 5 CM

LEAF TEMPERATURES FOR RESISTANCES=   TRANSPIRATION EXP 6 FOR RES =

TA	RH	**0*	**1*	**2*	**5*	*10*	*20*	INF*	**0*	**1*	**2*	**5*	*10*	*20*
0	0	-3.7	0.3	1.1	1.9	2.2	2.3	2.5	9.9	3.6	2.2	1.0	0.5	0.3
0	100	1.6	2.2	2.3	2.4	2.5	2.5	2.5	1.5	0.6	0.3	0.2	0.1	0.0
10	0	2.2	7.7	9.1	10.3	10.8	11.0	11.3	14.9	5.9	3.7	1.8	1.0	0.5
10	100	10.7	11.1	11.2	11.3	11.3	11.3	11.3	1.1	0.5	0.3	0.1	0.1	0.0
20	0	7.3	14.6	16.5	18.3	19.1	19.6	20.1	21.0	9.1	5.9	2.9	1.6	0.8
20	100	20.0	20.1	20.0	20.1	20.1	20.1	20.1	0.1	0.0	0.0	0.0	0.0	0.0
30	0	11.9	20.9	23.5	26.0	27.2	27.9	28.7	28.1	13.2	8.9	4.5	2.5	1.3
30	100													
40	0	15.9	26.6	29.9	33.3	35.0	36.0	37.2	36.0	18.3	12.7	6.8	3.8	2.1
40	100													

DIMENSION ALONG AIRFLOW = 20 CM   DIMENSION ACROSS AIRFLOW = 5 CM

LEAF TEMPERATURES FOR RESISTANCES=   TRANSPIRATION EXP 6 FOR RES =

TA	RH	**0*	**1*	**2*	**5*	*10*	*20*	INF*	**0*	**1*	**2*	**5*	*10*	*20*
0	0	-2.7	1.1	2.4	3.7	4.3	4.6	5.0	6.1	3.2	2.1	1.1	0.6	0.3
0	100	3.0	3.9	4.3	4.6	4.8	4.9	5.0	1.7	0.9	0.6	0.3	0.2	0.1
10	0	2.2	7.0	8.7	10.6	11.5	12.0	12.6	8.6	4.7	3.3	1.7	1.0	0.5
10	100	11.2	11.8	12.1	12.3	12.5	12.6	12.6	1.2	0.7	0.5	0.3	0.1	0.1
20	0	6.4	12.3	14.6	17.1	18.4	19.2	20.1	11.4	6.6	4.7	2.6	1.5	0.8
20	100	20.1	20.1	20.1	20.1	20.1	20.1	20.1	0.1	0.0	0.0	0.0	0.0	0.0
30	0	10.3	17.2	20.0	23.3	25.0	26.1	27.5	14.6	8.9	6.5	3.7	2.2	1.2
30	100													
40	0	13.7	21.6	24.9	29.0	31.3	32.8	34.7	18.1	11.5	8.6	5.1	3.1	1.7
40	100													

AIRSPEED = 100. CM/SEC   RADIATION ABSORBED = 0.4 EXP 6 ERGS/CM2/SEC
DIMENSION ALONG AIRFLOW = 1 CM   DIMENSION ACROSS AIRFLOW = 10 CM

TA	RH	**0*	**1*	**2*	**5*	*10*	*20*	INF*	**0*	**1*	**2*	**5*	*10*	*20*
		\multicolumn{7}{} LEAF TEMPERATURES FOR RESISTANCES=							TRANSPIRATION EXP 6 FOR RES =					
0	0	-3.5	0.1	0.6	1.0	1.2	1.3	1.4	14.4	3.9	2.2	1.0	0.5	0.3
0	100	0.9	1.2	1.3	1.3	1.3	1.3	1.4	1.2	0.3	0.2	0.1	0.0	0.0
10	0	3.1	8.5	9.4	10.1	10.4	10.6	10.7	22.7	6.8	4.0	1.8	0.9	0.5
10	100	10.4	10.6	10.7	10.7	10.7	10.7	10.7	0.9	0.3	0.2	0.1	0.0	0.0
20	0	9.0	16.4	17.8	19.0	19.5	19.8	20.0	33.4	11.1	6.7	3.1	1.6	0.8
20	100	20.0	20.0	20.0	20.0	20.0	20.0	20.0	0.1	0.0	0.0	0.0	0.0	0.0
30	0	14.2	23.8	25.8	27.7	28.4	28.8	29.3	46.2	17.0	10.7	5.1	2.7	1.4
30	100													
40	0	18.7	30.6	33.4	36.0	37.1	37.8	38.5	60.9	24.8	16.1	7.9	4.3	2.3
40	100													

DIMENSION ALONG AIRFLOW = 5 CM   DIMENSION ACROSS AIRFLOW = 10 CM

TA	RH	**0*	**1*	**2*	**5*	*10*	*20*	INF*	**0*	**1*	**2*	**5*	*10*	*20*
		\multicolumn{7}{} LEAF TEMPERATURES FOR RESISTANCES=							TRANSPIRATION EXP 6 FOR RES =					
0	0	-3.1	0.4	1.3	2.1	2.4	2.6	2.8	8.4	3.4	2.2	1.0	0.5	0.3
0	100	1.8	2.4	2.6	2.7	2.8	2.8	2.8	1.4	0.6	0.4	0.2	0.1	0.0
10	0	2.8	7.7	9.0	10.3	10.9	11.2	11.5	12.6	5.5	3.6	1.8	0.9	0.5
10	100	10.8	11.2	11.3	11.4	11.4	11.5	11.5	1.0	0.5	0.3	0.2	0.1	0.0
20	0	7.9	14.4	16.3	18.2	19.0	19.5	20.1	17.8	8.4	5.6	2.8	1.6	0.8
20	100	20.0	20.1	20.1	20.1	20.1	20.1	20.1	0.1	0.0	0.0	0.0	0.0	0.0
30	0	12.5	20.5	23.0	25.7	26.9	27.7	28.5	23.8	12.2	8.4	4.4	2.5	1.3
30	100													
40	0	16.6	26.0	29.2	32.7	34.5	35.6	36.9	30.5	16.7	11.8	6.4	3.7	2.0
40	100													

AIRSPEED = 100. CM/SEC   RADIATION ABSORBED = 0.4 EXP 6 ERGS/CM2/SEC

DIMENSION ALONG AIRFLOW = 10 CM   DIMENSION ACROSS AIRFLOW = 10 CM

LEAF TEMPERATURES FOR RESISTANCES=   TRANSPIRATION EXP 6 FOR RES =

TA	RH	**0*	**1*	**2*	**5*	*10*	*20*	INF*	**0*	**1*	**2*	**5*	*10*	*20*
0	0	-2.6	0.8	1.8	2.8	3.3	3.5	3.8	6.8	3.2	2.1	1.1	0.6	0.3
0	100	2.4	3.1	3.3	3.6	3.7	3.7	3.8	1.5	0.7	0.5	0.2	0.1	0.1
10	0	2.8	7.4	8.9	10.4	11.1	11.6	12.0	9.9	5.0	3.4	1.7	1.0	0.5
10	100	11.0	11.5	11.6	11.8	11.9	12.0	12.0	1.1	0.6	0.4	0.2	0.1	0.1
20	0	7.6	13.5	15.5	17.7	18.7	19.4	20.1	13.7	7.3	5.1	2.7	1.5	0.8
20	100	20.0	20.1	20.1	20.1	20.1	20.1	20.1	0.1	0.0	0.0	0.0	0.0	0.0
30	0	11.9	19.0	21.6	24.5	26.0	27.0	28.1	18.0	10.2	7.3	4.0	2.3	1.3
30	100													
40	0	15.8	24.0	27.2	31.0	33.0	34.3	35.9	22.8	13.7	10.1	5.7	3.4	1.9
40	100													

DIMENSION ALONG AIRFLOW = 20 CM   DIMENSION ACROSS AIRFLOW = 10 CM

LEAF TEMPERATURES FOR RESISTANCES=   TRANSPIRATION EXP 6 FOR RES =

TA	RH	**0*	**1*	**2*	**5*	*10*	*20*	INF*	**0*	**1*	**2*	**5*	*10*	*20*
0	0	-2.0	1.3	2.5	3.7	4.3	4.6	5.0	5.6	3.0	2.1	1.1	0.6	0.3
0	100	3.1	4.0	4.3	4.6	4.8	4.9	5.0	1.5	0.9	0.6	0.3	0.2	0.1
10	0	3.0	7.2	8.8	10.6	11.5	12.0	12.6	7.9	4.5	3.2	1.7	1.0	0.5
10	100	11.3	11.8	12.1	12.3	12.5	12.5	12.6	1.1	0.7	0.5	0.3	0.1	0.1
20	0	7.4	12.6	14.7	17.2	18.4	19.2	20.1	10.6	6.3	4.6	2.5	1.5	0.8
20	100	20.1	20.1	20.1	20.1	20.1	20.1	20.1	0.1	0.0	0.0	0.0	0.0	0.0
30	0	11.4	17.6	20.2	23.3	25.0	26.1	27.5	13.7	8.5	6.3	3.6	2.1	1.2
40	0	15.0	22.0	25.1	29.1	31.3	32.8	34.7	17.0	11.1	8.4	5.0	3.0	1.7

AIRSPEED = 100. CM/SEC   RADIATION ABSORBED = 0.6 EXP 6 ERGS/CM2/SEC

DIMENSION ALONG AIRFLOW = 1 CM   DIMENSION ACROSS AIRFLOW = 1 CM

TA	RH	**0*	**1*	**2*	**5*	*10*	*20*	INF*	**0*	**1*	**2*	**5*	*10*	*20*
		LEAF TEMPERATURES FOR RESISTANCES=							TRANSPIRATION EXP 6 FOR RES =					
0	0	-3.9	1.5	2.0	2.3	2.4	2.5	2.6	30.3	4.8	2.6	1.1	0.6	0.3
0	100	1.6	2.4	2.5	2.5	2.5	2.5	2.6	4.6	0.8	0.4	0.2	0.1	0.0
10	0	2.3	10.4	11.2	11.7	11.9	12.0	12.2	46.6	8.6	4.8	2.0	1.0	0.5
10	100	11.1	11.9	12.0	12.1	12.1	12.1	12.2	5.3	1.1	0.6	0.3	0.1	0.1
20	0	7.7	18.7	20.0	21.0	21.3	21.5	21.7	66.7	14.3	8.2	3.6	1.8	0.9
20	100	20.6	21.4	21.6	21.6	21.7	21.7	21.7	5.3	1.3	0.8	0.3	0.2	0.1
30	0	12.5	26.6	28.5	30.0	30.6	30.9	31.2	90.2	22.5	13.2	5.9	3.1	1.6
30	100	30.3	30.9	31.1	31.1	31.2	31.2	31.2	4.4	1.4	0.8	0.4	0.2	0.1
40	0	16.7	33.9	36.6	38.8	39.7	40.2	40.7	116.4	33.4	20.3	9.4	5.0	2.6
40	100	40.1	40.5	40.6	40.6	40.7	40.7	40.7	2.8	1.1	0.7	0.3	0.2	0.1

DIMENSION ALONG AIRFLOW = 5 CM   DIMENSION ACROSS AIRFLOW = 1 CM

TA	RH	**0*	**1*	**2*	**5*	*10*	*20*	INF*	**0*	**1*	**2*	**5*	*10*	*20*
		LEAF TEMPERATURES FOR RESISTANCES=							TRANSPIRATION EXP 6 FOR RES =					
0	0	-2.9	3.2	4.2	4.9	5.2	5.3	5.5	18.5	5.0	2.9	1.3	0.7	0.3
0	100	3.1	4.8	5.1	5.3	5.4	5.4	5.5	5.3	1.5	0.9	0.4	0.2	0.1
10	0	2.5	10.9	12.4	13.6	14.1	14.3	14.6	26.9	8.2	4.9	2.3	1.2	0.6
10	100	12.0	13.7	14.0	14.3	14.4	14.5	14.6	5.8	2.0	1.2	0.6	0.3	0.2
20	0	7.2	18.1	20.2	22.0	22.8	23.2	23.6	36.8	12.7	7.9	3.7	2.0	1.0
20	100	21.2	22.6	23.0	23.3	23.5	23.5	23.6	5.6	2.3	1.5	0.7	0.4	0.2
30	0	11.4	24.6	27.4	30.1	31.2	31.9	32.6	48.1	18.5	11.9	5.8	3.2	1.7
30	100	30.6	31.6	31.9	32.3	32.4	32.5	32.6	4.6	2.3	1.5	0.8	0.4	0.2
40	0	15.1	30.5	34.2	37.8	39.4	40.4	41.4	60.4	25.7	17.1	8.8	4.9	2.6
40	100	40.2	40.8	41.0	41.2	41.3	41.4	41.4	2.9	1.6	1.1	0.6	0.3	0.2

AIRSPEED = 100. CM/SEC   RADIATION ABSORBED = 0.6 EXP 6 ERGS/CM2/SEC

DIMENSION ALONG AIRFLOW = 1 CM   DIMENSION ACROSS AIRFLOW = 5 CM

		LEAF TEMPERATURES FOR RESISTANCES=							TRANSPIRATION EXP 6 FOR RES =				
TA	RH	**0*	**1*	**2*	**5*	*10*	*20*	INF*	**0*	**1*	**2*	**5*	*10*	*20*
0	0	-2.6	1.6	2.0	2.3	2.4	2.5	2.6	24.1	4.6	2.6	1.1	0.6	0.3
0	100	1.8	2.4	2.5	2.5	2.5	2.5	2.6	3.7	0.7	0.4	0.2	0.1	0.0
10	0	4.1	10.4	11.2	11.7	11.9	12.0	12.2	38.1	8.3	4.7	2.0	1.0	0.5
10	100	11.2	11.9	12.0	12.1	12.1	12.1	12.2	4.5	1.0	0.6	0.3	0.1	0.1
20	0	10.0	18.8	20.1	21.0	21.3	21.5	21.7	56.0	13.8	8.0	3.5	1.8	0.9
20	100	20.8	21.4	21.6	21.6	21.7	21.7	21.7	4.6	1.3	0.8	0.3	0.2	0.1
30	0	15.2	26.8	28.6	30.0	30.6	30.9	31.2	77.3	21.8	13.0	5.9	3.1	1.6
30	100	30.4	30.9	31.1	31.1	31.1	31.2	31.2	4.0	1.4	0.8	0.4	0.2	0.1
40	0	19.8	34.1	36.7	38.8	39.7	40.2	40.7	101.6	32.4	19.9	9.3	5.0	2.6
40	100	40.2	40.5	40.6	40.6	40.7	40.7	40.7	2.6	1.1	0.7	0.3	0.2	0.1

DIMENSION ALONG AIRFLOW = 5 CM   DIMENSION ACROSS AIRFLOW = 5 CM

		LEAF TEMPERATURES FOR RESISTANCES=							TRANSPIRATION EXP 6 FOR RES =				
TA	RH	**0*	**1*	**2*	**5*	*10*	*20*	INF*	**0*	**1*	**2*	**5*	*10*	*20*
0	0	-1.3	3.3	4.2	4.9	5.2	5.3	5.5	15.0	4.7	2.8	1.3	0.7	0.3
0	100	3.5	4.8	5.1	5.3	5.4	5.4	5.5	4.4	1.4	0.9	0.4	0.2	0.1
10	0	4.5	11.1	12.5	13.6	14.1	14.3	14.6	22.3	7.8	4.8	2.2	1.2	0.6
10	100	12.3	13.7	14.1	14.3	14.4	14.5	14.6	5.1	1.9	1.2	0.6	0.3	0.2
20	0	9.7	18.3	20.3	22.0	22.8	23.2	23.6	31.3	12.1	7.7	3.7	2.0	1.0
20	100	21.4	22.6	23.0	23.3	23.5	23.5	23.6	5.0	2.2	1.4	0.7	0.4	0.2
30	0	14.3	24.9	27.6	30.1	31.2	31.9	32.6	41.7	17.7	11.6	5.8	3.2	1.7
30	100	30.7	31.6	32.0	32.3	32.4	32.5	32.6	4.3	2.2	1.5	0.7	0.4	0.2
40	0	18.4	30.9	34.4	37.8	39.4	40.4	41.4	53.2	24.7	16.7	8.6	4.8	2.6
40	100	40.3	40.8	41.0	41.2	41.3	41.4	41.4	2.7	1.6	1.1	0.6	0.3	0.2

AIRSPEED = 100. CM/SEC   RADIATION ABSORBED = 0.6 EXP 6 ERGS/CM2/SEC

		DIMENSION ALONG AIRFLOW = 10 CM							DIMENSION ACROSS AIRFLOW = 5 CM					
		LEAF TEMPERATURES FOR RESISTANCES=							TRANSPIRATION EXP 6 FOR RES =					
TA	RH	**0*	**1*	**2*	***5*	*10*	*20*	INF*	**0*	**1*	**2*	***5*	*10*	*20*
0	0	-0.3	4.5	5.6	6.6	7.0	7.2	7.5	12.6	4.8	3.0	1.4	0.7	0.4
0	100	4.6	6.3	6.7	7.1	7.3	7.4	7.5	4.7	1.9	1.2	0.6	0.3	0.2
10	0	5.1	11.7	13.3	14.8	15.5	15.8	16.2	18.2	7.6	4.9	2.4	1.3	0.7
10	100	13.1	14.8	15.3	15.8	16.0	16.1	16.2	5.3	2.4	1.5	0.8	0.4	0.2
20	0	9.9	18.2	20.5	22.7	23.7	24.3	24.9	24.9	11.3	7.5	3.8	2.1	1.1
20	100	21.8	23.3	23.8	24.4	24.6	24.8	24.9	5.2	2.7	1.8	0.9	0.5	0.3
30	0	14.2	24.1	27.1	30.2	31.6	32.5	33.5	32.4	16.0	10.9	5.7	3.2	1.7
30	100	31.0	32.0	32.4	32.9	33.2	33.3	33.5	4.3	2.5	1.8	1.0	0.5	0.3
40	0	18.0	29.5	33.2	37.2	39.3	40.5	42.0	40.8	21.5	15.2	8.3	4.8	2.6
40	100	40.4	40.9	41.2	41.5	41.7	41.8	42.0	2.7	1.8	1.3	0.8	0.4	0.2

		DIMENSION ALONG AIRFLOW = 20 CM							DIMENSION ACROSS AIRFLOW = 5 CM					
		LEAF TEMPERATURES FOR RESISTANCES=							TRANSPIRATION EXP 6 FOR RES =					
TA	RH	**0*	**1*	**2*	***5*	*10*	*20*	INF*	**0*	**1*	**2*	***5*	*10*	*20*
0	0	3.4	8.5	10.4	12.5	13.5	14.1	14.8	9.3	5.2	3.6	1.9	1.1	0.6
0	100	8.2	11.0	12.1	13.4	14.0	14.3	14.8	5.4	3.1	2.2	1.2	0.7	0.4
10	0	7.6	13.8	16.1	18.9	20.3	21.2	22.2	12.3	7.2	5.2	2.9	1.7	0.9
10	100	15.4	18.0	19.1	20.5	21.2	21.7	22.2	5.8	3.6	2.7	1.5	0.9	0.5
20	0	11.3	18.5	21.4	24.9	26.8	28.0	29.5	15.6	9.6	7.1	4.1	2.4	1.3
20	100	23.3	25.3	26.3	27.7	28.4	28.9	29.5	5.5	3.7	2.8	1.7	1.0	0.5
30	0	14.6	22.8	26.2	30.5	33.0	34.6	36.7	19.1	12.3	9.3	5.5	3.3	1.9
30	100	31.7	33.1	33.8	34.9	35.6	36.1	36.7	4.5	3.3	2.6	1.6	1.0	0.6
40	0	17.7	26.7	30.7	35.8	38.8	40.9	43.7	23.0	15.3	11.9	7.3	4.5	2.6
40	100	40.7	41.4	41.8	42.4	42.9	43.2	43.7	2.8	2.2	1.8	1.2	0.7	0.4

AIRSPEED = 100. CM/SEC   RADIATION ABSORBED = 0.6 EXP 6 ERGS/CM2/SEC

DIMENSION ALONG AIRFLOW = 1 CM   DIMENSION ACROSS AIRFLOW = 10 CM
LEAF TEMPERATURES FOR RESISTANCES=   TRANSPIRATION EXP 6 FOR RES =

TA	RH	**0*	**1*	**2*	**5*	*10*	*20*	INF*	**0*	**1*	**2*	**5*	*10*	*20*
0	0	-1.5	2.5	3.2	3.7	3.8	3.9	4.0	16.5	4.6	2.7	1.2	0.6	0.3
0	100	-2.8	3.7	3.8	4.0	4.0	4.0	4.0	3.8	1.1	0.6	0.3	0.1	0.1
10	0	4.9	10.8	11.9	12.7	13.0	13.2	13.4	25.6	7.8	4.7	2.1	1.1	0.6
10	100	11.9	12.9	13.1	13.3	13.3	13.4	13.4	4.5	1.5	0.9	0.4	0.2	0.1
20	0	10.6	18.6	20.2	21.5	22.1	22.4	22.7	36.9	12.6	7.7	3.6	1.9	1.0
20	100	21.2	22.1	22.3	22.5	22.6	22.6	22.7	4.7	1.8	1.1	0.5	0.3	0.1
30	0	15.5	25.8	28.1	30.1	30.9	31.4	31.9	50.2	19.1	12.1	5.8	3.1	1.6
30	100	30.6	31.3	31.5	31.7	31.8	31.9	31.9	4.0	1.8	1.2	0.6	0.3	0.2
40	0	20.0	32.4	35.4	38.3	39.6	40.3	41.1	65.4	27.3	17.9	8.9	4.9	2.6
40	100	40.3	40.7	40.8	40.9	41.0	41.0	41.1	2.6	1.4	0.9	0.5	0.3	0.1

DIMENSION ALONG AIRFLOW = 5 CM   DIMENSION ACROSS AIRFLOW = 10 CM
LEAF TEMPERATURES FOR RESISTANCES=   TRANSPIRATION EXP 6 FOR RES =

TA	RH	**0*	**1*	**2*	**5*	*10*	*20*	INF*	**0*	**1*	**2*	**5*	*10*	*20*
0	0	0.7	5.2	6.3	7.4	7.9	8.1	8.4	11.0	4.7	3.0	1.5	0.8	0.4
0	100	5.3	7.0	7.5	8.0	8.2	8.3	8.4	4.5	2.0	1.3	0.6	0.3	0.2
10	0	6.2	12.0	13.7	15.4	16.1	16.5	17.0	15.8	7.3	4.8	2.4	1.3	0.7
10	100	13.6	15.3	15.9	16.4	16.7	16.8	17.0	5.1	2.5	1.7	0.8	0.5	0.2
20	0	11.0	18.4	20.7	23.0	24.1	24.8	25.5	21.5	10.7	7.3	3.8	2.1	1.1
20	100	22.2	23.7	24.2	24.8	25.1	25.3	25.5	5.0	2.8	1.9	1.0	0.6	0.3
30	0	15.2	24.1	27.0	30.2	31.8	32.8	33.9	28.0	15.0	10.5	5.6	3.2	1.7
30	100	31.2	32.2	32.7	33.2	33.5	33.7	33.9	4.2	2.6	1.9	1.0	0.6	0.3
40	0	19.0	29.3	32.9	37.0	39.2	40.6	42.2	35.2	20.0	14.4	8.1	4.7	2.6
40	100	40.5	41.0	41.3	41.7	41.9	42.0	42.2	2.7	1.8	1.4	0.8	0.5	0.3

AIRSPEED = 100. CM/SEC   RADIATION ABSORBED = 0.6 EXP 6 ERGS/CM2/SEC

DIMENSION ALONG AIRFLOW = 10 CM   DIMENSION ACROSS AIRFLOW = 10 CM

TA	RH	LEAF TEMPERATURES FOR RESISTANCES=							TRANSPIRATION EXP 6 FOR RES =					
		**0*	**1*	**2*	**5*	*10*	*20*	INF*	**0*	**1*	**2*	**5*	*10*	*20*
0	0	2.3	6.8	8.3	9.7	10.4	10.8	11.2	9.6	4.8	3.2	1.7	0.9	0.5
0	100	6.9	9.0	9.7	10.5	10.8	11.0	11.2	4.8	2.5	1.7	0.9	0.5	0.2
10	0	7.2	12.9	14.9	17.0	18.1	18.7	19.4	13.3	7.1	4.9	2.6	1.5	0.8
10	100	14.6	16.7	17.5	18.3	18.8	19.0	19.4	5.3	3.0	2.1	1.1	0.6	0.3
20	0	11.6	18.5	21.0	23.9	25.4	26.3	27.3	17.6	10.0	7.1	3.9	2.2	1.2
20	100	22.8	24.5	25.3	26.2	26.7	27.0	27.3	5.1	3.2	2.4	1.3	0.8	0.4
30	0	15.4	23.5	26.7	30.4	32.4	33.7	35.2	22.3	13.3	9.8	5.6	3.3	1.8
30	100	31.5	32.7	33.3	34.1	34.5	34.8	35.2	4.3	2.9	2.2	1.3	0.8	0.4
40	0	18.9	28.1	31.9	36.4	39.0	40.7	42.9	27.5	17.2	13.0	7.6	4.6	2.6
40	100	40.6	41.2	41.6	42.1	42.4	42.6	42.9	2.7	2.0	1.6	1.0	0.6	0.3

DIMENSION ALONG AIRFLOW = 20 CM   DIMENSION ACROSS AIRFLOW = 10 CM

TA	RH	LEAF TEMPERATURES FOR RESISTANCES=							TRANSPIRATION EXP 6 FOR RES =					
		**0*	**1*	**2*	**5*	*10*	*20*	INF*	**0*	**1*	**2*	**5*	*10*	*20*
0	0	4.3	8.8	10.6	12.5	13.5	14.1	14.8	8.6	5.0	3.5	1.9	1.1	0.6
0	100	8.7	11.2	12.2	13.4	14.0	14.3	14.8	5.1	3.0	2.2	1.2	0.7	0.4
10	0	8.6	14.1	16.3	18.9	20.3	21.2	22.2	11.4	6.9	5.0	2.8	1.6	0.9
10	100	15.8	18.2	19.2	20.5	21.2	21.7	22.2	5.4	3.5	2.6	1.5	0.9	0.5
20	0	12.5	18.9	21.6	25.0	26.8	28.0	29.5	14.6	9.2	6.9	4.0	2.4	1.3
20	100	23.6	25.4	26.4	27.7	28.4	28.9	29.5	5.2	3.6	2.8	1.6	1.0	0.5
30	0	15.9	23.2	26.5	30.6	33.0	34.6	36.7	18.0	11.9	9.1	5.5	3.3	1.9
30	100	31.9	33.2	33.9	35.0	35.6	36.1	36.7	4.3	3.2	2.5	1.6	1.0	0.6
40	0	19.1	27.2	30.9	35.9	38.9	40.9	43.7	21.8	14.9	11.6	7.2	4.5	2.6
40	100	40.8	41.4	41.8	42.5	42.9	43.2	43.7	2.7	2.1	1.8	1.2	0.7	0.4

4

AIRSPEED = 100. CM/SEC   RADIATION ABSORBED = 0.8 EXP 6 ERGS/CM2/SEC

DIMENSION ALONG AIRFLOW = 1 CM   DIMENSION ACROSS AIRFLOW = 1 CM

LEAF TEMPERATURES FOR RESISTANCES=   TRANSPIRATION EXP 6 FOR RES =

TA	RH	**0*	**1*	**2*	**5*	*10*	*20*	INF*	**0*	**1*	**2*	**5*	*10*	*20*
0	0	-2.7	3.1	3.6	4.0	4.1	4.2	4.3	32.9	5.3	2.9	1.2	0.6	0.3
0	100	2.6	4.0	4.1	4.2	4.2	4.2	4.3	7.8	1.3	0.7	0.3	0.2	0.1
10	0	3.3	11.9	12.8	13.4	13.6	13.7	13.8	49.9	9.4	5.3	2.3	1.2	0.6
10	100	11.9	13.4	13.6	13.8	13.8	13.8	13.8	9.6	2.0	1.1	0.5	0.2	0.1
20	0	8.6	20.2	21.6	22.6	23.0	23.2	23.4	70.6	15.6	8.9	3.9	2.0	1.0
20	100	21.2	22.8	23.1	23.3	23.4	23.4	23.4	10.5	2.8	1.6	0.7	0.4	0.2
30	0	13.2	28.0	30.0	31.6	32.2	32.6	32.9	94.6	24.2	14.3	6.5	3.4	1.7
30	100	30.8	32.2	32.5	32.7	32.8	32.9	32.9	10.5	3.4	2.0	0.9	0.5	0.2
40	0	17.3	35.2	38.0	40.3	41.3	41.8	42.4	121.3	35.6	21.8	10.2	5.4	2.8
40	100	40.4	41.6	41.9	42.1	42.2	42.3	42.4	9.6	3.8	2.4	1.1	0.6	0.3

DIMENSION ALONG AIRFLOW = 5 CM   DIMENSION ACROSS AIRFLOW = 1 CM

LEAF TEMPERATURES FOR RESISTANCES=   TRANSPIRATION EXP 6 FOR RES =

TA	RH	**0*	**1*	**2*	**5*	*10*	*20*	INF*	**0*	**1*	**2*	**5*	*10*	*20*
0	0	-0.7	6.3	7.5	8.4	8.7	8.9	9.1	21.6	6.1	3.6	1.6	0.8	0.4
0	100	5.0	7.8	8.3	8.7	8.9	9.0	9.1	9.1	2.7	1.6	0.7	0.4	0.2
10	0	4.5	13.8	15.5	16.9	17.5	17.8	18.2	30.6	9.8	6.0	2.8	1.5	0.8
10	100	13.5	16.5	17.1	17.7	17.9	18.0	18.2	10.6	3.8	2.3	1.1	0.6	0.3
20	0	9.0	20.7	23.1	25.2	26.1	26.6	27.2	41.1	14.8	9.4	4.5	2.4	1.2
20	100	22.3	25.1	25.8	26.5	26.8	27.0	27.2	11.3	4.8	3.1	1.5	0.8	0.4
30	0	12.9	27.0	30.2	33.2	34.5	35.3	36.1	52.8	21.2	13.9	6.9	3.8	2.0
30	100	31.4	33.7	34.5	35.3	35.7	35.9	36.1	11.0	5.5	3.7	1.9	1.0	0.5
40	0	16.5	32.7	36.7	40.7	42.6	43.7	44.9	65.6	28.9	19.5	10.2	5.7	3.0
40	100	40.8	42.6	43.2	44.0	44.4	44.7	44.9	9.9	5.7	4.0	2.2	1.2	0.7

AIRSPEED = 100. CM/SEC   RADIATION ABSORBED = 0.8 EXP 6 ERGS/CM2/SEC

DIMENSION ALONG AIRFLOW = 1 CM   DIMENSION ACROSS AIRFLOW = 5 CM

TA	RH	**0*	**1*	**2*	**5*	*10*	*20*	INF*	**0*	**1*	**2*	***5*	*10*	*20*
		LEAF TEMPERATURES FOR RESISTANCES=							TRANSPIRATION EXP 6 FOR RES =					
0	0	-1.3	3.2	3.7	4.0	4.1	4.2	4.3	26.3	5.2	2.9	1.2	0.6	0.3
0	100	2.9	4.0	4.1	4.2	4.2	4.2	4.3	6.3	1.3	0.7	0.3	0.2	0.1
10	0	5.2	11.9	12.8	13.4	13.6	13.7	13.8	41.0	9.1	5.2	2.2	1.2	0.6
10	100	12.2	13.4	13.6	13.8	13.8	13.8	13.8	8.1	1.9	1.1	0.5	0.2	0.1
20	0	11.0	20.3	21.6	22.6	23.0	23.2	23.4	59.5	15.1	8.8	3.9	2.0	1.0
20	100	21.5	22.8	23.1	23.3	23.4	23.4	23.4	9.3	2.7	1.6	0.7	0.4	0.2
30	0	16.1	28.1	30.0	31.6	32.2	32.6	32.9	81.4	23.5	14.0	6.4	3.4	1.7
30	100	31.0	32.2	32.5	32.7	32.8	32.9	32.9	9.6	3.3	2.0	0.9	0.5	0.2
40	0	20.5	35.4	38.1	40.3	41.3	41.8	42.4	106.2	34.6	21.4	10.1	5.4	2.8
40	100	40.6	41.6	41.9	42.1	42.2	42.3	42.4	8.9	3.7	2.3	1.1	0.6	0.3

DIMENSION ALONG AIRFLOW = 5 CM   DIMENSION ACROSS AIRFLOW = 5 CM

TA	RH	**0*	**1*	**2*	**5*	*10*	*20*	INF*	**0*	**1*	**2*	***5*	*10*	*20*
		LEAF TEMPERATURES FOR RESISTANCES=							TRANSPIRATION EXP 6 FOR RES =					
0	0	1.1	6.5	7.5	8.4	8.7	8.9	9.1	17.7	5.8	3.5	1.6	0.8	0.4
0	100	5.7	7.9	8.4	8.8	8.9	9.0	9.1	7.6	2.6	1.6	0.7	0.4	0.2
10	0	6.7	14.0	15.6	17.0	17.5	17.8	18.2	25.7	9.3	5.8	2.7	1.5	0.8
10	100	14.1	16.6	17.2	17.7	17.9	18.0	18.2	9.2	3.6	2.3	1.1	0.6	0.3
20	0	11.6	21.0	23.2	25.3	26.1	26.6	27.2	35.3	14.2	9.1	4.4	2.4	1.2
20	100	22.8	25.2	25.9	26.5	26.8	27.0	27.2	10.2	4.6	3.0	1.5	0.8	0.4
30	0	16.0	27.4	30.3	33.2	34.5	35.3	36.1	46.1	20.3	13.5	6.8	3.8	2.0
30	100	31.8	33.8	34.6	35.3	35.7	35.9	36.1	10.2	5.3	3.6	1.9	1.0	0.5
40	0	19.8	33.2	36.9	40.7	42.6	43.7	44.9	58.1	27.8	19.1	10.0	5.7	3.0
40	100	41.0	42.6	43.3	44.0	44.4	44.7	44.9	9.3	5.5	3.9	2.1	1.2	0.7

AIRSPEED = 100. CM/SEC   RADIATION ABSORBED = 0.8 EXP 6 ERGS/CM2/SEC

DIMENSION ALONG AIRFLOW = 10 CM   DIMENSION ACROSS AIRFLOW = 5 CM

		LEAF TEMPERATURES FOR RESISTANCES=							TRANSPIRATION EXP 6 FOR RES =					
TA	RH	**0*	**1*	**2*	**5*	*10*	*20*	INF*	**0*	**1*	**2*	**5*	*10*	*20*
0	0	2.8	8.6	10.0	11.2	11.8	12.1	12.4	15.6	6.2	4.0	1.9	1.0	0.5
0	100	7.4	10.3	11.1	11.7	12.0	12.2	12.4	8.2	3.4	2.2	1.0	0.6	0.3
10	0	7.9	15.4	17.4	19.3	20.1	20.6	21.1	21.8	9.5	6.2	3.1	1.7	0.9
10	100	15.3	18.4	19.3	20.2	20.6	20.9	21.1	9.7	4.6	3.0	1.5	0.8	0.4
20	0	12.4	21.6	24.3	26.9	28.2	28.9	29.7	29.0	13.8	9.3	4.8	2.7	1.4
20	100	23.6	26.4	27.5	28.6	29.1	29.4	29.7	10.5	5.6	3.9	2.0	1.1	0.6
30	0	16.4	27.2	30.6	34.2	35.9	37.0	38.2	37.0	19.0	13.2	7.1	4.0	2.2
30	100	32.3	34.7	35.7	36.8	37.4	37.8	38.2	10.4	6.2	4.5	2.5	1.4	0.8
40	0	19.9	32.3	36.4	41.0	43.4	44.9	46.6	45.8	25.0	18.0	10.0	5.8	3.2
40	100	41.3	43.1	44.0	45.1	45.7	46.1	46.6	9.4	6.2	4.7	2.7	1.6	0.9

DIMENSION ALONG AIRFLOW = 20 CM   DIMENSION ACROSS AIRFLOW = 5 CM

		LEAF TEMPERATURES FOR RESISTANCES=							TRANSPIRATION EXP 6 FOR RES =					
TA	RH	**0*	**1*	**2*	**5*	*10*	*20*	INF*	**0*	**1*	**2*	**5*	*10*	*20*
0	0	8.7	15.1	17.7	20.6	22.2	23.1	24.3	13.2	7.8	5.7	3.2	1.8	1.0
0	100	12.8	17.3	19.2	21.4	22.6	23.4	24.3	9.8	6.0	4.4	2.5	1.4	0.8
10	0	12.3	19.7	22.8	26.5	28.6	29.9	31.6	16.5	10.3	7.7	4.4	2.6	1.5
10	100	19.2	23.5	25.5	28.0	29.4	30.4	31.6	10.8	7.1	5.4	3.2	1.9	1.0
20	0	15.5	23.9	27.5	32.0	34.7	36.4	38.7	20.2	13.1	10.0	6.0	3.7	2.1
20	100	26.2	30.0	31.9	34.5	36.1	37.2	38.7	11.2	7.9	6.2	3.8	2.3	1.3
30	0	18.5	27.7	31.8	37.2	40.4	42.6	45.7	24.1	16.2	12.6	7.8	4.9	2.8
30	100	33.9	36.9	38.6	41.1	42.8	44.0	45.7	10.8	8.1	6.5	4.2	2.7	1.6
40	0	21.2	31.2	35.8	41.9	45.8	48.6	52.5	28.2	19.6	15.6	10.0	6.4	3.8
40	100	42.3	44.5	45.8	48.0	49.6	50.8	52.5	9.6	7.6	6.4	4.3	2.8	1.7

AIRSPEED = 100. CM/SEC   RADIATION ABSORBED = 0.8 EXP 6 ERGS/CM2/SEC

DIMENSION ALONG AIRFLOW = 1 CM   DIMENSION ACROSS AIRFLOW = 10 CM

TA	RH	LEAF TEMPERATURES FOR RESISTANCES=							TRANSPIRATION EXP 6 FOR RES =					
		**0*	**1*	**2*	**5*	*10*	*20*	INF*	**0*	**1*	**2*	**5*	*10*	*20*
0	0	0.4	4.9	5.7	6.3	6.5	6.6	6.7	18.9	5.4	3.1	1.4	0.7	0.4
0	100	4.5	6.1	6.4	6.6	6.6	6.7	6.7	6.6	1.9	1.1	0.5	0.3	0.1
10	0	6.6	13.1	14.3	15.3	15.6	15.9	16.1	28.6	9.0	5.4	2.5	1.3	0.7
10	100	13.3	15.1	15.5	15.8	15.9	16.0	16.1	8.3	2.8	1.7	0.8	0.4	0.2
20	0	12.0	20.7	22.5	24.0	24.6	25.0	25.3	40.5	14.3	8.8	4.1	2.2	1.1
20	100	22.3	24.1	24.6	25.0	25.2	25.2	25.3	9.4	3.7	2.3	1.1	0.6	0.3
30	0	16.9	27.7	30.2	32.5	33.4	34.0	34.6	54.4	21.3	13.6	6.6	3.6	1.9
30	100	31.5	33.1	33.6	34.1	34.3	34.4	34.6	9.6	4.4	2.9	1.4	0.8	0.4
40	0	21.1	34.2	37.4	40.6	42.0	42.8	43.7	70.0	30.0	19.9	10.0	5.5	2.9
40	100	40.9	42.2	42.7	43.2	43.4	43.6	43.7	8.9	4.7	3.2	1.7	0.9	0.5

DIMENSION ALONG AIRFLOW = 5 CM   DIMENSION ACROSS AIRFLOW = 10 CM

TA	RH	LEAF TEMPERATURES FOR RESISTANCES=							TRANSPIRATION EXP 6 FOR RES =					
		**0*	**1*	**2*	**5*	*10*	*20*	INF*	**0*	**1*	**2*	**5*	*10*	*20*
0	0	4.3	9.6	11.1	12.6	13.2	13.5	13.9	14.0	6.3	4.1	2.0	1.1	0.6
0	100	8.5	11.4	12.3	13.1	13.5	13.7	13.9	8.0	3.7	2.4	1.2	0.7	0.3
10	0	9.3	16.2	18.2	20.3	21.3	21.8	22.5	19.4	9.4	6.3	3.2	1.8	0.9
10	100	16.2	19.2	20.3	21.2	21.8	22.2	22.5	9.4	4.9	3.3	1.7	0.9	0.5
20	0	13.7	22.1	24.8	27.7	29.1	29.9	30.9	25.6	13.3	9.3	4.9	2.8	1.5
20	100	24.2	27.1	28.2	29.5	30.1	30.5	30.9	10.2	5.9	4.2	2.2	1.3	0.7
30	0	17.7	27.5	30.9	34.7	36.6	37.8	39.2	32.6	18.1	12.9	7.1	4.1	2.2
30	100	32.7	35.1	36.2	37.5	38.2	38.7	39.2	10.2	6.4	4.8	2.7	1.6	0.9
40	0	21.2	32.4	36.4	41.2	43.7	45.4	47.4	40.1	23.6	17.3	9.9	5.9	3.3
40	100	41.6	43.4	44.3	45.6	46.3	46.8	47.4	9.2	6.4	5.0	3.0	1.8	1.0

AIRSPEED = 100. CM/SEC   RADIATION ABSORBED = 0.8 EXP 6 ERGS/CM2/SEC

DIMENSION ALONG AIRFLOW = 10 CM   DIMENSION ACROSS AIRFLOW = 10 CM

LEAF TEMPERATURES FOR RESISTANCES=   TRANSPIRATION EXP 6 FOR RES =

TA	RH	**0*	**1*	**2*	**5*	*10*	*20*	INF*	**0*	**1*	**2*	**5*	*10*	*20*
0	0	6.8	12.4	14.3	16.4	17.3	17.9	18.6	12.9	6.9	4.8	2.5	1.4	0.7
0	100	10.8	14.4	15.7	17.1	17.7	18.1	18.6	8.6	4.7	3.3	1.7	1.0	0.5
10	0	11.2	18.0	20.5	23.3	24.7	25.6	26.6	17.1	9.7	6.9	3.7	2.1	1.2
10	100	17.8	21.4	22.8	24.5	25.4	26.0	26.6	9.9	5.9	4.2	2.3	1.3	0.7
20	0	15.1	23.1	26.2	29.8	31.7	33.0	34.4	21.8	13.0	9.5	5.4	3.1	1.7
20	100	25.3	28.6	30.1	31.9	33.0	33.6	34.4	10.5	6.8	5.1	2.9	1.7	1.0
30	0	18.6	27.7	31.4	35.9	38.4	40.1	42.2	27.0	16.9	12.6	7.4	4.5	2.5
30	100	33.4	36.1	37.4	39.3	40.4	41.2	42.2	10.3	7.2	5.6	3.4	2.1	1.2
40	0	21.8	31.9	36.2	41.6	44.6	46.9	49.8	32.5	21.2	16.3	9.9	6.1	3.5
40	100	42.1	44.0	45.1	46.8	47.9	48.7	49.8	9.3	7.0	5.7	3.6	2.3	1.3

DIMENSION ALONG AIRFLOW = 20 CM   DIMENSION ACROSS AIRFLOW = 10 CM

LEAF TEMPERATURES FOR RESISTANCES=   TRANSPIRATION EXP 6 FOR RES =

TA	RH	**0*	**1*	**2*	**5*	*10*	*20*	INF*	**0*	**1*	**2*	**5*	*10*	*20*
0	0	9.7	15.5	17.9	20.7	22.2	23.1	24.3	12.3	7.5	5.5	3.1	1.8	1.0
0	100	13.6	17.6	19.3	21.5	22.6	23.4	24.3	9.2	5.8	4.3	2.4	1.4	0.8
10	0	13.5	20.1	23.0	26.6	28.6	29.9	31.6	15.5	10.0	7.5	4.4	2.6	1.5
10	100	19.8	23.7	25.6	28.0	29.5	30.4	31.6	10.3	6.9	5.3	3.1	1.9	1.0
20	0	16.9	24.4	27.8	32.1	34.7	36.4	38.7	19.1	12.7	9.8	5.9	3.6	2.1
20	100	26.7	30.2	32.0	34.6	36.2	37.3	38.7	10.7	7.6	6.0	3.7	2.3	1.3
30	0	19.9	28.3	32.1	37.3	40.4	42.7	45.7	22.9	15.8	12.4	7.8	4.9	2.8
30	100	34.3	37.1	38.7	41.2	42.8	44.0	45.7	10.4	7.9	6.4	4.2	2.7	1.5
40	0	22.7	31.8	36.1	42.1	45.9	48.6	52.5	26.9	19.1	15.3	9.9	6.3	3.7
40	100	42.6	44.6	45.9	48.0	49.6	50.8	52.5	9.4	7.5	6.3	4.3	2.8	1.7

AIRSPEED = 100. CM/SEC   RADIATION ABSORBED = 1.0 EXP 6 ERGS/CM2/SEC

DIMENSION ALONG AIRFLOW = 1 CM   DIMENSION ACROSS AIRFLOW = 1 CM

LEAF TEMPERATURES FOR RESISTANCES=   TRANSPIRATION EXP 6 FOR RES =

TA	RH	**0*	**1*	**2*	**5*	*10*	*20*	INF*	**0*	**1*	**2*	**5*	*10*	*20*
0	0	-1.6	4.7	5.3	5.7	5.8	5.9	6.0	35.6	5.9	3.3	1.4	0.7	0.4
0	100	3.6	5.5	5.7	5.9	5.9	5.9	6.0	11.1	2.0	1.1	0.5	0.2	0.1
10	0	4.3	13.4	14.3	15.0	15.3	15.4	15.5	53.3	10.4	5.8	2.5	1.3	0.7
10	100	12.6	14.9	15.2	15.4	15.5	15.5	15.5	13.9	3.0	1.7	0.7	0.4	0.2
20	0	9.5	21.6	23.1	24.2	24.6	24.9	25.1	74.6	16.9	9.7	4.3	2.2	1.1
20	100	21.8	24.2	24.6	24.9	25.0	25.0	25.1	15.8	4.2	2.5	1.1	0.6	0.3
30	0	14.0	29.3	31.4	33.2	33.8	34.2	34.6	99.2	26.0	15.5	7.0	3.7	1.9
30	100	31.2	33.5	33.9	34.3	34.4	34.5	34.6	16.6	5.5	3.3	1.5	0.8	0.4
40	0	18.0	36.4	39.3	41.8	42.9	43.4	44.0	126.3	38.0	23.3	11.0	5.8	3.0
40	100	40.8	42.7	43.2	43.6	43.8	43.9	44.0	16.3	6.6	4.2	2.0	1.1	0.5

DIMENSION ALONG AIRFLOW = 5 CM   DIMENSION ACROSS AIRFLOW = 1 CM

LEAF TEMPERATURES FOR RESISTANCES=   TRANSPIRATION EXP 6 FOR RES =

TA	RH	**0*	**1*	**2*	**5*	*10*	*20*	INF*	**0*	**1*	**2*	**5*	*10*	*20*
0	0	1.4	9.4	10.7	11.8	12.2	12.4	12.7	25.0	7.4	4.4	2.0	1.1	0.5
0	100	6.8	10.8	11.6	12.0	12.5	12.5	12.7	13.1	4.2	2.5	1.1	0.6	0.3
10	0	6.3	16.6	18.6	20.3	21.0	21.3	21.7	34.6	11.7	7.2	3.4	1.8	0.9
10	100	14.9	19.2	20.2	21.0	21.3	21.5	21.7	15.6	5.8	3.6	1.7	0.9	0.5
20	0	10.6	23.3	26.0	28.4	29.5	30.1	30.7	45.6	17.2	11.0	5.3	2.9	1.5
20	100	23.3	27.5	28.6	29.7	30.2	30.4	30.7	17.1	7.5	4.9	2.4	1.3	0.7
30	0	14.4	29.3	32.8	36.2	37.7	38.6	39.6	57.8	24.1	16.0	8.1	4.5	2.4
30	100	32.2	35.8	37.0	38.3	38.8	39.2	39.6	17.5	9.0	6.1	3.2	1.8	0.9
40	0	17.8	34.8	39.1	43.5	45.7	46.9	48.4	70.9	32.3	22.1	11.7	6.6	3.6
40	100	41.4	44.3	45.5	46.8	47.5	47.9	48.4	16.9	9.9	7.1	3.9	2.2	1.2

95

AIRSPEED = 100. CM/SEC   RADIATION ABSORBED = 1.0 EXP 6 ERGS/CM2/SEC

DIMENSION ALONG AIRFLOW = 1 CM   DIMENSION ACROSS AIRFLOW = 5 CM

TA	RH	LEAF TEMPERATURES FOR RESISTANCES=							TRANSPIRATION EXP 6 FOR RES =					
		**0*	**1*	**2*	**5*	*10*	*20*	INF*	**0*	**1*	**2*	**5*	*10*	*20*
0	0	-0.1	4.7	5.3	5.7	5.8	5.9	6.0	28.6	5.7	3.2	1.4	0.7	0.4
0	100	4.0	5.6	5.7	5.9	5.9	5.9	6.0	9.1	1.9	1.1	0.5	0.2	0.1
10	0	6.3	13.5	14.4	15.0	15.3	15.4	15.5	44.0	10.0	5.7	2.5	1.3	0.7
10	100	13.1	14.9	15.2	15.4	15.5	15.5	15.5	11.9	2.9	1.7	0.7	0.4	0.2
20	0	11.9	21.7	23.1	24.2	24.6	24.9	25.1	63.1	16.4	9.6	4.3	2.2	1.1
20	100	22.2	24.2	24.6	24.9	25.0	25.0	25.1	14.0	4.1	2.4	1.1	0.6	0.3
30	0	16.9	29.4	31.5	33.2	33.8	34.2	34.6	85.6	25.2	15.2	7.0	3.7	1.9
30	100	31.5	33.5	33.9	34.3	34.4	34.5	34.6	15.2	5.3	3.3	1.5	0.8	0.4
40	0	21.3	36.6	39.4	41.9	43.0	43.4	44.0	110.9	36.9	22.9	10.9	5.8	3.0
40	100	41.0	42.7	43.2	43.6	43.8	43.9	44.0	15.3	6.4	4.1	2.0	1.0	0.5

DIMENSION ALONG AIRFLOW = 5 CM   DIMENSION ACROSS AIRFLOW = 5 CM

TA	RH	LEAF TEMPERATURES FOR RESISTANCES=							TRANSPIRATION EXP 6 FOR RES =					
		**0*	**1*	**2*	**5*	*10*	*20*	INF*	**0*	**1*	**2*	**5*	*10*	*20*
0	0	3.4	9.5	10.8	11.8	12.2	12.4	12.7	20.7	7.0	4.3	2.0	1.0	0.5
0	100	7.7	10.9	11.6	12.2	12.4	12.5	12.7	11.1	4.0	2.4	1.1	0.6	0.3
10	0	8.7	16.9	18.7	20.3	21.0	21.3	21.7	29.3	11.1	7.0	3.3	1.8	0.9
10	100	15.7	19.3	20.2	21.0	21.3	21.5	21.7	13.6	5.6	3.5	1.7	0.9	0.5
20	0	13.4	23.6	26.1	28.4	29.5	30.1	30.7	39.4	16.4	10.7	5.3	2.9	1.5
20	100	24.1	27.6	28.7	29.7	30.2	30.4	30.7	15.4	7.2	4.8	2.4	1.3	0.7
30	0	17.6	29.7	33.0	36.2	37.7	38.6	39.6	50.7	23.1	15.5	8.0	4.4	2.4
30	100	32.7	35.9	37.1	38.3	38.9	39.2	39.6	16.2	8.7	6.0	3.1	1.7	0.9
40	0	21.3	35.3	39.4	43.6	45.7	46.9	48.4	63.1	31.1	21.6	11.6	6.6	3.5
40	100	41.8	44.4	45.5	46.8	47.5	47.9	48.4	15.9	9.6	7.0	3.8	2.2	1.2

AIRSPEED = 100. CM/SEC RADIATION ABSORBED = 1.6 EXP 6 ERGS/CM2/SEC

DIMENSION ALONG AIRFLOW = 10 CM   DIMENSION ACROSS AIRFLOW = 5 CM

LEAF TEMPERATURES FOR RESISTANCES=   TRANSPIRATION EXP 6 FOR RES =

TA	RH	**0*	**1*	**2*	***5*	*10*	*20*	INF*	**0*	**1*	**2*	***5*	*10*	*20*
0	0	5.7	12.5	14.2	15.8	16.5	16.9	17.3	19.0	8.0	5.1	2.5	1.4	0.7
0	100	10.0	14.1	15.2	16.3	16.7	17.0	17.3	12.1	5.3	3.4	1.7	0.9	0.5
10	0	10.5	18.9	21.3	23.6	24.7	25.3	25.9	25.7	11.8	7.9	4.0	2.2	1.1
10	100	17.4	21.7	23.1	24.5	25.1	25.5	25.9	14.4	7.1	4.8	2.4	1.3	0.7
20	0	14.7	24.8	27.9	31.0	32.6	33.5	34.5	33.4	16.6	11.4	6.0	3.4	1.8
20	100	25.2	29.4	30.9	32.6	33.4	33.9	34.5	16.0	8.8	6.2	3.3	1.9	1.0
30	0	18.4	30.1	33.9	38.1	40.1	41.4	43.0	41.8	22.2	15.8	8.6	5.0	2.7
30	100	33.5	37.2	38.7	40.6	41.6	42.2	43.0	16.6	10.2	7.4	4.2	2.4	1.3
40	0	21.8	35.0	39.5	44.6	47.4	49.1	51.3	51.0	28.8	21.0	12.0	7.1	3.9
40	100	42.3	45.2	46.7	48.6	49.7	50.4	51.3	16.2	10.9	8.3	4.9	2.9	1.6

DIMENSION ALONG AIRFLOW = 20 CM   DIMENSION ACROSS AIRFLOW = 5 CM

LEAF TEMPERATURES FOR RESISTANCES=   TRANSPIRATION EXP 6 FOR RES =

TA	RH	**0*	**1*	**2*	***5*	*10*	*20*	INF*	**0*	**1*	**2*	***5*	*10*	*20*
0	0	13.2	21.0	24.2	28.1	30.3	31.8	33.6	17.6	11.1	8.3	4.9	2.9	1.6
0	100	16.9	22.9	25.5	28.9	30.8	32.0	33.6	14.5	9.4	7.1	4.2	2.5	1.4
10	0	16.4	25.0	28.8	33.5	36.3	38.2	40.7	21.3	14.0	10.7	6.5	4.0	2.3
10	100	22.5	28.3	31.1	34.9	37.1	38.6	40.7	16.1	11.1	8.6	5.3	3.3	1.9
20	0	19.3	28.8	33.0	38.6	42.0	44.4	47.6	25.3	17.2	13.4	8.4	5.3	3.1
20	100	28.8	34.1	36.9	40.8	43.2	45.1	47.6	17.1	12.4	10.0	6.4	4.0	2.4
30	0	21.9	32.2	36.8	43.2	47.3	50.2	54.4	29.4	20.6	16.4	10.6	6.9	4.1
30	100	36.0	40.4	43.0	46.8	49.5	51.5	54.4	17.2	13.2	10.9	7.3	4.8	2.8
40	0	24.3	35.3	40.4	47.6	52.3	55.8	61.1	33.8	24.3	19.7	13.1	8.7	5.2
40	100	43.9	47.3	49.5	53.1	55.7	57.8	61.1	16.5	13.3	11.3	7.9	5.3	3.2

AIRSPEED = 100. CM/SEC   RADIATION ABSORBED = 1.0 EXP 6 ERGS/CM2/SEC

DIMENSION ALONG AIRFLOW = 1 CM   DIMENSION ACROSS AIRFLOW = 10 CM

TA	RH	**0*	**1*	**2*	***5*	*10*	*20*	INF*	**0*	**1*	**2*	***5*	*10*	*20*
		LEAF TEMPERATURES FOR RESISTANCES=							TRANSPIRATION EXP 6 FOR RES =					
0	0	2.3	7.3	8.2	8.9	9.1	9.3	9.4	21.4	6.3	3.7	1.7	0.9	0.4
0	100	6.2	8.5	8.8	9.2	9.3	9.4	9.4	9.6	2.9	1.7	0.8	0.4	0.2
10	0	8.2	15.3	16.7	17.8	18.2	18.5	18.7	31.8	10.4	6.3	2.9	1.5	0.8
10	100	14.7	17.3	17.9	18.3	18.5	18.6	18.7	12.0	4.3	2.6	1.2	0.6	0.3
20	0	13.5	22.8	24.8	26.5	27.2	27.6	28.0	44.3	16.1	10.0	4.8	2.5	1.3
20	100	23.4	26.1	26.8	27.4	27.7	27.8	28.0	14.2	5.8	3.6	1.7	0.9	0.5
30	0	18.1	29.6	32.3	34.8	35.9	36.5	37.2	58.7	23.6	15.2	7.5	4.0	2.1
30	100	32.3	34.9	35.7	36.4	36.8	37.0	37.2	15.3	7.2	4.7	2.3	1.3	0.7
40	0	22.3	35.9	39.4	42.8	44.4	45.3	46.3	74.8	32.9	22.0	11.2	6.2	3.3
40	100	41.5	43.7	44.5	45.4	45.8	46.0	46.3	15.3	8.2	5.7	3.0	1.6	0.9

DIMENSION ALONG AIRFLOW = 5 CM   DIMENSION ACROSS AIRFLOW = 10 CM

TA	RH	**0*	**1*	**2*	***5*	*10*	*20*	INF*	**0*	**1*	**2*	***5*	*10*	*20*
		LEAF TEMPERATURES FOR RESISTANCES=							TRANSPIRATION EXP 6 FOR RES =					
0	0	7.6	13.9	15.7	17.6	18.4	18.9	19.4	17.4	8.2	5.4	2.7	1.5	0.8
0	100	11.4	15.5	16.8	18.1	18.7	19.0	19.4	11.8	5.7	3.9	1.9	1.1	0.6
10	0	12.2	20.0	22.5	25.1	26.3	27.1	27.9	23.3	11.8	8.1	4.2	2.4	1.3
10	100	18.6	22.9	24.4	26.1	26.9	27.4	27.9	14.0	7.6	5.2	2.8	1.5	0.8
20	0	16.3	25.6	28.8	32.2	33.9	35.0	36.3	30.0	16.3	11.5	6.3	3.6	1.9
20	100	26.1	30.3	31.9	34.0	34.9	35.5	36.3	15.6	9.2	6.7	3.7	2.1	1.1
30	0	20.0	30.7	34.5	38.9	41.2	42.7	44.5	37.3	21.5	15.7	8.9	5.2	2.9
30	100	34.1	37.8	39.5	41.6	42.8	43.6	44.5	16.2	10.5	7.9	4.6	2.7	1.5
40	0	23.3	35.2	39.7	45.1	48.1	50.1	52.6	45.3	27.4	20.5	12.1	7.3	4.1
40	100	42.7	45.7	47.2	49.3	50.6	51.5	52.6	15.9	11.2	8.8	5.4	3.3	1.8

AIRSPEED = 100. CM/SEC   RADIATION ABSORBED = 1.0 EXP 6 ERGS/CM2/SEC

| | | DIMENSION ALONG AIRFLOW = 10 CM | | | | | | | DIMENSION ACROSS AIRFLOW = 10 CM | | | | | |
| | | LEAF TEMPERATURES FOR RESISTANCES= | | | | | | | TRANSPIRATION EXP 6 FOR RES = | | | | | |
TA	RH	**0*	**1*	**2*	***5*	*10*	*20*	INF*	**0*	**1*	**2*	***5*	*10*	*20*
0	0	10.8	17.5	20.0	22.7	24.0	24.9	25.8	16.7	9.4	6.7	3.6	2.1	1.1
0	100	14.4	19.3	21.2	23.3	24.4	25.1	25.8	12.8	7.4	5.3	2.9	1.6	0.9
10	0	14.7	22.6	25.7	29.2	31.1	32.3	33.7	21.4	12.7	9.2	5.2	3.0	1.7
10	100	20.8	25.7	27.8	30.4	31.8	32.6	33.7	14.7	9.2	6.8	3.9	2.3	1.2
20	0	18.3	27.3	30.9	35.3	37.8	39.4	41.4	26.5	16.5	12.3	7.2	4.3	2.4
20	100	27.7	32.3	34.5	37.3	39.0	40.1	41.4	16.0	10.8	8.2	4.9	3.0	1.7
30	0	21.5	31.5	35.7	41.1	44.2	46.3	49.1	32.0	20.7	15.9	9.7	5.9	3.4
30	100	35.2	39.2	41.3	44.2	46.1	47.4	49.1	16.5	11.8	9.4	5.9	3.6	2.1
40	0	24.4	35.4	40.1	46.4	50.2	52.8	56.5	37.8	25.4	19.9	12.5	7.9	4.6
40	100	43.4	46.6	48.4	51.2	53.1	54.5	56.5	16.0	12.2	10.0	6.6	4.2	2.5

| | | DIMENSION ALONG AIRFLOW = 20 CM | | | | | | | DIMENSION ACROSS AIRFLOW = 10 CM | | | | | |
| | | LEAF TEMPERATURES FOR RESISTANCES= | | | | | | | TRANSPIRATION EXP 6 FOR RES = | | | | | |
TA	RH	**0*	**1*	**2*	***5*	*10*	*20*	INF*	**0*	**1*	**2*	***5*	*10*	*20*
0	0	14.5	21.4	24.4	28.2	30.4	31.8	33.6	16.5	10.7	8.1	4.8	2.9	1.6
0	100	17.8	23.2	25.7	28.9	30.8	32.0	33.6	13.7	9.1	7.0	4.1	2.5	1.4
10	0	17.8	25.5	29.0	33.6	36.4	38.2	40.7	20.1	13.6	10.5	6.4	4.0	2.3
10	100	23.4	28.7	31.3	34.9	37.1	38.7	40.7	15.4	10.8	8.5	5.2	3.2	1.9
20	0	20.7	29.3	33.3	38.7	42.0	44.4	47.6	24.0	16.7	13.2	8.3	5.3	3.1
20	100	29.6	34.5	37.1	40.9	43.3	45.1	47.6	16.4	12.1	9.8	6.3	4.0	2.3
30	0	23.5	32.8	37.2	43.3	47.3	50.2	54.4	28.1	20.1	16.1	10.5	6.8	4.0
30	100	36.6	40.7	43.1	46.9	49.5	51.5	54.4	16.7	12.9	10.7	7.2	4.7	2.8
40	0	26.0	35.9	40.8	47.7	52.3	55.8	61.1	32.4	23.7	19.3	13.0	8.6	5.2
40	100	44.3	47.6	49.7	53.1	55.7	57.8	61.1	16.2	13.1	11.1	7.8	5.3	3.2

AIRSPEED = 200. CM/SEC   RADIATION ABSORBED = 0.4 EXP 6 ERGS/CM2/SEC
DIMENSION ALONG AIRFLOW = 1 CM   DIMENSION ACROSS AIRFLOW = 1 CM

LEAF TEMPERATURES FOR RESISTANCES=   TRANSPIRATION EXP 6 FOR RES =

TA	RH	**0*	**1*	**2*	**5*	*10*	*20*	INF*	**0*	**1*	**2*	**5*	*10*	*20*
0	0	-5.4	-0.1	0.3	0.5	0.5	0.6	0.6	39.7	4.5	2.4	1.0	0.5	0.3
0	100	0.4	0.6	0.6	0.6	0.6	0.6	0.6	1.5	0.2	0.1	0.0	0.0	0.0
10	0	0.9	9.1	9.7	10.1	10.2	10.3	10.3	62.1	8.2	4.4	1.9	0.9	0.5
10	100	10.2	10.3	10.3	10.3	10.3	10.3	10.3	1.1	0.2	0.1	0.0	0.0	0.0
20	0	6.5	17.9	18.9	19.5	19.8	19.9	20.0	90.0	14.1	7.8	3.3	1.7	0.9
20	100	20.0	20.0	20.0	20.0	20.0	20.0	20.0	0.1	0.0	0.0	0.0	0.0	0.0
30	0	11.3	26.3	27.8	28.9	29.2	29.5	29.7	122.8	22.9	12.9	5.6	2.9	1.5
30	100													
40	0	15.6	34.2	36.3	38.0	38.6	38.9	39.3	159.8	35.1	20.4	9.1	4.7	2.4
40	100													

DIMENSION ALONG AIRFLOW = 5 CM   DIMENSION ACROSS AIRFLOW = 1 CM

LEAF TEMPERATURES FOR RESISTANCES=   TRANSPIRATION EXP 6 FOR RES =

TA	RH	**0*	**1*	**2*	**5*	*10*	*20*	INF*	**0*	**1*	**2*	**5*	*10*	*20*
0	0	-5.9	-0.1	0.6	1.0	1.2	1.2	1.3	21.8	4.2	2.3	1.0	0.5	0.3
0	100	0.7	1.2	1.3	1.3	1.3	1.3	1.3	1.7	0.4	0.2	0.1	0.0	0.0
10	0	-0.1	8.3	9.4	10.1	10.4	10.6	10.7	33.0	7.4	4.2	1.8	1.0	0.5
10	100	10.3	10.6	10.7	10.7	10.7	10.7	10.7	1.2	0.3	0.2	0.1	0.0	0.0
20	0	5.0	16.2	17.8	19.0	19.5	19.8	20.0	46.4	12.0	7.1	3.2	1.7	0.8
20	100	20.0	20.0	20.0	20.0	20.0	20.0	20.0	0.1	0.0	0.0	0.0	0.0	0.0
30	0	9.4	23.5	25.8	27.7	28.4	28.9	29.3	61.9	18.4	11.2	5.2	2.8	1.4
30	100													
40	0	13.3	30.2	33.3	36.0	37.2	37.8	38.5	79.0	26.7	16.9	8.1	4.4	2.3
40	100													

AIRSPEED = 200. CM/SEC   RADIATION ABSORBED = 0.4 EXP 6 ERGS/CM2/SEC
DIMENSION ALONG AIRFLOW = 1 CM   DIMENSION ACROSS AIRFLOW = 5 CM
LEAF TEMPERATURES FOR RESISTANCES=   TRANSPIRATION EXP 6 FOR RES =

TA	RH	**0*	**1*	**2*	**5*	*10*	*20*	INF*	**0*	**1*	**2*	**5*	*10*	*20*
0	0	-4.2	-0.0	0.3	0.5	0.5	0.6	0.6	31.5	4.3	2.3	1.0	0.5	0.3
0	100	0.4	0.6	0.6	0.6	0.6	0.6	0.6	1.2	0.2	0.1	0.0	0.0	0.0
10	0	2.7	9.1	9.7	10.1	10.2	10.3	10.3	50.7	8.0	4.4	1.8	0.9	0.5
10	100	10.2	10.3	10.3	10.3	10.3	10.3	10.3	1.0	0.2	0.1	0.0	0.0	0.0
20	0	8.7	18.0	18.9	19.5	19.8	19.9	20.0	75.4	13.8	7.7	3.3	1.7	0.9
20	100	20.0	20.0	20.0	20.0	20.0	20.0	20.0	0.1	0.0	0.0	0.0	0.0	0.0
30	0	14.0	26.4	27.8	28.9	29.3	29.5	29.7	105.2	22.4	12.7	5.6	2.9	1.5
30	100													
40	0	18.7	34.3	36.4	38.0	38.6	38.9	39.3	139.4	34.3	20.1	9.0	4.7	2.4
40	100													

DIMENSION ALONG AIRFLOW = 5 CM   DIMENSION ACROSS AIRFLOW = 5 CM
LEAF TEMPERATURES FOR RESISTANCES=   TRANSPIRATION EXP 6 FOR RES =

TA	RH	**0*	**1*	**2*	**5*	*10*	*20*	INF*	**0*	**1*	**2*	**5*	*10*	*20*
0	0	-4.5	-0.0	0.6	1.0	1.2	1.2	1.3	17.5	4.0	2.3	1.0	0.5	0.3
0	100	0.8	1.2	1.3	1.3	1.3	1.3	1.3	1.4	0.4	0.2	0.1	0.0	0.0
10	0	1.8	8.4	9.4	10.1	10.4	10.6	10.7	27.2	7.1	4.1	1.8	0.9	0.5
10	100	10.4	10.6	10.7	10.7	10.7	10.7	10.7	1.1	0.3	0.2	0.1	0.0	0.0
20	0	7.3	16.3	17.8	19.0	19.5	19.8	20.0	39.3	11.6	6.9	3.1	1.6	0.8
20	100	20.0	20.0	20.0	20.0	20.0	20.0	20.0	0.1	0.0	0.0	0.0	0.0	0.0
30	0	12.2	23.7	25.8	27.7	28.4	28.9	29.3	53.4	17.8	11.0	5.1	2.7	1.4
30	100													
40	0	16.4	30.4	33.4	36.0	37.2	37.8	38.5	69.4	25.9	16.5	8.0	4.3	2.3
40	100													

AIRSPEED = 200. CM/SEC   RADIATION ABSORBED = 0.4 EXP 6 ERGS/CM2/SEC

DIMENSION ALONG AIRFLOW = 10 CM   DIMENSION ACROSS AIRFLOW = 5 CM

		LEAF TEMPERATURES FOR RESISTANCES=							TRANSPIRATION EXP 6 FOR RES =					
TA	RH	**0*	**1*	**2*	**5*	*10*	*20*	INF*	**0*	**1*	**2*	**5*	*10*	*20*
0	0	-4.5	0.1	0.8	1.4	1.6	1.7	1.8	13.8	3.9	2.3	1.0	0.5	0.3
0	100	1.1	1.6	1.7	1.8	1.8	1.8	1.8	1.5	0.5	0.3	0.1	0.1	0.0
10	0	1.5	8.0	9.2	10.2	10.6	10.8	11.0	21.0	6.6	4.0	1.8	0.9	0.5
10	100	10.8	10.9	10.9	10.9	11.0	11.0	11.0	1.1	0.4	0.2	0.1	0.1	0.0
20	0	6.8	15.4	17.2	18.7	19.3	19.7	20.0	29.8	10.5	6.5	3.1	1.6	0.8
20	100	20.0	20.0	20.0	20.0	20.0	20.0	20.0	0.1	0.0	0.0	0.0	0.0	0.0
30	0	11.4	22.2	24.7	26.9	27.9	28.4	29.0	40.0	15.7	10.0	4.9	2.6	1.4
30	100													
40	0	15.5	28.4	31.7	34.8	36.2	37.0	37.9	51.5	22.2	14.7	7.5	4.1	2.2
40	100													

DIMENSION ALONG AIRFLOW = 20 CM   DIMENSION ACROSS AIRFLOW = 5 CM

		LEAF TEMPERATURES FOR RESISTANCES=							TRANSPIRATION EXP 6 FOR RES =					
TA	RH	**0*	**1*	**2*	**5*	*10*	*20*	INF*	**0*	**1*	**2*	**5*	*10*	*20*
0	0	-4.0	0.5	1.7	2.8	3.2	3.5	3.8	8.2	3.5	2.2	1.1	0.6	0.3
0	100	2.2	3.1	3.3	3.6	3.7	3.7	3.8	1.7	0.8	0.5	0.2	0.1	0.1
10	0	1.1	7.1	8.8	10.4	11.1	11.5	12.0	11.7	5.4	3.6	1.8	1.0	0.5
10	100	10.9	11.4	11.6	11.8	11.9	12.0	12.0	1.2	0.6	0.4	0.2	0.1	0.1
20	0	5.6	13.0	15.3	17.6	18.7	19.4	20.1	15.8	7.8	5.3	2.8	1.5	0.8
20	100	20.0	20.1	20.1	20.1	20.1	20.1	20.1	0.1	0.0	0.0	0.0	0.0	0.0
30	0	9.6	18.4	21.3	24.5	26.0	27.0	28.1	20.5	10.9	7.6	4.1	2.3	1.3
30	100													
40	0	13.2	23.3	26.9	30.9	33.0	34.3	35.9	25.6	14.5	10.4	5.8	3.4	1.9
40	100													

AIRSPEED = 200. CM/SEC   RADIATION ABSORBED = 0.4 EXP 6 ERGS/CM2/SEC

DIMENSION ALONG AIRFLOW = 1 CM   DIMENSION ACROSS AIRFLOW = 10 CM

LEAF TEMPERATURES FOR RESISTANCES=   TRANSPIRATION EXP 6 FOR RES =

TA	RH	**0*	**1*	**2*	**5*	*10*	*20*	INF*	**0*	**1*	**2*	**5*	*10*	*20*
0	0	-4.0	-0.0	0.4	0.7	0.9	0.9	1.0	20.3	4.1	2.3	1.0	0.5	0.3
0	100	0.7	0.9	0.9	1.0	1.0	1.0	1.0	1.3	0.3	0.1	0.1	0.0	0.0
10	0	2.7	8.8	9.5	10.1	10.3	10.4	10.5	32.4	7.4	4.2	1.8	0.9	0.5
10	100	10.3	10.5	10.5	10.5	10.5	10.5	10.5	1.0	0.2	0.1	0.1	0.0	0.0
20	0	8.6	17.1	18.3	19.3	19.6	19.8	20.0	47.8	12.4	7.2	3.2	1.7	0.8
20	100	20.0	20.0	20.0	20.0	20.0	20.0	20.0	0.1	0.0	0.0	0.0	0.0	0.0
30	0	13.8	24.9	26.8	28.2	28.8	29.2	29.5	66.2	19.5	11.7	5.3	2.8	1.4
30	100													
40	0	18.4	32.2	34.8	36.9	37.9	38.4	38.9	87.4	29.0	18.0	8.5	4.5	2.3
40	100													

DIMENSION ALONG AIRFLOW = 5 CM   DIMENSION ACROSS AIRFLOW = 10 CM

LEAF TEMPERATURES FOR RESISTANCES=   TRANSPIRATION EXP 6 FOR RES =

TA	RH	**0*	**1*	**2*	**5*	*10*	*20*	INF*	**0*	**1*	**2*	**5*	*10*	*20*
0	0	-3.9	0.2	0.9	1.6	1.8	1.9	2.1	11.6	3.7	2.2	1.0	0.5	0.3
0	100	1.3	1.8	1.9	2.0	2.0	2.1	2.1	1.5	0.5	0.3	0.1	0.1	0.0
10	0	2.1	7.9	9.2	10.2	10.6	10.9	11.1	17.7	6.3	3.8	1.8	0.9	0.5
10	100	10.6	10.9	11.0	11.0	11.1	11.1	11.1	1.1	0.4	0.3	0.1	0.1	0.0
20	0	7.4	15.2	17.0	18.6	19.3	19.6	20.1	25.1	9.8	6.2	3.0	1.6	0.8
20	100	20.0	20.0	20.0	20.0	20.1	20.1	20.1	0.1	0.0	0.0	0.0	0.0	0.0
30	0	12.1	21.8	24.3	26.6	27.7	28.3	28.9	33.8	14.6	9.5	4.7	2.6	1.4
30	100													
40	0	16.2	27.8	31.0	34.3	35.8	36.7	37.7	43.6	20.5	13.9	7.2	4.0	2.1
40	100													

AIRSPEED = 200. CM/SEC   RADIATION ABSORBED = 0.4 EXP 6 ERGS/CM2/SEC

DIMENSION ALONG AIRFLOW = 10 CM   DIMENSION ACROSS AIRFLOW = 10 CM
LEAF TEMPERATURES FOR RESISTANCES=   TRANSPIRATION EXP 6 FOR RES =

TA	RH	**0*	**1*	**2*	**5*	*10*	*20*	INF*	***0*	***1*	***2*	***5*	*10*	*20*
0	0	-3.7	0.3	1.3	2.1	2.4	2.6	2.8	9.3	3.5	2.2	1.0	0.6	0.3
0	100	1.7	2.4	2.6	2.7	2.8	2.8	2.8	1.5	0.6	0.4	0.2	0.1	0.0
10	0	2.0	7.6	9.0	10.3	10.9	11.2	11.5	13.8	5.7	3.7	1.8	1.0	0.5
10	100	10.7	11.2	11.3	11.4	11.4	11.5	11.5	1.1	0.5	0.3	0.2	0.1	0.0
20	0	7.0	14.2	16.2	18.2	19.0	19.5	20.1	19.2	8.7	5.7	2.9	1.6	0.8
20	100	20.0	20.1	20.1	20.1	20.1	20.1	20.1	0.1	0.0	0.0	0.0	0.0	0.0
30	0	11.4	20.3	22.9	25.6	26.9	27.7	28.5	25.4	12.5	8.5	4.4	2.5	1.3
30	100													
40	0	15.3	25.7	29.1	32.7	34.5	35.6	36.9	32.4	17.1	12.0	6.5	3.7	2.0
40	100													

DIMENSION ALONG AIRFLOW = 20 CM   DIMENSION ACROSS AIRFLOW = 10 CM
LEAF TEMPERATURES FOR RESISTANCES=   TRANSPIRATION EXP 6 FOR RES =

TA	RH	**0*	**1*	**2*	**5*	*10*	*20*	INF*	***0*	***1*	***2*	***5*	*10*	*20*
0	0	-3.3	0.6	1.8	2.8	3.3	3.5	3.8	7.5	3.3	2.2	1.1	0.6	0.3
0	100	2.3	3.1	3.3	3.6	3.7	3.7	3.8	1.6	0.8	0.5	0.2	0.1	0.1
10	0	2.0	7.2	8.8	10.4	11.1	11.5	12.0	10.8	5.2	3.5	1.8	1.0	0.5
10	100	11.0	11.5	11.6	11.8	11.9	12.0	12.0	1.1	0.6	0.4	0.2	0.1	0.1
20	0	6.6	13.2	15.4	17.7	18.7	19.4	20.1	14.7	7.6	5.2	2.7	1.5	0.8
20	100	20.0	20.1	20.1	20.1	20.1	20.1	20.1	0.1	0.0	0.0	0.0	0.0	0.0
30	0	10.8	18.7	21.5	24.5	26.0	27.0	28.1	19.2	10.6	7.5	4.1	2.3	1.3
30	100													
40	0	14.5	23.6	27.0	30.9	33.0	34.3	35.9	24.2	14.1	10.3	5.8	3.4	1.9
40	100													

AIRSPEED = 200. CM/SEC   RADIATION ABSORBED = 0.6 EXP 6 ERGS/CM2/SEC

DIMENSION ALONG AIRFLOW = 1 CM   DIMENSION ACROSS AIRFLOW = 1 CM

LEAF TEMPERATURES FOR RESISTANCES=   TRANSPIRATION EXP 6 FOR RES =

TA	RH	**0*	**1*	**2*	**5*	*10*	*20*	INF*	**0*	**1*	**2*	**5*	*10*	*20*
0	0	-4.6	1.1	1.4	1.7	1.7	1.8	1.8	42.1	4.8	2.6	1.1	0.5	0.3
0	100	1.1	1.7	1.8	1.8	1.8	1.8	1.8	4.7	0.6	0.3	0.1	0.1	0.0
10	0	1.7	10.2	10.8	11.2	11.4	11.5	11.5	65.3	8.8	4.8	2.0	1.0	0.5
10	100	10.7	11.4	11.5	11.5	11.5	11.5	11.5	5.4	0.8	0.4	0.2	0.1	0.0
20	0	7.1	19.0	20.0	20.7	21.0	21.1	21.2	93.9	15.1	8.3	3.5	1.8	0.9
20	100	20.4	21.1	21.1	21.2	21.2	21.2	21.2	5.4	1.0	0.6	0.2	0.1	0.1
30	0	11.9	27.3	28.9	30.0	30.4	30.7	30.9	127.3	24.2	13.7	6.0	3.1	1.6
30	100	30.2	30.7	30.8	30.8	30.9	30.9	30.9	4.5	1.1	0.6	0.3	0.1	0.1
40	0	16.1	35.1	37.4	39.1	39.8	40.1	40.5	164.7	36.9	21.5	9.6	5.0	2.6
40	100	40.1	40.4	40.4	40.5	40.5	40.5	40.5	2.8	0.9	0.5	0.2	0.1	0.1

DIMENSION ALONG AIRFLOW = 5 CM   DIMENSION ACROSS AIRFLOW = 1 CM

LEAF TEMPERATURES FOR RESISTANCES=   TRANSPIRATION EXP 6 FOR RES =

TA	RH	**0*	**1*	**2*	**5*	*10*	*20*	INF*	**0*	**1*	**2*	**5*	*10*	*20*
0	0	-4.2	2.3	3.0	3.6	3.8	3.9	4.0	24.7	5.0	2.8	1.2	0.6	0.3
0	100	2.2	3.6	3.7	3.9	3.9	3.9	4.0	5.4	1.2	0.7	0.3	0.1	0.1
10	0	1.4	10.6	11.7	12.6	13.0	13.1	13.3	36.5	8.5	4.9	2.2	1.1	0.6
10	100	11.4	12.8	13.0	13.2	13.3	13.3	13.3	6.0	1.6	0.9	0.4	0.2	0.1
20	0	6.3	18.3	20.1	21.5	22.0	22.3	22.6	50.6	13.6	8.1	3.7	1.9	1.0
20	100	20.8	22.0	22.3	22.5	22.5	22.6	22.6	5.7	1.9	1.1	0.5	0.3	0.1
30	0	10.5	25.4	27.9	30.0	30.9	31.4	31.9	66.5	20.6	12.6	5.9	3.1	1.6
30	100	30.4	31.3	31.5	31.7	31.8	31.8	31.9	4.7	1.9	1.2	0.6	0.3	0.2
40	0	14.3	31.9	35.3	38.3	39.5	40.3	41.1	84.1	29.4	18.7	9.1	4.9	2.6
40	100	40.2	40.6	40.8	40.9	41.0	41.0	41.1	2.9	1.4	0.9	0.5	0.3	0.1

AIRSPEED = 200. CM/SEC   RADIATION ABSORBED = 0.6 EXP 6 ERGS/CM2/SEC

DIMENSION ALONG AIRFLOW = 1 CM   DIMENSION ACROSS AIRFLOW = 5 CM

		LEAF TEMPERATURES FOR RESISTANCES=							TRANSPIRATION EXP 6 FOR RES =					
TA	RH	**0*	**1*	**2*	**5*	*10*	*20*	INF*	**0*	**1*	**2*	**5*	*10*	*20*
0	0	-3.3	1.1	1.4	1.7	1.7	1.8	1.8	33.6	4.7	2.5	1.1	0.5	0.3
0	100	1.3	1.7	1.8	1.8	1.8	1.8	1.8	3.8	0.6	0.3	0.1	0.1	0.0
10	0	3.5	10.3	10.8	11.2	11.4	11.5	11.5	53.5	8.6	4.7	2.0	1.0	0.5
10	100	10.9	11.4	11.5	11.5	11.5	11.5	11.5	4.6	0.8	0.4	0.2	0.1	0.0
20	0	9.4	19.1	20.0	20.7	21.0	21.1	21.2	78.9	14.7	8.2	3.5	1.8	0.9
20	100	20.5	21.1	21.1	21.2	21.2	21.2	21.2	4.7	1.0	0.6	0.2	0.1	0.1
30	0	14.6	27.4	28.9	30.0	30.4	30.7	30.9	109.2	23.7	13.5	5.9	3.1	1.6
30	100	30.3	30.7	30.8	30.8	30.9	30.9	30.9	4.1	1.1	0.6	0.3	0.1	0.1
40	0	19.2	35.3	37.4	39.1	39.8	40.1	40.5	144.0	36.0	21.2	9.6	5.0	2.6
40	100	40.1	40.4	40.4	40.5	40.5	40.5	40.5	2.6	0.9	0.5	0.2	0.1	0.1

DIMENSION ALONG AIRFLOW = 5 CM   DIMENSION ACROSS AIRFLOW = 5 CM

		LEAF TEMPERATURES FOR RESISTANCES=							TRANSPIRATION EXP 6 FOR RES =					
TA	RH	**0*	**1*	**2*	**5*	*10*	*20*	INF*	**0*	**1*	**2*	**5*	*10*	*20*
0	0	-2.6	2.4	3.1	3.6	3.8	3.9	4.0	20.0	4.8	2.7	1.2	0.6	0.3
0	100	2.5	3.6	3.7	3.9	3.9	3.9	4.0	4.5	1.1	0.6	0.3	0.1	0.0
10	0	3.4	10.7	11.8	12.6	13.0	13.1	13.3	30.4	8.2	4.8	2.1	1.1	0.6
10	100	11.7	12.8	13.0	13.2	13.3	13.3	13.3	5.2	1.5	0.9	0.4	0.2	0.1
20	0	8.7	18.4	20.1	21.5	22.3	22.6	22.6	43.0	13.1	7.9	3.6	1.9	1.0
20	100	21.0	22.1	22.3	22.5	22.6	22.6	22.6	5.2	1.8	1.1	0.5	0.3	0.1
30	0	13.6	25.6	28.0	30.0	30.9	31.4	31.9	57.8	19.9	12.4	5.9	3.1	1.6
30	100	30.5	31.3	31.5	31.7	31.8	31.8	31.9	4.3	1.8	1.2	0.6	0.3	0.2
40	0	17.5	32.2	35.4	38.3	39.6	40.3	41.1	74.2	28.5	18.4	9.0	4.9	2.6
40	100	40.2	40.6	40.8	40.9	41.0	41.0	41.1	2.7	1.4	0.9	0.5	0.3	0.1

AIRSPEED = 200. CM/SEC   RADIATION ABSORBED = 0.6 EXP 6 ERGS/CM2/SEC

DIMENSION ALONG AIRFLOW = 10 CM   DIMENSION ACROSS AIRFLOW = 5 CM

		LEAF TEMPERATURES FOR RESISTANCES=							TRANSPIRATION EXP 6 FOR RES =					
TA	RH	***0*	***1*	***2*	***5*	*10*	*20*	INF*	***0*	***1*	***2*	***5*	*10*	*20*
0	0	-2.0	3.3	4.2	4.9	5.2	5.3	5.5	16.4	4.8	2.9	1.3	0.7	0.3
0	100	3.3	4.8	5.1	5.3	5.4	5.4	5.5	4.8	1.5	0.9	0.4	0.2	0.1
10	0	3.7	11.0	12.4	13.6	14.1	14.3	14.6	24.2	8.0	4.9	2.2	1.2	0.6
10	100	12.2	13.7	14.0	14.3	14.5	14.5	14.6	5.4	2.0	1.2	0.6	0.3	0.2
20	0	8.7	18.2	20.2	22.0	22.8	23.2	23.6	33.6	12.4	7.8	3.7	2.0	1.0
20	100	21.3	22.6	23.0	23.3	23.5	23.5	23.6	5.3	2.3	1.4	0.7	0.4	0.2
30	0	13.1	24.8	27.5	30.1	31.2	31.9	32.6	44.4	18.1	11.8	5.8	3.2	1.7
30	100	30.7	31.6	31.9	32.3	32.4	32.5	32.6	4.4	2.2	1.5	0.7	0.4	0.2
40	0	17.0	30.7	34.3	37.8	39.4	40.4	41.4	56.3	25.1	16.9	8.7	4.8	2.6
40	100	40.3	40.8	41.0	41.2	41.3	41.4	41.4	2.8	1.6	1.1	0.6	0.3	0.2

DIMENSION ALONG AIRFLOW = 20 CM   DIMENSION ACROSS AIRFLOW = 5 CM

		LEAF TEMPERATURES FOR RESISTANCES=							TRANSPIRATION EXP 6 FOR RES =					
TA	RH	***0*	***1*	***2*	***5*	*10*	*20*	INF*	***0*	***1*	***2*	***5*	*10*	*20*
0	0	0.7	6.5	8.1	9.7	10.4	10.8	11.2	11.4	5.2	3.4	1.7	0.9	0.5
0	100	6.1	8.8	9.6	10.4	10.8	11.0	11.2	5.5	2.7	1.8	0.9	0.5	0.3
10	0	5.2	12.5	14.7	17.0	18.0	18.7	19.4	15.4	7.6	5.1	2.7	1.5	0.8
10	100	14.0	16.5	17.4	18.3	18.8	19.0	19.4	5.9	3.2	2.2	1.2	0.6	0.3
20	0	9.3	17.9	20.8	23.8	25.4	26.3	27.3	20.0	10.6	7.4	4.0	2.3	1.2
20	100	22.4	24.3	25.2	26.1	26.7	27.0	27.3	5.6	3.4	2.4	1.3	0.8	0.4
30	0	12.8	22.9	26.4	30.3	32.3	33.6	35.2	25.1	14.1	10.2	5.7	3.3	1.8
30	100	31.2	32.6	33.2	34.0	34.5	34.8	35.2	4.6	3.1	2.3	1.3	0.8	0.4
40	0	16.1	27.3	31.5	36.3	39.0	40.7	42.9	30.6	18.1	13.4	7.8	4.7	2.6
40	100	40.5	41.1	41.5	42.0	42.4	42.6	42.9	2.9	2.1	1.6	1.0	0.6	0.3

AIRSPEED = 200. CM/SEC   RADIATION ABSORBED = 0.6 EXP 6 ERGS/CM2/SEC

DIMENSION ALONG AIRFLOW = 1 CM   DIMENSION ACROSS AIRFLOW = 10 CM

		LEAF TEMPERATURES FOR RESISTANCES=							TRANSPIRATION EXP 6 FOR RES =					
TA	RH	**0*	**1*	**2*	**5*	*10*	*20*	INF*	**0*	**1*	**2*	**5*	*10*	*20*
0	0	-2.5	1.8	2.3	2.6	2.8	2.9	2.9	22.5	4.6	2.6	1.1	0.6	0.3
0	100	2.0	2.7	2.8	2.9	2.9	2.9	2.9	3.9	0.8	0.5	0.2	0.1	0.1
10	0	4.0	10.5	11.3	12.0	12.2	12.3	12.5	35.3	8.2	4.7	2.1	1.1	0.5
10	100	11.4	12.2	12.3	12.4	12.4	12.4	12.5	4.6	1.2	0.7	0.3	0.2	0.1
20	0	9.7	18.7	20.1	21.1	21.5	21.7	21.9	51.3	13.6	8.0	3.6	1.9	0.9
20	100	20.8	21.6	21.7	21.9	21.9	21.9	21.9	4.8	1.4	0.8	0.4	0.2	0.1
30	0	14.8	26.0	28.4	30.0	30.7	31.0	31.4	70.3	21.2	12.8	5.9	3.1	1.6
30	100	30.4	31.0	31.2	31.3	31.3	31.4	31.4	4.1	1.5	0.9	0.4	0.2	0.1
40	0	19.3	33.6	36.3	38.7	39.7	40.2	40.8	91.9	31.2	19.5	9.2	4.9	2.6
40	100	40.2	40.5	40.6	40.7	40.7	40.8	40.8	2.6	1.2	0.7	0.4	0.2	0.1

DIMENSION ALONG AIRFLOW = 5 CM   DIMENSION ACROSS AIRFLOW = 10 CM

		LEAF TEMPERATURES FOR RESISTANCES=							TRANSPIRATION EXP 6 FOR RES =					
TA	RH	**0*	**1*	**2*	**5*	*10*	*20*	INF*	**0*	**1*	**2*	**5*	*10*	*20*
0	0	-1.1	3.8	4.7	5.5	5.8	6.0	6.2	14.2	4.8	2.9	1.3	0.7	0.4
0	100	3.8	5.4	5.7	5.9	6.1	6.1	6.2	4.6	1.6	1.0	0.4	0.2	0.1
10	0	4.6	11.3	12.8	14.0	14.6	14.9	15.2	20.9	7.7	4.8	2.3	1.2	0.6
10	100	12.6	14.1	14.5	15.0	15.1	15.1	15.2	5.2	2.1	1.3	0.6	0.3	0.2
20	0	9.6	18.2	20.3	22.3	23.1	23.6	24.1	28.9	11.8	7.6	3.7	2.0	1.0
20	100	21.5	22.9	23.3	23.7	23.9	24.0	24.1	5.2	2.4	1.6	0.8	0.4	0.2
30	0	14.0	24.6	27.4	30.1	31.4	32.1	32.9	38.2	17.1	11.4	5.8	3.2	1.7
30	100	30.8	31.6	32.1	32.5	32.7	32.8	32.9	4.3	2.3	1.6	0.8	0.5	0.2
40	0	17.9	30.3	33.9	37.6	39.4	40.4	41.6	48.4	23.5	16.2	8.5	4.8	2.6
40	100	40.3	40.8	41.1	41.3	41.5	41.5	41.6	2.7	1.7	1.2	0.7	0.4	0.2

AIRSPEED = 200. CM/SEC   RADIATION ABSORBED = 0.6 EXP 6 ERGS/CM2/SEC

DIMENSION ALONG AIRFLOW = 10 CM   DIMENSION ACROSS AIRFLOW = 10 CM

LEAF TEMPERATURES FOR RESISTANCES=   TRANSPIRATION EXP 6 FOR RES =

TA	RH	**0*	**1*	**2*	**5*	*10*	*20*	INF*	**0*	**1*	**2*	**5*	*10*	*20*
0	0	0.0	5.0	6.3	7.4	7.9	8.4	8.4	12.0	4.9	3.1	1.5	0.8	0.4
0	100	5.0	7.0	7.5	8.0	8.2	8.3	8.4	4.9	2.1	1.3	0.6	0.3	0.2
10	0	5.3	11.9	13.7	15.4	16.1	16.5	17.0	17.1	7.5	4.9	2.4	1.3	0.7
10	100	13.3	15.3	15.8	16.4	16.7	16.8	17.0	5.4	2.6	1.7	0.9	0.5	0.2
20	0	9.9	18.1	20.6	23.0	24.1	24.8	25.5	23.1	11.0	7.4	3.8	2.1	1.1
20	100	22.0	23.6	24.2	24.8	25.1	25.3	25.5	5.3	2.9	2.0	1.0	0.6	0.3
30	0	14.0	23.8	26.9	30.2	31.8	32.8	33.9	29.8	15.4	10.7	5.7	3.2	1.7
30	100	31.1	32.2	32.7	33.2	33.5	33.7	33.9	4.4	2.7	1.9	1.1	0.6	0.3
40	0	17.6	29.0	32.8	37.0	39.2	40.6	42.2	37.2	20.5	14.7	8.1	4.7	2.6
40	100	40.4	41.0	41.3	41.7	41.9	42.0	42.2	2.8	1.9	1.4	0.8	0.5	0.3

DIMENSION ALONG AIRFLOW = 20 CM   DIMENSION ACROSS AIRFLOW = 10 CM

LEAF TEMPERATURES FOR RESISTANCES=   TRANSPIRATION EXP 6 FOR RES =

TA	RH	**0*	**1*	**2*	**5*	*10*	*20*	INF*	**0*	**1*	**2*	**5*	*10*	*20*
0	0	1.5	6.6	8.2	9.7	10.4	10.8	11.2	10.5	5.0	3.3	1.7	0.9	0.5
0	100	6.5	8.9	9.7	10.5	10.8	11.0	11.2	5.2	2.6	1.7	0.9	0.5	0.3
10	0	6.2	12.7	14.8	17.0	18.0	18.7	19.4	14.3	7.4	5.0	2.6	1.5	0.8
10	100	14.3	16.6	17.4	18.3	18.8	19.0	19.4	5.6	3.1	2.2	1.1	0.6	0.3
20	0	10.4	18.2	20.9	23.9	25.4	26.3	27.3	18.8	10.3	7.3	3.9	2.2	1.2
20	100	22.6	24.4	25.2	26.2	26.7	27.0	27.3	5.4	3.3	2.4	1.3	0.8	0.4
30	0	14.2	23.2	26.5	30.3	32.4	33.6	35.2	23.7	13.7	10.0	5.6	3.3	1.8
30	100	31.3	32.6	33.2	34.0	34.5	34.8	35.2	4.5	3.0	2.3	1.3	0.8	0.4
40	0	17.5	27.7	31.6	36.4	39.0	40.7	42.9	29.0	17.7	13.2	7.7	4.6	2.6
40	100	40.6	41.2	41.5	42.1	42.4	42.6	42.9	2.8	2.1	1.6	1.0	0.6	0.3

AIRSPEED = 200. CM/SEC   RADIATION ABSORBED = 0.8 EXP 6 ERGS/CM2/SEC

DIMENSION ALONG AIRFLOW = 1 CM   DIMENSION ACROSS AIRFLOW = 1 CM

TA	RH	LEAF TEMPERATURES FOR RESISTANCES=							TRANSPIRATION EXP 6 FOR RES =					
		**0*	**1*	**2*	**5*	*10*	*20*	INF*	**0*	**1*	**2*	**5*	*10*	*20*
0	0	-3.8	2.3	2.6	2.9	3.0	3.0	3.0	44.7	5.2	2.8	1.2	0.6	0.3
0	100	1.9	2.9	3.0	3.0	3.0	3.0	3.0	7.9	1.0	0.5	0.2	0.1	0.1
10	0	2.4	11.3	12.0	12.4	12.6	12.7	12.8	68.6	9.4	5.1	2.2	1.1	0.6
10	100	11.3	12.5	12.6	12.7	12.7	12.7	12.8	9.7	1.5	0.8	0.3	0.2	0.1
20	0	7.8	20.1	21.1	21.9	22.1	22.3	22.4	97.8	16.0	8.9	3.8	1.9	1.0
20	100	20.9	22.1	22.3	22.4	22.4	22.4	22.4	10.7	2.1	1.2	0.5	0.3	0.1
30	0	12.4	28.3	30.0	31.2	31.6	31.8	32.1	131.7	25.6	14.5	6.4	3.3	1.7
30	100	30.5	31.7	31.9	32.0	32.0	32.1	32.1	10.6	2.7	1.5	0.7	0.3	0.2
40	0	16.6	36.1	38.4	40.2	40.9	41.3	41.7	169.6	38.7	22.7	10.2	5.3	2.7
40	100	40.3	41.3	41.4	41.6	41.6	41.7	41.7	9.6	3.1	1.8	0.8	0.4	0.2

DIMENSION ALONG AIRFLOW = 5 CM   DIMENSION ACROSS AIRFLOW = 1 CM

TA	RH	LEAF TEMPERATURES FOR RESISTANCES=							TRANSPIRATION EXP 6 FOR RES =					
		**0*	**1*	**2*	**5*	*10*	*20*	INF*	**0*	**1*	**2*	**5*	*10*	*20*
0	0	-2.6	4.7	5.5	6.1	6.4	6.5	6.6	27.8	5.8	3.3	1.4	0.7	0.4
0	100	3.6	5.9	6.2	6.4	6.5	6.5	6.6	9.2	2.1	1.2	0.5	0.3	0.1
10	0	2.8	12.8	14.1	15.1	15.5	15.7	15.9	40.2	9.8	5.7	2.5	1.3	0.7
10	100	12.5	15.0	15.4	15.7	15.8	15.9	15.9	10.8	3.0	1.7	0.8	0.4	0.2
20	0	7.5	20.3	22.3	23.9	24.5	24.9	25.2	54.8	15.4	9.2	4.2	2.2	1.1
20	100	21.6	24.0	24.5	24.9	25.0	25.1	25.2	11.5	3.9	2.4	1.1	0.6	0.3
30	0	11.6	27.3	30.0	32.4	33.3	33.9	34.5	71.3	22.9	14.2	6.7	3.6	1.9
30	100	31.0	33.0	33.5	34.0	34.2	34.3	34.5	11.2	4.6	2.9	1.4	0.8	0.4
40	0	15.3	33.6	37.2	40.5	41.9	42.7	43.6	89.3	32.2	20.7	10.2	5.6	2.9
40	100	40.6	42.1	42.6	43.1	43.3	43.5	43.6	10.0	4.9	3.3	1.7	0.9	0.5

AIRSPEED = 200. CM/SEC   RADIATION ABSORBED = 0.8 EXP 6 ERGS/CM2/SEC

DIMENSION ALONG AIRFLOW = 1 CM   DIMENSION ACROSS AIRFLOW = 5 CM

TA	RH	**0*	**1*	**2*	**5*	*10*	*20*	INF*	**0*	**1*	**2*	**5*	*10*	*20*
		LEAF TEMPERATURES FOR RESISTANCES=							TRANSPIRATION EXP 6 FOR RES =					
0	0	-2.4	2.3	2.6	2.9	3.0	3.0	3.0	35.7	5.1	2.7	1.2	0.6	0.3
0	100	2.1	2.9	3.0	3.0	3.0	3.0	3.0	6.4	1.0	0.5	0.2	0.1	0.1
10	0	4.3	11.4	12.0	12.4	12.6	12.7	12.8	56.3	9.2	5.0	2.1	1.1	0.6
10	100	11.5	12.5	12.6	12.7	12.7	12.7	12.8	8.2	1.5	0.8	0.3	0.2	0.1
20	0	10.1	20.1	21.1	21.9	22.2	22.3	22.4	82.4	15.6	8.7	3.8	1.9	1.0
20	100	21.0	22.1	22.3	22.4	22.4	22.4	22.4	9.4	2.0	1.2	0.5	0.3	0.1
30	0	15.2	28.4	30.0	31.2	31.6	31.8	32.1	113.4	25.0	14.4	6.3	3.3	1.7
30	100	30.7	31.7	31.9	32.0	32.0	32.1	32.1	9.7	2.6	1.5	0.7	0.3	0.2
40	0	19.8	36.2	38.5	40.2	40.9	41.3	41.7	148.6	37.9	22.4	10.1	5.3	2.7
40	100	40.4	41.3	41.4	41.6	41.6	41.6	41.7	9.0	3.0	1.8	0.8	0.4	0.2

DIMENSION ALONG AIRFLOW = 5 CM   DIMENSION ACROSS AIRFLOW = 5 CM

TA	RH	**0*	**1*	**2*	**5*	*10*	*20*	INF*	**0*	**1*	**2*	**5*	*10*	*20*
		LEAF TEMPERATURES FOR RESISTANCES=							TRANSPIRATION EXP 6 FOR RES =					
0	0	-0.9	4.8	5.5	6.1	6.4	6.5	6.6	22.7	5.6	3.2	1.4	0.7	0.4
0	100	4.1	5.9	6.2	6.4	6.5	6.5	6.6	7.7	2.0	1.1	0.5	0.3	0.1
10	0	5.0	12.9	14.2	15.1	15.5	15.7	15.9	33.7	9.4	5.5	2.5	1.3	0.7
10	100	12.9	15.0	15.4	15.7	15.8	15.9	15.9	9.4	2.9	1.7	0.8	0.4	0.2
20	0	10.1	20.5	22.4	23.9	24.5	24.9	25.2	47.0	14.8	9.0	4.2	2.2	1.1
20	100	22.0	24.0	24.5	24.9	25.0	25.1	25.2	10.3	3.8	2.3	1.1	0.6	0.3
30	0	14.6	27.5	30.1	32.4	33.3	33.9	34.5	62.2	22.1	13.9	6.6	3.6	1.9
30	100	31.2	33.1	33.6	34.0	34.2	34.3	34.5	10.3	4.5	2.9	1.4	0.8	0.4
40	0	18.6	33.9	37.3	40.5	41.9	42.7	43.6	79.1	31.2	20.3	10.1	5.5	2.9
40	100	40.7	42.1	42.6	43.1	43.3	43.5	43.6	9.4	4.8	3.2	1.6	0.9	0.5

111

AIRSPEED = 200. CM/SEC   RADIATION ABSORBED = 0.8 EXP 6 ERGS/CM2/SEC

DIMENSION ALONG AIRFLOW = 10 CM   DIMENSION ACROSS AIRFLOW = 5 CM

TA	RH	LEAF TEMPERATURES FOR RESISTANCES=							TRANSPIRATION EXP 6 FOR RES =					
		**0*	**1*	**2*	**5*	*10*	*20*	INF*	**0*	**1*	**2*	**5*	*10*	*20*
0	0	0.3	6.4	7.5	8.4	8.7	8.9	9.1	19.3	5.9	3.5	1.6	0.8	0.4
0	100	5.4	7.9	8.4	8.8	8.9	9.0	9.1	8.3	2.7	1.6	0.7	0.4	0.2
10	0	5.8	13.9	15.6	17.0	17.5	17.8	18.2	27.8	9.6	5.9	2.7	1.5	0.8
10	100	13.8	16.5	17.1	17.7	17.9	18.0	18.2	9.9	3.7	2.3	1.1	0.6	0.3
20	0	10.5	20.9	23.2	25.3	26.1	26.6	27.2	37.7	14.5	9.2	4.4	2.4	1.2
20	100	22.5	25.1	25.9	26.5	26.8	27.0	27.2	10.7	4.7	3.0	1.5	0.8	0.4
30	0	14.7	27.2	30.3	33.2	34.5	35.3	36.1	49.0	20.7	13.7	6.9	3.8	2.0
30	100	31.6	33.8	34.5	35.3	35.7	35.9	36.1	10.6	5.4	3.7	1.9	1.0	0.5
40	0	18.4	32.9	36.8	40.7	42.6	43.7	44.9	61.3	28.3	19.3	10.1	5.7	3.0
40	100	40.9	42.6	43.3	44.0	44.4	44.7	44.9	9.6	5.6	4.0	2.2	1.2	0.7

DIMENSION ALONG AIRFLOW = 20 CM   DIMENSION ACROSS AIRFLOW = 5 CM

TA	RH	LEAF TEMPERATURES FOR RESISTANCES=							TRANSPIRATION EXP 6 FOR RES =					
		**0*	**1*	**2*	**5*	*10*	*20*	INF*	**0*	**1*	**2*	**5*	*10*	*20*
0	0	4.8	11.9	14.1	16.3	17.3	17.9	18.6	15.0	7.3	5.0	2.6	1.4	0.7
0	100	9.7	14.1	15.5	17.0	17.7	18.1	18.6	9.8	5.0	3.4	1.8	1.0	0.5
10	0	8.9	17.4	20.3	23.2	24.7	25.6	26.6	19.6	10.3	7.2	3.8	2.2	1.2
10	100	16.8	21.1	22.7	24.5	25.4	25.9	26.6	11.0	6.2	4.4	2.4	1.4	0.7
20	0	12.5	22.4	25.9	29.7	31.7	33.0	34.4	24.6	13.8	9.9	5.5	3.2	1.7
20	100	24.5	28.3	29.9	31.9	32.9	33.6	34.4	11.4	7.1	5.3	3.0	1.7	1.0
30	0	15.8	26.9	31.0	35.8	38.4	40.1	42.2	30.1	17.7	13.1	7.6	4.5	2.5
30	100	32.8	35.8	37.3	39.3	40.4	41.2	42.2	11.0	7.5	5.8	3.5	2.1	1.2
40	0	18.7	31.0	35.7	41.4	44.7	46.9	49.8	35.9	22.2	16.8	10.1	6.2	3.5
40	100	41.7	43.8	45.0	46.7	47.9	48.7	49.8	9.8	7.3	5.8	3.7	2.3	1.3

AIRSPEED = 200. CM/SEC   RADIATION ABSORBED = 0.8 EXP 6 ERGS/CM2/SEC

DIMENSION ALONG AIRFLOW = 1 CM   DIMENSION ACROSS AIRFLOW = 10 CM

TA	RH	**0*	**1*	**2*	**5*	*10*	*20*	INF*	**0*	**1*	**2*	**5*	*10*	*20*
		LEAF TEMPERATURES FOR RESISTANCES=							TRANSPIRATION EXP 6 FOR RES =					
0	0	-1.2	3.6	4.1	4.5	4.7	4.8	4.9	24.8	5.2	2.9	1.3	0.7	0.3
0	100		3.2	4.5	4.7	4.8	4.8	4.9	6.7	1.5	0.8	0.4	0.2	0.1
10	0	5.2	12.2	13.1	13.8	14.1	14.2	14.4	38.2	9.1	5.2	2.3	1.2	0.6
10	100	12.4	13.9	14.1	14.3	14.3	14.3	14.4	8.4	2.2	1.3	0.6	0.3	0.1
20	0	10.8	20.4	21.8	22.9	23.4	23.6	23.9	54.9	15.0	8.8	4.0	2.1	1.1
20	100	21.6	23.2	23.5	23.7	23.8	23.8	23.9	9.5	3.0	1.8	0.8	0.4	0.2
30	0	15.7	28.0	30.1	31.8	32.5	32.9	33.3	74.5	23.0	14.0	6.5	3.4	1.8
30	100	31.0	32.5	32.8	33.1	33.2	33.2	33.3	9.8	3.6	2.2	1.0	0.6	0.3
40	0	20.1	35.0	37.9	40.4	41.5	42.0	42.7	96.6	33.5	21.1	10.1	5.4	2.8
40	100	40.6	41.8	42.1	42.4	42.5	42.6	42.7	9.0	4.0	2.6	1.3	0.7	0.4

DIMENSION ALONG AIRFLOW = 5 CM   DIMENSION ACROSS AIRFLOW = 10 CM

TA	RH	**0*	**1*	**2*	**5*	*10*	*20*	INF*	**0*	**1*	**2*	**5*	*10*	*20*
		LEAF TEMPERATURES FOR RESISTANCES=							TRANSPIRATION EXP 6 FOR RES =					
0	0	1.6	7.2	8.4	9.4	9.8	10.0	10.3	17.1	6.0	3.7	1.7	0.9	0.5
0	100	6.2	8.8	9.4	9.8	10.0	10.2	10.3	8.0	2.9	1.8	0.8	0.4	0.2
10	0	6.9	14.5	16.3	17.8	18.5	18.8	19.2	24.4	9.5	6.0	2.9	1.5	0.8
10	100	14.5	17.2	18.0	18.6	18.9	19.1	19.2	9.5	4.0	2.6	1.2	0.7	0.3
20	0	11.7	21.2	23.6	25.9	26.9	27.5	28.1	33.0	14.1	9.2	4.6	2.5	1.3
20	100	23.0	25.6	26.5	27.3	27.6	27.9	28.1	10.4	5.0	3.3	1.7	0.9	0.5
30	0	15.9	27.3	30.4	33.6	35.0	35.9	36.9	42.7	19.9	13.4	6.9	3.8	2.0
30	100	31.9	34.1	35.0	35.9	36.3	36.6	36.9	10.3	5.7	4.0	2.1	1.2	0.6
40	0	19.6	32.8	36.7	40.8	42.9	44.1	45.6	53.3	26.8	18.7	10.0	5.7	3.1
40	100	41.1	42.8	43.6	44.4	44.9	45.2	45.6	9.4	5.8	4.3	2.4	1.4	0.7

AIRSPEED = 200. CM/SEC   RADIATION ABSORBED = 0.8 EXP 6 ERGS/CM2/SEC

DIMENSION ALONG AIRFLOW = 10 CM   DIMENSION ACROSS AIRFLOW = 10 CM

		LEAF TEMPERATURES FOR RESISTANCES=							TRANSPIRATION EXP 6 FOR RES =					
TA	RH	**0*	**1*	**2*	**5*	*10*	*20*	INF*	**0*	**1*	**2*	**5*	*10*	*20*
0	0	3.5	9.5	11.1	12.5	13.2	13.5	13.9	15.2	6.5	4.2	2.0	1.1	0.6
0	100	8.1	11.3	12.2	13.1	13.5	13.7	13.9	8.6	3.8	2.5	1.2	0.7	0.3
10	0	8.3	16.0	18.2	20.3	21.3	21.8	22.5	20.9	9.7	6.5	3.3	1.8	0.9
10	100	15.8	19.1	20.2	21.3	21.8	22.1	22.5	10.0	5.0	3.4	1.7	0.9	0.5
20	0	12.5	21.8	24.7	27.7	29.1	29.9	30.9	27.3	13.7	9.4	4.9	2.8	1.5
20	100	23.9	27.0	28.1	29.4	30.1	30.5	30.9	10.7	6.0	4.2	2.3	1.3	0.7
30	0	16.4	27.2	30.7	34.6	36.6	37.8	39.2	34.5	18.5	13.2	7.2	4.1	2.2
30	100	32.4	35.0	36.1	37.5	38.2	38.7	39.2	10.5	6.6	4.9	2.7	1.6	0.9
40	0	19.8	32.0	36.2	41.1	43.7	45.4	47.4	42.3	24.1	17.6	10.0	5.9	3.3
40	100	41.4	43.3	44.3	45.6	46.3	46.8	47.4	9.5	6.5	5.0	3.0	1.8	1.0

DIMENSION ALONG AIRFLOW = 20 CM   DIMENSION ACROSS AIRFLOW = 10 CM

		LEAF TEMPERATURES FOR RESISTANCES=							TRANSPIRATION EXP 6 FOR RES =					
TA	RH	**0*	**1*	**2*	**5*	*10*	*20*	INF*	**0*	**1*	**2*	**5*	*10*	*20*
0	0	5.8	12.1	14.2	16.3	17.3	17.9	18.6	14.0	7.1	4.9	2.5	1.4	0.7
0	100	10.3	14.2	15.6	17.0	17.7	18.1	18.6	9.2	4.9	3.4	1.8	1.0	0.5
10	0	10.0	17.7	20.4	23.3	24.7	25.6	26.6	18.3	10.0	7.0	3.8	2.2	1.2
10	100	17.3	21.2	22.8	24.5	25.4	25.9	26.6	10.4	6.1	4.3	2.4	1.3	0.7
20	0	13.8	22.7	26.0	29.8	31.7	33.0	34.4	23.2	13.4	9.7	5.4	3.2	1.7
20	100	24.9	28.4	30.0	31.9	33.0	33.6	34.4	11.0	7.0	5.2	3.0	1.7	1.0
30	0	17.2	27.3	31.2	35.8	38.4	40.1	42.2	28.5	17.3	12.9	7.5	4.5	2.5
30	100	33.1	35.9	37.4	39.3	40.4	41.2	42.2	10.7	7.4	5.7	3.4	2.1	1.2
40	0	20.3	31.4	35.9	41.5	44.7	46.9	49.8	34.2	21.7	16.5	10.0	6.1	3.5
40	100	41.8	43.9	45.0	46.8	47.9	48.7	49.8	9.6	7.1	5.7	3.6	2.3	1.3

AIRSPEED = 200. CM/SEC   RADIATION ABSORBED = 1.0 EXP 6 ERGS/CM2/SEC

DIMENSION ALONG AIRFLOW = 1 CM   DIMENSION ACROSS AIRFLOW = 1 CM

TA	RH	LEAF TEMPERATURES FOR RESISTANCES=							TRANSPIRATION EXP 6 FOR RES =					
		**0*	**1*	**2*	**5*	*10*	*20*	INF*	**0*	**1*	**2*	**5*	*10*	*20*
0	0	-3.0	3.4	3.8	4.1	4.2	4.2	4.3	47.4	5.6	3.0	1.3	0.6	0.3
0	100	2.6	4.0	4.2	4.2	4.3	4.3	4.3	11.2	1.4	0.8	0.3	0.2	0.1
10	0	3.1	12.5	13.1	13.6	13.8	13.9	14.0	72.0	10.1	5.5	2.3	1.2	0.6
10	100	11.9	13.6	13.8	13.9	13.9	14.0	14.0	14.1	2.2	1.2	0.5	0.3	0.1
20	0	8.4	21.1	22.2	23.0	23.3	23.5	23.6	101.8	17.1	9.5	4.1	2.1	1.1
20	100	21.3	23.2	23.4	23.5	23.6	23.6	23.6	16.0	3.2	1.8	0.8	0.4	0.2
30	0	13.0	29.3	31.0	32.3	32.8	33.0	33.3	136.3	27.1	15.4	6.8	3.5	1.8
30	100	30.8	32.7	32.9	33.1	33.2	33.2	33.3	16.8	4.3	2.5	1.1	0.6	0.3
40	0	17.1	37.0	39.4	41.3	42.1	42.5	42.9	174.6	40.6	23.9	10.8	5.6	2.9
40	100	40.5	42.1	42.4	42.7	42.8	42.8	42.9	16.4	5.3	3.2	1.4	0.8	0.4

DIMENSION ALONG AIRFLOW = 5 CM   DIMENSION ACROSS AIRFLOW = 1 CM

TA	RH	LEAF TEMPERATURES FOR RESISTANCES=							TRANSPIRATION EXP 6 FOR RES =					
		**0*	**1*	**2*	**5*	*10*	*20*	INF*	**0*	**1*	**2*	**5*	*10*	*20*
0	0	-1.0	7.0	8.0	8.7	8.9	9.1	9.2	31.0	6.8	3.8	1.7	0.9	0.4
0	100	4.9	8.2	8.6	9.0	9.1	9.1	9.2	13.1	3.1	1.8	0.8	0.4	0.2
10	0	4.2	15.0	16.5	17.6	18.2	18.3	18.5	44.1	11.2	6.5	2.9	1.5	0.8
10	100	13.5	17.1	17.7	18.2	18.4	18.4	18.5	15.7	4.5	2.7	1.2	0.6	0.3
20	0	8.7	22.3	24.5	26.3	27.0	27.4	27.8	59.3	17.3	10.5	4.8	2.5	1.3
20	100	22.3	25.9	26.6	27.3	27.5	27.7	27.8	17.3	6.1	3.7	1.7	0.9	0.5
30	0	12.7	29.1	32.1	34.7	35.8	36.4	37.0	76.2	25.3	15.8	7.6	4.1	2.1
30	100	31.5	34.7	35.5	36.3	36.6	36.8	37.0	17.7	7.5	4.8	2.3	1.3	0.7
40	0	16.2	35.3	39.1	42.7	44.3	45.2	46.2	94.5	35.1	22.8	11.4	6.2	3.3
40	100	40.9	43.5	44.4	45.3	45.7	45.9	46.2	17.0	8.6	5.8	2.9	1.6	0.9

AIRSPEED = 200. CM/SEC   RADIATION ABSORBED = 1.0 EXP 6 ERGS/CM2/SEC

DIMENSION ALONG AIRFLOW = 1 CM   DIMENSION ACROSS AIRFLOW = 5 CM

		LEAF TEMPERATURES FOR RESISTANCES=							TRANSPIRATION EXP 6 FOR RES =					
TA	RH	**0*	**1*	**2*	**5*	*10*	*20*	INF*	**0*	**1*	**2*	**5*	*10*	*20*
0	0	-1.5	3.4	3.8	4.1	4.2	4.2	4.3	38.0	5.5	3.0	1.2	0.6	0.3
0	100	2.9	4.1	4.2	4.2	4.2	4.3	4.3	9.2	1.4	0.7	0.3	0.2	0.1
10	0	5.0	12.5	13.2	13.6	13.8	13.9	14.0	59.3	9.9	5.4	2.3	1.2	0.6
10	100	12.2	13.6	13.8	13.9	13.9	14.0	14.0	12.0	2.2	1.2	0.5	0.3	0.1
20	0	10.8	21.2	22.3	23.0	23.3	23.5	23.6	86.0	16.6	9.3	4.0	2.1	1.1
20	100	21.5	23.2	23.4	23.5	23.6	23.6	23.6	14.2	3.1	1.8	0.8	0.4	0.2
30	0	15.8	29.4	31.1	32.3	32.8	33.0	33.3	117.5	26.4	15.2	6.7	3.5	1.8
30	100	31.0	32.7	32.9	33.1	33.2	33.2	33.3	15.4	4.2	2.4	1.1	0.6	0.3
40	0	20.3	37.1	39.5	41.4	42.1	42.5	42.9	153.3	39.7	23.6	10.7	5.6	2.9
40	100	40.7	42.2	42.4	42.7	42.8	42.8	42.9	15.4	5.2	3.1	1.4	0.8	0.4

DIMENSION ALONG AIRFLOW = 5 CM   DIMENSION ACROSS AIRFLOW = 5 CM

		LEAF TEMPERATURES FOR RESISTANCES=							TRANSPIRATION EXP 6 FOR RES =					
TA	RH	**0*	**1*	**2*	**5*	*10*	*20*	INF*	**0*	**1*	**2*	**5*	*10*	*20*
0	0	0.9	7.1	8.0	8.7	8.9	9.1	9.2	25.5	6.5	3.8	1.7	0.9	0.4
0	100	5.6	8.2	8.7	9.0	9.1	9.1	9.2	11.1	3.0	1.7	0.8	0.4	0.2
10	0	6.5	15.1	16.5	17.6	18.1	18.3	18.5	37.2	10.7	6.4	2.9	1.5	0.8
10	100	14.1	17.2	17.7	18.2	18.4	18.4	18.5	13.7	4.3	2.6	1.2	0.6	0.3
20	0	11.4	22.5	24.6	26.3	27.0	27.4	27.8	51.0	16.7	10.2	4.8	2.5	1.3
20	100	22.9	26.0	26.7	27.3	27.5	27.5	27.8	15.6	5.9	3.6	1.7	0.9	0.5
30	0	15.8	29.4	32.2	34.7	35.8	36.4	37.0	66.7	24.5	15.5	7.5	4.0	2.1
30	100	31.9	34.8	35.6	36.3	36.6	36.8	37.0	16.4	7.3	4.7	2.3	1.3	0.7
40	0	19.7	35.6	39.3	42.7	44.3	45.2	46.2	84.1	34.1	22.4	11.3	6.2	3.3
40	100	41.2	43.6	44.4	45.3	45.7	45.9	46.2	16.1	8.4	5.7	2.9	1.6	0.9

AIRSPEED = 200. CM/SEC   RADIATION ABSORBED = 1.0 EXP 6 ERGS/CM2/SEC

DIMENSION ALONG AIRFLOW = 10 CM   DIMENSION ACROSS AIRFLOW = 5 CM

LEAF TEMPERATURES FOR RESISTANCES=   TRANSPIRATION EXP 6 FOR RES =

TA	RH	**0*	**1*	**2*	**5*	*10*	*20*	INF*	**0*	**1*	**2*	**5*	*10*	*20*
0	0	2.6	9.5	10.7	11.8	12.2	12.4	12.7	22.5	7.2	4.4	2.0	1.1	0.5
0	100	7.3	10.9	11.6	12.2	12.4	12.5	12.7	12.0	4.0	2.5	1.1	0.6	0.3
10	0	7.7	16.8	18.6	20.3	21.0	21.3	21.7	31.6	11.3	7.1	3.3	1.8	0.9
10	100	15.4	19.2	20.2	21.0	21.3	21.5	21.7	14.5	5.7	3.6	1.7	0.9	0.5
20	0	12.2	23.4	26.0	28.4	29.5	30.2	30.7	42.0	16.8	10.8	5.3	2.9	1.5
20	100	23.7	27.5	28.6	29.7	30.2	30.4	30.7	16.2	7.4	4.8	2.4	1.3	0.7
30	0	16.2	29.5	32.9	36.2	37.7	38.6	39.6	53.7	23.6	15.7	8.0	4.4	2.4
30	100	32.5	35.9	37.0	38.0	38.9	39.2	39.6	16.8	8.8	6.1	3.1	1.8	0.9
40	0	19.8	35.1	39.3	43.6	45.7	46.9	48.4	66.4	31.6	21.8	11.6	6.6	3.5
40	100	41.6	44.3	45.5	46.8	47.5	47.9	48.4	16.4	9.7	7.0	3.9	2.2	1.2

DIMENSION ALONG AIRFLOW = 20 CM   DIMENSION ACROSS AIRFLOW = 5 CM

LEAF TEMPERATURES FOR RESISTANCES=   TRANSPIRATION EXP 6 FOR RES =

TA	RH	**0*	**1*	**2*	**5*	*10*	*20*	INF*	**0*	**1*	**2*	**5*	*10*	*20*
0	0	8.5	17.0	19.7	22.6	24.0	24.9	25.8	19.1	10.0	6.9	3.7	2.1	1.1
0	100	12.9	18.9	21.0	23.3	24.4	25.1	25.8	14.4	7.8	5.5	2.9	1.7	0.9
10	0	12.2	22.0	25.4	29.1	31.0	32.3	33.7	24.1	13.4	9.6	5.3	3.1	1.7
10	100	19.4	25.3	27.6	30.3	31.7	32.6	33.7	16.3	9.7	7.1	3.9	2.3	1.3
20	0	15.5	26.5	30.5	35.2	37.8	39.4	41.4	29.5	17.3	12.8	7.4	4.4	2.4
20	100	26.5	31.9	34.3	37.2	38.9	40.1	41.4	17.4	11.3	8.5	5.0	3.0	1.7
30	0	18.5	30.7	35.3	40.9	44.1	46.3	49.1	35.3	21.8	16.4	9.8	6.0	3.4
30	100	34.3	38.8	41.1	44.1	46.0	47.3	49.1	17.6	12.3	9.6	6.0	3.7	2.1
40	0	21.2	34.4	39.6	46.2	50.1	52.8	56.5	41.4	26.6	20.5	12.7	8.0	4.6
40	100	42.8	46.2	48.2	51.2	53.1	54.5	56.5	16.8	12.7	10.3	6.7	4.3	2.5

117

AIRSPEED = 200. CM/SEC   RADIATION ABSORBED = 1.0 EXP 6 ERGS/CM2/SEC

DIMENSION ALONG AIRFLOW = 1 CM   DIMENSION ACROSS AIRFLOW = 10 CM

		LEAF TEMPERATURES FOR RESISTANCES=							TRANSPIRATION EXP 6 FOR RES =					
TA	RH	**0*	**1*	**2*	**5*	*10*	*20*	INF*	**0*	**1*	**2*	**5*	*10*	*20*
0	0	0.2	5.4	6.0	6.4	6.6	6.7	6.8	27.3	5.9	3.3	1.4	0.7	0.4
0	100	4.5	6.3	6.5	6.7	6.7	6.8	6.8	9.6	2.2	1.2	0.5	0.3	0.1
10	0	6.4	13.9	14.9	15.7	16.0	16.1	16.3	41.4	10.2	5.9	2.6	1.3	0.7
10	100	13.4	15.5	15.9	16.1	16.2	16.3	16.3	12.3	3.3	1.9	0.8	0.4	0.2
20	0	11.9	21.9	23.5	24.8	25.2	25.5	25.8	58.7	16.4	9.7	4.4	2.3	1.2
20	100	22.4	24.7	25.1	25.5	25.6	25.7	25.8	14.4	4.6	2.7	1.2	0.6	0.3
30	0	16.7	29.4	31.7	33.6	34.3	34.8	35.2	78.8	25.0	15.3	7.1	3.8	1.9
30	100	31.6	33.9	34.4	34.8	35.0	35.1	35.2	15.5	5.9	3.7	1.7	0.9	0.5
40	0	20.9	36.3	39.4	42.1	43.2	43.9	44.6	101.4	36.0	22.8	11.0	5.9	3.1
40	100	41.1	43.0	43.6	44.1	44.3	44.4	44.6	15.5	7.0	4.5	2.2	1.2	0.6

DIMENSION ALONG AIRFLOW = 5 CM   DIMENSION ACROSS AIRFLOW = 10 CM

		LEAF TEMPERATURES FOR RESISTANCES=							TRANSPIRATION EXP 6 FOR RES =					
TA	RH	**0*	**1*	**2*	**5*	*10*	*20*	INF*	**0*	**1*	**2*	**5*	*10*	*20*
0	0	4.1	10.6	12.0	13.3	13.8	14.0	14.3	20.2	7.4	4.6	2.2	1.2	0.6
0	100	8.5	12.1	12.9	13.7	14.0	14.2	14.3	11.6	4.5	2.8	1.3	0.7	0.4
10	0	9.2	17.6	19.6	21.5	22.3	22.8	23.3	28.1	11.4	7.3	3.6	1.9	1.0
10	100	16.3	20.2	21.3	22.3	22.7	23.0	23.3	14.1	6.2	4.0	1.9	1.1	0.5
20	0	13.6	24.0	26.7	29.4	30.6	31.3	32.1	37.3	16.6	11.0	5.5	3.0	1.6
20	100	24.4	28.3	29.5	30.8	31.4	31.7	32.1	15.7	7.9	5.3	2.7	1.5	0.8
30	0	17.6	29.8	33.3	36.9	38.6	39.6	40.8	47.4	22.9	15.7	8.2	4.6	2.5
30	100	32.9	36.4	37.7	39.2	39.9	40.3	40.8	16.4	9.3	6.6	3.5	2.0	1.1
40	0	21.1	35.1	39.4	44.0	46.3	47.7	49.5	58.4	30.3	21.4	11.7	6.8	3.7
40	100	41.9	44.7	46.0	47.5	48.3	48.8	49.5	16.1	10.2	7.5	4.2	2.5	1.4

AIRSPEED = 200. CM/SEC   RADIATION ABSORBED = 1.0 EXP 6 ERGS/CM2/SEC

		DIMENSION ALONG AIRFLOW = 10 CM							DIMENSION ACROSS AIRFLOW = 10 CM					
		LEAF TEMPERATURES FOR RESISTANCES=							TRANSPIRATION EXP 6 FOR RES =					
TA	RH	**0*	**1*	**2*	***5*	*10*	*20*	INF*	**0*	**1*	**2*	***5*	*10*	*20*
0	0	6.6	13.7	15.7	17.6	18.4	18.9	19.4	18.7	8.4	5.6	2.8	1.5	0.8
0	100	10.9	15.4	16.8	18.1	18.7	19.0	19.4	12.6	5.9	3.9	2.0	1.1	0.6
10	0	11.1	19.8	22.4	25.1	26.3	27.1	27.9	24.9	12.2	8.3	4.3	2.4	1.3
10	100	18.0	22.8	24.4	26.1	26.9	27.3	27.9	14.8	7.8	5.3	2.8	1.6	0.8
20	0	15.0	25.3	28.6	32.2	33.9	35.0	36.3	31.9	16.7	11.7	6.3	3.6	1.9
20	100	25.6	30.1	31.9	33.9	34.9	35.5	36.3	16.3	9.5	6.8	3.7	2.1	1.1
30	0	18.6	30.3	34.3	38.8	41.2	42.7	44.5	39.4	22.0	15.9	8.9	5.2	2.9
30	100	33.8	37.7	39.4	41.6	42.8	43.6	44.5	16.8	10.8	8.0	4.6	2.7	1.5
40	0	21.8	34.9	39.5	45.1	48.1	50.1	52.6	47.5	28.0	20.8	12.2	7.3	4.1
40	100	42.4	45.5	47.1	49.3	50.6	51.5	52.6	16.3	11.4	8.9	5.4	3.3	1.9

		DIMENSION ALONG AIRFLOW = 20 CM							DIMENSION ACROSS AIRFLOW = 10 CM					
		LEAF TEMPERATURES FOR RESISTANCES=							TRANSPIRATION EXP 6 FOR RES =					
TA	RH	**0*	**1*	**2*	***5*	*10*	*20*	INF*	**0*	**1*	**2*	***5*	*10*	*20*
0	0	9.7	17.2	19.8	22.6	24.0	24.9	25.8	17.9	9.7	6.8	3.7	2.1	1.1
0	100	13.7	19.1	21.1	23.3	24.4	25.1	25.8	13.6	7.6	5.4	2.9	1.7	0.9
10	0	13.5	22.3	25.5	29.2	31.1	32.3	33.7	22.7	13.1	9.4	5.3	3.1	1.7
10	100	20.1	25.5	27.7	30.3	31.8	32.6	33.7	15.5	9.4	6.9	3.9	2.3	1.2
20	0	16.9	26.9	30.7	35.3	37.8	39.4	41.4	28.0	16.9	12.6	7.3	4.4	2.4
20	100	27.1	32.1	34.4	37.3	38.9	40.1	41.4	16.7	11.0	8.4	4.9	3.0	1.7
30	0	20.0	31.1	35.5	41.0	44.1	46.3	49.1	33.6	21.3	16.2	9.7	6.0	3.4
30	100	34.8	39.0	41.2	44.2	46.1	47.3	49.1	17.0	12.1	9.5	5.9	3.7	2.1
40	0	22.8	34.9	39.9	46.3	50.1	52.8	56.5	39.6	26.0	20.2	12.6	7.9	4.6
40	100	43.1	46.4	48.3	51.2	53.1	54.5	56.5	16.5	12.5	10.2	6.6	4.3	2.5

AIRSPEED = 400. CM/SEC   RADIATION ABSORBED = 0.4 EXP 6 ERGS/CM2/SEC

DIMENSION ALONG AIRFLOW = 1 CM   DIMENSION ACROSS AIRFLOW = 1 CM

TA	RH	**0*	**1*	**2*	**5*	*10*	*20*	INF*	**0*	**1*	**2*	**5*	*10*	*20*
		\multicolumn{7}{LEAF TEMPERATURES FOR RESISTANCES=}		TRANSPIRATION EXP 6 FOR RES =					
0	0	-5.7	-0.1	0.2	0.3	0.4	0.4	0.4	56.8	4.6	2.4	1.0	0.5	0.2
0	100	0.3	0.4	0.4	0.4	0.4	0.4	0.4	1.6	0.1	0.1	0.0	0.0	0.0
10	0	0.6	9.3	9.8	10.0	10.1	10.2	10.2	89.0	8.5	4.5	1.9	0.9	0.5
10	100	10.1	10.2	10.2	10.2	10.2	10.2	10.2	1.2	0.1	0.1	0.0	0.0	0.0
20	0	6.2	18.4	19.2	19.7	19.8	19.9	20.0	129.1	14.9	8.0	3.4	1.7	0.9
20	100	20.0	20.0	20.0	20.0	20.0	20.0	20.0	0.1	0.0	0.0	0.0	0.0	0.0
30	0	11.0	27.2	28.4	29.2	29.5	29.6	29.8	176.0	24.6	13.5	5.7	2.9	1.5
30	100													
40	0	15.2	35.5	37.3	38.5	39.0	39.2	39.5	228.9	38.5	21.7	9.4	4.8	2.5
40	100													

DIMENSION ALONG AIRFLOW = 5 CM   DIMENSION ACROSS AIRFLOW = 1 CM

TA	RH	**0*	**1*	**2*	**5*	*10*	*20*	INF*	**0*	**1*	**2*	**5*	*10*	*20*
		\multicolumn{7}{LEAF TEMPERATURES FOR RESISTANCES=}		TRANSPIRATION EXP 6 FOR RES =					
0	0	-6.4	-0.1	0.4	0.7	0.8	0.9	1.0	30.9	4.4	2.4	1.0	0.5	0.3
0	100	0.5	0.9	0.9	0.9	0.9	0.9	1.0	1.8	0.3	0.2	0.1	0.0	0.0
10	0	-0.5	8.7	9.5	10.1	10.3	10.4	10.5	46.8	7.9	4.3	1.9	0.9	0.5
10	100	10.2	10.5	10.5	10.5	10.5	10.5	10.5	1.3	0.2	0.1	0.1	0.0	0.0
20	0	4.6	17.0	18.3	19.3	19.6	19.8	20.0	66.1	13.2	7.5	3.3	1.7	0.9
20	100	20.0	20.0	20.0	20.0	20.0	20.0	20.0	0.1	0.0	0.0	0.0	0.0	0.0
30	0	9.0	24.8	26.7	28.3	28.8	29.2	29.5	88.3	20.7	12.1	5.4	2.8	1.4
30	100													
40	0	12.9	32.0	34.7	37.0	37.9	38.4	38.9	112.9	30.7	18.6	8.6	4.6	2.3
40	100													

AIRSPEED = 400. CM/SEC   RADIATION ABSORBED = 0.4 EXP 6 ERGS/CM2/SEC

DIMENSION ALONG AIRFLOW = 1 CM   DIMENSION ACROSS AIRFLOW = 5 CM

LEAF TEMPERATURES FOR RESISTANCES= TRANSPIRATION EXP 6 FOR RES =

TA	RH	**0*	**1*	**2*	**5*	*10*	*20*	INF*	**0*	**1*	**2*	**5*	*10*	*20*
0	0	-4.5	-0.0	0.2	0.3	0.4	0.4	0.4	45.1	4.5	2.4	1.0	0.5	0.2
0	100	0.3	0.4	0.4	0.4	0.4	0.4	0.4	1.3	0.1	0.1	0.0	0.0	0.0
10	0	2.4	9.3	9.8	10.0	10.1	10.2	10.2	72.8	8.4	4.5	1.9	0.9	0.5
10	100	10.1	10.2	10.2	10.2	10.2	10.2	10.2	1.0	0.1	0.1	0.0	0.0	0.0
20	0	8.4	18.5	19.2	19.7	19.8	19.9	20.0	108.3	14.6	7.9	3.3	1.7	0.9
20	100	20.0	20.0	20.0	20.0	20.0	20.0	20.0	0.1	0.0	0.0	0.0	0.0	0.0
30	0	13.7	27.2	28.4	29.2	29.5	29.6	29.8	151.1	24.2	13.4	5.7	2.9	1.5
30	100													
40	0	18.3	35.6	37.3	38.5	39.0	39.2	39.5	200.1	37.9	21.5	9.4	4.8	2.5
40	100													

DIMENSION ALONG AIRFLOW = 5 CM   DIMENSION ACROSS AIRFLOW = 5 CM

LEAF TEMPERATURES FOR RESISTANCES= TRANSPIRATION EXP 6 FOR RES =

TA	RH	**0*	**1*	**2*	**5*	*10*	*20*	INF*	**0*	**1*	**2*	**5*	*10*	*20*
0	0	-4.9	-0.1	0.4	0.7	0.8	0.9	1.0	24.8	4.2	2.3	1.0	0.5	0.3
0	100	0.6	0.9	0.9	0.9	0.9	0.9	1.0	1.5	0.3	0.1	0.1	0.0	0.0
10	0	1.4	8.7	9.5	10.1	10.3	10.4	10.5	38.7	7.6	4.3	1.8	0.9	0.5
10	100	10.3	10.5	10.5	10.5	10.5	10.5	10.5	1.1	0.2	0.1	0.1	0.0	0.0
20	0	6.9	17.1	18.3	19.3	19.6	19.8	20.0	56.1	12.8	7.3	3.2	1.7	0.9
20	100	20.0	20.0	20.0	20.0	20.0	20.0	20.0	0.1	0.0	0.0	0.0	0.0	0.0
30	0	11.8	24.9	26.8	28.3	28.9	29.2	29.5	76.4	20.1	11.9	5.4	2.8	1.4
30	100													
40	0	16.1	32.2	34.8	37.0	37.9	38.4	38.9	99.4	30.0	18.3	8.6	4.5	2.3
40	100													

5

AIRSPEED = 400. CM/SEC   RADIATION ABSORBED = 0.4 EXP 6 ERGS/CM2/SEC

DIMENSION ALONG AIRFLOW = 10 CM   DIMENSION ACROSS AIRFLOW = 5 CM

TA	RH	**0*	**1*	**2*	**5*	*10*	*20*	INF*	**0*	**1*	**2*	**5*	*10*	*20*
		LEAF TEMPERATURES FOR RESISTANCES=							TRANSPIRATION EXP 6 FOR RES =					
0	0	-5.1	-0.0	0.6	1.0	1.2	1.2	1.3	19.3	4.1	2.3	1.0	0.5	0.3
0	100	0.8	1.2	1.3	1.3	1.3	1.3	1.3	1.6	0.4	0.2	0.1	0.0	0.0
10	0	1.0	8.4	9.4	10.1	10.4	10.6	10.7	29.6	7.2	4.1	1.8	0.9	0.5
10	100	10.3	10.6	10.7	10.7	10.7	10.7	10.7	1.1	0.3	0.2	0.1	0.0	0.0
20	0	6.3	16.3	17.8	19.0	19.5	19.8	20.0	42.3	11.8	7.0	3.2	1.7	0.8
20	100	20.0	20.0	20.0	20.0	20.0	20.0	20.0	0.1	0.0	0.0	0.0	0.0	0.0
30	0	11.0	23.6	25.8	27.7	28.4	28.9	29.3	57.0	18.1	11.1	5.2	2.7	1.4
30	100													
40	0	15.1	30.3	33.3	36.0	37.2	37.8	38.5	73.5	26.3	16.7	8.1	4.4	2.3
40	100													

DIMENSION ALONG AIRFLOW = 20 CM   DIMENSION ACROSS AIRFLOW = 5 CM

TA	RH	**0*	**1*	**2*	**5*	*10*	*20*	INF*	**0*	**1*	**2*	**5*	*10*	*20*
		LEAF TEMPERATURES FOR RESISTANCES=							TRANSPIRATION EXP 6 FOR RES =					
0	0	-5.0	0.2	1.2	2.1	2.4	2.6	2.8	11.1	3.8	2.3	1.1	0.6	0.3
0	100	1.6	2.4	2.5	2.7	2.8	2.8	2.8	1.8	0.7	0.4	0.2	0.1	0.1
10	0	0.3	7.3	8.9	10.3	10.8	11.2	11.5	16.2	6.1	3.8	1.8	1.0	0.5
10	100	10.6	11.1	11.3	11.4	11.4	11.5	11.5	1.3	0.5	0.3	0.2	0.1	0.0
20	0	4.9	13.9	16.1	18.1	19.0	19.5	20.1	22.1	9.2	5.9	2.9	1.6	0.8
20	100	20.0	20.1	20.1	20.1	20.1	20.1	20.1	0.1	0.0	0.0	0.0	0.0	0.0
30	0	9.0	19.8	22.7	25.6	26.9	27.7	28.5	28.9	13.1	8.8	4.5	2.5	1.3
30	100													
40	0	12.6	25.2	28.8	32.6	34.5	35.6	36.9	36.3	17.9	12.4	6.6	3.7	2.0
40	100													

AIRSPEED = 400. CM/SEC   RADIATION ABSORBED = 0.4 EXP 6 ERGS/CM2/SEC

DIMENSION ALONG AIRFLOW = 1 CM   DIMENSION ACROSS AIRFLOW = 10 CM

LEAF TEMPERATURES FOR RESISTANCES=   TRANSPIRATION EXP 6 FOR RES =

TA	RH	**0*	**1*	**2*	**5*	*10*	*20*	INF*	**0*	**1*	**2*	**5*	*10*	*20*
0	0	-4.3	-0.0	0.3	0.5	0.6	0.7	0.7	29.0	4.3	2.3	1.0	0.5	0.3
0	100	0.5	0.7	0.7	0.7	0.7	0.7	0.7	1.3	0.2	0.1	0.0	0.0	0.0
10	0	2.4	9.0	9.6	10.1	10.2	10.3	10.4	46.3	7.9	4.3	1.8	0.9	0.5
10	100	10.2	10.3	10.4	10.4	10.4	10.4	10.4	1.0	0.2	0.1	0.0	0.0	0.0
20	0	8.3	17.7	18.7	19.5	19.7	19.9	20.0	68.5	13.5	7.6	3.3	1.7	0.9
20	100	20.0	20.0	20.0	20.0	20.0	20.0	20.0	0.1	0.0	0.0	0.0	0.0	0.0
30	0	13.5	26.0	27.5	28.7	29.1	29.4	29.6	95.0	21.7	12.5	5.5	2.9	1.5
30	100													
40	0	18.1	33.7	36.0	37.7	38.4	38.8	39.2	125.3	33.0	19.6	8.9	4.7	2.4
40	100													

DIMENSION ALONG AIRFLOW = 5 CM   DIMENSION ACROSS AIRFLOW = 10 CM

LEAF TEMPERATURES FOR RESISTANCES=   TRANSPIRATION EXP 6 FOR RES =

TA	RH	**0*	**1*	**2*	**5*	*10*	*20*	INF*	**0*	**1*	**2*	**5*	*10*	*20*
0	0	-4.6	0.0	0.6	1.1	1.3	1.4	1.5	16.2	4.0	2.3	1.0	0.5	0.3
0	100	0.9	1.4	1.4	1.5	1.5	1.5	1.5	1.5	0.4	0.2	0.1	0.1	0.0
10	0	1.6	8.3	9.3	10.1	10.5	10.6	10.8	24.9	6.9	4.1	1.8	0.9	0.5
10	100	10.4	10.7	10.7	10.8	10.8	10.8	10.8	1.1	0.3	0.2	0.1	0.0	0.0
20	0	6.9	16.0	17.6	18.9	19.4	19.7	20.0	35.7	11.2	6.8	3.1	1.6	0.8
20	100	20.0	20.0	20.0	20.0	20.0	20.0	20.0	0.1	0.0	0.0	0.0	0.0	0.0
30	0	11.7	23.1	25.4	27.4	28.2	28.7	29.2	48.3	17.0	10.6	5.1	2.7	1.4
30	100													
40	0	15.8	29.6	32.7	35.6	36.8	37.5	38.3	62.4	24.5	15.9	7.8	4.3	2.2
40	100													

AIRSPEED = 400. CM/SEC   RADIATION ABSORBED = 0.4 EXP 6 ERGS/CM2/SEC

DIMENSION ALONG AIRFLOW = 10 CM   DIMENSION ACROSS AIRFLOW = 10 CM

LEAF TEMPERATURES FOR RESISTANCES=   TRANSPIRATION EXP 6 FOR RES =

TA	RH	**0*	**1*	**2*	**5*	*10*	*20*	INF*	**0*	**1*	**2*	**5*	*10*	*20*
0	0	-4.5	0.1	0.9	1.6	1.8	1.9	2.1	12.8	3.8	2.3	1.0	0.5	0.3
0	100	1.3	1.8	1.9	2.0	2.0	2.1	2.1	1.6	0.5	0.3	0.1	0.1	0.0
10	0	1.3	7.9	9.1	10.2	10.6	10.9	11.1	19.2	6.4	3.9	1.8	1.0	0.5
10	100	10.5	10.9	11.0	11.0	11.1	11.1	11.1	1.1	0.4	0.3	0.1	0.1	0.0
20	0	6.4	15.0	16.9	18.6	19.3	19.6	20.1	27.1	10.1	6.3	3.0	1.6	0.8
20	100	20.0	20.0	20.0	20.0	20.1	20.1	20.1	0.1	0.0	0.0	0.0	0.0	0.0
30	0	10.9	21.6	24.2	26.6	27.7	28.2	28.9	36.1	14.9	9.7	4.8	2.6	1.4
30	100													
40	0	14.9	27.6	30.9	34.2	35.8	36.7	37.7	46.2	20.9	14.0	7.2	4.0	2.1
40	100													

DIMENSION ALONG AIRFLOW = 20 CM   DIMENSION ACROSS AIRFLOW = 10 CM

LEAF TEMPERATURES FOR RESISTANCES=   TRANSPIRATION EXP 6 FOR RES =

TA	RH	**0*	**1*	**2*	**5*	*10*	*20*	INF*	**0*	**1*	**2*	**5*	*10*	*20*
0	0	-4.3	0.3	1.3	2.1	2.4	2.6	2.8	10.2	3.7	2.2	1.0	0.6	0.3
0	100	1.7	2.4	2.5	2.7	2.8	2.8	2.8	1.7	0.6	0.4	0.2	0.1	0.0
10	0	1.1	7.4	9.0	10.3	10.8	11.2	11.5	14.9	5.9	3.7	1.8	1.0	0.5
10	100	10.7	11.1	11.3	11.4	11.4	11.5	11.5	1.2	0.5	0.3	0.2	0.1	0.0
20	0	6.0	14.0	16.1	18.1	19.0	19.5	20.1	20.6	8.9	5.8	2.9	1.6	0.8
20	100	20.0	20.1	20.1	20.1	20.1	20.1	20.1	0.1	0.0	0.0	0.0	0.0	0.0
30	0	10.2	20.0	22.8	25.6	26.9	27.7	28.5	27.1	12.8	8.7	4.5	2.5	1.3
30	100													
40	0	14.0	25.5	29.0	32.7	34.5	35.6	36.9	34.4	17.5	12.2	6.5	3.7	2.0
40	100													

AIRSPEED = 400. CM/SEC   RADIATION ABSORBED = 0.6 EXP 6 ERGS/CM2/SEC

DIMENSION ALONG AIRFLOW = 1 CM   DIMENSION ACROSS AIRFLOW = 1 CM

TA	RH	**0*	**1*	**2*	**5*	*10*	*20*	INF*	**0*	**1*	**2*	**5*	*10*	*20*
		LEAF TEMPERATURES FOR RESISTANCES=							TRANSPIRATION EXP 6 FOR RES =					
0	0	-5.1	0.8	1.0	1.2	1.2	1.3	1.3	59.3	4.8	2.5	1.0	0.5	0.3
0	100	0.8	1.3	1.3	1.3	1.3	1.3	1.3	4.8	0.4	0.2	0.1	0.0	0.0
10	0	1.1	10.1	10.6	10.9	11.0	11.0	11.1	92.2	9.0	4.7	2.0	1.0	0.5
10	100	10.5	11.0	11.1	11.1	11.1	11.1	11.1	5.5	0.6	0.3	0.1	0.1	0.0
20	0	6.6	19.2	20.0	20.5	20.7	20.8	20.9	133.0	15.6	8.4	3.5	1.8	0.9
20	100	20.3	20.8	20.8	20.9	20.9	20.9	20.9	5.4	0.8	0.4	0.2	0.1	0.0
30	0	11.4	27.9	29.2	30.0	30.3	30.5	30.6	180.5	25.7	14.1	6.0	3.1	1.6
30	100	30.2	30.5	30.6	30.6	30.6	30.6	30.6	4.5	0.9	0.5	0.2	0.1	0.1
40	0	15.6	36.2	38.0	39.3	39.8	40.1	40.4	233.8	39.9	22.5	9.8	5.0	2.6
40	100	40.1	40.3	40.3	40.3	40.3	40.4	40.4	2.8	0.7	0.4	0.2	0.1	0.0

DIMENSION ALONG AIRFLOW = 5 CM   DIMENSION ACROSS AIRFLOW = 1 CM

TA	RH	**0*	**1*	**2*	**5*	*10*	*20*	INF*	**0*	**1*	**2*	**5*	*10*	*20*
		LEAF TEMPERATURES FOR RESISTANCES=							TRANSPIRATION EXP 6 FOR RES =					
0	0	-5.2	1.7	2.2	2.6	2.7	2.8	2.8	33.7	4.9	2.7	1.1	0.6	0.3
0	100	1.6	2.6	2.7	2.8	2.8	2.8	2.8	5.5	0.9	0.5	0.2	0.1	0.1
10	0	0.5	10.4	11.3	11.9	12.2	12.3	12.4	50.4	8.7	4.8	2.1	1.1	0.5
10	100	11.0	12.1	12.2	12.3	12.4	12.4	12.4	6.1	1.2	0.7	0.3	0.1	0.1
20	0	5.5	18.6	20.0	21.1	21.5	21.7	21.9	70.3	14.5	8.2	3.6	1.9	0.9
20	100	20.6	21.6	21.7	21.8	21.9	21.9	21.9	5.8	1.5	0.9	0.4	0.2	0.1
30	0	9.8	26.2	28.4	30.0	30.7	31.0	31.4	93.0	22.5	13.2	6.0	3.1	1.6
30	100	30.3	31.0	31.2	31.3	31.3	31.3	31.4	4.7	1.5	0.9	0.4	0.2	0.1
40	0	13.6	33.3	36.3	38.7	39.7	40.2	40.8	118.0	33.0	20.1	9.4	5.0	2.6
40	100	40.1	40.5	40.6	40.7	40.7	40.7	40.8	2.9	1.2	0.7	0.4	0.2	0.1

AIRSPEED = 400. CM/SEC   RADIATION ABSORBED = 0.6 EXP 6 ERGS/CM2/SEC

DIMENSION ALONG AIRFLOW = 1 CM   DIMENSION ACROSS AIRFLOW = 5 CM

TA	RH	LEAF TEMPERATURES FOR RESISTANCES=							TRANSPIRATION EXP 6 FOR RES =					
		**0*	**1*	**2*	**5*	*10*	*20*	INF*	**0*	**1*	**2*	***5*	*10*	*20*
0	0	-3.8	0.8	1.0	1.2	1.2	1.3	1.3	47.3	4.7	2.5	1.0	0.5	0.3
0	100	0.9	1.3	1.3	1.3	1.3	1.3	1.3	3.9	0.4	0.2	0.1	0.0	0.0
10	0	3.0	10.2	10.6	10.9	11.0	11.0	11.1	75.6	8.8	4.7	2.0	1.0	0.5
10	100	10.6	11.0	11.1	11.1	11.1	11.1	11.1	4.7	0.6	0.3	0.1	0.1	0.0
20	0	8.9	19.3	20.0	20.5	20.7	20.8	20.9	111.8	15.4	8.3	3.5	1.8	0.9
20	100	20.4	20.8	20.8	20.9	20.9	20.9	20.9	4.8	0.8	0.4	0.2	0.1	0.0
30	0	14.1	28.0	29.2	30.0	30.3	30.5	30.6	155.2	25.2	14.0	6.0	3.1	1.6
30	100	30.2	30.5	30.6	30.6	30.6	30.6	30.6	4.1	0.8	0.5	0.2	0.1	0.1
40	0	18.7	36.3	38.0	39.3	39.8	40.1	40.4	204.7	39.3	22.3	9.8	5.0	2.6
40	100	40.1	40.3	40.3	40.3	40.3	40.4	40.4	2.7	0.7	0.4	0.2	0.1	0.0

DIMENSION ALONG AIRFLOW = 5 CM   DIMENSION ACROSS AIRFLOW = 5 CM

TA	RH	LEAF TEMPERATURES FOR RESISTANCES=							TRANSPIRATION EXP 6 FOR RES =					
		**0*	**1*	**2*	***5*	*10*	*20*	INF*	**0*	**1*	**2*	***5*	*10*	*20*
0	0	-3.6	1.7	2.2	2.6	2.7	2.8	2.8	27.3	4.8	2.6	1.1	0.6	0.3
0	100	1.8	2.6	2.7	2.8	2.8	2.8	2.8	4.6	0.8	0.5	0.2	0.1	0.1
10	0	2.5	10.4	11.3	11.9	12.2	12.3	12.4	41.9	8.5	4.8	2.1	1.1	0.5
10	100	11.2	12.1	12.2	12.3	12.4	12.4	12.4	5.3	1.2	0.7	0.3	0.1	0.1
20	0	8.0	18.7	20.0	21.1	21.5	21.7	21.9	59.9	14.1	8.1	3.6	1.9	0.9
20	100	20.7	21.6	21.7	21.8	21.9	21.9	21.9	5.3	1.5	0.8	0.4	0.2	0.1
30	0	12.7	26.4	28.4	30.0	30.7	31.0	31.4	80.8	21.9	13.0	5.9	3.1	1.6
30	100	30.4	31.0	31.2	31.3	31.3	31.3	31.4	4.4	1.5	0.9	0.4	0.2	0.1
40	0	16.9	33.5	36.3	38.7	39.7	40.2	40.8	104.2	32.2	19.9	9.3	5.0	2.6
40	100	40.1	40.5	40.6	40.7	40.7	40.7	40.8	2.8	1.2	0.7	0.4	0.2	0.1

AIRSPEED = 400. CM/SEC   RADIATION ABSORBED = 0.6 EXP 6 ERGS/CM2/SEC

DIMENSION ALONG AIRFLOW = 10 CM   DIMENSION ACROSS AIRFLOW = 5 CM
LEAF TEMPERATURES FOR RESISTANCES=   TRANSPIRATION EXP 6 FOR RES =

TA	RH	**0*	**1*	**2*	**5*	*10*	*20*	INF*	**0*	**1*	**2*	**5*	*10*	*20*
0	0	-3.3	2.4	3.1	3.6	3.8	3.9	4.0	22.0	4.8	2.7	1.2	0.6	0.3
0	100	2.4	3.6	3.7	3.9	3.9	3.9	4.0	4.9	1.1	0.6	0.3	0.1	0.1
10	0	2.6	10.6	11.8	12.6	13.0	13.1	13.3	32.9	8.3	4.8	2.1	1.1	0.6
10	100	11.6	12.8	13.0	13.2	13.3	13.3	13.3	5.5	1.6	0.9	0.4	0.2	0.1
20	0	7.7	18.4	20.1	21.6	22.0	22.3	22.6	46.2	13.4	8.0	3.6	1.9	1.0
20	100	20.9	22.0	22.3	22.5	22.5	22.6	22.6	5.4	1.9	1.1	0.5	0.3	0.1
30	0	12.2	25.5	28.0	30.0	30.9	31.4	31.9	61.5	20.2	12.5	5.9	3.1	1.6
30	100	30.5	31.3	31.5	31.7	31.8	31.8	31.9	4.5	1.9	1.2	0.6	0.3	0.2
40	0	16.2	32.1	35.3	38.3	39.5	40.3	41.1	78.4	28.9	18.5	9.1	4.9	2.6
40	100	40.2	40.6	40.8	40.9	41.0	41.0	41.1	2.8	1.4	0.9	0.5	0.3	0.1

DIMENSION ALONG AIRFLOW = 20 CM   DIMENSION ACROSS AIRFLOW = 5 CM
LEAF TEMPERATURES FOR RESISTANCES=   TRANSPIRATION EXP 6 FOR RES =

TA	RH	**0*	**1*	**2*	**5*	*10*	*20*	INF*	**0*	**1*	**2*	**5*	*10*	*20*
0	0	-1.5	4.8	6.2	7.4	7.9	8.1	8.4	14.2	5.1	3.2	1.5	0.8	0.4
0	100	4.5	6.9	7.5	8.0	8.2	8.3	8.4	5.6	2.2	1.4	0.6	0.3	0.2
10	0	3.3	11.6	13.6	15.3	16.1	16.5	17.0	19.9	8.0	5.1	2.5	1.3	0.7
10	100	12.9	15.2	15.8	16.4	16.7	16.9	17.0	6.1	2.7	1.8	0.9	0.5	0.2
20	0	7.6	17.8	20.4	23.0	24.1	24.8	25.5	26.4	11.6	7.7	3.9	2.1	1.1
20	100	21.7	23.5	24.2	24.8	25.1	25.3	25.5	5.8	3.0	2.0	1.0	0.6	0.3
30	0	11.4	23.3	26.7	30.2	31.8	32.8	33.9	33.5	16.1	11.0	5.8	3.2	1.7
30	100	30.9	32.1	32.6	33.2	33.5	33.7	33.9	4.7	2.8	2.0	1.1	0.6	0.3
40	0	14.8	28.4	32.5	36.9	39.2	40.5	42.2	41.4	21.3	15.1	8.3	4.8	2.6
40	100	40.3	41.0	41.3	41.7	41.9	42.0	42.2	2.9	1.9	1.4	0.8	0.5	0.3

AIRSPEED = 400. CM/SEC   RADIATION ABSORBED = 0.6 EXP 6 ERGS/CM2/SEC

DIMENSION ALONG AIRFLOW = 1 CM   DIMENSION ACROSS AIRFLOW = 10 CM

TA	RH	LEAF TEMPERATURES FOR RESISTANCES=							TRANSPIRATION EXP 6 FOR RES =					
		**0*	**1*	**2*	**5*	*10*	*20*	INF*	**0*	**1*	**2*	**5*	*10*	*20*
0	0	-3.3	1.3	1.6	1.9	2.0	2.0	2.1	31.2	4.7	2.6	1.1	0.5	0.3
0	100	1.4	2.0	2.0	2.1	2.1	2.1	2.1	4.0	0.6	0.3	0.1	0.1	0.0
10	0	3.3	10.3	11.0	11.4	11.6	11.7	11.8	49.2	8.5	4.7	2.0	1.0	0.5
10	100	11.0	11.6	11.7	11.7	11.7	11.7	11.8	4.7	0.9	0.5	0.2	0.1	0.1
20	0	9.1	19.0	20.0	20.8	21.1	21.2	21.4	72.0	14.5	8.2	3.5	1.8	0.9
20	100	20.6	21.2	21.3	21.4	21.4	21.4	21.4	4.9	1.1	0.6	0.3	0.1	0.1
30	0	14.2	27.1	28.8	30.0	30.5	30.7	31.0	99.1	23.1	13.4	5.9	3.1	1.6
30	100	30.3	30.8	30.9	31.0	31.0	31.0	31.0	4.2	1.2	0.7	0.3	0.2	0.1
40	0	18.7	34.8	37.1	39.0	39.7	40.1	40.6	129.9	34.9	20.8	9.5	5.0	2.6
40	100	40.1	40.4	40.5	40.5	40.6	40.6	40.6	2.7	0.9	0.6	0.3	0.1	0.1

DIMENSION ALONG AIRFLOW = 5 CM   DIMENSION ACROSS AIRFLOW = 10 CM

TA	RH	LEAF TEMPERATURES FOR RESISTANCES=							TRANSPIRATION EXP 6 FOR RES =					
		**0*	**1*	**2*	**5*	*10*	*20*	INF*	**0*	**1*	**2*	**5*	*10*	*20*
0	0	-2.5	2.7	3.5	4.0	4.3	4.4	4.5	18.8	4.8	2.8	1.2	0.6	0.3
0	100	2.8	4.0	4.2	4.4	4.4	4.5	4.5	4.7	1.3	0.7	0.3	0.2	0.1
10	0	3.4	10.8	12.0	13.0	13.4	13.6	13.8	28.2	8.1	4.8	2.2	1.1	0.6
10	100	11.8	13.2	13.4	13.6	13.7	13.7	13.8	5.3	1.7	1.0	0.5	0.2	0.1
20	0	8.5	18.3	20.1	21.7	22.3	22.6	23.0	39.5	12.9	7.9	3.7	1.9	1.0
20	100	21.1	22.3	22.5	22.8	22.9	22.9	23.0	5.3	2.0	1.2	0.6	0.3	0.2
30	0	13.0	25.3	27.8	30.1	31.0	31.6	32.1	52.6	19.2	12.2	5.8	3.1	1.6
30	100	30.6	31.4	31.7	31.9	32.0	32.1	32.1	4.4	2.0	1.3	0.6	0.3	0.2
40	0	17.1	31.6	35.0	38.1	39.5	40.3	41.2	67.2	27.2	17.8	8.9	4.9	2.6
40	100	40.2	40.7	40.8	41.0	41.1	41.1	41.2	2.8	1.5	1.0	0.5	0.3	0.1

AIRSPEED = 400. CM/SEC   RADIATION ABSORBED = 0.6 EXP 6 ERGS/CM2/SEC

DIMENSION ALONG AIRFLOW = 10 CM   DIMENSION ACROSS AIRFLOW = 10 CM

TA	RH	LEAF TEMPERATURES FOR RESISTANCES=							TRANSPIRATION EXP 6 FOR RES =					
		**0*	**1*	**2*	**5*	*10*	*20*	INF*	**0*	**1*	**2*	***5*	*10*	*20*
0	0	-1.8	3.7	4.7	5.5	5.8	6.0	6.2	15.5	4.9	2.9	1.3	0.7	0.4
0	100	3.7	5.3	5.7	5.9	6.1	6.1	6.2	5.0	1.6	1.0	0.5	0.2	0.1
10	0	3.7	11.2	12.7	14.0	14.6	14.9	15.2	22.6	7.9	4.9	2.3	1.2	0.6
10	100	12.4	14.1	14.5	14.9	15.0	15.1	15.2	5.6	2.2	1.3	0.6	0.3	0.2
20	0	8.5	18.1	20.3	22.2	23.1	23.6	24.1	31.0	12.1	7.7	3.7	2.0	1.0
20	100	21.4	22.9	23.3	23.7	23.9	24.0	24.1	5.4	2.5	1.6	0.8	0.4	0.2
30	0	12.8	24.4	27.3	30.1	31.4	32.1	32.9	40.6	17.5	11.5	5.8	3.2	1.7
30	100	30.7	31.8	32.1	32.5	32.7	32.8	32.9	4.5	2.4	1.6	0.8	0.5	0.2
40	0	16.6	30.1	33.8	37.6	39.3	40.4	41.6	51.1	24.0	16.4	8.6	4.8	2.6
40	100	40.3	40.8	41.1	41.3	41.5	41.5	41.6	2.8	1.7	1.2	0.7	0.4	0.2

DIMENSION ALONG AIRFLOW = 20 CM   DIMENSION ACROSS AIRFLOW = 10 CM

TA	RH	LEAF TEMPERATURES FOR RESISTANCES=							TRANSPIRATION EXP 6 FOR RES =					
		**0*	**1*	**2*	***5*	*10*	*20*	INF*	**0*	**1*	**2*	***5*	*10*	*20*
0	0	-0.7	5.0	6.2	7.4	7.9	8.1	8.4	13.1	5.0	3.1	1.5	0.8	0.4
0	100	4.8	6.9	7.5	8.0	8.2	8.3	8.4	5.3	2.1	1.3	0.6	0.3	0.2
10	0	4.3	11.7	13.6	15.4	16.1	16.5	17.0	18.5	7.8	5.0	2.5	1.3	0.7
10	100	13.1	15.2	15.8	16.4	16.7	16.9	17.0	5.8	2.7	1.7	0.9	0.5	0.2
20	0	8.8	17.9	20.5	23.0	24.1	24.8	25.5	24.7	11.3	7.6	3.8	2.1	1.1
20	100	21.8	23.6	24.2	24.8	25.1	25.3	25.5	5.5	2.9	2.0	1.0	0.6	0.3
30	0	12.7	23.6	26.8	30.2	31.8	32.8	33.9	31.7	15.7	10.9	5.7	3.2	1.7
30	100	30.9	32.1	32.6	33.2	33.5	33.7	33.9	4.6	2.7	2.0	1.1	0.6	0.3
40	0	16.2	28.7	32.6	37.0	39.2	40.5	42.2	39.3	20.9	14.9	8.2	4.7	2.6
40	100	40.4	41.0	41.3	41.7	41.9	42.0	42.2	2.8	1.9	1.4	0.8	0.5	0.3

AIRSPEED = 400. CM/SEC   RADIATION ABSORBED = 0.8 EXP 6 ERGS/CM2/SEC

DIMENSION ALONG AIRFLOW = 1 CM   DIMENSION ACROSS AIRFLOW = 1 CM
LEAF TEMPERATURES FOR RESISTANCES=   TRANSPIRATION EXP 6 FOR RES =

TA	RH	**0*	**1*	**2*	**5*	*10*	*20*	INF*	**0*	**1*	**2*	**5*	*10*	*20*
0	0	-4.6	1.6	1.9	2.1	2.1	2.1	2.2	61.9	5.1	2.7	1.1	0.6	0.3
0	100	1.3	2.1	2.1	2.2	2.2	2.2	2.2	8.0	0.7	0.4	0.2	0.1	0.0
10	0	1.7	11.0	11.4	11.7	11.9	11.9	12.0	95.5	9.4	5.0	2.1	1.1	0.5
10	100	10.9	11.8	11.9	11.9	12.0	12.0	12.0	9.8	1.1	0.6	0.2	0.1	0.1
20	0	7.1	20.0	20.8	21.3	21.5	21.6	21.7	136.9	16.4	8.8	3.7	1.9	0.9
20	100	20.6	21.6	21.6	21.7	21.7	21.7	21.7	10.8	1.6	0.8	0.4	0.2	0.1
30	0	11.8	28.7	30.0	30.8	31.2	31.3	31.5	185.0	26.8	14.7	6.3	3.2	1.6
30	100	30.4	31.3	31.4	31.4	31.5	31.5	31.5	10.7	2.0	1.1	0.5	0.2	0.1
40	0	15.9	36.9	38.8	40.2	40.7	40.9	41.2	238.7	41.4	23.4	10.2	5.3	2.7
40	100	40.2	41.0	41.1	41.2	41.2	41.2	41.2	9.7	2.4	1.4	0.6	0.3	0.2

DIMENSION ALONG AIRFLOW = 5 CM   DIMENSION ACROSS AIRFLOW = 1 CM
LEAF TEMPERATURES FOR RESISTANCES=   TRANSPIRATION EXP 6 FOR RES =

TA	RH	**0*	**1*	**2*	**5*	*10*	*20*	INF*	**0*	**1*	**2*	**5*	*10*	*20*
0	0	-4.0	3.4	4.0	4.4	4.6	4.7	4.7	36.7	5.6	3.0	1.3	0.7	0.3
0	100	2.6	4.4	4.5	4.7	4.7	4.7	4.7	9.3	1.5	0.8	0.4	0.2	0.1
10	0	1.6	12.0	13.0	13.7	14.0	14.1	14.3	54.1	9.7	5.4	2.3	1.2	0.6
10	100	11.7	13.8	14.0	14.2	14.2	14.2	14.3	10.9	2.3	1.3	0.5	0.3	0.1
20	0	6.4	20.1	21.7	22.9	23.3	23.5	23.8	74.6	15.9	9.1	4.0	2.1	1.1
20	100	21.1	23.1	23.4	23.6	23.7	23.7	23.8	11.6	3.1	1.8	0.8	0.4	0.2
30	0	10.6	27.7	30.0	31.7	32.5	32.8	33.2	97.7	24.4	14.4	6.5	3.4	1.8
30	100	30.7	32.4	32.7	33.0	33.1	33.2	33.2	11.3	3.8	2.3	1.0	0.5	0.3
40	0	14.3	34.7	37.8	40.4	41.4	42.0	42.6	123.1	35.4	21.8	10.2	5.4	2.8
40	100	40.4	41.7	42.0	42.3	42.5	42.5	42.6	10.1	4.1	2.6	1.2	0.7	0.3

AIRSPEED = 400. CM/SEC   RADIATION ABSORBED = 0.8 EXP 6 ERGS/CM2/SEC
DIMENSION ALONG AIRFLOW = 1 CM   DIMENSION ACROSS AIRFLOW = 5 CM

TA	RH	LEAF TEMPERATURES FOR RESISTANCES=							TRANSPIRATION EXP 6 FOR RES =					
		**0*	**1*	**2*	**5*	*10*	*20*	INF*	**0*	**1*	**2*	**5*	*10*	*20*
0	0	-3.2	1.6	1.9	2.1	2.1	2.1	2.2	49.4	5.0	2.7	1.1	0.6	0.3
0	100	1.5	2.1	2.1	2.2	2.2	2.2	2.2	6.5	0.7	0.4	0.2	0.1	0.0
10	0	3.5	11.0	11.4	11.7	11.9	11.9	12.0	78.5	9.3	5.0	2.1	1.0	0.5
10	100	11.1	11.9	11.9	11.9	12.0	12.0	12.0	8.4	1.1	0.6	0.2	0.1	0.1
20	0	9.4	20.0	20.8	21.4	21.5	21.6	21.7	115.4	16.1	8.7	3.7	1.9	0.9
20	100	20.7	21.6	21.7	21.7	21.7	21.7	21.7	9.6	1.5	0.8	0.4	0.2	0.1
30	0	14.6	28.7	30.0	30.8	31.2	31.3	31.5	159.3	26.3	14.6	6.3	3.2	1.6
30	100	30.5	31.3	31.4	31.4	31.5	31.5	31.5	9.8	2.0	1.1	0.5	0.2	0.1
40	0	19.1	37.0	38.8	40.2	40.7	40.9	41.2	209.3	40.8	23.2	10.2	5.3	2.7
40	100	40.3	41.0	41.1	41.2	41.2	41.2	41.2	9.1	2.4	1.4	0.6	0.3	0.2

DIMENSION ALONG AIRFLOW = 5 CM   DIMENSION ACROSS AIRFLOW = 5 CM

TA	RH	LEAF TEMPERATURES FOR RESISTANCES=							TRANSPIRATION EXP 6 FOR RES =					
		**0*	**1*	**2*	**5*	*10*	*20*	INF*	**0*	**1*	**2*	**5*	*10*	*20*
0	0	-2.3	3.5	4.0	4.4	4.6	4.7	4.7	29.9	5.4	3.0	1.3	0.7	0.3
0	100	2.9	4.4	4.5	4.7	4.7	4.7	4.7	7.7	1.5	0.8	0.4	0.2	0.1
10	0	3.7	12.1	13.0	13.7	14.0	14.1	14.3	45.2	9.4	5.3	2.3	1.2	0.6
10	100	12.1	13.8	14.0	14.2	14.2	14.2	14.3	9.5	2.2	1.2	0.5	0.3	0.1
20	0	8.9	20.2	21.7	22.9	23.3	23.5	23.8	63.8	15.4	8.9	4.0	2.1	1.1
20	100	21.4	23.1	23.4	23.6	23.7	23.7	23.8	10.5	3.0	1.7	0.8	0.4	0.2
30	0	13.5	27.8	30.0	31.8	32.4	32.8	33.2	85.2	23.7	14.2	6.5	3.4	1.8
30	100	30.9	32.4	32.7	33.0	33.1	33.2	33.2	10.5	3.7	2.2	1.0	0.5	0.3
40	0	17.6	34.9	37.8	40.4	41.4	42.0	42.6	109.1	34.6	21.5	10.1	5.4	2.8
40	100	40.5	41.7	42.0	42.3	42.5	42.5	42.6	9.5	4.0	2.6	1.2	0.7	0.3

AIRSPEED = 400. CM/SEC   RADIATION ABSORBED = 0.8 EXP 6 ERGS/CM2/SEC

DIMENSION ALONG AIRFLOW = 10 CM   DIMENSION ACROSS AIRFLOW = 5 CM

		LEAF TEMPERATURES FOR RESISTANCES=							TRANSPIRATION EXP 6 FOR RES =					
TA	RH	**0*	**1*	**2*	**5*	*10*	*20*	INF*	**0*	**1*	**2*	**5*	*10*	*20*
0	0	-1.6	4.7	5.5	6.1	6.4	6.5	6.6	24.8	5.7	3.2	1.4	0.7	0.4
0	100	3.9	5.9	6.2	6.4	6.5	6.5	6.6	8.3	2.0	1.2	0.5	0.3	0.1
10	0	4.1	12.9	14.1	15.1	15.5	15.7	15.9	36.4	9.6	5.6	2.5	1.3	0.7
10	100	12.7	15.0	15.4	15.7	15.8	15.9	15.9	10.0	2.9	1.7	0.8	0.4	0.2
20	0	9.0	20.4	22.3	23.9	24.5	24.9	25.2	50.3	15.1	9.1	4.2	2.2	1.1
20	100	21.8	24.0	24.5	24.9	25.1	25.1	25.2	10.8	3.8	2.3	1.1	0.6	0.3
30	0	13.4	27.4	30.1	32.4	33.3	33.9	34.5	66.1	22.4	14.0	6.7	3.6	1.9
30	100	31.1	33.0	33.6	34.0	34.2	34.3	34.5	10.7	4.6	2.9	1.4	0.8	0.4
40	0	17.2	33.8	37.3	40.5	41.9	42.7	43.6	83.4	31.7	20.5	10.1	5.5	2.9
40	100	40.7	42.1	42.6	43.1	43.3	43.5	43.6	9.7	4.9	3.3	1.7	0.9	0.5

DIMENSION ALONG AIRFLOW = 20 CM   DIMENSION ACROSS AIRFLOW = 5 CM

		LEAF TEMPERATURES FOR RESISTANCES=							TRANSPIRATION EXP 6 FOR RES =					
TA	RH	**0*	**1*	**2*	**5*	*10*	*20*	INF*	**0*	**1*	**2*	**5*	*10*	*20*
0	0	1.6	9.2	11.0	12.5	13.2	13.5	13.9	17.7	6.9	4.3	2.1	1.1	0.6
0	100	7.2	11.2	12.2	13.1	13.5	13.7	13.9	9.8	4.0	2.6	1.2	0.7	0.3
10	0	6.1	15.6	18.0	20.3	21.3	21.8	22.5	23.9	10.2	6.7	3.3	1.8	0.9
10	100	15.0	19.0	20.1	21.3	21.8	22.1	22.5	11.1	5.3	3.5	1.7	1.0	0.5
20	0	10.1	21.4	24.5	27.6	29.1	29.9	30.9	30.9	14.4	9.7	5.0	2.8	1.5
20	100	23.2	26.8	28.1	29.4	30.1	30.5	30.9	11.6	6.3	4.4	2.3	1.3	0.7
30	0	13.6	26.6	30.5	34.5	36.6	37.8	39.2	38.5	19.3	13.5	7.3	4.2	2.3
30	100	32.0	34.8	36.0	37.5	38.2	38.7	39.2	11.2	6.8	5.0	2.8	1.6	0.9
40	0	16.8	31.4	35.9	41.0	43.7	45.4	47.4	46.6	25.0	18.0	10.2	6.0	3.3
40	100	41.2	43.2	44.2	45.6	46.3	46.8	47.4	10.0	6.7	5.1	3.0	1.8	1.0

AIRSPEED = 400. CM/SEC   RADIATION ABSORBED = 0.8 EXP 6 ERGS/CM2/SEC

DIMENSION ALONG AIRFLOW = 1 CM   DIMENSION ACROSS AIRFLOW = 10 CM

LEAF TEMPERATURES FOR RESISTANCES= | TRANSPIRATION EXP 6 FOR RES =

TA	RH	**0*	**1*	**2*	**5*	*10*	*20*	INF*	**0*	**1*	**2*	**5*	*10*	*20*
0	0	-2.3	2.6	3.0	3.3	3.4	3.4	3.5	33.5	5.1	2.8	1.2	0.6	0.3
0	100	2.3	3.3	3.4	3.4	3.5	3.5	3.5	6.7	1.1	0.6	0.2	0.1	0.1
10	0	4.2	11.6	12.3	12.8	13.0	13.0	13.1	52.0	9.2	5.1	2.2	1.1	0.6
10	100	11.7	12.9	13.0	13.1	13.1	13.1	13.1	8.5	1.7	0.9	0.4	0.2	0.1
20	0	9.9	20.2	21.3	22.1	22.4	22.6	22.8	75.7	15.5	8.8	3.8	2.0	1.0
20	100	21.1	22.4	22.6	22.7	22.7	22.8	22.8	9.7	2.3	1.3	0.6	0.3	0.1
30	0	14.9	28.3	30.0	31.3	31.8	32.1	32.4	103.3	24.6	14.3	6.4	3.3	1.7
30	100	30.7	31.9	32.1	32.2	32.3	32.3	32.4	9.9	2.9	1.7	0.8	0.4	0.2
40	0	19.3	35.8	38.3	40.3	41.1	41.5	41.9	134.6	36.9	22.1	10.1	5.3	2.7
40	100	40.4	41.4	41.6	41.8	41.9	41.9	41.9	9.1	3.3	2.0	0.9	0.5	0.3

DIMENSION ALONG AIRFLOW = 5 CM   DIMENSION ACROSS AIRFLOW = 10 CM

LEAF TEMPERATURES FOR RESISTANCES= | TRANSPIRATION EXP 6 FOR RES =

TA	RH	**0*	**1*	**2*	**5*	*10*	*20*	INF*	**0*	**1*	**2*	**5*	*10*	*20*
0	0	-0.6	5.4	6.2	6.9	7.2	7.3	7.5	21.6	5.7	3.3	1.5	0.8	0.4
0	100	4.5	6.6	7.0	7.3	7.4	7.4	7.5	8.0	2.2	1.3	0.6	0.3	0.2
10	0	5.1	13.3	14.7	15.8	16.2	16.5	16.7	31.6	9.5	5.7	2.6	1.4	0.7
10	100	13.2	15.6	16.0	16.4	16.6	16.6	16.7	9.7	3.2	1.9	0.9	0.5	0.2
20	0	10.0	20.6	22.7	24.4	25.1	25.5	25.9	43.5	14.7	9.1	4.3	2.3	1.2
20	100	22.1	24.4	25.0	25.5	25.7	25.8	25.9	10.6	4.1	2.6	1.2	0.7	0.3
30	0	14.4	27.4	30.2	32.7	33.8	34.4	35.0	57.2	21.6	13.8	6.7	3.6	1.9
30	100	31.3	33.3	33.9	34.5	34.7	34.9	35.0	10.5	4.9	3.2	1.6	0.9	0.4
40	0	18.3	33.5	37.1	40.6	42.2	43.1	44.1	72.1	30.1	20.0	10.1	5.6	2.9
40	100	40.8	42.3	42.9	43.5	43.7	43.9	44.1	9.5	5.1	3.5	1.8	1.0	0.5

AIRSPEED = 400. CM/SEC   RADIATION ABSORBED = 0.8 EXP 6 ERGS/CM2/SEC

DIMENSION ALONG AIRFLOW = 10 CM   DIMENSION ACROSS AIRFLOW = 10 CM
LEAF TEMPERATURES FOR RESISTANCES=   TRANSPIRATION EXP 6 FOR RES =

TA	RH	**0*	**1*	**2*	**5*	*10*	*20*	INF*	**0*	**1*	**2*	**5*	*10*	*20*
0	0	0.8	7.2	8.4	9.4	9.8	10.0	10.3	18.6	6.1	3.7	1.7	0.9	0.5
0	100	5.9	8.8	9.3	9.8	10.0	10.2	10.3	8.6	3.0	1.8	0.8	0.4	0.2
10	0	6.0	14.0	16.2	17.8	18.5	18.8	19.2	26.3	9.7	6.1	2.9	1.5	0.8
10	100	14.2	17.2	17.9	18.6	18.9	19.1	19.2	10.1	4.1	2.6	1.2	0.7	0.3
20	0	10.5	21.0	23.5	25.9	26.9	27.5	28.1	35.2	14.4	9.3	4.6	2.5	1.3
20	100	22.8	25.6	26.4	27.3	27.6	27.9	28.1	10.9	5.1	3.4	1.7	0.9	0.5
30	0	14.5	27.1	30.3	33.5	35.0	35.9	36.9	45.3	20.3	13.6	7.0	3.9	2.0
30	100	31.7	34.1	34.9	35.9	36.3	36.6	36.9	10.7	5.8	4.0	2.1	1.2	0.6
40	0	18.1	32.5	36.6	40.8	42.9	44.1	45.6	56.2	27.3	18.9	10.1	5.7	3.1
40	100	41.0	42.8	43.5	44.4	44.9	45.2	45.6	9.6	5.9	4.3	2.4	1.4	0.7

DIMENSION ALONG AIRFLOW = 20 CM   DIMENSION ACROSS AIRFLOW = 10 CM
LEAF TEMPERATURES FOR RESISTANCES=   TRANSPIRATION EXP 6 FOR RES =

TA	RH	**0*	**1*	**2*	**5*	*10*	*20*	INF*	**0*	**1*	**2*	**5*	*10*	*20*
0	0	2.6	9.4	11.0	12.5	13.2	13.5	13.9	16.4	6.7	4.3	2.1	1.1	0.6
0	100	7.6	11.2	12.2	13.1	13.5	13.7	13.9	9.2	3.9	2.5	1.2	0.7	0.3
10	0	7.2	15.8	18.1	20.3	21.3	21.8	22.5	22.4	10.0	6.6	3.3	1.8	0.9
10	100	15.4	19.0	20.2	21.3	21.8	22.1	22.5	10.6	5.1	3.4	1.7	1.0	0.5
20	0	11.3	21.6	24.6	27.6	29.1	29.9	30.9	29.1	14.1	9.6	5.0	2.8	1.5
20	100	23.5	26.9	28.1	29.4	30.1	30.5	30.9	11.2	6.1	4.3	2.3	1.3	0.7
30	0	15.0	26.9	30.6	34.6	36.6	37.8	39.2	36.5	19.0	13.3	7.2	4.2	2.2
30	100	32.2	34.9	36.1	37.5	38.2	38.7	39.2	10.9	6.7	4.9	2.7	1.6	0.9
40	C	18.3	31.7	36.1	41.1	43.7	45.4	47.4	44.5	24.6	17.8	10.1	5.9	3.3
40	100	41.3	43.3	44.2	45.6	46.3	46.8	47.4	9.7	6.6	5.1	3.0	1.8	1.0

AIRSPEED = 400. CM/SEC   RADIATION ABSORBED = 1.0 EXP 6 ERGS/CM2/SEC

DIMENSION ALONG AIRFLOW = 1 CM   DIMENSION ACROSS AIRFLOW = 1 CM

LEAF TEMPERATURES FOR RESISTANCES=   TRANSPIRATION EXP 6 FOR RES =

TA	RH	**0*	**1*	**2*	**5*	*10*	*20*	INF*	**0*	**1*	**2*	**5*	*10*	*20*
0	0	-4.0	2.5	2.7	2.9	3.0	3.0	3.0	64.5	5.4	2.8	1.2	0.6	0.3
0	100	1.8	2.9	3.0	3.0	3.0	3.0	3.0	11.3	1.0	0.5	0.2	0.1	0.1
10	0	2.2	11.8	12.3	12.6	12.7	12.8	12.8	98.9	9.9	5.3	2.0	1.1	0.6
10	100	11.3	12.7	12.7	12.8	12.8	12.8	12.8	14.2	1.6	0.9	0.4	0.2	0.1
20	0	7.5	20.8	21.6	22.2	22.4	22.5	22.6	140.9	17.1	9.2	3.9	2.0	1.0
20	100	20.9	22.4	22.5	22.5	22.6	22.6	22.6	16.2	2.4	1.3	0.5	0.3	0.1
30	0	12.2	29.4	30.7	31.7	32.0	32.3	32.4	189.5	27.9	15.4	6.6	3.4	1.7
30	100	30.6	32.0	32.2	32.3	32.3	32.3	32.4	17.0	3.3	1.8	0.8	0.4	0.2
40	0	16.3	37.6	39.6	41.0	41.5	41.8	42.1	243.7	43.0	24.3	10.6	5.5	2.8
40	100	40.4	41.6	41.8	42.0	42.0	42.0	42.1	16.6	4.1	2.4	1.0	0.5	0.3

DIMENSION ALONG AIRFLOW = 5 CM   DIMENSION ACROSS AIRFLOW = 1 CM

LEAF TEMPERATURES FOR RESISTANCES=   TRANSPIRATION EXP 6 FOR RES =

TA	RH	**0*	**1*	**2*	**5*	*10*	*20*	INF*	**0*	**1*	**2*	**5*	*10*	*20*
0	0	-2.8	5.2	5.8	6.3	6.5	6.5	6.6	39.9	6.2	3.4	1.5	0.7	0.4
0	100	3.5	6.1	6.3	6.5	6.6	6.6	6.6	13.2	2.2	1.2	0.5	0.3	0.1
10	0	2.6	13.7	14.8	15.6	15.9	16.0	16.2	57.9	10.8	6.0	2.6	1.3	0.7
10	100	12.5	15.4	15.7	16.0	16.1	16.1	16.2	15.9	3.4	1.9	0.8	0.4	0.2
20	0	7.3	21.7	23.4	24.6	25.1	25.4	25.7	78.9	17.3	10.0	4.4	2.3	1.2
20	100	21.7	24.6	25.0	25.4	25.5	25.6	25.7	17.5	4.7	2.8	1.2	0.6	0.3
30	0	11.4	29.1	31.5	33.5	34.2	34.7	35.1	102.6	26.3	15.7	7.2	3.8	1.9
30	100	31.1	33.7	34.3	34.7	34.9	35.0	35.1	17.9	6.1	3.7	1.7	0.9	0.5
40	0	15.0	36.0	39.2	42.0	43.2	43.8	44.5	128.4	37.9	23.5	11.1	5.9	3.1
40	100	40.7	42.9	43.5	44.0	44.2	44.3	44.5	17.2	7.2	4.6	2.2	1.2	0.6

AIRSPEED = 400. CM/SEC   RADIATION ABSORBED = 1.0 EXP 6 ERGS/CM2/SEC

DIMENSION ALONG AIRFLOW = 1 CM   DIMENSION ACROSS AIRFLOW = 5 CM

LEAF TEMPERATURES FOR RESISTANCES=   TRANSPIRATION EXP 6 FOR RES =

TA	RH	**0*	***1*	**2*	***5*	*10*	*20*	INF*	**0*	***1*	**2*	***5*	*10*	*20*
0	0	-2.6	2.5	2.7	2.9	3.0	3.0	3.0	51.7	5.3	2.8	1.2	0.6	0.3
0	100	-2.0	2.9	3.0	3.0	3.0	3.0	3.0	9.3	1.0	0.5	0.2	0.1	0.1
10	0	4.1	11.8	12.3	12.6	12.7	12.8	12.8	81.5	9.8	5.2	2.2	1.1	0.6
10	100	11.5	12.7	12.7	12.8	12.8	12.8	12.8	12.2	1.6	0.9	0.4	0.2	0.1
20	0	9.9	20.8	21.6	22.2	22.4	22.5	22.6	119.0	16.8	9.2	3.9	2.0	1.0
20	100	21.1	22.4	22.5	22.5	22.6	22.6	22.6	14.4	2.3	1.3	0.5	0.3	0.1
30	0	15.0	29.5	30.8	31.7	32.0	32.2	32.4	163.5	27.4	15.2	6.5	3.4	1.7
30	100	30.7	32.0	32.2	32.3	32.3	32.3	32.4	15.6	3.2	1.8	0.8	0.4	0.2
40	0	19.5	37.7	39.6	41.0	41.5	41.8	42.1	214.0	42.3	24.1	10.6	5.5	2.8
40	100	40.5	41.7	41.8	42.0	42.0	42.0	42.1	15.6	4.1	2.4	1.0	0.5	0.3

DIMENSION ALONG AIRFLOW = 5 CM   DIMENSION ACROSS AIRFLOW = 5 CM

LEAF TEMPERATURES FOR RESISTANCES=   TRANSPIRATION EXP 6 FOR RES =

TA	RH	**0*	***1*	**2*	***5*	*10*	*20*	INF*	**0*	***1*	**2*	***5*	*10*	*20*
0	0	-1.1	5.2	5.8	6.3	6.5	6.5	6.6	32.6	6.1	3.4	1.4	0.7	0.4
0	100	4.0	6.1	6.3	6.5	6.6	6.6	6.6	11.1	2.2	1.2	0.5	0.3	0.1
10	0	4.8	13.7	14.8	15.6	15.9	16.0	16.2	48.6	10.4	5.9	2.6	1.3	0.7
10	100	12.9	15.4	15.7	16.0	16.1	16.1	16.2	13.9	3.3	1.9	0.8	0.4	0.2
20	0	9.9	21.8	23.4	24.6	25.1	25.4	25.7	67.8	16.9	9.8	4.4	2.3	1.2
20	100	22.0	24.6	25.0	25.4	25.5	25.6	25.7	15.8	4.6	2.7	1.2	0.6	0.3
30	0	14.4	29.3	31.6	33.5	34.2	34.7	35.1	89.8	25.7	15.5	7.1	3.8	1.9
30	100	31.3	33.8	34.3	34.7	34.9	35.0	35.1	16.6	5.9	3.6	1.7	0.9	0.5
40	0	18.4	36.2	39.3	42.0	43.2	43.8	44.5	114.1	37.0	23.1	11.0	5.9	3.1
40	100	40.9	42.9	43.5	44.0	44.2	44.3	44.5	16.3	7.0	4.5	2.2	1.2	0.6

AIRSPEED = 400. CM/SEC   RADIATION ABSORBED = 1.0 EXP 6 ERGS/CM2/SEC

DIMENSION ALONG AIRFLOW = 10 CM   DIMENSION ACROSS AIRFLOW = 5 CM

TA	RH	LEAF TEMPERATURES FOR RESISTANCES=							TRANSPIRATION EXP 6 FOR RES =					
		**0*	**1*	**2*	**5*	*10*	*20*	INF*	**0*	**1*	**2*	**5*	*10*	*20*
0	0	0.1	7.1	8.0	8.7	8.9	9.1	9.2	27.8	6.6	3.8	1.7	0.9	0.4
0	100	5.3	8.2	8.6	9.0	9.1	9.1	9.2	11.9	3.0	1.7	0.8	0.4	0.2
10	0	5.5	15.0	16.5	17.6	18.1	18.3	18.5	40.1	10.9	6.4	2.9	1.5	0.8
10	100	13.9	17.1	17.7	18.2	18.4	18.4	18.5	14.6	4.4	2.6	1.2	0.6	0.3
20	0	10.3	22.4	24.6	26.3	27.0	27.4	27.8	54.5	17.0	10.3	4.8	2.5	1.3
20	100	22.6	25.9	26.7	27.3	27.5	27.7	27.8	16.3	6.0	3.7	1.7	0.9	0.5
30	0	14.5	29.3	32.1	34.7	35.8	36.4	37.0	70.8	24.8	15.7	7.5	4.1	2.1
30	100	31.7	34.7	35.5	36.3	36.6	36.8	37.0	17.0	7.4	4.8	2.3	1.3	0.7
40	0	18.2	35.5	39.2	42.7	44.3	45.2	46.2	88.6	34.6	22.6	11.3	6.2	3.3
40	100	41.1	43.6	44.4	45.3	45.7	45.9	46.2	16.5	8.4	5.7	2.9	1.6	0.9

DIMENSION ALONG AIRFLOW = 20 CM   DIMENSION ACROSS AIRFLOW = 5 CM

TA	RH	LEAF TEMPERATURES FOR RESISTANCES=							TRANSPIRATION EXP 6 FOR RES =					
		**0*	**1*	**2*	**5*	*10*	*20*	INF*	**0*	**1*	**2*	**5*	*10*	*20*
0	0	4.6	13.4	15.6	17.5	18.4	18.9	19.4	21.6	8.9	5.8	2.8	1.5	0.8
0	100	9.7	15.2	16.7	18.1	18.7	19.0	19.4	14.3	6.2	4.1	2.0	1.1	0.6
10	0	8.7	19.4	22.3	25.0	26.3	27.0	27.9	28.3	12.8	8.5	4.4	2.4	1.3
10	100	16.9	22.5	24.3	26.0	26.9	27.3	27.9	16.4	8.1	5.5	2.8	1.6	0.8
20	0	12.4	24.8	28.4	32.1	33.9	35.0	36.3	35.7	17.5	12.1	6.4	3.6	2.0
20	100	24.7	29.9	31.7	33.8	34.9	35.5	36.3	17.6	9.8	7.0	3.8	2.1	1.2
30	0	15.7	29.7	34.0	38.7	41.2	42.7	44.5	43.7	22.9	16.3	9.1	5.3	2.9
30	100	33.1	37.4	39.3	41.5	42.8	43.6	44.5	17.8	11.1	8.2	4.7	2.8	1.5
40	0	18.6	34.2	39.2	45.0	48.1	50.1	52.6	52.1	29.1	21.3	12.3	7.4	4.1
40	100	41.9	45.3	47.0	49.2	50.6	51.5	52.6	17.1	11.7	9.1	5.5	3.3	1.9

AIRSPEED = 400. CM/SEC   RADIATION ABSORBED = 1.0 EXP 6 ERGS/CM2/SEC

DIMENSION ALONG AIRFLOW = 1 CM
DIMENSION ACROSS AIRFLOW = 10 CM

		LEAF TEMPERATURES FOR RESISTANCES=							TRANSPIRATION EXP 6 FOR RES =					
TA	RH	**0*	**1*	**2*	**5*	*10*	*20*	INF**	**0*	**1*	**2*	**5*	*10*	*20*
0	0	-1.4	3.9	4.3	4.6	4.7	4.8	4.9	35.8	5.6	3.1	1.3	0.7	0.3
0	100	3.2	4.6	4.7	4.8	4.8	4.8	4.9	9.6	1.6	0.9	0.4	0.2	0.1
10	0	5.0	12.8	13.6	14.1	14.3	14.4	14.5	55.3	10.0	5.5	2.4	1.2	0.6
10	100	12.4	14.1	14.3	14.4	14.5	14.5	14.5	12.5	2.5	1.4	0.6	0.3	0.2
20	0	10.6	21.3	22.6	23.5	23.8	24.0	24.2	79.4	16.7	9.5	4.1	2.1	1.1
20	100	21.7	23.6	23.8	24.0	24.1	24.1	24.2	14.6	3.5	2.0	0.9	0.5	0.2
30	0	15.5	29.4	31.2	32.6	33.2	33.5	33.7	107.6	26.2	15.3	6.8	3.6	1.8
30	100	31.1	33.0	33.3	33.5	33.6	33.7	33.7	15.7	4.7	2.8	1.2	0.6	0.3
40	0	19.9	36.9	39.4	41.5	42.4	42.8	43.3	139.4	38.9	23.4	10.8	5.7	2.9
40	100	40.7	42.4	42.7	43.0	43.2	43.2	43.3	15.6	5.7	3.5	1.6	0.9	0.4

DIMENSION ALONG AIRFLOW = 5 CM
DIMENSION ACROSS AIRFLOW = 10 CM

		LEAF TEMPERATURES FOR RESISTANCES=							TRANSPIRATION EXP 6 FOR RES =					
TA	RH	**0*	**1*	**2*	**5*	*10*	*20*	INF**	**0*	**1*	**2*	**5*	*10*	*20*
0	0	1.3	8.0	9.0	9.8	10.1	10.3	10.5	24.6	6.8	4.0	1.8	0.9	0.5
0	100	6.2	9.2	9.7	10.1	10.3	10.4	10.5	11.6	3.4	2.0	0.9	0.5	0.2
10	0	6.7	15.7	17.3	18.6	19.1	19.4	19.7	35.2	11.0	6.6	3.1	1.6	0.8
10	100	14.5	17.9	18.6	19.2	19.4	19.6	19.7	14.2	4.9	3.0	1.4	0.7	0.4
20	0	11.5	22.8	25.1	27.1	27.9	28.4	28.9	47.7	16.8	10.5	5.0	2.7	1.4
20	100	23.1	26.6	27.4	28.2	28.5	28.7	28.9	15.9	6.5	4.1	2.0	1.0	0.5
30	0	15.7	29.4	32.4	35.3	36.5	37.2	38.0	61.8	24.2	15.6	7.7	4.2	2.2
30	100	32.1	35.2	36.1	37.0	37.5	37.7	38.0	16.7	7.9	5.2	2.6	1.4	0.8
40	0	19.4	35.4	39.2	43.0	44.8	45.8	47.0	77.2	33.2	22.2	11.4	6.3	3.4
40	100	41.3	43.9	44.8	45.8	46.3	46.6	47.0	16.3	8.9	6.2	3.3	1.8	1.0

AIRSPEED = 400. CM/SEC   RADIATION ABSORBED = 1.0 EXP 6 ERGS/CM2/SEC

DIMENSION ALONG AIRFLOW = 10 CM   DIMENSION ACROSS AIRFLOW = 10 CM

TA	RH	**0*	**1*	**2*	**5*	*10*	*20*	INF*	**0*	**1*	**2*	**5*	*10*	*20*
		LEAF TEMPERATURES FOR RESISTANCES=							TRANSPIRATION EXP 6 FOR RES =					
0	0	3.2	10.5	12.0	13.2	13.8	14.0	14.3	21.9	7.6	4.7	2.2	1.2	0.6
0	100	8.0	12.0	12.9	13.7	14.0	14.2	14.3	12.5	4.6	2.8	1.3	0.7	0.4
10	0	8.1	17.5	19.6	21.5	22.3	22.8	23.3	30.2	11.7	7.4	3.6	1.9	1.0
10	100	15.9	20.1	21.3	22.3	22.7	23.0	23.3	14.9	6.3	4.1	2.0	1.1	0.6
20	0	12.4	23.8	26.7	29.4	30.6	31.3	32.1	39.7	16.9	11.1	5.6	3.1	1.6
20	100	24.0	28.2	29.5	30.6	31.4	31.7	32.1	16.5	8.0	5.4	2.7	1.5	0.8
30	0	16.2	29.6	33.2	36.9	38.6	39.6	40.8	50.1	23.3	15.9	8.3	4.6	2.5
30	100	32.7	36.3	37.7	39.1	39.9	40.3	40.8	17.0	9.5	6.6	3.5	2.0	1.1
40	0	19.6	34.8	39.2	43.9	46.3	47.7	49.5	61.4	30.8	21.7	11.8	6.8	3.7
40	100	41.7	44.6	45.9	47.5	48.3	48.8	49.5	16.5	10.3	7.6	4.3	2.5	1.4

DIMENSION ALONG AIRFLOW = 20 CM   DIMENSION ACROSS AIRFLOW = 10 CM

TA	RH	**0*	**1*	**2*	**5*	*10*	*20*	INF*	**0*	**1*	**2*	**5*	*10*	*20*
		LEAF TEMPERATURES FOR RESISTANCES=							TRANSPIRATION EXP 6 FOR RES =					
0	0	5.6	13.5	15.6	17.6	18.4	18.9	19.4	20.2	8.7	5.7	2.8	1.5	0.8
0	100	10.3	15.3	16.7	18.1	18.7	19.0	19.4	13.4	6.1	4.0	2.0	1.1	0.6
10	0	9.9	19.6	22.3	25.0	26.3	27.1	27.9	26.6	12.5	8.4	4.3	2.4	1.3
10	100	17.5	22.6	24.3	26.1	26.9	27.3	27.9	15.6	8.0	5.4	2.8	1.6	0.8
20	0	13.7	25.1	28.5	32.1	33.9	35.0	36.3	33.8	17.1	11.9	6.4	3.6	1.9
20	100	25.2	30.0	31.8	33.8	34.9	35.5	36.3	17.0	9.7	6.9	3.7	2.1	1.2
30	0	17.1	30.0	34.2	38.8	41.2	42.7	44.5	41.5	22.5	16.1	9.0	5.2	2.9
30	100	33.4	37.5	39.3	41.6	42.8	43.6	44.5	17.3	11.0	8.1	4.7	2.7	1.5
40	0	20.2	34.5	39.4	45.0	48.1	50.1	52.6	49.8	28.6	21.1	12.2	7.3	4.1
40	100	42.2	45.4	47.1	49.3	50.6	51.5	52.6	16.7	11.6	9.0	5.4	3.3	1.9

AIRSPEED = 800. CM/SEC   RADIATION ABSORBED = 0.4 EXP 6 ERGS/CM2/SEC

DIMENSION ALONG AIRFLOW = 1 CM   DIMENSION ACROSS AIRFLOW = 1 CM

LEAF TEMPERATURES FOR RESISTANCES= / TRANSPIRATION EXP 6 FOR RES =

TA	RH	**0*	**1*	**2*	**5*	*10*	*20*	INF*	**0*	**1*	**2*	**5*	*10*	*20*
0	0	-6.0	-0.0	0.1	0.2	0.3	0.3	0.3	81.6	4.7	2.4	1.0	0.5	0.2
0	100	0.2	0.3	0.3	0.3	0.3	0.3	0.3	1.6	0.1	0.1	0.0	0.0	0.0
10	0	0.3	9.5	9.8	10.0	10.1	10.1	10.2	127.8	8.8	4.6	1.9	0.9	0.5
10	100	10.1	10.2	10.2	10.2	10.2	10.2	10.2	1.2	0.1	0.0	0.0	0.0	0.0
20	0	5.9	18.8	19.4	19.8	19.9	19.9	20.0	185.3	15.5	8.2	3.4	1.7	0.9
20	100	20.0	20.0	20.0	20.0	20.0	20.0	20.0	0.1	0.0	0.0	0.0	0.0	0.0
30	0	10.7	27.9	28.8	29.4	29.6	29.7	29.8	252.4	26.1	14.0	5.8	3.0	1.5
30	100													
40	0	14.9	36.6	38.0	38.9	39.3	39.5	39.6	327.8	41.4	22.7	9.6	4.9	2.5
40	100													

DIMENSION ALONG AIRFLOW = 5 CM   DIMENSION ACROSS AIRFLOW = 1 CM

LEAF TEMPERATURES FOR RESISTANCES= / TRANSPIRATION EXP 6 FOR RES =

TA	RH	**0*	**1*	**2*	**5*	*10*	*20*	INF*	**0*	**1*	**2*	**5*	*10*	*20*
0	0	-6.8	-0.1	0.3	0.5	0.6	0.6	0.7	43.9	4.5	2.4	1.0	0.5	0.3
0	100	-0.4	0.7	0.7	0.7	0.7	0.7	0.7	1.8	0.2	0.1	0.0	0.0	0.0
10	0	-0.9	9.0	9.6	10.1	10.2	10.3	10.4	66.7	8.2	4.4	1.9	0.9	0.5
10	100	10.1	10.3	10.4	10.4	10.4	10.4	10.4	1.3	0.2	0.1	0.0	0.0	0.0
20	0	4.2	17.7	18.7	19.5	19.7	19.9	20.0	94.4	14.1	7.8	3.3	1.7	0.9
20	100	20.0	20.0	20.0	20.0	20.0	20.0	20.0	0.1	0.0	0.0	0.0	0.0	0.0
30	0	8.6	25.9	27.5	28.7	29.2	29.4	29.6	126.1	22.7	12.8	5.6	2.9	1.5
30	100													
40	0	12.5	33.6	36.0	37.8	38.5	38.8	39.2	161.2	34.5	20.1	9.0	4.7	2.4
40	100													

AIRSPEED = 800. CM/SEC   RADIATION ABSORBED = 0.4 EXP 6 ERGS/CM2/SEC

DIMENSION ALONG AIRFLOW = 1 CM   DIMENSION ACROSS AIRFLOW = 5 CM

LEAF TEMPERATURES FOR RESISTANCES=   TRANSPIRATION EXP 6 FOR RES =

TA	RH	**0*	**1*	**2*	**5*	*10*	*20*	INF*	**0*	**1*	**2*	**5*	*10*	*20*
0	0	-4.7	-0.0	0.1	0.2	0.3	0.3	0.3	64.9	4.6	2.4	1.0	0.5	0.2
0	100	0.2	0.3	0.3	0.3	0.3	0.3	0.3	1.3	0.1	0.1	0.0	0.0	0.0
10	0	2.1	9.5	9.8	10.0	10.1	10.1	10.2	104.7	8.6	4.5	1.9	0.9	0.5
10	100	10.1	10.2	10.2	10.2	10.1	10.2	10.2	1.0	0.1	0.0	0.0	0.0	0.0
20	0	8.1	18.9	19.4	19.8	19.9	19.9	20.0	155.8	15.3	8.1	3.4	1.7	0.9
20	100	20.0	20.0	20.0	20.0	20.0	20.0	20.0	0.1	0.0	0.0	0.0	0.0	0.0
30	0	13.4	27.9	28.8	29.4	29.6	29.7	29.8	217.1	25.7	13.9	5.8	3.0	1.5
30	100													
40	0	18.0	36.6	38.0	38.9	39.3	39.5	39.6	287.1	40.9	22.5	9.6	4.9	2.5
40	100													

DIMENSION ALONG AIRFLOW = 5 CM   DIMENSION ACROSS AIRFLOW = 5 CM

LEAF TEMPERATURES FOR RESISTANCES=   TRANSPIRATION EXP 6 FOR RES =

TA	RH	**0*	**1*	**2*	**5*	*10*	*20*	INF*	**0*	**1*	**2*	**5*	*10*	*20*
0	0	-5.3	-0.1	0.3	0.5	0.6	0.6	0.7	35.4	4.4	2.4	1.0	0.5	0.3
0	100	0.4	0.6	0.7	0.7	0.7	0.7	0.7	1.5	0.2	0.1	0.0	0.0	0.0
10	0	1.0	9.0	9.6	10.1	10.2	10.3	10.4	55.3	8.1	4.4	1.9	0.9	0.5
10	100	10.2	10.3	10.4	10.4	10.4	10.4	10.4	1.1	0.2	0.1	0.0	0.0	0.0
20	0	6.6	17.7	18.8	19.5	19.7	19.9	20.0	80.2	13.8	7.7	3.3	1.7	0.9
20	100	20.0	20.0	20.0	20.0	20.0	20.0	20.0	0.1	0.0	0.0	0.0	0.0	0.0
30	0	11.4	26.0	27.6	28.7	29.2	29.4	29.6	109.4	22.3	12.7	5.6	2.9	1.5
30	100													
40	0	15.7	33.7	36.0	37.8	38.5	38.8	39.2	142.3	33.9	19.9	9.0	4.7	2.4
40	100													

AIRSPEED = 800. CM/SEC   RADIATION ABSORBED = 0.4 EXP 6 ERGS/CM2/SEC

DIMENSION ALONG AIRFLOW = 10 CM   DIMENSION ACROSS AIRFLOW = 5 CM

TA	RH	**0*	**1*	**2*	**5*	*10*	*20*	INF*	**0*	**1*	**2*	**5*	*10*	*20*
		LEAF TEMPERATURES FOR RESISTANCES=							TRANSPIRATION EXP 6 FOR RES =					
0	0	-5.5	-0.1	0.4	0.7	0.8	0.9	1.0	27.3	4.3	2.4	1.0	0.5	0.3
0	100	0.6	0.9	0.9	0.9	0.9	0.9	1.0	1.6	0.3	0.1	0.1	0.0	0.0
10	0	0.6	8.7	9.5	10.1	10.3	10.4	10.5	42.1	7.7	4.3	1.8	0.9	0.5
10	100	10.2	10.5	10.5	10.5	10.5	10.5	10.5	1.2	0.2	0.1	0.1	0.0	0.0
20	0	5.9	17.0	18.3	19.3	19.6	19.8	20.0	60.3	13.0	7.4	3.2	1.7	0.9
20	100	20.0	20.0	20.0	20.0	20.0	20.0	20.0	0.1	0.0	0.0	0.0	0.0	0.0
30	0	10.6	24.8	26.8	28.3	28.9	29.2	29.5	81.5	20.4	12.0	5.4	2.8	1.4
30	100													
40	0	14.7	32.1	34.8	37.0	37.9	38.4	38.9	105.1	30.3	18.5	8.6	4.5	2.3
40	100													

DIMENSION ALONG AIRFLOW = 20 CM   DIMENSION ACROSS AIRFLOW = 5 CM

TA	RH	**0*	**1*	**2*	**5*	*10*	*20*	INF*	**0*	**1*	**2*	**5*	*10*	*20*
		LEAF TEMPERATURES FOR RESISTANCES=							TRANSPIRATION EXP 6 FOR RES =					
0	0	-5.9	0.0	0.9	1.5	1.8	1.9	2.1	15.3	4.0	2.3	1.0	0.5	0.3
0	100	1.1	1.8	1.9	2.0	2.0	2.1	2.1	1.9	0.5	0.3	0.1	0.1	0.0
10	0	-0.4	7.7	9.1	10.2	10.6	10.9	11.1	22.5	6.7	4.0	1.8	1.0	0.5
10	100	10.5	10.9	11.0	11.0	11.1	11.1	11.1	1.3	0.4	0.3	0.1	0.1	0.0
20	0	4.3	14.8	16.8	18.6	19.3	19.6	20.1	31.1	10.5	6.5	3.1	1.6	0.8
20	100	20.0	20.0	20.0	20.0	20.1	20.1	20.1	0.1	0.0	0.0	0.0	0.0	0.0
30	0	8.5	21.3	24.1	26.6	27.6	28.3	28.9	40.9	15.5	9.9	4.8	2.6	1.4
30	100													
40	0	12.2	27.2	30.8	34.2	35.8	36.7	37.7	51.6	21.6	14.3	7.3	4.0	2.1
40	100													

AIRSPEED = 800. CM/SEC   RADIATION ABSORBED = 0.4 EXP 6 ERGS/CM2/SEC

DIMENSION ALONG AIRFLOW = 1 CM   DIMENSION ACROSS AIRFLOW = 10 CM

LEAF TEMPERATURES FOR RESISTANCES=   TRANSPIRATION EXP 6 FOR RES =

TA	RH	**0*	**1*	**2*	**5*	*10*	*20*	INF*	***0*	***1*	***2*	***5*	*10*	*20*
0	0	-4.7	-0.1	0.2	0.4	0.4	0.5	0.5	41.5	4.5	2.4	1.0	0.5	0.2
0	100	0.3	0.5	0.5	0.5	0.5	0.5	0.5	1.3	0.1	0.1	0.0	0.0	0.0
10	0	2.1	9.3	9.7	10.0	10.2	10.2	10.3	66.5	8.3	4.4	1.9	0.9	0.5
10	100	10.1	10.3	10.3	10.3	10.3	10.3	10.3	1.0	0.1	0.1	0.0	0.0	0.0
20	0	8.0	18.3	19.1	19.6	19.8	19.9	20.0	98.3	14.4	7.9	3.3	1.7	0.9
20	100	20.0	20.0	20.0	20.0	20.0	20.0	20.0	0.0	0.0	0.0	0.0	0.0	0.0
30	0	13.2	26.9	28.2	29.1	29.4	29.6	29.7	136.4	23.7	13.2	5.7	2.9	1.5
30	100													
40	0	17.7	35.1	36.9	38.3	38.9	39.1	39.4	179.8	36.7	21.0	9.3	4.8	2.4
40	100													

DIMENSION ALONG AIRFLOW = 5 CM   DIMENSION ACROSS AIRFLOW = 10 CM

LEAF TEMPERATURES FOR RESISTANCES=   TRANSPIRATION EXP 6 FOR RES =

TA	RH	**0*	**1*	**2*	**5*	*10*	*20*	INF*	***0*	***1*	***2*	***5*	*10*	*20*
0	0	-5.1	-0.0	0.5	0.8	0.9	1.0	1.1	22.9	4.2	2.3	1.0	0.5	0.3
0	100	0.7	1.0	1.0	1.1	1.1	1.1	1.1	1.5	0.3	0.2	0.1	0.0	0.0
10	0	1.1	8.6	9.5	10.1	10.3	10.5	10.6	35.4	7.5	4.2	1.8	0.9	0.5
10	100	10.3	10.5	10.5	10.6	10.6	10.6	10.6	1.1	0.3	0.2	0.1	0.0	0.0
20	0	6.5	16.8	18.1	19.2	19.6	19.8	20.0	50.8	12.4	7.2	3.2	1.7	0.8
20	100	20.0	20.0	20.0	20.0	20.0	20.0	20.0	0.1	0.0	0.0	0.0	0.0	0.0
30	0	11.3	24.4	26.4	28.1	28.7	29.1	29.4	68.9	19.4	11.6	5.3	2.8	1.4
30	100													
40	0	15.4	31.4	34.2	36.6	37.6	38.2	38.8	89.2	28.6	17.7	8.4	4.5	2.3
40	100													

AIRSPEED = 800. CM/SEC RADIATION ABSORBED = 0.4 EXP 6 ERGS/CM2/SEC

DIMENSION ALONG AIRFLOW = 10 CM   DIMENSION ACROSS AIRFLOW = 10 CM

TA	RH	**0*	**1*	**2*	**5*	*10*	*20*	INF*	**0*	**1*	**2*	**5*	*10*	*20*
		LEAF TEMPERATURES FOR RESISTANCES=							TRANSPIRATION EXP 6 FOR RES =					
0	0	-5.2	-0.0	0.6	1.1	1.3	1.4	1.5	17.8	4.1	2.3	1.0	0.5	0.3
0	100	0.9	1.4	1.4	1.5	1.5	1.5	1.5	1.6	0.4	0.2	0.1	0.1	0.0
10	0	0.7	8.2	9.3	10.1	10.5	10.6	10.8	27.1	7.1	4.1	1.8	0.9	0.5
10	100	10.4	10.7	10.7	10.8	10.8	10.8	10.8	1.2	0.3	0.2	0.1	0.0	0.0
20	0	5.9	15.9	17.6	18.9	19.4	19.7	20.0	38.4	11.4	6.8	3.1	1.6	0.8
20	100	20.0	20.0	20.0	20.0	20.0	20.0	20.0	0.1	0.0	0.0	0.0	0.0	0.0
30	0	10.5	23.0	25.4	27.4	28.2	28.7	29.2	51.4	17.3	10.8	5.1	2.7	1.4
30	100													
40	0	14.5	29.5	32.7	35.5	36.8	37.5	38.3	66.0	24.9	16.0	7.9	4.3	2.2
40	100													

DIMENSION ALONG AIRFLOW = 20 CM   DIMENSION ACROSS AIRFLOW = 10 CM

TA	RH	**0*	**1*	**2*	**5*	*10*	*20*	INF*	**0*	**1*	**2*	**5*	*10*	*20*
		LEAF TEMPERATURES FOR RESISTANCES=							TRANSPIRATION EXP 6 FOR RES =					
0	0	-5.2	0.1	0.9	1.5	1.8	1.9	2.1	14.0	3.9	2.3	1.0	0.5	0.3
0	100	1.2	1.8	1.9	2.0	2.0	2.1	2.1	1.7	0.5	0.3	0.1	0.1	0.0
10	0	0.5	7.8	9.1	10.2	10.6	10.9	11.1	20.8	6.6	4.0	1.8	1.0	0.5
10	100	10.5	10.9	11.0	11.0	11.1	11.1	11.1	1.2	0.4	0.3	0.1	0.1	0.0
20	0	5.4	14.9	16.9	18.6	19.3	19.6	20.1	29.1	10.3	6.4	3.0	1.6	0.8
20	100	20.0	20.0	20.0	20.1	20.1	20.1	20.1	0.1	0.0	0.0	0.0	0.0	0.0
30	0	9.7	21.5	24.1	26.6	27.7	28.3	28.9	38.5	15.2	9.8	4.8	2.6	1.4
30	100													
40	0	13.5	27.4	30.9	34.2	35.8	36.7	37.7	48.9	21.3	14.2	7.3	4.0	2.1
40	100													

AIRSPEED = 800. CM/SEC RADIATION ABSORBED = 0.6 EXP 6 ERGS/CM2/SEC
DIMENSION ALONG AIRFLOW = 1 CM   DIMENSION ACROSS AIRFLOW = 1 CM

TA	RH	LEAF TEMPERATURES FOR RESISTANCES=							TRANSPIRATION EXP 6 FOR RES =					
		**0*	**1*	**2*	**5*	*10*	*20*	INF*	**0*	**1*	**2*	**5*	*10*	*20*
0	0	-5.6	0.6	0.7	0.8	0.9	0.9	0.9	84.1	4.8	2.5	1.0	0.5	0.3
0	100	-0.6	0.9	0.9	0.9	0.9	0.9	0.9	4.8	0.3	0.2	0.1	0.0	0.0
10	0	0.7	10.1	10.4	10.6	10.7	10.7	10.8	131.1	9.1	4.7	1.9	1.0	0.5
10	100	10.4	10.8	10.8	10.8	10.8	10.8	10.8	5.6	0.4	0.2	0.1	0.0	0.0
20	0	6.2	19.4	20.0	20.4	20.5	20.6	20.6	189.2	16.1	8.5	3.5	1.8	0.9
20	100	20.2	20.6	20.6	20.6	20.6	20.6	20.6	5.5	0.6	0.3	0.1	0.1	0.0
30	0	10.9	28.4	29.4	30.0	30.2	30.3	30.4	256.9	26.9	14.4	6.0	3.1	1.5
30	100	30.1	30.4	30.4	30.4	30.4	30.3	30.4	4.6	0.6	0.3	0.1	0.1	0.0
40	0	15.1	37.1	38.5	39.5	39.9	40.1	40.3	332.8	42.6	23.3	9.9	5.1	2.6
40	100	40.0	40.2	40.2	40.2	40.2	40.3	40.3	2.9	0.5	0.3	0.1	0.1	0.0

DIMENSION ALONG AIRFLOW = 5 CM   DIMENSION ACROSS AIRFLOW = 1 CM

TA	RH	LEAF TEMPERATURES FOR RESISTANCES=							TRANSPIRATION EXP 6 FOR RES =					
		**0*	**1*	**2*	**5*	*10*	*20*	INF*	**0*	**1*	**2*	**5*	*10*	*20*
0	0	-5.9	1.2	1.6	1.9	1.9	2.0	2.0	46.7	4.9	2.6	1.1	0.6	0.3
0	100	1.1	1.9	2.0	2.0	2.0	2.0	2.0	5.6	0.6	0.3	0.1	0.1	0.0
10	0	-0.2	10.2	10.9	11.4	11.5	11.6	11.7	70.3	8.9	4.8	2.0	1.0	0.5
10	100	10.7	11.6	11.6	11.7	11.7	11.7	11.7	6.2	0.9	0.5	0.2	0.1	0.1
20	0	4.8	18.9	20.0	20.8	21.1	21.2	21.4	98.6	15.1	8.4	3.6	1.8	0.9
20	100	20.4	21.2	21.3	21.3	21.3	21.4	21.4	5.9	1.1	0.6	0.3	0.1	0.1
30	0	9.2	27.0	28.7	30.0	30.5	30.7	31.0	130.8	24.2	13.7	6.0	3.1	1.6
30	100	30.2	30.8	30.9	30.9	31.0	31.0	31.0	4.8	1.2	0.7	0.3	0.2	0.1
40	0	13.0	34.7	37.1	39.0	39.7	40.1	40.6	166.4	36.5	21.4	9.6	5.0	2.6
40	100	40.1	40.4	40.5	40.5	40.5	40.5	40.6	3.0	1.0	0.6	0.3	0.1	0.1

AIRSPEED = 800. CM/SEC   RADIATION ABSORBED = 0.6 EXP 6 ERGS/CM2/SEC

DIMENSION ALONG AIRFLOW = 1 CM   DIMENSION ACROSS AIRFLOW = 5 CM

LEAF TEMPERATURES FOR RESISTANCES=   TRANSPIRATION EXP 6 FOR RES =

TA	RH	**0*	**1*	**2*	**5*	*10*	*20*	INF*	**0*	**1*	**2*	**5*	*10*	*20*
0	0	-4.3	0.6	0.7	0.9	0.9	0.9	0.9	67.1	4.8	2.5	1.0	0.5	0.3
0	100	0.6	0.9	0.9	0.9	0.9	0.9	0.9	4.0	0.3	0.2	0.1	0.0	0.0
10	0	2.5	10.1	10.4	10.6	10.7	10.7	10.8	107.6	9.0	4.7	1.9	1.0	0.5
10	100	10.4	10.8	10.8	10.8	10.8	10.8	10.8	4.7	0.4	0.2	0.1	0.0	0.0
20	0	8.5	19.4	20.0	20.4	20.5	20.6	20.6	159.3	15.9	8.4	3.5	1.8	0.9
20	100	20.3	20.6	20.6	20.6	20.6	20.6	20.6	4.9	0.6	0.3	0.1	0.1	0.0
30	0	13.7	28.5	29.4	30.0	30.2	30.3	30.4	221.2	26.5	14.3	6.0	3.1	1.5
30	100	30.1	30.4	30.4	30.4	30.4	30.4	30.4	4.2	0.6	0.3	0.1	0.1	0.0
40	0	18.3	37.1	38.5	39.5	39.9	40.1	40.3	291.8	42.0	23.2	9.9	5.1	2.6
40	100	40.1	40.2	40.2	40.2	40.3	40.3	40.3	2.7	0.5	0.3	0.1	0.1	0.0

DIMENSION ALONG AIRFLOW = 5 CM   DIMENSION ACROSS AIRFLOW = 5 CM

LEAF TEMPERATURES FOR RESISTANCES=   TRANSPIRATION EXP 6 FOR RES =

TA	RH	**0*	**1*	**2*	**5*	*10*	*20*	INF*	**0*	**1*	**2*	**5*	*10*	*20*
0	0	-4.4	1.2	1.6	1.9	1.9	2.0	2.0	37.8	4.8	2.6	1.1	0.5	0.3
0	100	1.3	1.9	2.0	2.0	2.0	2.0	2.0	4.6	0.6	0.3	0.1	0.1	0.0
10	0	1.9	10.3	10.9	11.4	11.5	11.6	11.7	58.5	8.7	4.8	2.0	1.0	0.5
10	100	10.8	11.6	11.6	11.7	11.7	11.7	11.7	5.3	0.9	0.5	0.2	0.1	0.1
20	0	7.3	18.9	20.0	20.8	21.1	21.2	21.4	84.0	14.8	8.3	3.6	1.8	0.9
20	100	20.5	21.2	21.3	21.3	21.3	21.4	21.4	5.3	1.1	0.6	0.3	0.1	0.1
30	0	12.1	27.1	28.8	30.0	30.5	30.7	31.0	113.8	23.7	13.6	6.0	3.1	1.6
30	100	30.3	30.8	30.9	30.9	31.0	31.0	31.0	4.5	1.2	0.7	0.3	0.2	0.1
40	0	16.3	34.8	37.1	39.0	39.7	40.1	40.6	147.2	35.8	21.1	9.6	5.0	2.6
40	100	40.1	40.4	40.5	40.5	40.5	40.5	40.6	2.8	0.9	0.6	0.3	0.1	0.1

AIRSPEED = 800. CM/SEC   RADIATION ABSORBED = 0.6 EXP 6 ERGS/CM2/SEC

DIMENSION ALONG AIRFLOW = 10 CM   DIMENSION ACROSS AIRFLOW = 5 CM

		LEAF TEMPERATURES FOR RESISTANCES=							TRANSPIRATION EXP 6 FOR RES =					
TA	RH	**0*	**1*	**2*	**5*	*10*	*20*	INF*	**0*	**1*	**2*	**5*	*10*	*20*
0	0	-4.3	1.7	2.2	2.6	2.7	2.8	2.8	30.0	4.9	2.7	1.1	0.6	0.3
0	100	1.7	2.6	2.7	2.8	2.8	2.8	2.8	4.9	0.9	0.5	0.2	0.1	0.1
10	0	1.7	10.4	11.3	11.9	12.2	12.3	12.4	45.4	8.6	4.8	2.1	1.1	0.5
10	100	11.1	12.1	12.2	12.3	12.4	12.4	12.4	5.6	1.2	0.7	0.3	0.1	0.1
20	0	6.9	18.6	20.0	21.1	21.5	21.7	21.9	64.3	14.2	8.2	3.6	1.9	0.9
20	100	20.6	21.6	21.7	21.8	21.9	21.9	21.9	5.5	1.5	0.9	0.4	0.2	0.1
30	0	11.5	26.3	28.4	30.0	30.7	31.0	31.4	85.9	22.2	13.1	5.9	3.1	1.6
30	100	30.3	31.0	31.2	31.3	31.3	31.3	31.4	4.6	1.5	0.9	0.4	0.2	0.1
40	0	15.5	33.4	36.3	38.7	39.7	40.2	40.8	110.1	32.6	20.0	9.4	5.0	2.6
40	100	40.1	40.5	40.6	40.7	40.7	40.7	40.8	2.8	1.2	0.7	0.4	0.2	0.1

DIMENSION ALONG AIRFLOW = 20 CM   DIMENSION ACROSS AIRFLOW = 5 CM

		LEAF TEMPERATURES FOR RESISTANCES=							TRANSPIRATION EXP 6 FOR RES =					
TA	RH	**0*	**1*	**2*	**5*	*10*	*20*	INF*	**0*	**1*	**2*	**5*	*10*	*20*
0	0	-3.3	3.6	4.6	5.5	5.8	6.0	6.2	18.4	5.1	3.0	1.3	0.7	0.4
0	100	3.3	5.3	5.7	6.0	6.1	6.1	6.2	5.8	1.7	1.0	0.5	0.2	0.1
10	0	1.8	11.0	12.7	14.0	14.6	14.9	15.2	26.3	8.3	5.0	2.3	1.2	0.6
10	100	12.1	14.1	14.5	14.9	15.0	15.1	15.2	6.2	2.2	1.4	0.6	0.3	0.2
20	0	6.3	17.9	20.2	22.2	23.1	23.6	24.1	35.4	12.6	7.9	3.8	2.0	1.1
20	100	21.2	22.8	23.3	23.7	23.9	24.0	24.1	5.9	2.5	1.6	0.8	0.4	0.2
30	0	10.2	24.1	27.2	30.1	31.4	32.1	32.9	45.6	18.1	11.8	5.9	3.2	1.7
30	100	30.6	31.7	32.1	32.5	32.7	32.8	32.9	4.8	2.4	1.7	0.8	0.5	0.2
40	0	13.7	29.7	33.6	37.5	39.3	40.4	41.6	56.7	24.8	16.7	8.7	4.8	2.6
40	100	40.2	40.8	41.0	41.3	41.5	41.5	41.6	2.9	1.7	1.2	0.7	0.4	0.2

AIRSPEED = 800. CM/SEC   RADIATION ABSORBED = 0.6 EXP 6 ERGS/CM2/SEC

DIMENSION ALONG AIRFLOW = 1 CM   DIMENSION ACROSS AIRFLOW = 10 CM

LEAF TEMPERATURES FOR RESISTANCES=   TRANSPIRATION EXP 6 FOR RES =

TA	RH	**0*	**1*	**2*	***5*	*10*	*20*	INF*	**0*	**1*	**2*	***5*	*10*	*20*
0	0	-3.9	0.9	1.2	1.4	1.4	1.5	1.5	43.7	4.8	2.5	1.0	0.5	0.3
0	100	1.0	1.4	1.5	1.5	1.5	1.5	1.5	4.1	0.5	0.2	0.1	0.1	0.0
10	0	2.7	10.2	10.7	11.0	11.1	11.2	11.3	69.4	8.8	4.7	2.0	1.0	0.5
10	100	10.7	11.2	11.2	11.2	11.2	11.3	11.3	4.8	0.7	0.4	0.2	0.1	0.0
20	0	8.5	19.2	20.0	20.6	20.8	20.9	21.0	101.9	15.2	8.3	3.5	1.8	0.9
20	100	20.4	20.9	20.9	21.0	21.0	21.0	21.0	4.9	0.9	0.5	0.2	0.1	0.1
30	0	13.7	27.8	29.1	30.0	30.4	30.5	30.7	140.5	24.8	13.9	6.0	3.1	1.6
30	100	30.2	30.6	30.7	30.7	30.7	30.7	30.7	4.2	0.9	0.5	0.2	0.1	0.1
40	0	18.2	35.9	37.8	39.3	39.8	40.1	40.4	184.5	38.3	22.0	9.7	5.0	2.6
40	100	40.1	40.3	40.4	40.4	40.4	40.4	40.4	2.7	0.8	0.4	0.2	0.1	0.1

DIMENSION ALONG AIRFLOW = 5 CM   DIMENSION ACROSS AIRFLOW = 10 CM

LEAF TEMPERATURES FOR RESISTANCES=   TRANSPIRATION EXP 6 FOR RES =

TA	RH	**0*	**1*	**2*	***5*	*10*	*20*	INF*	**0*	**1*	**2*	***5*	*10*	*20*
0	0	-3.6	1.9	2.5	2.9	3.1	3.2	3.2	25.4	4.8	2.7	1.2	0.6	0.3
0	100	2.0	3.0	3.1	3.2	3.2	3.2	3.2	4.7	1.0	0.5	0.2	0.1	0.1
10	0	2.4	10.5	11.5	12.2	12.4	12.6	12.7	38.6	8.4	4.8	2.1	1.1	0.5
10	100	11.3	12.4	12.5	12.6	12.7	12.7	12.7	5.4	1.3	0.8	0.3	0.2	0.1
20	0	7.6	18.5	20.1	21.2	21.7	21.9	22.2	54.7	13.8	8.1	3.6	1.9	1.0
20	100	20.8	21.7	21.9	22.1	22.1	22.1	22.2	5.4	1.6	0.9	0.4	0.2	0.1
30	0	12.3	26.0	28.2	30.0	30.7	31.1	31.5	73.4	21.3	12.8	5.9	3.1	1.6
30	100	30.4	31.1	31.3	31.4	31.5	31.5	31.5	4.5	1.7	1.0	0.5	0.2	0.1
40	0	16.3	32.9	35.9	38.5	39.6	40.2	40.9	94.1	31.0	19.4	9.2	4.9	2.6
40	100	40.2	40.6	40.7	40.8	40.8	40.8	40.9	2.8	1.3	0.8	0.4	0.2	0.1

AIRSPEED = 800. CM/SEC   RADIATION ABSORBED = 0.6 EXP 6 ERGS/CM2/SEC

DIMENSION ALONG AIRFLOW = 10 CM   DIMENSION ACROSS AIRFLOW = 10 CM

LEAF TEMPERATURES FOR RESISTANCES=   TRANSPIRATION EXP 6 FOR RES =

TA	RH	**0*	**1*	**2*	***5*	*10*	*20*	INF*	**0*	**1*	**2*	***5*	*10*	*20*
0	0	-3.2	2.7	3.5	4.0	4.3	4.4	4.5	20.6	4.9	2.8	1.2	0.6	0.3
0	100	2.6	4.0	4.2	4.4	4.4	4.5	4.5	5.0	1.3	0.7	0.3	0.2	0.1
10	0	2.5	10.7	12.0	13.0	13.4	13.6	13.8	30.5	8.3	4.9	2.2	1.1	0.6
10	100	11.7	13.1	13.4	13.6	13.7	13.7	13.8	5.7	1.7	1.0	0.5	0.2	0.1
20	0	7.4	18.2	20.1	21.7	22.3	22.6	23.0	42.4	13.1	8.0	3.7	1.9	1.0
20	100	21.0	22.3	22.5	22.8	22.9	22.9	23.0	5.5	2.0	1.3	0.6	0.3	0.2
30	0	11.8	25.1	27.8	30.0	31.0	31.6	32.1	56.0	19.6	12.3	5.9	3.2	1.6
30	100	30.5	31.4	31.7	31.9	32.0	32.1	32.1	4.6	2.0	1.3	0.6	0.3	0.2
40	0	15.7	31.5	34.9	38.1	39.5	40.3	41.2	71.0	27.7	18.0	9.0	4.9	2.6
40	100	40.2	40.7	40.8	41.0	41.1	41.1	41.2	2.8	1.5	1.0	0.5	0.3	0.1

DIMENSION ALONG AIRFLOW = 20 CM   DIMENSION ACROSS AIRFLOW = 10 CM

LEAF TEMPERATURES FOR RESISTANCES=   TRANSPIRATION EXP 6 FOR RES =

TA	RH	**0*	**1*	**2*	***5*	*10*	*20*	INF*	**0*	**1*	**2*	***5*	*10*	*20*
0	0	-2.5	3.6	4.7	5.5	5.8	6.0	6.2	16.9	5.0	3.0	1.3	0.7	0.4
0	100	3.5	5.3	5.7	6.0	6.1	6.1	6.2	5.4	1.7	1.0	0.5	0.2	0.1
10	0	2.8	11.1	12.7	14.0	14.6	14.9	15.2	24.4	8.1	5.0	2.3	1.2	0.6
10	100	12.2	14.1	14.5	14.9	15.0	15.1	15.2	5.9	2.2	1.4	0.6	0.3	0.2
20	0	7.4	18.0	20.2	22.2	23.1	23.6	24.1	33.2	12.4	7.8	3.8	2.0	1.1
20	100	21.3	22.9	23.3	23.7	23.9	24.0	24.1	5.7	2.5	1.6	0.8	0.4	0.2
30	0	11.5	24.2	27.2	30.1	31.4	32.1	32.9	43.1	17.8	11.7	5.8	3.2	1.7
30	100	30.7	31.7	32.1	32.5	32.7	32.8	32.9	4.6	2.4	1.6	0.8	0.5	0.2
40	0	15.1	29.9	33.7	37.5	39.3	40.4	41.6	53.9	24.4	16.5	8.6	4.8	2.6
40	100	40.3	40.8	41.1	41.3	41.4	41.5	41.6	2.9	1.7	1.2	0.7	0.4	0.2

AIRSPEED = 800. CM/SEC   RADIATION ABSORBED = 0.8 EXP 6 ERGS/CM2/SEC
DIMENSION ALONG AIRFLOW = 1 CM   DIMENSION ACROSS AIRFLOW = 1 CM

TA	RH	LEAF TEMPERATURES FOR RESISTANCES=							TRANSPIRATION EXP 6 FOR RES =					
		**0*	**1*	**2*	**5*	*10*	*20*	INF*	**0*	**1*	**2*	**5*	*10*	*20*
0	0	-5.2	1.2	1.3	1.5	1.5	1.5	1.5	86.7	5.1	2.6	1.1	0.5	0.3
0	100	0.9	1.5	1.5	1.5	1.5	1.5	1.5	8.1	0.5	0.3	0.1	0.1	0.0
10	0	1.1	10.7	11.0	11.2	11.3	11.4	11.4	134.4	9.4	4.9	2.0	1.0	0.5
10	100	10.6	11.3	11.4	11.4	11.4	11.4	11.4	10.0	0.8	0.4	0.2	0.1	0.0
20	0	6.5	20.0	20.6	21.0	21.1	21.2	21.2	193.2	16.6	8.8	3.6	1.8	0.9
20	100	20.4	21.2	21.2	21.2	21.2	21.2	21.2	11.0	1.2	0.6	0.3	0.1	0.1
30	0	11.2	29.0	30.0	30.6	30.8	30.9	31.1	261.4	27.7	14.9	6.2	3.2	1.6
30	100	30.3	30.9	31.0	31.0	31.1	31.1	31.1	10.9	1.5	0.8	0.3	0.2	0.1
40	0	15.4	37.6	39.1	40.1	40.5	40.7	40.9	337.8	43.7	24.0	10.2	5.2	2.6
40	100	40.1	40.7	40.8	40.8	40.9	40.9	40.9	9.8	1.8	1.0	0.4	0.2	0.1

DIMENSION ALONG AIRFLOW = 5 CM   DIMENSION ACROSS AIRFLOW = 1 CM

TA	RH	LEAF TEMPERATURES FOR RESISTANCES=							TRANSPIRATION EXP 6 FOR RES =					
		**0*	**1*	**2*	**5*	*10*	*20*	INF*	**0*	**1*	**2*	**5*	*10*	*20*
0	0	-5.1	2.5	2.9	3.2	3.3	3.3	3.4	49.7	5.4	2.9	1.2	0.6	0.3
0	100	1.8	3.2	3.3	3.4	3.4	3.4	3.4	9.4	1.1	0.6	0.2	0.1	0.1
10	0	0.6	11.5	12.2	12.7	12.9	13.0	13.1	74.0	9.6	5.2	2.2	1.1	0.6
10	100	11.2	12.8	12.9	13.0	13.0	13.1	13.1	11.1	1.7	0.9	0.4	0.2	0.1
20	0	5.5	20.0	21.2	22.1	22.4	22.6	22.7	102.9	16.2	9.0	3.9	2.0	1.0
20	100	20.8	22.3	22.5	22.6	22.7	22.7	22.7	11.8	2.3	1.3	0.6	0.3	0.1
30	0	9.7	28.1	29.9	31.3	31.8	32.0	32.3	135.6	25.7	14.6	6.4	3.3	1.7
30	100	30.5	31.8	32.0	32.2	32.3	32.3	32.3	11.7	3.0	1.7	0.8	0.4	0.2
40	0	13.5	35.7	38.2	40.2	41.0	41.4	41.9	171.6	38.5	22.6	10.2	5.4	2.7
40	100	40.3	41.4	41.6	41.7	41.8	41.8	41.9	10.1	3.4	2.0	0.9	0.5	0.2

AIRSPEED = 800. CM/SEC   RADIATION ABSORBED = 0.8 EXP 6 ERGS/CM2/SEC

DIMENSION ALONG AIRFLOW = 1 CM   DIMENSION ACROSS AIRFLOW = 5 CM

		LEAF TEMPERATURES FOR RESISTANCES=							TRANSPIRATION EXP 6 FOR RES =					
TA	RH	**0*	**1*	**2*	**5*	*10*	*20*	INF*	**0*	**1*	**2*	**5*	*10*	*20*
0	0	-3.8	1.2	1.3	1.5	1.5	1.5	1.5	69.3	5.0	2.6	1.1	0.5	0.3
0	100	1.0	1.5	1.5	1.5	1.5	1.5	1.5	6.7	0.5	0.3	0.1	0.1	0.0
10	0	2.9	10.7	11.0	11.2	11.3	11.4	11.4	110.5	9.3	4.9	2.0	1.0	0.5
10	100	10.8	11.3	11.4	11.4	11.4	11.4	11.4	8.5	0.8	0.4	0.2	0.1	0.0
20	0	8.8	20.0	20.6	21.0	21.1	21.2	21.2	162.9	16.4	8.7	3.6	1.8	0.9
20	100	20.5	21.2	21.2	21.2	21.2	21.2	21.2	9.7	1.1	0.6	0.3	0.1	0.1
30	0	14.0	29.0	30.0	30.6	30.8	30.9	31.1	225.4	27.4	14.8	6.2	3.2	1.6
30	100	30.3	30.9	31.0	31.0	31.0	31.1	31.1	10.0	1.5	0.8	0.3	0.2	0.1
40	0	18.5	37.7	39.1	40.1	40.5	40.7	40.9	296.5	43.2	23.8	10.2	5.2	2.6
40	100	40.2	40.7	40.8	40.9	40.9	40.9	40.9	9.2	1.8	1.0	0.4	0.2	0.1

DIMENSION ALONG AIRFLOW = 5 CM   DIMENSION ACROSS AIRFLOW = 5 CM

		LEAF TEMPERATURES FOR RESISTANCES=							TRANSPIRATION EXP 6 FOR RES =					
TA	RH	**0*	**1*	**2*	**5*	*10*	*20*	INF*	**0*	**1*	**2*	**5*	*10*	*20*
0	0	-3.5	2.5	2.9	3.2	3.3	3.3	3.4	40.4	5.3	2.8	1.2	0.6	0.3
0	100	2.1	3.2	3.3	3.4	3.4	3.4	3.4	7.9	1.1	0.6	0.2	0.1	0.1
10	0	2.7	11.5	12.2	12.7	12.9	13.0	13.1	61.8	9.4	5.2	2.2	1.1	0.6
10	100	11.5	12.8	12.9	13.0	13.0	13.1	13.1	9.7	1.7	0.9	0.4	0.2	0.1
20	0	8.0	20.1	21.3	22.1	22.4	22.5	22.7	88.0	15.9	8.9	3.8	2.0	1.0
20	100	21.0	22.3	22.5	22.6	22.7	22.7	22.7	10.6	2.3	1.3	0.6	0.3	0.1
30	0	12.7	28.2	30.0	31.3	31.8	32.0	32.3	118.3	25.2	14.5	6.4	3.3	1.7
30	100	30.6	31.8	32.0	32.2	32.3	32.3	32.3	10.6	2.9	1.7	0.7	0.4	0.2
40	0	16.8	35.8	38.3	40.3	41.0	41.5	41.9	152.1	37.8	22.4	10.2	5.3	2.7
40	100	40.3	41.4	41.6	41.7	41.8	41.9	41.9	9.6	3.3	2.0	0.9	0.5	0.2

151

AIRSPEED = 800. CM/SEC   RADIATION ABSORBED = 0.8 EXP 6 ERGS/CM2/SEC

DIMENSION ALONG AIRFLOW = 10 CM   DIMENSION ACROSS AIRFLOW = 5 CM

TA	RH	**0*	**1*	**2*	**5*	*10*	*20*	INF*	**0*	**1*	**2*	**5*	*10*	*20*
		LEAF TEMPERATURES FOR RESISTANCES=							TRANSPIRATION EXP 6 FOR RES =					
0	0	-3.0	3.5	4.0	4.4	4.6	4.7	4.7	32.7	5.5	3.0	1.3	0.7	0.3
0	100	2.8	4.4	4.5	4.7	4.7	4.7	4.7	8.4	1.5	0.8	0.4	0.2	0.1
10	0	2.8	12.1	13.0	13.7	14.0	14.1	14.3	48.9	9.6	5.4	2.3	1.2	0.6
10	100	11.9	13.8	14.0	14.2	14.2	14.3	14.3	10.1	2.2	1.3	0.5	0.3	0.1
20	0	7.9	20.2	21.7	22.9	23.3	23.5	23.8	68.3	15.6	9.0	4.0	2.1	1.1
20	100	21.3	23.1	23.4	23.6	23.7	23.7	23.8	11.0	3.0	1.8	0.8	0.4	0.2
30	0	12.3	27.8	30.0	31.8	32.5	32.8	33.2	90.6	24.0	14.3	6.5	3.4	1.8
30	100	30.8	32.4	32.7	33.0	33.1	33.2	33.2	10.8	3.7	2.2	1.0	0.5	0.3
40	0	16.2	34.8	37.8	40.4	41.4	42.0	42.6	115.1	35.0	21.6	10.2	5.4	2.8
40	100	40.5	41.7	42.0	42.3	42.5	42.5	42.6	9.8	4.1	2.6	1.2	0.7	0.3

DIMENSION ALONG AIRFLOW = 20 CM   DIMENSION ACROSS AIRFLOW = 5 CM

TA	RH	**0*	**1*	**2*	**5*	*10*	*20*	INF*	**0*	**1*	**2*	**5*	*10*	*20*
		LEAF TEMPERATURES FOR RESISTANCES=							TRANSPIRATION EXP 6 FOR RES =					
0	0	-0.9	7.0	8.3	9.4	9.8	10.0	10.3	21.8	6.4	3.8	1.7	0.9	0.5
0	100	5.3	8.7	9.3	9.8	10.0	10.2	10.3	9.9	3.1	1.9	0.9	0.4	0.2
10	0	3.9	14.2	16.1	17.8	18.5	18.8	19.2	30.3	10.1	6.2	2.9	1.5	0.8
10	100	13.6	17.1	17.9	18.6	18.9	19.1	19.2	11.3	4.3	2.7	1.3	0.7	0.3
20	0	8.1	20.7	23.4	25.8	26.9	27.5	28.1	39.9	14.9	9.5	4.6	2.5	1.3
20	100	22.3	25.5	26.4	27.3	27.6	27.9	28.1	11.8	5.3	3.5	1.7	0.9	0.5
30	0	11.8	26.7	30.2	33.5	35.0	35.9	36.9	50.5	21.0	13.9	7.0	3.9	2.1
30	100	31.4	34.0	34.9	35.8	36.3	36.6	36.9	11.4	6.0	4.1	2.1	1.2	0.6
40	0	15.2	32.1	36.4	40.7	42.8	44.1	45.6	62.0	28.1	19.3	10.2	5.8	3.1
40	100	40.8	42.7	43.5	44.4	44.9	45.2	45.6	10.1	6.1	4.4	2.4	1.4	0.7

AIRSPEED = 800. CM/SEC   RADIATION ABSORBED = 0.8 EXP 6 ERGS/CM2/SEC

DIMENSION ALONG AIRFLOW = 1 CM   DIMENSION ACROSS AIRFLOW = 10 CM

TA	RH	LEAF TEMPERATURES FOR RESISTANCES=							TRANSPIRATION EXP 6 FOR RES =					
		**0*	**1*	**2*	**5*	*10*	*20*	INF*	**0*	**1*	**2*	**5*	*10*	*20*
0	0	-3.2	1.9	2.1	2.3	2.4	2.4	2.5	46.0	5.1	2.7	1.1	0.6	0.3
0	100	1.6	2.4	2.4	2.5	2.5	2.5	2.5	6.8	0.8	0.4	0.2	0.1	0.0
10	0	3.3	11.1	11.6	12.0	12.1	12.2	12.2	72.4	9.3	5.0	2.1	1.1	0.5
10	100	11.2	12.1	12.2	12.2	12.2	12.2	12.2	8.7	1.2	0.7	0.3	0.1	0.1
20	0	9.1	20.1	20.9	21.5	21.8	21.9	22.0	105.5	16.0	8.8	3.7	1.9	1.0
20	100	20.8	21.8	21.9	21.9	22.0	22.0	22.0	9.8	1.7	1.0	0.4	0.2	0.1
30	0	14.1	28.6	30.0	31.0	31.3	31.5	31.7	144.8	26.0	14.5	6.3	3.2	1.6
30	100	30.5	31.4	31.6	31.6	31.7	31.7	31.7	10.0	2.3	1.3	0.6	0.3	0.1
40	0	18.6	36.7	38.7	40.2	40.8	41.1	41.4	189.2	39.9	23.0	10.2	5.3	2.7
40	100	40.3	41.1	41.2	41.3	41.3	41.3	41.4	9.2	2.6	1.5	0.7	0.4	0.2

DIMENSION ALONG AIRFLOW = 5 CM   DIMENSION ACROSS AIRFLOW = 10 CM

TA	RH	LEAF TEMPERATURES FOR RESISTANCES=							TRANSPIRATION EXP 6 FOR RES =					
		**0*	**1*	**2*	**5*	*10*	*20*	INF*	**0*	**1*	**2*	**5*	*10*	*20*
0	0	-2.2	3.9	4.6	5.0	5.2	5.3	5.4	28.2	5.5	3.1	1.3	0.7	0.3
0	100	3.2	4.9	5.1	5.3	5.3	5.4	5.4	8.1	1.7	0.9	0.4	0.2	0.1
10	0	3.6	12.4	13.4	14.2	14.6	14.7	14.9	42.0	9.5	5.4	2.4	1.2	0.6
10	100	12.3	14.2	14.5	14.7	14.8	14.8	14.9	9.8	2.5	1.4	0.6	0.3	0.2
20	0	8.7	20.3	21.9	23.2	23.7	24.0	24.3	58.7	15.3	9.0	4.1	2.1	1.1
20	100	21.5	23.4	23.8	24.1	24.2	24.2	24.3	10.7	3.3	2.0	0.9	0.5	0.2
30	0	13.2	27.7	30.0	32.0	32.8	33.2	33.7	77.9	23.3	14.2	6.6	3.5	1.8
30	100	30.9	32.6	33.0	33.4	33.5	33.6	33.7	10.6	4.0	2.5	1.2	0.6	0.3
40	0	17.2	34.4	37.6	40.4	41.6	42.3	43.0	99.1	33.5	21.1	10.2	5.5	2.8
40	100	40.5	41.9	42.3	42.6	42.8	42.9	43.0	9.6	4.4	2.8	1.4	0.7	0.4

6

AIRSPEED = 800. CM/SEC   RADIATION ABSORBED = 0.8 EXP 6 ERGS/CM2/SEC

DIMENSION ALONG AIRFLOW = 10 CM   DIMENSION ACROSS AIRFLOW = 10 CM

		LEAF TEMPERATURES FOR RESISTANCES=							TRANSPIRATION EXP 6 FOR RES =					
TA	RH	**0*	**1*	**2*	**5*	*10*	*20*	INF*	**0*	**1*	**2*	**5*	*10*	*20*
0	0	-1.3	5.3	6.2	6.9	7.2	7.3	7.5	23.5	5.8	3.4	1.5	0.8	0.4
0	100	4.3	6.6	7.0	7.3	7.4	7.4	7.5	8.7	2.3	1.3	0.6	0.3	0.2
10	0	4.1	13.2	14.6	15.8	16.2	16.5	16.7	34.1	9.7	5.7	2.6	1.4	0.7
10	100	13.0	15.6	16.0	16.4	16.6	16.6	16.7	10.3	3.3	1.9	0.9	0.5	0.2
20	0	8.9	20.5	22.6	24.4	25.1	25.5	25.9	46.6	15.0	9.2	4.3	2.3	1.2
20	100	22.0	24.4	25.0	25.5	25.7	25.8	25.9	11.0	4.2	2.6	1.2	0.7	0.3
30	0	13.1	27.2	30.1	32.7	33.8	34.4	35.0	60.6	22.0	14.0	6.8	3.6	1.9
30	100	31.2	33.3	33.9	34.5	34.7	34.7	35.0	10.9	4.9	3.2	1.6	0.9	0.4
40	0	16.8	33.4	37.1	40.6	42.2	43.1	44.1	76.0	30.6	20.1	10.2	5.6	3.0
40	100	40.7	42.3	42.9	43.5	43.7	43.7	44.1	9.8	5.2	3.6	1.8	1.0	0.5

DIMENSION ALONG AIRFLOW = 20 CM   DIMENSION ACROSS AIRFLOW = 10 CM

		LEAF TEMPERATURES FOR RESISTANCES=							TRANSPIRATION EXP 6 FOR RES =					
TA	RH	**0*	**1*	**2*	**5*	*10*	*20*	INF*	**0*	**1*	**2*	**5*	*10*	*20*
0	0	-0.0	7.1	8.4	9.4	9.8	10.0	10.3	20.1	6.3	3.8	1.7	0.9	0.5
0	100	5.6	8.7	9.3	9.8	10.0	10.2	10.3	9.2	3.1	1.9	0.9	0.4	0.2
10	0	5.0	14.3	16.2	17.8	18.5	18.8	19.2	28.2	9.9	6.1	2.9	1.5	0.8
10	100	13.9	17.1	17.9	18.6	18.9	19.1	19.2	10.7	4.2	2.6	1.2	0.7	0.3
20	0	9.3	20.9	23.5	25.8	26.9	27.5	28.1	37.5	14.7	9.4	4.6	2.5	1.3
20	100	22.5	25.5	26.4	27.3	27.6	27.9	28.1	11.4	5.2	3.4	1.7	0.9	0.5
30	0	13.2	26.9	30.3	33.5	35.0	35.9	36.9	47.9	20.6	13.8	7.0	3.9	2.1
30	100	31.6	34.0	34.9	35.9	36.3	36.6	36.9	11.1	5.9	4.1	2.1	1.2	0.6
40	0	16.6	32.3	36.5	40.8	42.8	44.1	45.6	59.1	27.7	19.1	10.2	5.8	3.1
40	100	40.9	42.7	43.5	44.4	44.9	45.2	45.6	9.9	6.0	4.3	2.4	1.4	0.7

AIRSPEED = 800. CM/SEC   RADIATION ABSORBED = 1.0 EXP 6 ERGS/CM2/SEC

DIMENSION ALONG AIRFLOW = 1 CM   DIMENSION ACROSS AIRFLOW = 1 CM

LEAF TEMPERATURES FOR RESISTANCES=   TRANSPIRATION EXP 6 FOR RES =

TA	RH	**0*	**1*	**2*	**5*	*10*	*20*	INF*	**0*	**1*	**2*	**5*	*10*	*20*
0	0	-4.7	1.8	2.0	2.1	2.1	2.1	2.2	89.4	5.3	2.7	1.1	0.6	0.3
0	100	1.3	2.1	2.1	2.2	2.2	2.2	2.2	11.5	0.7	0.4	0.2	0.1	0.0
10	0	1.4	11.3	11.6	11.9	11.9	12.0	12.0	137.8	9.8	5.1	2.1	1.1	0.5
10	100	10.9	11.9	12.0	12.0	12.0	12.0	12.0	14.4	1.2	0.6	0.2	0.1	0.1
20	0	6.8	20.6	21.2	21.6	21.7	21.8	21.9	197.2	17.2	9.1	3.8	1.9	1.0
20	100	20.6	21.7	21.8	21.8	21.8	21.8	21.9	16.4	1.8	0.9	0.4	0.2	0.1
30	0	11.5	29.5	30.5	31.2	31.4	31.6	31.7	266.0	28.5	15.3	6.4	3.3	1.6
30	100	30.4	31.5	31.6	31.6	31.7	31.7	31.7	17.1	2.5	1.3	0.6	0.3	0.1
40	0	15.6	38.2	39.7	40.7	41.1	41.3	41.5	342.7	44.9	24.7	10.5	5.4	2.7
40	100	40.3	41.2	41.3	41.4	41.5	41.5	41.5	16.7	3.2	1.8	0.7	0.4	0.2

DIMENSION ALONG AIRFLOW = 5 CM   DIMENSION ACROSS AIRFLOW = 1 CM

LEAF TEMPERATURES FOR RESISTANCES=   TRANSPIRATION EXP 6 FOR RES =

TA	RH	**0*	**1*	**2*	**5*	*10*	*20*	INF*	**0*	**1*	**2*	**5*	*10*	*20*
0	0	-4.2	3.8	4.2	4.5	4.6	4.7	4.8	52.8	5.9	3.1	1.3	0.7	0.3
0	100	2.5	4.5	4.6	4.7	4.7	4.7	4.8	13.3	1.6	0.9	0.4	0.2	0.1
10	0	1.3	12.7	13.5	14.0	14.2	14.3	14.4	77.8	10.4	5.7	2.4	1.2	0.6
10	100	11.7	14.0	14.2	14.3	14.3	14.4	14.4	16.0	2.5	1.4	0.6	0.3	0.1
20	0	6.1	21.2	22.5	23.4	23.7	23.9	24.1	107.2	17.4	9.7	4.1	2.1	1.1
20	100	21.2	23.5	23.7	23.9	24.0	24.0	24.1	17.7	3.6	2.0	0.9	0.4	0.2
30	0	10.3	29.2	31.1	32.5	33.1	33.4	33.7	140.4	27.3	15.6	6.9	3.6	1.8
30	100	30.7	32.9	33.2	33.5	33.6	33.6	33.7	18.0	4.8	2.8	1.2	0.6	0.3
40	0	14.0	36.7	39.4	41.5	42.3	42.8	43.2	176.8	40.5	24.0	10.9	5.7	2.9
40	100	40.5	42.3	42.7	43.0	43.1	43.2	43.2	17.3	5.8	3.5	1.6	0.8	0.4

AIRSPEED = 800. CM/SEC   RADIATION ABSORBED = 1.0 EXP 6 ERGS/CM2/SEC
DIMENSION ALONG AIRFLOW = 1 CM   DIMENSION ACROSS AIRFLOW = 5 CM

TA	RH	**0*	**1*	**2*	***5*	*10*	*20*	INF*	**0*	**1*	**2*	***5*	*10*	*20*
		\multicolumn{7}{LEAF TEMPERATURES FOR RESISTANCES=}		TRANSPIRATION EXP 6 FOR RES =					
0	0	-3.4	1.8	2.0	2.1	2.1	2.1	2.2	71.5	5.2	2.7	1.1	0.6	0.3
0	100	1.4	2.1	2.1	2.2	2.2	2.2	2.2	9.4	0.7	0.4	0.2	0.1	0.0
10	0	3.3	11.3	11.6	11.9	11.9	12.0	12.0	113.5	9.7	5.1	2.1	1.1	0.5
10	100	11.1	11.9	12.0	12.0	12.0	12.0	12.0	12.3	1.2	0.6	0.2	0.1	0.1
20	0	9.2	20.6	21.2	21.6	21.7	21.8	21.9	166.5	17.0	9.0	3.8	1.9	1.0
20	100	20.8	21.7	21.8	21.8	21.8	21.8	21.9	14.6	1.7	0.9	0.4	0.2	0.1
30	0	14.3	29.6	30.5	31.2	31.4	31.6	31.7	229.6	28.2	15.2	6.4	3.3	1.6
30	100	30.5	31.5	31.6	31.6	31.7	31.7	31.7	15.7	2.4	1.3	0.6	0.3	0.1
40	0	18.8	38.2	39.7	40.7	41.1	41.3	41.5	301.2	44.4	24.5	10.5	5.4	2.7
40	100	40.3	41.2	41.4	41.4	41.5	41.5	41.5	15.7	3.1	1.7	0.7	0.4	0.2

DIMENSION ALONG AIRFLOW = 5 CM   DIMENSION ACROSS AIRFLOW = 5 CM

TA	RH	**0*	**1*	**2*	***5*	*10*	*20*	INF*	**0*	**1*	**2*	***5*	*10*	*20*
		\multicolumn{7}{LEAF TEMPERATURES FOR RESISTANCES=}		TRANSPIRATION EXP 6 FOR RES =					
0	0	-2.6	3.8	4.2	4.5	4.6	4.7	4.8	43.1	5.7	3.1	1.3	0.7	0.3
0	100	2.9	4.5	4.6	4.7	4.7	4.7	4.8	11.2	1.6	0.8	0.4	0.2	0.1
10	0	3.5	12.7	13.5	14.0	14.2	14.3	14.4	65.2	10.2	5.6	2.4	1.2	0.6
10	100	12.1	14.0	14.2	14.3	14.4	14.4	14.4	14.0	2.5	1.3	0.6	0.3	0.1
20	0	8.7	21.3	22.5	23.4	23.7	23.9	24.1	92.0	17.0	9.5	4.1	2.1	1.1
20	100	21.4	23.5	23.7	23.9	24.0	24.0	24.1	16.0	3.5	2.0	0.9	0.4	0.2
30	0	13.3	29.3	31.2	32.6	33.1	33.4	33.7	122.8	26.7	15.4	6.8	3.6	1.8
30	100	30.9	32.9	33.2	33.5	33.6	33.6	33.7	16.8	4.7	2.7	1.2	0.6	0.3
40	0	17.3	36.8	39.4	41.5	42.3	42.8	43.2	157.1	39.8	23.7	10.8	5.7	2.9
40	100	40.6	42.3	42.7	43.0	43.1	43.2	43.2	16.4	5.7	3.5	1.6	0.8	0.4

AIRSPEED = 800. CM/SEC   RADIATION ABSORBED = 1.0 EXP 6 ERGS/CM2/SEC

DIMENSION ALONG AIRFLOW = 10 CM   DIMENSION ACROSS AIRFLOW = 5 CM

TA	RH	**0*	**1*	**2*	**5*	*10*	*20*	INF*	**0*	**1*	**2*	**5*	*10*	*20*
		LEAF TEMPERATURES FOR RESISTANCES=							TRANSPIRATION EXP 6 FOR RES =					
0	0	-1.8	5.2	5.8	6.3	6.5	6.5	6.6	35.7	6.1	3.4	1.4	0.7	0.4
0	100	3.8	6.1	6.3	6.5	6.6	6.6	6.6	12.0	2.2	1.2	0.5	0.3	0.1
10	0	3.9	13.7	14.8	15.6	15.9	16.0	16.2	52.5	10.6	6.0	2.6	1.3	0.7
10	100	12.7	15.4	15.7	16.0	16.1	16.1	16.2	14.8	3.3	1.9	0.8	0.4	0.2
20	0	8.8	21.7	23.4	24.6	25.1	25.4	25.7	72.5	17.1	9.9	4.4	2.3	1.2
20	100	21.9	24.6	25.0	25.4	25.5	25.6	25.7	16.5	4.7	2.7	1.2	0.6	0.3
30	0	13.1	29.2	31.6	33.5	34.2	34.7	35.1	95.3	26.0	15.6	7.1	3.8	1.9
30	100	31.2	33.7	34.3	34.7	34.9	35.0	35.1	17.2	6.0	3.7	1.7	0.9	0.5
40	0	16.9	36.1	39.3	42.0	43.2	43.8	44.5	120.2	37.5	23.3	11.1	5.9	3.1
40	100	40.8	42.9	43.5	44.0	44.2	44.3	44.5	16.7	7.1	4.5	2.2	1.2	0.6

DIMENSION ALONG AIRFLOW = 20 CM   DIMENSION ACROSS AIRFLOW = 5 CM

TA	RH	**0*	**1*	**2*	**5*	*10*	*20*	INF*	**0*	**1*	**2*	**5*	*10*	*20*
		LEAF TEMPERATURES FOR RESISTANCES=							TRANSPIRATION EXP 6 FOR RES =					
0	0	1.4	10.3	11.9	13.2	13.8	14.0	14.3	25.5	7.9	4.8	2.2	1.2	0.6
0	100	7.1	11.9	12.9	13.7	14.0	14.2	14.3	14.2	4.8	2.9	1.3	0.7	0.4
10	0	5.9	17.2	19.5	21.5	22.3	22.8	23.3	34.5	12.1	7.6	3.6	1.9	1.0
10	100	15.0	20.0	21.2	22.2	22.7	23.0	23.3	16.5	6.6	4.2	2.0	1.1	0.6
20	0	9.9	23.5	26.6	29.4	30.6	31.3	32.1	44.6	17.5	11.4	5.6	3.1	1.6
20	100	23.4	28.1	29.4	30.8	31.4	31.7	32.1	17.8	8.3	5.5	2.8	1.5	0.8
30	0	13.4	29.2	33.1	36.8	38.6	39.6	40.8	55.7	24.1	16.2	8.4	4.7	2.5
30	100	32.2	36.2	37.6	39.1	39.9	40.3	40.8	18.0	9.7	6.8	3.6	2.0	1.1
40	0	16.5	34.4	39.0	43.9	46.3	47.7	49.5	67.4	31.7	22.1	11.9	6.8	3.7
40	100	41.4	44.5	45.9	47.5	48.3	48.8	49.5	17.2	10.6	7.7	4.3	2.5	1.4

AIRSPEED = 800. CM/SEC   RADIATION ABSORBED = 1.0 EXP 6 ERGS/CM2/SEC

DIMENSION ALONG AIRFLOW = 1 CM   DIMENSION ACROSS AIRFLOW = 10 CM

LEAF TEMPERATURES FOR RESISTANCES=   TRANSPIRATION EXP 6 FOR RES =

TA	RH	**0*	**1*	**2*	**5*	*10*	*20*	INF*	**0*	**1*	**2*	**5*	*10*	*20*
0	0	-2.5	2.8	3.1	3.3	3.4	3.4	3.5	48.3	5.4	2.9	1.2	0.6	0.3
0	100	2.3	3.3	3.4	3.4	3.5	3.5	3.5	9.7	1.1	0.6	0.3	0.1	0.1
10	0	4.0	12.0	12.6	13.0	13.1	13.2	13.2	75.4	9.9	5.3	2.2	1.1	0.6
10	100	11.7	13.0	13.1	13.2	13.2	13.2	13.2	12.6	1.8	1.0	0.4	0.2	0.1
20	0	9.6	20.9	21.9	22.5	22.7	22.8	23.0	109.2	16.9	9.2	3.9	2.0	1.0
20	100	21.2	22.7	22.8	22.9	22.9	23.0	23.0	14.8	2.7	1.5	0.6	0.3	0.2
30	0	14.6	29.4	30.9	31.9	32.3	32.5	32.7	149.0	27.2	15.3	6.6	3.4	1.7
30	100	30.8	32.3	32.4	32.6	32.7	32.7	32.7	15.9	3.6	2.0	0.9	0.5	0.2
40	0	19.0	37.5	39.5	41.1	41.7	42.0	42.4	193.9	41.5	24.0	10.6	5.5	2.8
40	100	40.5	41.8	42.1	42.2	42.3	42.3	42.4	15.8	4.5	2.7	1.2	0.6	0.3

DIMENSION ALONG AIRFLOW = 5 CM   DIMENSION ACROSS AIRFLOW = 10 CM

LEAF TEMPERATURES FOR RESISTANCES=   TRANSPIRATION EXP 6 FOR RES =

TA	RH	**0*	**1*	**2*	**5*	*10*	*20*	INF*	**0*	**1*	**2*	**5*	*10*	*20*
0	0	-0.8	5.9	6.6	7.1	7.3	7.4	7.5	31.0	6.3	3.5	1.5	0.8	0.4
0	100	4.5	6.9	7.2	7.4	7.5	7.5	7.5	11.6	2.5	1.4	0.6	0.3	0.2
10	0	4.9	14.2	15.4	16.3	16.6	16.8	17.0	45.6	10.7	6.1	2.7	1.4	0.7
10	100	13.2	16.0	16.4	16.8	16.9	16.9	17.0	14.3	3.7	2.1	0.9	0.5	0.2
20	0	9.8	22.0	23.8	25.2	25.8	26.1	26.4	62.9	16.9	10.0	4.5	2.4	1.2
20	100	22.2	25.1	25.6	26.1	26.2	26.3	26.4	16.1	5.1	3.1	1.4	0.7	0.4
30	0	14.2	29.2	31.8	34.0	34.8	35.3	35.8	82.5	25.4	15.6	7.3	3.9	2.0
30	100	31.5	34.1	34.7	35.3	35.5	35.6	35.8	16.9	6.5	4.1	1.9	1.0	0.5
40	0	18.0	35.9	39.3	42.3	43.6	44.3	45.1	104.1	36.2	23.0	11.1	6.0	3.1
40	100	40.9	43.2	43.8	44.5	44.7	44.9	45.1	16.5	7.6	5.0	2.5	1.3	0.7

AIRSPEED = 800. CM/SEC   RADIATION ABSORBED = 1.0 EXP 6 ERGS/CM2/SEC

DIMENSION ALONG AIRFLOW = 10 CM   DIMENSION ACROSS AIRFLOW = 10 CM

LEAF TEMPERATURES FOR RESISTANCES=   TRANSPIRATION EXP 6 FOR RES =

TA	RH	**0*	**1*	**2*	**5*	*10*	*20*	INF*	**0*	**1*	**2*	**5*	*10*	*20*
0	0	0.5	7.9	9.0	9.8	10.1	10.3	10.5	26.7	6.9	4.0	1.8	0.9	0.5
0	100	5.9	9.2	9.7	10.1	10.3	10.4	10.5	12.4	3.4	2.0	0.9	0.5	0.2
10	0	5.7	15.6	17.3	18.6	19.1	19.4	19.7	37.9	11.2	6.7	3.1	1.6	0.8
10	100	14.2	17.9	18.6	19.2	19.4	19.6	19.7	15.0	4.9	3.0	1.4	0.7	0.4
20	0	10.3	22.7	25.1	27.1	27.9	28.4	28.9	50.9	17.1	10.6	5.0	2.7	1.4
20	100	22.9	26.5	27.4	28.2	28.5	28.7	28.9	16.7	6.6	4.1	2.0	1.0	0.5
30	0	14.3	29.3	32.4	35.2	36.5	37.2	38.0	65.4	24.6	15.8	7.7	4.2	2.2
30	100	31.9	35.1	36.1	37.0	37.4	37.7	38.0	17.2	8.0	5.3	2.6	1.4	0.8
40	0	17.9	35.2	39.2	43.0	44.8	45.8	47.0	81.2	33.7	22.4	11.5	6.4	3.4
40	100	41.2	43.9	44.8	45.8	46.3	46.6	47.0	16.7	9.1	6.3	3.3	1.8	1.0

DIMENSION ALONG AIRFLOW = 20 CM   DIMENSION ACROSS AIRFLOW = 10 CM

LEAF TEMPERATURES FOR RESISTANCES=   TRANSPIRATION EXP 6 FOR RES =

TA	RH	**0*	**1*	**2*	**5*	*10*	*20*	INF*	**0*	**1*	**2*	**5*	*10*	*20*
0	0	2.3	10.4	12.0	13.2	13.8	14.0	14.3	23.7	7.8	4.7	2.2	1.2	0.6
0	100	7.6	12.0	12.9	13.7	14.0	14.2	14.3	13.4	4.7	2.9	1.3	0.7	0.4
10	0	7.0	17.3	19.5	21.5	22.3	22.8	23.3	32.3	11.9	7.5	3.6	1.9	1.0
10	100	15.4	20.1	21.2	22.3	22.7	23.0	23.3	15.7	6.4	4.1	2.0	1.1	0.6
20	0	11.1	23.7	26.6	29.4	30.6	31.3	32.1	42.1	17.2	11.3	5.6	3.1	1.6
20	100	23.7	28.1	29.4	30.8	31.4	31.7	32.1	17.2	8.2	5.4	2.7	1.5	0.8
30	0	14.8	29.4	33.1	36.9	38.6	39.6	40.8	52.9	23.7	16.0	8.3	4.7	2.5
30	100	32.4	36.2	37.6	39.1	39.9	40.3	40.8	17.5	9.6	6.7	3.6	2.0	1.1
40	0	18.1	34.6	39.1	43.9	46.3	47.7	49.5	64.4	31.3	21.9	11.9	6.8	3.7
40	100	41.5	44.6	45.9	47.5	48.3	48.8	49.5	16.9	10.4	7.7	4.3	2.5	1.4

THE GRAPHS

The graphs are two-dimensional slices through the multidimensional space of leaf temperature, transpiration rate, amount of radiation absorbed by a plant leaf, air temperature, wind speed, relative humidity, leaf dimension, and internal diffusion resistance to water vapor. A total of 110 graphs are presented. Many more might have been included, but were omitted in order to save space. Most graphs shown are for a leaf of dimensions 5 × 5 cm, but when there are interesting features with dimension, other dimensions are given as well. The general functional relations are easily visualized from the graphs for leaves larger or smaller than 5 × 5 cm, whereby the dependent variables are shifted in absolute value only.

Leaf temperature versus air temperature

Graphs 1 through 4 show the temperature of a 5 × 5 cm leaf as a function of the air temperature for wind speeds of 10 and 100 cm sec^{-1} and for internal diffusion resistances to water vapor of 1 and 10 sec cm^{-1}. The leaf temperature increases monotonically with the air temperature at a given amount of absorbed radiation and at a constant relative humidity. Incomplete lines terminate at the point that the transpiration rate becomes zero.

Graphs 5 and 6 illustrate changes that occur in leaf temperature with other dimensions. The temperature of the small leaf (1 × 1 cm) is very closely coupled to the air temperature regardless of the amount of radiation absorbed or the humidity of the air. But the temperature of the large leaf (10 × 10 cm) is affected significantly by the amount of radiation absorbed.

Transpiration rate versus air temperature

Graphs 7 through 18 show the transpiration rate of a leaf as a function of the air temperature for wind speeds of 10 and 100 cm sec^{-1} and for internal diffusion resistances to water vapor of 1 and 10 sec cm^{-1}. Curves that begin at an air temperature greater than $-10°C$ begin at the point where leaf temperature is equal to 0°C. The transpiration rate always increases monotonically with the air temperature for dry air, but for very humid air the transpiration rate may increase with increasing air temperature at low air temperatures but may decrease with increasing air temperature at high air temperatures. As the leaf temperature increases at a constant relative humidity, the water vapor density of the air increases. In very moist air the water vapor density of the air increases more rapidly than does the leaf temperature and the difference $_sd_l(T_l) -$ r.h. $_sd_a(T_a)$ begins to diminish above a certain air temperature. For a larger leaf, whose temperature is not so close to the air temperature, the same effect is apparent in moderately humid air.

Leaf temperature versus air speed

Graphs 19 through 24 show the leaf temperature as a function of the air speed for internal diffusion resistances of 1 and 10 sec cm^{-1} at radiation absorbed of 0.4×10^6 and 1.0×10^6 ergs cm^{-2} sec^{-1} and a relative humidity of 50%. All curves begin at an air speed of 10 cm sec^{-1} which we consider representative of still air or free convection conditions. A change of relative humidity to 0 or 100% would not shift the curves as much as does the change of 5°C air temperature. It is noteworthy that the greatest change of leaf temperature occurs with the change from still air (10 cm sec^{-1}) to a wind speed of about 100 cm sec^{-1} (2.2 mph). The very gentlest breezes in nature are the most significant as far as leaf temperature is concerned. It is these low air movements which are so very common in the natural environment. Note the fact that at high amounts of absorbed radiation (1.0×10^6 ergs cm^{-2} sec^{-1}) the leaf temperature always decreases with an increase of wind speed, but that at low amounts of absorbed radiation (0.4×10^6 ergs cm^{-2} sec^{-1}) the leaf temperature may decrease or it may increase with an increase of wind speed. At airspeed above 100 cm sec^{-1} a small leaf (1×1 cm) maintains a temperature close to air temperature. A large leaf (10×10 cm) remains cooler than the air at high air temperatures and warmer than the air at low air temperatures.

Transpiration rate versus air speed

Graphs 25 through 32 show the transpiration rate of a 5×5 cm leaf as a function of the air speed for internal diffusion resistances of 1 and 10 sec cm^{-1} with 0.4×10^6 and 1.0×10^6 ergs cm^{-2} sec^{-1} of absorbed radiation at a relative humidity of 60 and 100%. The effect of humidity on the variation of transpiration rate with wind speed is so dramatic that it was deemed important to give sets of curves at both 60 and 100% relative humidity. When the air temperature is -5°C there is no line drawn if the leaf temperature is below the freezing point of water, 0°C. When the internal diffusion resistance of a leaf is low (1.0 sec cm^{-1}) and the relative humidity is 60% as in Graph 29, an increase of air speed with a constant high amount of radiation absorbed (1.0×10^6 ergs cm^{-2} sec^{-1}) will increase the rate of transpiration from a leaf if the air temperature is high and will decrease the rate of transpiration if the air temperature is low. For an air temperature of about 30°C a change of wind speed produces essentially no change in the rate of water loss from a leaf at an amount of radiation absorbed of 1.0×10^6 ergs cm^{-2} sec^{-1} and 60% relative humidity. On the other hand, if the internal diffusion resistance is medium to high (e.g. 10 sec cm^{-1} as in Graph 30), an increase of wind speed only decreases the transpiration rate for an amount of radiation absorbed of 1.0×10^6 ergs cm^{-2} sec^{-1} and a relative humidity of 60%. At high humidity and high radiation absorbed (Graphs 31 and 32) an increase of wind speed only decreases the rate of water loss from a leaf. As with the leaf temperature the transpiration rate is affected most strongly at low wind speeds.

Graphs 33 through 38 show the change in transpiration rate with a change in leaf dimension. In a low radiation environment the transpiration rate of a small leaf with moderate internal resistance (Graph 33) is greater than that of a large leaf with moderate internal resistance (Graph 36). As the amount of radiation absorbed increases, the transpiration rate of the large leaf increases faster than that of the small leaf (Graph 35 compared to Graph 38).

Leaf temperature versus water vapor density

Graphs 39 through 46 show the leaf temperature as a function of the water vapor density of the air for internal diffusion resistances of 1 and 10 sec cm^{-1} for amounts of radiation absorbed of 0.4×10^6 and 1.0×10^6 ergs cm^{-2} sec^{-1} and for air speeds of 10 and 100 cm sec^{-1}. All curves end at the point where the relative humidity exceeds 100%. In every case the leaf temperature increases monotonically with an increase of the water vapor density of the air. In order to facilitate the use of these graphs, Table 1 is an abbreviated listing of water vapor density as a function of the relative humidity and the air temperature.

Graphs 47 and 48 show leaf temperature as a function of the water vapor density of the air for leaves of dimensions 1×1 cm at low and high amounts of radiation absorbed respectively. Graphs 49 and 50 show leaf temperature as a function of the water vapor density of the air for leaves of dimensions 10×10 cm. As noted before, the temperature of the small leaf is close to the air temperature. The temperature of the large leaf is cooler than the air temperature in a low radiation environment, and warmer than the air temperature in a high radiation environment.

Transpiration rate versus water vapor density

Graphs 51 through 62 show the transpiration rate of a leaf as a function of the water vapor density of the air for internal diffusion resistances of

1 and 10 sec cm^{-1} for amounts of radiation absorbed of 0.4 × 10^6 and 1.0 × 10^6 ergs cm^{-2} sec^{-1} and for air speeds of 10 and 100 cm sec^{-1}. Holding internal diffusion resistance and air speed constant, and setting the amount of radiation absorbed equal to 0.4 × 10^6 ergs cm^{-2} sec^{-1}, leaves of all sizes transpire about the same at low air temperatures (see Graphs 52, 59, and 61). The large leaf transpires the least at high air temperatures. When the amount of radiation is increased to 1.0 × 10^6 ergs cm^{-2} sec^{-1}, the small leaf transpires the least at low air temperatures as well as the most at high air temperatures (Graphs 60 and 62). Holding air speed and the amount of radiation absorbed constant, the transpiration rate decreases by a constant amount as the internal diffusion resistance increases; for example, compare Graph 61 with Graph 63. Holding radiation absorbed and internal diffusion resistance constant, then increasing the air speed increases transpiration rates as shown in Graphs 61 and 62. For all cases the range of values of transpiration rates for large leaves are less than the range of values for small ones. All curves end at the point where the relative humidity exceeds 100%. In every case the rate of water loss from a leaf decreases monotonically with an increase of the water vapor density of the air. In going from one graph to another note the change in scale used for the transpiration rate. In order to facilitate the use of these graphs, Table 1 is an abbreviated listing of water vapor density as a function of the relative humidity and the air temperature.

Leaf temperature versus internal diffusion resistance

Graphs 63 through 68 show the leaf temperature as a function of the internal diffusion resistance of the leaf to water vapor for wind speeds of 10 and 100 cm sec^{-1} at air temperatures of 20 and 40°C for amounts of absorbed radiation of 0.4 × 10^6, 0.6 × 10^6, 0.8 × 10^6, and 1.0 × 10^6 ergs cm^{-2} sec^{-1} for relative humidities of 20, 60, and 100%. In Graphs 65 and 66 at an air temperature of 40°C the lines for 100% relative humidity and 0.4 × 10^6 ergs cm^{-2} sec^{-1} are omitted because transpiration has become condensation due to a reversal of the pressure gradient for water vapor. All graphs show a monotonic increase of leaf temperature with increasing internal diffusion resistance.

Transpiration rate versus internal diffusion resistance

Graphs 69 through 74 show the transpiration rate of a leaf as a function of the internal diffusion resistance of the leaf to water vapor for wind speeds of 10 and 100 cm sec^{-1} at air temperatures of 20 and 40°C for amounts of absorbed radiation of 0.4 × 10^6, 0.6 × 10^6, 0.8 × 10^6, and 1.0 × 10^6 ergs cm^{-2} sec^{-1} for relative humidities of 20, 60, and

100%. In Graphs 71 and 72 at an air temperature of 40°C the lines for 100% relative humidity and 0.4×10^6 ergs cm^{-2} sec^{-1} are omitted because transpiration has become condensation due to a reversal of the pressure gradient for water vapor. All graphs show a monotonic decrease of transpiration rate with increasing internal diffusion resistance.

Leaf temperature versus leaf dimension along air flow

Graphs 75 through 82 show the leaf temperature as a function of the characteristic dimension of the leaf in the direction of the air flow at internal diffusion resistances of 1 and 10 sec cm^{-1} for air temperatures of 20 and 40°C and wind speeds of 10 and 100 cm sec^{-1}. Families of curves are given at constant radiation absorbed of 0.4×10^6, 0.7×10^6, 1.0×10^6 ergs cm^{-2} sec^{-1} and relative humidities of 20, 60, and 100%. The line representing 100% relative humidity and radiation absorbed of 0.4×10^6 ergs cm^{-2} sec^{-1} is missing in some figures because transpiration has become zero or changed to condensation. Note the changes of scale of transpiration rate used for these graphs.

Usually an increase of leaf dimension results in an increase of leaf temperature if all other factors remain constant. However, with small amounts of absorbed radiation, here 0.4×10^6 ergs cm^{-2} sec^{-1} (small compared to the blackbody radiation at the air temperature), there may be a decrease of leaf temperature with increasing leaf dimension. The effect becomes more pronounced at an air temperature of 40°C than at 20°C. If a leaf has a low internal diffusion resistance of water vapor then an increase of leaf dimension produces a significant increase in leaf temperature only in still air and at high amounts of absorbed radiation. Leaves with intermediate to high internal diffusion resistance ($r_l = 10$ sec cm^{-1}) respond strongly by leaf temperature increase with increases of leaf size with low wind speed and high amounts of radiation absorbed. If a plant grows best at 30°C then for large quantities of incident radiation the leaf will either need to be small or else orient in such a way as to absorb as little radiation as possible. Likewise if the plant proteins denature when leaf temperatures exceed 45°C one can see quickly that a leaf with intermediate to high internal diffusion resistance must either not absorb much radiation, be as small as possible, or both.

All eight graphs are for a 5 × 5 cm leaf. No significant change occurs in the curves for an increase or decrease in dimension across the direction of air flow.

Transpiration rate versus leaf dimension along air flow

Graphs 83 through 93 show the transpiration rate as a function of the characteristic dimension of a leaf along the direction of air flow at internal diffusion resistances 1 and 10 sec cm^{-1} for air temperatures of 20 and 40°C, 5 cm dimension across the direction of air flow, and wind speeds of 10 and 100 cm sec^{-1}. Families of curves are given at constant radiation absorbed of 0.4×10^6, 0.7×10^6, 1.0×10^6 ergs cm^{-2} sec^{-1} and relative humidities of 20, 60 and 100%. The line representing 100% relative humidity and radiation absorbed of 0.4×10^6 ergs cm^{-2} sec^{-1} is missing in some figures because transpiration has become zero or changed to condensation. Note the changes of scale of transpiration rate used for these graphs.

Many interesting effects show up within this set of graphs. Often the leaf size has relatively little influence on the transpiration rate, sometimes an increase of leaf size produces an increased rate of water loss from the leaf and sometimes it results in a decreased rate of water loss. The most perceptible change is for a resistance of 10 sec cm^{-1}, air temperature of 40°C and windspeed of 10 cm sec^{-1}. Graphs 91 and 92 for these conditions are included to show the maximum amount of change in transpiration rate that can be expected with change in dimension across the direction of air flow.

Transpiration rate versus leaf temperature

Graphs 93 through 110 show the transpiration rate of a leaf and the leaf temperature, each considered as a dependent variable, as a function of the internal diffusion resistance of the leaf to water vapor and of the leaf dimension along the direction of air flow. There are nine graphs at 20°C for air speeds of 10, 100 and 1000 cm sec^{-1} and for relative humidities of 20, 50, and 80% and nine graphs at 40°C for the same set of air speeds and relative humidities. All graphs are for a $Q_{abs} = 0.70 \times 10^6$ ergs cm^{-2} sec^{-1} (1.00 cal cm^{-2} min^{-1}).

Many interesting features concerning the energy budgets of plant leaves are seen within these figures. At a given air temperature as the wind speed increases the lines at constant leaf dimension crowd together and approach a leaf temperature equal to the air temperature. As humidity increases the transpiration rate decreases and leaf temperature increases. The reader should note the change of scale of ordinate on some of the graphs. It is interesting to observe the convergence and "cross over" of the lines of constant leaf dimension when the air temperature is high. At moderate to high resistance an increase in leaf size usually results in an increase of leaf temperature and an increase of transpiration rate, while at low resistance an increase of leaf size results in a decrease of transpiration rate and a decrease of leaf temperature.

TABLE 1. *Water vapor density as a function of the relative humidity and air temperature*

Water Vapor Density (gm cm^{-3} x 10^6)	Relative Humidity (%)	Air Temperature (°C)
3.46	20	20
10.38	60	20
17.30	100	20
6.08	20	30
18.23	60	30
30.38	100	30
10.24	20	40
30.17	60	40
51.19	100	40

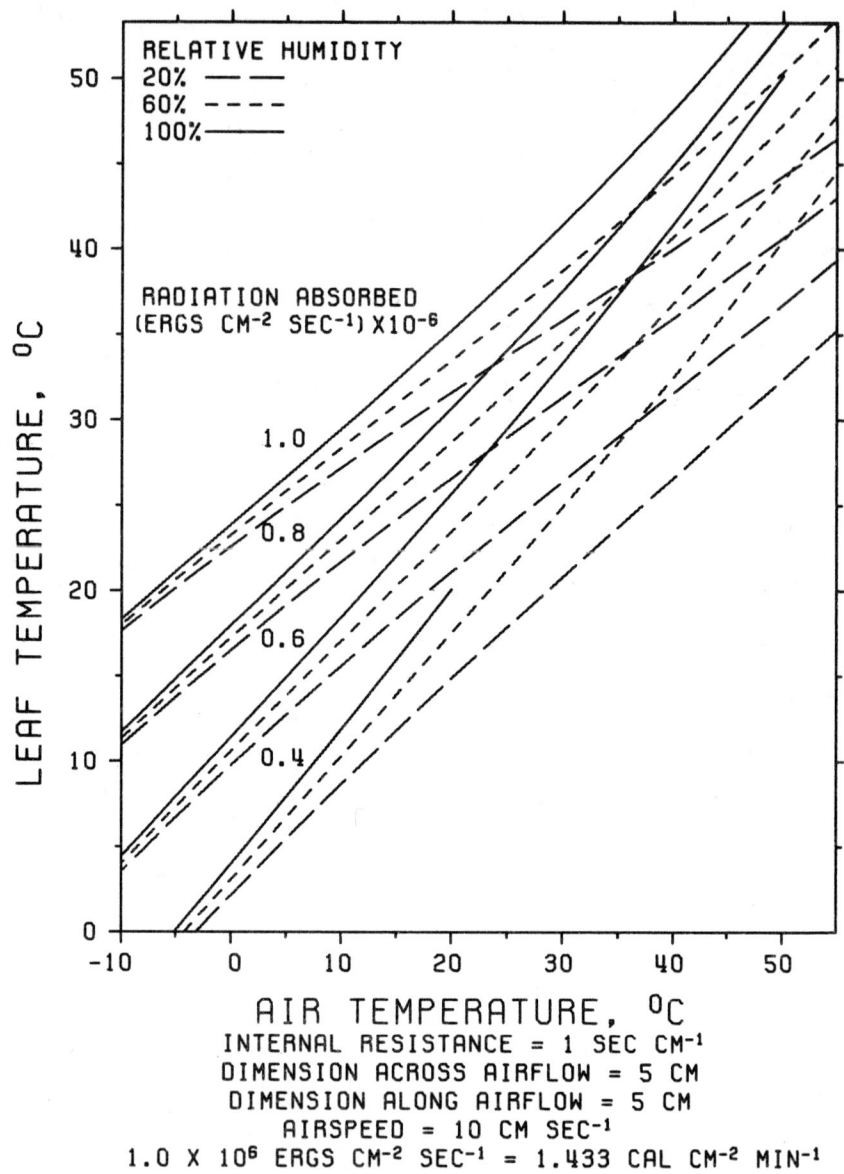

RELATIVE HUMIDITY
20% — —
60% - - - -
100%———

RADIATION ABSORBED
(ERGS CM^{-2} SEC^{-1}) X10^{-6}

1.0

0.8

0.6

0.4

LEAF TEMPERATURE, ^{0}C

AIR TEMPERATURE, ^{0}C
INTERNAL RESISTANCE = 1 SEC CM^{-1}
DIMENSION ACROSS AIRFLOW = 5 CM
DIMENSION ALONG AIRFLOW = 5 CM
AIRSPEED = 10 CM SEC^{-1}
1.0 X 10^{6} ERGS CM^{-2} SEC^{-1} = 1.433 CAL CM^{-2} MIN^{-1}

GRAPH 1

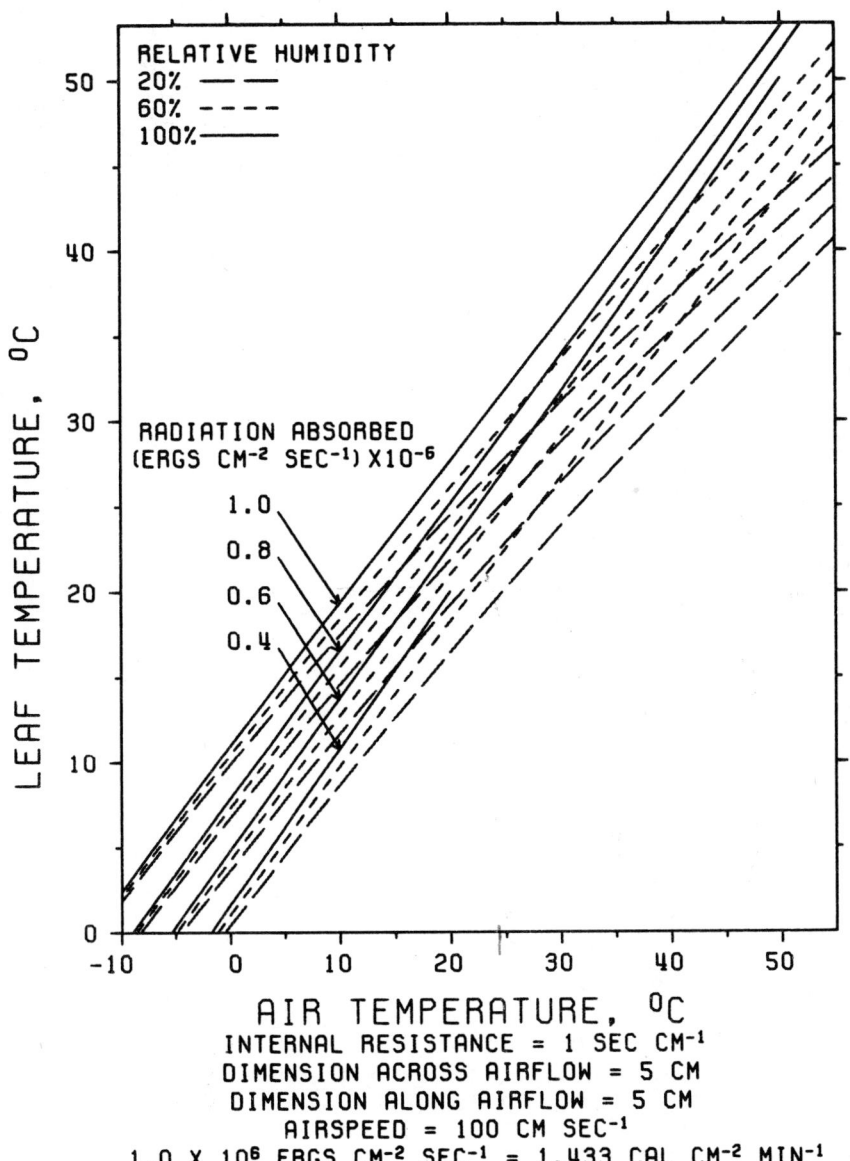

GRAPH 2

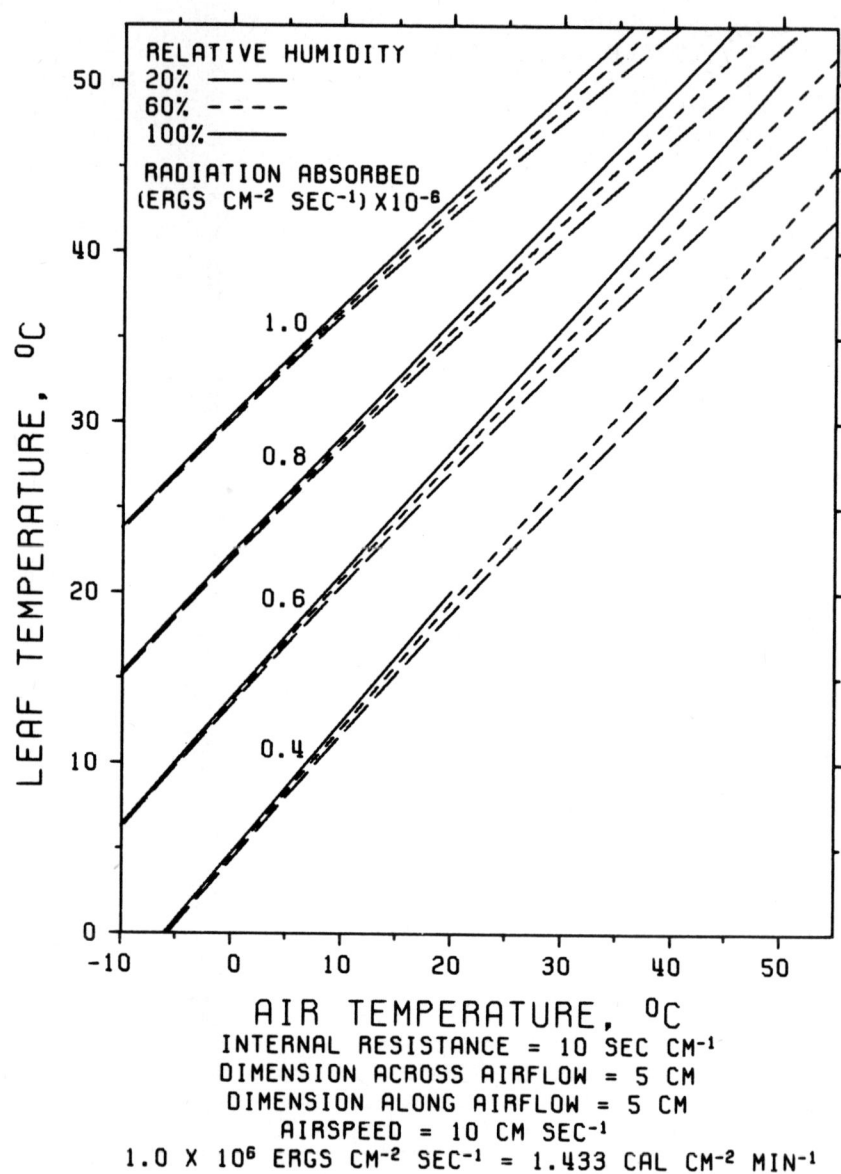

GRAPH 3

170

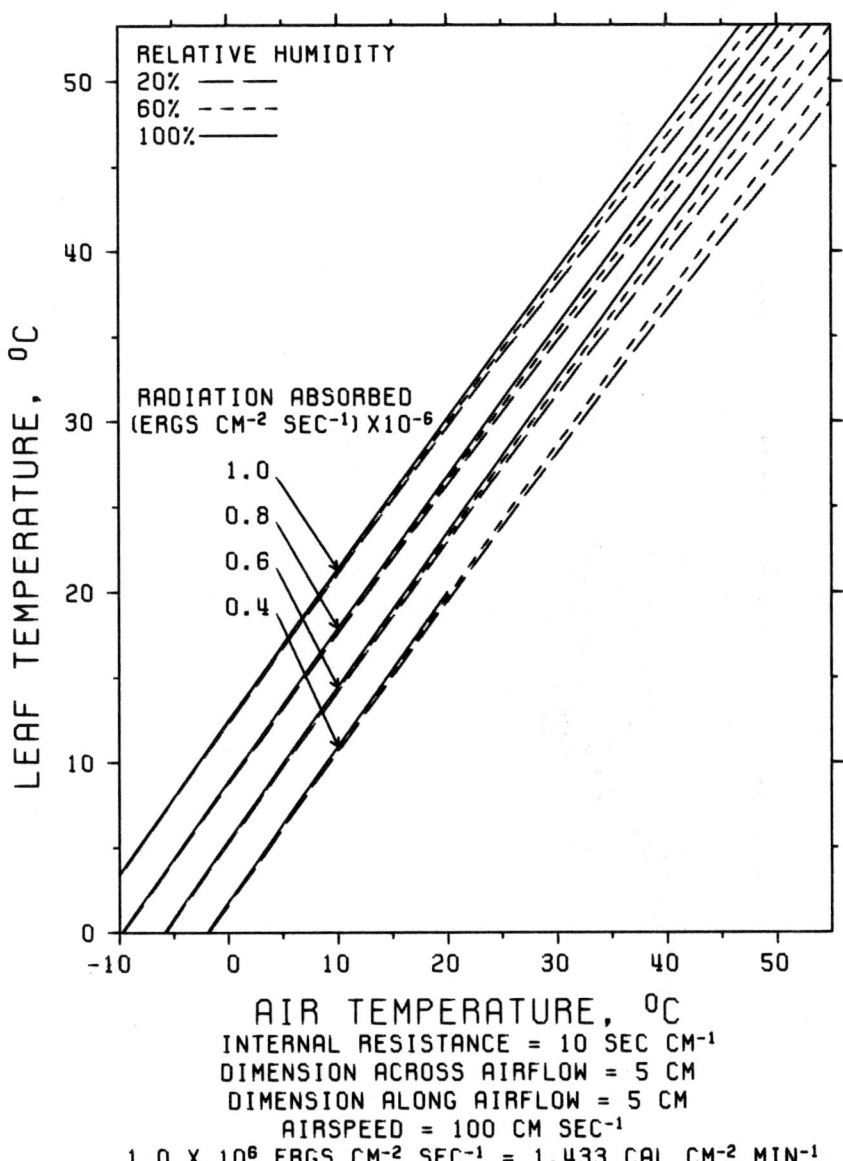

GRAPH 4

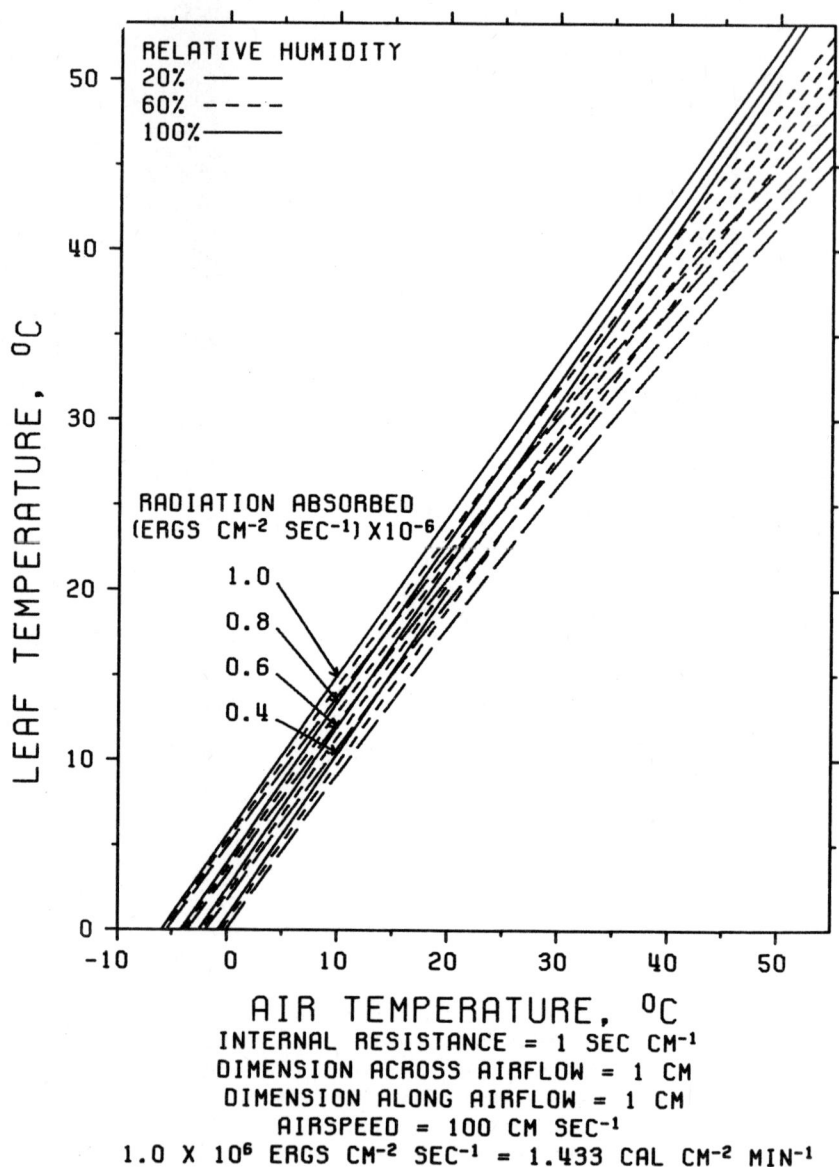

GRAPH 5

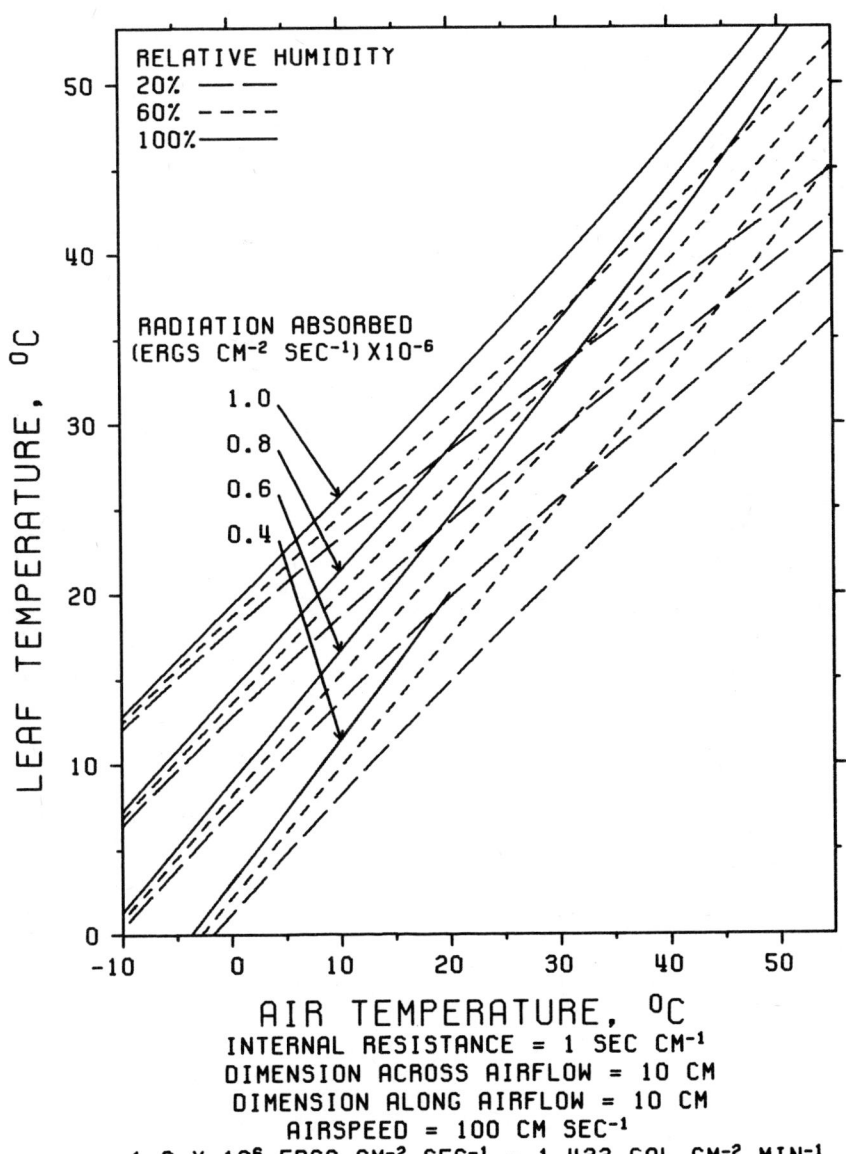

GRAPH 6

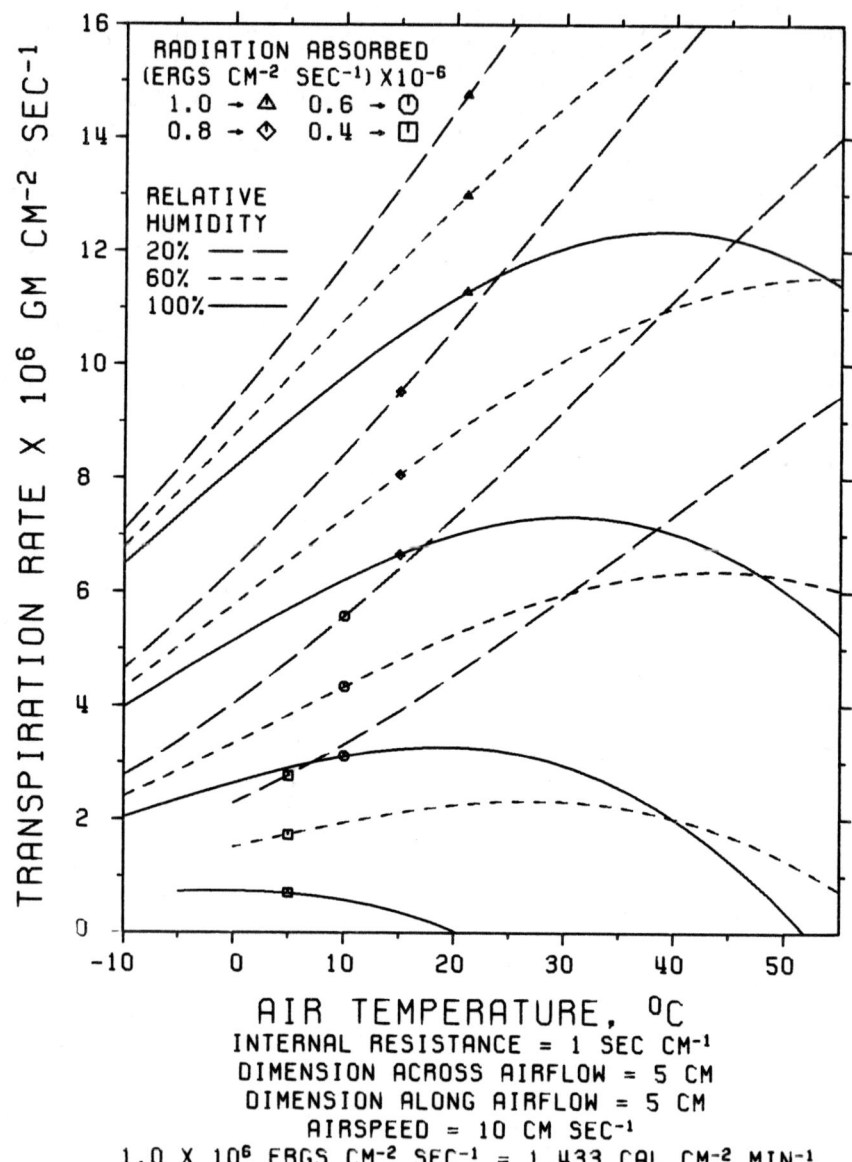

GRAPH 7

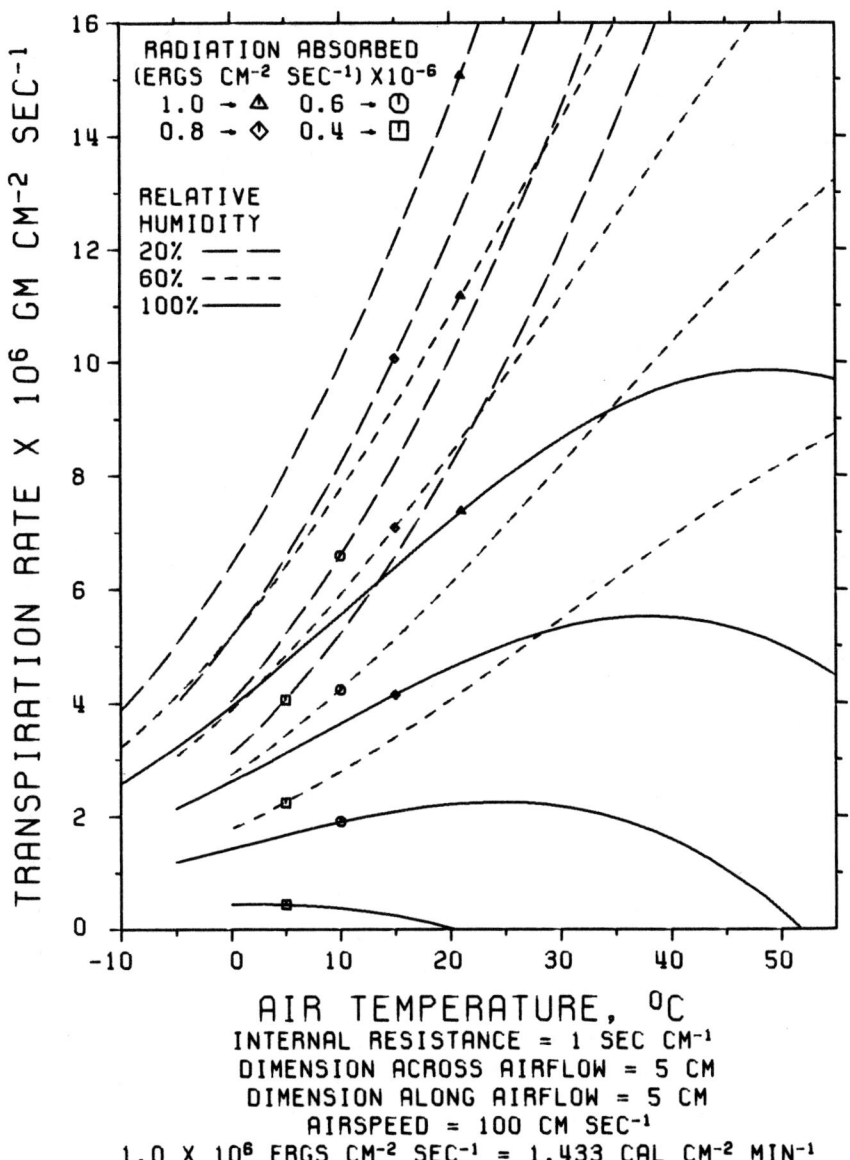

GRAPH 8

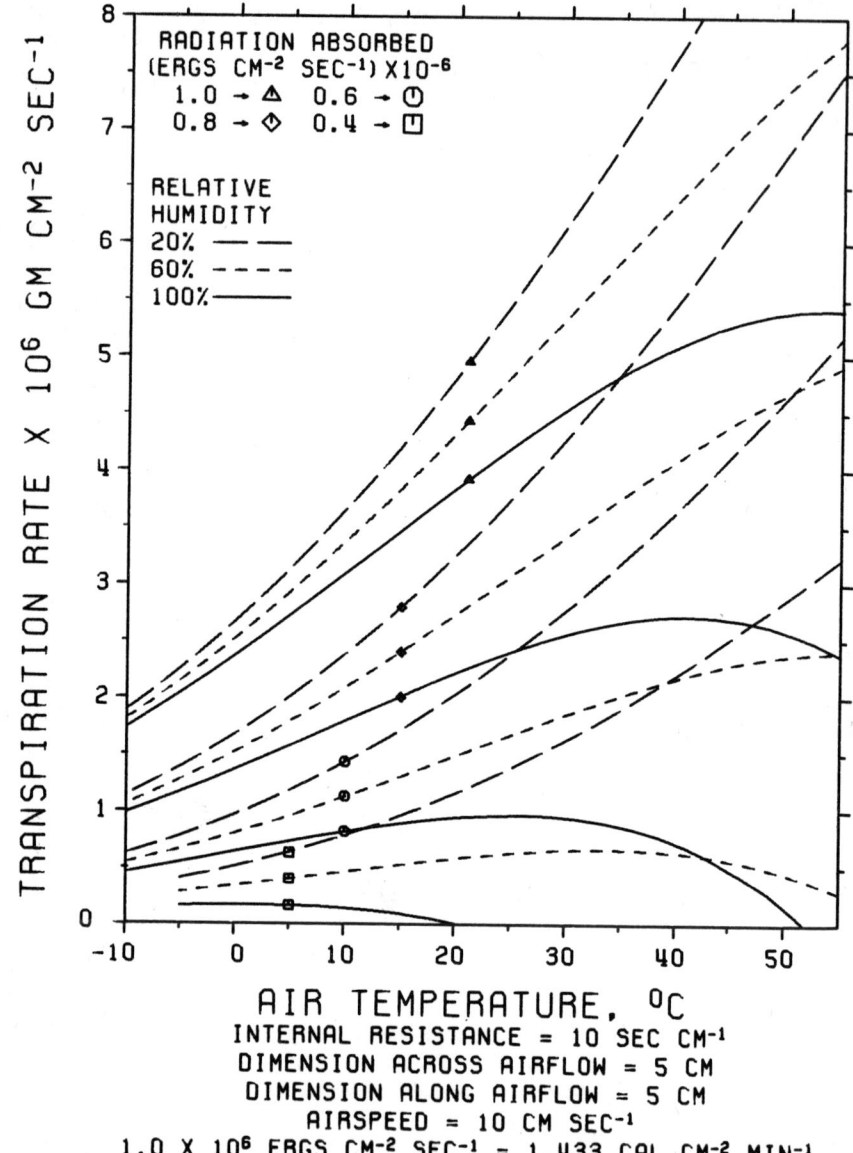

GRAPH 9

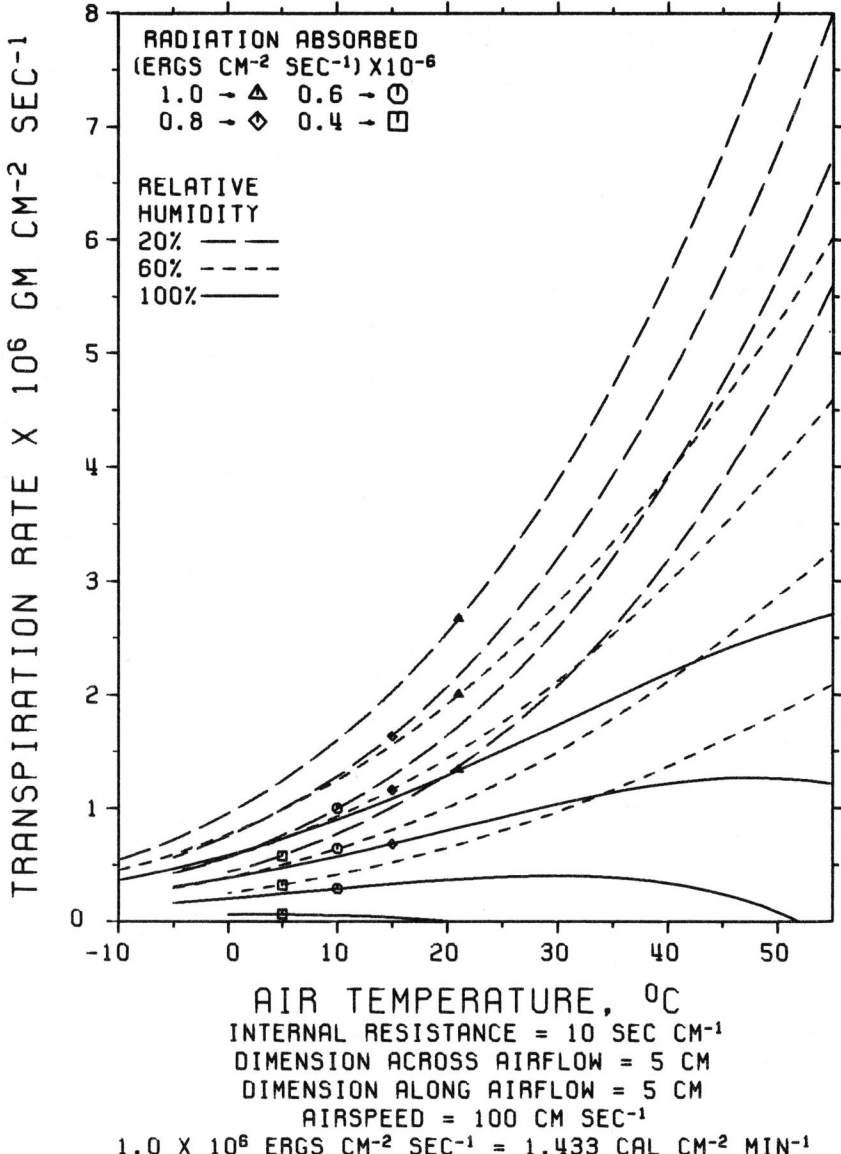

RADIATION ABSORBED
(ERGS CM⁻² SEC⁻¹) X10⁻⁶
1.0 → △ 0.6 → ☉
0.8 → ◇ 0.4 → ▢

RELATIVE
HUMIDITY
20% ⸺ ⸺
60% - - - -
100%⸺⸺

TRANSPIRATION RATE X 10⁶ GM CM⁻² SEC⁻¹

AIR TEMPERATURE, °C
INTERNAL RESISTANCE = 10 SEC CM⁻¹
DIMENSION ACROSS AIRFLOW = 5 CM
DIMENSION ALONG AIRFLOW = 5 CM
AIRSPEED = 100 CM SEC⁻¹
1.0 X 10⁶ ERGS CM⁻² SEC⁻¹ = 1.433 CAL CM⁻² MIN⁻¹

GRAPH 10

177

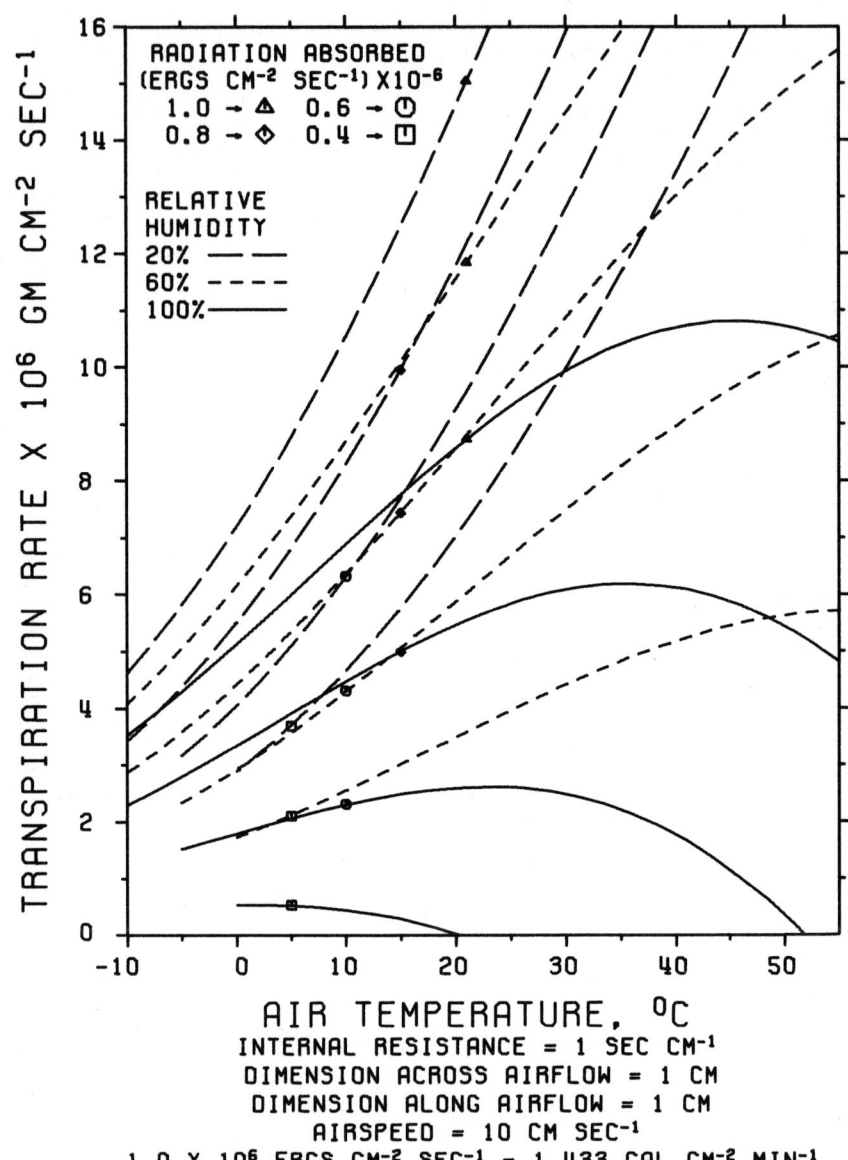

GRAPH 11

178

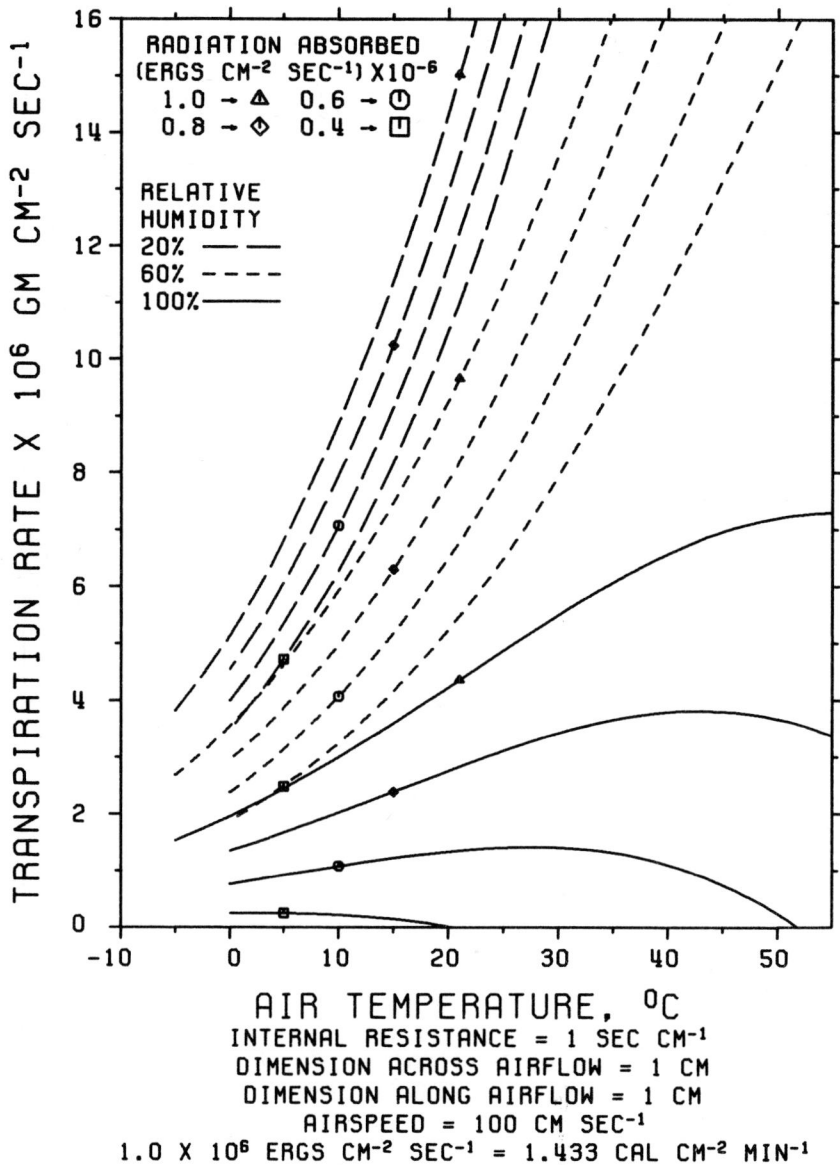

GRAPH 12

179

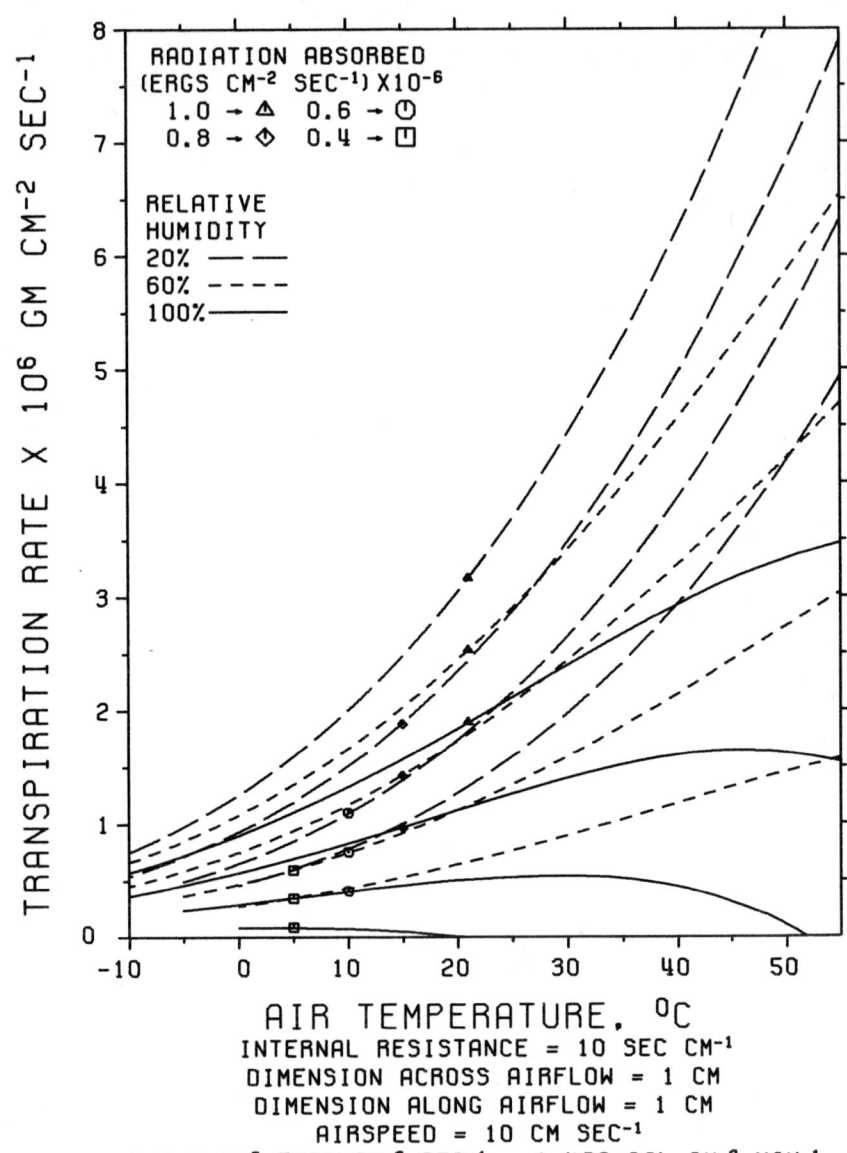

GRAPH 13

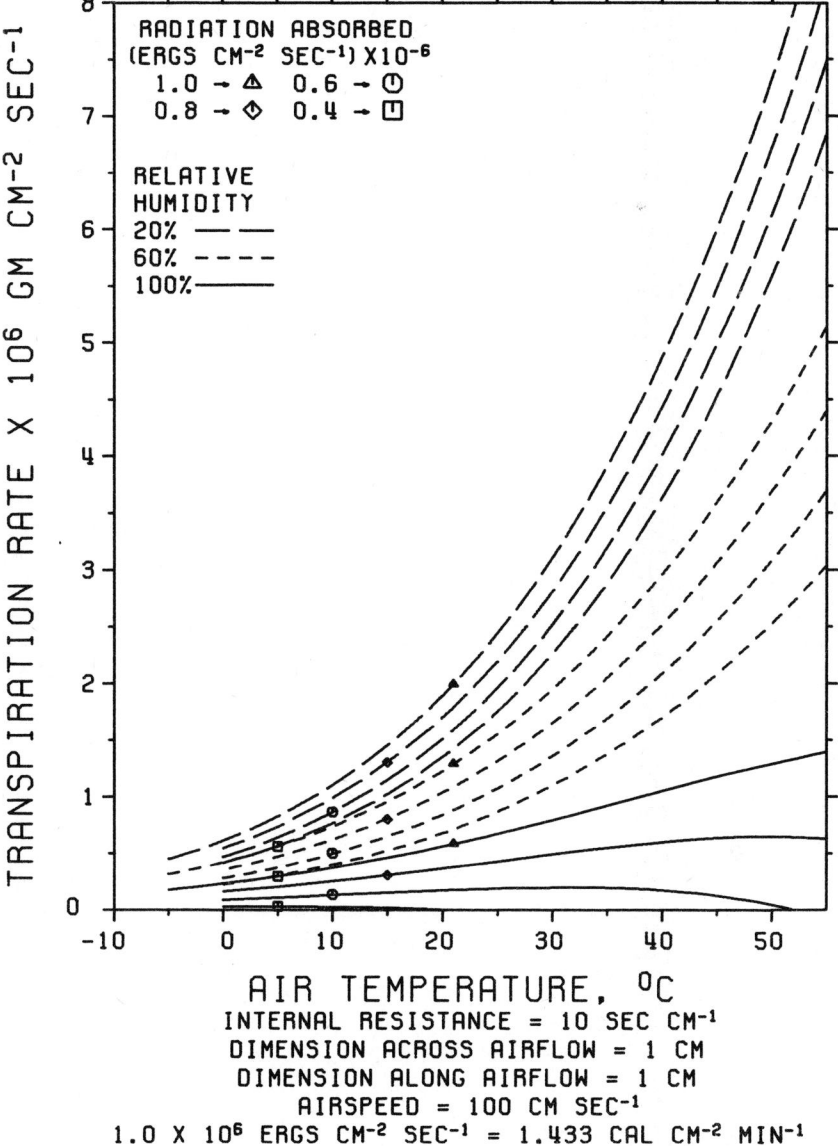

GRAPH 14

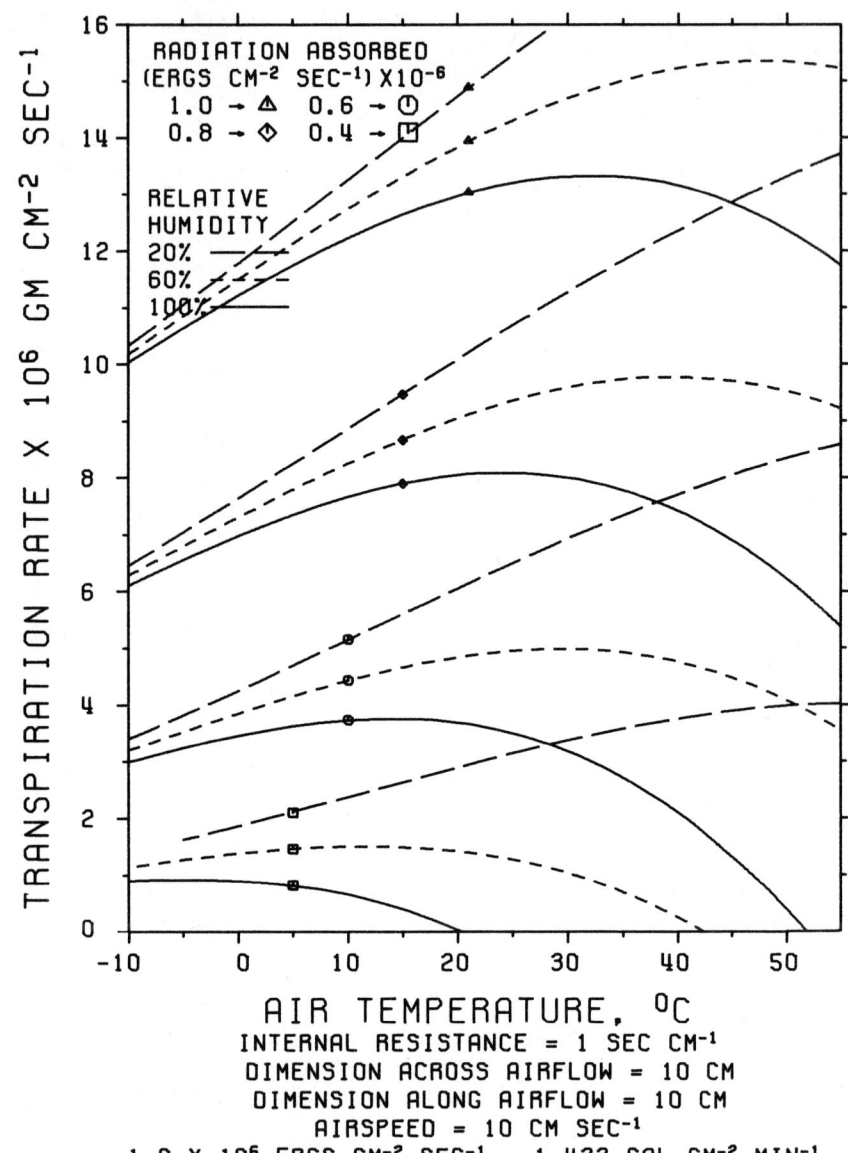

GRAPH 15

182

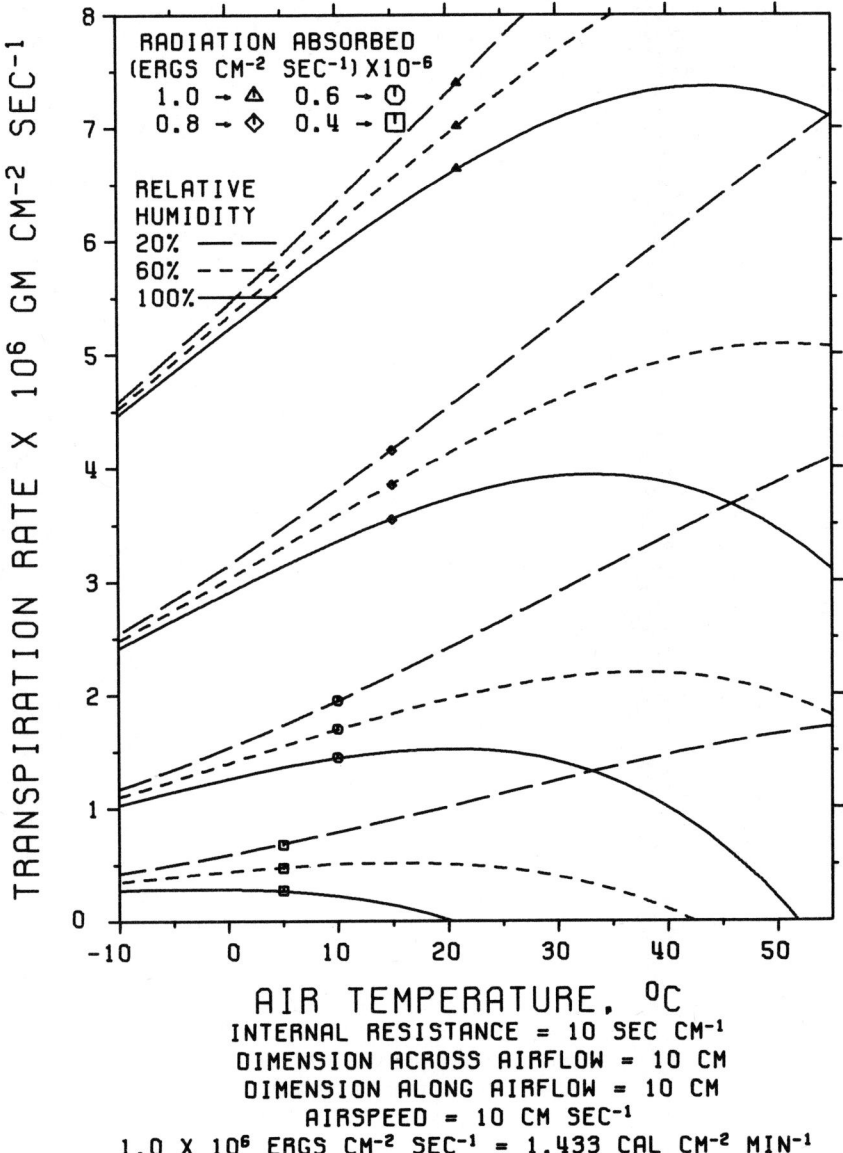

GRAPH 16

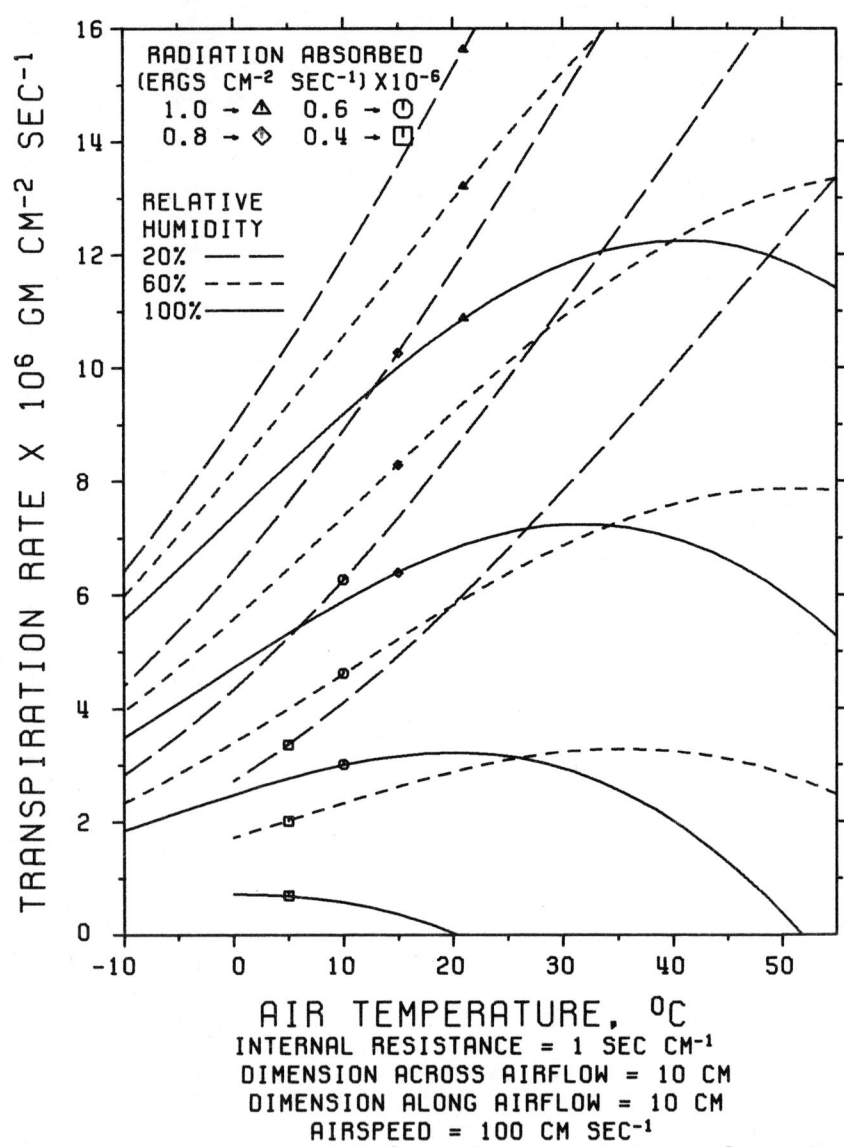

AIR TEMPERATURE, °C

INTERNAL RESISTANCE = 1 SEC CM⁻¹
DIMENSION ACROSS AIRFLOW = 10 CM
DIMENSION ALONG AIRFLOW = 10 CM
AIRSPEED = 100 CM SEC⁻¹
1.0 X 10⁶ ERGS CM⁻² SEC⁻¹ = 1.433 CAL CM⁻² MIN⁻¹

GRAPH 17

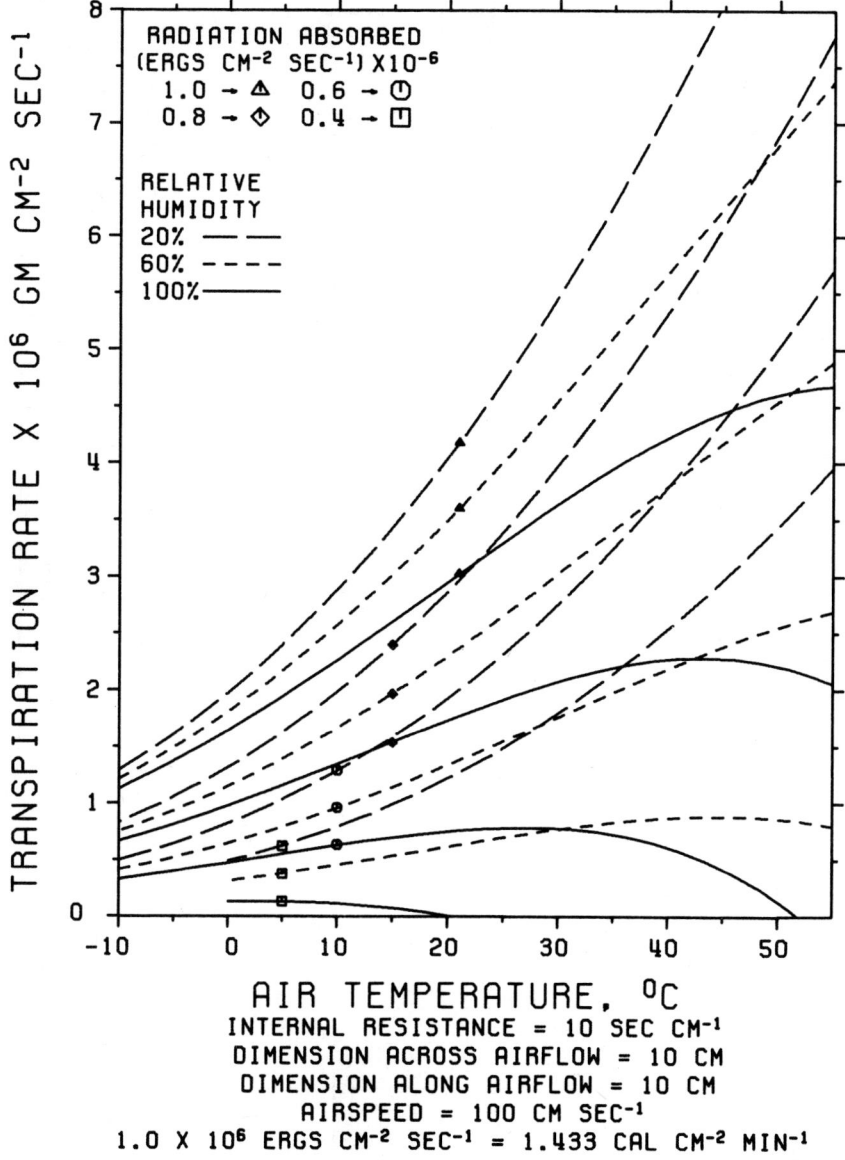

GRAPH 18

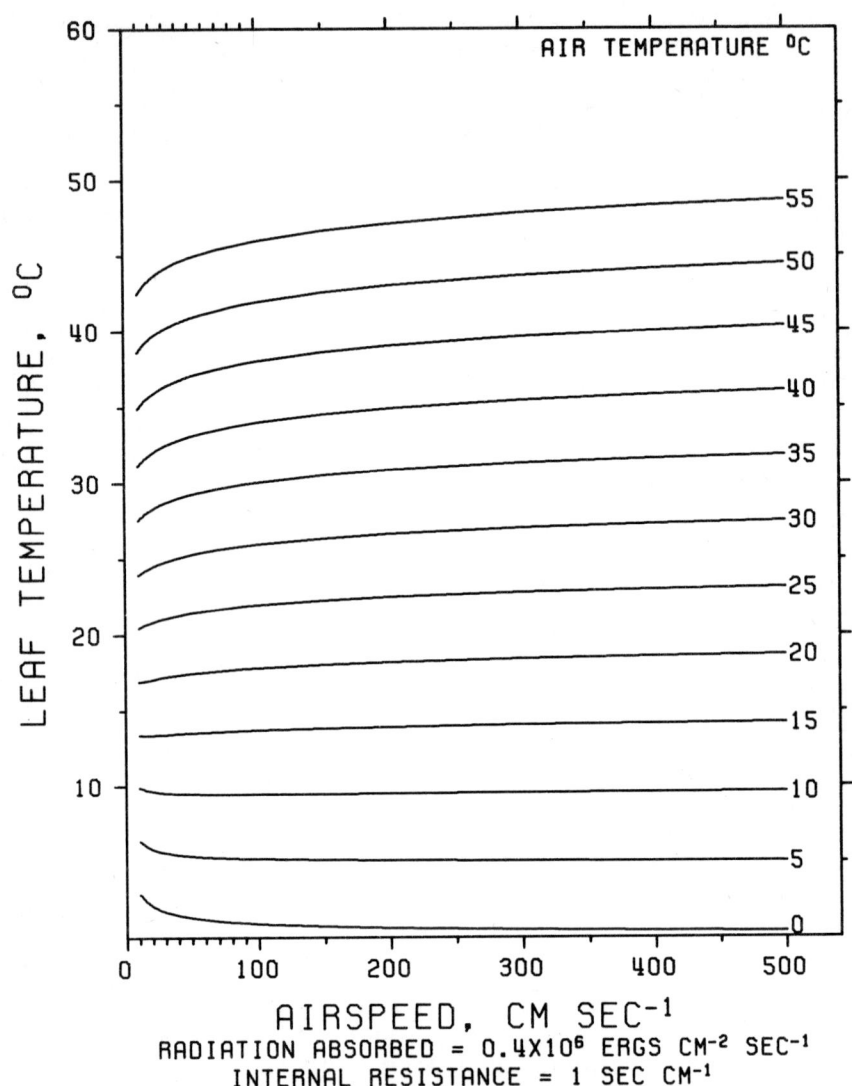

AIRSPEED, CM SEC^{-1}
RADIATION ABSORBED = 0.4X10^6 ERGS CM^{-2} SEC^{-1}
INTERNAL RESISTANCE = 1 SEC CM^{-1}
DIMENSION ACROSS AIRFLOW = 5 CM
DIMENSION ALONG AIRFLOW = 5 CM
RELATIVE HUMIDITY = 50 %
0.4 X 10^6 ERGS CM^{-2} SEC^{-1} = 0.573 CAL CM^{-2} MIN^{-1}

GRAPH 19

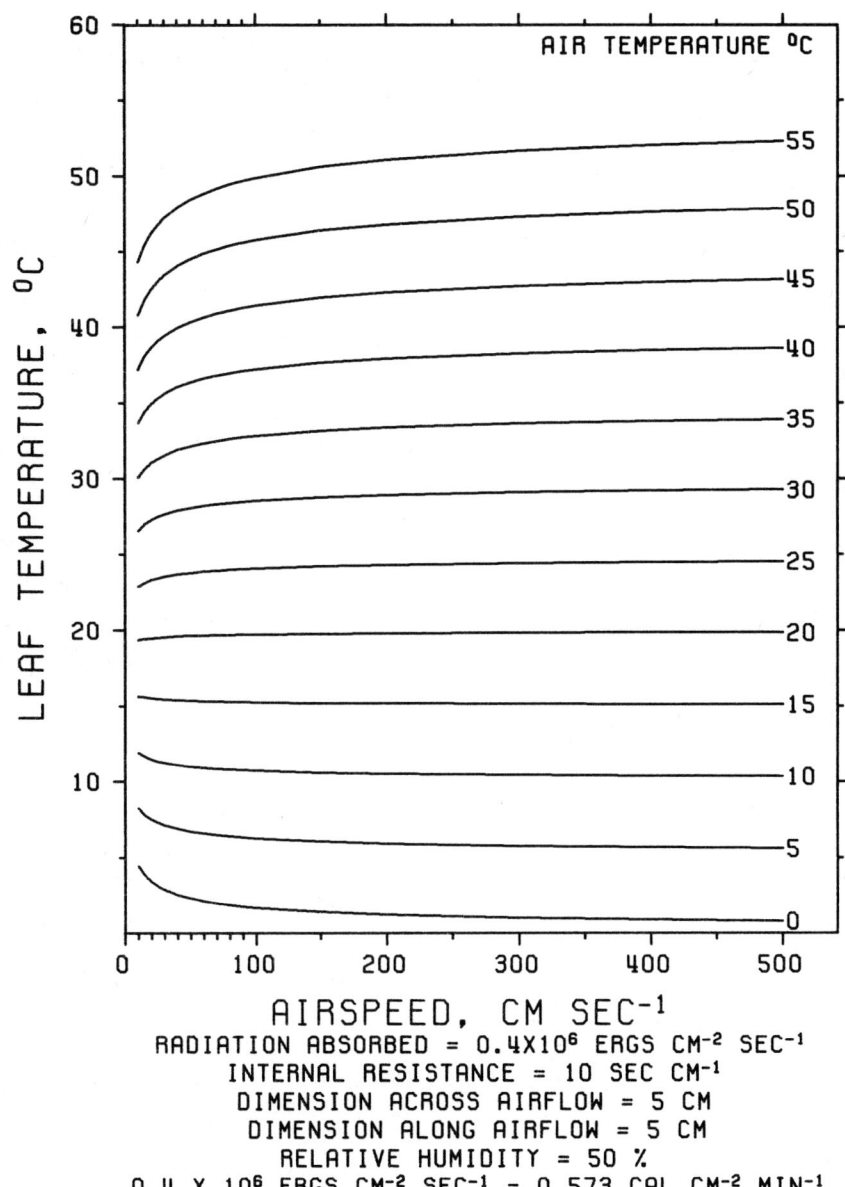

AIRSPEED, CM SEC⁻¹

RADIATION ABSORBED = 0.4X10⁶ ERGS CM⁻² SEC⁻¹
INTERNAL RESISTANCE = 10 SEC CM⁻¹
DIMENSION ACROSS AIRFLOW = 5 CM
DIMENSION ALONG AIRFLOW = 5 CM
RELATIVE HUMIDITY = 50 %
0.4 X 10⁶ ERGS CM⁻² SEC⁻¹ = 0.573 CAL CM⁻² MIN⁻¹

GRAPH 20

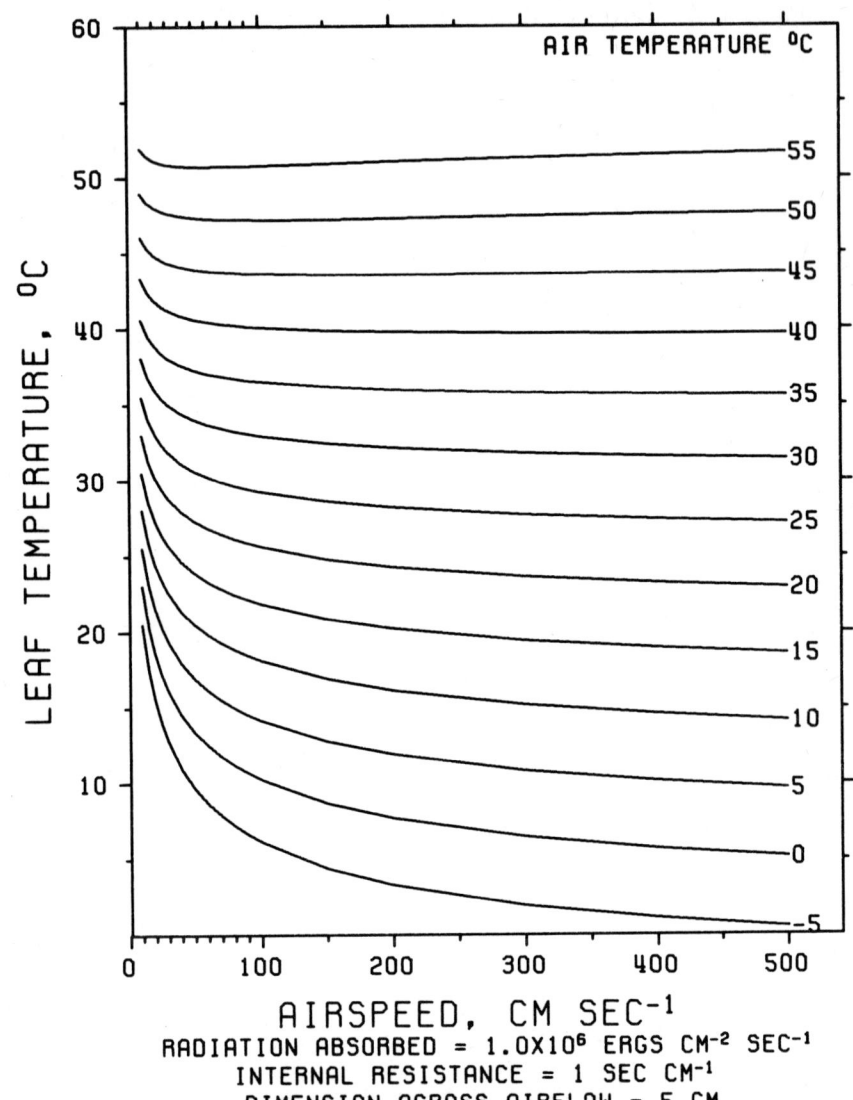

AIRSPEED, CM SEC^{-1}

RADIATION ABSORBED = 1.0X10^6 ERGS CM^{-2} SEC^{-1}
INTERNAL RESISTANCE = 1 SEC CM^{-1}
DIMENSION ACROSS AIRFLOW = 5 CM
DIMENSION ALONG AIRFLOW = 5 CM
RELATIVE HUMIDITY = 50 %
1.0 X 10^6 ERGS CM^{-2} SEC^{-1} = 1.433 CAL CM^{-2} MIN^{-1}

GRAPH 21

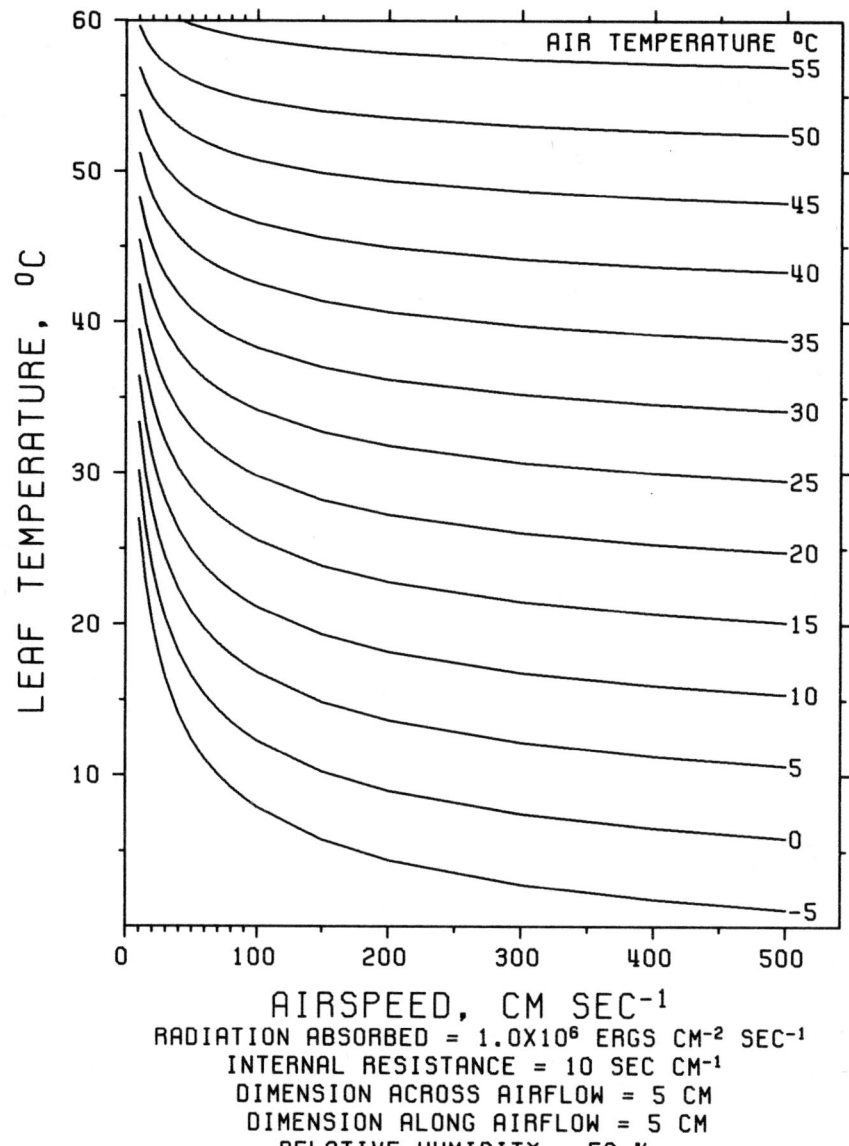

AIR TEMPERATURE °C

AIRSPEED, CM SEC⁻¹

RADIATION ABSORBED = 1.0X10⁶ ERGS CM⁻² SEC⁻¹
INTERNAL RESISTANCE = 10 SEC CM⁻¹
DIMENSION ACROSS AIRFLOW = 5 CM
DIMENSION ALONG AIRFLOW = 5 CM
RELATIVE HUMIDITY = 50 %
1.0 X 10⁶ ERGS CM⁻² SEC⁻¹ = 1.433 CAL CM⁻² MIN⁻¹

GRAPH 22

189

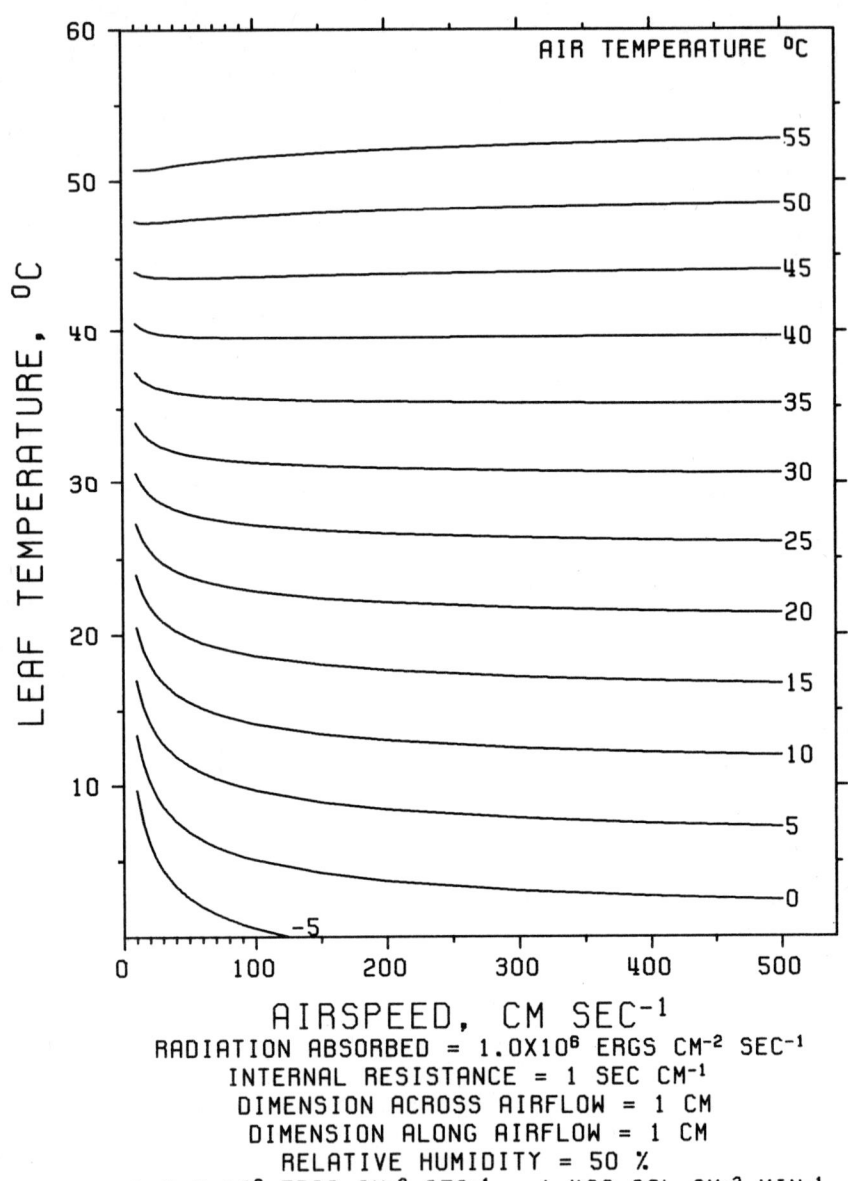

AIRSPEED, CM SEC⁻¹
RADIATION ABSORBED = 1.0X10⁶ ERGS CM⁻² SEC⁻¹
INTERNAL RESISTANCE = 1 SEC CM⁻¹
DIMENSION ACROSS AIRFLOW = 1 CM
DIMENSION ALONG AIRFLOW = 1 CM
RELATIVE HUMIDITY = 50 %
1.0 X 10⁶ ERGS CM⁻² SEC⁻¹ = 1.433 CAL CM⁻² MIN⁻¹

GRAPH 23

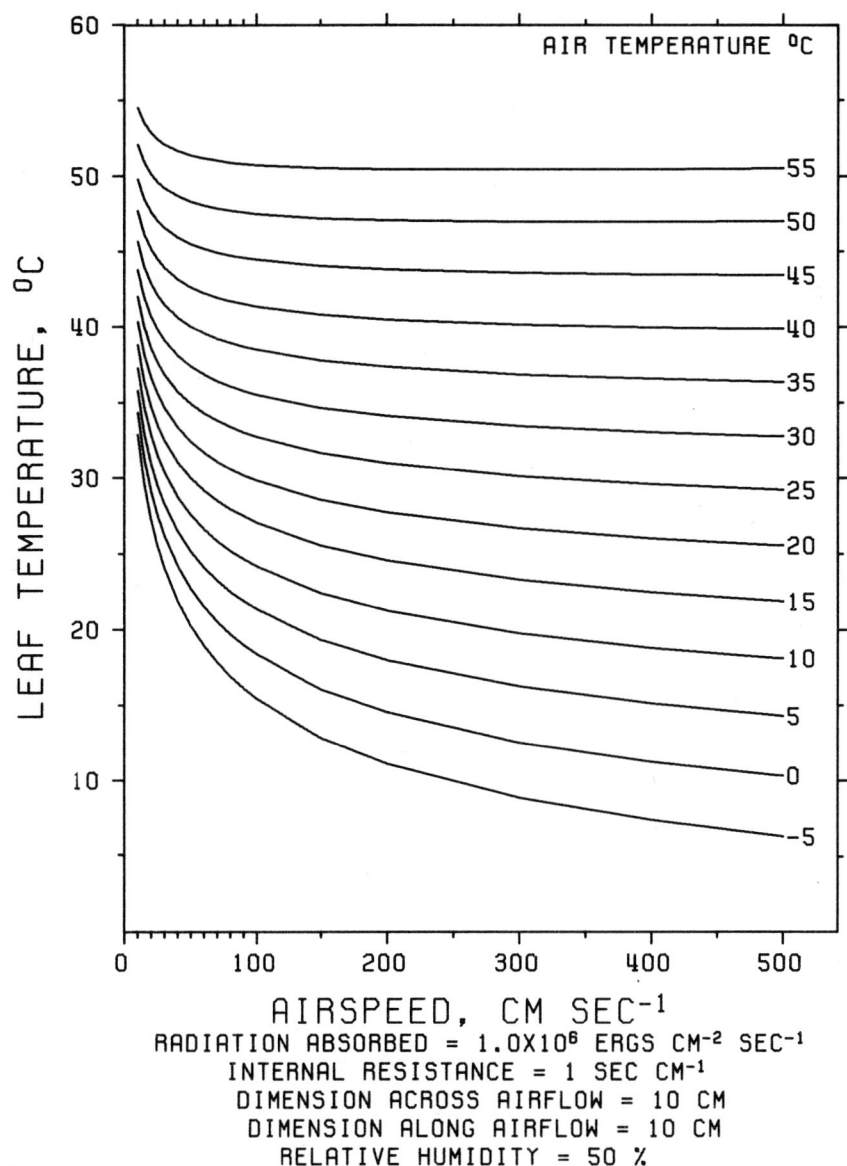

AIRSPEED, CM SEC^{-1}

RADIATION ABSORBED = 1.0X10^6 ERGS CM^{-2} SEC^{-1}
INTERNAL RESISTANCE = 1 SEC CM^{-1}
DIMENSION ACROSS AIRFLOW = 10 CM
DIMENSION ALONG AIRFLOW = 10 CM
RELATIVE HUMIDITY = 50 %
1.0 X 10^6 ERGS CM^{-2} SEC^{-1} = 1.433 CAL CM^{-2} MIN^{-1}

GRAPH 24

191

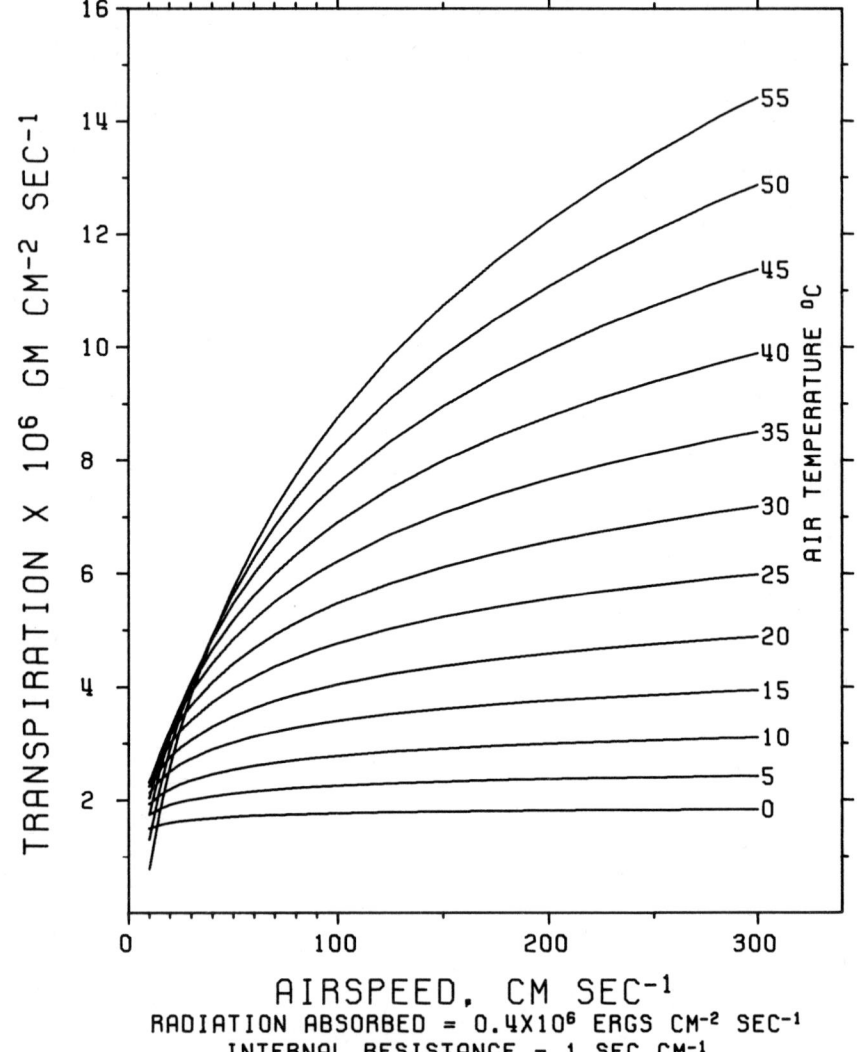

AIRSPEED, CM SEC⁻¹

RADIATION ABSORBED = 0.4X10⁶ ERGS CM⁻² SEC⁻¹
INTERNAL RESISTANCE = 1 SEC CM⁻¹
DIMENSION ACROSS AIRFLOW = 5 CM
DIMENSION ALONG AIRFLOW = 5 CM
RELATIVE HUMIDITY = 60 %
0.4 X 10⁶ ERGS CM⁻² SEC⁻¹ = 0.573 CAL CM⁻² MIN⁻¹

GRAPH 25

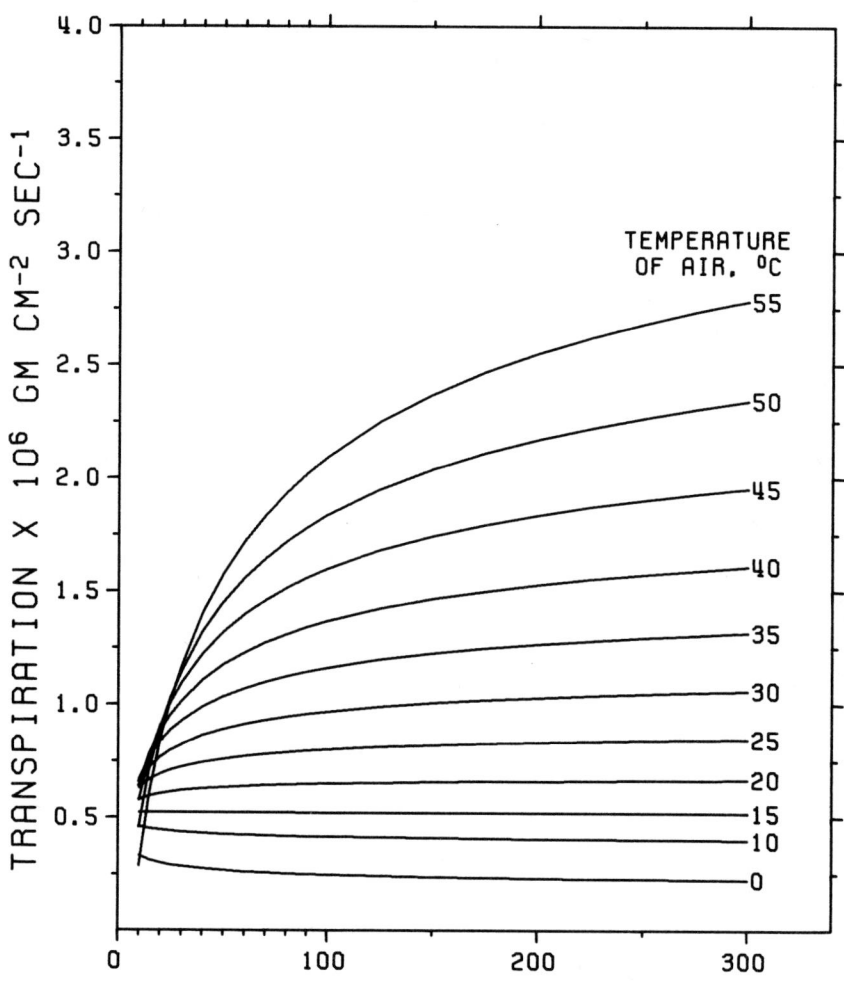

AIRSPEED, CM SEC⁻¹

RADIATION ABSORBED = 0.4X10⁶ ERGS CM⁻² SEC⁻¹
INTERNAL RESISTANCE = 10 SEC CM⁻¹
DIMENSION ACROSS AIRFLOW = 5 CM
DIMENSION ALONG AIRFLOW = 5 CM
RELATIVE HUMIDITY = 60 %
0.4 X 10⁶ ERGS CM⁻² SEC⁻¹ = 0.573 CAL CM⁻² MIN⁻¹

GRAPH 26

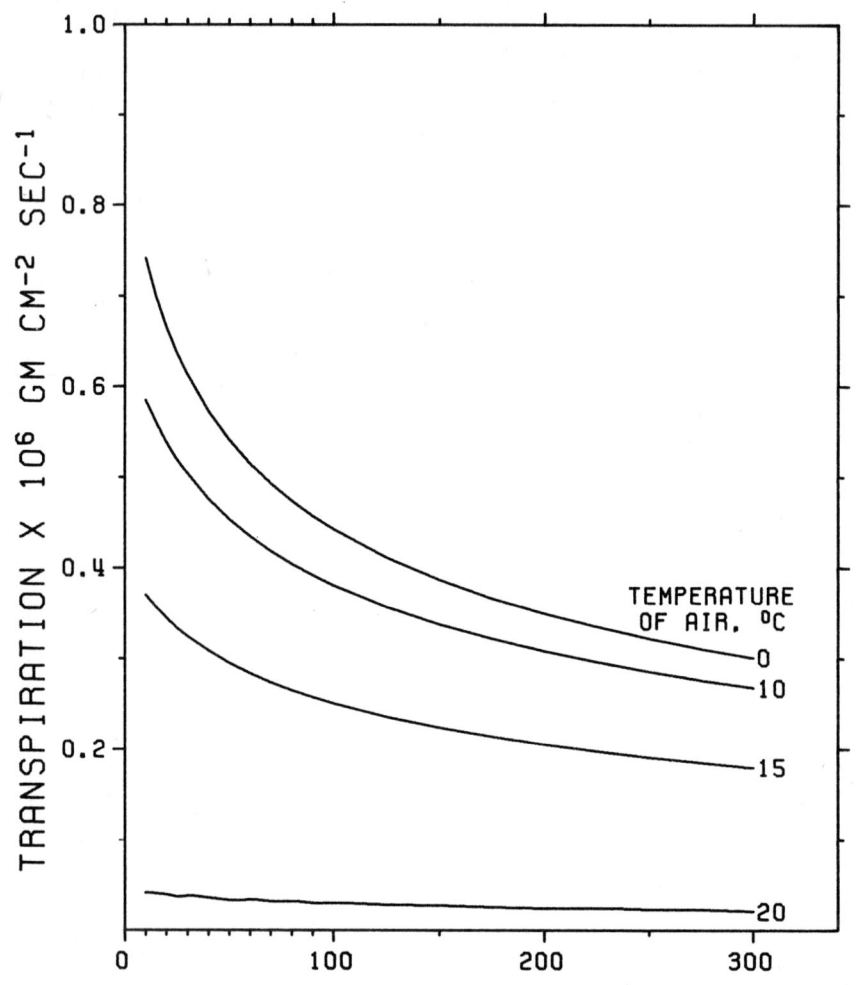

AIRSPEED, CM SEC⁻¹

RADIATION ABSORBED = 0.4X10⁶ ERGS CM⁻² SEC⁻¹
INTERNAL RESISTANCE = 1 SEC CM⁻¹
DIMENSION ACROSS AIRFLOW = 5 CM
DIMENSION ALONG AIRFLOW = 5 CM
RELATIVE HUMIDITY = 100 %
0.4 X 10⁶ ERGS CM⁻² SEC⁻¹ = 0.573 CAL CM⁻² MIN⁻¹

GRAPH 27

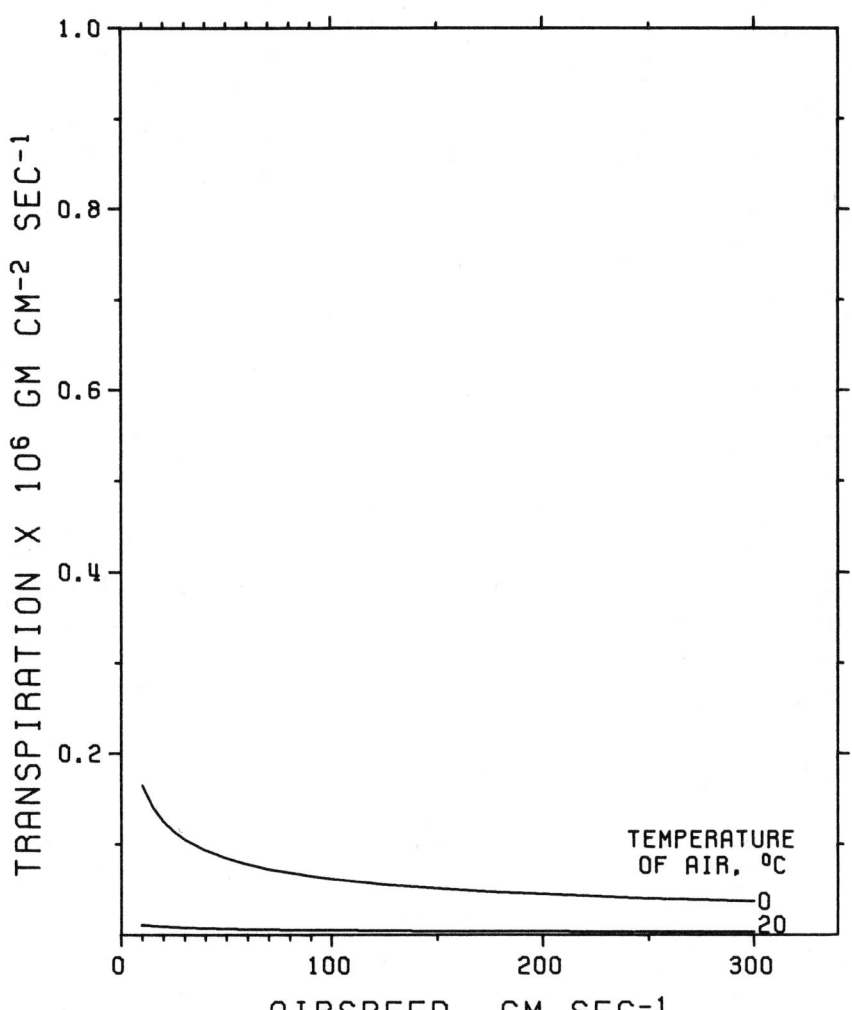

AIRSPEED, CM SEC⁻¹

RADIATION ABSORBED = 0.4X10⁶ ERGS CM⁻² SEC⁻¹
INTERNAL RESISTANCE = 10 SEC CM⁻¹
DIMENSION ACROSS AIRFLOW = 5 CM
DIMENSION ALONG AIRFLOW = 5 CM
RELATIVE HUMIDITY = 100 %
0.4 X 10⁶ ERGS CM⁻² SEC⁻¹ = 0.573 CAL CM⁻² MIN⁻¹

GRAPH 28

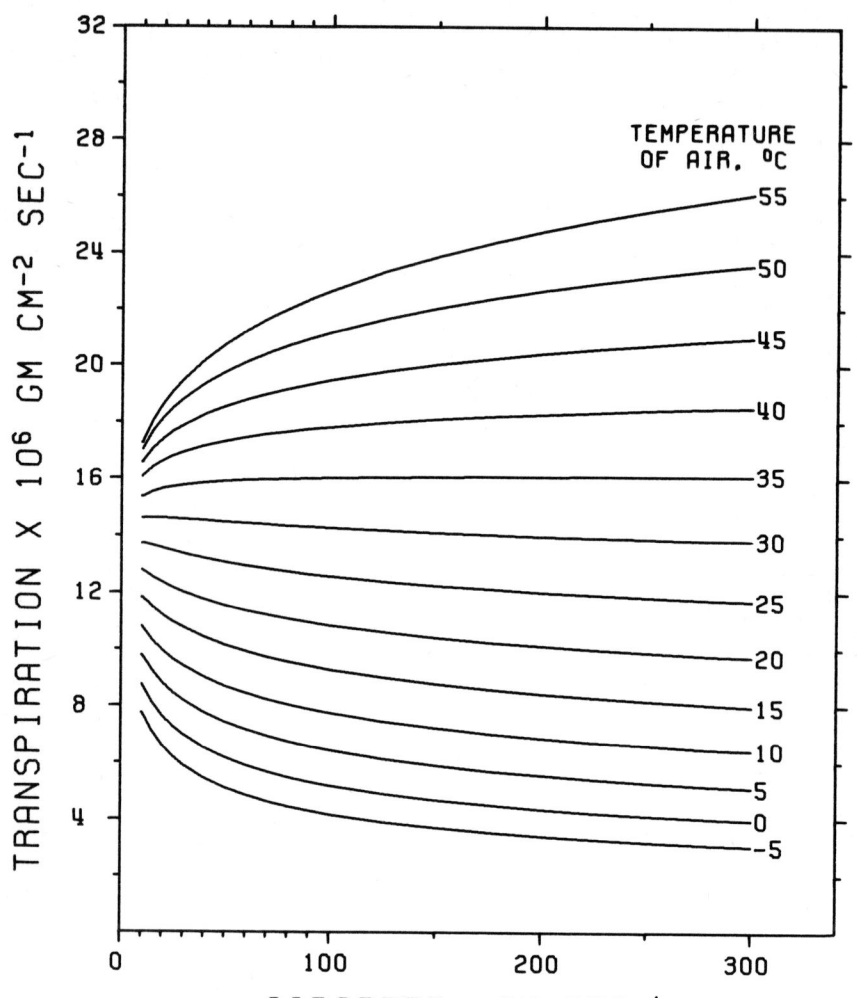

AIRSPEED, CM SEC⁻¹

RADIATION ABSORBED = 1.0X10⁶ ERGS CM⁻² SEC⁻¹
INTERNAL RESISTANCE = 1 SEC CM⁻¹
DIMENSION ACROSS AIRFLOW = 5 CM
DIMENSION ALONG AIRFLOW = 5 CM
RELATIVE HUMIDITY = 60 %
1.0 X 10⁶ ERGS CM⁻² SEC⁻¹ = 1.433 CAL CM⁻² MIN⁻¹

GRAPH 29

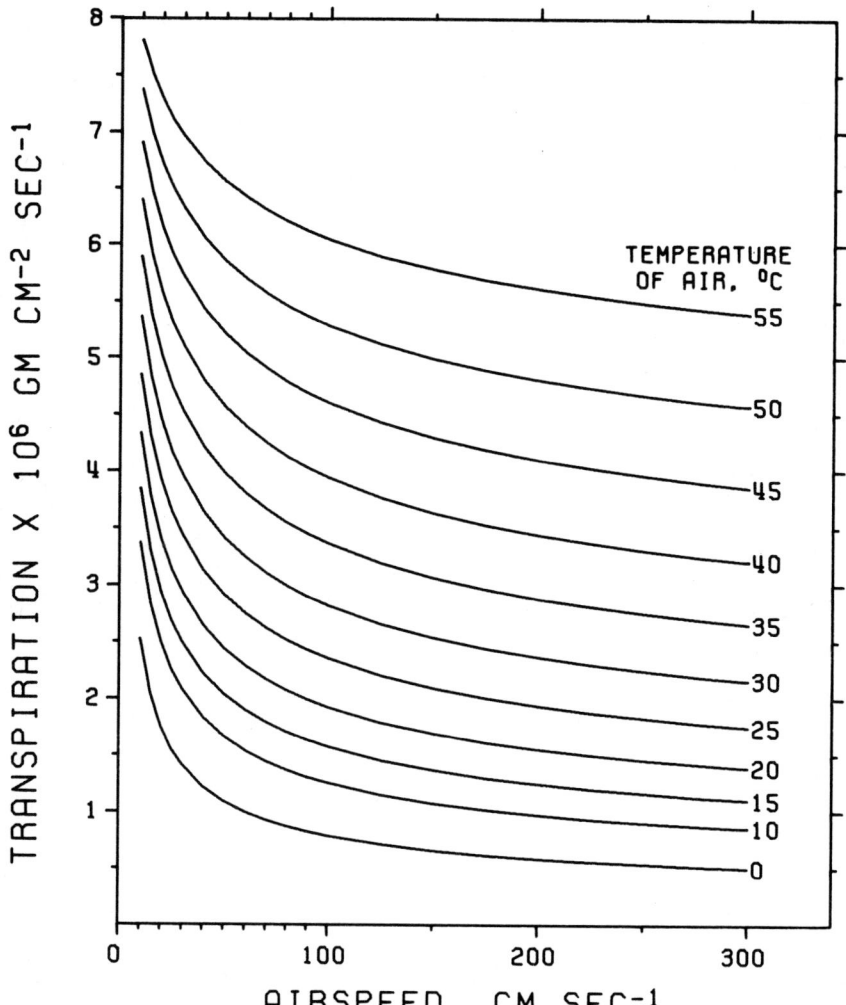

AIRSPEED, CM SEC⁻¹
RADIATION ABSORBED = 1.0X10⁶ ERGS CM⁻² SEC⁻¹
INTERNAL RESISTANCE = 10 SEC CM⁻¹
DIMENSION ACROSS AIRFLOW = 5 CM
DIMENSION ALONG AIRFLOW = 5 CM
RELATIVE HUMIDITY = 60 %
1.0 X 10⁶ ERGS CM⁻² SEC⁻¹ = 1.433 CAL CM⁻² MIN⁻¹

GRAPH 30

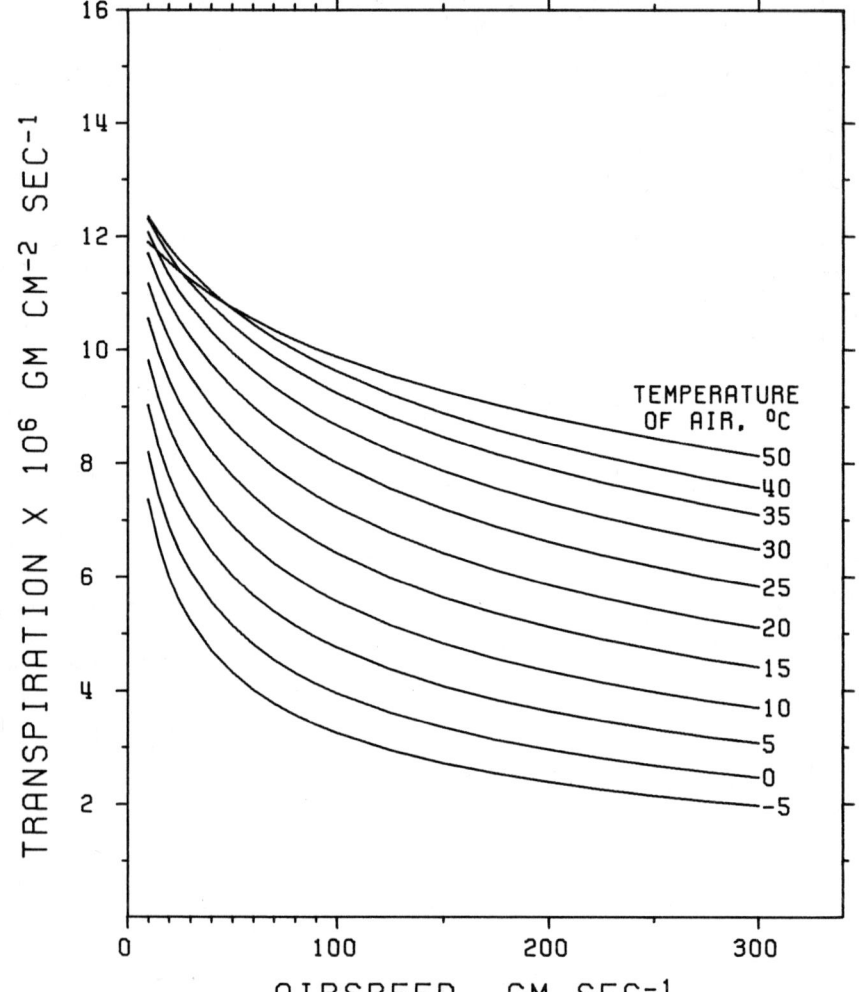

AIRSPEED, CM SEC⁻¹

RADIATION ABSORBED = 1.0X10⁶ ERGS CM⁻² SEC⁻¹
INTERNAL RESISTANCE = 1 SEC CM⁻¹
DIMENSION ACROSS AIRFLOW = 5 CM
DIMENSION ALONG AIRFLOW = 5 CM
RELATIVE HUMIDITY = 100 %
1.0 X 10⁶ ERGS CM⁻² SEC⁻¹ = 1.433 CAL CM⁻² MIN⁻¹

GRAPH 31

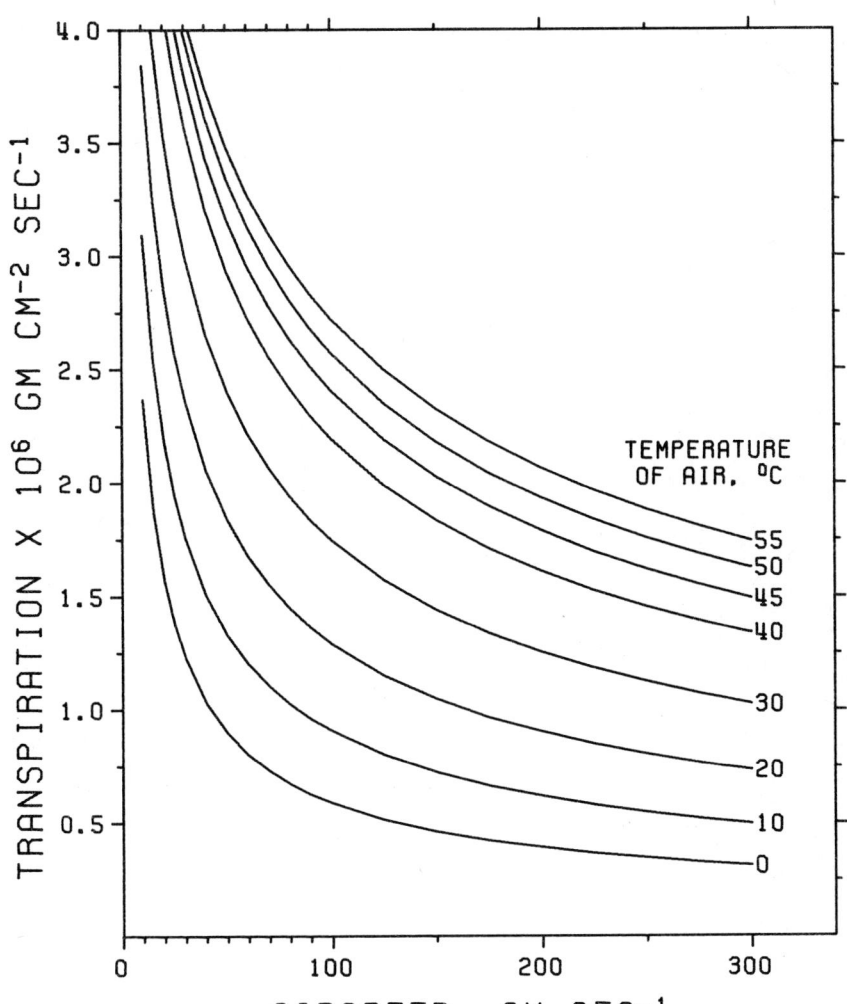

AIRSPEED, CM SEC⁻¹

RADIATION ABSORBED = 1.0×10⁶ ERGS CM⁻² SEC⁻¹
INTERNAL RESISTANCE = 10 SEC CM⁻¹
DIMENSION ACROSS AIRFLOW = 5 CM
DIMENSION ALONG AIRFLOW = 5 CM
RELATIVE HUMIDITY = 100 %
1.0 × 10⁶ ERGS CM⁻² SEC⁻¹ = 1.433 CAL CM⁻² MIN⁻¹

GRAPH 32

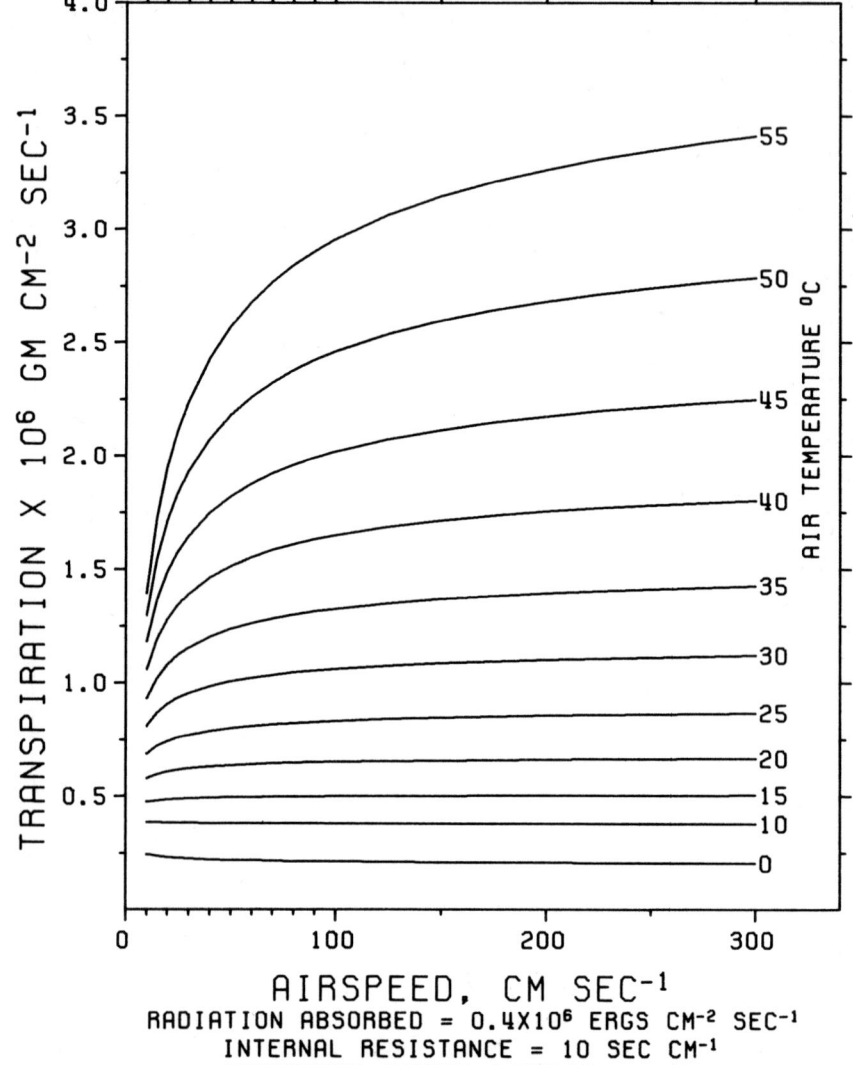

AIRSPEED, CM SEC^{-1}

RADIATION ABSORBED = 0.4X10^6 ERGS CM^{-2} SEC^{-1}
INTERNAL RESISTANCE = 10 SEC CM^{-1}
DIMENSION ACROSS AIRFLOW = 1 CM
DIMENSION ALONG AIRFLOW = 1 CM
RELATIVE HUMIDITY = 60 %
0.4 X 10^6 ERGS CM^{-2} SEC^{-1} = 0.537 CAL CM^{-2} MIN^{-1}

GRAPH 33

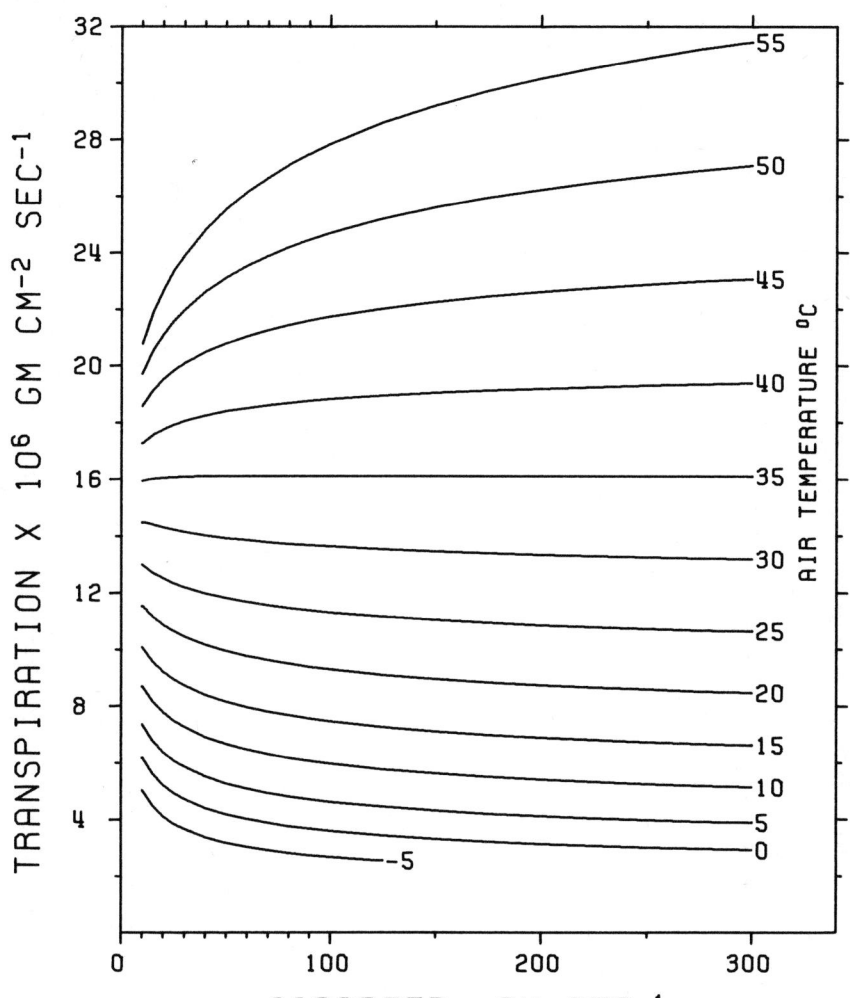

AIRSPEED, CM SEC⁻¹
RADIATION ABSORBED = 1.0×10^6 ERGS CM⁻² SEC⁻¹
INTERNAL RESISTANCE = 1 SEC CM⁻¹
DIMENSION ACROSS AIRFLOW = 1 CM
DIMENSION ALONG AIRFLOW = 1 CM
RELATIVE HUMIDITY = 60 %
1.0×10^6 ERGS CM⁻² SEC⁻¹ = 1.433 CAL CM⁻² MIN⁻¹

GRAPH 34

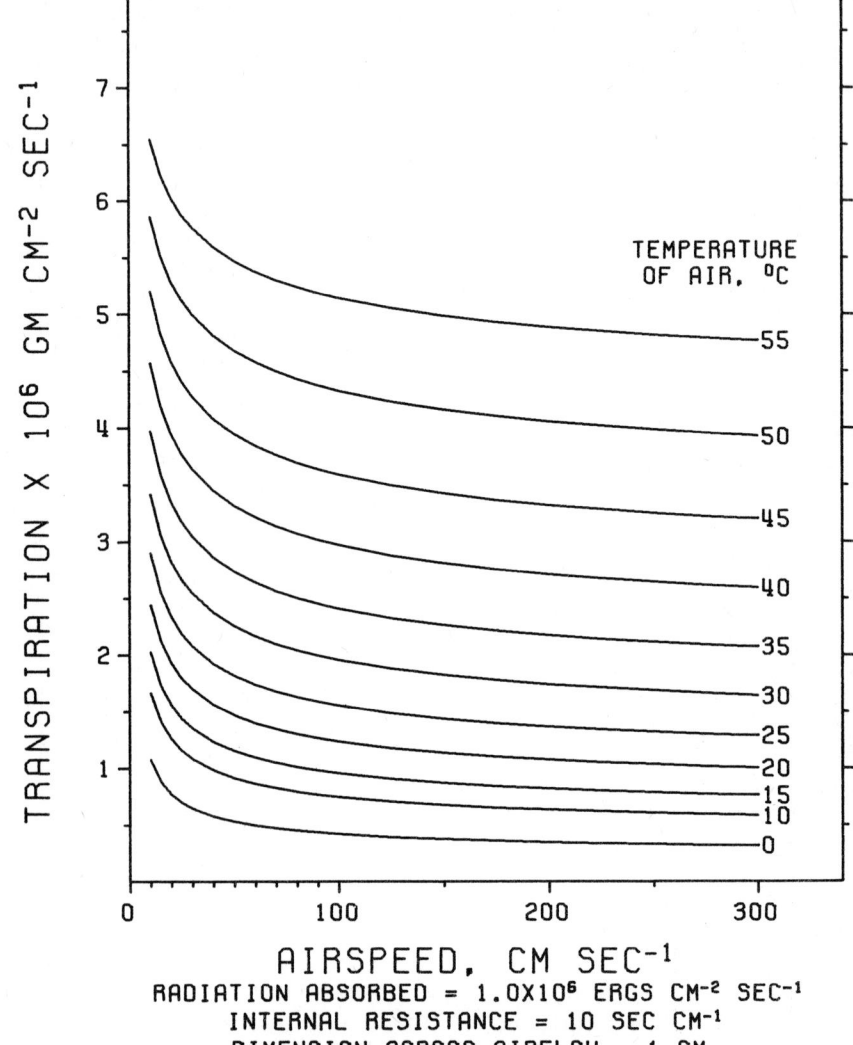

AIRSPEED, CM SEC⁻¹
RADIATION ABSORBED = 1.0X10⁶ ERGS CM⁻² SEC⁻¹
INTERNAL RESISTANCE = 10 SEC CM⁻¹
DIMENSION ACROSS AIRFLOW = 1 CM
DIMENSION ALONG AIRFLOW = 1 CM
RELATIVE HUMIDITY = 60 %
1.0 X 10⁶ ERGS CM⁻² SEC⁻¹ = 1.433 CAL CM⁻² MIN⁻¹

Graph 35

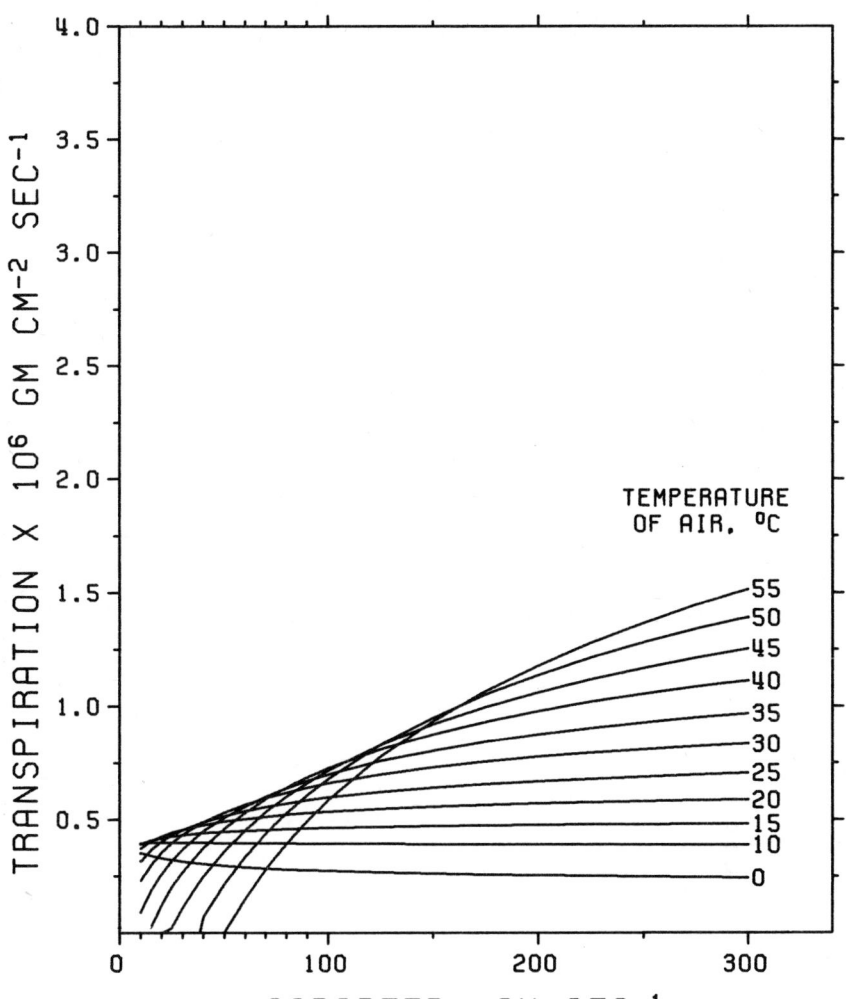

GRAPH 36

203

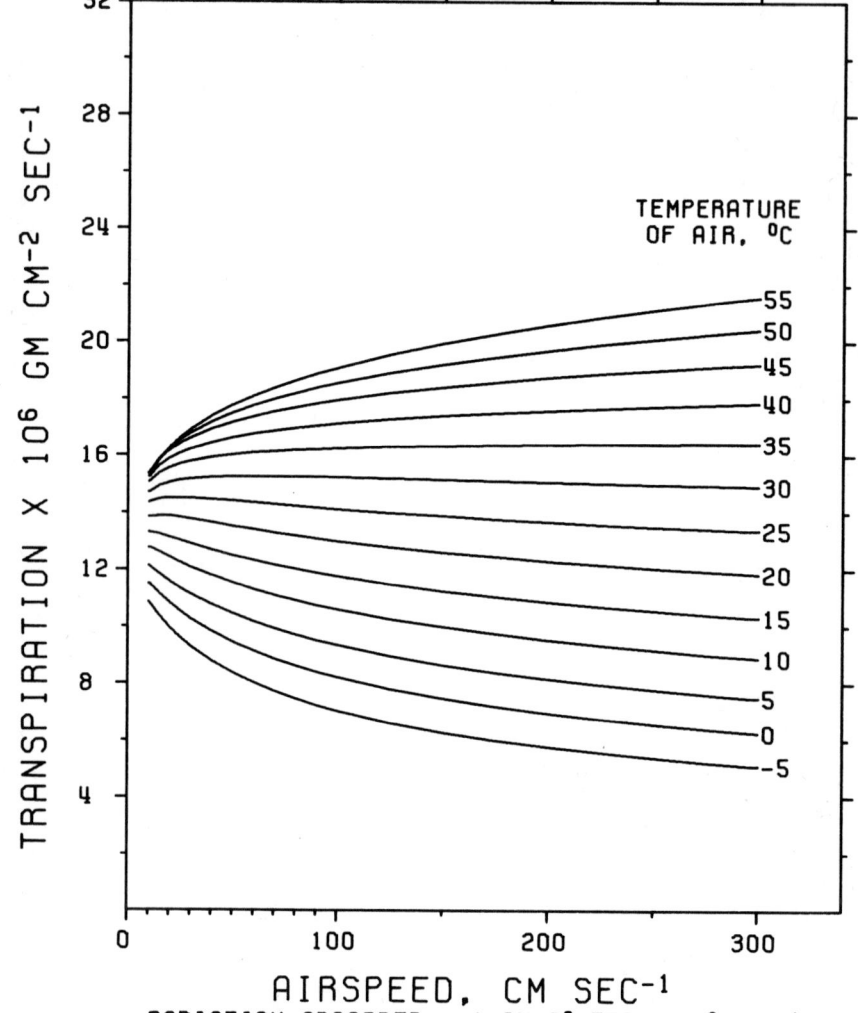

AIRSPEED, CM SEC⁻¹

RADIATION ABSORBED = 1.0X10⁶ ERGS CM⁻² SEC⁻¹
INTERNAL RESISTANCE = 1 SEC CM⁻¹
DIMENSION ACROSS AIRFLOW = 10 CM
DIMENSION ALONG AIRFLOW = 10 CM
RELATIVE HUMIDITY = 60 %
1.0 X 10⁶ ERGS CM⁻² SEC⁻¹ = 1.433 CAL CM⁻² MIN⁻¹

GRAPH 37

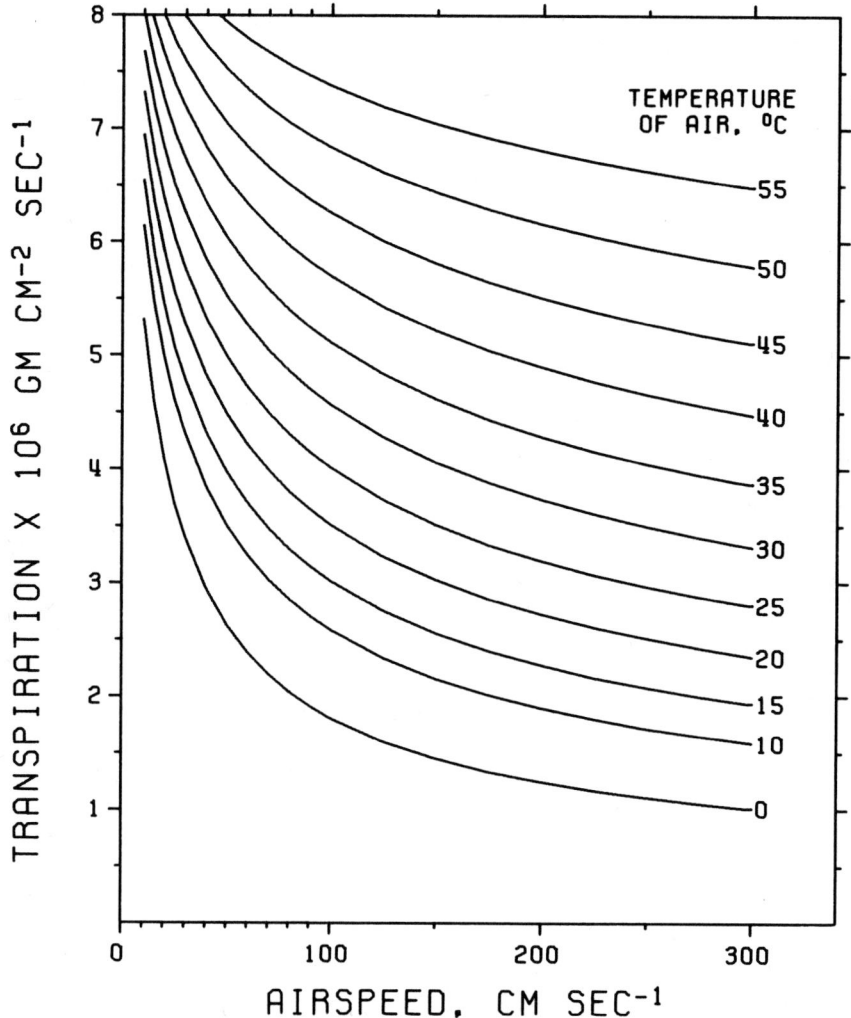

AIRSPEED, CM SEC⁻¹

RADIATION ABSORBED = 1.0X10⁶ ERGS CM⁻² SEC⁻¹
INTERNAL RESISTANCE = 10 SEC CM⁻¹
DIMENSION ACROSS AIRFLOW = 10 CM
DIMENSION ALONG AIRFLOW = 10 CM
RELATIVE HUMIDITY = 60 %
1.0 X 10⁶ ERGS CM⁻² SEC⁻¹ = 1.433 CAL CM⁻² MIN⁻¹

GRAPH 38

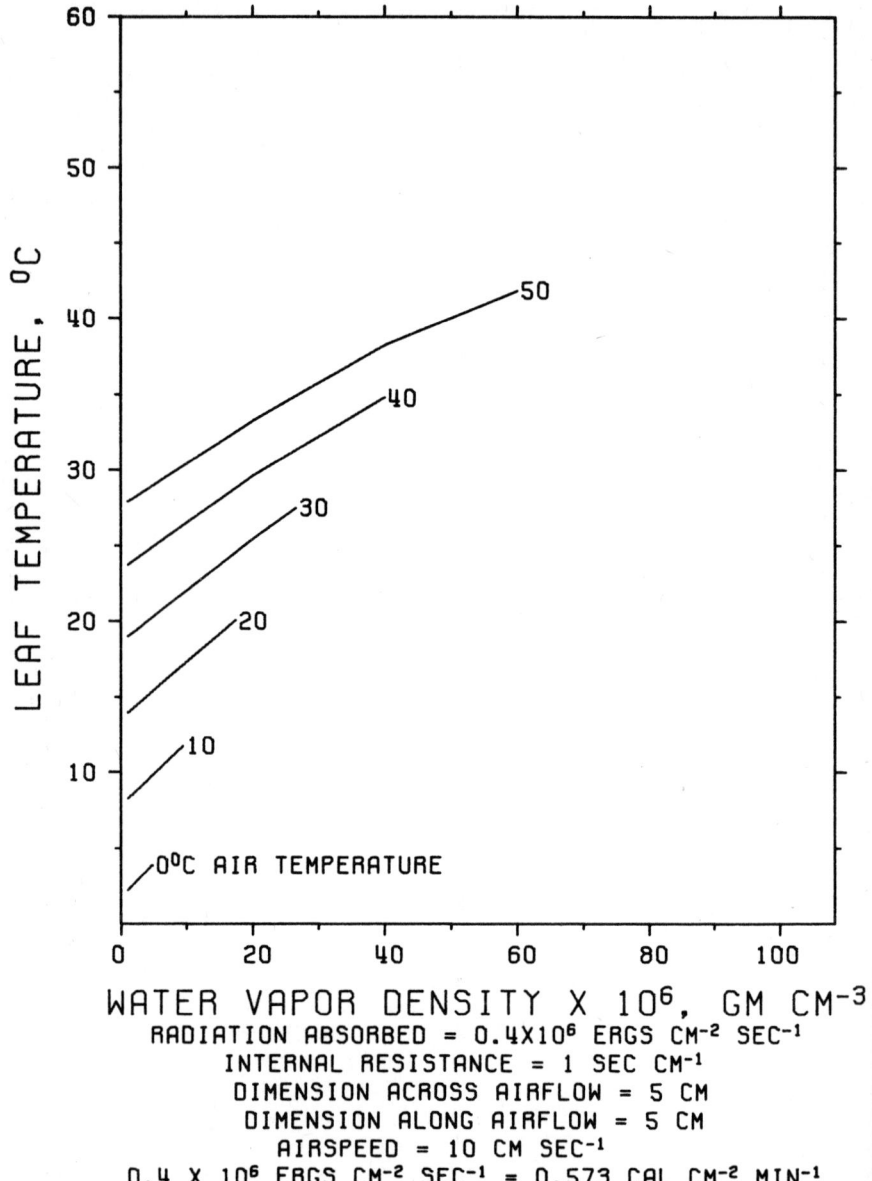

WATER VAPOR DENSITY X 10⁶, GM CM⁻³
RADIATION ABSORBED = 0.4X10⁶ ERGS CM⁻² SEC⁻¹
INTERNAL RESISTANCE = 1 SEC CM⁻¹
DIMENSION ACROSS AIRFLOW = 5 CM
DIMENSION ALONG AIRFLOW = 5 CM
AIRSPEED = 10 CM SEC⁻¹
0.4 X 10⁶ ERGS CM⁻² SEC⁻¹ = 0.573 CAL CM⁻² MIN⁻¹

GRAPH 39

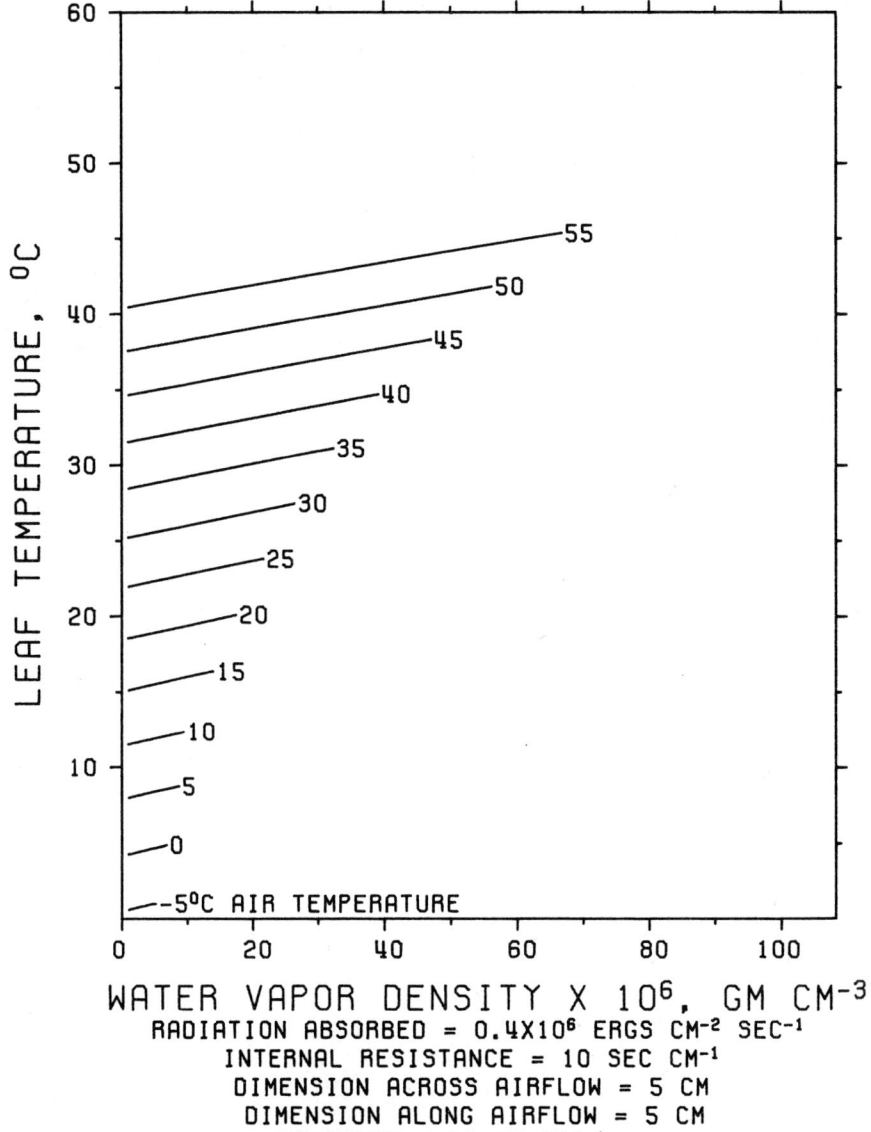

WATER VAPOR DENSITY X 10⁶, GM CM⁻³

RADIATION ABSORBED = 0.4X10⁶ ERGS CM⁻² SEC⁻¹
INTERNAL RESISTANCE = 10 SEC CM⁻¹
DIMENSION ACROSS AIRFLOW = 5 CM
DIMENSION ALONG AIRFLOW = 5 CM
AIRSPEED = 10 CM SEC⁻¹
0.4 X 10⁶ ERGS CM⁻² SEC⁻¹ = 0.573 CAL CM⁻² MIN⁻¹

GRAPH 40

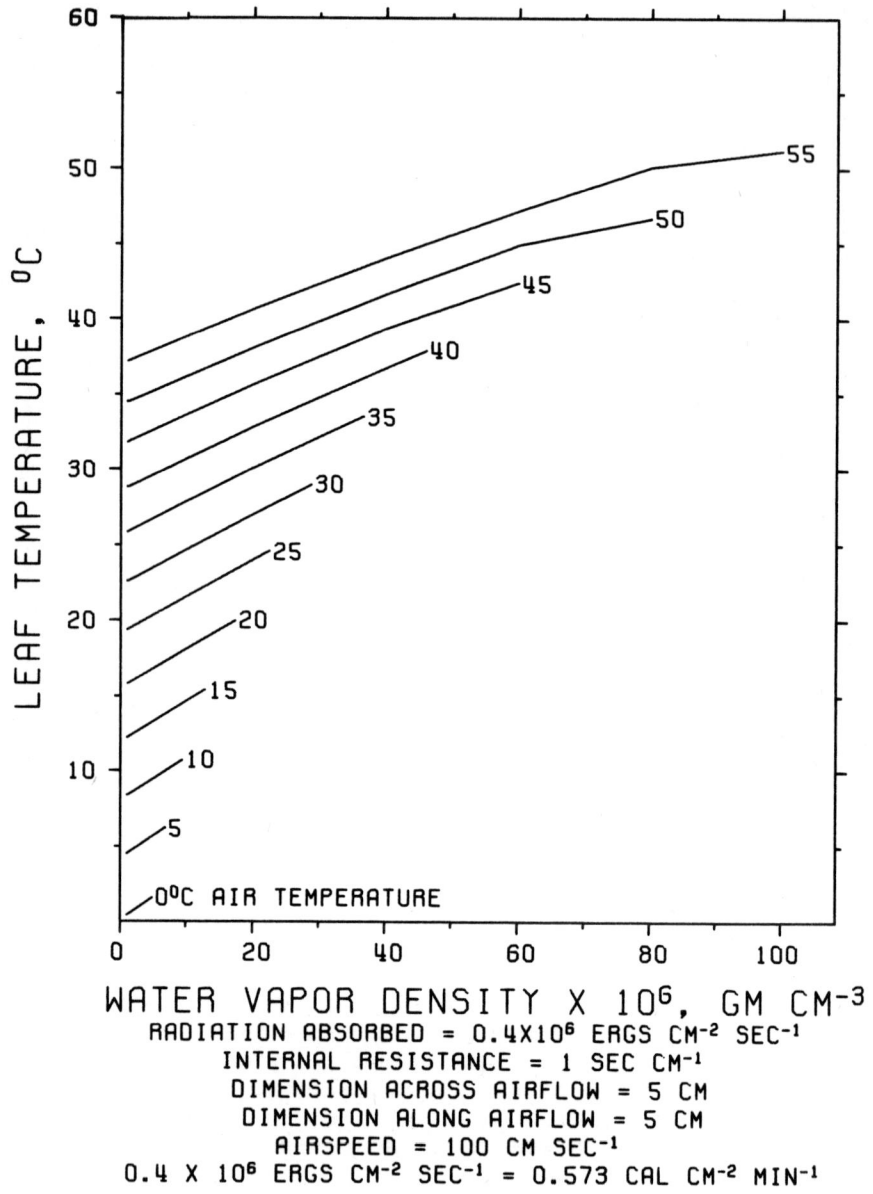

WATER VAPOR DENSITY X 10⁶, GM CM⁻³
RADIATION ABSORBED = 0.4X10⁶ ERGS CM⁻² SEC⁻¹
INTERNAL RESISTANCE = 1 SEC CM⁻¹
DIMENSION ACROSS AIRFLOW = 5 CM
DIMENSION ALONG AIRFLOW = 5 CM
AIRSPEED = 100 CM SEC⁻¹
0.4 X 10⁶ ERGS CM⁻² SEC⁻¹ = 0.573 CAL CM⁻² MIN⁻¹

GRAPH 41

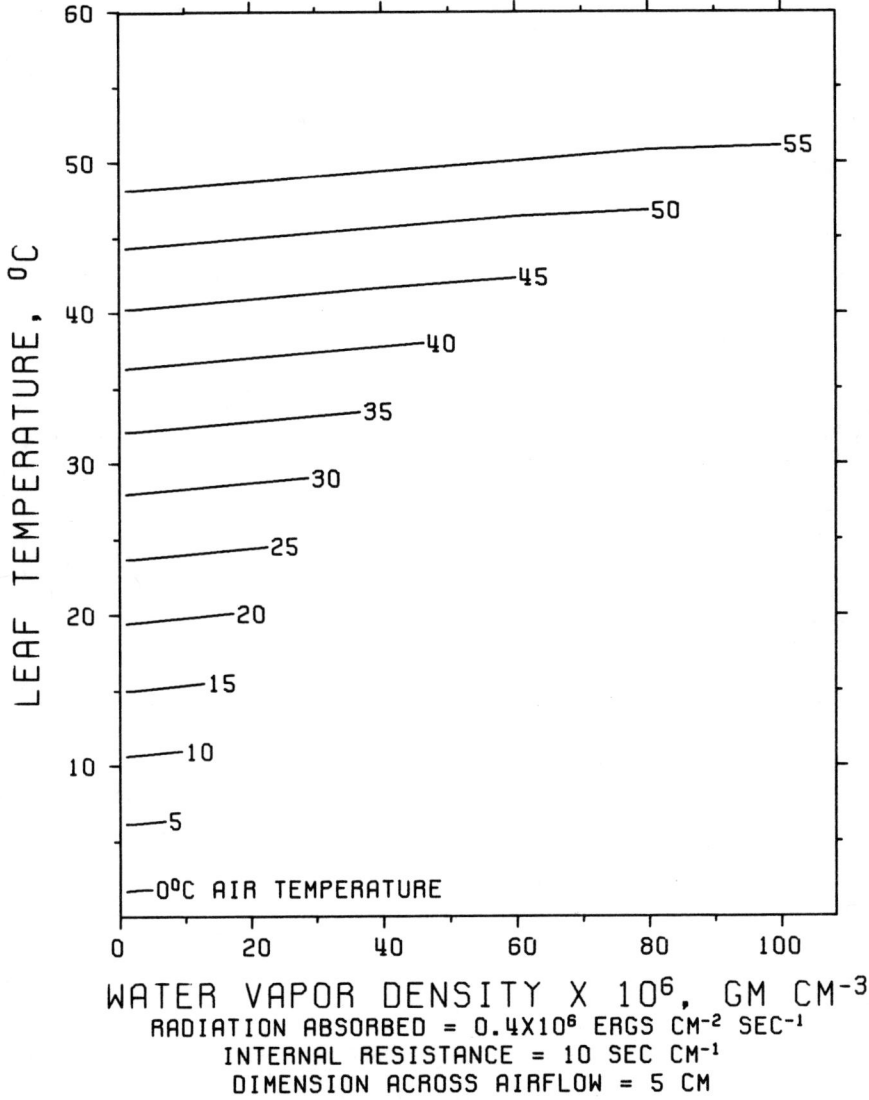

WATER VAPOR DENSITY X 10^6, GM CM^{-3}

RADIATION ABSORBED = 0.4X10^6 ERGS CM^{-2} SEC^{-1}
INTERNAL RESISTANCE = 10 SEC CM^{-1}
DIMENSION ACROSS AIRFLOW = 5 CM
DIMENSION ALONG AIRFLOW = 5 CM
AIRSPEED = 100 CM SEC^{-1}
0.4 X 10^6 ERGS CM^{-2} SEC^{-1} = 0.573 CAL CM^{-2} MIN^{-1}

GRAPH 42

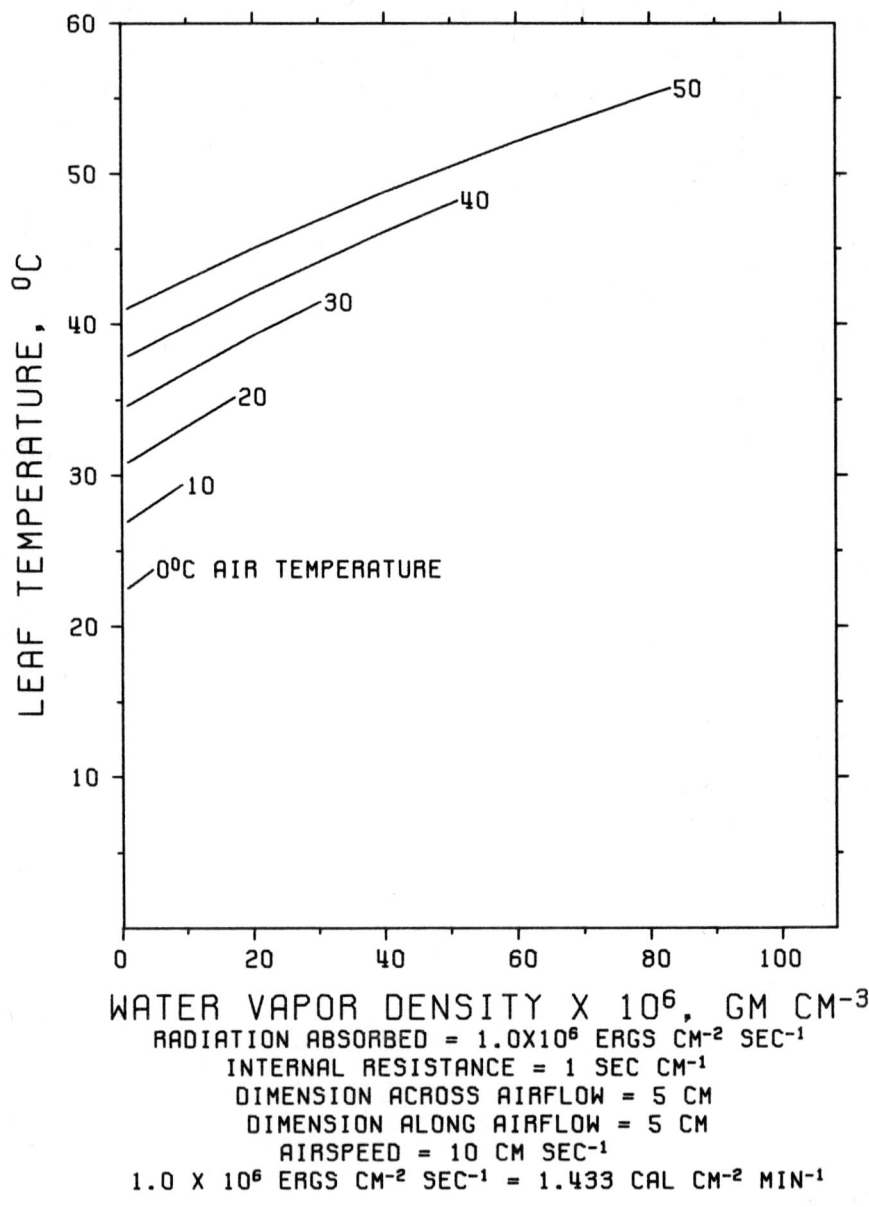

WATER VAPOR DENSITY X 10⁶, GM CM⁻³
RADIATION ABSORBED = 1.0X10⁶ ERGS CM⁻² SEC⁻¹
INTERNAL RESISTANCE = 1 SEC CM⁻¹
DIMENSION ACROSS AIRFLOW = 5 CM
DIMENSION ALONG AIRFLOW = 5 CM
AIRSPEED = 10 CM SEC⁻¹
1.0 X 10⁶ ERGS CM⁻² SEC⁻¹ = 1.433 CAL CM⁻² MIN⁻¹

GRAPH 43

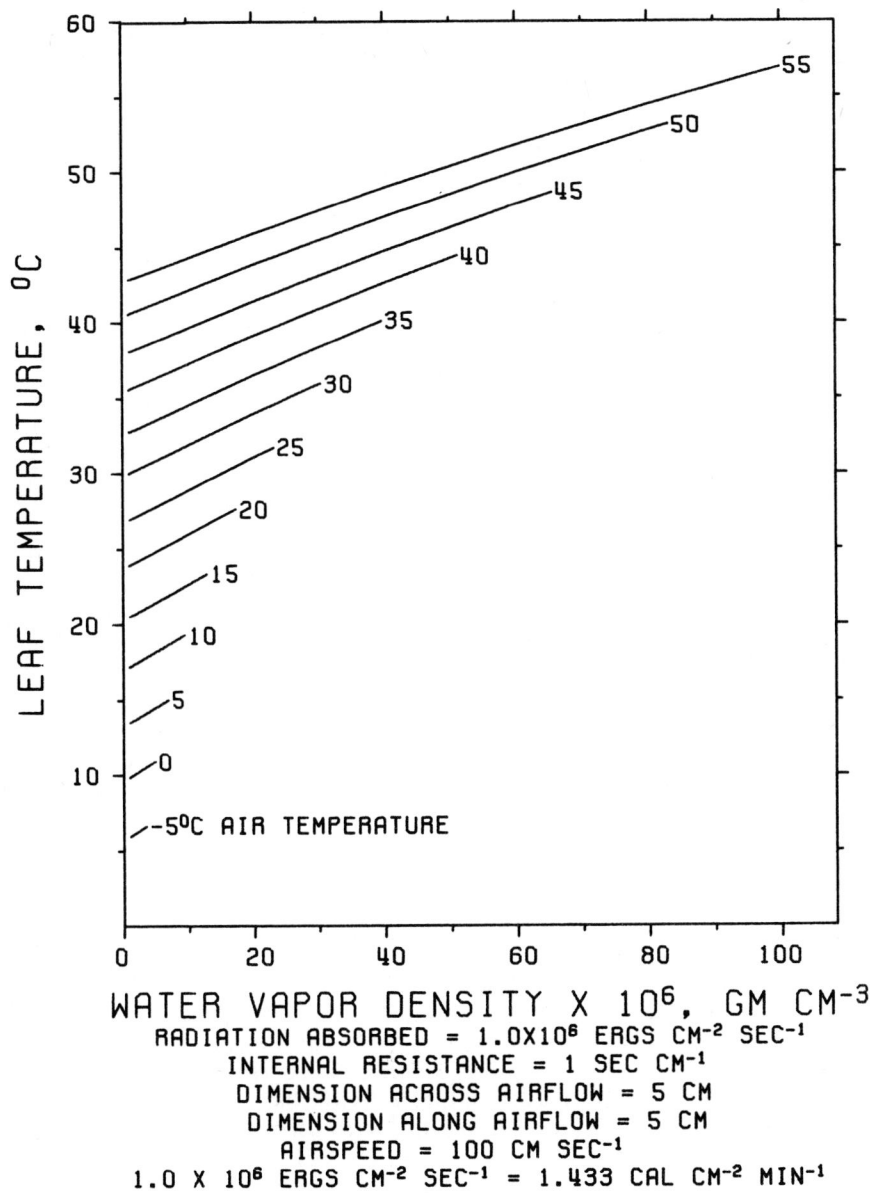

WATER VAPOR DENSITY X 10⁶, GM CM⁻³

RADIATION ABSORBED = 1.0×10^6 ERGS CM⁻² SEC⁻¹
INTERNAL RESISTANCE = 1 SEC CM⁻¹
DIMENSION ACROSS AIRFLOW = 5 CM
DIMENSION ALONG AIRFLOW = 5 CM
AIRSPEED = 100 CM SEC⁻¹
1.0×10^6 ERGS CM⁻² SEC⁻¹ = 1.433 CAL CM⁻² MIN⁻¹

GRAPH 44

211

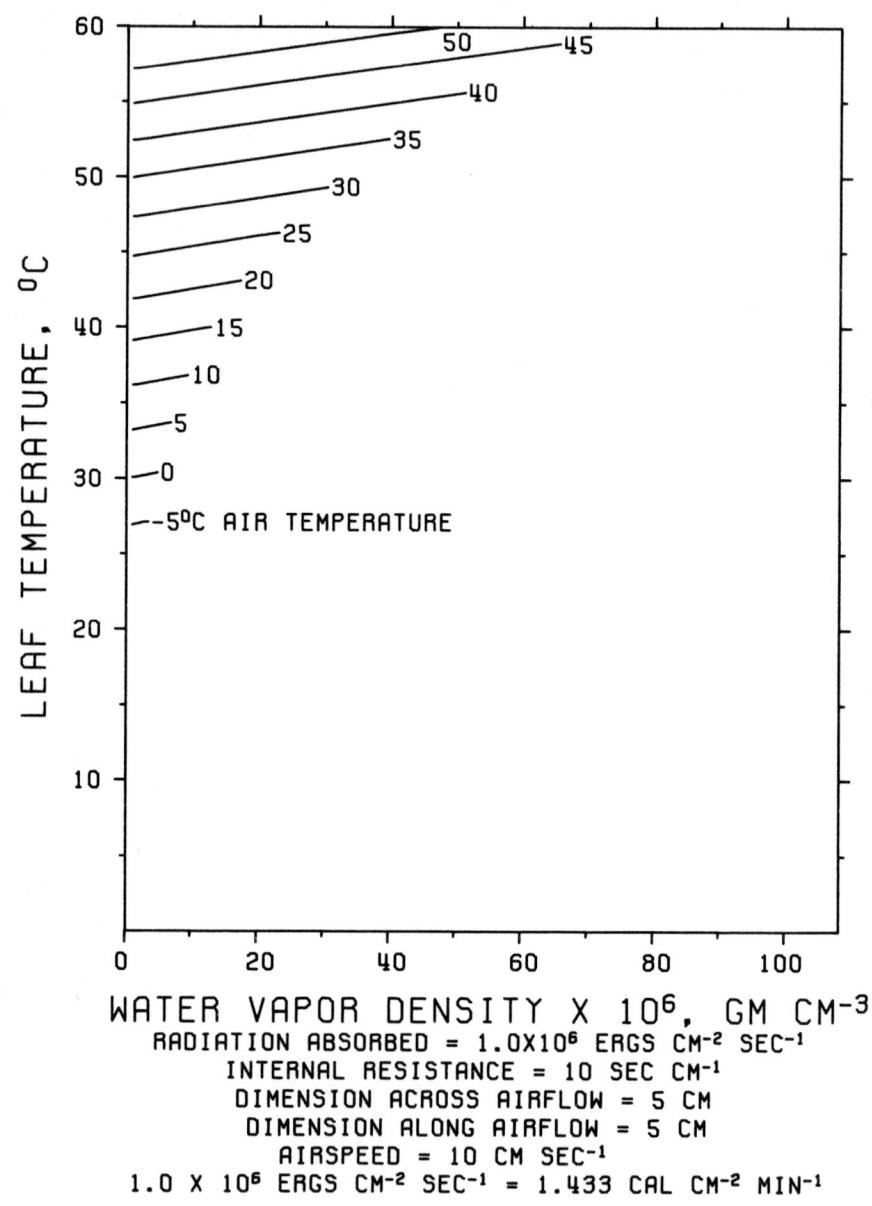

WATER VAPOR DENSITY X 10⁶, GM CM⁻³

RADIATION ABSORBED = 1.0X10⁶ ERGS CM⁻² SEC⁻¹
INTERNAL RESISTANCE = 10 SEC CM⁻¹
DIMENSION ACROSS AIRFLOW = 5 CM
DIMENSION ALONG AIRFLOW = 5 CM
AIRSPEED = 10 CM SEC⁻¹
1.0 X 10⁶ ERGS CM⁻² SEC⁻¹ = 1.433 CAL CM⁻² MIN⁻¹

GRAPH 45

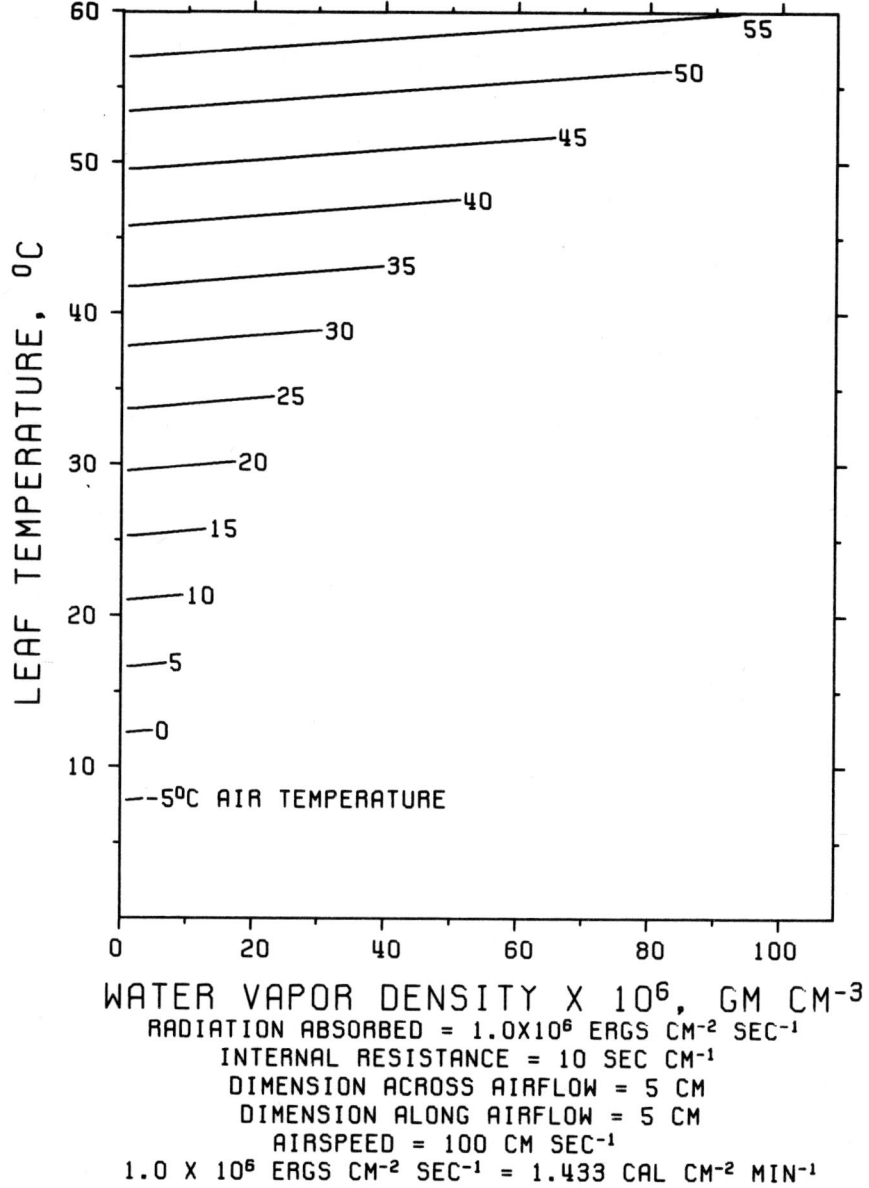

WATER VAPOR DENSITY X 10^6, GM CM^{-3}

RADIATION ABSORBED = 1.0X10^6 ERGS CM^{-2} SEC^{-1}
INTERNAL RESISTANCE = 10 SEC CM^{-1}
DIMENSION ACROSS AIRFLOW = 5 CM
DIMENSION ALONG AIRFLOW = 5 CM
AIRSPEED = 100 CM SEC^{-1}
1.0 X 10^6 ERGS CM^{-2} SEC^{-1} = 1.433 CAL CM^{-2} MIN^{-1}

GRAPH 46

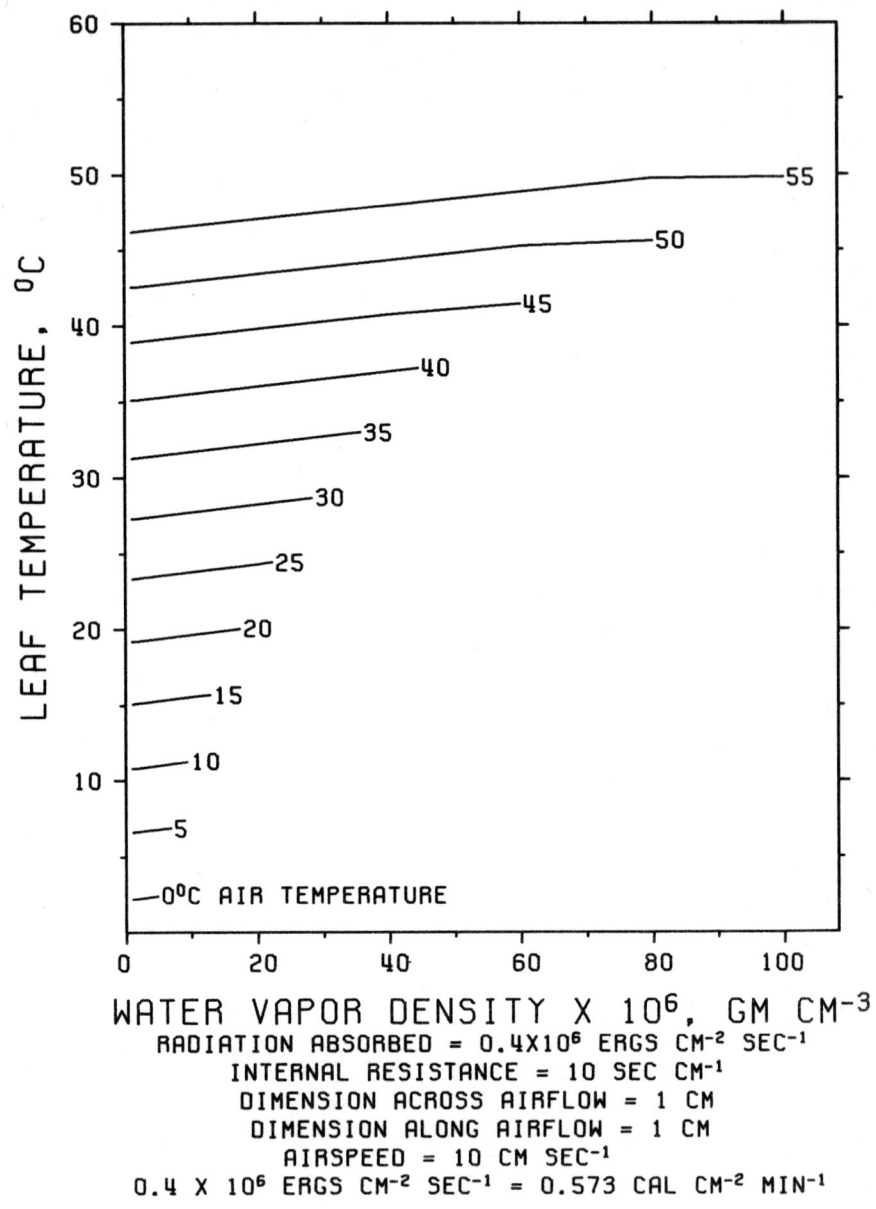

WATER VAPOR DENSITY X 10^6, GM CM^{-3}

RADIATION ABSORBED = $0.4X10^6$ ERGS CM^{-2} SEC^{-1}
INTERNAL RESISTANCE = 10 SEC CM^{-1}
DIMENSION ACROSS AIRFLOW = 1 CM
DIMENSION ALONG AIRFLOW = 1 CM
AIRSPEED = 10 CM SEC^{-1}
$0.4 X 10^6$ ERGS CM^{-2} SEC^{-1} = 0.573 CAL CM^{-2} MIN^{-1}

GRAPH 47

214

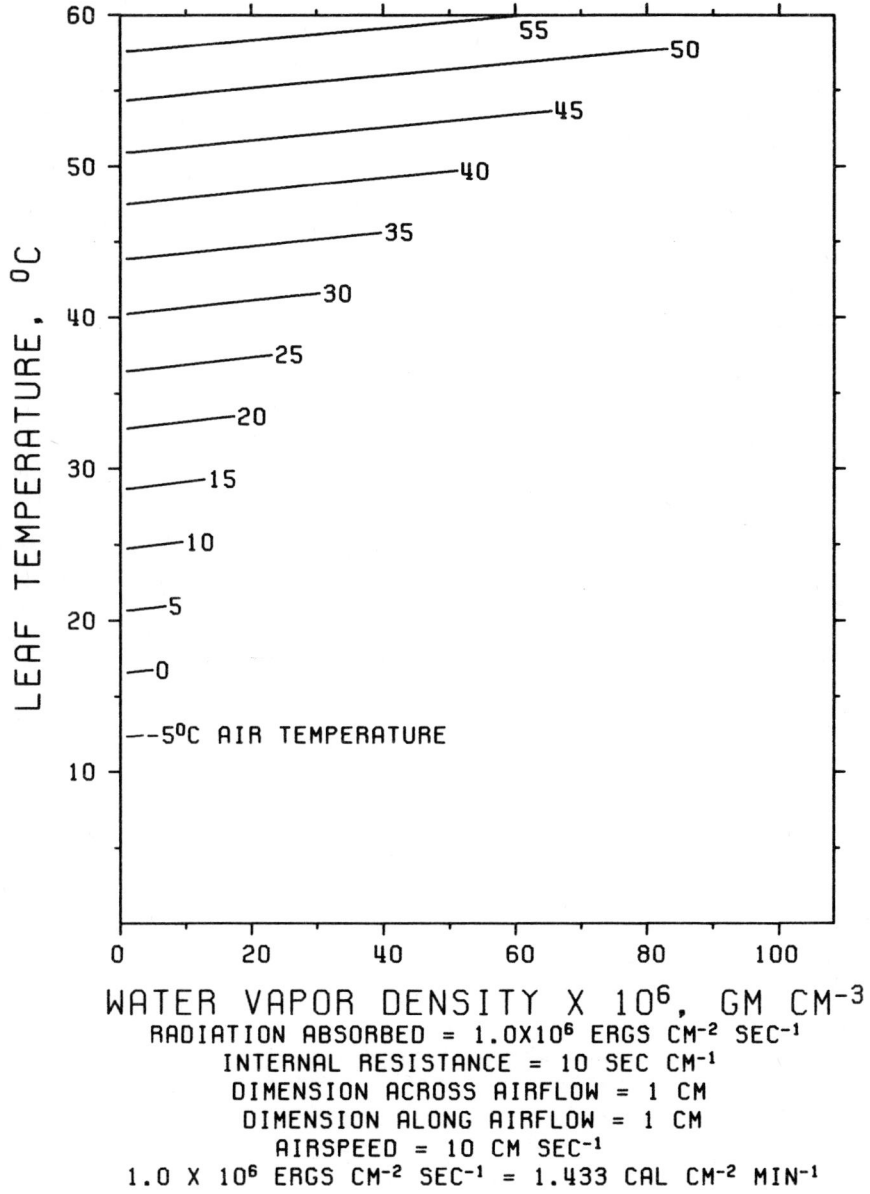

WATER VAPOR DENSITY X 10⁶, GM CM⁻³

RADIATION ABSORBED = 1.0X10⁶ ERGS CM⁻² SEC⁻¹
INTERNAL RESISTANCE = 10 SEC CM⁻¹
DIMENSION ACROSS AIRFLOW = 1 CM
DIMENSION ALONG AIRFLOW = 1 CM
AIRSPEED = 10 CM SEC⁻¹
1.0 X 10⁶ ERGS CM⁻² SEC⁻¹ = 1.433 CAL CM⁻² MIN⁻¹

GRAPH 48

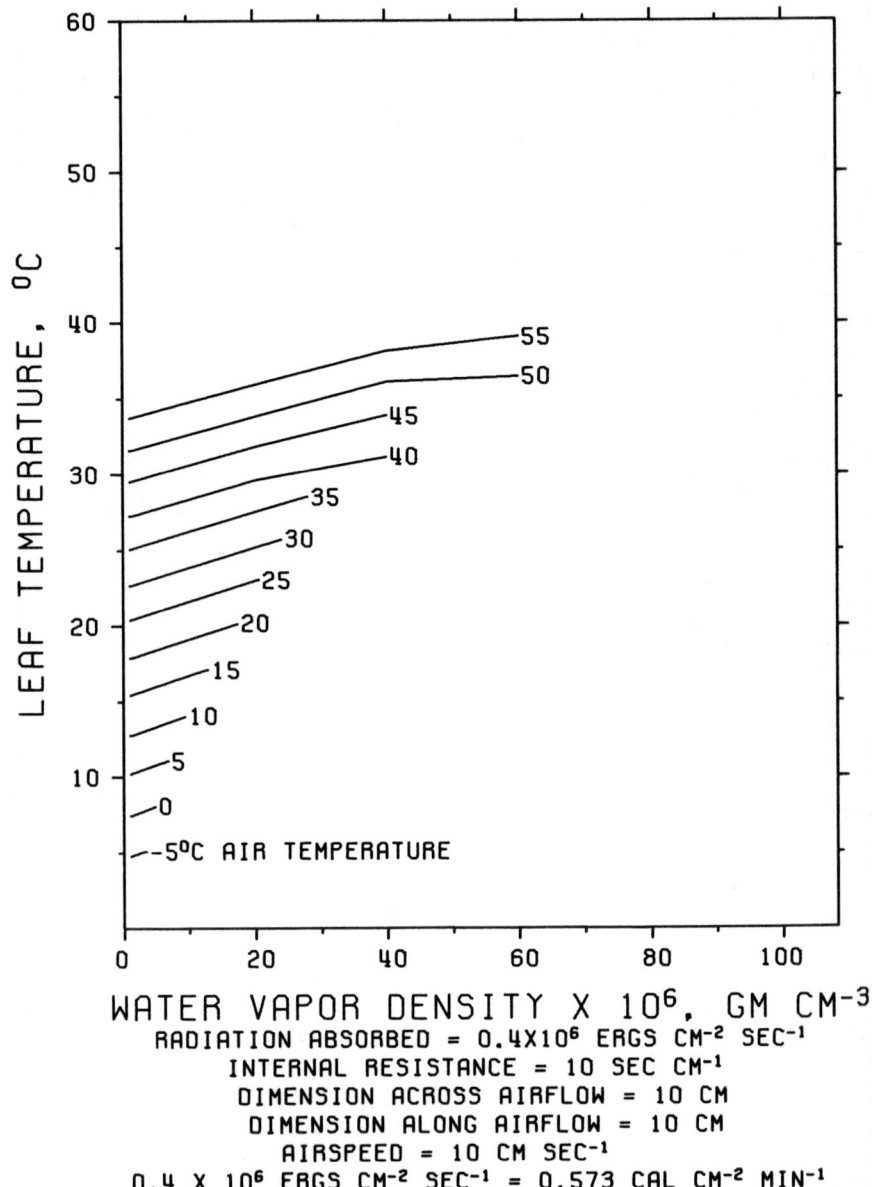

GRAPH 49

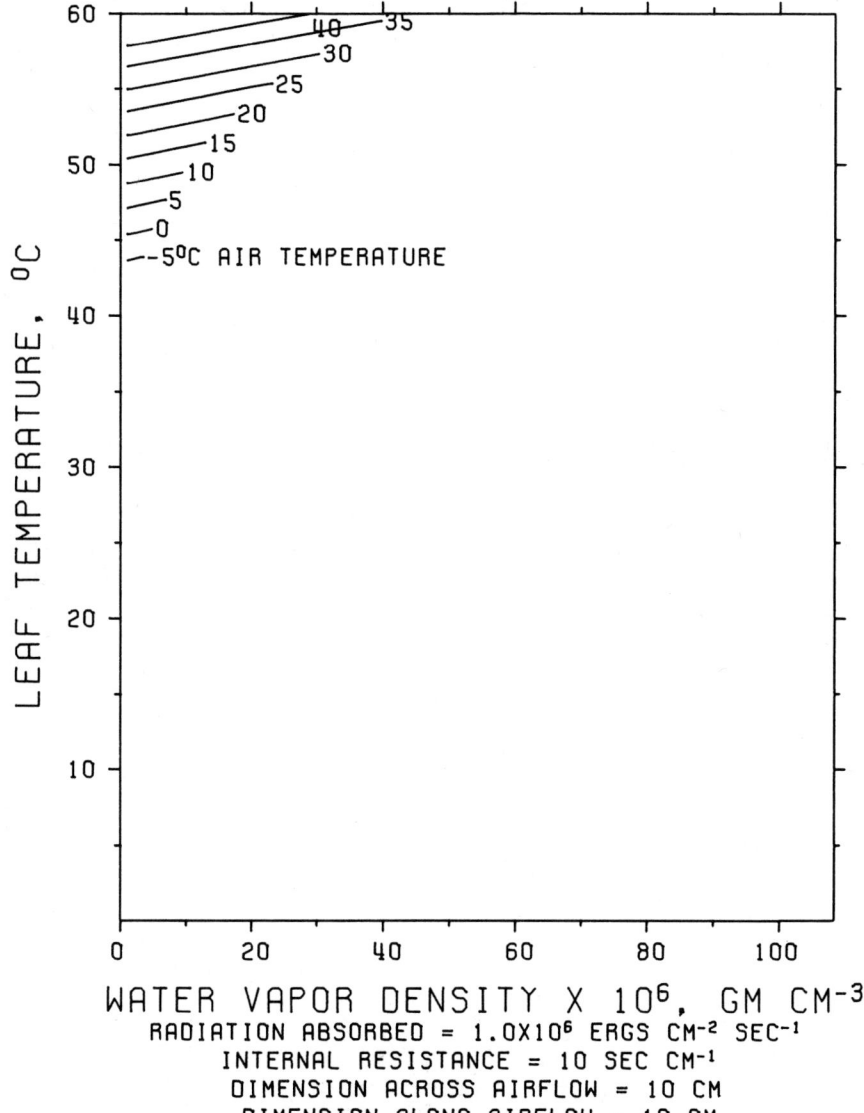

LEAF TEMPERATURE, °C

40 35
30
25
20
15
10
5
0
-5°C AIR TEMPERATURE

WATER VAPOR DENSITY X 10⁶, GM CM⁻³
RADIATION ABSORBED = 1.0X10⁶ ERGS CM⁻² SEC⁻¹
INTERNAL RESISTANCE = 10 SEC CM⁻¹
DIMENSION ACROSS AIRFLOW = 10 CM
DIMENSION ALONG AIRFLOW = 10 CM
AIRSPEED = 10 CM SEC⁻¹
1.0 X 10⁶ ERGS CM⁻² SEC⁻¹ = 1.433 CAL CM⁻² MIN⁻¹

GRAPH 50

8

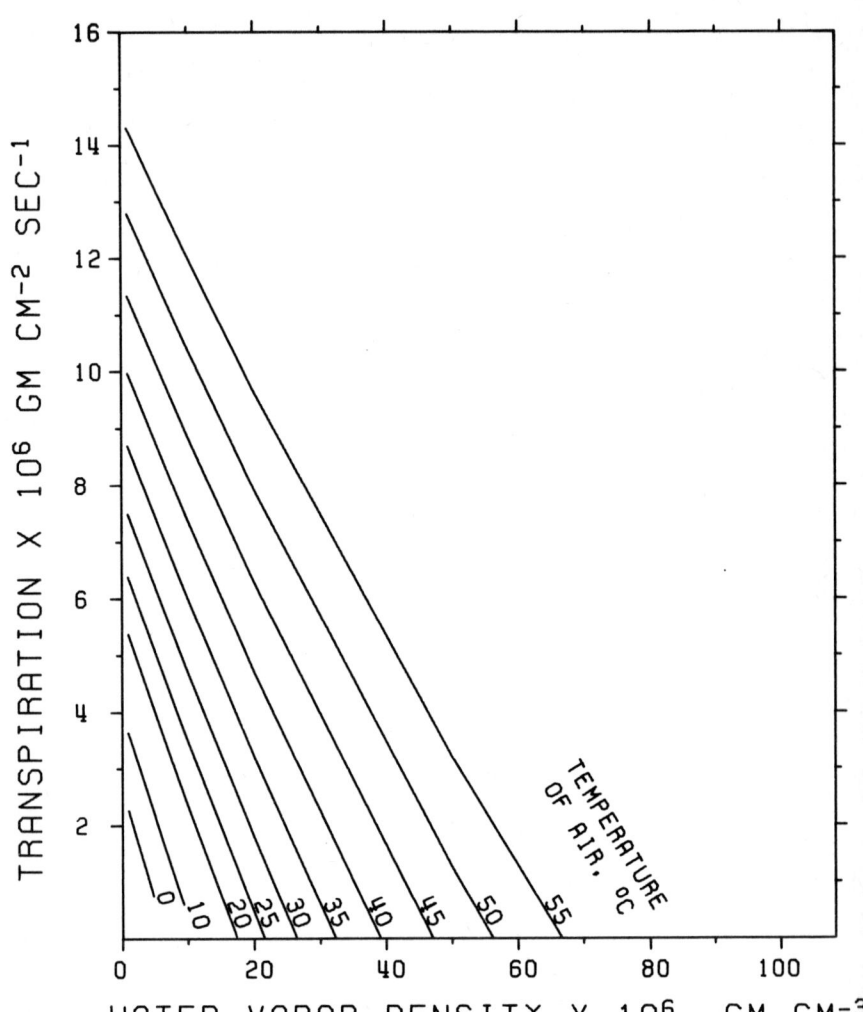

WATER VAPOR DENSITY X 10⁶, GM CM⁻³

RADIATION ABSORBED = 0.4X10⁶ ERGS CM⁻² SEC⁻¹
INTERNAL RESISTANCE = 1 SEC CM⁻¹
DIMENSION ACROSS AIRFLOW = 5 CM
DIMENSION ALONG AIRFLOW = 5 CM
AIRSPEED = 10 CM SEC⁻¹
0.4 X 10⁶ ERGS CM⁻² SEC⁻¹ = 0.573 CAL CM⁻² MIN⁻¹

GRAPH 51

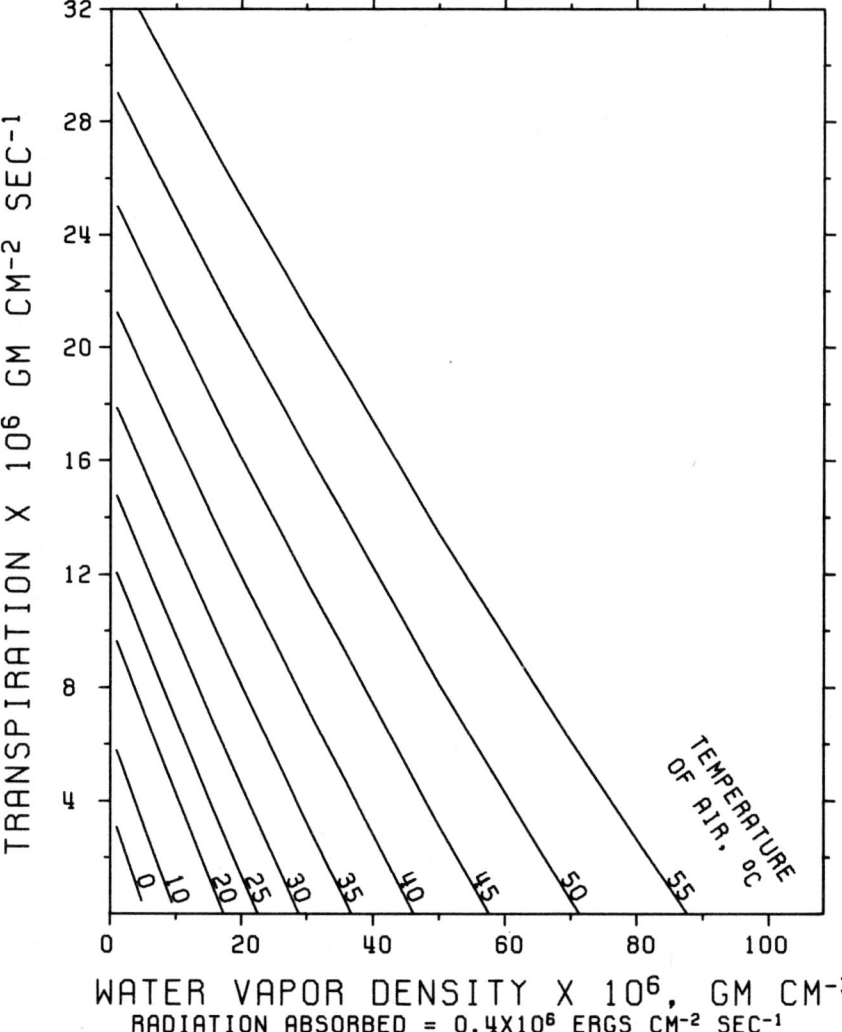

WATER VAPOR DENSITY X 10^6, GM CM^{-3}

RADIATION ABSORBED = 0.4X10^6 ERGS CM^{-2} SEC^{-1}
INTERNAL RESISTANCE = 1 SEC CM^{-1}
DIMENSION ACROSS AIRFLOW = 5 CM
DIMENSION ALONG AIRFLOW = 5 CM
AIRSPEED = 100 CM SEC^{-1}
0.4 X 10^6 ERGS CM^{-2} SEC^{-1} = 0.573 CAL CM^{-2} MIN^{-1}

GRAPH 52

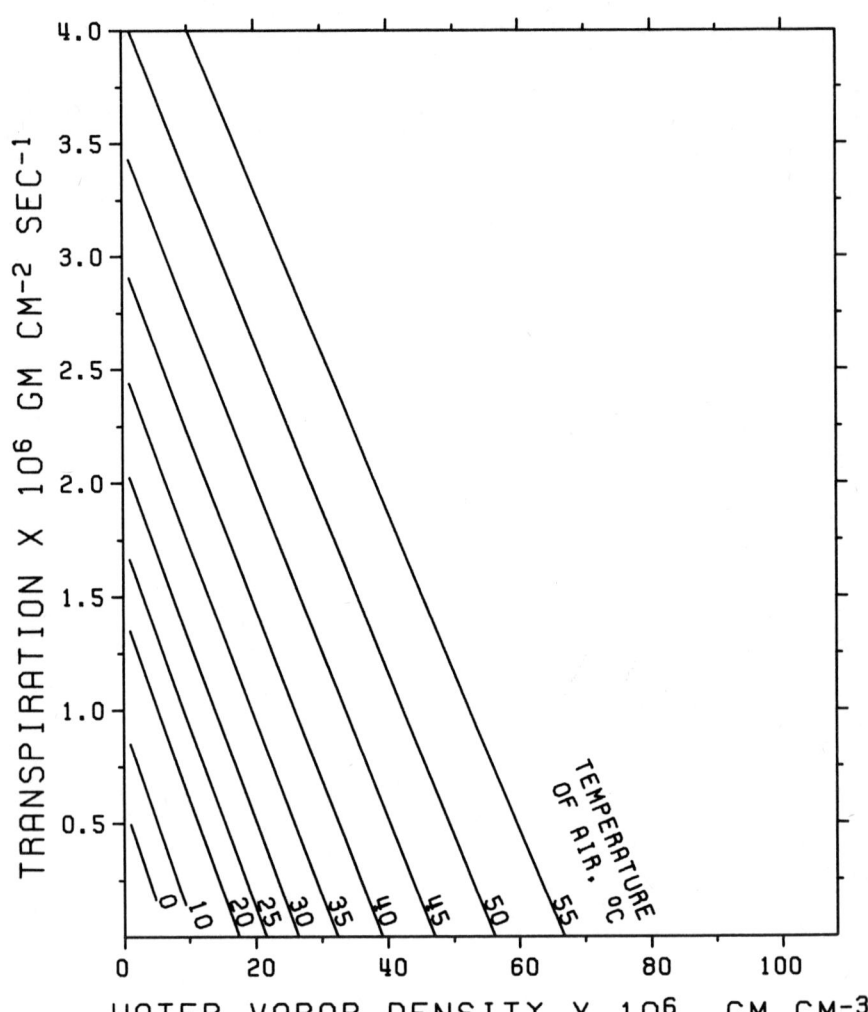

WATER VAPOR DENSITY X 10⁶, GM CM⁻³

RADIATION ABSORBED = 0.4X10⁶ ERGS CM⁻² SEC⁻¹
INTERNAL RESISTANCE = 10 SEC CM⁻¹
DIMENSION ACROSS AIRFLOW = 5 CM
DIMENSION ALONG AIRFLOW = 5 CM
AIRSPEED = 10 CM SEC⁻¹
0.4 X 10⁶ ERGS CM⁻² SEC⁻¹ = 0.573 CAL CM⁻² MIN⁻¹

GRAPH 53

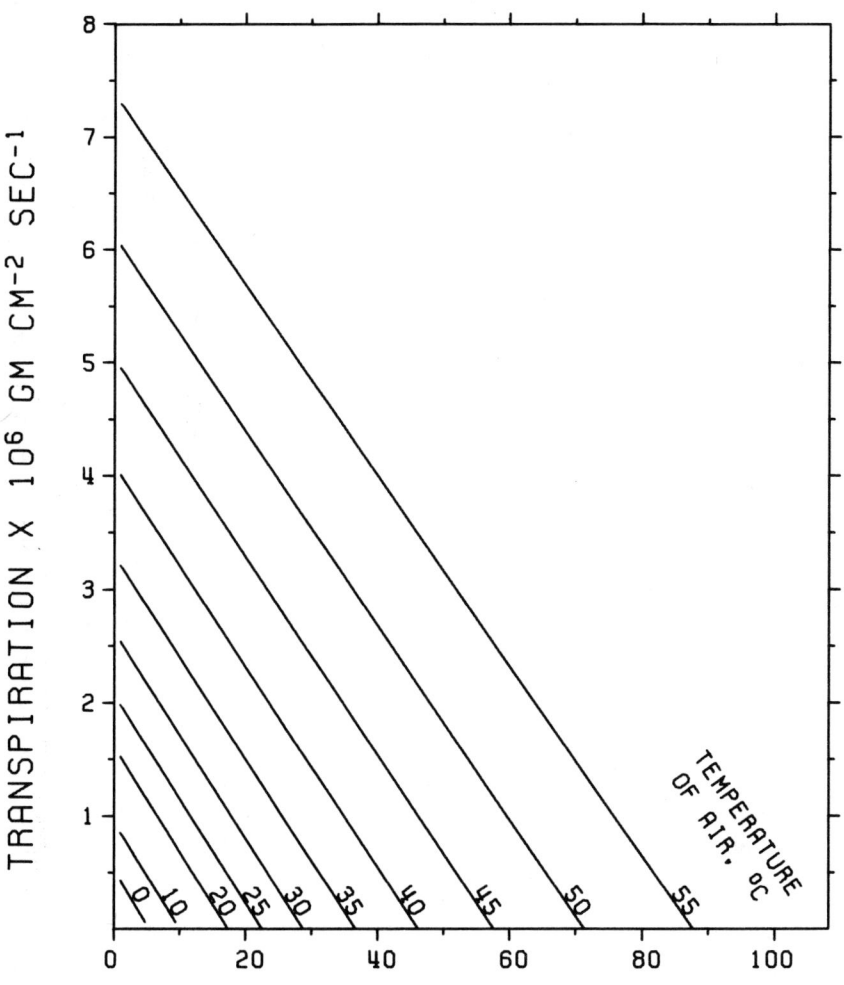

WATER VAPOR DENSITY X 10^6, GM CM^{-3}

RADIATION ABSORBED = 0.4X10^6 ERGS CM^{-2} SEC^{-1}
INTERNAL RESISTANCE = 10 SEC CM^{-1}
DIMENSION ACROSS AIRFLOW = 5 CM
DIMENSION ALONG AIRFLOW = 5 CM
AIRSPEED = 100 CM SEC^{-1}
0.4 X 10^6 ERGS CM^{-2} SEC^{-1} = 0.573 CAL CM^{-2} MIN^{-1}

GRAPH 54

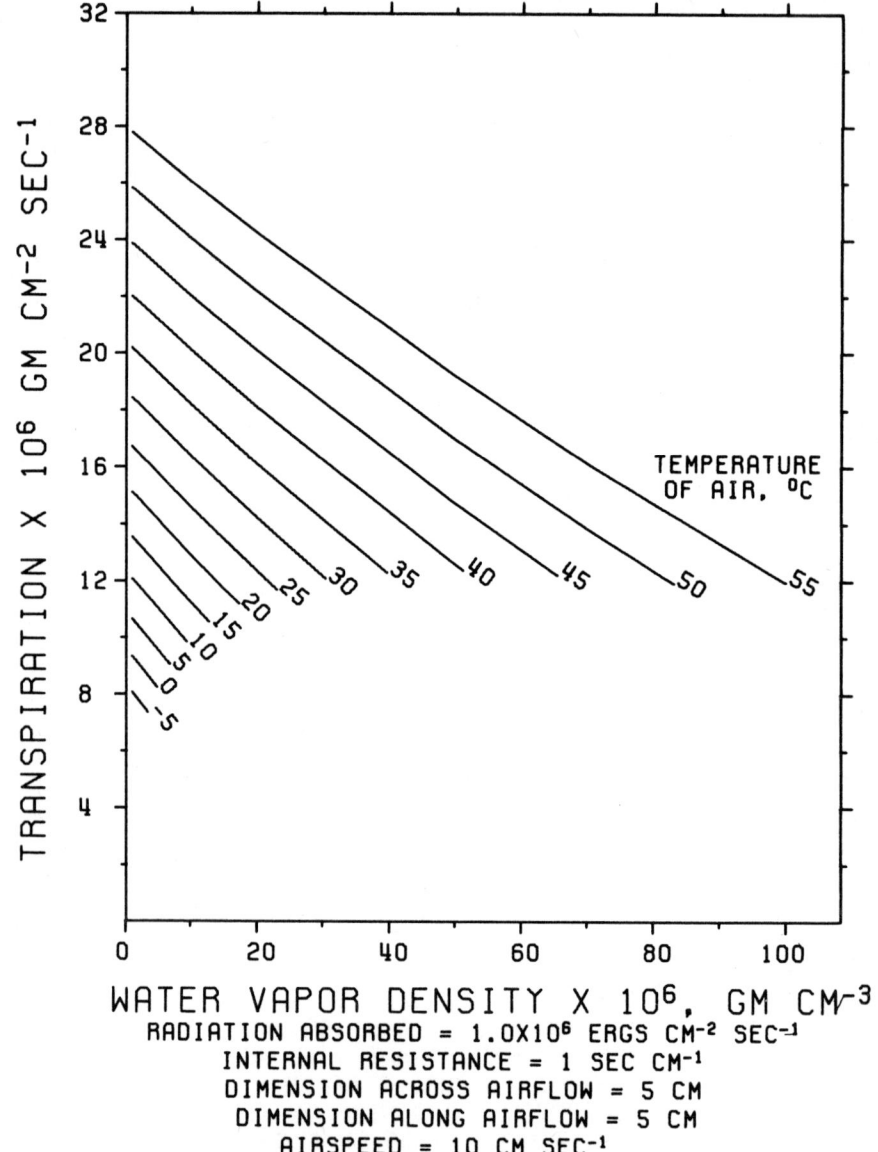

WATER VAPOR DENSITY X 10^6, GM CM^{-3}

RADIATION ABSORBED = 1.0×10^6 ERGS CM^{-2} SEC^{-1}
INTERNAL RESISTANCE = 1 SEC CM^{-1}
DIMENSION ACROSS AIRFLOW = 5 CM
DIMENSION ALONG AIRFLOW = 5 CM
AIRSPEED = 10 CM SEC^{-1}
1.0×10^6 ERGS CM^{-2} SEC^{-1} = 1.433 CAL CM^{-2} MIN^{-1}

GRAPH 55

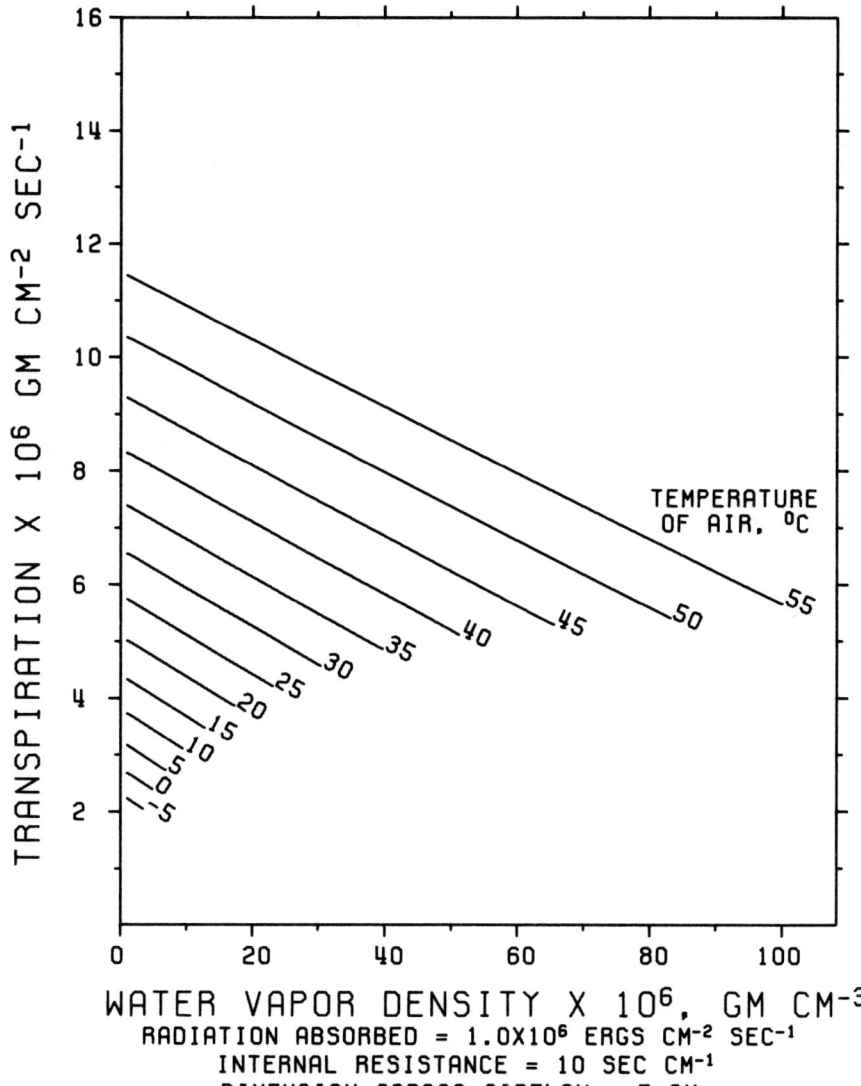

WATER VAPOR DENSITY X 10^6, GM CM^{-3}

RADIATION ABSORBED = 1.0X10^6 ERGS CM^{-2} SEC^{-1}
INTERNAL RESISTANCE = 10 SEC CM^{-1}
DIMENSION ACROSS AIRFLOW = 5 CM
DIMENSION ALONG AIRFLOW = 5 CM
AIRSPEED = 10 CM SEC^{-1}
1.0 X 10^6 ERGS CM^{-2} SEC^{-1} = 1.433 CAL CM^{-2} MIN^{-1}

GRAPH 56

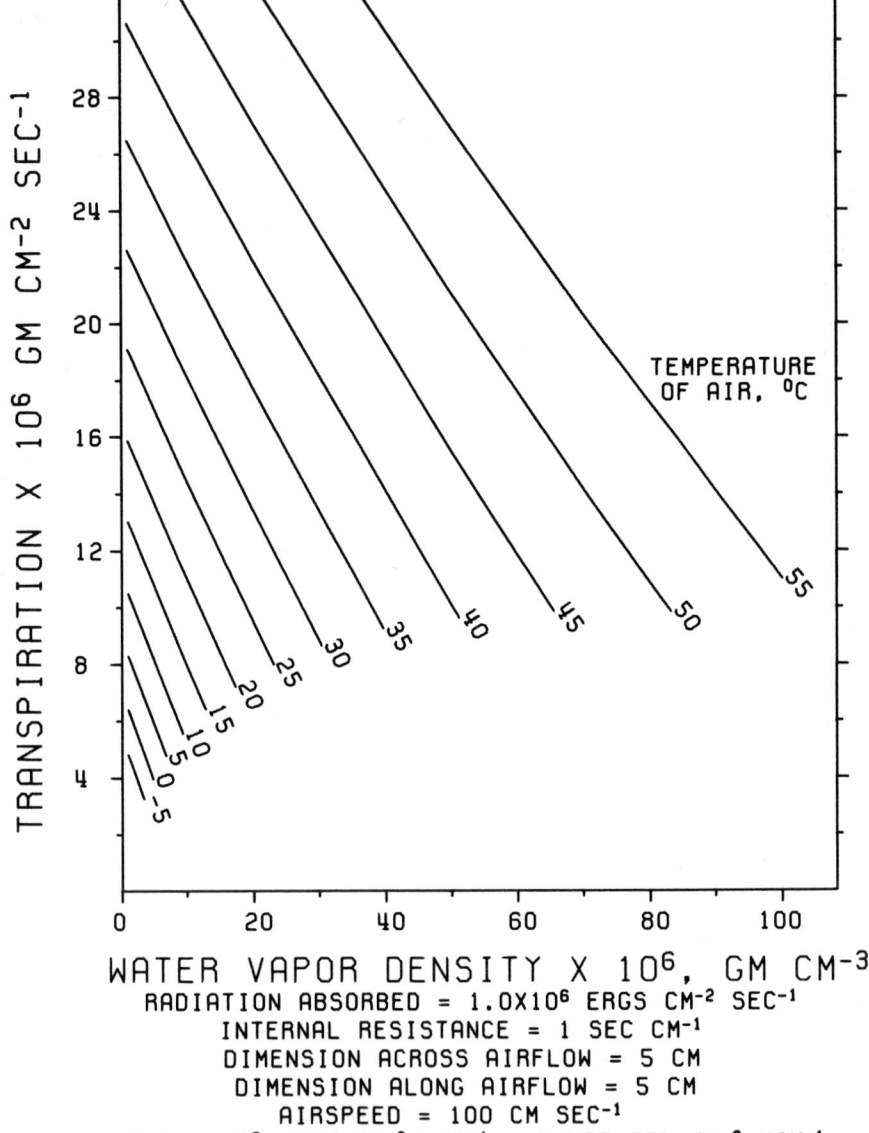

WATER VAPOR DENSITY X 10⁶, GM CM⁻³
RADIATION ABSORBED = 1.0X10⁶ ERGS CM⁻² SEC⁻¹
INTERNAL RESISTANCE = 1 SEC CM⁻¹
DIMENSION ACROSS AIRFLOW = 5 CM
DIMENSION ALONG AIRFLOW = 5 CM
AIRSPEED = 100 CM SEC⁻¹
1.0 X 10⁶ ERGS CM⁻² SEC⁻¹ = 1.433 CAL CM⁻² MIN⁻¹

GRAPH 57

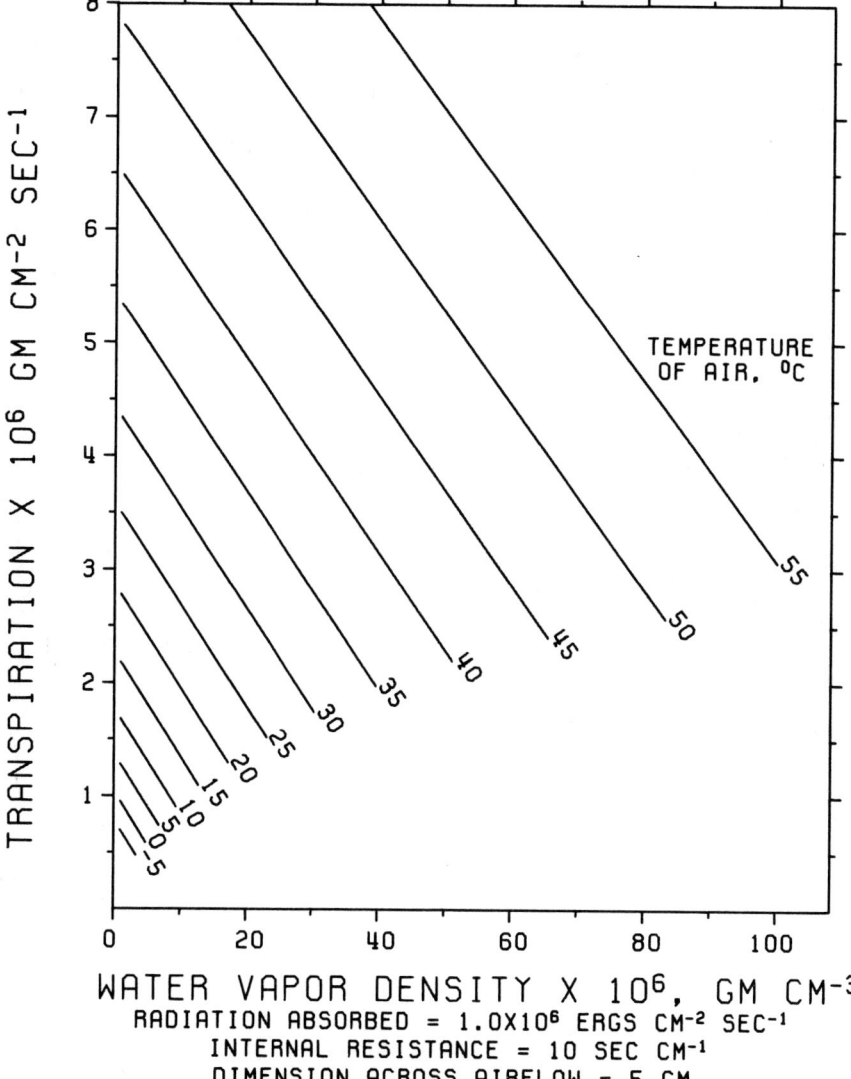

WATER VAPOR DENSITY X 10⁶, GM CM⁻³

RADIATION ABSORBED = 1.0X10⁶ ERGS CM⁻² SEC⁻¹
INTERNAL RESISTANCE = 10 SEC CM⁻¹
DIMENSION ACROSS AIRFLOW = 5 CM
DIMENSION ALONG AIRFLOW = 5 CM
AIRSPEED = 100 CM SEC⁻¹
1.0 X 10⁶ ERGS CM⁻² SEC⁻¹ = 1.433 CAL CM⁻² MIN⁻¹

GRAPH 58

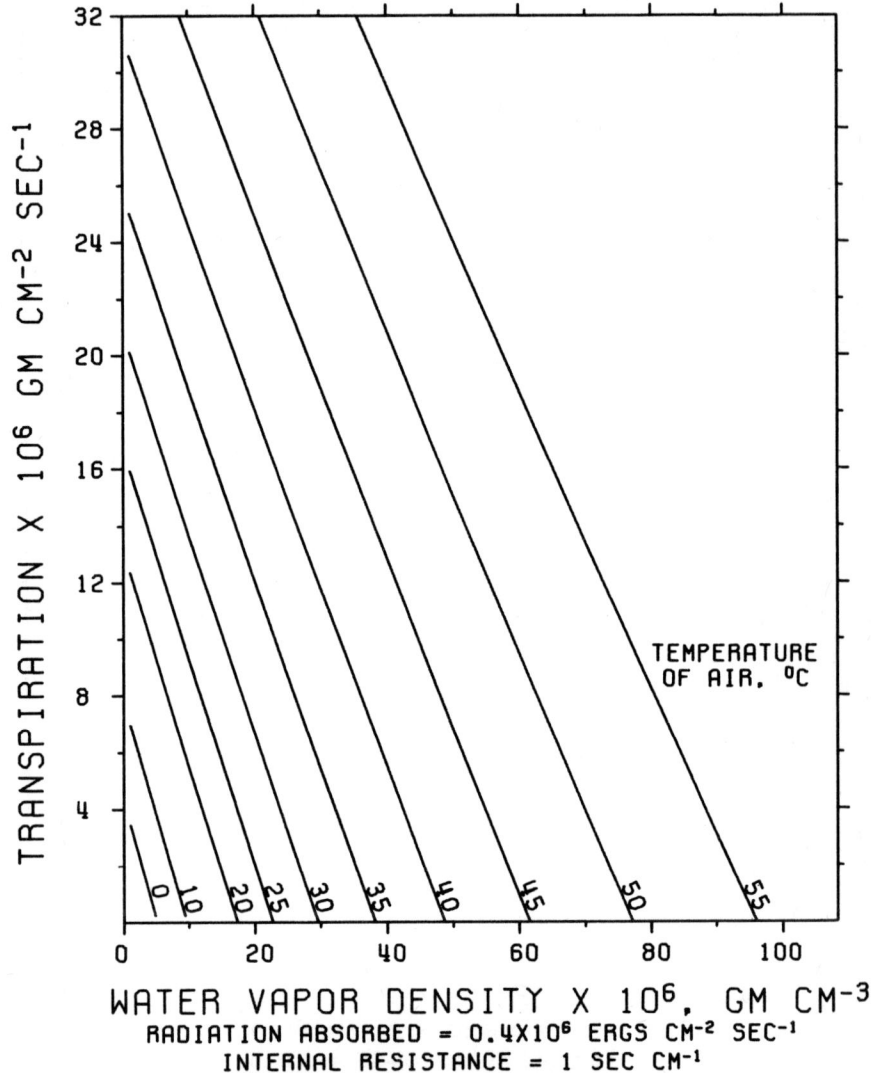

WATER VAPOR DENSITY X 10⁶, GM CM⁻³

RADIATION ABSORBED = 0.4X10⁶ ERGS CM⁻² SEC⁻¹
INTERNAL RESISTANCE = 1 SEC CM⁻¹
DIMENSION ACROSS AIRFLOW = 1 CM
DIMENSION ALONG AIRFLOW = 1 CM
AIRSPEED = 100 CM SEC⁻¹
0.4 X 10⁶ ERGS CM⁻² SEC⁻¹ = 0.573 CAL CM⁻² MIN⁻¹

Graph 59

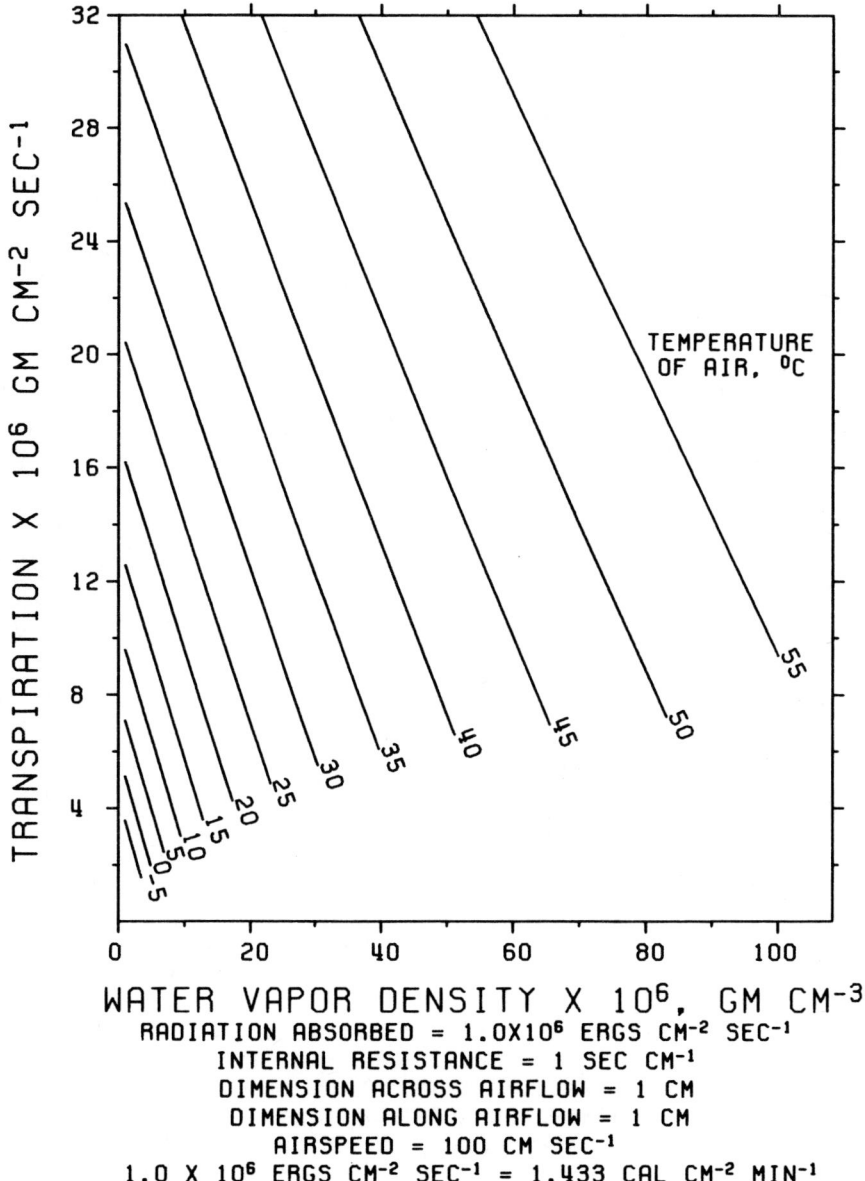

WATER VAPOR DENSITY X 10⁶, GM CM⁻³

RADIATION ABSORBED = 1.0X10⁶ ERGS CM⁻² SEC⁻¹
INTERNAL RESISTANCE = 1 SEC CM⁻¹
DIMENSION ACROSS AIRFLOW = 1 CM
DIMENSION ALONG AIRFLOW = 1 CM
AIRSPEED = 100 CM SEC⁻¹
1.0 X 10⁶ ERGS CM⁻² SEC⁻¹ = 1.433 CAL CM⁻² MIN⁻¹

GRAPH 60

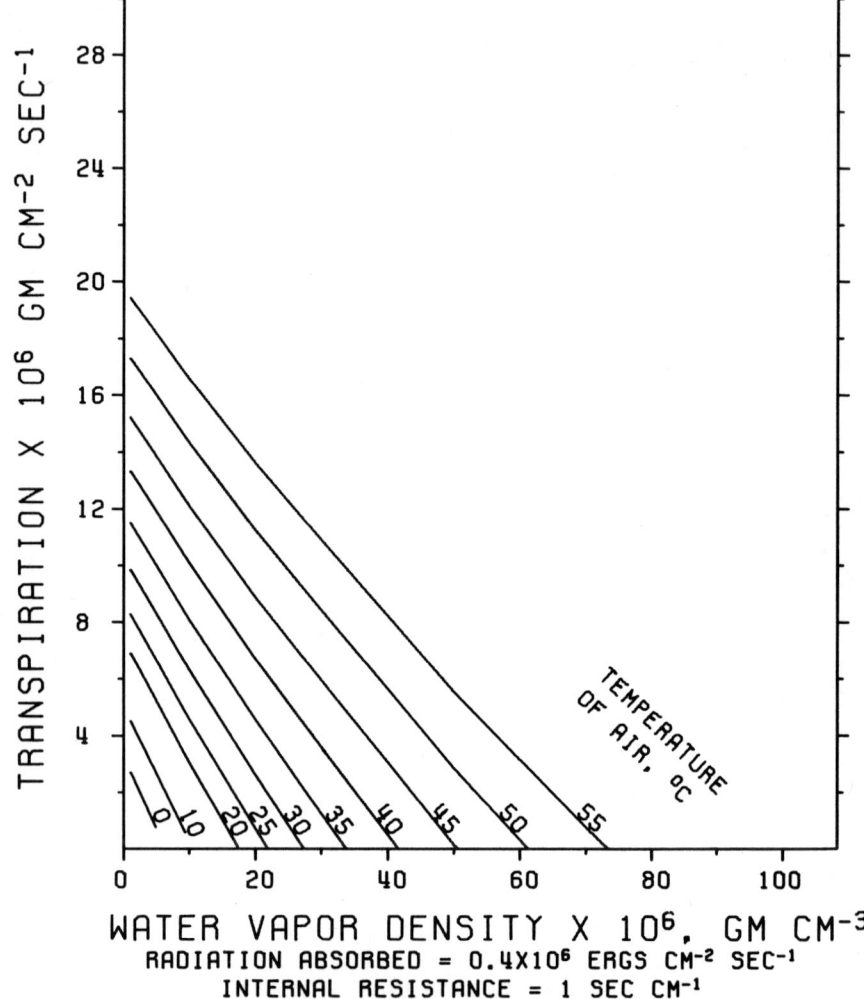

WATER VAPOR DENSITY X 10⁶, GM CM⁻³
RADIATION ABSORBED = 0.4X10⁶ ERGS CM⁻² SEC⁻¹
INTERNAL RESISTANCE = 1 SEC CM⁻¹
DIMENSION ACROSS AIRFLOW = 10 CM
DIMENSION ALONG AIRFLOW = 10 CM
AIRSPEED = 100 CM SEC⁻¹
0.4 X 10⁶ ERGS CM⁻² SEC⁻¹ = 0.573 CAL CM⁻² MIN⁻¹

GRAPH 61

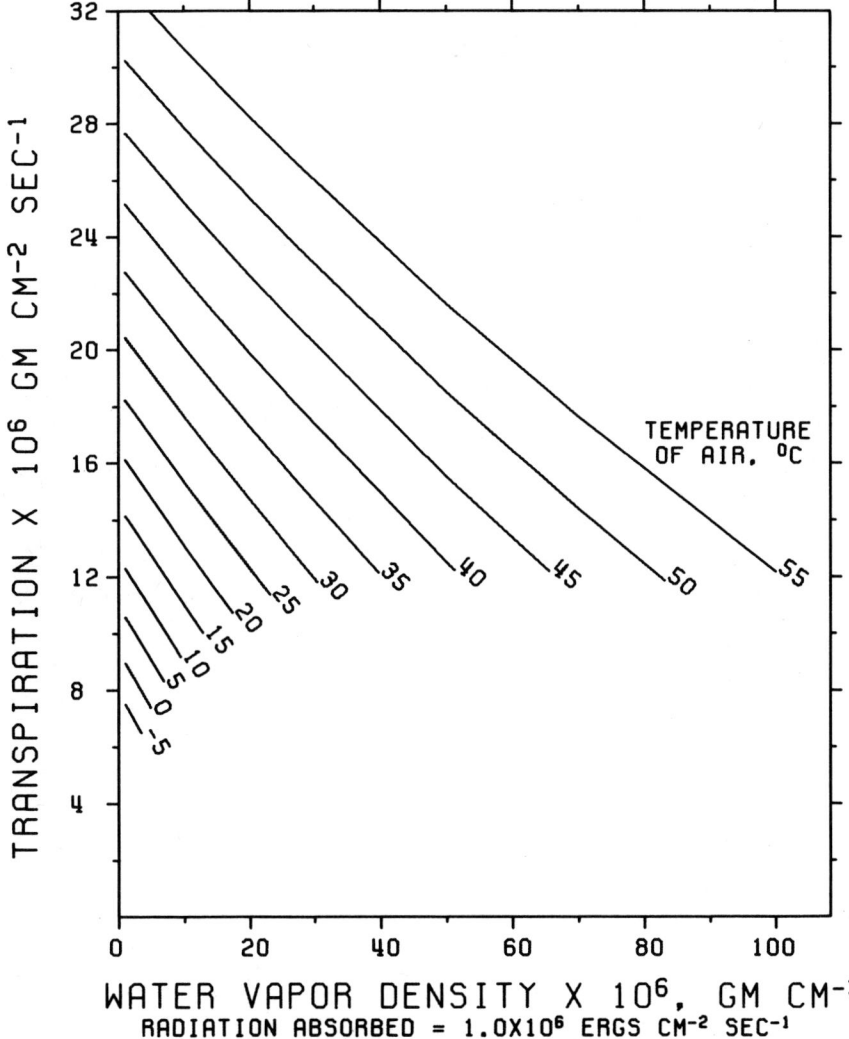

WATER VAPOR DENSITY X 10⁶, GM CM⁻³
RADIATION ABSORBED = 1.0X10⁶ ERGS CM⁻² SEC⁻¹
INTERNAL RESISTANCE = 1 SEC CM⁻¹
DIMENSION ACROSS AIRFLOW = 10 CM
DIMENSION ALONG AIRFLOW = 10 CM
AIRSPEED = 100 CM SEC⁻¹
1.0 X 10⁶ ERGS CM⁻² SEC⁻¹ = 1.433 CAL CM⁻² MIN⁻¹

GRAPH 62

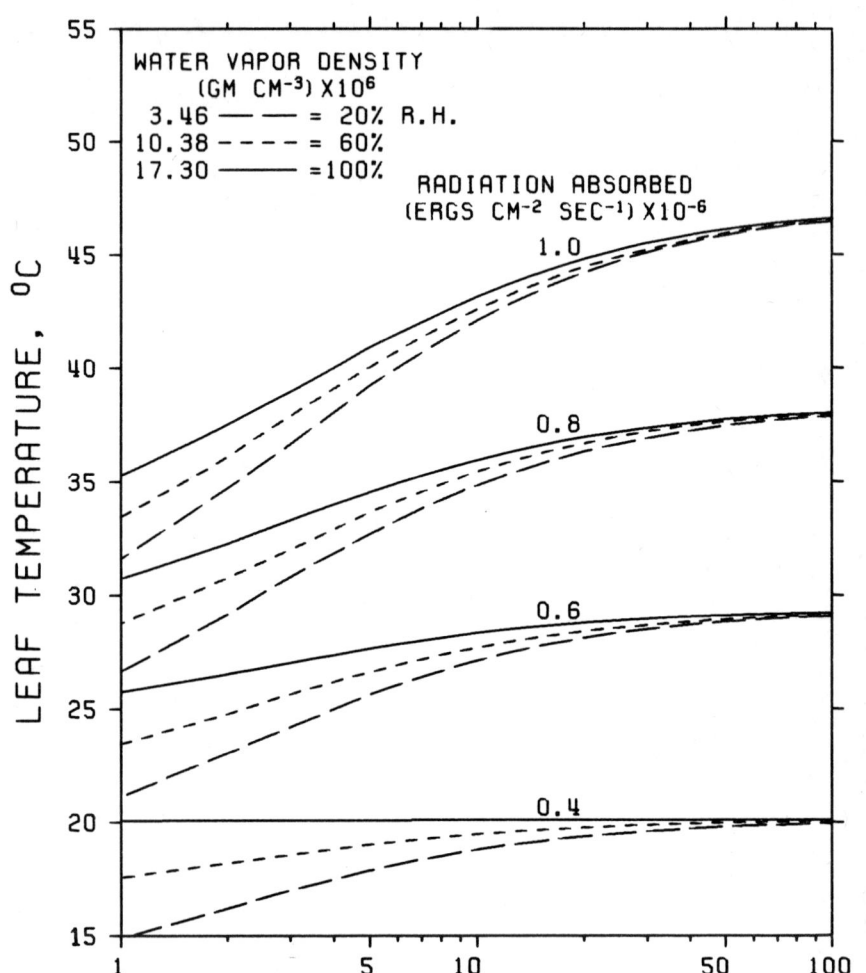

WATER VAPOR DENSITY
(GM CM⁻³) X10⁶

3.46	— —	= 20% R.H.
10.38	- - -	= 60%
17.30	——	=100%

RADIATION ABSORBED
(ERGS CM⁻² SEC⁻¹) X10⁻⁶

1.0

0.8

0.6

0.4

LEAF TEMPERATURE, ⁰C

INTERNAL DIFFUSION RESISTANCE, SEC CM

DIMENSION ACROSS AIRFLOW = 5 CM
DIMENSION ALONG AIRFLOW = 5 CM
AIR TEMPERATURE = 20 ⁰C
AIRSPEED = 10 CM SEC⁻¹
1.0 X 10⁶ ERGS CM⁻² SEC⁻¹ = 1.433 CAL CM⁻² MIN⁻¹

GRAPH 63

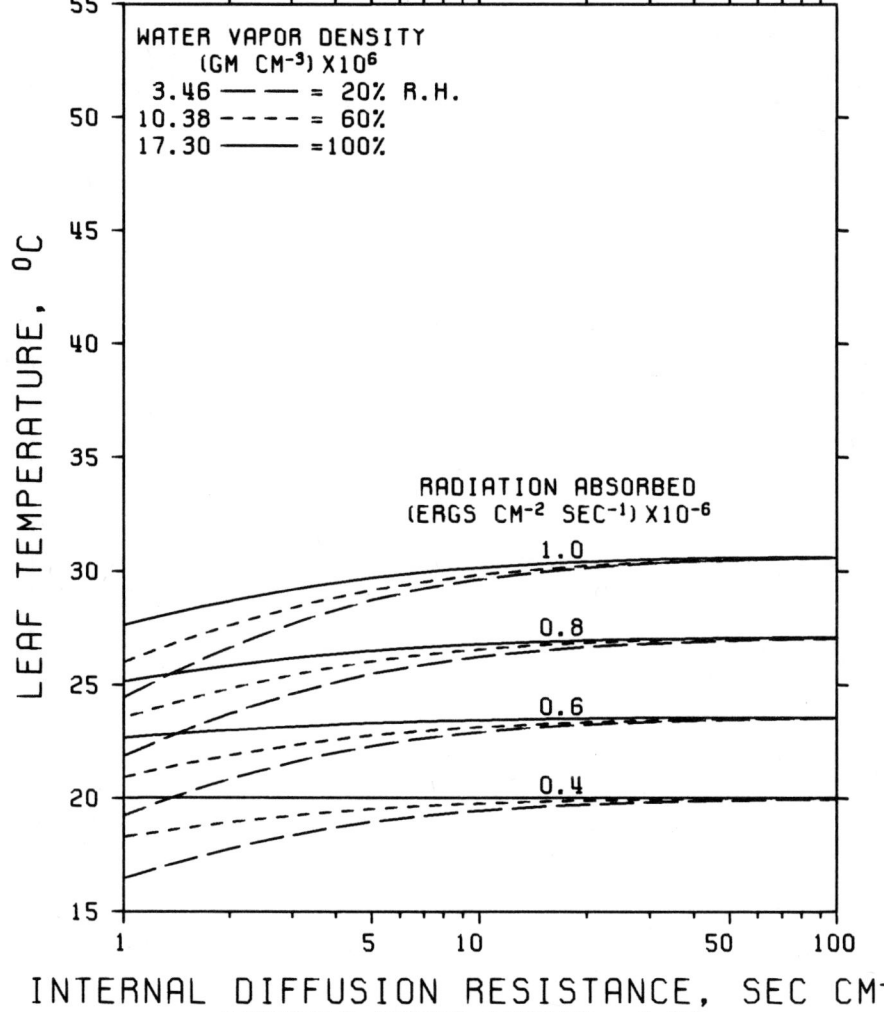

GRAPH 64

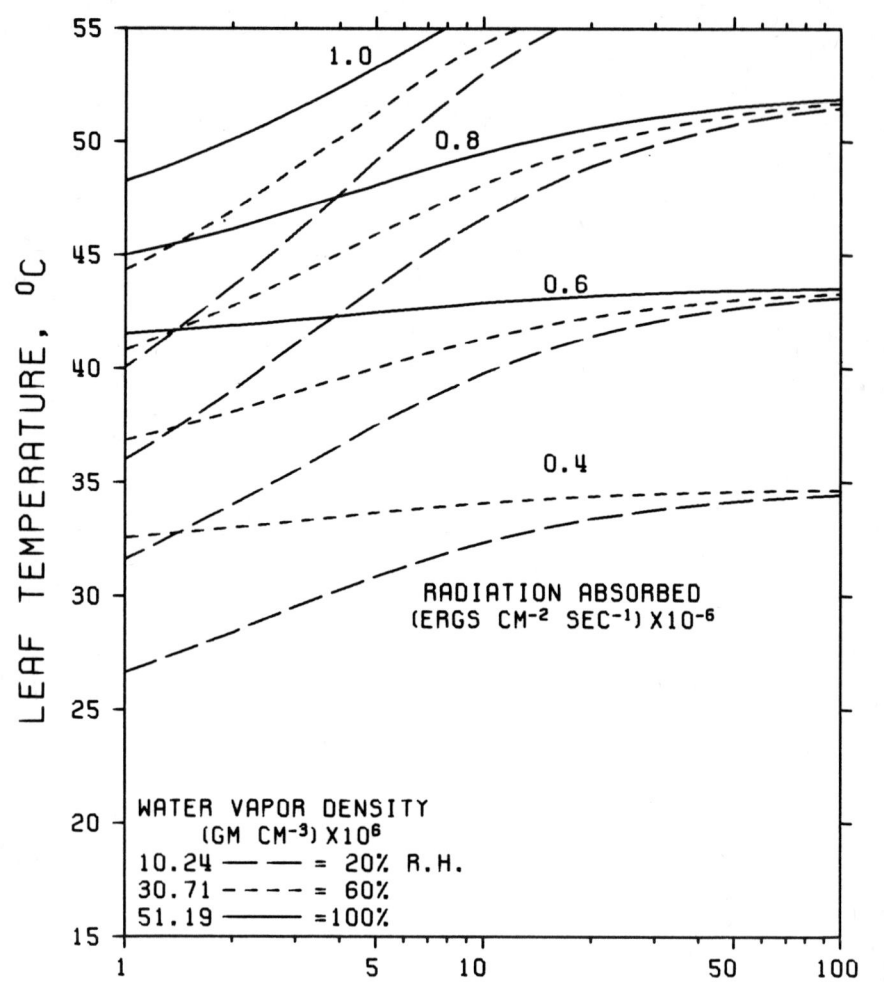

LEAF TEMPERATURE, °C

1.0

0.8

0.6

0.4

RADIATION ABSORBED
(ERGS CM⁻² SEC⁻¹) X10⁻⁶

WATER VAPOR DENSITY
(GM CM⁻³) X10⁶
10.24 —— = 20% R.H.
30.71 ---- = 60%
51.19 —— =100%

INTERNAL DIFFUSION RESISTANCE, SEC CM⁻
DIMENSION ACROSS AIRFLOW = 5 CM
DIMENSION ALONG AIRFLOW = 5 CM
AIR TEMPERATURE = 40 °C
AIRSPEED = 10 CM SEC⁻¹
1.0 X 10⁶ ERGS CM⁻² SEC⁻¹ = 1.433 CAL CM⁻² MIN⁻¹

GRAPH 65

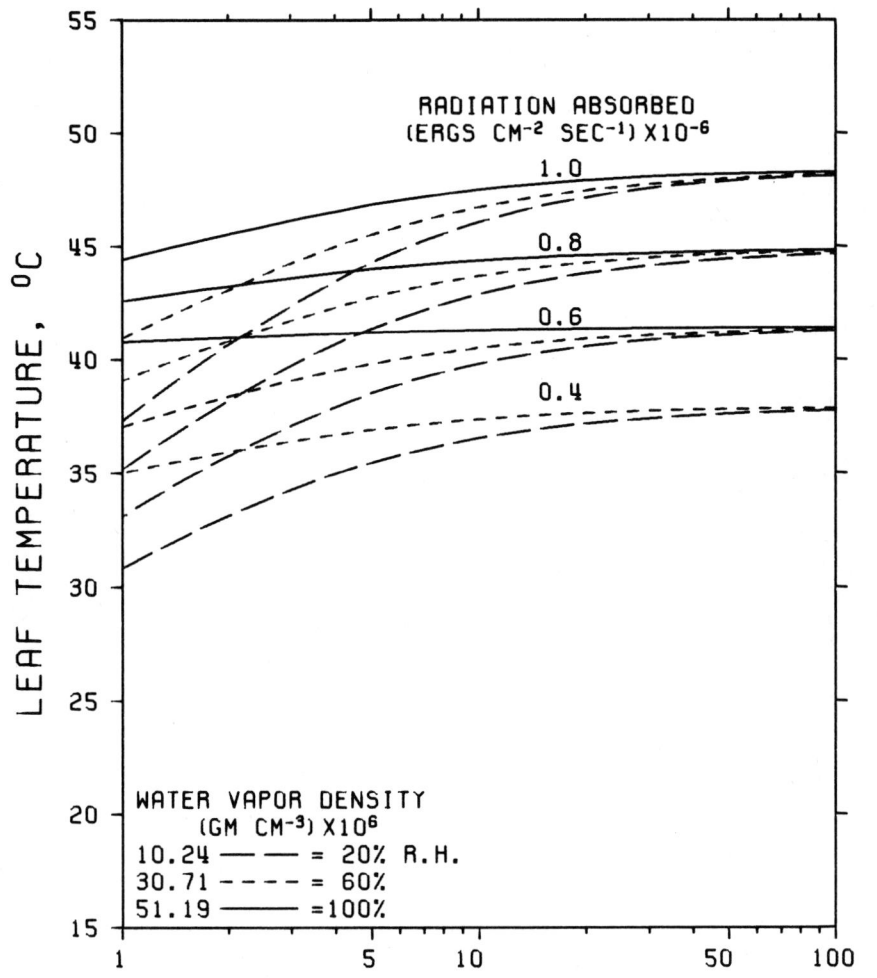

INTERNAL DIFFUSION RESISTANCE, SEC CM^{-1}

DIMENSION ACROSS AIRFLOW = 5 CM
DIMENSION ALONG AIRFLOW = 5 CM
AIR TEMPERATURE = 40 $^{\circ}$C
AIRSPEED = 100 CM SEC^{-1}
1.0 X 10^6 ERGS CM^{-2} SEC^{-1} = 1.433 CAL CM^{-2} MIN^{-1}

GRAPH 66

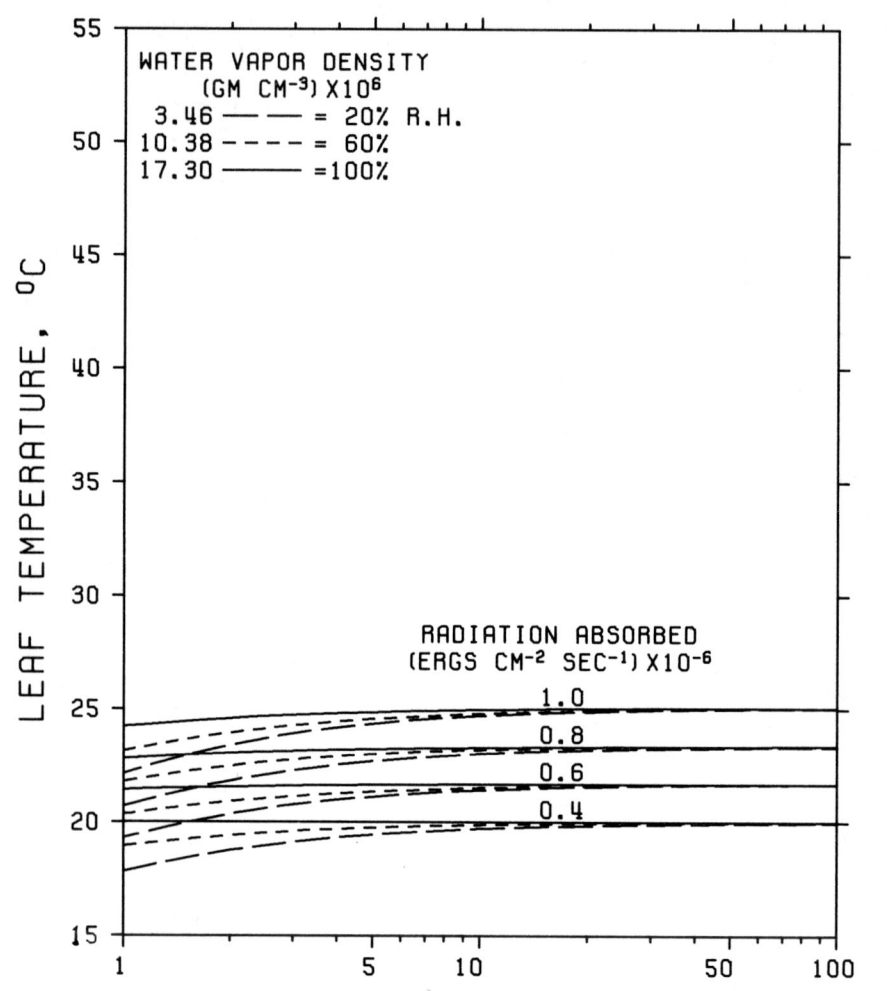

GRAPH 67

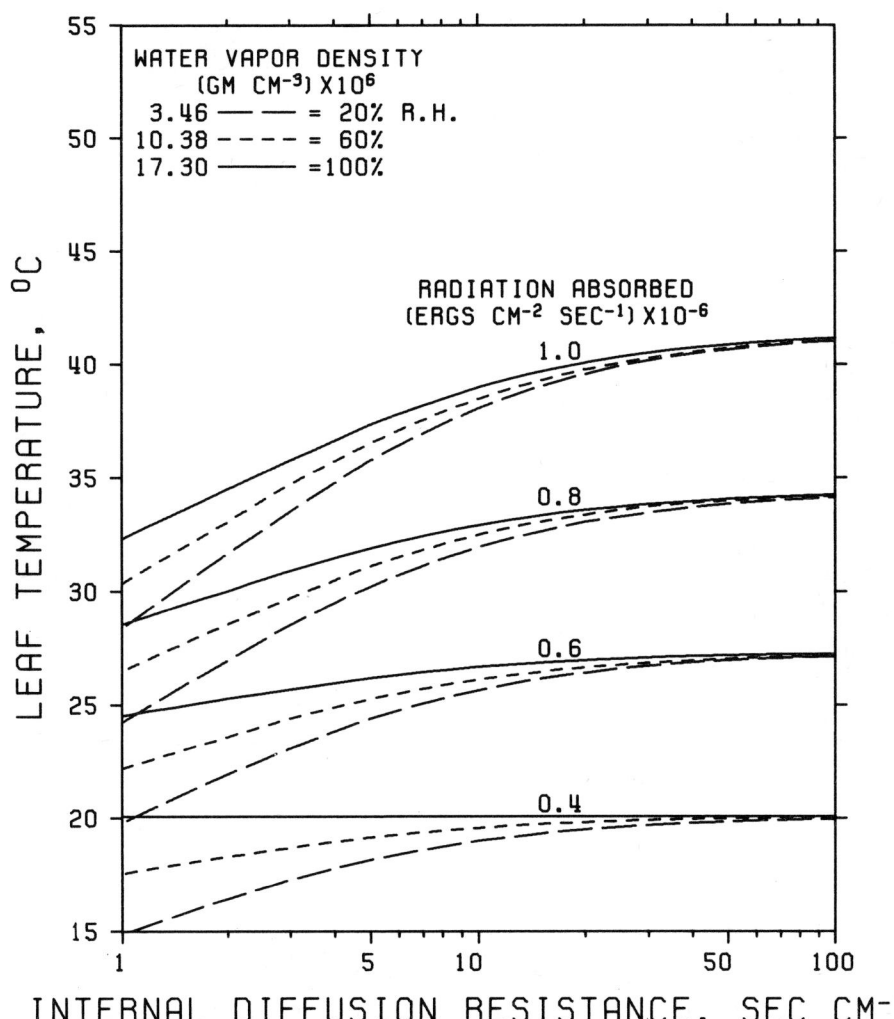

WATER VAPOR DENSITY
(GM CM^{-3}) X10^6
3.46 ———— = 20% R.H.
10.38 ----- = 60%
17.30 ——— =100%

RADIATION ABSORBED
(ERGS CM^{-2} SEC^{-1}) X10^{-6}

1.0

0.8

0.6

0.4

LEAF TEMPERATURE, ^{0}C

INTERNAL DIFFUSION RESISTANCE, SEC CM^{-1}
DIMENSION ACROSS AIRFLOW = 10 CM
DIMENSION ALONG AIRFLOW = 10 CM
AIR TEMPERATURE = 20 ^{0}C
AIRSPEED = 100 CM SEC^{-1}
1.0 X 10^6 ERGS CM^{-2} SEC^{-1} = 1.433 CAL CM^{-2} MIN^{-1}

GRAPH 68

235

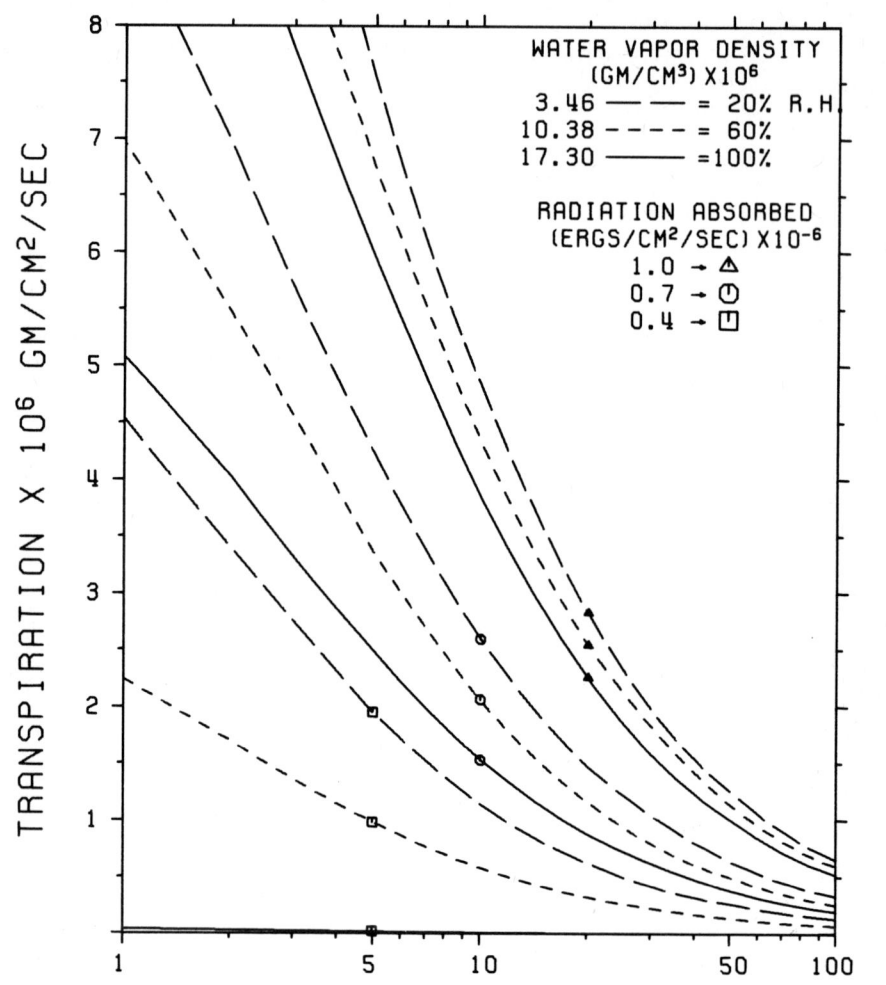

INTERNAL DIFFUSION RESISTANCE, SEC/CM
DIMENSION ACROSS AIRFLOW = 5 CM
DIMENSION ALONG AIRFLOW = 5 CM
AIR TEMPERATURE = 20 ⁰C
AIRSPEED = 10 CM/SEC
1.0 X 10⁶ ERGS/CM²/SEC = 1.433 CAL/CM²/MIN

GRAPH 69

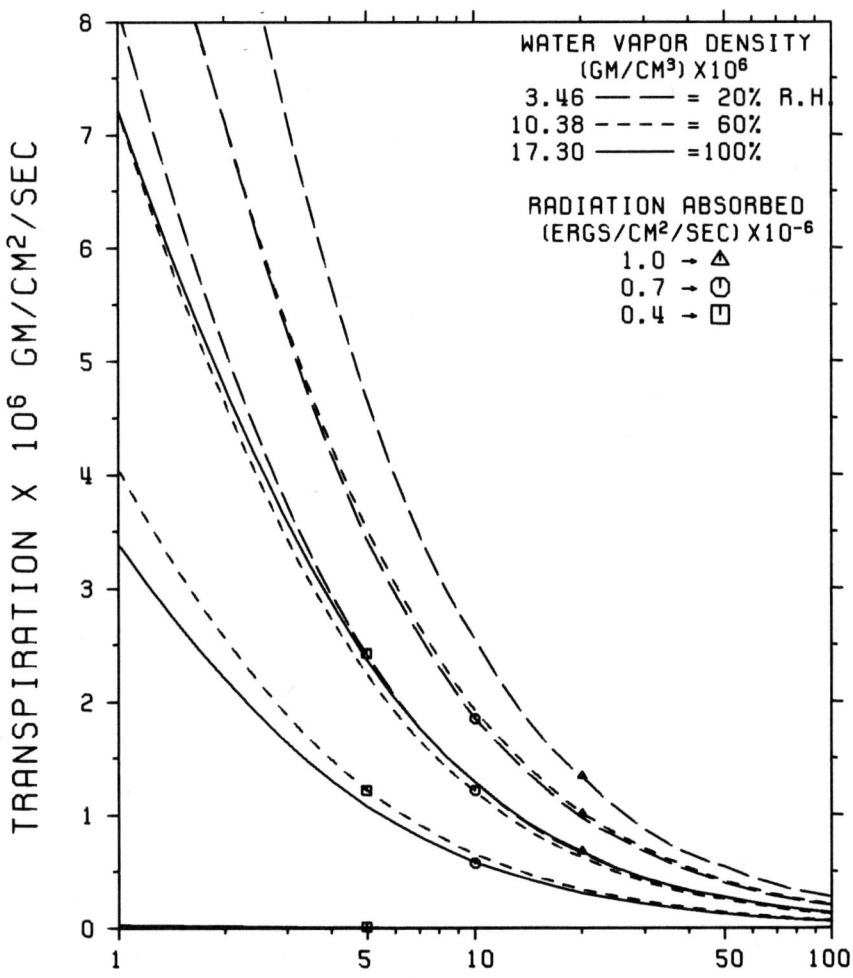

INTERNAL DIFFUSION RESISTANCE, SEC/CM
DIMENSION ACROSS AIRFLOW = 5 CM
DIMENSION ALONG AIRFLOW = 5 CM
AIR TEMPERATURE = 20 °C
AIRSPEED = 100 CM/SEC
1.0 X 10⁶ ERGS/CM²/SEC = 1.433 CAL/CM²/MIN

GRAPH 70

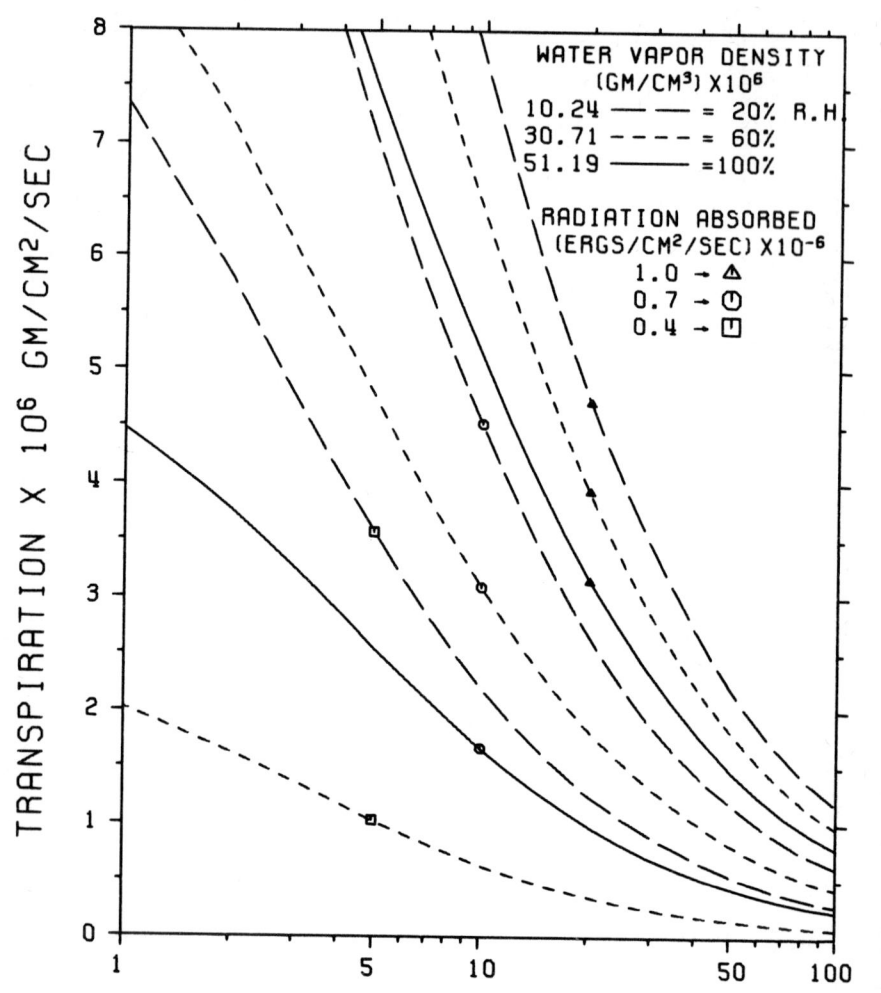

INTERNAL DIFFUSION RESISTANCE, SEC/CM

DIMENSION ACROSS AIRFLOW = 5 CM
DIMENSION ALONG AIRFLOW = 5 CM
AIR TEMPERATURE = 40 °C
AIRSPEED = 10 CM/SEC
1.0 X 10⁶ ERGS/CM²/SEC = 1.433 CAL/CM²/MIN

GRAPH 71

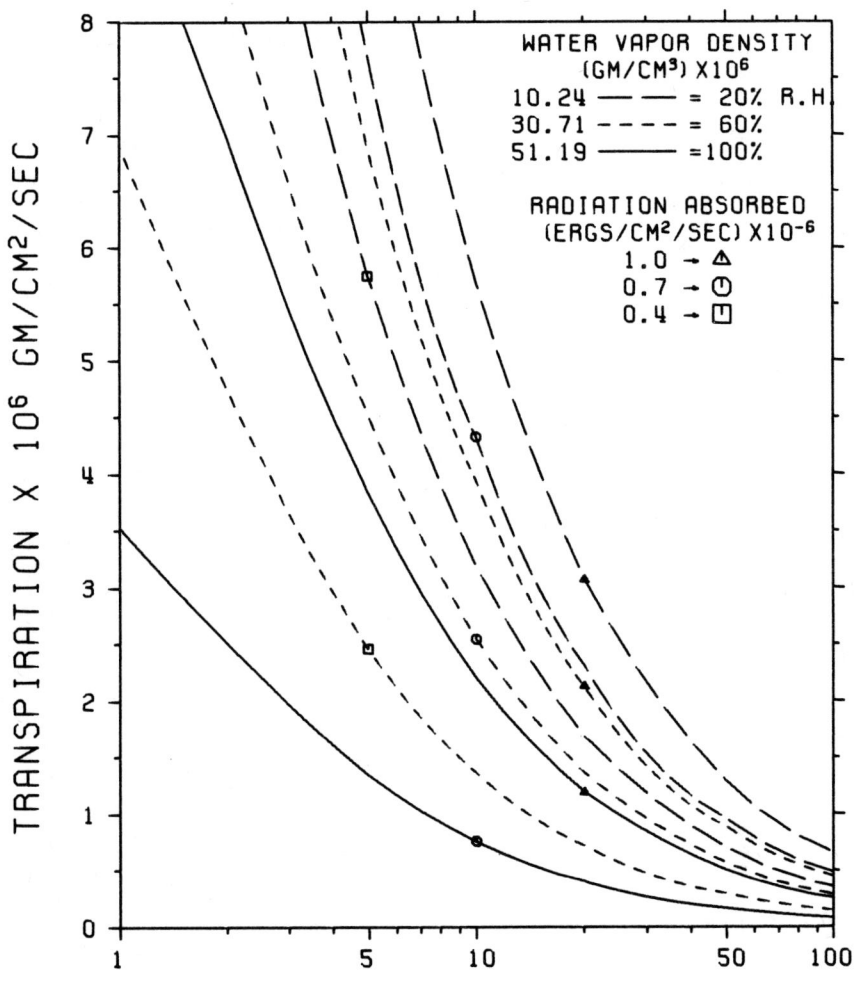

INTERNAL DIFFUSION RESISTANCE, SEC/CM
DIMENSION ACROSS AIRFLOW = 5 CM
DIMENSION ALONG AIRFLOW = 5 CM
AIR TEMPERATURE = 40 °C
AIRSPEED = 100 CM/SEC
1.0 X 10⁶ ERGS/CM²/SEC = 1.433 CAL/CM²/MIN

GRAPH 72

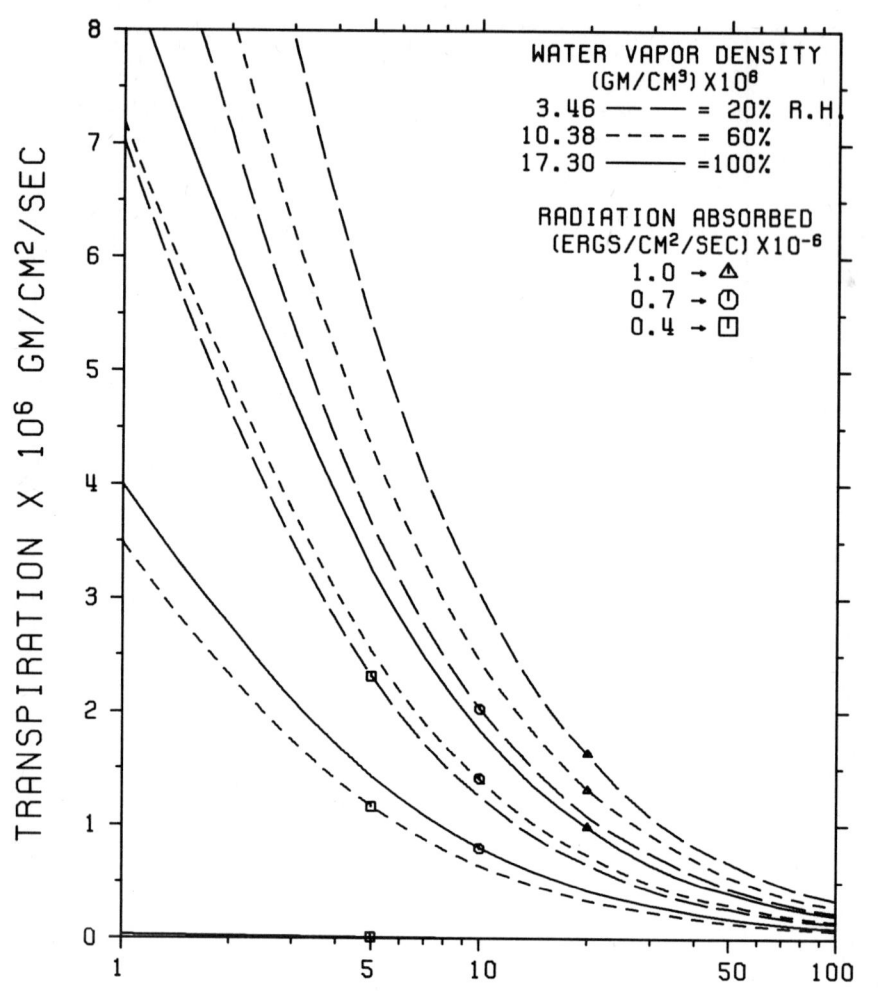

WATER VAPOR DENSITY
(GM/CM³) X10⁸
3.46 —— —— = 20% R.H.
10.38 - - - - = 60%
17.30 —————— =100%

RADIATION ABSORBED
(ERGS/CM²/SEC) X10⁻⁶
1.0 → △
0.7 → ☉
0.4 → ☐

INTERNAL DIFFUSION RESISTANCE, SEC/CM

DIMENSION ACROSS AIRFLOW = 1 CM
DIMENSION ALONG AIRFLOW = 1 CM
AIR TEMPERATURE = 20 ⁰C
AIRSPEED = 10 CM/SEC
1.0 X 10⁶ ERGS/CM²/SEC = 1.433 CAL/CM²/MIN

Graph 73

240

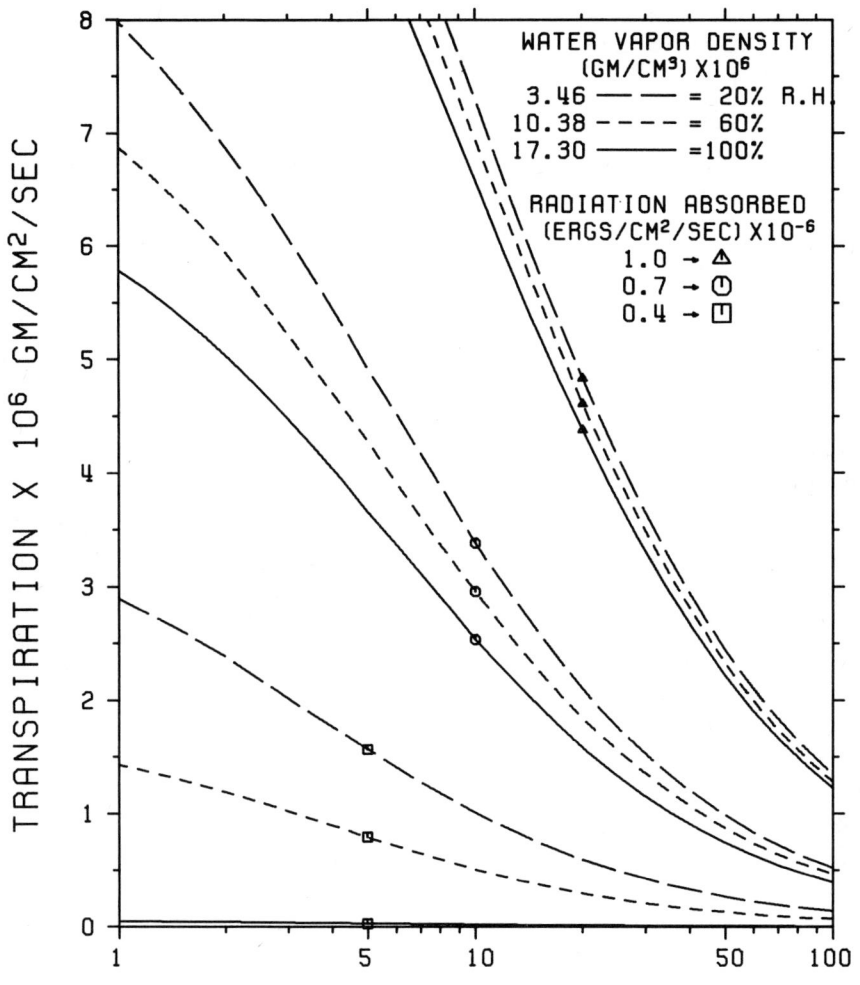

INTERNAL DIFFUSION RESISTANCE, SEC/CM
DIMENSION ACROSS AIRFLOW = 10 CM
DIMENSION ALONG AIRFLOW = 10 CM
AIR TEMPERATURE = 20 °C
AIRSPEED = 10 CM/SEC
1.0 X 10⁶ ERGS/CM²/SEC = 1.433 CAL/CM²/MIN

GRAPH 74

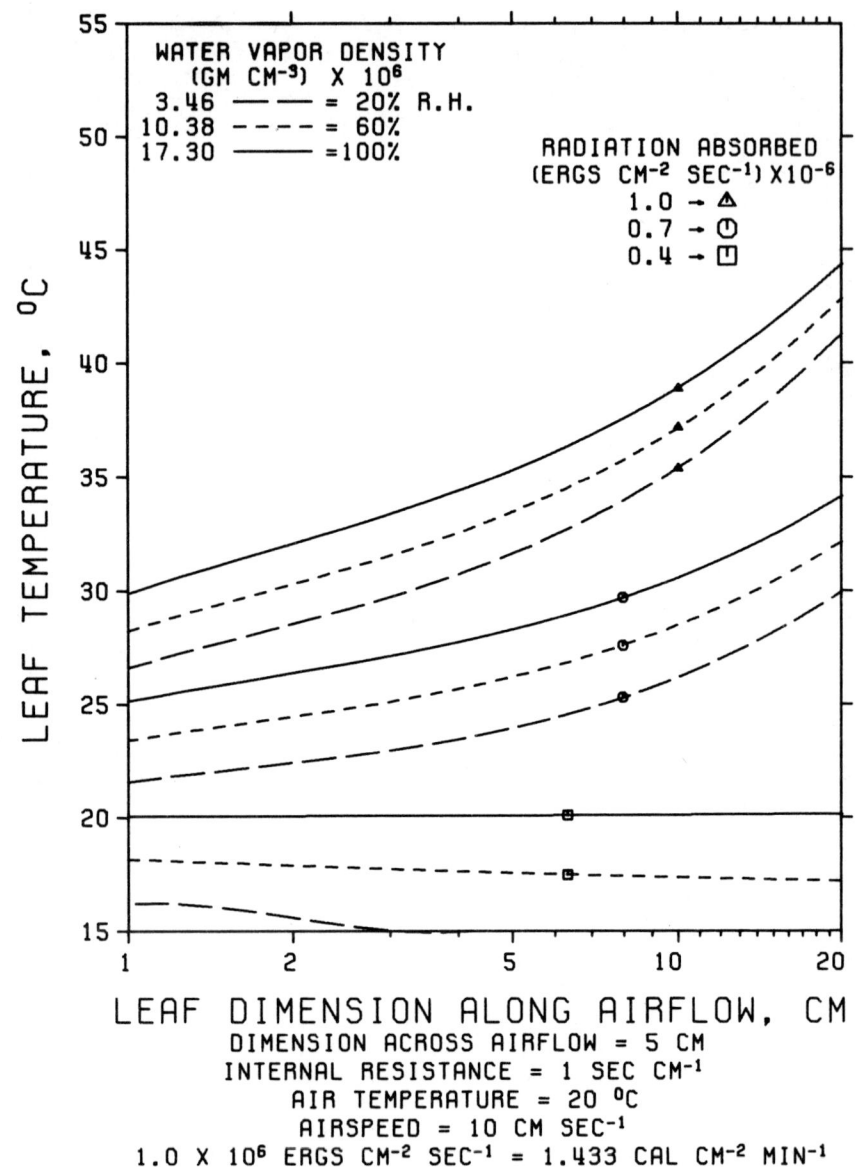

LEAF DIMENSION ALONG AIRFLOW, CM

DIMENSION ACROSS AIRFLOW = 5 CM
INTERNAL RESISTANCE = 1 SEC CM^{-1}
AIR TEMPERATURE = 20 ^{0}C
AIRSPEED = 10 CM SEC^{-1}
1.0 X 10^{6} ERGS CM^{-2} SEC^{-1} = 1.433 CAL CM^{-2} MIN^{-1}

GRAPH 75

242

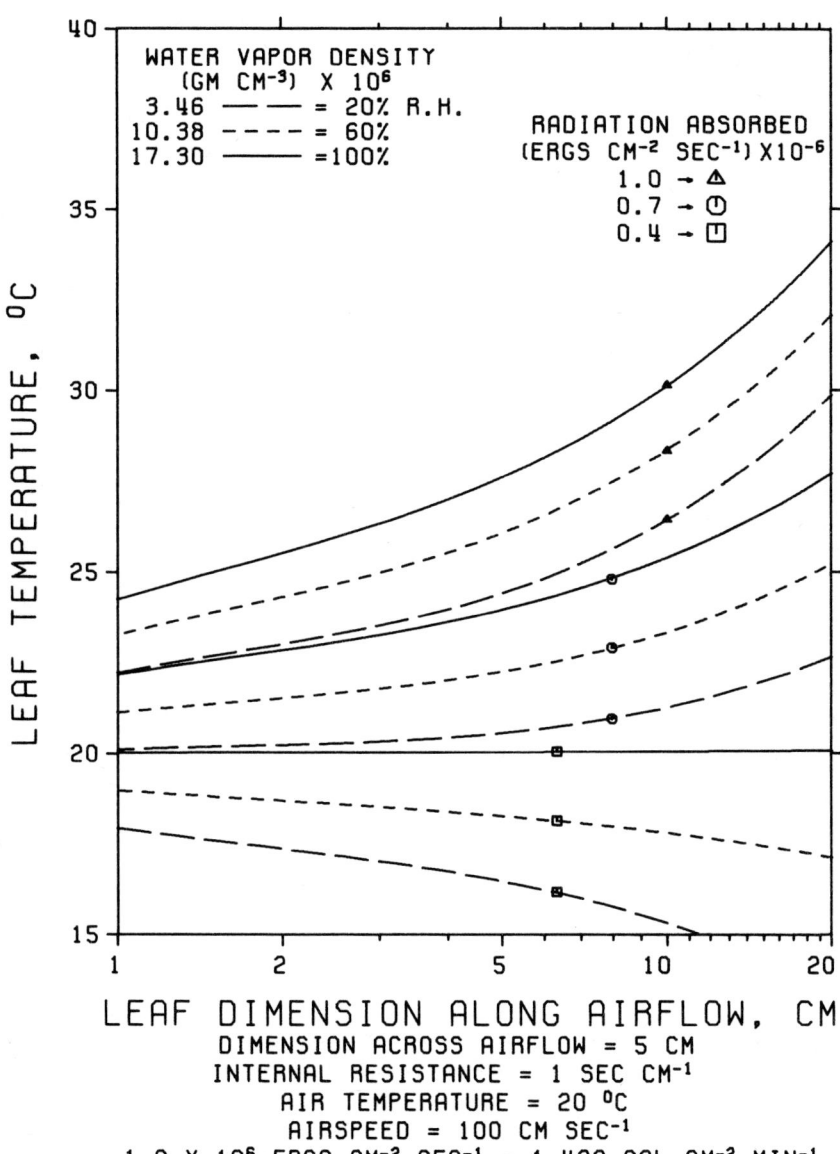

LEAF DIMENSION ALONG AIRFLOW, CM
DIMENSION ACROSS AIRFLOW = 5 CM
INTERNAL RESISTANCE = 1 SEC CM⁻¹
AIR TEMPERATURE = 20 °C
AIRSPEED = 100 CM SEC⁻¹
1.0 X 10⁶ ERGS CM⁻² SEC⁻¹ = 1.433 CAL CM⁻² MIN⁻¹

GRAPH 76

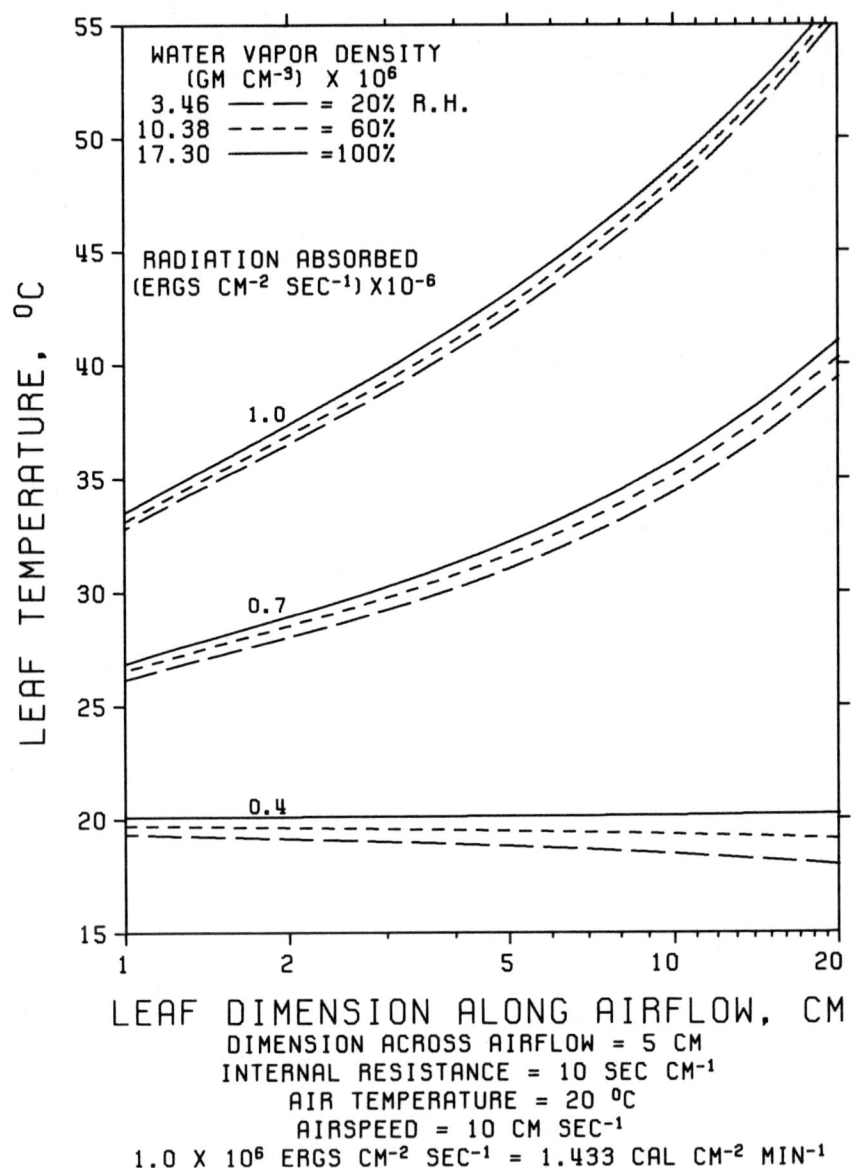

LEAF DIMENSION ALONG AIRFLOW, CM

DIMENSION ACROSS AIRFLOW = 5 CM
INTERNAL RESISTANCE = 10 SEC CM⁻¹
AIR TEMPERATURE = 20 ⁰C
AIRSPEED = 10 CM SEC⁻¹
1.0 X 10⁶ ERGS CM⁻² SEC⁻¹ = 1.433 CAL CM⁻² MIN⁻¹

GRAPH 77

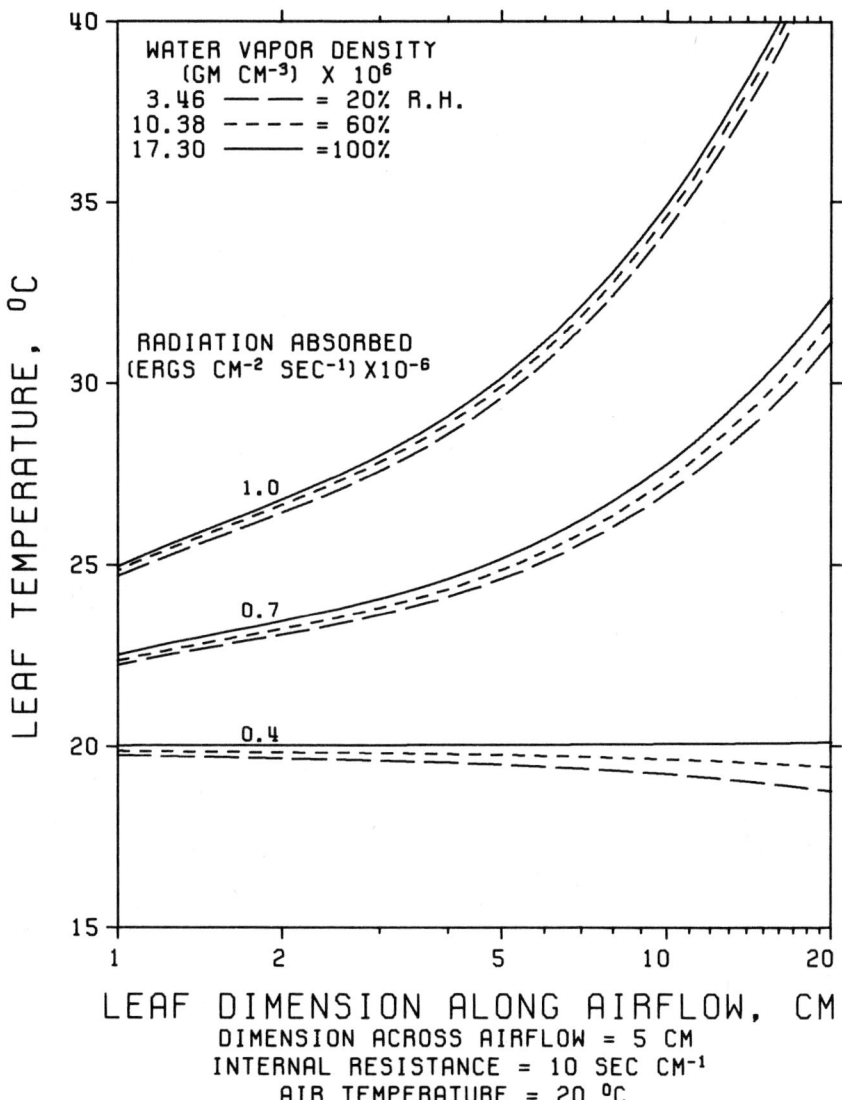

WATER VAPOR DENSITY
(GM CM^{-3}) X 10^6
3.46 — — = 20% R.H.
10.38 - - - - = 60%
17.30 ———— =100%

RADIATION ABSORBED
(ERGS CM^{-2} SEC^{-1}) X10^{-6}

1.0

0.7

0.4

LEAF TEMPERATURE, ^{0}C

LEAF DIMENSION ALONG AIRFLOW, CM
DIMENSION ACROSS AIRFLOW = 5 CM
INTERNAL RESISTANCE = 10 SEC CM^{-1}
AIR TEMPERATURE = 20 ^{0}C
AIRSPEED = 100 CM SEC^{-1}
1.0 X 10^6 ERGS CM^{-2} SEC^{-1} = 1.433 CAL CM^{-2} MIN^{-1}

GRAPH 78

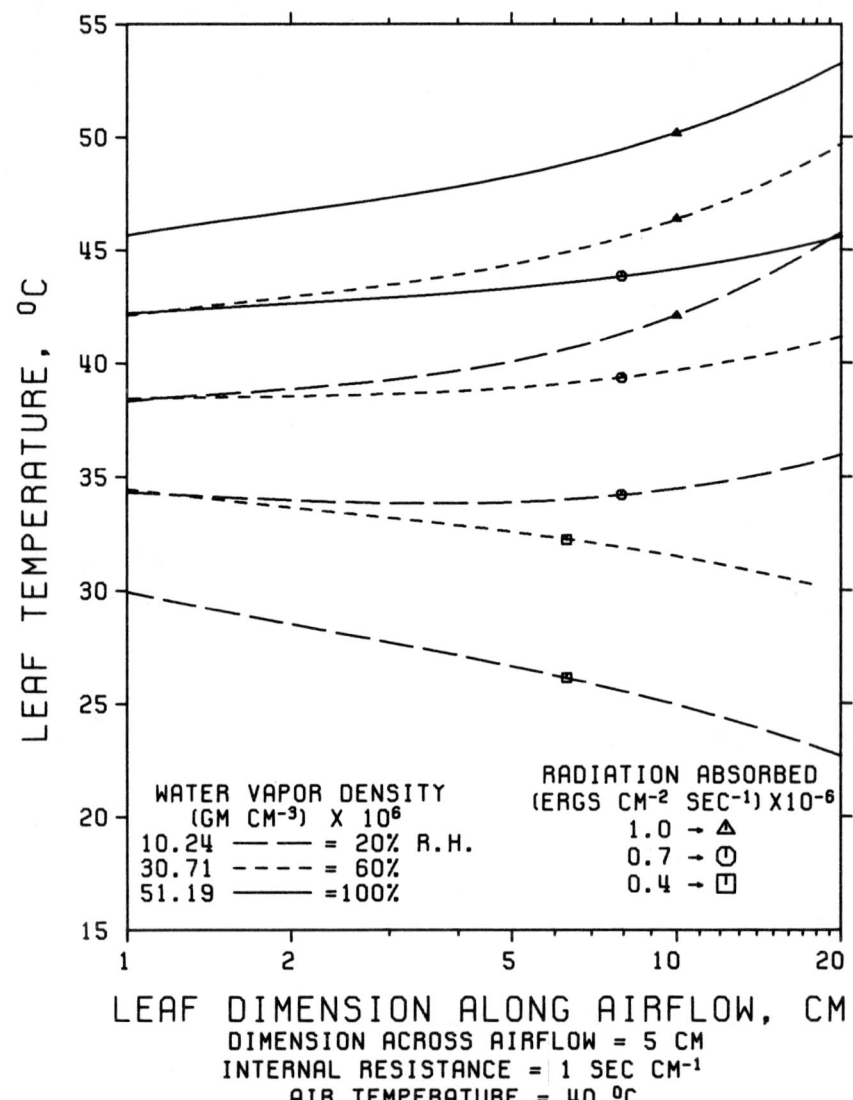

LEAF TEMPERATURE, °C

55

50

45

40

35

30

25

20

15

WATER VAPOR DENSITY
(GM CM⁻³) X 10⁶
10.24 ——— = 20% R.H.
30.71 ----- = 60%
51.19 ——— =100%

RADIATION ABSORBED
(ERGS CM⁻² SEC⁻¹) X10⁻⁶
1.0 → △
0.7 → ⊙
0.4 → ⊡

1   2   5   10   20

LEAF DIMENSION ALONG AIRFLOW, CM
DIMENSION ACROSS AIRFLOW = 5 CM
INTERNAL RESISTANCE = 1 SEC CM⁻¹
AIR TEMPERATURE = 40 °C
AIRSPEED = 10 CM SEC⁻¹
1.0 X 10⁶ ERGS CM⁻² SEC⁻¹ = 1.433 CAL CM⁻² MIN⁻¹

GRAPH 79

246

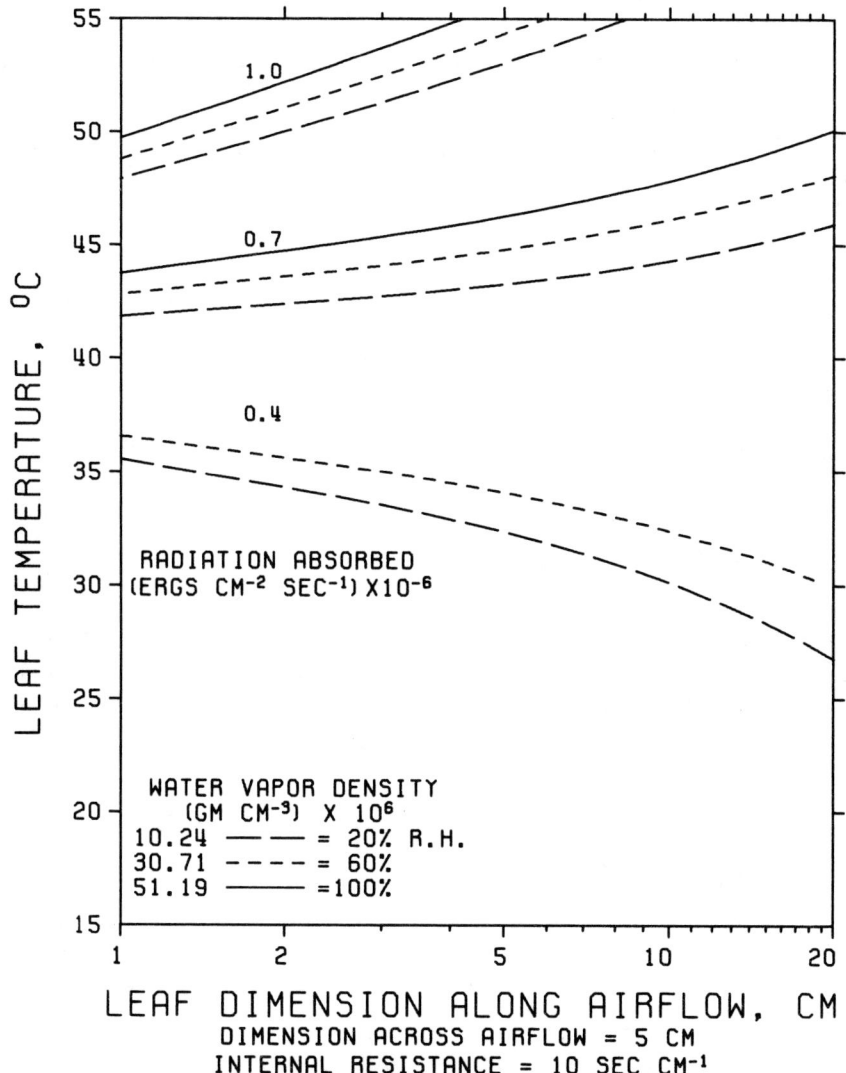

LEAF DIMENSION ALONG AIRFLOW, CM
DIMENSION ACROSS AIRFLOW = 5 CM
INTERNAL RESISTANCE = 10 SEC CM⁻¹
AIR TEMPERATURE = 40 °C
AIRSPEED = 10 CM SEC⁻¹
1.0 X 10⁶ ERGS CM⁻² SEC⁻¹ = 1.433 CAL CM⁻² MIN⁻¹

GRAPH 80

247

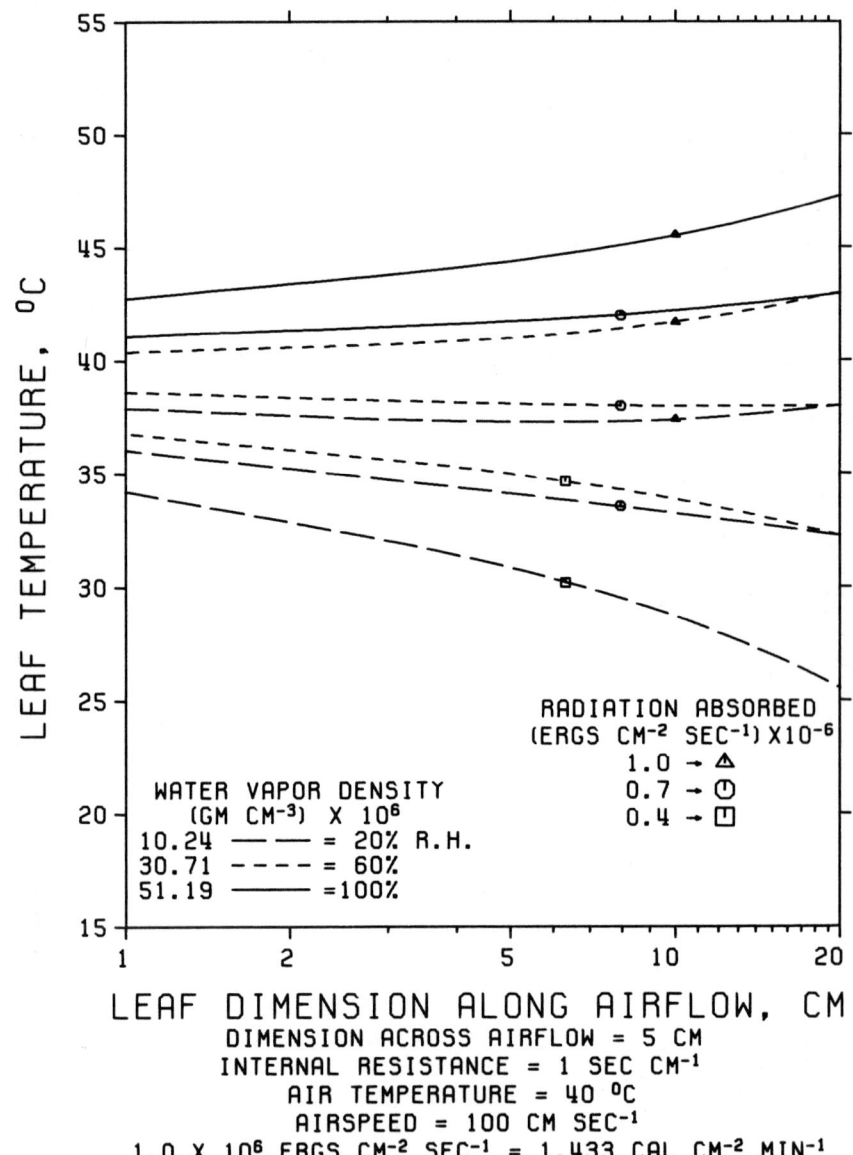

LEAF DIMENSION ALONG AIRFLOW, CM
DIMENSION ACROSS AIRFLOW = 5 CM
INTERNAL RESISTANCE = 1 SEC CM⁻¹
AIR TEMPERATURE = 40 °C
AIRSPEED = 100 CM SEC⁻¹
1.0 X 10⁶ ERGS CM⁻² SEC⁻¹ = 1.433 CAL CM⁻² MIN⁻¹

GRAPH 81

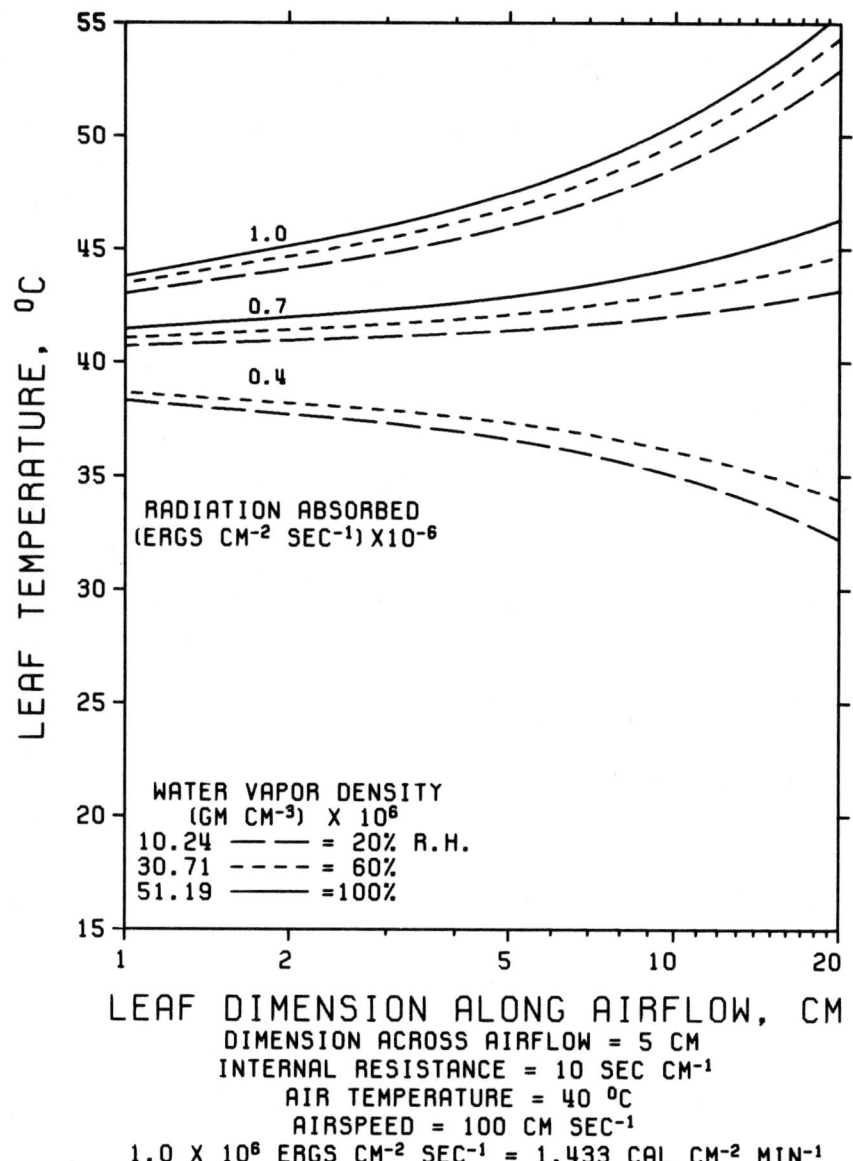

GRAPH 82

9

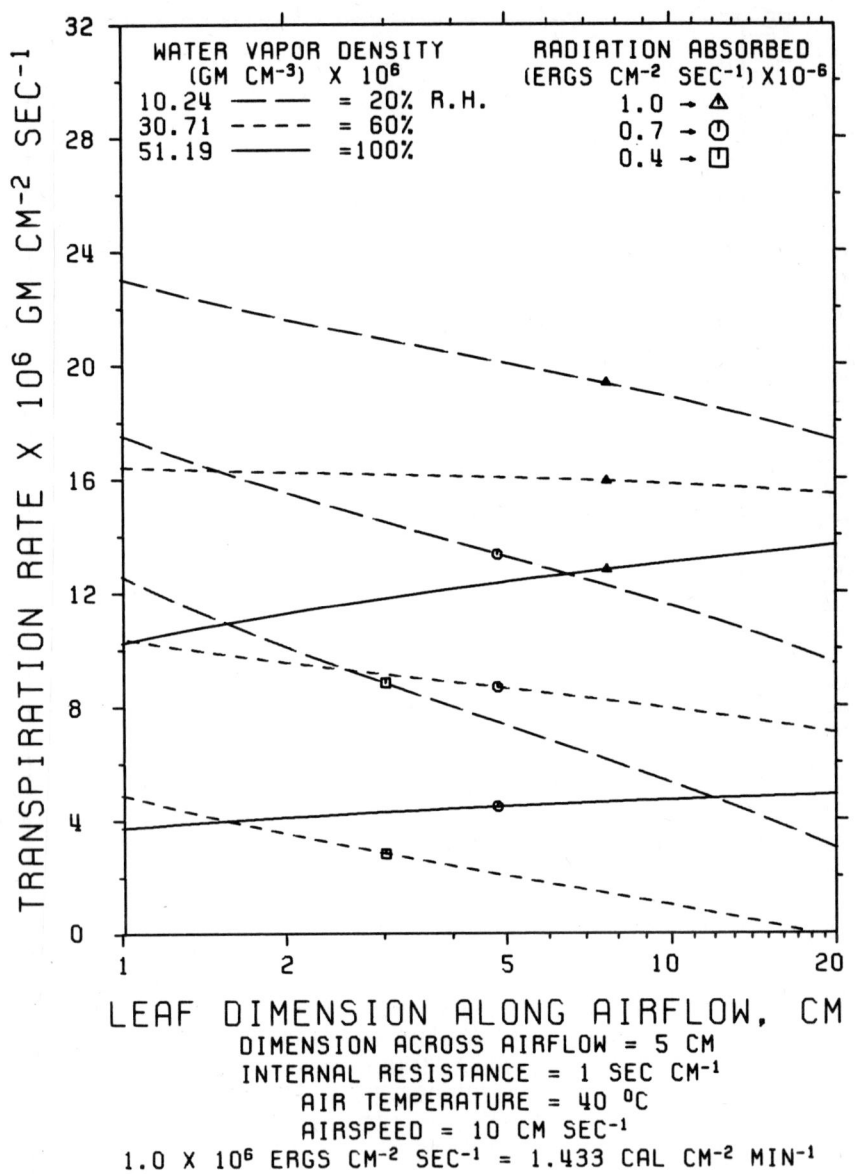

LEAF DIMENSION ALONG AIRFLOW, CM
DIMENSION ACROSS AIRFLOW = 5 CM
INTERNAL RESISTANCE = 1 SEC CM⁻¹
AIR TEMPERATURE = 40 °C
AIRSPEED = 10 CM SEC⁻¹
1.0 X 10⁶ ERGS CM⁻² SEC⁻¹ = 1.433 CAL CM⁻² MIN⁻¹

GRAPH 83

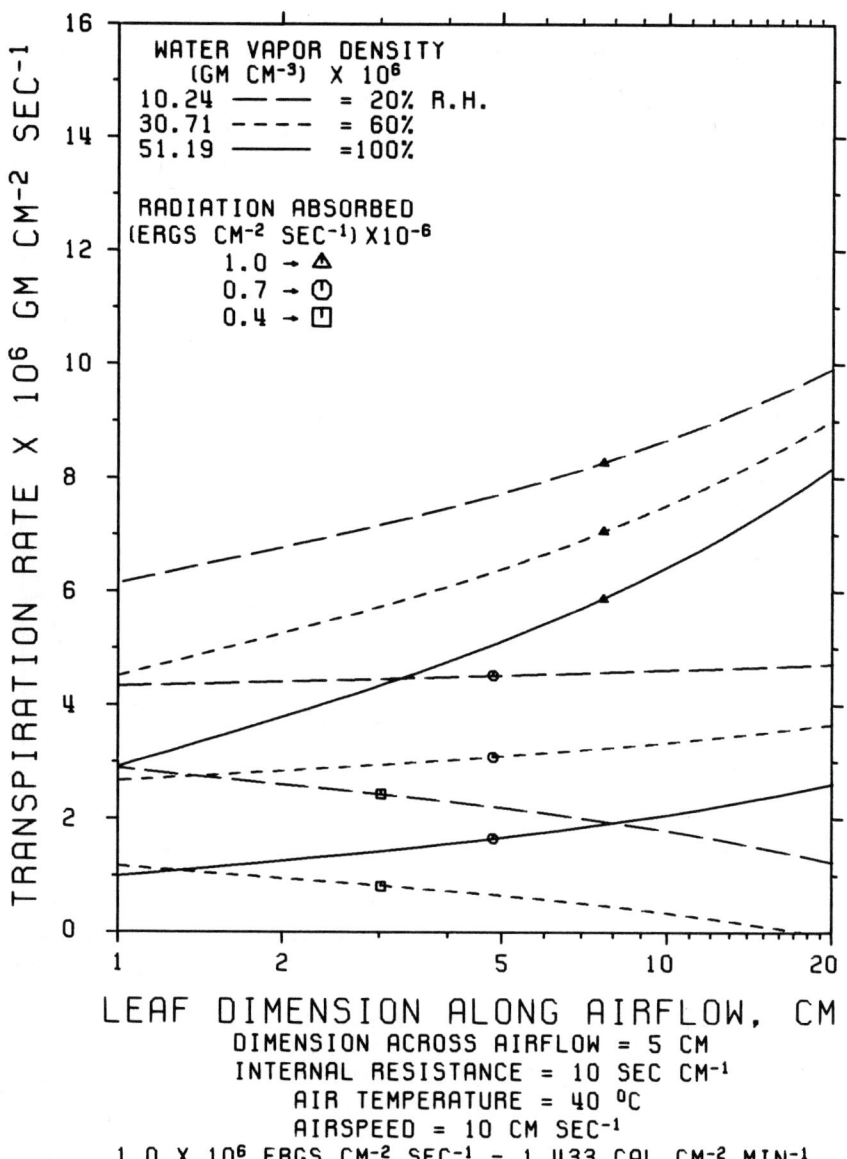

LEAF DIMENSION ALONG AIRFLOW, CM
DIMENSION ACROSS AIRFLOW = 5 CM
INTERNAL RESISTANCE = 10 SEC CM⁻¹
AIR TEMPERATURE = 40 °C
AIRSPEED = 10 CM SEC⁻¹
1.0 X 10⁶ ERGS CM⁻² SEC⁻¹ = 1.433 CAL CM⁻² MIN⁻¹

GRAPH 84

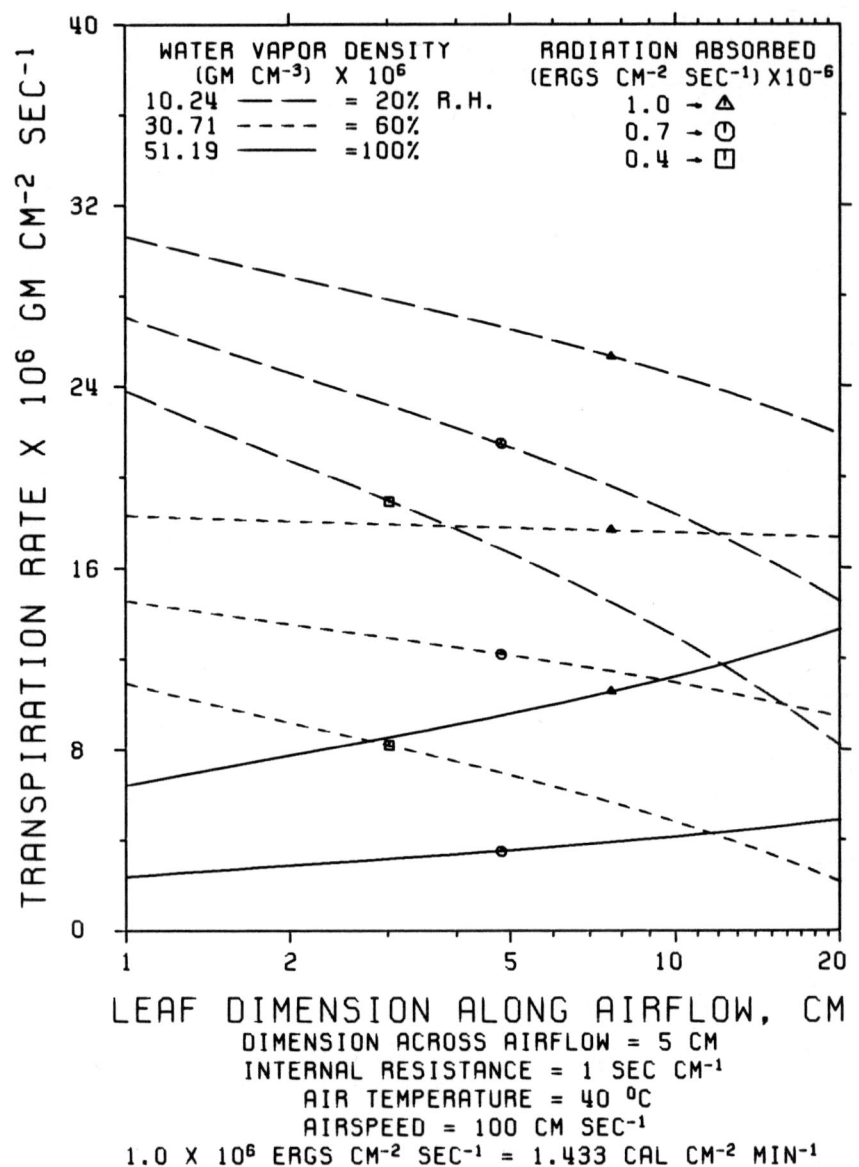

GRAPH 85

252

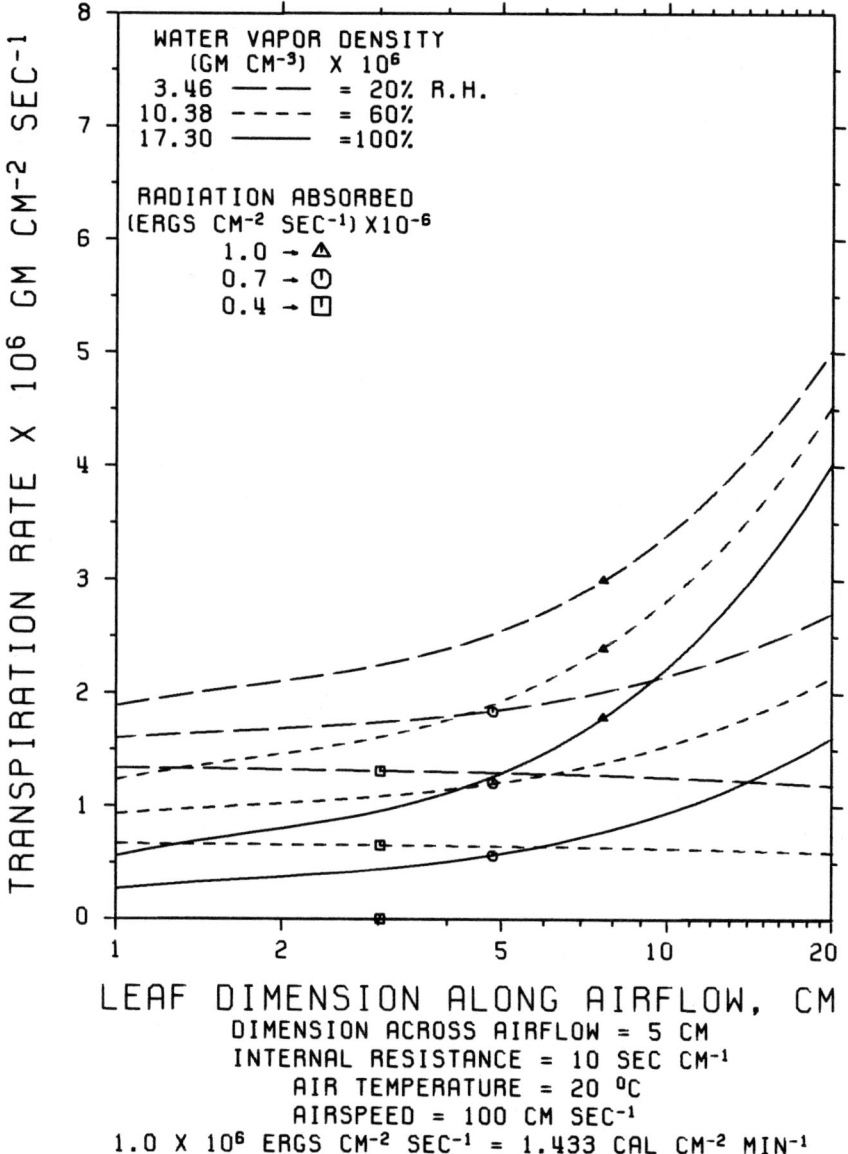

LEAF DIMENSION ALONG AIRFLOW, CM
DIMENSION ACROSS AIRFLOW = 5 CM
INTERNAL RESISTANCE = 10 SEC CM⁻¹
AIR TEMPERATURE = 20 ºC
AIRSPEED = 100 CM SEC⁻¹
1.0 X 10⁶ ERGS CM⁻² SEC⁻¹ = 1.433 CAL CM⁻² MIN⁻¹

GRAPH 86

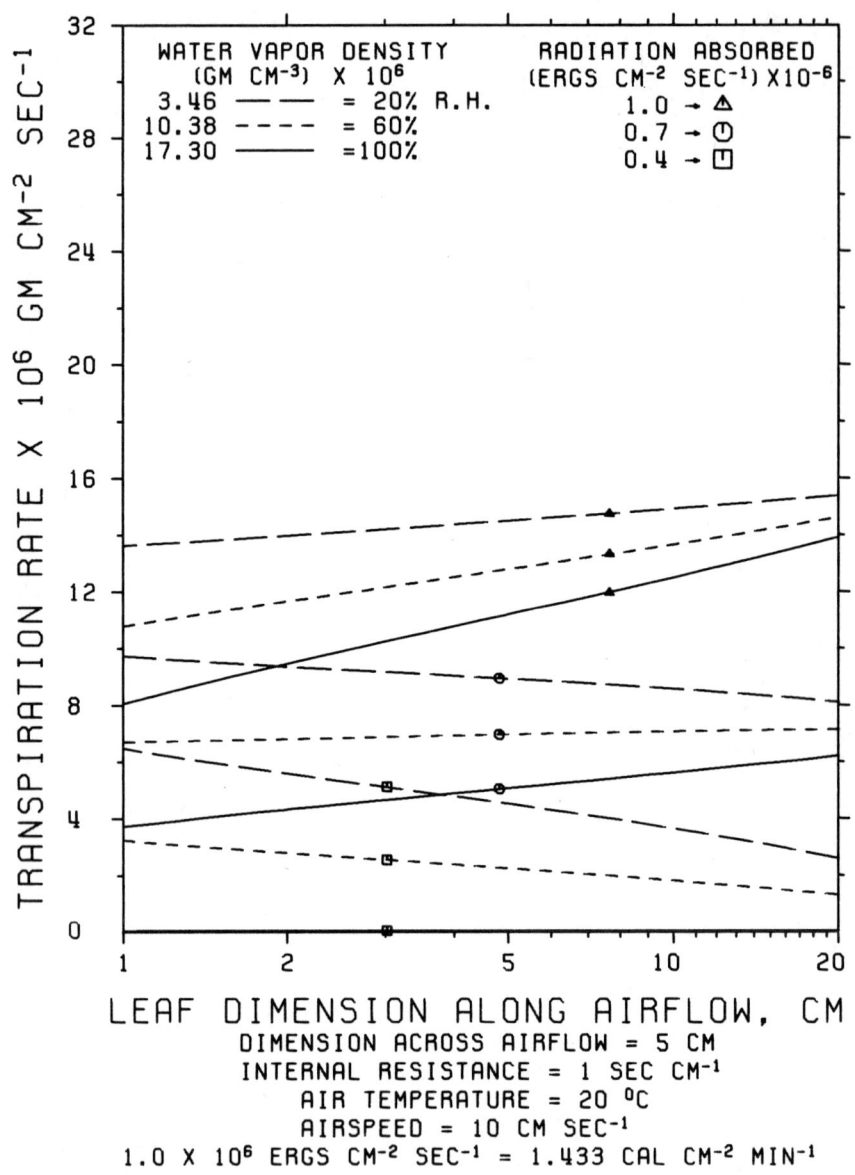

WATER VAPOR DENSITY
(GM CM^{-3}) X 10^6
3.46 — — = 20% R.H.
10.38 - - - - = 60%
17.30 ——— =100%

RADIATION ABSORBED
(ERGS CM^{-2} SEC^{-1}) X10^{-6}
1.0 → △
0.7 → ◔
0.4 → ▢

TRANSPIRATION RATE X 10^6 GM CM^{-2} SEC^{-1}

LEAF DIMENSION ALONG AIRFLOW, CM
DIMENSION ACROSS AIRFLOW = 5 CM
INTERNAL RESISTANCE = 1 SEC CM^{-1}
AIR TEMPERATURE = 20 °C
AIRSPEED = 10 CM SEC^{-1}
1.0 X 10^6 ERGS CM^{-2} SEC^{-1} = 1.433 CAL CM^{-2} MIN^{-1}

GRAPH 87

254

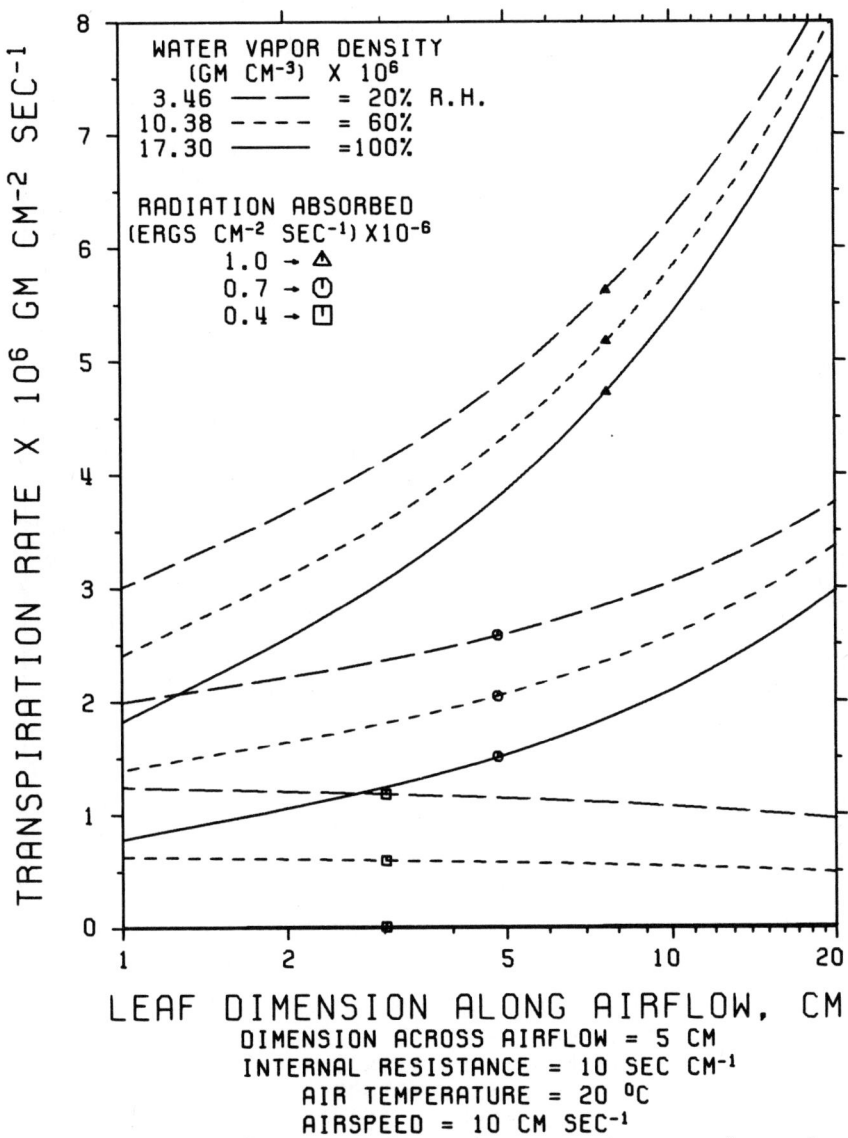

LEAF DIMENSION ALONG AIRFLOW, CM
DIMENSION ACROSS AIRFLOW = 5 CM
INTERNAL RESISTANCE = 10 SEC CM⁻¹
AIR TEMPERATURE = 20 °C
AIRSPEED = 10 CM SEC⁻¹
1.0 X 10⁶ ERGS CM⁻² SEC⁻¹ = 1.433 CAL CM⁻² MIN⁻¹

GRAPH 88

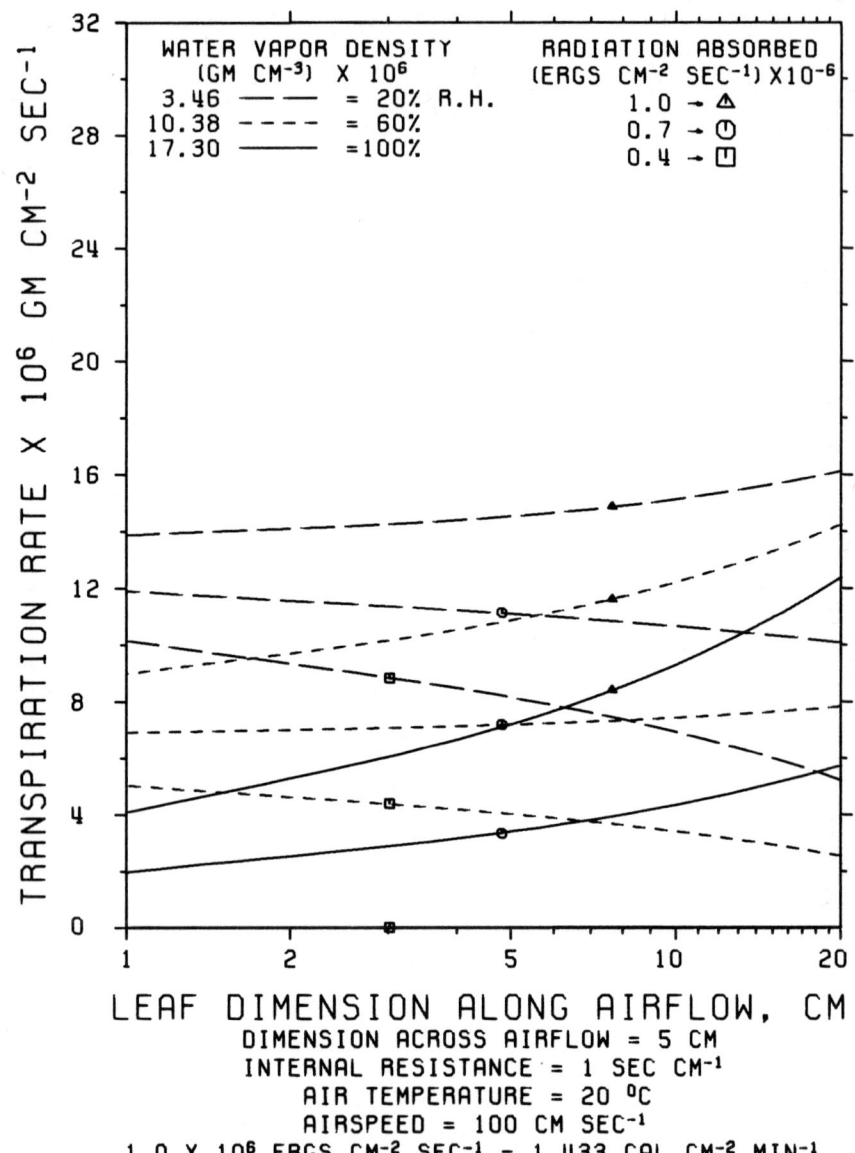

WATER VAPOR DENSITY
(GM CM⁻³) X 10⁶
3.46 — — = 20% R.H.
10.38 — — — — = 60%
17.30 ———— =100%

RADIATION ABSORBED
(ERGS CM⁻² SEC⁻¹) X10⁻⁶
1.0 → △
0.7 → ◐
0.4 → ☐

LEAF DIMENSION ALONG AIRFLOW, CM
DIMENSION ACROSS AIRFLOW = 5 CM
INTERNAL RESISTANCE = 1 SEC CM⁻¹
AIR TEMPERATURE = 20 ⁰C
AIRSPEED = 100 CM SEC⁻¹
1.0 X 10⁶ ERGS CM⁻² SEC⁻¹ = 1.433 CAL CM⁻² MIN⁻¹

GRAPH 89

256

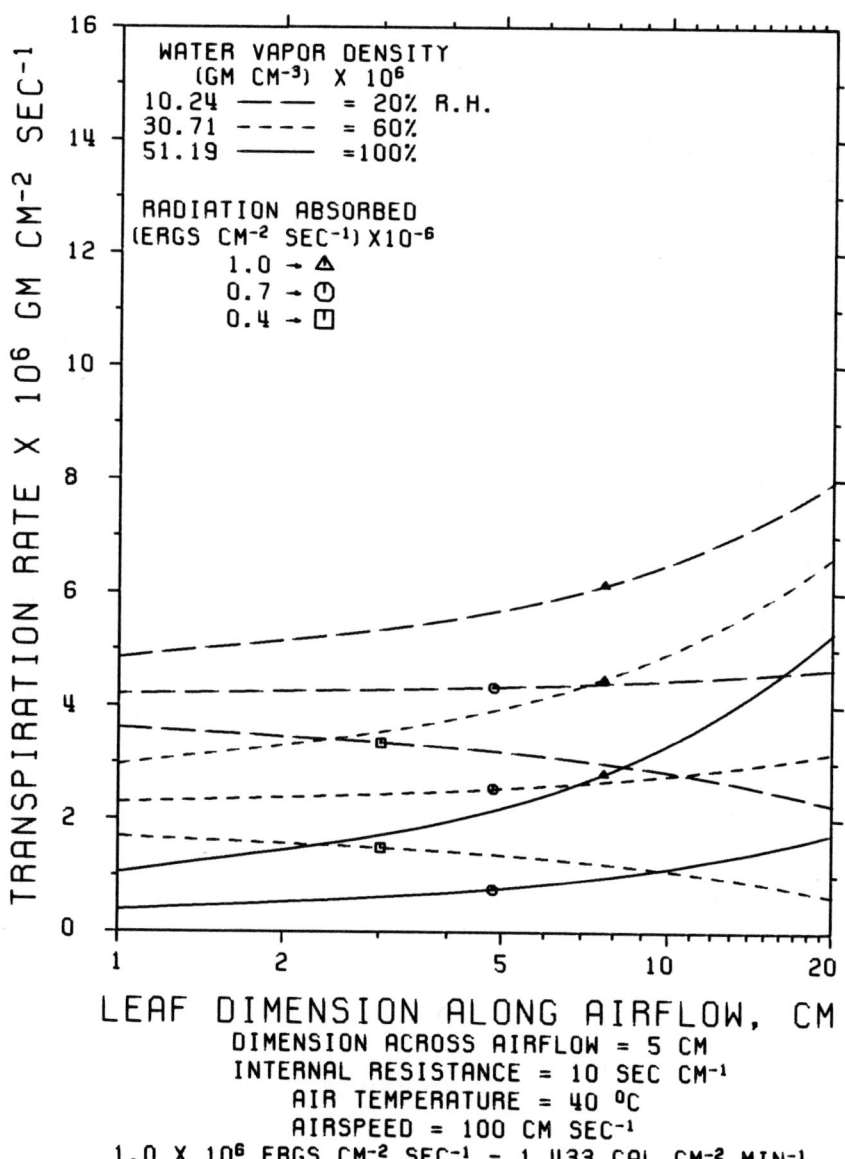

GRAPH 90

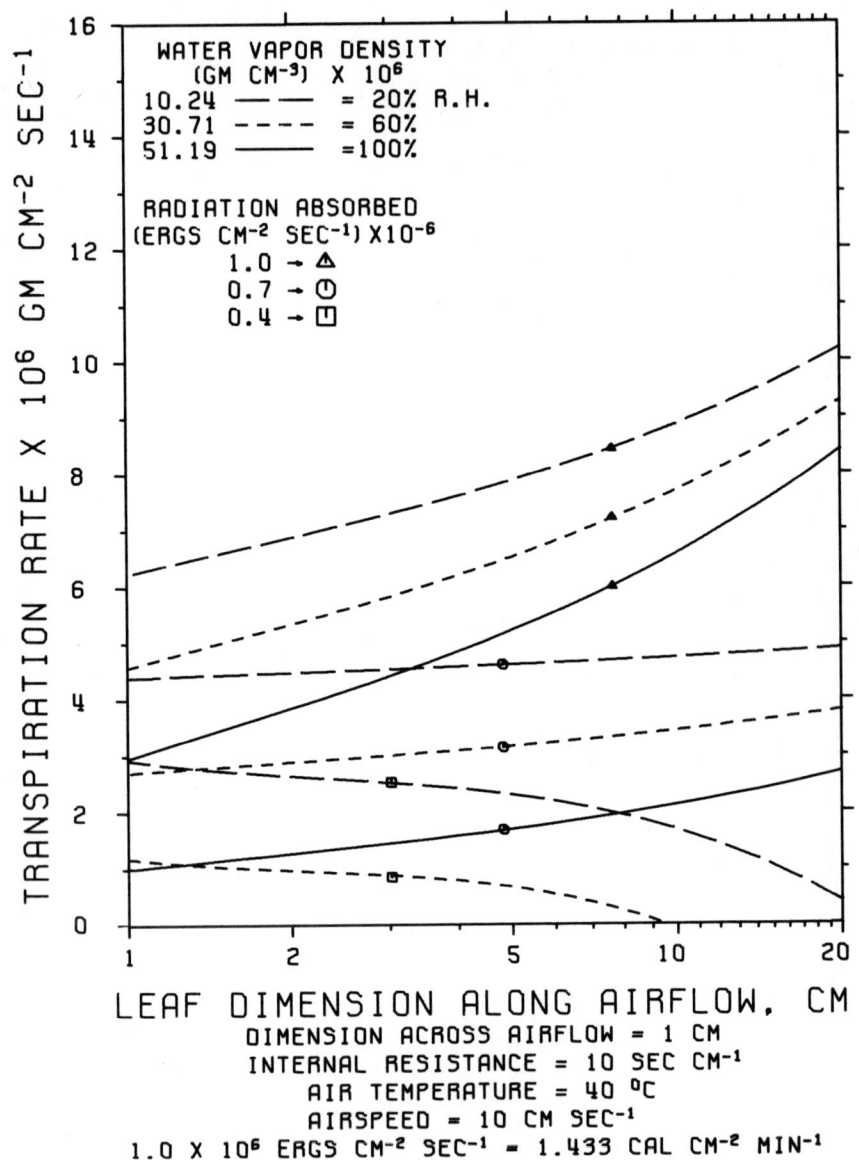

WATER VAPOR DENSITY
(GM CM⁻³) X 10⁶
10.24 — — = 20% R.H.
30.71 — — — — = 60%
51.19 ———— =100%

RADIATION ABSORBED
(ERGS CM⁻² SEC⁻¹) X10⁻⁶
1.0 → △
0.7 → ⊙
0.4 → ⊡

LEAF DIMENSION ALONG AIRFLOW, CM
DIMENSION ACROSS AIRFLOW = 1 CM
INTERNAL RESISTANCE = 10 SEC CM⁻¹
AIR TEMPERATURE = 40 °C
AIRSPEED = 10 CM SEC⁻¹
1.0 X 10⁶ ERGS CM⁻² SEC⁻¹ = 1.433 CAL CM⁻² MIN⁻¹

Graph 91

258

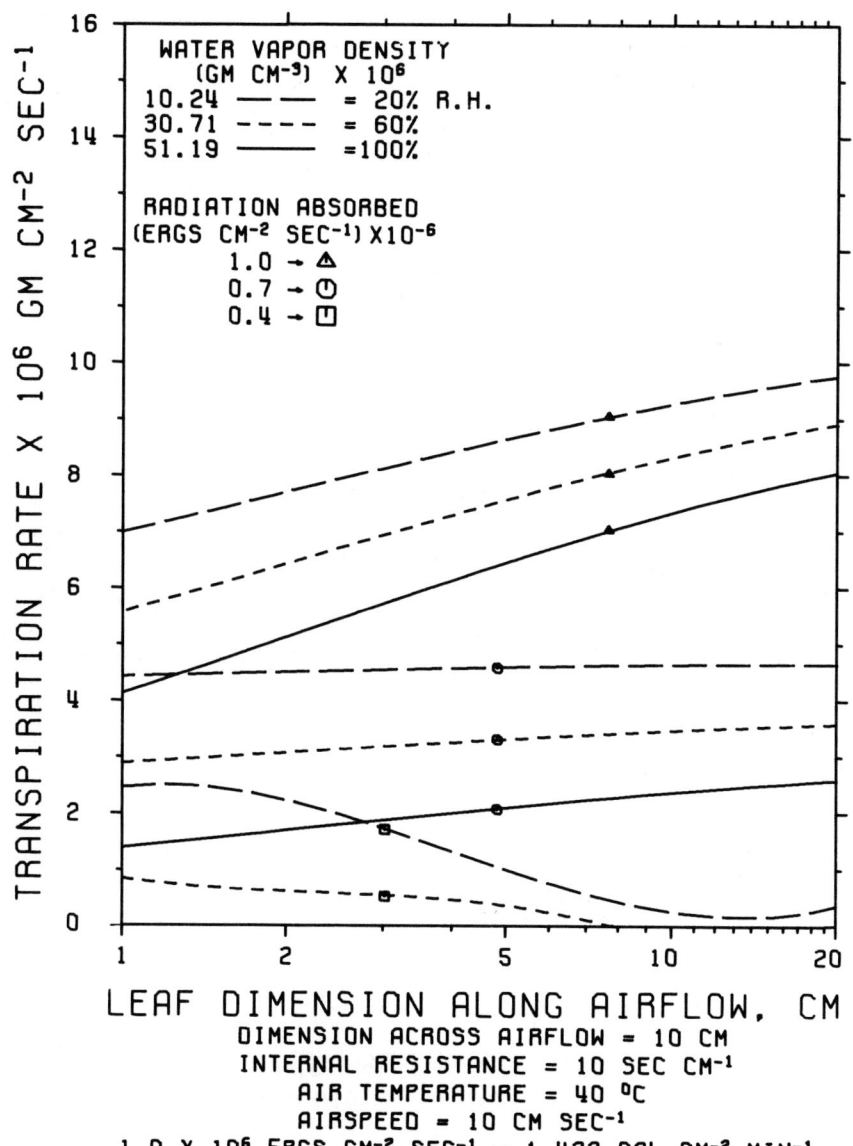

GRAPH 92

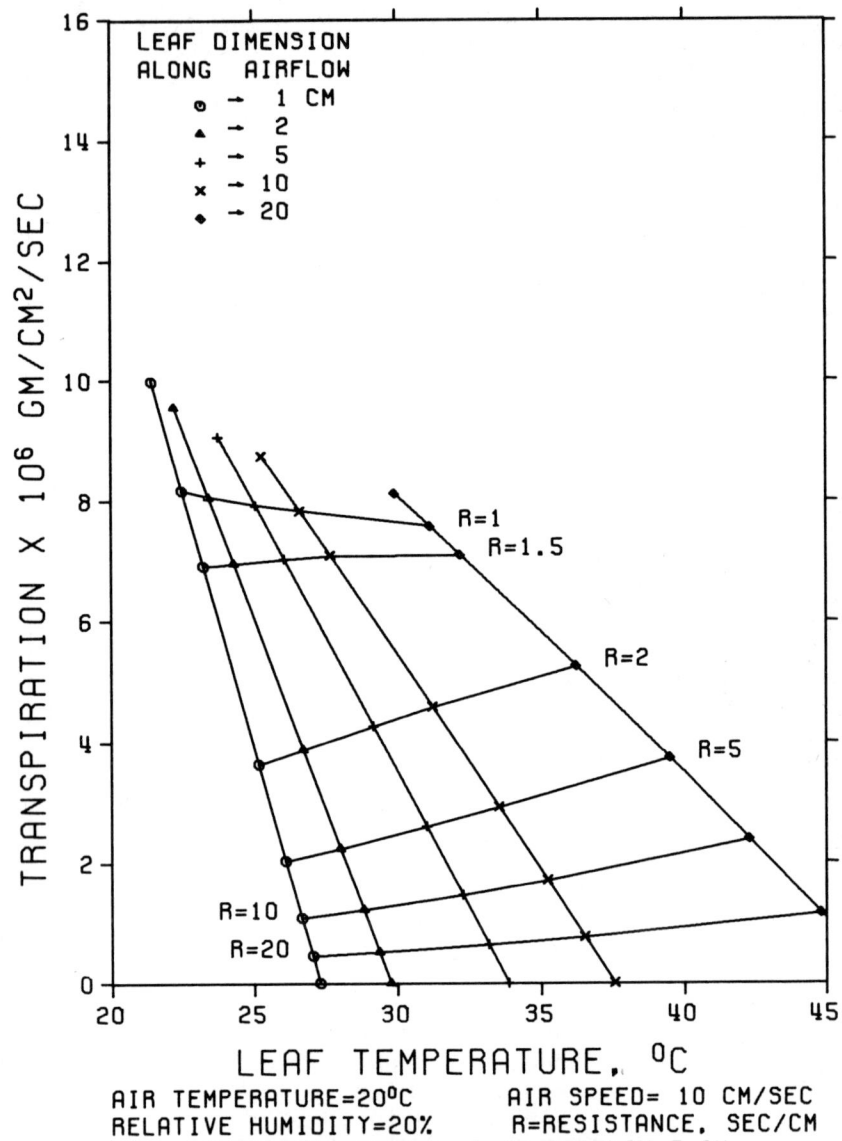

LEAF DIMENSION
ALONG AIRFLOW
- → 1 CM
- → 2
- → 5
- → 10
- → 20

R=1
R=1.5
R=2
R=5
R=10
R=20

TRANSPIRATION X 10^6 GM/CM^2/SEC

LEAF TEMPERATURE, ^{0}C

AIR TEMPERATURE=20^{0}C   AIR SPEED= 10 CM/SEC
RELATIVE HUMIDITY=20%   R=RESISTANCE, SEC/CM
LEAF DIMENSION ACROSS AIRFLOW=5 CM
RADIATION ABSORBED =
1.003 CAL/CM^2/MIN   OR   0.7 X 10^6 ERGS/CM^2/SEC

GRAPH 93

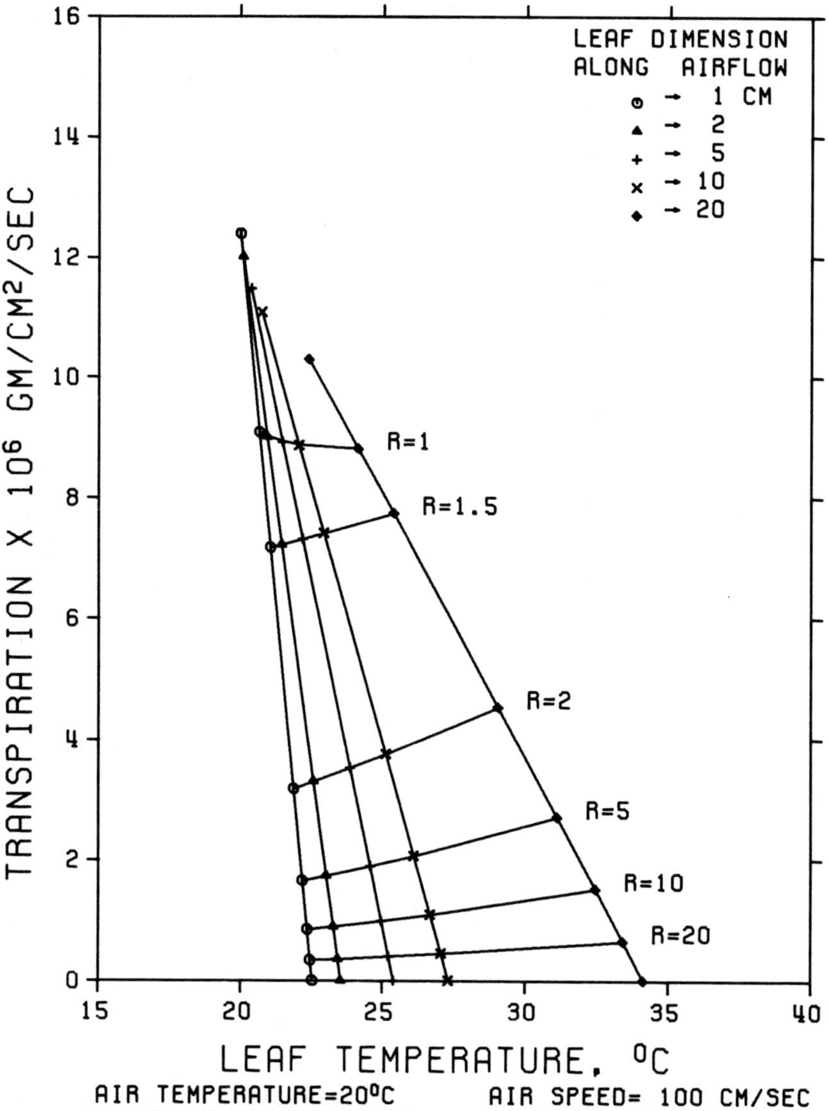
LEAF DIMENSION
ALONG AIRFLOW
→ 1 CM
→ 2
→ 5
→ 10
→ 20
R=1
R=1.5
R=2
R=5
R=10
R=20
16
14
12
10
8
6
4
2
0
15
20
25
30
35
40
TRANSPIRATION X 10⁶ GM/CM²/SEC
LEAF TEMPERATURE, °C

AIR TEMPERATURE=20°C AIR SPEED= 100 CM/SEC
RELATIVE HUMIDITY=20% R=RESISTANCE, SEC/CM
LEAF DIMENSION ACROSS AIRFLOW=5 CM
RADIATION ABSORBED =
1.003 CAL/CM²/MIN OR 0.7 X 10^6 ERGS/CM²/SEC

GRAPH 94

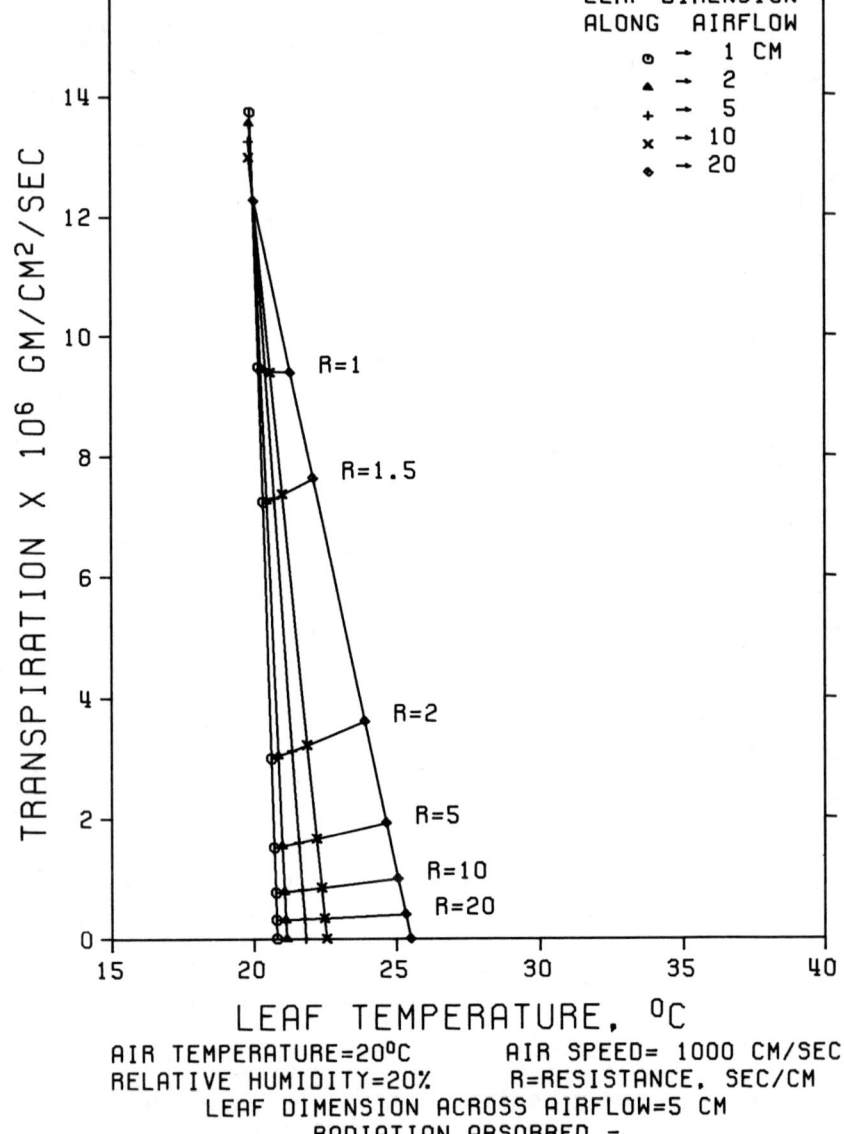

LEAF DIMENSION
ALONG AIRFLOW
⊕ → 1 CM
▲ → 2
+ → 5
× → 10
◆ → 20

R=1

R=1.5

R=2

R=5

R=10

R=20

TRANSPIRATION X 10^6 GM/CM²/SEC

LEAF TEMPERATURE, °C

AIR TEMPERATURE=20°C   AIR SPEED= 1000 CM/SEC
RELATIVE HUMIDITY=20%   R=RESISTANCE, SEC/CM
LEAF DIMENSION ACROSS AIRFLOW=5 CM
RADIATION ABSORBED =
1.003 CAL/CM²/MIN   OR   0.7 X 10^6 ERGS/CM²/SEC

GRAPH 95

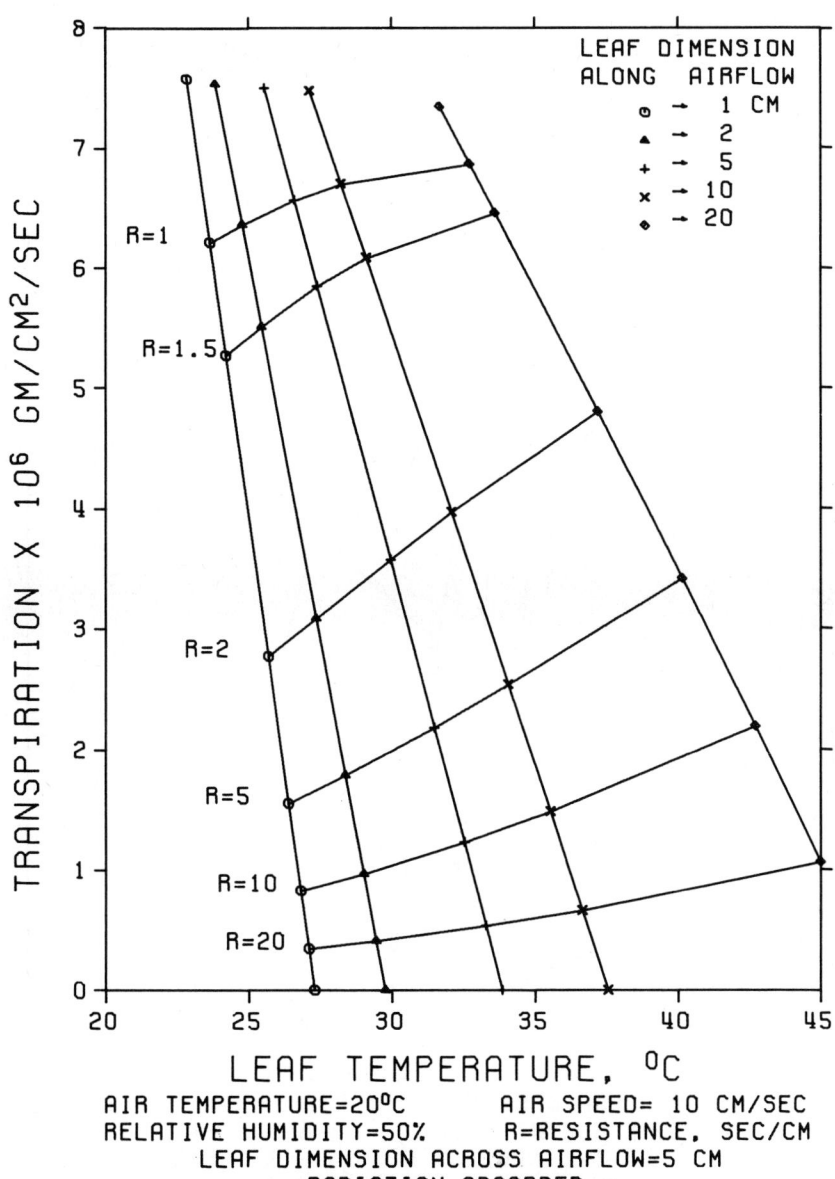

LEAF DIMENSION
ALONG AIRFLOW
⊙ → 1 CM
▲ → 2
+ → 5
× → 10
◆ → 20

R=1
R=1.5
R=2
R=5
R=10
R=20

TRANSPIRATION X 10^6 GM/CM^2/SEC

LEAF TEMPERATURE, ^{0}C

AIR TEMPERATURE=20^{0}C   AIR SPEED= 10 CM/SEC
RELATIVE HUMIDITY=50%   R=RESISTANCE, SEC/CM
LEAF DIMENSION ACROSS AIRFLOW=5 CM
RADIATION ABSORBED =
1.003 CAL/CM^2/MIN   OR   0.7 X 10^6 ERGS/CM^2/SEC

GRAPH 96

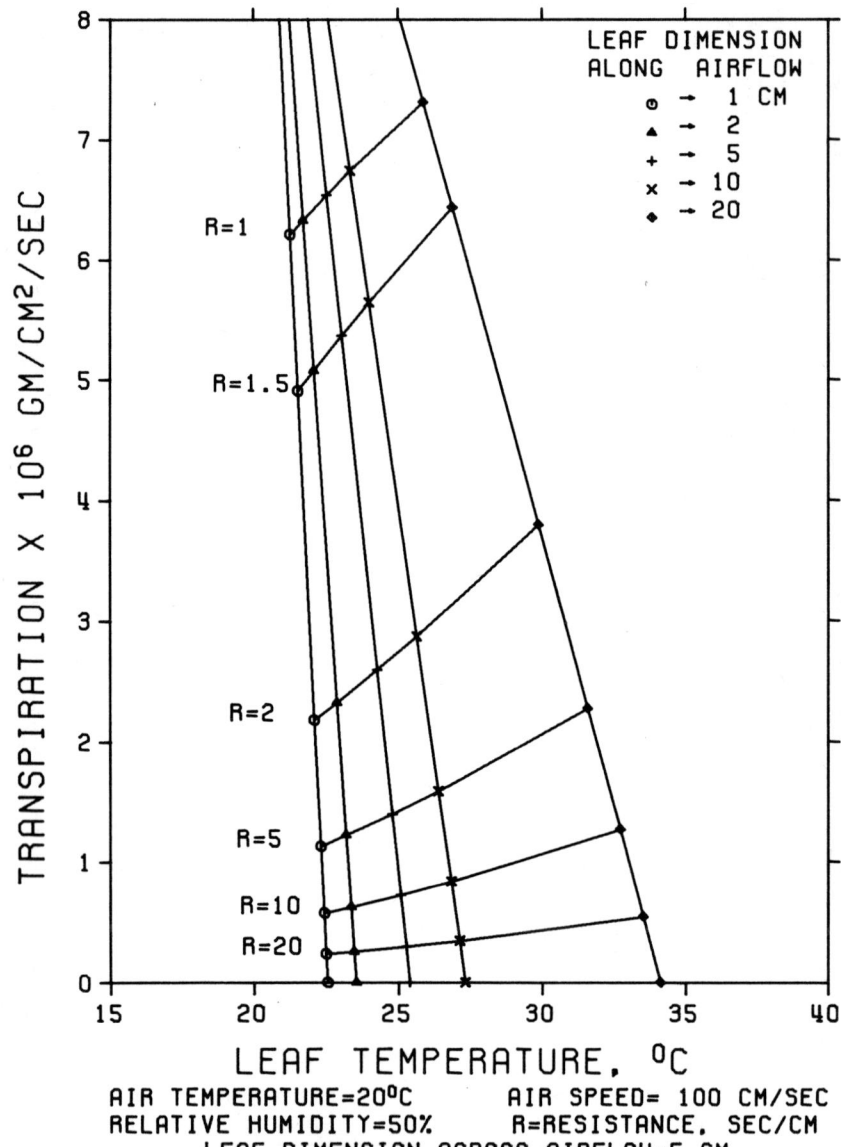

GRAPH 97

AIR TEMPERATURE=20⁰C   AIR SPEED= 100 CM/SEC
RELATIVE HUMIDITY=50%   R=RESISTANCE, SEC/CM
LEAF DIMENSION ACROSS AIRFLOW=5 CM
RADIATION ABSORBED =
1.003 CAL/CM²/MIN   OR   0.7 X 10⁶ ERGS/CM²/SEC

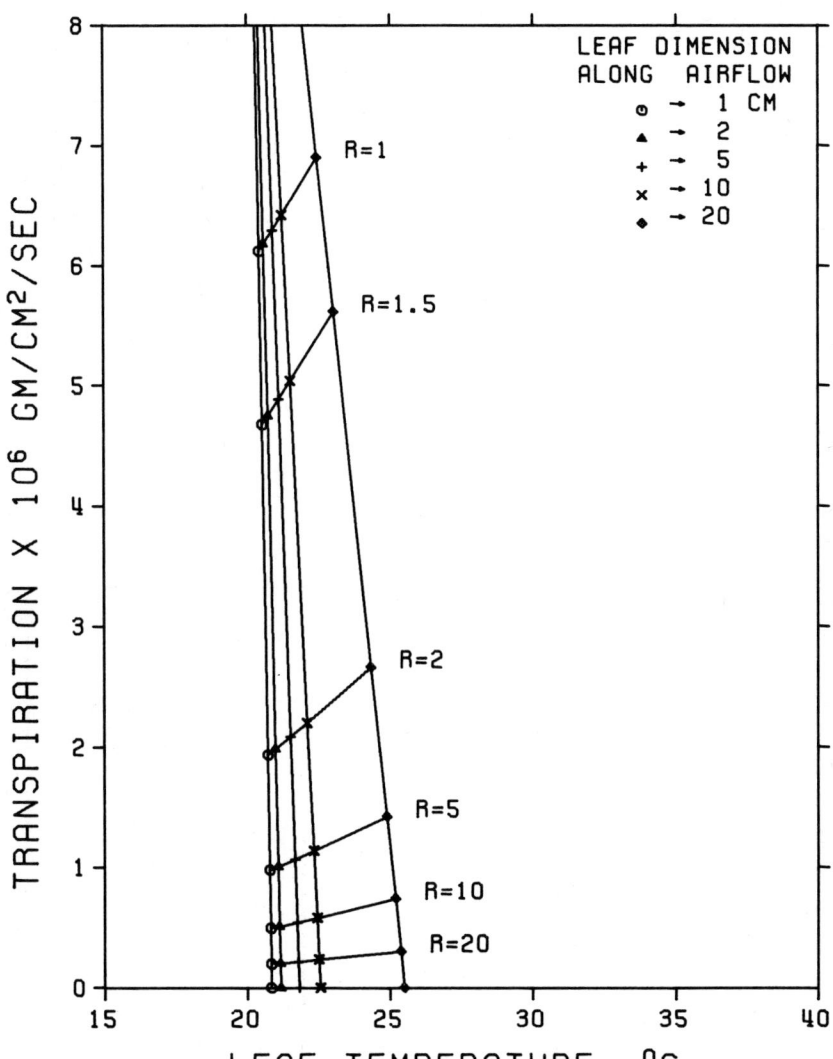

GRAPH 98

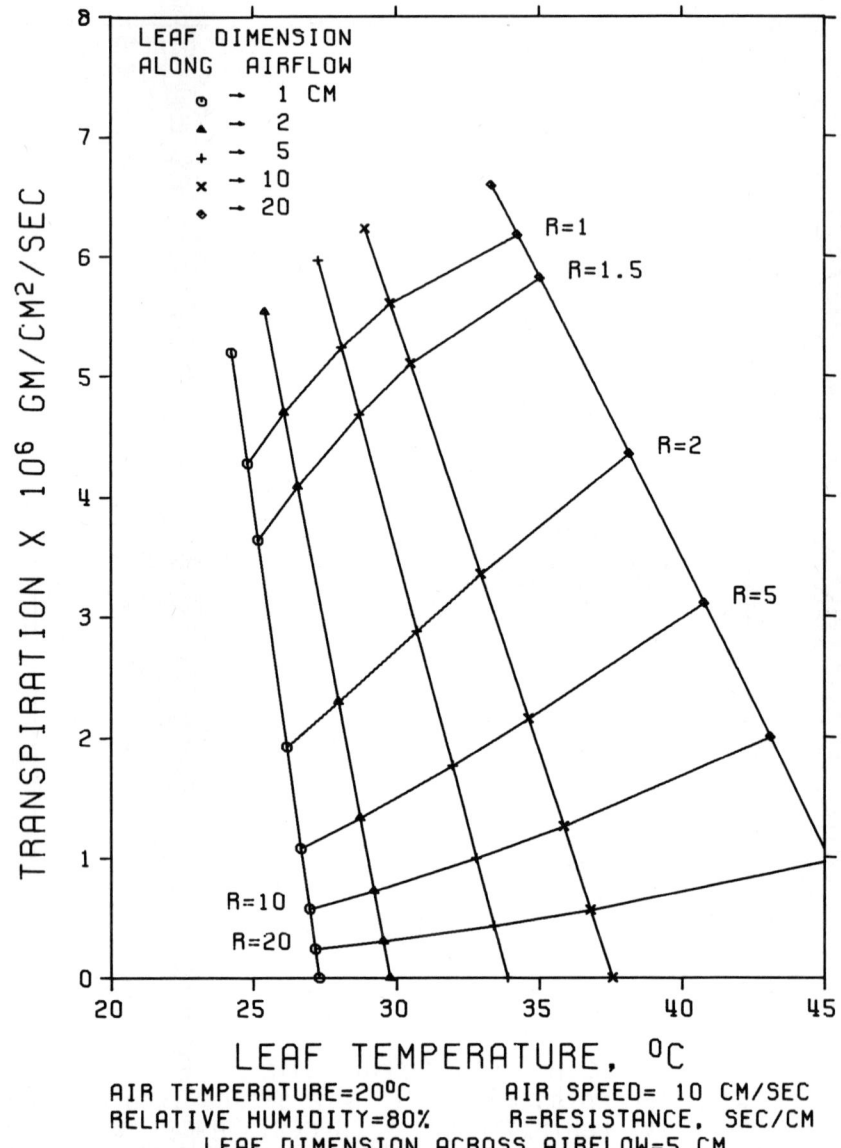

GRAPH 99

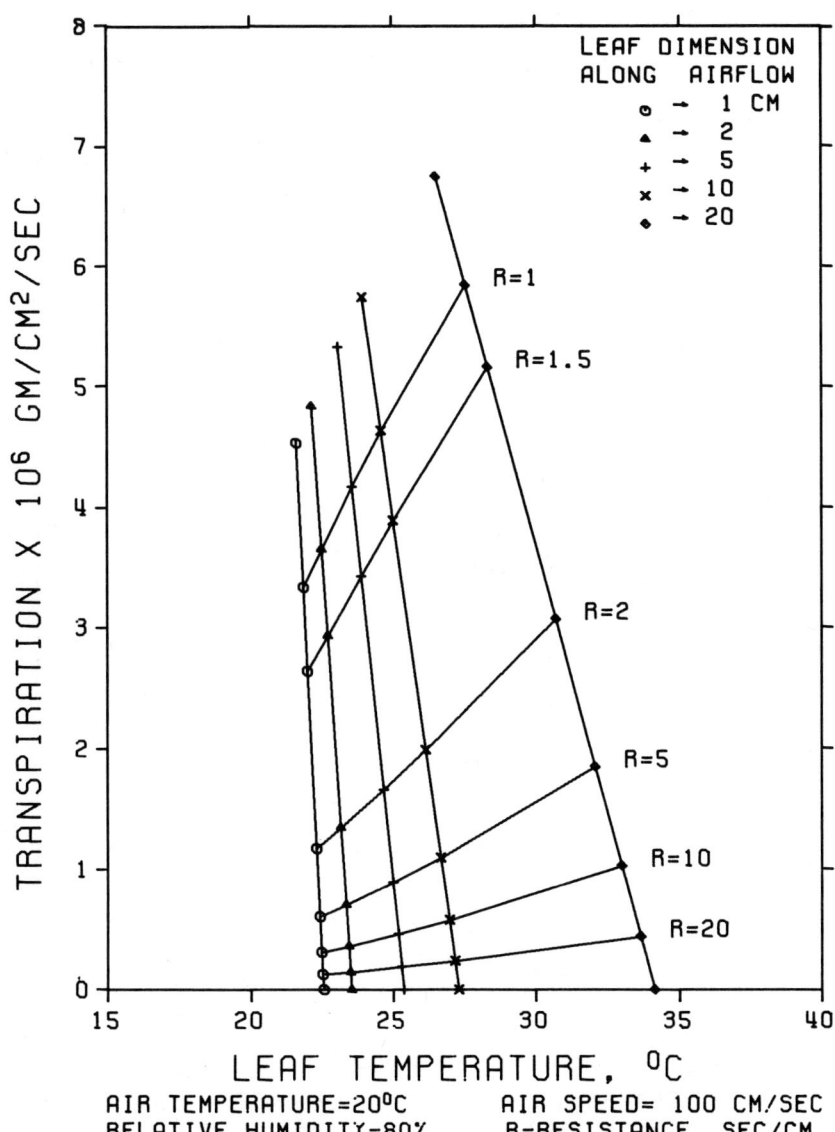

GRAPH 100

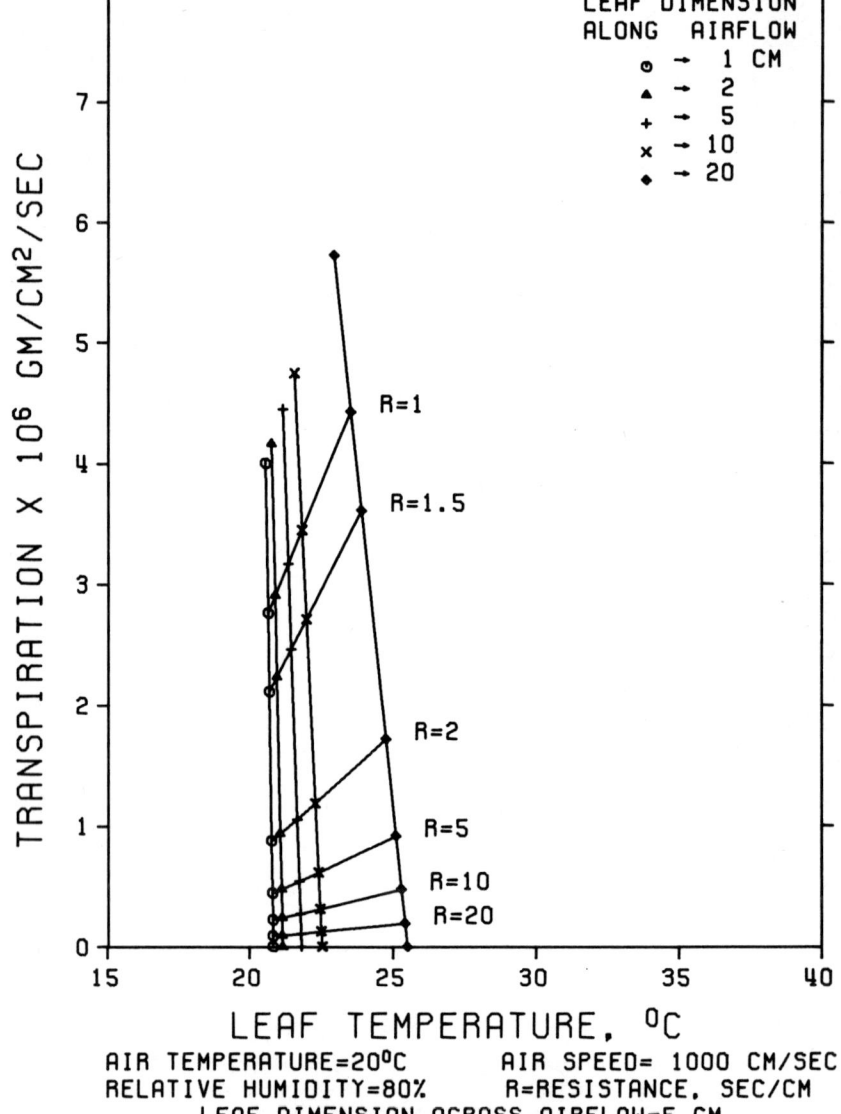

LEAF DIMENSION
ALONG AIRFLOW
⊙ → 1 CM
▲ → 2
+ → 5
× → 10
◆ → 20

R=1
R=1.5
R=2
R=5
R=10
R=20

TRANSPIRATION X 10⁶ GM/CM²/SEC

LEAF TEMPERATURE, °C

AIR TEMPERATURE=20°C   AIR SPEED= 1000 CM/SEC
RELATIVE HUMIDITY=80%   R=RESISTANCE, SEC/CM
LEAF DIMENSION ACROSS AIRFLOW=5 CM
RADIATION ABSORBED =
1.003 CAL/CM²/MIN   OR   0.7 X 10⁶ ERGS/CM²/SEC

GRAPH 101

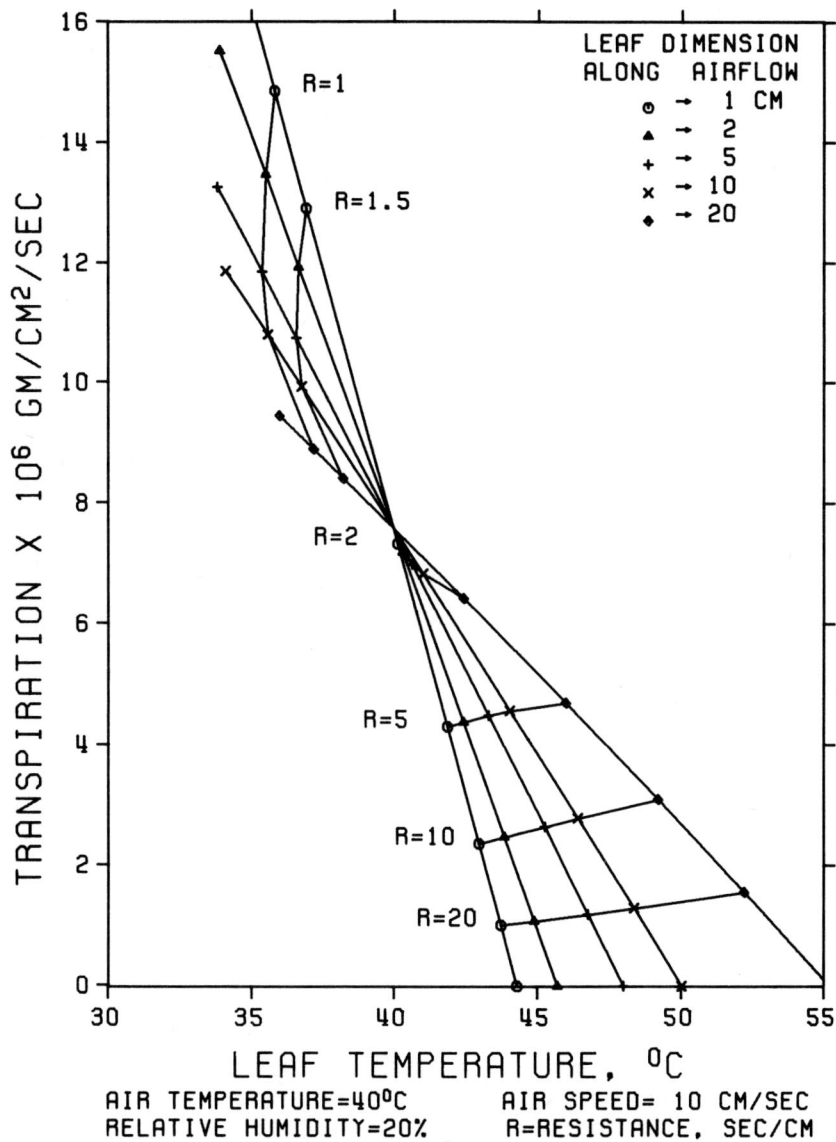

GRAPH 102

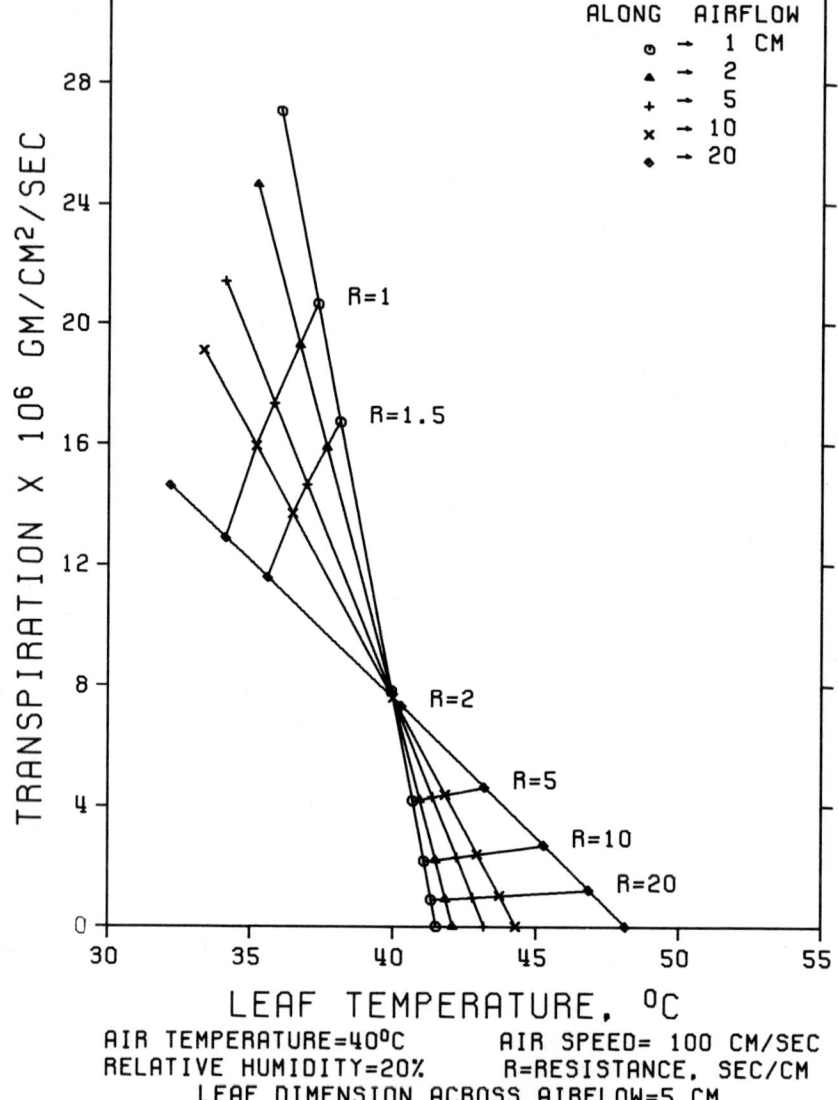

LEAF DIMENSION
ALONG AIRFLOW
⊙ → 1 CM
▲ → 2
+ → 5
× → 10
◆ → 20

R=1
R=1.5
R=2
R=5
R=10
R=20

TRANSPIRATION X 10^6 GM/CM²/SEC

LEAF TEMPERATURE, °C

AIR TEMPERATURE=40°C   AIR SPEED= 100 CM/SEC
RELATIVE HUMIDITY=20%   R=RESISTANCE, SEC/CM
LEAF DIMENSION ACROSS AIRFLOW=5 CM
RADIATION ABSORBED =
1.003 CAL/CM²/MIN   OR   0.7 X 10^6 ERGS/CM²/SEC

GRAPH 103

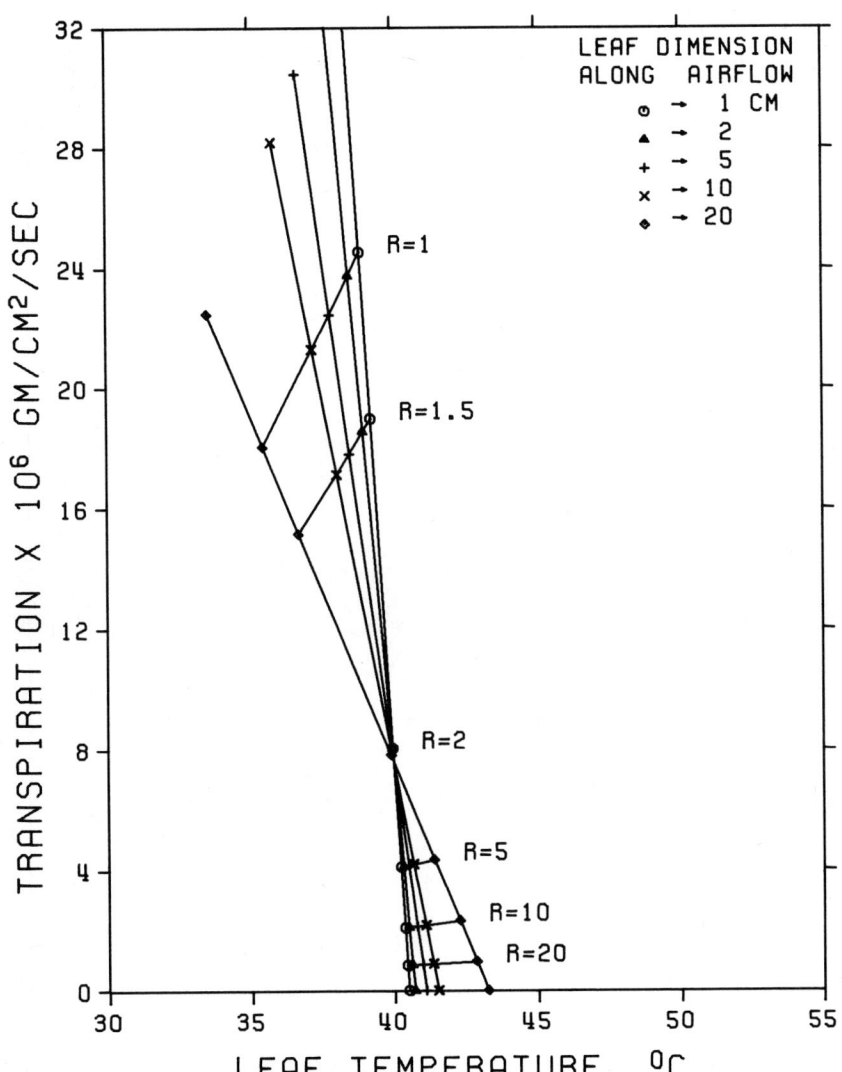

LEAF DIMENSION
ALONG AIRFLOW
⊙ → 1 CM
▲ → 2
+ → 5
× → 10
◆ → 20

R=1

R=1.5

R=2

R=5

R=10

R=20

TRANSPIRATION X 10⁶ GM/CM²/SEC

LEAF TEMPERATURE, °C

AIR TEMPERATURE=40°C   AIR SPEED= 1000 CM/SEC
RELATIVE HUMIDITY=20%   R=RESISTANCE, SEC/CM
LEAF DIMENSION ACROSS AIRFLOW=5 CM
RADIATION ABSORBED =
1.003 CAL/CM²/MIN   OR   0.7 X 10⁶ ERGS/CM²/SEC

GRAPH 104

271

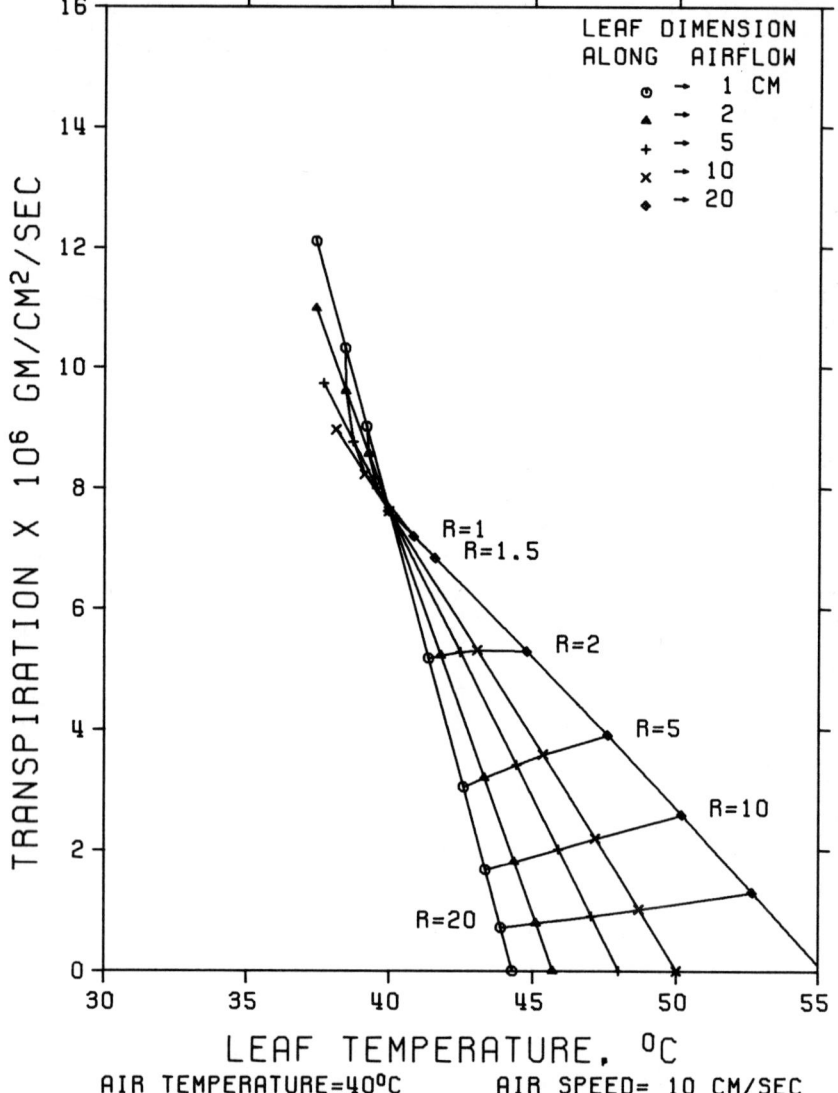

GRAPH 105

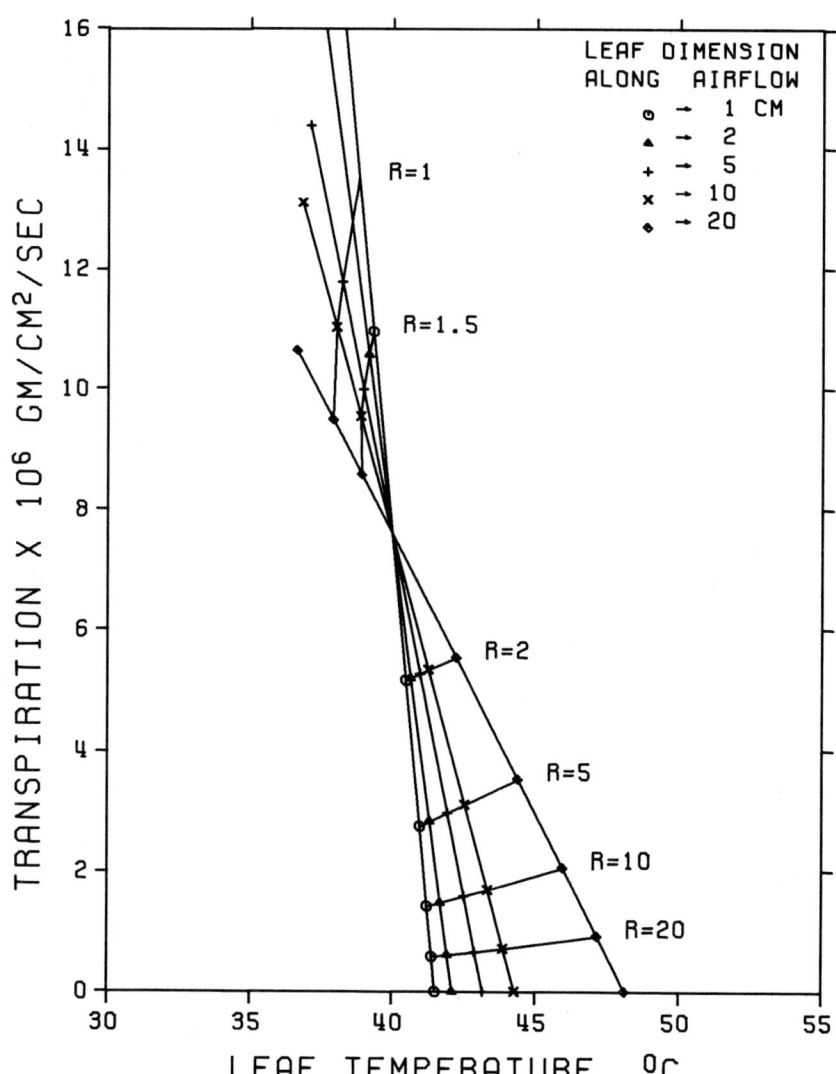

GRAPH 106

AIR TEMPERATURE=40°C   AIR SPEED= 100 CM/SEC
RELATIVE HUMIDITY=50%   R=RESISTANCE, SEC/CM
LEAF DIMENSION ACROSS AIRFLOW=5 CM
RADIATION ABSORBED =
1.003 CAL/CM²/MIN   OR   0.7 X 10⁶ ERGS/CM²/SEC

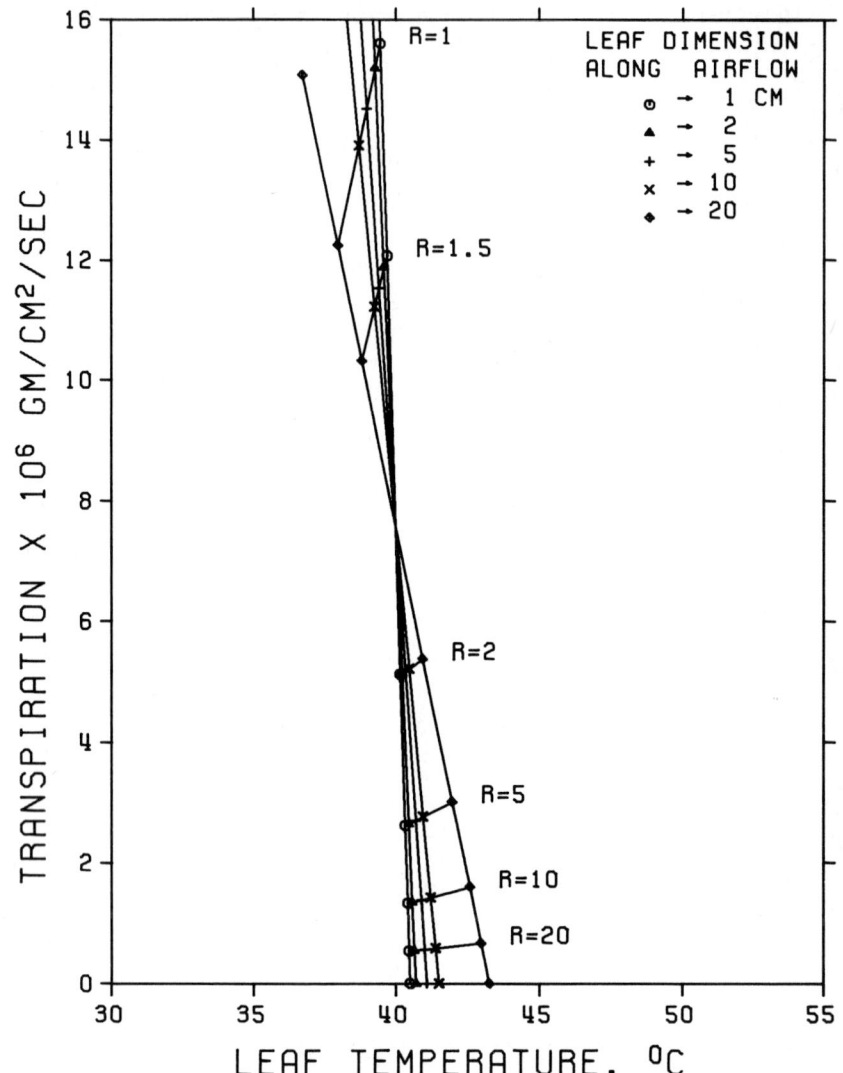

LEAF DIMENSION
ALONG AIRFLOW
⊙ → 1 CM
▲ → 2
+ → 5
× → 10
◆ → 20

R=1
R=1.5
R=2
R=5
R=10
R=20

TRANSPIRATION X 10⁶ GM/CM²/SEC

LEAF TEMPERATURE, °C

AIR TEMPERATURE=40°C   AIR SPEED= 1000 CM/SEC
RELATIVE HUMIDITY=50%   R=RESISTANCE, SEC/CM
LEAF DIMENSION ACROSS AIRFLOW=5 CM
RADIATION ABSORBED =
1.003 CAL/CM²/MIN   OR   0.7 X 10⁶ ERGS/CM²/SEC

GRAPH 107

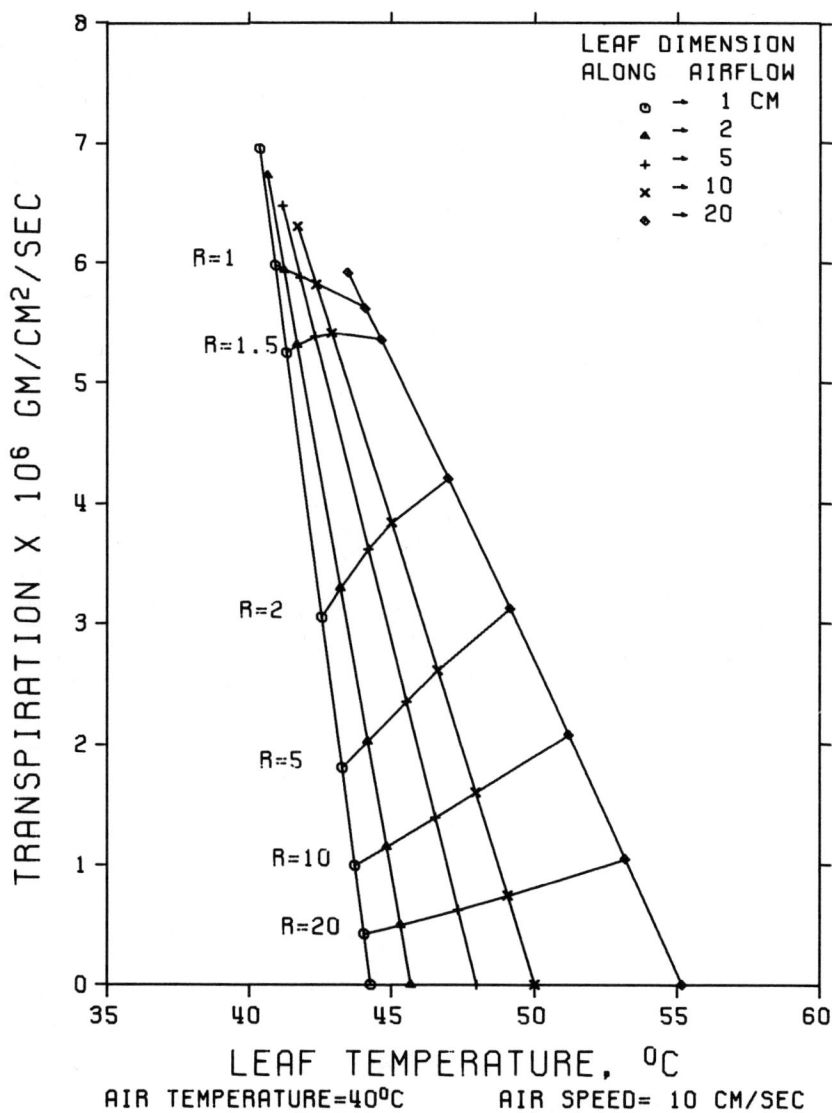

LEAF DIMENSION
ALONG AIRFLOW
⊕ → 1 CM
▲ → 2
+ → 5
× → 10
◆ → 20

R=1
R=1.5
R=2
R=5
R=10
R=20

LEAF TEMPERATURE, °C

TRANSPIRATION X 10⁶ GM/CM²/SEC

AIR TEMPERATURE=40°C   AIR SPEED= 10 CM/SEC
RELATIVE HUMIDITY=80%   R=RESISTANCE, SEC/CM
LEAF DIMENSION ACROSS AIRFLOW=5 CM
RADIATION ABSORBED =
1.003 CAL/CM²/MIN   OR   0.7 X 10⁶ ERGS/CM²/SEC

GRAPH 108

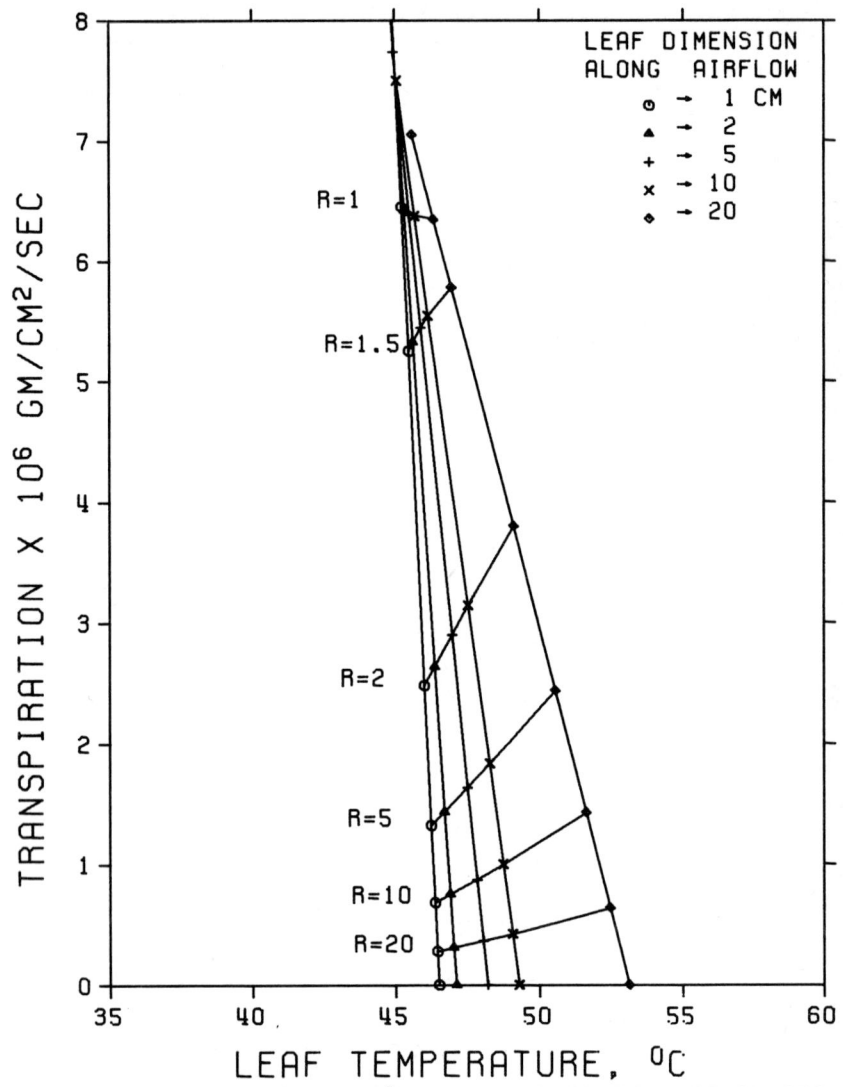

GRAPH 109

AIR TEMPERATURE=40°C   AIR SPEED= 100 CM/SEC
RELATIVE HUMIDITY=80%   R=RESISTANCE, SEC/CM
LEAF DIMENSION ACROSS AIRFLOW=5 CM
RADIATION ABSORBED =
1.003 CAL/CM²/MIN   OR   0.7 X 10⁶ ERGS/CM²/SEC

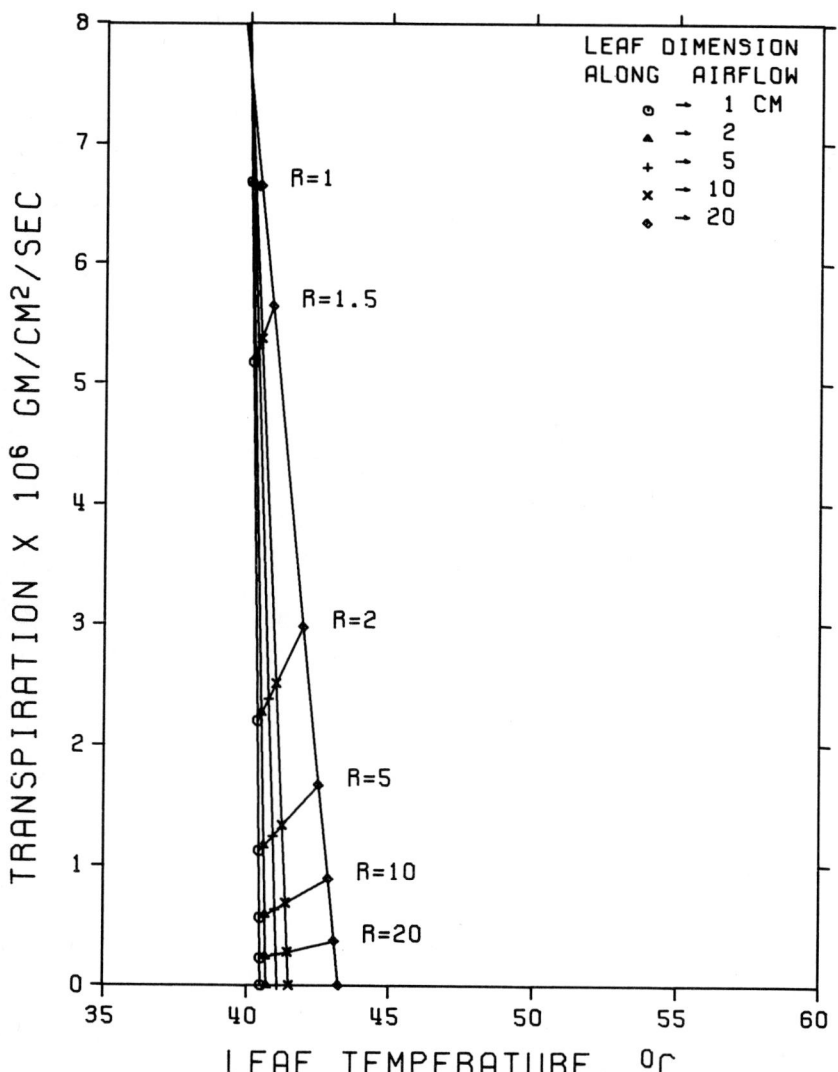

GRAPH 110

BIBLIOGRAPHY

Gates, D. M. (1962). "Energy Exchange in the Biosphere". Harper-Row Inc., p. 160.
Gates, D. M. (1965). A. Heat, Radiant and Sensible. Chapter I. Radiant Energy, its Receipt and Disposal. *Meteorological Monographs* **6**, 28, 1–26.
Gates, D. M. (1968). Transpiration and Leaf Temperature. *Annual Review of Plant Physiology* **19**, 211–238.
Gates, D. M., Alderfer, R. and Taylor, E. (1968). Leaf Temperatures of Desert Plants. *Science, N.Y.* **159**, 3818, 994–995.
Parkhurst, D. F., Duncan, P. R., Gates, D. M. and Kreith, F. (1968). Wind-Tunnel Modelling of Convection of Heat Between Air and Broad Leaves of Plants. *Agricultural Meteorology* **5**, 33–47.
Raschke, K. (1956). Über die Physikalischen Beziehungen Zwischen Wärmeübergangszahl, Strahlungsaustausch, Temperatur und Transpiration eines Blättes. *Planta* **48**, 200–238.
Raschke, K. (1960). Heat transfer between the Plants and the Environment. *Annual Review of Plant Physiology* **11**, 111–126.